Legal Issues in
HOMELAND
SECURITY

U.S. Supreme Court Cases
Commentary and Questions

TERRENCE P. DWYER, J.D.

Looseleaf
Law Publications, Inc.

43-08 162nd Street
Flushing, NY 11358
www.LooseleafLaw.com
800-647-5547

Library of Congress - Cataloging-in-Publication Data

Dwyer, Terrence P., author.
  Legal issues in homeland security : U.S. Supreme Court cases, commentary, and questions / Terrence P. Dwyer.
      pages cm
  Includes bibliographical references and index.
  ISBN 978-1-60885-070-9 -- ISBN 978-1-60885-129-4 (mobi, epub)
  1. National security--Law and legislation--United States. 2. Internal security--United States. 3. Terrorism--United States--Prevention. 4. Habeas corpus--United States. 5. Civil rights--United States. 6. Border security--Law and legislation--United States. 7. National security--Law and legislation--United States--Cases. I. United States. Supreme Court. II. Title.
  KF4850.D89 2015
  343.73'01--dc23

                                                          2014032678

Cover by *Sans Serif,* Saline, Michigan

43-08 162nd Street
Flushing, NY 11358
www.LooseleafLaw.com   Info@LooseleafLaw.com

Table of Contents

DEDICATION

For Joan, who through her love makes all things in
my world possible.

For Brian, Siobhan and Deirdre, who are the reasons
I dare the impossible.

ABOUT THE AUTHOR

Terrence P. Dwyer is an Associate Professor of Legal Studies in the Division of Justice and Law Administration at Western Connecticut State University and an attorney in private practice.

Prior to joining the faculty at Western Connecticut State University, he was an Investigator in the New York State Police Bureau of Criminal Investigation (BCI). At the time of his retirement in 2007 he was assigned to the Violent Crimes Investigation Team (Major Crimes Unit). As a 22-year member of the State Police, he served 17½ years as an Investigator. The bulk of his investigative experience focused on organized crime, street gang and homicide investigations. During his time in the New York State Police BCI, he worked many high profile investigations that included cases with the FBI, U.S. Secret Service, U.S. Department of State, New York Joint Terrorism Task Force, NYPD and Department of Homeland Security. As an attorney in private practice, he represents police officers in critical incidents, disciplinary and employment related cases.

Professor Dwyer holds a bachelor of arts degree from Fordham University and a juris doctorate degree from Pace University School of Law, as well as a postgraduate certificate in Labor Studies from Cornell University. He is admitted to practice law in New York and Connecticut, the Southern and Eastern Districts of New York, and the United States Supreme Court.

INTRODUCTION

"Right, as the world goes, is only in question between equals in power, while the strong do what they can and the weak suffer what they must."
— Thucydides, *History of the Peloponnesian War*

When United Airlines Flight 11 struck Tower One of the World Trade Center at 8:46 a.m. on September 11, 2001, I was at my desk at a New York State Police barracks 75 miles north of New York City. I was one of seven Investigators assigned to the detective bureau of the State Police, the Bureau of Criminal Investigation, who were less than a half hour into our workday; we were reviewing teletypes, checking previous tour patrol activities and going through case files for the day's work ahead. A television was on in the room and we were soon riveted to the news of a plane striking the World Trade Center. Immediately, the suspicions of the assembled members in the room turned to something more sinister than a random private plane striking the tower as initially reported. Those suspicions were confirmed minutes later when, at 9:03 a.m., United Flight 175 struck the second tower. Terrorism had struck the mainland of the United States in a manner unprecedented in our country's history. Subsequent reports of a plane crashing into the Pentagon and a downed plane in a field in Shanksville, Pennsylvania signified that America was under attack. The haunting scar that was Pearl Harbor nearly 60 years earlier seemed to peel open. How did this happen? What did the government know? Why weren't we prepared? Could it have been prevented? My own thoughts went immediately to February 26, 1993, the date of the first World Trade Center attack when a truck bomb exploded in the garage beneath the North Tower. I was in east Harlem at the time with several members of my state police unit, supervising a surveillance operation. We had just ended the surveillance after several hours and were debriefing at a local firehouse when we heard the citywide alarm about an explosion at the World Trade Center. The 911 call was originally reported as a transformer explosion but I knew from my college days of working in building maintenance at the Towers that the possibility seemed remote. By the time we returned to our original early morning meeting point at a NYPD Queens precinct house, we were notified from State Police Headquarters in Albany, New York of a possible terrorist attack and that we were on indefinite standby duty. Several conspirators were subsequently apprehended, indicted and convicted in federal court. Chief among the conspirators was Ramzi Yousef, the nephew of Khaled Sheikh Mohammed, who masterminded the 1993 attack. Mohammed, or KSM, as he came to be referred to by the government, would also be credited with being the architect of the 9/11 plots. In replaying the scene from 1993 I wondered how we were caught so unaware. Suddenly, the news events I had watched with detachment along with other State Police members at various times while dealing with caseloads, prisoners and administrative matters, seemed to fit into a pattern. The varied pieces of fabric had become whole cloth—the 1998 U.S. Embassy bombings in Tanzania, Dar es Salaam and Nairobi, the 2000 attack on the USS *Cole* in Yemen. Still, the question persisted—how could the government not have known?

In the hours after the planes hit there was numbness. Any work planned for the day became secondary. During the following week, I, along with other Investigators across the state, would track down the thousands of leads that poured in; we joined forces with local FBI agents to locate and interview males of Middle Eastern descent who in some instances would be taken into federal custody under immigration violations or as material witnesses. At that point in my law enforcement career I had served for 18 years and the one unassailable fact I took from the days, weeks and months following 9/11 was that domestic law enforcement would forever be changed by the awful events of that day. I witnessed this at a macrolevel but also at a more intimate microlevel because I had been working a confidential informant, an Egyptian national, since January 2001. My investigation into a large-scale immigration fraud involving Middle Eastern males dating back at least a decade seemed to be more significant in the aftermath. In the nine months since I had registered my informant with the New York State Police I recorded many hours of conversation between the informant and several other Egyptian nationals connected to the immigration fraud. Some of my criminal targets were former Egyptian army members with specialties in explosive ordnance, radar and electronic tracking and armored vehicles. I would discover another suspect who falsely entered the United States under a fake student visa, married an American woman, obtained a hazardous materials commercial vehicle operator's license and attempted to obtain aviation lessons at a local airport. All of these activities were red flags the federal government would later present as suspicious indicators of potential terrorist activity.

During the early evening of September 11, 2001, I met with my informant to question him about the day's events. We reviewed the hours of tape recordings we made over the past several months and went through our suspect list. Information was forwarded to the FBI and to the Joint Terrorism Task Force in New York City. The months that followed would bring more urgency to the investigation and more interest from my State Police supervisors and outside agencies. But aside from the increased interest in what I was doing there was a new paradigm to American policing that was developing. This new paradigm would take hold in a way that would lead to the present debates over the militarization of the police. Antiterrorism and homeland security efforts were no longer to be confined to the federal government or intelligence agencies. Local law enforcement had a new and active role in the endeavor. Police officers and other law enforcement professionals became the boots on the ground in the domestic efforts. Eventually the United States would take military action in Afghanistan and then Iraq. At this writing, more than a decade later, there are still American service men and women serving and fighting, some being injured others dying in those far-off countries.

It so happened that in the fall of 2001 I had also begun my sixth year as an adjunct professor at Mercy College in Westchester County, New York. I was teaching two courses, Criminal Procedure Law and White Collar Crime. During that time, discussions in class concerning the attacks were unavoidable. Nor was there any reason to avoid the subject; it was an event that in many respects would define a generation. However, as a professor I tried to bring some relevance of the discussion to the subject at hand, which was not difficult with the two subjects I was teaching. In Criminal Procedure Law that semester the class discussed the due process rights for any conspirators or accomplices the government may apprehend in the terror plot. This was a relevant inquiry, especially for those studying the law, even if the country was still in mourning. We also debated whether terrorism in general and the 9/11 attacks in particular were crimes or acts of war. In White Collar Crime we explored the relationships of companies doing business with the bin Laden Group and other organizations that could be deemed to have supported in word, deed or financially the efforts of radical Islamic groups and what their complicity may have been. Of course, all of this was ad hoc, a way of trying to get through the early part of the semester, provide a discussion outlet for students and bring the poignancy of the issues to light. My own perspective at the time that I shared with the students was that although I was immersed in the daily media concerning investigation of the attacks and the ensuing political and military actions taken by our government, I would be more interested in the stories we would read 5 and 10 years after the 9/11 attacks. These, I suggested, would be a closer approximation to the full story of what had happened—the successes, the failures, the reasons why, and so many more of the as-of-then unanswered questions.

But other questions and concerns would become more topical immediately, and these had to do with individual rights and liberties, the hard fought protections we as a nation secured throughout our long history, and the sudden, fell swoop with which the government seemingly limited them overnight as a result of 9/11. The most visible manifestation of this concern was the USA PATRIOT Act (more fully known in its Senate bill manifestation and final full title as Uniting and Strengthening America by Providing Appropriate Tools Required to Intercept and Obstruct Terrorism[1]), which was signed into law by President Bush on October 26, 2001, after a near unanimous vote in the Senate and a super-majority in the House. What did the Act seek to do and control in its voluminous pages? There were five key areas the Patriot Act addressed and strengthened in the fight against terrorism: 1) increased surveillance capabilities of law enforcement in the investigation of suspected terrorist activity, which included relaxed intelligence-gathering standards; 2) increased scrutiny of financial transactions that may aid terrorist activity; 3) defining the crime of terrorism, which in this definition includes acts of domestic terrorism; 4) enhanced border security and increased law enforcement discretion in detaining suspected immigration law violators; 5) the increase of information sharing among federal, state and local law enforcement agencies. Many of the elected politicians who voted for the Act felt the necessity for it to protect the country from further harm, yet their shortsighted goal did not consider the long-term civil liberty effects of their votes. During World War II this same logic was used to intern in camps a whole race of U.S. citizens. The logic of that decision would be upheld by the U.S. Supreme Court and remain precedential law in a case that ranks with *Dred Scott v. Sandford* and *Plessy v. Ferguson* as one of the darkest moments in Supreme Court history and American jurisprudence. My own experiences in the days, months and years after 9/11 would see an increase in efforts aimed at homeland security but which came with questionable infringements upon individual liberties, chief of which were those of privacy. New York State instituted Operation Safeguard, coordinated by the New York State Police as the primary agency, that sought to involve business owners and private citizens in the collective effort to gather information on potential suspicious activities which could lead to rooting out terrorist plans. The problem with the implementation of the program was that some activities came dangerously close to law enforcement gathering intelligence on citizens and selected groups without any suspicion of criminality,[2] a government activity that the courts clearly held as illegal in the aftermath of the Vietnam War and period covering the 1960s and 1970s.[3]

Just shy of six years after that awful day of 9/11/01, I retired from the New York State Police in 2007. By then I had witnessed the transformation in law enforcement since 9/11. I had been to homeland security training courses, massive crime scene management courses and intelligence-gathering courses. I had been to the intelligence fusion centers and regional intelligence meetings that had sprung up post-9/11, and I experienced an interagency cooperation, specifically with federal agencies, previously unknown. Now as a full-time professor teaching legal studies at Western Connecticut State University's Division of Justice and Law Administration, I see the large number of students who want to enter law enforcement for the noble profession it is and as a means to not only serve their community but their country. I see some of those same students who are back in the classroom after serving one or multiple tours of duty in the combat zones of Afghanistan and Iraq. There is one constant I continuously remind my classes of, which is that the criminal justice system is only as good as the ingrained ethics and integrity of its individual members. The same can be said for our government. This is why it is important to understand the events of 9/11 and the concept of homeland security from the broader legal prism of U.S. Supreme Court cases that have tackled various constitutional issues on the subject. How we react as a country, a free and democratic republican form of government, to national emergencies confronting us and those who would not agree with us, even attempt to harm us, defines the legitimacy of our constitutional system. As a country we have not always been perfect but we have sustained that which above all we cherish, the rule of law. Aristotle wrote in **Politics**: *"It is more proper that law should govern than any one of the citizens: upon the same principle, if it is advantageous to place the supreme power in some particular persons, they should be appointed to be only guardians, and the servants of the laws."* The servants of the laws title applies to all who serve the public will—the president, Congress, the courts, all state and local political bodies, the military and its commanders, and law enforcement. Preservation of our legal heritage begins with a knowledge and understanding followed by an appreciation for and commitment to its preservation. The chapters that follow with the various Supreme Court cases, commentary and questions are an attempt at such knowledge, understanding, commitment and preservation.

The student will quickly see that homeland security is not new, a post-9/11 invention, but a continuation of a long stream of government action in the best interests of the country. Sometimes, however, these best interests have not served the better interests of all persons or groups and have pitted citizen against citizen. Yet, the fabric of our country remains, sometimes a little tattered and worn, though sure to endure. We are largely a country that has learned from and corrected its mistakes. We are also a country that has repeated some of those mistakes. However, it is our sense of justice—that overriding

American value—that eventually enables us to ensure that injustice, even our own, does not permeate our national soul. The Preamble to the U.S. Constitution reads as follows:

> *"We the people of the United States, in order to form a more perfect union, establish justice, insure domestic tranquility, provide for the common defense, promote the general welfare, and secure the blessings of liberty to ourselves and our posterity, do ordain and establish this Constitution for the United States of America."*

For these words to have their ordained meaning, the provisions of the Constitution that follow that opening Preamble have to be read, judged, interpreted and applied so that the country remains the representative democracy it was crafted to be. Throughout our nation's history the U.S. Supreme Court has stood as the watchdog over that ideal and no where has this duty been more relevant than in the many difficult cases it has handled over the years in dealing with matters of national security. Your reading of the cases and the commentary that precedes and follows will allow you to explore the depth and breadth of this nation's struggle with the many legal issues surrounding this not-so-new concept of homeland security.

Text Format

The text is separated into ten chapters, each dealing with a relevant aspect of homeland security and the law. The chapters begin with a discussion of the subject matter to be covered and its background material before the text of the U.S. Supreme Court cases to be studied within the chapter is provided. Each Supreme Court case has been edited with certain nonrelevant parts of the case removed. Also removed are any footnote references from the original decision because these distract from the substantive case material and add little in way of overall understanding of the particular case and the subject matter in general. With some cases I have left more of the decisions intact and excised little because I felt the material was too important to winnow down to a few readable pages. The bulk of the cases that I left intact, and thus run a bit longer than other chapter cases, can be found in chapters 3 and 4 and deal with habeas corpus, military tribunals and civilian access to courts. The reason for this is that these particular cases have historically and in present time drawn the most attention and need to be digested more whole than piecemeal. After the cases, I have provided sections of additional commentary that provide a fuller understanding of the material and some necessary historical and legal background for the particular chapter material. Included with this commentary are questions for reflection and review to put the prior case reading in context and assist the student with discerning the relevance of the material. Because the subject matter material is quite voluminous and can be overwhelming for the student and reader I have organized the chapters into areas that I feel more easily lead to overall comprehension and understanding of the subject. Although there is going to be some overlap between chapter material, the cases are contained in the chapters that best highlight and explain them and provide the proper topical context for the student and reader.

Case Briefing

As indicated from the prior section, the bulk of this text is comprised of relevant U.S. Supreme Court cases dealing with homeland security issues. Additionally, there are excerpts from other relevant federal and state cases and statutory material. One of the traditional ways in which law school students were taught the law was by way of the Socratic Method, which had students read case law and then come to class prepared to discuss those cases and solve proposed legal problems based on their case law readings. This was the way I was trained in the law, it is the way my father was trained in the law, and based on first year law books I have in my possession from 1929 it was the way my granduncle from Ireland was trained in the law at Fordham University. I must admit that after four years of undergraduate study there was a big adjustment to this type of learning during my first year of law school. Yet, learn it I did and in doing so developed my critical thinking skills. Admittedly, there were times when I wondered if there wasn't a better way to teach and learn the law. Upon embarking on my own career as a college and university professor, I found that I tended to teach using the case method as well as more traditional classroom methods. There has been criticism among law faculty over the past decade as to how to better train the next generation of lawyers, and many law schools have made the shift from a total Socratic Method to one that also emphasizes core legal principles and statutory analysis along with policy discussion.[4] To this end, I have developed this text in the style as indicated above so as to accommodate these varied learning objectives. Still, I do believe in the merits of teaching students of the law, whether they are undergraduate, graduate or 1L to 3Ls, the case method for several reasons. First, the law is about problem solving and developing critical thinking skills—having students read cases, discuss and apply the legal concepts gleaned from those cases is essential to this skill set. Second, those employed in the legal profession, and in this I include not just lawyers, judges and paralegals but those who actually apply aspects of the law every day in their professions, such as criminal justice system workers (police, corrections, probation, parole), as well as a diverse and myriad field of other professions that in some way touch upon the law (social workers and health care professionals for instance), need to know how to read and understand case law because it impacts their jobs. Third, reading cases and writing out case briefs attunes students to the language of the law and develops the ability to apply legal reasoning. Fourth, there is generally some good writing that can be found in court decisions, especially those coming out of the U.S. Supreme Court. Past Justices such as Oliver Wendell Holmes, Benjamin Cardozo and Robert Jackson have been known for the quality of writing found in their opinions. Reading such well-crafted decisions expands the reader's own ability to communicate and do it well.

To properly read a court decision it is necessary to know what to look for in the decision and how to break down the decision into its core components. This is part of the fundamentals all aspiring lawyers are taught in law school and, despite the criticisms, how they learn to think in the law. The ability to brief court cases assists the student in learning how to get to the guts of a case. I have taught all my students how to do case briefs and there is not a semester that goes by that my undergraduate students are not doing several case briefs in each of my law classes. Once they learn how to do it properly, the students become better able to read the cases and get to the issues and the resolution of those issues. So, how do you brief a case?

To brief a case means to break it down into the several components that make up the whole of a court's decision. It is an indispensable tool in summarizing and simplifying the sometimes complex legal issues that surround a conflict between two parties. Just as every good detective begins an investigation with inquiry into the *who, what, when, where, why* and *how*, the same questions should be applied when reading and briefing a court's decision:

Who – are the parties to the conflict?
What – is the issue in conflict?
When – did the conflict arise?
Where – is the case conflict being presented? (Is it a trial court or appellate court decision? Is it in state or federal court?)
Why – are the parties in conflict at odds with each other?
How – does the court reconcile the legal issue between the parties?

If you can answer each of these questions when reading a court's decision, you have effectively begun the first step in briefing the case. Although the briefing of a case is a little more involved than what is outlined above, it is a good starting point to present these six questions *(Who? What? When? Where? Why? How?)* as you read the case. With the answers to these questions, you can discuss any case by being able to recite the FACTS, LEGAL ISSUE(S), COURT'S DECISION, and the RULE OF LAW resulting from the court's decision. There are a few different ways how professors prefer their case briefs to be done, and formats may vary among professors, but the basic format is as follows: **Facts, Procedural History, Issue, Holding** and **Rationale**. A case brief should begin with the header, which includes the case name followed by the case citation beneath it.

For example: *Miranda v. Arizona*
            348 U.S. 436 (1966)

The case citation is important because it is the location of where the case is reported. The first number indicates the volume number, the page number of where the case begins follows the case reporter designation (e.g., U.S.), which is followed by the year the decision was issued. To look for the above case in a library, the student would go to where the U.S. Supreme Court volumes are kept (there are three reported volumes for the U.S. Supreme Court)—the official reporter for U.S. Supreme Court decisions is the *United States Reports* (designated by *U.S.* after the volume number and preceding the page number). Unofficial reporters are the *Lawyers' Edition of the Supreme Court Reports (L.Ed.)* and the *Supreme Court Reporter (S.Ct.)*. In a law library the above

Miranda decision would be found in volume 348 of the *United States Reports* at page 436. If a student were to look for the case online through Lexis or WestLaw the citation would provide direct access to the case.

Now let's take a look at each separate part of the case brief:

Facts—A court's decision can go on for a number of pages, many the length of a short novel (the full decision in *Miranda v. Arizona* was close to 100 pages), and much of it may contain an extensive recitation of the background facts to the case. It is not necessary in the case brief to include all the facts, only the relevant facts pertinent to the legal analysis should be included. These are the key facts that are essential to forming a legal conclusion and that aid in establishing elements of a rule of law to be applied.

Procedural History—The majority of cases a student will read are appellate court cases, which means that the case began somewhere else in a state or federal court of general jurisdiction. Cases generally come to appellate courts after trial in a court of general jurisdiction or sometimes on what is known as an interlocutory appeal. An interlocutory appeal is rare because it is a request by a litigant for an appellate court to review an aspect of the case before the conclusion of the trial. Appellate courts are reluctant to allow such fractured litigation, but there are circumstances under which such an appeal will be taken. The subject of the interlocutory appeal must be separate from the merits of the case, and it must be unreviewable on appeal from a final judgment. But whether the case is a direct or inter-locutory appeal, the Procedural History will provide a synopsis of the route the case took to its present destination in the court from which the decision is being read. It is, as I often tell my students, the road map of a case— where has it been and how did it get to the appellate court? The Procedural History will also tell which side won at the lower court, who is appealing and the reason for the appeal. A typical Procedural History might read as follows: *"Petitioner appeals from an appellate court decision which reversed a trial court order suppressing a gun found in petitioner's possession when pulled over for speeding. At trial the court suppressed the gun based on a lack of probable cause for the search and a violation of the petitioner's 4th Amendment rights. The intermediate appellate reversed finding that the fact of petitioner operating with a suspended license would have necessitated impound of petitioner's vehicle and a related inventory of the vehicle's contents which would have disclosed the gun."* The preceding tells someone reading the brief all they would need to know about the progress of the case through the courts.

Issue—The law is about problem solving and every case involves a problem or issue for resolution presented before the court. The Issue is simply the question for resolution placed before the court by the relevant legal facts that must be answered in light of the applicable rule of law. The Issue in a brief is framed as a question, much the same way appeals to the U.S. Supreme Court are framed as "Questions Presented" for the Court's determination. A typical issue in a case brief might read as follows: *"Whether the police had sufficient probable cause to justify a warrantless search of petitioner's vehicle?"* The Issue should cut to the core of the legal question presented to the appellate court and be as simple and straightforward as possible. Some cases may involve multiple issues and thus the Issue section in the case brief should reflect that by posing a second or third issue before the court. But it should be remembered that appellate courts try to limit the issues brought before them and narrow the argument to one or two salient points.

Holding—The Holding is essentially the court's answer to the question presented by the Issue. The Holding, if the Issue has been properly framed, will be a simple Yes or No response to the Issue's question presented followed by a declaratory sentence of the court's application of the rule of law followed to decide the conflict.

Rationale—This section, along with the Facts section, should be the case brief's longest parts. The Facts and Rationale comprise what I like to refer to as the "meat" of the case brief with the other sections comprising the "bone." The Rationale is simply the part where the court's reasoning for its Holding is explained. The Rationale should highlight the basis for the court's justification for its decision and why it held as it did. In doing so the student should avoid relying on court dicta, which are parts of a decision that are not considered authoritative or binding and represent merely a judge's explanation or material that is informative or instructive in nature. If the opinion goes into areas not directly on point to the issue in the case or the facts in dispute then this is considered dicta. The word itself comes from the Latin *obiter dictum*, which translates to *"said in passing."*

In putting all of these components together, the student will have a case brief in hand and will have learned an initial skillset taught to all first-year law students. After reading several cases and writing out case briefs, the student will also have a better understanding of the language of the law and how to apply legal reasoning. The cases within should provide plenty of opportunity for students to apply their case-briefing skills.

Endnotes

1   Senate Bill 1510, 107th Congress, 2001.

2   See e.g., *NAACP v. Alabama*, 357 U.S. 449 (1958) regarding the Court's denial of government attempts to subpoena lists of a group's membership.

3   See e.g., *Handschu v. Special Services Division*, 605 F. Supp. 1389 (DCNY, 1988) regarding the limiting of a police department's intelligence gathering.

4   Slawson, W.D. (2000). Changing How We Teach: A Critique of the Case Method. *Southern California Law Review, 343–346.*

Chapter One

HOMELAND SECURITY:
INTRODUCTION AND HISTORICAL CONTEXT

What Is Homeland Security?

Prior to any discussion regarding legal issues involved in homeland security it is best to define the main subject and begin by asking, *"What is homeland security?"* On September 10, 2001, it was a term many Americans had not heard or considered in their busy lives. More than a decade removed from the events of 9/11, it is a term familiar to most grade school children and an area wherein many college students are seeking careers in government service. Homeland security has been defined by the White House's National Strategy for Homeland Security as *"a concerted national effort to prevent terrorist attacks within the United States, reduce America's vulnerability to terrorism, and minimize the damage and recover from attacks that do occur."*[1] Specifically, homeland security has come to represent the federal cabinet position created after 9/11 that consolidated several diverse federal agencies and placed them within one comprehensive cabinet level organization. The Homeland Security Act of 2002 in section 101(b)(1) defines the mission of the Department of Homeland Security as: (A) prevent terrorist attacks within the United States; (B) reduce the vulnerability of the United States to terrorism; and (C) minimize the damage, and assist in the recovery, from terrorist attacks that do occur within the United States.[2] Still, the Homeland Security Act itself does not provide a concrete definition of homeland security. Although most would agree homeland security is concerned with thwarting, preventing and responding to terror threats against our national government there have been diverse interests involved within the sphere of homeland security protection and mitigation. Defining homeland security is not a simple matter, especially in our expansive government system based on federalism. The federalist system in the United States focuses on the relationship between the states and the federal government. It is a system, in the words of James Madison, in which the states and national government *"are in fact but different agents and trustees of the people, constituted with different powers."*[3] Local, state and the federal government exercise diverse authority for the benefit of citizens. This authority is further fragmented among diverse public agencies. Therefore, the definition for homeland security may vary according to agency and function, according to political subdivision and particular threat risk. One scholar has suggested seven definitions relating to homeland security:[4] 1) terrorism, 2) national security, 3) metahazards,[5] 4) jurisdictional hazards,[6] 5) all hazards,[7] 6) terrorism and catastrophe, 7) security over everything.[8] No matter how many different ways it may be defined, homeland security in the United States has become a centralizing aspect of government response to threat, external and internal, coordinated at a national level through the Department of Homeland Security. Such coordination was reflected in an April 2004 press release through the U.S. Department of Homeland Security's Science and Technology Directorate, which announced the development of the SAFECOM program providing interoperability of wireless communications among 50,000 public service agencies across the United States. As noted in the press release, "the Department has undertaken this unprecedented step toward defining the nation's interoperability challenges for the future. This approach not only complements the grant guidance we have in place but also provides a roadmap for our interoperability goals and brings government and public safety officials together under a common mission."[9] The significant part of this announcement and other related integrations between the federal government and local governments is the level of cooperation and interoperation between the two with homeland security being the tie that binds. But this only begs the follow-up question to our beginning inquiry—is this a new phenomena or has it been an evolving concern in response to more modern, technologically advanced threats? Concern over the security of our nation has been part of government since the country's founding. Though not necessarily termed homeland security, the protections sought and the threats contemplated were no less significant. Borders had to be secured, treason punished, admission of occupants regulated and, of course, funding secured for the national security. No sooner did the Founding Fathers establish a separate and free nation than the initial political debates surrounding political concerns relating to homeland security began to stir.

The Birth of Homeland Security

The Preamble to the U.S. Constitution states that one of its purposes is to insure domestic tranquility and to provide for the common defense. This is the earliest provision for homeland security in the United States. Throughout the text of the Constitution are other examples of the inherent authority of the government to provide for the national defense which, includes the power to declare and wage war, maintain and support an army and navy, and enter into treaties with foreign governments. The Constitution also provides for intergovernmental checks and balances between the branches of government as well as a Bill of Rights so that the might of the government does not become the very threat the Founders so carefully sought to protect against. The Supreme Court acts as a fulcrum in the balance between the sometimes competing interests of the Executive and Legislative branches in the national defense. Ideally it also acts as a neutral party in disputes between the rights of citizens and government intervention. From the latter part of the 18th century up to the present day, the Court has maintained its role in assuring this overall balance.

Even though the term homeland security may be fairly new in our collective lexicon the concept is as old as the United States. The Alien and Sedition Acts of 1798 are an example of early legislation aimed at American security. These four bills, passed by the fifth U.S. Congress during the French Revolution, sought to protect the United States from the effects of the revolution that were finding their way to North America. The Acts were signed into law by President John Adams, a Federalist, under much criticism from opposition Republicans, chief among them being Adams's political rival and Vice President Thomas Jefferson. The pro-French Revolution Jefferson, like other Republicans, viewed the Acts as unconstitutional. The four Acts were as follows: The Naturalization Act, The Sedition Act, The Alien Act and The Alien Enemies Act. The

Naturalization Act extended the residency requirement for U.S. citizenship from five years to fourteen years, whereas The Sedition Act made it a crime to publish false or malicious comments about government officials or the government in general. Government officials' fear of insurrection prompted by criticism of the government would continue as a common theme in United States history during times of emergency or war. The Sedition Act of 1918 would follow the Espionage Act of 1917 and place broader restrictions on speech and opinion that was negative toward the government. Both of these acts of Congress were in response to American involvement in World War I. The constitutional progression of First Amendment rights to the modern understanding wherein criticism of the government, even in times of national crisis, is tolerated has made its way through two world wars, Communist scares and hysteria after both world wars, the Korean Conflict and the Vietnam War. Yet, the protection of First Amendment rights has remained no less of a concern in the government's 21st century global war on terror.

The Alien Act and The Alien Enemies Act would also be the introductory legislation in a long history of anti-immigrant behavior and sentiment in the name of national security and defense. Section 1 of the Alien Act of 1798 provided:

> "Be it enacted by the Senate and House of Representatives of the United States of America, in Congress assembled, That it shall be lawful for the President of the United States, at any time during the continuance of this act, to order all such aliens as he. shall judge dangerous to the peace and safety of the United States, or shall have reasonable grounds to suspect are concerned in any treasonable or secret machinations against the government thereof, to depart out of the territory of the United States within such time as shall be expressed in such order ..."

An alien ordered to depart who was subsequently found in the United States would, upon conviction, be imprisoned for three years and forever barred from obtaining citizenship. The Act also provided for the jurisdiction of such cases to reside in the district and circuit courts and for the captain of any ship entering a port to account the customs officer of any aliens on board his ship.

The Alien Enemies Act of 1798 provided the president more power with respect to immigrants whose country was at war with the United States:

> "Be it enacted by the Senate and House of Representatives of the United States of America, in Congress assembled, That whenever there shall be a declared war between the United States and any foreign nation or government, or any invasion or predatory incursion shall be perpetrated, attempted, or threatened against the territory of the United States, by any foreign nation or government, and the President of the United States shall make public proclamation of the event, all natives, citizens, denizens, or subjects of the hostile nation or government, being males of the age of fourteen years and upwards, who shall be within the United States, and not actually naturalized, shall be liable to be apprehended, restrained, secured and removed, as alien enemies ... and to establish any other

regulations which shall be found necessary in the premises and for the public safety ..."

The recognition of the ability of the government, specifically the president, to expel those inhabitants who were deemed to be a danger to the country in a time of war is also the earliest statutory expression, aside from the enumerated powers of the Constitution, of such homeland security authority. The more controversial and criticized of the Alien and Sedition Acts of 1798 was the sedition statute that Republican critics blasted as unconstitutional. Yet, in this early legislation of a partisan Congress, we find a common course of action when it comes to internal security in times of either actual or perceived national emergency, and that is the distrust of those considered foreigners within the country and the stifling of speech considered critical of the government and potentially inflammatory.

The ensuing Quasi-War with France would eventually provide further development of America's right of security and national protection. This would come in the form of early U.S. Supreme Court cases concerning the capture of enemy vessels. The term "prize" referred to a claim under admiralty law wherein an enemy ship and its cargo are captured and taken during armed conflict. The seized ship would be made the subject of an "in rem" court proceeding to determine the legal right and ownership of the captured prize. A finding of a valid prize claim would convert title to the seizing party. The prize determination was made in the courts of the seizing authority's country. Under original prize law the commanders and crew of the ship seizing the opposing vessel retained a split share of the prize. The Quasi-War with France, as the title would suggest, was not a Congress-declared war as contemplated under Article I, section 8 of the U.S. Constitution. The extent of the right of American vessels to claim prize against foreign vessels in an undeclared war would be, along with jurisdictional issues regarding such claims, early considerations for the U.S. Supreme Court as the developing nation had to consider conflict and security beyond its own borders. These are the concerns of the following two cases:

Glass v. The Betsey
3 U.S. 3 Dall. 6 (1794)

Mr. Chief Justice Jay delivered the following unanimous opinion of the Court.

The judges being decidedly of opinion that every district court in the United States possesses all the powers of a court of admiralty, whether considered as an instance or as a prize court, and that the plea of the aforesaid appellee, Pierre Arcade Johannene, to the jurisdiction of the District Court of Maryland, is insufficient.

Therefore, it is considered by the Supreme Court aforesaid, and now finally decreed and adjudged by the same that the said plea be and the same is hereby overruled and dismissed, and that the decree of the said District Court of Maryland founded thereon be and the same is hereby revoked, reversed, and annulled.

And the said Supreme Court, being further clearly of opinion that the District Court of Maryland aforesaid has jurisdiction competent to inquire and to decide whether, in the present case, restitution ought to be made to the claimants, or either of them, in whole or in part (that is, whether such restitution can be made consistently with the laws of nations and the treaties and laws of the United States) therefore it is ordered and adjudged that the said District Court of Maryland do proceed to determine upon the libel of the said Alexander S. Glass and others, agreeably to law and right, the said plea to the jurisdiction of the said court notwithstanding.

And the Supreme Court being further of opinion that no foreign power can of right institute or erect any court of judicature of any kind within the jurisdiction of the United States but such only as may be warranted by and be in pursuance of treaties, it is therefore

Decreed and adjudged that the admiralty jurisdiction which has been exercised in the United States by the consuls of France, not being so warranted, is not of right.

It is further ordered by the said Supreme Court that this cause be and it is hereby remanded to the District Court for the Maryland District for a final decision, and that the several parties to the same do each pay their own costs.

Bas v. Tingy
4 U. S. 37 (1800)

The Judges delivered their opinions *seriatim* in the following manner:

Justice Moore.

This case depends on the construction of the act for the regulation of the navy. It is objected, indeed, that the act applies only to future wars, but its provisions are obviously applicable to the present situation of things, and there is nothing to prevent an immediate commencement of its operation.

It is, however, more particularly urged that the word "enemy" cannot be applied to the French, because the section in which it is used, is confined to such a state of war, as would authorize a recapture of property belonging to a nation in amity with the United States, and such a state of war, it is said, does not exist between America and France. A number of books have been cited to furnish a glossary on the word enemy; yet our situation is so extraordinary that I doubt whether a parallel case can be traced in the history of nations. But if words are the representatives of ideas, let me ask by what other word the idea of the relative situation of America and France could be communicated, than by that of hostility, or war? And how can the characters of the parties engaged in hostility or war be otherwise described than by the denomination of enemies? It is for the honor and dignity of both nations, therefore, that they should be called enemies, for it is by that description alone that either could justify or excuse the scene of bloodshed, depredation, and confiscation which has unhappily occurred, and surely Congress could only employ the language of the act of June 13, 1798, towards a nation whom she considered as an enemy.

***

During the present hostilities it affects the case of recaptured property belonging to our own citizens, and in the event of a future war it might also be applied to the case of recaptured property belonging to a nation in amity with the United States. But it is further to be remarked that all the expressions of the act may be satisfied, even at this very time, for by former laws, the recapture of property, belonging to persons resident within the United States is authorized; those residents may be aliens, and if they are subjects of a nation in amity with the United States, they answer completely the description of the law.

On these grounds I am clearly of opinion that the decree of the circuit court ought to be affirmed.

Justice Washington.

The decision of this question must depend upon another, which is whether, at the time of passing the Act of Congress of 2 March, 1799, there subsisted a state of war between the two nations? It may, I believe, be safely laid down that every contention by force between two nations in external matters, under the authority of their respective governments, is not only war, but public war. If it be declared in form, it is called solemn and is of the perfect kind; because one whole nation is at war with another whole nation, and all the members of the nation declaring war, are authorized to commit hostilities against all the members of the other, in every place, and under every circumstance. In such a war, all the members act under a general authority, and all the rights and consequences of war attach to their condition.

But hostilities may subsist between two nations more confined in its nature and extent, being limited as to places, persons, and things, and this is more properly termed imperfect war; because not solemn, and because those who are authorized to commit hostilities, act under special authority, and can go no further than to the extent of their commission. Still, however, it is public war, because it is an external contention by force between some of the members of the two nations, authorized by the legitimate powers. It is a war between the two nations, though all the members are not authorized to commit hostilities such as in a solemn war, where the government restrain the general power.

Now if this be the true definition of war, let us see what was the situation of the United States in relation to France. In March, 1799, Congress had raised an army, stopped all intercourse with France, dissolved our treaty, built and equipped ships of war, and commissioned private armed ships, enjoining the former, and authorizing the latter, to defend themselves against the armed ships of France, to attack them on the high seas, to subdue and take them as prize, and to recapture armed vessels found in their possession. Here, then, let me ask what were the technical characters of an American and French armed vessel combating on the high seas with a view the one to subdue the other and to make prize of his property? They certainly were not friends, because there was a contention by force; nor were they private enemies, because the contention was external, and authorized by the legitimate authority of the two governments. If they were not our enemies, I know not what constitutes an enemy.

***

But secondly it is said that a war of the imperfect kind is more properly called acts of hostility, or reprisal, and that Congress did not mean to consider the hostility subsisting between France and the United States, as constituting a state of war.

In support of this position it has been observed that in no law prior to March, 1799, is France styled our enemy, nor are we said to be at war. This is true, but neither of these things was necessary to be done, because as to France, she was sufficiently described by the title of the French Republic, and as to America, the degree of hostility meant to be carried on was sufficiently described without declaring war or declaring that we were at war. Such a declaration by Congress might have constituted a perfect state of war, which was not intended by the government.

… It has likewise been said that the 7th section of the act of March 1799, embraces cases which, according to preexisting laws, could not then take place, because no authority had been given to recapture friendly vessels from the French, and this argument was strongly and forcibly pressed.

But because every case provided for by this law was not then existing, it does not follow that the law should not operate upon such as did exist and upon the rest whenever they should arise. It is a permanent law, embracing a variety of subjects, not made in relation to the present war with France only but in relation to any future war with her or with any other nation. It might then very properly allow salvage for recapturing of American vessels from France, which had previously been authorized by law, though it could not immediately apply to the vessels of friends, and whenever such a war should exist between the United States and France, or any other nation, as according to the law of nations or special authority would justify the recapture of friendly vessels, it might on that event, with similar propriety, apply to them, which furnishes, I think, the true construction of the act.

The opinion which I delivered at New York in *Talbot v. Seeman* was that although an American vessel could not justify the retaking of a neutral vessel from the French, because neither the sort of war that subsisted, nor the special commission under which the American acted, authorized the proceeding; yet that the 7th sec. of the act of 1799, applied to recaptures from France as an enemy, in all cases authorized by Congress. And on both points my opinion remains unshaken, or rather has been confirmed by the very able discussion which the subject has lately undergone in this Court on the appeal from my decree. Another reason has been assigned by the defendant's counsel why the former law is not to be regarded as repealed by the latter, to-wit: that a subsequent affirmative general law cannot repeal a former affirmative special law, if both may stand together. This ground is not taken, because such an effect involves an indecent censure upon the legislature for passing contradictory laws, since the censure only applies where the contradiction appears in the same law, and it does not follow that a provision which is proper at one time may not be improper at another when circumstances are changed, but the ground of argument is that a change ought not to be presumed. Yet if there is sufficient evidence of such a change in the legislative will, and the two laws are in collision, we are forced to presume it.

What then is the evidence of legislative will? In fact and in law, we are at war: an American vessel fighting with a French vessel, to subdue and make her prize, is fighting with an enemy accurately and technically speaking, and if this be not sufficient evidence of the legislative mind, it is explained in the same law. The sixth and the ninth sections of the act speak of prizes, which can only be of property taken at sea from an enemy *jure belli*, and the 9th section speaks of prizes as taken from an enemy, in so many words, alluding to prizes which had been previously taken; but no prize could have been then taken except from France; prizes taken from France were therefore taken from the enemy. This, then, is a legislative interpretation of the word "enemy," and if the enemy as to prizes, surely they preserve the same character as to recaptures. Besides, it may be fairly asked, why should the rate of salvage be different in such a war as the present, from the salvage in a war more solemn or general? And it must be recollected that the occasion of making the law of March, 1799, was not only to raise the salvage, but to apportion it to the hazard in which the property retaken was placed, a circumstance for which the former salvage law had not provided.

The two laws, upon the whole, cannot be rendered consistent unless the court could wink so hard as not to see and know that in fact, in the view of Congress, and to every intent and purpose, the possession by a French armed vessel of an American vessel was the possession of an enemy, and therefore, in my opinion, the decree of the circuit court ought to be affirmed.

Justice Chase.

The judges agreeing unanimously in their opinion, I presumed that the sense of the Court would have been delivered by the President, and therefore I have not prepared a formal argument on the occasion. I find no difficulty, however, in assigning the general reasons which induce me to concur in affirming the decree of the circuit court.

An American public vessel of war recaptures an American merchant vessel from a French privateer, after 96 hours' possession, and the question is stated what salvage ought to be allowed? There are two laws on the subject, by the first of which only one-eighth of the value of the recaptured property is allowed, but by the second, the recaptor is entitled to a moiety. The recapture happened after the passing of the latter law, and the whole controversy turns on the single question whether France was at that time an enemy. If France was an enemy, then the law obliges us to decree one-half of the value of ship and cargo for salvage, but if France was not an enemy, then no more than one-eighth can be allowed.

The decree of the circuit court (in which I presided) passed by consent; but although I never gave an opinion, I have never entertained a doubt on the subject. Congress is empowered to declare a general war, or Congress may wage a limited war, limited in place, in objects, and in time. If a general war is declared, its extent and operations are only restricted and regulated by the *jus belli*, forming a part of the law of nations, but if a partial war is waged, its extent and operation depend on our municipal laws.

What, then, is the nature of the contest subsisting between American and France? In my judgment it is a limited partial war. Congress has not declared war in general terms, but Congress has authorized hostilities on the high seas by certain persons in certain cases. There is no authority given to commit hostilities on land, to capture unarmed French vessels, nor even to capture French armed vessels lying in a French port, and the authority is not given indiscriminately to every citizen of America against every citizen of France; but only to citizens appointed by commissions or exposed to immediate outrage and violence. So far it is unquestionably a partial war; but nevertheless it is a public war, on account of the public authority from which it emanates.

There are four acts authorized by our government that are demonstrative of a state of war. A belligerent power has a right, by the law of nations, to search a neutral vessel, and, upon suspicion of a violation of her neutral obligations, to seize and carry her into port for further examination. But by the acts of Congress, an American vessel it authorized: 1st, to resist the search of a French public vessel; 2d, to capture any vessel that should attempt, by force, to compel submission to a search; 3d, to recapture any American vessel seized by a French vessel, and 4th, to capture any French armed vessel wherever found on the high seas. This suspension of the law of nations, this right of capture and recapture, can only be authorized by an act of the government, which is, in itself, an act of hostility. But still it is a restrained or limited hostility, and there are undoubtedly many rights attached to a general war which do not attach to this modification of the powers of defense and aggression.

***

As there may be a public general war, and a public qualified war, so there may, upon correspondent principles, be a general enemy, and a partial enemy. The designation of "enemy" extends to a case of perfect war; but as a general designation, it surely includes the less, as well as the greater, species of warfare. If Congress had chosen to declare a general war, France would have been a general enemy, having chosen to wage a partial war, France was, at the time of the capture, only a partial enemy, but still she was an enemy.

It has been urged, however, that Congress did not intend the provisions of the act of March 1799, for the case of our subsisting qualified hostility with France, but for the case of a future state of general war with any nation. I think, however, that the contrary appears from the terms of the law itself, and from the subsequent repeal. In the 9th section, it is said that all the money accruing, "or which has already accrued from the sale of prizes," shall constitute a fund for the half pay of officers and seamen. Now at the time of making this appropriation, no prizes (which *ex vi termini* implies a capture in a state of war) had been taken from any nation but France, those which had been taken were not taken from France as a friend, they must consequently have been taken from her as an enemy, and the retrospective provision of the law can only operate on such prizes. Besides, when the 13th section regulates "the bounty given by the United States on any national ship of war, taken from the enemy, and brought into port," it is obvious that even if the bounty has no relation to previous captures, it must operate from the moment of passing the act, and embraces the case of a national ship of war taken from France as an enemy, according to the existing qualified state of hostilities. But the repealing act, passed on 3 March, 1800 (subsequent to the recapture in the present case) ought to silence all doubt as to the intention of the legislature, for, if the act of March 1799, did not apply to the French Republic, as an enemy, there could be no reason for altering or repealing that part of it which regulates the rate of salvage on recaptures.

The acts of Congress have been analyzed to show that a war is not openly denounced against France, and that France is nowhere expressly called the enemy of America, but this only proves the circumspection and prudence of the legislature. Considering our national prepossessions in favor of the French Republic, Congress had an arduous task to perform, even in preparing for necessary defense, and just retaliation. As the temper of the people rose, however, in resentment of accumulated wrongs, the language and the measures of the government became more and more energetic and indignant; though hitherto the popular feeling may not have been ripe for a solemn declaration of war; and an active and powerful opposition in our public councils, has postponed, if not prevented that decisive event, which many thought would have best suited the interest, as well as the honor of the United States. The progress of our contest with France, indeed, resembles much the progress of our revolutionary contest, in which, watching the current of public sentiment, the patriots of that day proceeded, step by step, from the supplicatory language of petitions for a redress of grievances, to the bold and noble declaration of national independence.

Having, then, no hesitation in pronouncing, that a partial war exists between America and France, and that France was an enemy within the meaning of the act of March 1799, my voice must be given for affirming the decree of the circuit court.

Justice Paterson.

... The United States and the French republic are in a qualified state of hostility. An imperfect war, or a war, as to certain objects, and to a certain extent, exists between the two nations, and this modified warfare is authorized by the constitutional authority of our country. It is a war *quoad hoc*. As far as Congress tolerated and authorized the war on our part, so far may we proceed in hostile operations. It is a maritime war; a war at sea as to certain purposes. The national armed vessels of France attack and capture the national armed vessels of the United States, and the national armed vessels of the United States are expressly authorized and directed to attack, subdue, and take the national armed vessels of France, and also to recapture American vessels. It is therefore a public war between the two nations, qualified, on our part, in the manner prescribed by the constitutional organ of our country. In such a state of things, it is scarcely necessary to add that the term "enemy," applies; it is the appropriate expression, to be limited in its signification, import, and use, by the qualified nature and operation of the war on our part. The word "enemy" proceeds the full length of the war, and no further ... The word "prizes" in this section can apply to the French, and the French only. This is decisive on the subject of legislative intention.

By the Court:

Let the decree of the circuit court be affirmed.

Commentary and Questions

1. In the *Glass* case, the sloop *Betsey* was captured by the French privateer *The Citizen Genet* whose captain declared the captured sloop as prize and had it sailed to the port in Baltimore. Glass was an American businessman who had a financial interest in the sloop *Betsey*, a ship also owned by citizens of Sweden that sailed under the Swedish flag. Sweden was a neutral party at the time. Both Glass and the Swedish owners brought the action for restoration of their ownership rights to the ship and its cargo in the District Court of Maryland. The French commander sought to have the prize claim determined by French consuls in America. What is the significance of Chief Justice Jay's opinion with regard to American jurisdiction over foreign nations?

2. The U.S Supreme Court was still relatively new and ineffective in 1794 at the time of the *Glass* case. The seminal decision of *Marbury v. Madison*, 5 U.S. 137 (1803) would be nine years away. The fourth Chief Justice, John Marshall, established the concept of judicial review and asserted the Article III powers of the Court in *Marbury* thereby establishing his place in our legal and constitutional history. Yet, the simple opinion of Chief Justice Jay in *Glass* won him much praise at the time. That same year he would be sent to London by President Washington to negotiate an agreement with the British regarding issues unresolved since the Treaty of Paris of 1783, which ended the War for Independence with Britain. The Jay Treaty, as it became known, was an agreement regarding commerce and admiralty matters between the two countries.[10] The treaty was important because of the un-settled atmosphere abroad with the United States' former ally France's ongoing revolution and the increasing hostility between the United States and Britain. The Jay Treaty was a major step in assuring American security at home and in commerce. As part of the negotiated agreement the British government would vacate the remaining forts the country occupied in the western part of the United States. Additionally, both governments agreed to compensate each country's ship owners whose vessels were destroyed or captured by the opposing side and disagreements over any remaining wartime debts were to be submitted to arbitration. Britain was also given most favored nation trade status and the United States agreed not to interfere with anti-French maritime policies adopted by Britain. These were but a number of agreements entered into by the two countries that provided a measure of stability and security for the United States and was recognition by Britain of its former colonies as a world power. Article XVII of the treaty provided a procedure for when vessels were captured and suspected of possessing enemy property on board: *"It is agreed, that in all cases where vessels shall be captured or detained on just suspicion of having on board*

enemy's property, or of carrying to the enemy any of the articles which are contraband of war; the said vessel shall be brought to the nearest or most convenient port; and if any property of an enemy shall be found on board such vessel, that part of which belongs to the enemy shall be made prize, and the vessel shall be at liberty to proceed with the remainder without an impediment. And it is agreed, that all proper measures shall be taken to prevent delay, in deciding the cases of ships or cargoes so brought in for adjudication; and in payment or recovery of any indemnification, adjudged or agreed to be paid to the masters or owners of such ships."[11]

Treaties have the force and effect of law. Authority to enter into and make treaties resides with the president under Article II, section 2, clause 2 of the Constitution. The president, however, must act with the advice and consent of the Senate. What did the Court state in *Glass v. The Betsey* with regard to the existence of treaties in connection with the dispute between Alexander Glass and *Citizen Genet* Captain Pierre Arcade Johannene?

3. *Bas v. Tingy* was also a prize case before the U.S. Supreme Court, but the threshold question in the case differed from the jurisdictional consideration before Chief Justice Jay in *Glass v. The Betsey*. What was the constitutional question the Court had to consider in *Bas v. Tingy*?

4. At issue in *Bas v. Tingy* was a dispute over payment on a seized ship according to the law of prize. Bas, the appellant in the case, was the owner of the ship *Eliza*, an American vessel that had been captured by the French. Tingy, captain of the *Ganges*, reclaimed the ship. Congress passed an Act of June 28, 1798, which declared: *"That whenever any vessel the property of or employed by any citizen of the United States or person resident therein or any goods or effects belonging to any such citizen or resident shall be recaptured by any public armed vessel of the United States, the same shall be restored to the former owner or owners upon due proof, he or they paying and allowing, as and for salvage to the recaptors, one-eighth part of the value of such vessel, goods, and effects, free from all deduction and expenses."* A little less than a year later by an Act of March 2, 1799, Congress passed a superseding Act: *"That for the ships or goods belonging to the citizens of the United States or to the citizens or subjects of any nation in amity with the United States, if retaken from the enemy within twenty-four hours, the owners are to allow one-eighth part of the whole value for salvage, ... and if above ninety-six hours one-half all of which is to be paid without any deduction whatsoever ...."* A later section of the 1799 Act provided for one-half compensation for the officers and seaman who recaptured the vessel. Although the compensation was at the core of the dispute, with Bas seeking to make the lesser payment to the crew of the *Ganges*, the U.S. Supreme Court had to consider the congressional shift in language from the 1798 Act to the inclusion of the word "enemy" in the 1799 Act. Why was the inclusion of the word "enemy" in the later act so critical? What did the Court say with respect to the existence of a war? Are there modern parallels to the reasoning of the Court?

5. How did each of the Justices address the issue differently in the *Bas* opinion?

Ex Parte Bollman and Ex Parte Swartwout
8 U. S. 75 (1807)

Mr. Chief Justice Marshall delivered the opinion of the Court.

The prisoners having been brought before this Court on a writ of habeas corpus, and the testimony on which they were committed having been fully examined and attentively considered, the Court is now to declare the law upon their case.

This being a mere inquiry, which, without deciding upon guilt, precedes the institution of a prosecution, the question to be determined is whether the accused shall be discharged or held to trial, and if the latter in what place they are to be tried, and whether they shall be confined or admitted to bail. "If," says a very learned and accurate commentator, "upon this inquiry it manifestly appears that no such crime has been committed, or that the suspicion entertained of the prisoner was wholly groundless, in such cases only is it lawful totally to discharge him. Otherwise he must either be committed to prison or give bail."

The specific charge brought against the prisoners is treason in levying war against the United States.

As there is no crime which can more excite and agitate the passions of men than treason, no charge demands more from the tribunal before which it is made a deliberate and temperate inquiry. Whether this inquiry be directed to the fact or to the law, none can be more solemn, none more important to the citizen or to the government; none can more affect the safety of both.

To prevent the possibility of those calamities which result from the extension of treason to offenses of minor importance, that great fundamental law which defines and limits the various departments of our government has given a rule on the subject both to the legislature and the courts of America, which neither can be permitted to transcend.

"Treason against the United States shall consist only in levying war against them, or in adhering to their enemies, giving them aid and comfort."

To constitute that specific crime for which the prisoners now before the court have been committed, war must be actually levied against the United States. However flagitious may be the crime of conspiring to subvert by force the government of our country, such conspiracy is not treason. To conspire to levy war, and actually to levy war, the distinct offenses. The first must be brought into operation by the assemblage of men for a purpose treasonable in itself or the fact of levying war cannot have been committed.

***

It is not the intention of the Court to say that no individual can be guilty of this crime who has not appeared in arms against his country. On the contrary, if war be actually levied—that is if a body of men be actually assembled for the purpose of effecting by force a treasonable purpose—all those who perform any part, however minute or however remote from the scene of action, and who are actually leagued in the general conspiracy, are to be considered as traitors. But there must be an actual assembling of men for the treasonable purpose to constitute a levying of war.

Crimes so atrocious as those which have for their object the subversion by violence of those laws and those institutions which have been ordained in order to secure the peace and happiness of society are not to escape punishment because they have not ripened into treason. The wisdom of the legislature is competent to provide for the case, and the framers of our Constitution, who not only defined and limited the crime but with jealous circumspection attempted to protect their limitation by providing that no person should be convicted of it unless on the testimony of two witnesses to the same overt act or on confession in open court, must have conceived it more safe that punishment in such cases should be ordained by general laws, formed upon deliberation, under the influence of no resentments, and without knowing on whom they were to operate than that it should be inflicted under the influence of those passions which the occasion seldom fails to excite and which a flexible definition of the crime or a construction which would render it flexible might bring into operation. It is therefore more safe as well as more consonant to the principles of our Constitution that the crime of treason should not be extended by construction to doubtful cases, and that crimes not clearly within the constitutional definition should receive such punishment as the legislature in its wisdom may provide.

To complete the crime of levying war against the United States, there must be an actual assemblage of men for the purpose of executing a treasonable design. In the case now before the Court, a design to overturn the government of the United States in New Orleans by force would have been unquestionably a design which, if carried into execution, would have been treason, and the assemblage of a body of men for the purpose of carrying it into execution would amount to levying of war against the United States; but no conspiracy for this object, no enlisting of men to effect it, would be an actual levying of war.

In conformity with the principles now laid down have been the decisions heretofore made by the judges of the United States.

***

The application of these general principles to the particular case before the Court will depend on the testimony which has been exhibited against the accused.

The first deposition to be considered is that of General Eaton. This gentleman connects in one statement the purport of numerous conversations held with Colonel Burr throughout the last winter. In the course of these conversations were communicated various criminal projects which seem to have been revolving in the mind of the projector. An expedition against Mexico seems to have been the first and most matured part of his plan, if indeed it did not constitute a distinct and separate plan, upon the success of which other schemes still more culpable, but not yet well digested, might depend. Maps and other information preparatory to its execution, and which would rather indicate that it was the immediate object, had been procured, and for a considerable time, in repeated conversations, the whole efforts of Colonel Burr were directed to prove to the witness, who was to have held a high command under him, the practicability of the enterprise, and in explaining to him the means by which it was to be effected.

This deposition exhibits the various schemes of Col. Burr, and its materiality depends on connecting the prisoners at the bar in such of those schemes as were treasonable. For this purpose the affidavit of General Wilkinson, comprehending in its body the substance of a letter from Colonel Burr, has been offered, and was received by the circuit court. To the admission of this testimony great and serious objections have been made. It has been urged that it is a voluntary, or rather an extrajudicial, affidavit, made before a person not appearing to be a magistrate, and contains the substance only of a letter, of which the original is retained by the person who made the affidavit.

The objection that the affidavit is extrajudicial resolves itself into the question whether one magistrate may commit on an affidavit taken before another magistrate. For if he may, an affidavit made as the foundation of a commitment ceases to be extrajudicial, and the person who makes it would be as liable to a prosecution for perjury as if the warrant of commitment had been issued by the magistrate before whom the affidavit was made.

To decide that an affidavit made before one magistrate would not justify a commitment by another might in many cases be productive of great inconvenience, and does not appear susceptible of abuse if the verity of the certificate be established. Such an affidavit seems admissible on the principle that before the accused is put upon his trial, all the proceedings are *ex parte*. The Court therefore overrules this objection.

That which questions the character of the person who has on this occasion administered the oath is next to be considered.

The certificate from the Office of the Department of State has been deemed insufficient by the counsel for the prisoners because the law does not require the appointment of magistrates for the territory of New Orleans to be certified to that office, because the certificate is in itself informal, and because it does not appear that the magistrate had taken the oath required by the act of Congress.

The first of these objections is not supported by the law of the case, and the second may be so readily corrected that the Court has proceeded to consider the subject as if it were corrected, retaining however any final decision, if against the prisoners, until the correction shall be made. With regard to the third, the magistrate must be presumed to have taken the requisite oaths, since he is found acting as a magistrate.

On the admissibility of that part of the affidavit which purports to be as near the substance of the letter from Colonel Burr to General Wilkinson as the latter could interpret it, a division of opinion has taken place in the Court. Two judges are of opinion that as such testimony delivered in the presence of the prisoner on his trial would be totally inadmissible, neither can it be considered as a foundation for a commitment. Although in making a commitment the magistrate does not decide on the guilt of the prisoner, yet he does decide on the probable cause, and a long and painful imprisonment may be the consequence of his decision. This probable cause, therefore, ought to be proved by testimony in itself legal, and which, though from the nature of the case it must be *ex parte*, ought in many other respects to be such as a court and jury might hear.

Two judges are of opinion that in this incipient stage of the prosecution an affidavit stating the general purport of a letter may be read, particularly where the person in possession of it is at too great a distance to admit of its being obtained, and that a commitment may be founded on it.

Under this embarrassment it was deemed necessary to look into the affidavit for the purpose of discovering whether, if admitted, it contains matter which would justify the commitment of the prisoners at the bar on the charge of treason.

That the letter from Colonel Burr to General Wilkinson relates to a military enterprise mediated by the former has not been questioned. If this enterprise was against Mexico, it would amount to a high misdemeanor; if against any of the territories of the United States or if in its progress the subversion of the government of the United States in any of their territories was a means clearly and necessarily to be employed, if such means formed a substantive part of the plan, the assemblage of a body of men to effect it would be levying war against the United States.

The letter is in language which furnishes no distinct view of the design of the writer. The cooperation, however, which is stated to have been secured points strongly to some expedition against the territories of Spain. After making these general statements, the writer becomes rather more explicit and says "Burr's plan of operations is to move down rapidly from the falls on 15 November with the first 500 or 1,000 men in light boats now constructing for that purpose, to be at Natchez between 5 and 15 December, there to meet Wilkinson; then to determine whether it will be expedient in the first instance to seize on or to pass by Baton Rouge. The people of the country to which we are going are prepared to receive us. Their agents now with Burr say that if we will protect their religion and will not subject them to a foreign power, in three weeks all will be settled."

There is no expression in these sentences which would justify a suspicion that any territory of the United States was the object of the expedition.

For what purpose seize on Baton Rouge; why engage Spain against this enterprise if it was designed against the United States?

"The people of the country to which we are going are prepared to receive us." This language is peculiarly appropriate to a foreign country. It will not be contended that the terms would be inapplicable to a territory of the United States, but other terms would more aptly convey the idea, and Burr seems to consider himself as giving information of which Wilkinson was not possessed. When it is recollected that he was the governor of a territory adjoining that which must have been threatened if a territory of the United States was threatened, and that he commanded the army, a part of which was stationed in that territory, the probability that the information communicated related to a foreign country, it must be admitted, gains strength.

"Their agents now with Burr say that if we will protect their religion and will not subject them to a foreign power, in three weeks all will be settled."

This is apparently the language of a people who, from the contemplated change in their political situation, feared for their religion and feared that they would be made the subjects of a foreign power. That the Mexicans should entertain these apprehensions was natural, and would readily be believed. They were, if the representation made of their dispositions be correct, about to place themselves much in the power of men who professed a different faith from theirs and who, by making them dependent on England or the United States, would subject them to a foreign power.

That the people of New Orleans, as a people, if really engaged in the conspiracy, should feel the same apprehensions and require assurances on the same points is by no means so obvious.

There certainly is not in the letter delivered to Gen. Wilkinson, so far as that letter is laid before the Court, one syllable which has a necessary or a natural reference to an enterprise against any territory of the United States.

That the bearer of this letter must be considered as acquainted with its contents is not to be controverted. The letter and his own declarations evince the fact.

After stating himself to have passed through New York and the western states and territories without insinuating that he had performed on his route any act whatever which was connected with the enterprise, he states their object to be, "to carry an expedition into the Mexican provinces."

This statement may be considered as explanatory of the letter of Col. Burr if the expressions of that letter could be thought ambiguous.

But there are other declarations made by Mr. Swartwout which constitute the difficulty of this case. On an inquiry from General Wilkinson, he said "this territory would be revolutionized where the people were ready to join them, and that there would be some seizing, he supposed, at New Orleans."

If these words import that the government established by the United States in any of its territories was to be revolutionized by force, although merely as a step to or a means of executing some greater projects, the design was unquestionably treasonable, and any assemblage of men for that purpose would amount to a levying of war. But on the import of the words a difference of opinion exists. Some of the judges suppose they refer to the territory against which the expedition was intended; others to that in which the conversation was held. Some consider the words, if even applicable to a territory of the United States, as alluding to a revolution to be effected by the people, rather than by the party conducted by Col. Burr.

But whether this treasonable intention be really imputable to the plan or not, it is admitted that it must have been carried into execution by an open assemblage of men for that purpose previous to the arrest of the prisoner in order to consummate the crime as to him, and a majority of the Court is of opinion that the conversation of Mr. Swartwout affords no sufficient proof of such assembling.

The prisoner stated that "Col. Burr, with the support of a powerful association extending from New York to New Orleans, was levying an armed body of 7,000 men from the State of New York and the western states and territories, with a view to carry an expedition to the Mexican territories." That the association, whatever may be its purpose, is not treason has been already stated. That levying an army may or may not be treason, and that this depends on the intention with which it is levied and on the point to which the parties have advanced, has been also stated. The mere enlisting of men, without assembling them, is not levying war. The question then is whether this evidence proves Col. Burr to have advanced so far in levying an army as actually to have assembled them.

It is argued that since it cannot be necessary that the whole 7,000 men should have assembled, their commencing their march by detachments to the place of rendezvous must be sufficient to constitute the crime.

This position is correct, with some qualification. It cannot be necessary that the whole army should assemble and that the various parts which are to compose it should have combined. But it is necessary that there should be an actual assemblage, and therefore the evidence should make the fact unequivocal.

The traveling of individuals to the place of rendezvous would perhaps not be sufficient. This would be an equivocal act, and has no warlike appearance. The meeting of particular bodies of men and their marching from places of partial to a place of general rendezvous would be such an assemblage.

The particular words used by Mr. Swartwout are that Col. Burr "was levying an armed body of 7,000 men."

If the term "levying" in this place imports that they were assembled, then such fact would amount, if the intention be against the United States, to levying war. If it barely imports that he was enlisting or engaging them in his service, the fact would not amount to levying war.

It is thought sufficiently apparent that the latter is the sense in which the term was used. The fact alluded to, if taken in the former sense, is of a nature so to force itself upon the public view that if the army had then actually assembled, either together or in detachments, some evidence of such assembling would have been laid before the court.

The words used by the prisoner in reference to seizing at New Orleans and borrowing perhaps by force from the bank, though indicating a design to rob, and consequently importing a high offense, do not designate the specific crime of levying war against the United States.

It is therefore the opinion of a majority of the Court that in the case of Samuel Swartwout, there is not sufficient evidence of his levying war against the United States to justify his commitment on the charge of treason.

Against Erick Bollman there is still less testimony. Nothing has been said by him to support the charge that the enterprise in which he was engaged had any other object than was stated in the letter of Colonel Burr. Against him, therefore, there is no evidence to support a charge of treason.

That both of the prisoners were engaged in a most culpable enterprise against the dominions of a power at peace with the United States those who admit the affidavit of General Wilkinson cannot doubt. But that no part of this crime was committed in the District of Columbia is apparent. It is therefore the unanimous opinion of the court that they cannot be tried in this district.

The law read on the part of the prosecution is understood to apply only to offenses committed on the high seas or in any river, haven, basin, or bay not within the jurisdiction of any particular state. In those cases there is no court which has particular cognizance of the crime, and therefore the place in which the criminal shall be apprehended, or, if he be apprehended where no court has exclusive jurisdiction, that to which he shall be first brought, is substituted for the place in which the offense was committed.

But in this case, a tribunal for the trial of the offense, wherever it may have been committed, had been provided by Congress, and at the place where the prisoners were seized by the authority of the commander in chief there existed such a tribunal. It would, too, be extremely dangerous to say that because the prisoners were apprehended not by a civil magistrate, but by the military power, there could be given by law a right to try the persons so seized in any place which the general might select and to which he might direct them to be carried.

The act of Congress which the prisoners are supposed to have violated describes as offenders those who begin or set on foot, or provide, or prepare the means for any military expedition or enterprise to be carried on from thence against the dominions of a foreign prince or state with whom the United States is at peace.

There is a want of precision in the description of the offense which might produce some difficulty in deciding what cases would come within it. But several other questions arise which a Court consisting of four judges finds itself unable to decide, and therefore, as the crime with which the prisoners stand charged has not been committed, the Court can only direct them to be discharged. This is done with the less reluctance because the discharge does not acquit them from the offense which there is probable cause for supposing they have committed, and if those whose duty it is to protect the nation by prosecuting offenders against the laws shall suppose those who have been charged with treason to be proper objects for punishment, they will, when possessed of less exceptionable testimony and when able to say at what place the offense has been committed, institute fresh proceedings against them.

Martin v. Mott
25 U.S. (12 Wheat.) 19 (1827)

Mr. Justice Story delivered the opinion of the Court.

This is a writ of error to the judgment of the Court for the Trial of Impeachments and the Correction of Errors of the State of New York, being the highest court of that state, and is brought here in virtue of the 25th section of the Judiciary Act of 1789, ch. 20. The original action was a replevin for certain goods and chattels, to which the original defendant put in an avowry, and to that avowry there was a demurrer assigning nineteen distinct and special causes of demurrer. Upon a joinder in demurrer, the supreme court of the state gave judgment against the avowant, and that judgment was affirmed by the high court to which the present writ of error is addressed.

The avowry in substance asserts a justification of the taking of the goods and chattels to satisfy a fine and forfeiture imposed upon the original plaintiff by a court martial for a failure to enter the service of the United States as a militiaman, when thereto required by the President of the United States in pursuance of the Act of 28 February, 1795, c. 101. It is argued that this avowry is defective both in substance and form, and it will be our business to discuss the most material of these objections, and as to others, of which no particular notice is taken, it is to be understood that the Court is of opinion that they are either unfounded in fact or in law and do not require any separate examination.

For the more clear and exact consideration of the subject, it may be necessary to refer to the Constitution of the United States and some of the provisions of the act of 1795. The Constitution declares that Congress shall have power "to provide for calling forth the militia, to execute the laws of the Union, suppress insurrections, and repel invasions," and also "to provide for organizing, arming, and disciplining the militia and for governing such part of them as may be employed in the service of the United States." In pursuance of this authority, the act of 1795 has provided: "That whenever the United States shall be invaded or be in imminent danger of invasion from any foreign nation or Indian tribe, it shall be lawful for the President of the United States to call forth such number of the militia of the state or states most convenient to the place of danger or scene of action as he may judge necessary to repel such invasion, and to issue his order for that purpose to such officer or officers of the militia as he shall think proper."

And like provisions are made for the other cases stated in the Constitution. It has not been denied here that the act of 1795 is within the constitutional authority of Congress or that Congress may not lawfully provide for cases of imminent danger of invasion, as well as for cases where an invasion has actually taken place. In our opinion, there is no ground for a doubt on this point, even if it had been relied on, for the power to provide for repelling invasions includes the power to provide against the attempt and danger of invasion, as the necessary and proper means to effectuate the object. One of the best means to repel invasion is to provide the requisite force for action before the invader himself has reached the soil.

The power thus confided by Congress to the President is doubtless, of a very high and delicate nature. A free people are naturally jealous of the exercise of military power, and the power to call the militia into actual service is certainly felt to be one of no ordinary magnitude. But it is not a power which can be executed without a correspondent responsibility. It is, in its terms, a limited power, confined to cases of actual invasion or of imminent danger of invasion. If it be a limited power, the question arises by whom is the exigency to be judged of and decided? Is the President the sole and exclusive judge whether the exigency has arisen, or is it to be considered as an open question, upon which every officer to whom the orders of the President are addressed, may decide for himself, and equally open to be contested by every militiaman who shall refuse to obey the orders of the President? We are all of opinion that the authority to decide whether the exigency has arisen belongs exclusively to the President, and that his decision is conclusive upon all other persons. We think that this construction necessarily results from the nature of the power itself and from the manifest object contemplated by the act of Congress. The power itself is to be exercised upon sudden emergencies, upon great occasions of state, and under circumstances which may be vital to the existence of the Union. A prompt and unhesitating obedience to orders is indispensable to the complete attainment of the object.

***

If we look at the language of the act of 1795, every conclusion drawn from the nature of the power itself is strongly fortified. The words are "whenever the United States shall be invaded or be in imminent danger of invasion, &c., it shall be lawful for the President, &c., to call forth such number of the militia, &c., as he may judge necessary to repel such invasion."

The power itself is confided to the Executive of the Union, to him who is, by the Constitution, "the commander-in-chief of the militia, when called into the actual service of the United States," whose duty it is to "take care that the laws be faithfully executed," and whose responsibility for an honest discharge of his official obligations is secured by the highest sanctions. He is necessarily constituted the judge of the existence of the exigency in the first instance, and is bound to act according to his belief of the facts. If he does so act and decides to call forth the militia, his orders for this purpose are in strict conformity with the provisions of the law, and it would seem to follow as a necessary consequence that every act done by a subordinate officer in obedience to such orders is equally justifiable. The law contemplates that under such circumstances orders shall be given to carry the power into effect, and it cannot therefore be a correct inference that any other person has a just right to disobey them. The law does not provide for any appeal from the judgment of the President or for any right in subordinate officers to review his decision and in effect defeat it. Whenever a statute gives a discretionary power to any person to be exercised by him upon his own opinion of certain facts, it is a sound rule of construction that the statute constitutes him the sole and exclusive judge of the existence of those facts. And in the present case we are all of opinion that such is the true construction of the act of 1795. It is no answer that such a power may be abused, for there is no power which is not susceptible of abuse. The remedy for this, as well as for all other official misconduct, if it should occur, is to be found in the Constitution itself. In a free government, the danger must be remote, since in addition to the high qualities which the Executive must be presumed to possess, of public virtue, and honest devotion to the public interests, the frequency of elections, and the watchfulness of the representatives of the nation carry with them all the checks which can be useful to guard against usurpation or wanton tyranny.

***

But it is now contended, as it was contended in that case, that notwithstanding the judgment of the President is conclusive as to the existence of the exigency and may be given in evidence as conclusive proof thereof, yet that the avowry is fatally defective, because it omits to aver that the fact did exist. The argument is that the power confided to the President is a limited power, and can be exercised only in the cases pointed out in the statute, and therefore it is necessary to aver the facts which bring the exercise within the purview of the statute. In short, the same principles are sought to be applied to the delegation and exercise of this power entrusted to the Executive of the nation for great political purposes as might be applied to the humblest officer in the government, acting upon the most narrow and special authority. It is the opinion of the Court that this objection cannot be maintained. When the President exercises an authority confided to him by law, the presumption is that it is exercised in pursuance of law. Every public officer is presumed to act in obedience to his duty until the contrary is shown, and a fortiori this presumption ought to be favorably applied to the chief magistrate of the Union.

***

Another objection is that the orders of the President are not set forth, nor is it averred that he issued any orders, but only that the Governor of New York called out the militia upon the requisition of the President. The objection, so far as it proceeds upon a supposed difference between a requisition and an order, is untenable, for a requisition calling forth the militia is, in legal intendment, an order, and must be so interpreted in this avowry.

***

The next objection is that it does not sufficiently appear in the avowry that the court martial was a lawfully constituted court martial, having jurisdiction of the offense at the time of passing its sentence against the original plaintiff.

Various grounds have been assigned in support of this objection. In the first place it is said that the original plaintiff was never employed in the service of the United States, but refused to enter that service, and that consequently he was not liable to the rules and articles of war or to be tried for the offense by any court martial organized under the authority of the United States. The case of *Houston v. Moore*, 5 Wheat. 1, affords a conclusive answer to this suggestion. It was decided in that case that although a militiaman who refused to obey the orders of the President calling him into the public service was not, in the sense of the act of 1795, "employed in the service of the United States" so as to be subject to the rules and articles of war, yet that he was liable to be tried for the offense under the 5th section of the same act by a court martial called under the authority of the United States. The great doubt in that case was whether the delinquent was liable to be tried for the offense by a court martial organized under state authority.

In the next place it is said the court martial was not composed of the proper number of officers required by law. In order to understand the force of this objection it is necessary to advert to the terms of the act of 1795 and the rules and articles of war. The act of 1795 (s. 5) provides:

"That every officer, noncommissioned officer, or private of the militia who shall fail to obey the orders of the President of the United States ... shall forfeit a sum not exceeding one year's pay and not less than one month's pay, to be determined and adjudged by a court martial."

And it further provides (s. 6) "that courts martial for the trial of militia shall be composed of militia officers only." These are the only provisions in the act on this subject. It is not stated by whom the courts martial shall be called, nor in what manner, nor of what number they shall be composed. But the court is referred to the 64th and 65th of the rules and articles of war, enacted by the act of 10 April, 1806, ch. 20., which provide: "That general courts martial may consist of any number of commissioned officers from five to thirteen inclusively, but they shall not consist of less than thirteen where that number can be convened without manifest injury to the service," and that "any general officer commanding an army or colonel commanding a separate department may appoint general courts martial when necessary." Supposing these clauses applicable to the court martial in question, it is very clear that the act is merely directory to the officer appointing the court, and that his decision as to the number which can be convened without manifest injury to the service, being in a matter submitted to his sound discretion, must be conclusive. But the present avowry goes further and alleges not only that the court martial was appointed by a general officer commanding an army, that it was composed of militia officers, naming them, but it goes on to assign the reason why a number short of thirteen composed the court, in the very terms of the 64th article, and the truth of this allegation is admitted by the demurrer. Tried, therefore, by the very test which has been resorted to in support of the objection, it utterly fails.

But in strictness of law the propriety of this resort may admit of question. The rules and articles of war, by the very terms of the statute of 1806, are those "by which the armies of the United States shall be governed," and the act of 1795 has only provided: "That the militia employed in the service of the United States [not the militia ordered into the service of the United States] shall be subject to the same rules and articles of war as the troops of the United States," and this is in substance reenacted by the 97th of the rules and articles of war. It is not, therefore, admitted that any express authority is given by either statute that such a court martial as is contemplated for the trial of delinquents under the 5th section of the act of 1795 is to be composed of the same number of officers, organized in the same manner as these rules and articles contemplate for persons in actual service. If any resort is to be had to them, it can only be to guide the discretion of the officer ordering the court, as matter of usage and not as matter of positive institution. If, then, there be no mode pointed out for the formation of the court martial in these cases, it may be asked in what manner is such court to be appointed? The answer is according to the general usage of the military service, or what may not unfitly be called the customary military law. It is by the same law that courts martial, when duly organized, are bound to execute their duties and regulate their modes of proceeding in the absence of positive enactments. Upon any other principle, courts martial would be left without any adequate means to exercise the authority confided to them, for there could scarcely be framed a positive code to provide for the infinite variety of incidents applicable to them.

The Act of 18 April, 1814, ch. 141. which expired at the end of the late war, was in a great measure intended to obviate difficulties arising from the imperfection of the provisions of the act of 1795, and especially to aid courts martial in exercising jurisdiction over cases like the present. But whatever may have been the legislative intention, its terms do not extend to the declaration of the number of which such courts martial shall be composed. The first section provides

"That courts martial to be composed of militia officers alone, for the trial of militia drafted, detached, and called forth [not or called forth] for the service of the United States, whether acting in conjunction with the regular forces or otherwise, shall, when necessary, be appointed, held, and conducted in the manner prescribed by the rules and articles of war for appointing, holding, and conducting courts martial for the trial of delinquents in the Army of the United States."

This language is obviously confined to the militia in the actual service of the United States, and does not extend to such as are drafted and refuse to obey the call. So that the Court is driven back to the act of 1795 as the legitimate source for the ascertainment of the organization and jurisdiction of the court martial in the present case. And we are of opinion that nothing appears on the face of the avowry to lead to any doubt that it was a legal court martial, organized according to military usage and entitled to take cognizance of the delinquencies stated in the avowry.

***

Another objection to the proceedings of the court martial is that they took place, and the sentence was given, three years and more after the war was concluded, and in a time of profound peace. But the opinion of this Court is that a court martial, regularly called under the act of 1795, does not expire with the end of a war then existing, nor is its jurisdiction to try these offenses in any shape dependent upon the fact of war or peace. The act of 1795 is not confined in its operation to cases of refusal to obey the orders of the President in times of public war. On the contrary, that act authorizes the President to call forth the militia to suppress insurrections, and to enforce the laws of the United States, in times of peace. And courts martial are, under the 5th section of the act, entitled to take cognizance of, and to punish delinquencies in such cases, as well as in cases where the object is to repel invasion in times of war. It would be a strained construction of the act to limit the authority of the court to the mere time of the existence of the particular exigency, when it might be thereby unable to take cognizance of, and decide upon a single offense. It is sufficient for us to say, that there is no such limitation in the act itself.

***

Of the remaining causes of special demurrer, some are properly matters of defense before the court martial, and its sentence being upon a subject within its jurisdiction, is conclusive, and others turn upon niceties of pleading, to which no separate answers are deemed necessary. In general it may be said of them that the Court does not deem them well founded objections to the avowry.

Upon the whole, it is the opinion of the Court that the judgment of the Court for the Trial of Impeachments and the Correction of Errors ought to be *Reversed and that the cause be remanded to the same court with directions to cause a judgment to be entered upon the pleadings in favor of the avowant.*

Judgment. This cause came on ... consideration, whereof it is Considered and Adjudged that there is error in the judgment of the said Court for the Trial of Impeachments and the Correction of Errors, in this that upon the pleadings in the cause, judgment ought to have been rendered in favor of the avowant, whereas it was rendered in favor of the original plaintiff, and it is therefore further Considered and Adjudged that the same judgment be and the same hereby is Reversed and Annulled, and also that the judgment of the Supreme Court of Judicature of the State of New York, which was affirmed by the said Court for the Trial of Impeachments and the Correction of Errors be Reversed and Annulled, and that judgment be rendered, that the said avowry is good and sufficient in law to bar the plaintiff's action, and that the plaintiff take nothing by his writ; and that the cause be remanded to the said Court for the Trial of Impeachments and the Correction of Errors, if the record be now in the said court, and if not, then to the Supreme Court of Judicature of the state aforesaid, to which the same has been remitted, with directions to cause judgment to be entered upon the pleadings in favor of the avowant.

Pennsylvania v. Nelson
350 U.S. 497 (1956)

Mr. Chief Justice Warren delivered the opinion of the Court.

The respondent Steve Nelson, an acknowledged member of the Communist Party, was convicted in the Court of Quarter Sessions of Allegheny County, Pennsylvania, of a violation of the Pennsylvania Sedition Act and sentenced to imprisonment for twenty years and to a fine of $10,000 and to costs of prosecution in the sum of $13,000. The Superior Court affirmed the conviction. 172 Pa.Super. 125, 92 A.2d 431. The Supreme Court of Pennsylvania, recognizing but not reaching many alleged serious trial errors and conduct of the trial court infringing upon respondent's right to due process of law, decided the case on the narrow issue of supersession of the state law by the Federal Smith Act. In its opinion, the court stated:

And, while the Pennsylvania statute proscribes sedition against either the Government of the United States or the Government of Pennsylvania, it is only alleged sedition against the United States with which the instant case is concerned. Out of all the voluminous testimony, we have not found, nor has anyone pointed to, a single word indicating a seditious act or even utterance directed against the Government of Pennsylvania.

The precise holding of the court, and all that is before us for review, is that the Smith Act of 1940, as amended in 1948, which prohibits the knowing advocacy of the overthrow of the Government of the United States by force and violence, supersedes the enforceability of the Pennsylvania Sedition Act, which proscribes the same conduct.

Many State Attorneys General and the Solicitor General of the United States appeared as *amici curiae* for petitioner, and several briefs were filed on behalf of the respondent. Because of the important question of federal-state relationship involved, we granted certiorari. 348 U.S. 814.

It should be said at the outset that the decision in this case does not affect the right of States to enforce their sedition laws at times when the Federal Government has not occupied the field and is not protecting the entire country from seditious conduct. The distinction between the two situations was clearly recognized by the court below. Nor does it limit the jurisdiction of the States where the Constitution and Congress have specifically given them concurrent jurisdiction, as was done under the Eighteenth Amendment and the Volstead Act. **United States v. Lanza**, 260 U.S. 377. Neither does it limit the right of the State to protect itself at any time against sabotage or attempted violence of all kinds. Nor does it prevent the State from prosecuting where the same act constitutes both a federal offense and a state offense under the police power, as was done in **Fox v. Ohio**, 5 How. 410, and **Gilbert v. Minnesota**, 254 U.S. 325, relied upon by petitioner as authority herein. In neither of those cases did the state statute impinge on federal jurisdiction. In the **Fox** case, the federal offense was counterfeiting. The state offense was defrauding the person to whom the spurious money was passed. In the **Gilbert** case this Court, in upholding the enforcement of a state statute, proscribing conduct which would "interfere with or discourage the enlistment of men in the military or naval forces of the United States or of the State of Minnesota," treated it not as an act relating to "the raising of armies for the national defense, nor to rules and regulations for the government of those under arms [a constitutionally exclusive federal power]. It [was] simply a local police measure ..."

Where, as in the instant case, Congress has not stated specifically whether a federal statute has occupied a field in which the States are otherwise free to legislate, different criteria have furnished touchstones for decision. Thus, [t]his Court, in considering the validity of state laws in the light of ... federal laws touching the same subject, has made use of the following expressions: conflicting; contrary to; occupying the field; repugnance; difference; irreconcilability; inconsistency; violation; curtailment, and interference. But none of these expressions provides an infallible constitutional test or an exclusive constitutional yardstick. In the final analysis, there can be no one crystal clear distinctly marked formula. **Hines v. Davidowitz**, 312 U.S. 52,

67. *And see* **Rice v. Santa Fe Elevator Corp.**, 331 U.S. 218, 230-231. In this case, we think that each of several tests of supersession is met.

First, [t]he scheme of federal regulation [is] so pervasive as to make reasonable the inference that Congress left no room for the States to supplement it. **Rice v. Santa Fe Elevator Corp.**, 331 U.S. at 230. The Congress determined in 1940 that it was necessary for it to reenter the field of anti-subversive legislation, which had been abandoned by it in 1921. In that year, it enacted the Smith Act, which proscribes advocacy of the overthrow of any government—federal, state or local—by force and violence and organization of and knowing membership in a group which so advocates. Conspiracy to commit any of these acts is punishable under the general criminal conspiracy provisions in 18 U.S.C. § 371. The Internal Security Act of 1950 is aimed more directly at Communist organizations. It distinguishes between "Communist action organizations" and "Communist front organizations," requiring such organizations to register and to file annual reports with the Attorney General giving complete details as to their officers and funds. Members of Communist action organizations who have not been registered by their organization must register as individuals. Failure to register in accordance with the requirements of Sections 786-787 is punishable by a fine of not more than $10,000 for an offending organization and by a fine of not more than $10,000 or imprisonment for not more than five years or both for an individual offender—each day of failure to register constituting a separate offense. And the Act imposes certain sanctions upon both "action" and "front" organizations and their members. The Communist Control Act of 1954 declares "that the Communist Party of the United States, although purportedly a political party, is, in fact, an instrumentality of a conspiracy to overthrow the Government of the United States," and that "its role as the agency of a hostile foreign power renders its existence a clear present and continuing danger to the security of the United States."

It also contains a legislative finding that the Communist Party is a "Communist action organization" within the meaning of the Internal Security Act of 1950, and provides that "knowing" members of the Communist Party are "subject to all the provisions and penalties" of that Act. It furthermore sets up a new classification of "Communist-infiltrated organizations," and provides for the imposition of sanctions against them.

We examine these Acts only to determine the congressional plan. Looking to all of them in the aggregate, the conclusion is inescapable that Congress has intended to occupy the field of sedition. Taken as a whole, they evince a congressional plan which makes it reasonable to determine that no room has been left for the States to supplement it. Therefore, a state sedition statute is superseded regardless of whether it purports to supplement the federal law. As was said by Mr.

Justice Holmes in **Charleston & Western Carolina R. Co. v. Varnville Furniture Co.**, 237 U.S. 597, 604:

When Congress has taken the particular subject matter in hand, coincidence is as ineffective as opposition, and a state law is not to be declared a help because it attempts to go farther than Congress has seen fit to go.

Second, the federal statutes touch a field in which the federal interest is so dominant that the federal system [must] be assumed to preclude enforcement of state laws on the same subject. **Rice v. Santa Fe Elevator Corp.**, 331 U.S. at 230, citing **Hines v. Davidowitz**, supra. Congress has devised an all-embracing program for resistance to the various forms of totalitarian aggression. Our external defenses have been strengthened, and a plan to protect against internal subversion has been made by it. It has appropriated vast sums, not only for our own protection, but also to strengthen freedom throughout the world. It has charged the Federal Bureau of Investigation and the Central Intelligence Agency with responsibility for intelligence concerning Communist seditious activities against our Government, and has de-nominated such activities as part of a world conspiracy. It accordingly proscribed sedition against all government in the nation—national, state and local. Congress declared that these steps were taken to provide for the common defense, to preserve the sovereignty of the United States as an independent nation, and to guarantee to each State a republican form of government ...

Congress having thus treated seditious conduct as a matter of vital national concern, it is in no sense a local enforcement problem. As was said in the court below:

Sedition against the United States is not a local offense. It is a crime against the Nation. As such, it should be prosecuted and punished in the Federal courts, where this defendant has, in fact, been prosecuted and convicted and is now under sentence. It is not only important, but vital, that such prosecutions should be exclusively within the control of the Federal Government ...

Third, enforcement of state sedition acts presents a serious danger of conflict with the administration of the federal program. Since 1939, in order to avoid a hampering of uniform enforcement of its program by sporadic local prosecutions, the Federal Government has urged local authorities not to intervene in such matters, but to turn over to the federal authorities immediately and unevaluated all information concerning subversive activities. The President made such a request on September 6, 1939, when he placed the Federal Bureau of Investigation in charge of investigation in this field: The Attorney General has been requested by me to instruct the Federal Bureau of Investigation of the Department of Justice to take charge of investigative work in matters relating to espionage, sabotage, and violations of the neutrality regulations.

This task must be conducted in a comprehensive and effective manner on a national basis, and all information must be carefully sifted out and correlated in order to avoid confusion and irresponsibility.

To this end, I request all police officers, sheriffs, and all other law enforcement officers in the United States promptly to turn over to the nearest representative of the Federal Bureau of Investigation any information obtained by them relating to espionage, counterespionage, sabotage, subversive activities and violations of the neutrality laws.

And, in addressing the Federal-State Conference on Law Enforcement Problems of National Defense, held on August 5 and 6, 1940, only a few weeks after the passage of the Smith Act, the Director of the Federal Bureau of Investigation said:

The fact must not be overlooked that meeting the spy, the saboteur and the subverter is a problem that must be handled on a nationwide basis. An isolated incident in the middle west may be of little significance, but, when fitted into a national pattern of similar incidents, it may lead to an important revelation of subversive activity. It is for this reason that the President requested all of our citizens and law enforcing agencies to report directly to the Federal Bureau of Investigation any complaints or information dealing with espionage, sabotage or subversive activities. In such matters, time is of the essence. It is unfortunate that, in a few States, efforts have been made by individuals not fully acquainted with the far-flung ramifications of this problem to interject superstructures of agencies between local law enforcement and the FBI to sift what might be vital information, thus delaying its immediate reference to the FBI. This cannot be if our internal security is to be best served. This is no time for red tape or amateur handling of such vital matters. There must be a direct and free flow of contact between the local law enforcement agencies and the FBI. The job of meeting the spy or saboteur is one for experienced men of law enforcement.

Moreover, the Pennsylvania Statute presents a peculiar danger of interference with the federal program. For, as the court below observed:

Unlike the Smith Act, which can be administered only by federal officers acting in their official capacities, indictment for sedition under the Pennsylvania statute can be initiated upon an information made by a private individual. The opportunity thus present for the indulgence of personal spite and hatred or for furthering some selfish advantage or ambition need only be mentioned to be appreciated. Defense of the Nation by law, no less than by arms, should be a public, and not a private, undertaking. It is important that punitive sanctions for sedition against the United States be such as have been promulgated by the central governmental authority and administered under the supervision and review of that authority's judiciary. If that be done, sedition will be detected and punished no less, wherever it may be found, and the right of the individual to speak freely and without fear, even in criticism of the government, will, at the same time, be protected.

In his brief, the Solicitor General states that forty-two States plus Alaska and Hawaii have statutes which, in some form, prohibit advocacy of the violent overthrow of established government. These statutes are entitled anti-sedition statutes, criminal anarchy laws, criminal syndicalist laws, etc. Although all of them are primarily directed against the overthrow of the United States Government, they are in no sense uniform. And our attention has not been called to any case where the prosecution has been successfully directed against an attempt to destroy state or local government. Some of these Acts are studiously drawn, and purport to protect fundamental rights by appropriate definitions, standards of proof, and orderly procedures in keeping with the avowed congressional purpose "to protect freedom from those who would destroy it, without infringing upon the freedom of all our people." Others are vague, and are almost wholly without such safeguards. Some even purport to punish mere membership in subversive organizations, which the federal statutes do not punish where federal registration requirements have been fulfilled.

When we were confronted with a like situation in the field of labor-management relations, Mr. Justice Jackson wrote:

A multiplicity of tribunals and a diversity of procedures are quite as apt to produce incompatible or conflicting adjudications as are different rules of substantive law.

Should the States be permitted to exercise a concurrent jurisdiction in this area, federal enforcement would encounter not only the difficulties mentioned by Mr. Justice Jackson, but the added conflict engendered by different criteria of substantive offenses.

Since we find that Congress has occupied the field to the exclusion of parallel state legislation, that the dominant interest of the Federal Government precludes state intervention, and that administration of state Acts would conflict with the operation of the federal plan, we are convinced that the decision of the Supreme Court of Pennsylvania is unassailable.

We are not unmindful of the risk of compounding punishments which would be created by finding concurrent state power. In our view of the case, we do not reach the question whether double or multiple punishment for the same overt acts directed against the United States has constitutional sanction. Without compelling indication to the contrary, we will not assume that Congress intended to permit the possibility of double punishment. Cf. **Houston v. Moore**, 5 Wheat. 1, 31, 75; **Jerome v. United States**, 318 U.S. 101, 105.

The judgment of the Supreme Court of Pennsylvania is Affirmed.

APPENDIX

Pennsylvania Penal Code § 207

The word "sedition," as used in this section, shall mean:
Any writing, publication, printing, cut, cartoon, utterance, or conduct, either individually or in connection or combination with any other person, the intent of which is:

(a) To make or cause to be made any outbreak or demonstration of violence against this State or against the United States.

(b) To encourage any person to take any measures or engage in any conduct with a view of overthrowing or destroying or attempting to overthrow or destroy, by any force or show or threat of force, the Government of this State or of the United States.

(c) To incite or encourage any person to commit any overt act with a view to bringing the Government of this State or of the United States into hatred or contempt.

(d) To incite any person or persons to do or attempt to do personal injury or harm to any officer of this State or of the United States, or to damage or destroy any public property or the property of any public official because of his official position.

The word "sedition" shall also include:

(e) The actual damage to, or destruction of, any public property or the property of any public official, perpetrated because the owner or occupant is in official position.

(f) Any writing, publication, printing, cut, cartoon, or utterance which advocates or teaches the duty, necessity, or propriety of engaging in crime, violence, or any form of terrorism, as a means of accomplishing political reform or change in government.

(g) The sale, gift or distribution of any prints, publications, books, papers, documents, or written matter in any form, which advocates, furthers or teaches sedition as hereinbefore defined.

(h) Organizing or helping to organize or becoming a member of any assembly, society, or group, where any of the policies or purposes thereof are seditious as hereinbefore defined.

Sedition shall be a felony. Whoever is guilty of sedition shall, upon conviction thereof, be sentenced to pay a fine not exceeding ten thousand dollars ($10,000), or to undergo imprisonment not exceeding twenty (20) years, or both.

18 U.S.C. § 2385

Whoever knowingly or willfully advocates, abets, advises, or teaches the duty, necessity, desirability, or propriety of overthrowing or destroying the government of the United States or the government of any State, Territory, District or Possession thereof, or the government of any political subdivision therein, by force or violence, or by the assassination of any officer of any such government; or

Whoever, with intent to cause the overthrow or destruction of any such government, prints, publishes, edits, issues, circulates, sells, distributes, or publicly displays any written or printed matter advocating, advising, or teaching the duty, necessity, desirability, or propriety of overthrowing or destroying any government in the United States by force or violence, or attempts to do so; or

Whoever organizes or helps or attempts to organize any society, group, or assembly of persons who teach, advocate, or encourage the overthrow or destruction of any such government by force or violence; or becomes or is a member of, or affiliates with, any such society, group, or assembly of persons, knowing the purposes thereof—shall be fined not more than $10,000 or imprisoned not more than ten years, or both, and shall be ineligible for employment by the United States or any department or agency thereof, for the five years next following his conviction.

Commentary and Questions

6. *Ex Parte Bollman* is an early case that set the standard for treasonous conduct. Article III, section 3 of the Constitution provides: *"Treason against the United States, shall consist only in levying War against them, or in adhering to their Enemies, giving them Aid and Comfort."* Bollman and Swartwout were associates of former Vice President Aaron Burr. In 1806 Burr formulated a plan to lead an expedition to the western territories of the United States and establish a "separate confederacy."[12] The conspiracy was uncovered when one of the conspirators became a government informer. Bollman and Swartwout were both integral in the carrying of messages from Burr to other involved members, including a cipher letter which was used in the treason trial of Burr.[13] After their arrest both defendants sought habeas corpus relief in the U.S. Supreme Court. What did Chief Justice Marshall establish as the standard for treasonous action? What would a plan against Spain or any other government friendly to the United States at the time lead to for the defendants?

7. *Martin v. Mott* results from President James Madison's call-up of state militias during the War of 1812. New York's governor, Daniel Tompkins, complied with the Executive Order pursuant to the Militia Act of 1792 and the Act for Calling Forth the Militia of 1795.[14] When Jacob Mott, a private in the New York Militia refused the call-up he was court-martialed and fined.[15] Mott further refused to pay the fine and had his property seized by Martin, a Deputy U.S. Marshal. What did the Court in *Martin v. Mott* hold with regard to presidential power in time of war to call out a state's militia for service? Was the taking of property by the government from Jacob Mott, a private in the New York State Militia, a proper exercise of executive authority over the state?

8. Would a refusal to comply with military conscription, or as in Mott's case, the refusal of a militia member to obey and report for activation at the order of the president amount to treasonous activity? Could such activity be considered as adhering to the enemies of the United States under Article III, section 3 of the Constitution? What guidance does *Ex Parte Bollman* provide in this situation?

9. In *Pennsylvania v. Nelson* the Court heard the case of Steven Nelson, a Pennsylvania Communist Party member who was tried under the state's sedition law. What was the Court's reasoning in overturning Nelson's conviction under the state statute? What did Chief Justice Warren say about the state government's involvement in an area of national interest?

Endnotes

1   *Office of Homeland Security, National Strategy for Homeland Security* (Washington, DC: Office of Homeland Security, 2002), 2.

2   http://www.dhs.gov/xabout/laws/law_regulation_rule_0011.shtm

3   James Madison, "Federalist No. 46," in *The Federalist Papers*, para. 2 at http://thomas.loc.gov/home/fedpapers/fed_10.html.

4   *Changing Homeland Security: What is Homeland Security,* Christopher Bellavita, Homeland Security Affairs, Vol. IV, No. 2, June 2008.

5   Defined as "social trends or threats that can disrupt the long-term stability of the American way of life." *Id.*

6   Defined as "locally-directed effort to prevent and prepare for incidents most likely to threaten the safety and security of its citizens." *Id.*

7   This includes man-made and natural hazards. *Id.*

8   This is viewed as the least civil liberty-minded response to external threat and a means by which government gains further access and control over citizens' private lives.

9   http://www.dhs.gov/xnews/releases/press_release_0396.shtm

10   The actual name of the treaty was The Treaty of Amity, Commerce and Navigation between His Brittanic Majesty and the United States of America, by their President, with the Advice and Consent of their Senate. It was signed on November 19, 1794 and ratified on June 24, 1795.

11   *Treaty with Great Britain 1794,* p. 125, Library of Congress.

12   Hobson, C. (2006). *The Aaron Burr Treason Trial.* Washington D.C.: The Federal Judicial Center.

13   Id.

14   http://www.historyofsupremecourt.org/scripts/supremecourt/glossary.cgi?term=m &letter=yes

15   Id.

Chapter Two
PRESIDENTIAL POWER AND CONGRESSIONAL AUTHORITY

Article II, section 1 of the Constitution vests executive power in the president of the United States. Section 2 provides that the president is the commander in chief of the army and navy and state militias. Additional section 2 powers give the president the ability to make treaties with the advice and consent of the Senate. It is Article I, section 1 that creates the legislative body of Congress and its two branches, the Senate and House of Representatives. Article I, section 8 contains the enumerated powers of Congress that include providing for the common defense and general welfare of the country as well as the regulation of commerce with foreign nations. The additional powers of the Congress found in section 8 relate to the raising and funding of an army and navy, regulation of piracy, offenses on the high seas and those against the law of nations and the declaration of war. This enumeration and separation of powers are part of the brilliant construction, along with that third branch of government, the judiciary, created in Article III, which were bequeathed to following generations. As part of this construction of government, the early architects provided additional instructions that can be found in *The Federalist*, a collection of 85 essays written to promote ratification but also considered as an explanation of the document as a whole. Under the pseudonym of Publius, Alexander Hamilton, John Jay and James Madison provided explanation and support for the Constitution. In *Federalist No. 23*, Alexander Hamilton writes of the necessity for a unified national government: *"The principal purpose to be answered by union, are these: the common defence of the members; the preservation of the public peace, as well against internal convulsions as external attacks; the regulation of commerce with other nations, and between the states; the superintendence of our intercourse, political and commercial, with foreign countries .... The circumstances that endanger the safety of nations are infinite; and for this reason, no constitutional shackles can wisely be imposed on the power to which care of it is committed ... it must be admitted as a necessary consequence, that there can be no limitation of that authority, which is to provide for the defence and protection of the community, in any matter essential to its efficacy; that is, in any manner essential to the formation, direction or support of the national forces."*

The recognition of the necessity for national defense and the unification of that power are at the heart of *Federalist No. 23*. Later in *No. 70* and *No. 74* Hamilton would discuss the role of the executive in the government in general but more specifically in *No. 74* with regard to the executive's war power: *"The President of the United States, is to be commander 'in chief of the army and navy of the United States, and of the militia of the several states when called into actual service of the United States' ... The direction of war, implies the direction of the common strength: and the power of directing an employing the common strength, forms an usual and essential part in the definition of the executive authority."*

An earlier essay by James Madison, *No. 41*, speaks more to the powers of the general government and discusses those specific powers vested in the Congress. The roles of internal and external security of the nation are important factors in governing: *"Security against foreign danger is one of the primitive objects of civil society. It is an avowed and essential object of the American union. The powers requisite for attaining it, must be effectually confided to the federal councils."*

Despite the guidelines found in the pages of *The Federalist* and the enumerated powers contained in the Constitution, there has been disagreement concerning the respective powers of each branch. Nowhere is this disagreement more intense and susceptible to constitutional challenge than when the use of military force is implemented. Post 9/11, the Bush Administration policies in the conduct of the war in Afghanistan and the war in Iraq have undergone intense criticism. Similar criticism has been levied against the Obama Administration and the continuing war in Afghanistan and use of unmanned drone strikes. But President George W. Bush and President Barack Obama share similar criticism with other wartime presidents, going back to Abraham Lincoln during the Civil War and John Adams during the Quasi-War with France. The U.S. Supreme Court in its infancy would rule against Adams and the extension of Executive power in the 1804 case *Little v. Barreme*.[1] During the Quasi-War with France, Congress annually passed an act suspending any trade between the two nations. Section 5 of the act authorized the president of the United States *"to stop and examine any ship or vessel of the United States on the high sea which there may be reason to suspect to be engaged in any traffic or commerce contrary to the true tenor of the act, and if upon examination it should appear that such ship or vessel is bound or sailing to any or place within the territory of the French Republic or her dependencies, it is rendered lawful to seize such vessel and send her into the United States for adjudication."*[2] Captain Little of the USS *Boston* captured a Dutch Vessel, *The Flying Fish*, which was sailing from a French port. The capture was carried out on the orders of the Secretary of the Navy, on behalf of President Adams, who directed that seizure be made of any American ship sailing to or from a French port. Captain Little suspected the vessel was an American ship sailing under the neutral colors of the Dutch. Though the ship and cargo were ordered by the district court to be returned to the owner, damages for the capture and detention were refused. The circuit court allowed for damages on the basis that even if the ship were American it could not be seized since it was on "a voyage from, not to, a French port" and thus not subject to capture.[3] Chief Justice Marshall, writing for the Court, found Captain Little personally liable for damages owed to the owner of the Dutch vessel. This determination rested on the Court's finding that President Adams had no inherent power to issue an order to capture ships travelling from French ports.[4] As such, the acts of Captain Little, even though based on orders from the commander in chief, could not give lawful authority or protection to an unlawful act. From *Little v. Barreme* it is clear that once Congress has legislated in an area where it provides specific powers to the executive under that legislation the executive has no unilateral authority to extend those powers. Even if the argument can be made that those powers were extended in the national security interest the limit set by Congress controls. Yet, there are powers the executive retains as commander in chief and in the ability to make and enter into treaties that are superior to the representative branch of government. The extent of these powers will be evident in later cases within this chapter. However, it is interesting for the moment to consider what occurred in **Little v. Barreme** with regard to the seizure of a noncombatant's property and the limits placed on executive power. The case of **Youngstown Sheet & Tube Co. v. Sawyer**, also referred to as *"The Steel Seizure Cases,"* deals with a similar grasp of executive power in the name of national defense except this time it would occur nearly 150 years later during the Korean War and the administration of President Harry Truman. The U.S. Supreme Court similarly rebuked executive overreach when President Truman attempted to take over the operations and production of U.S. steel mills at the height of the Korean War.

Our tripartite system of government calls for a separation of powers, but a determination of those powers in the balance of national interest and national security are often controversial and left to the courts to decide. In the final examination it falls to the Supreme Court to "say what the law is."[5] The ultimate issues remain unchanged whether discussing 18th century admiralty seizures during a period of undeclared war but active aggression between nations and 21st century authorizations for use of force against unlawful enemy combatants. In *Federalist No. 41* Madison wrote: *"The means of security can only be regulated by the means and danger of attack. They will be forever determined by these rules, and by no others. It is in vain to oppose constitutional barriers to the impulse of self-preservation."*

Prize Cases
67 U.S. 635 (1863)

Mr. Justice Grier.

There are certain propositions of law which must necessarily affect the ultimate decision of these cases, and many others which it will be proper to discuss and decide before we notice the special facts peculiar to each.

They are,

1st. Had the President a right to institute a blockade of ports in possession of persons in armed rebellion against the Government, on the principles of international law, as known and acknowledged among civilized States?

2d. Was the property of persons domiciled or residing within those States a proper subject of capture on the sea as "enemies' property?"

I. Neutrals have a right to challenge the existence of a blockade de facto, and also the authority of the party exercising the right to institute it. They have a right to enter the ports of a friendly nation for the purposes of trade and commerce, but are bound to recognize the rights of a belligerent engaged in actual war, to use this mode of coercion, for the purpose of subduing the enemy.

That a blockade de facto actually existed, and was formally declared and notified by the President on the 27th and 30th of April, 1861, is an admitted fact in these cases.

That the President, as the Executive Chief of the Government and Commander-in-chief of the Army and Navy, was the proper person to make such notification has not been, and cannot be disputed.

The right of prize and capture has its origin in the "jus belli," and is governed and adjudged under the law of nations. To legitimate the capture of a neutral vessel or property on the high seas, a war must exist de facto, and the neutral must have knowledge or notice of the intention of one of the parties belligerent to use this mode of coercion against a port, city, or territory, in possession of the other.

Let us enquire whether, at the time this blockade was instituted, a state of war existed which would justify a resort to these means of subduing the hostile force.

War has been well defined to be, "That state in which a nation prosecutes its right by force."

The parties belligerent in a public war are independent nations. But it is not necessary, to constitute war, that both parties should be acknowledged as independent nations or sovereign States. A war may exist where one of the belligerents claims sovereign rights as against the other.

***

The laws of war, as established among nations, have their foundation in reason, and all tend to mitigate the cruelties and misery produced by the scourge of war. Hence the parties to a civil war usually concede to each other belligerent rights. They exchange prisoners, and adopt the other courtesies and rules common to public or national wars.

By the Constitution, Congress alone has the power to declare a national or foreign war. It cannot declare war against a State, or any number of States, by virtue of any clause in the Constitution. The Constitution confers on the President the whole Executive power. He is bound to take care that the laws be faithfully executed. He is Commander-in-chief of the Army and Navy of the United States, and of the militia of the several States when called into the actual service of the United States. He has no power to initiate or declare a war either against a foreign nation or a domestic State. But, by the Acts of Congress of February 28th, 1795, and 3d of March, 1807, he is authorized to call out the militia and use the military and naval forces of the United States in case of invasion by foreign nations and to suppress insurrection against the government of a State or of the United States.

If a war be made by invasion of a foreign nation, the President is not only authorized but bound to resist force by force. He does not initiate the war, but is bound to accept the challenge without waiting for any special legislative authority. And whether the hostile party be a foreign invader or States organized in rebellion, it is nonetheless a war although the declaration of it be "unilateral."

This greatest of civil wars... [T]he President was bound to meet it in the shape it presented itself, without waiting for Congress to baptize it with a name; and no name given to it by him or them could change the fact.

It is not the less a civil war, with belligerent parties in hostile array, because it may be called an "insurrection" by one side, and the insurgents be considered as rebels or traitors. It is not necessary that the independence of the revolted province or State be acknowledged in order to constitute it a party belligerent in a war according to the law of nations. Foreign nations acknowledge it as war by a declaration of neutrality. The condition of neutrality cannot exist unless there be two belligerent parties.

***

As soon as the news of the attack on Fort Sumter, and the organization of a government by the seceding States, assuming to act as belligerents, could become known in Europe, to-wit, on the 13th of May, 1861, the Queen of England issued her proclamation of neutrality, recognizing hostilities as existing between the Government of the United States of American and certain States styling themselves the Confederate States of America.

This was immediately followed by similar declarations or silent acquiescence by other nations. After such an official recognition by the sovereign, a citizen of a foreign State is estopped to deny the existence of a war with all its consequences as regards neutrals.

***

Whether the President, in fulfilling his duties as Commander-in-chief in suppressing an insurrection, has met with such armed hostile resistance and a civil war of such alarming proportions as will compel him to accord to them the character of belligerents is a question to be decided by him, and this Court must be governed by the decisions and acts of the political department of the Government to which this power was entrusted.... The proclamation of blockade is itself official and conclusive evidence to the Court that a state of war existed which demanded and authorized a recourse to such a measure under the circumstances peculiar to the case.

***

If it were necessary to the technical existence of a war that it should have a legislative sanction, we find it in almost every act passed at the extraordinary session of the Legislature of 1861, which was wholly employed in enacting laws to enable the Government to prosecute the war with vigor and efficiency.

***

The objection made to this act of ratification, that it is *ex post facto* and therefore unconstitutional and void, might possibly have some weight on the trial of an indictment in a criminal Court. But precedents from that source cannot be received as authoritative in a tribunal administering public and international law.

On this first question, therefore, we are of the opinion that the President had a right, *jure belli,* to institute a blockade of ports in possession of the States in rebellion which neutrals are bound to regard.

II. We come now to the consideration of the second question. What is included in the term "enemies' property?"

Is the property of all persons residing within the territory of the States now in rebellion, captured on the high seas, to be treated as "enemies' property," whether the owner be in arms against the Government or not?

The right of one belligerent not only to coerce the other by direct force, but also to cripple his resources by the seizure or destruction of his property, is a necessary result of a state of war. Money and wealth, the products of agriculture and commerce, are said to be the sinews of war, and as necessary in its conduct as numbers and physical force. Hence it is that the laws of war recognize the right of a belligerent to cut these sinews of the power of the enemy by capturing his property on the high seas.

The appellants contend that the term "enemy" is properly applicable to those only who are subjects or citizens of a foreign State at war with our own. They quote from the pages of the common law, which say "that persons who wage war against the King may be of two kinds, subjects or citizens. The former are not proper enemies, but rebels and traitors; the latter are those that come properly under the name of enemies."

***

They contend also that insurrection is the act of individuals, and not of a government or sovereignty; that the individuals engaged are subjects of law. That confiscation of their property can be effected only under a municipal law. That, by the law of the land, such confiscation cannot take place without the conviction of the owner of some offence, and finally that the secession ordinances are nullities, and ineffectual to release any citizen from his allegiance to the national Government, and consequently that the Constitution and Laws of the United States are still operative over persons in all the States for punishment, as well as protection.

***

Under the very peculiar Constitution of this Government, although the citizens owe supreme allegiance to the Federal Government, they owe also a qualified allegiance to the State in which they are domiciled. Their persons and property are subject to its laws.

Hence, in organizing this rebellion, they have acted as States claiming to be sovereign over all persons and property within their respective limits, and asserting a right to absolve their citizens from their allegiance to the Federal Government. Several of these States have combined to form a new confederacy, claiming to be acknowledged by the world as a sovereign State. Their right to do so is now being decided by wager of battle. The ports and territory of each of these States are held in hostility to the General Government. It is no loose, unorganized insurrection, having no defined boundary or possession. It has a boundary marked by lines of bayonets, and which can be crossed only by force—south of this line is enemies' territory, because it is claimed and held in possession by an organized, hostile and belligerent power.

All persons residing within this territory whose property may be used to increase the revenues of the hostile power are, in this contest, liable to be treated as enemies, though not foreigners. They have cast off their allegiance and made war on their Government, and are none-theless enemies because they are traitors.

***

Whether property be liable to capture as "enemies' property" does not in any manner depend on the personal allegiance of the owner.

It is the illegal traffic that stamps it as "enemies' property." It is of no consequence whether it belongs to an ally or a citizen .... The owner, *pro hac vice*, is an enemy .... The produce of the soil of the hostile territory, as well as other property engaged in the commerce of the hostile power, as the source of its wealth and strength, are always regarded as legitimate prize, without regard to the domicile of the owner, and much more so if he reside and trade within their territory.

Commentary and Questions

1. With the April 1861 attack of Fort Sumter by Confederate forces, President Lincoln declared a blockade of Southern ports; however, Congress did not authorize the president to declare a state of insurrection until July 13, 1861. Several ships were seized by the Union prior to the July 13th authorization from Congress. What did the Court say with respect to the president's ability to act in response to the attack on Fort Sumter and institute a blockade of Southern ports? Congress, the Court acknowledged, has the constitutional authority to declare war against a state or foreign nation. Where did the Court find the authority for the president's seizure of the vessels?

2. In 1837 a rebellion in Upper Canada, a British dominion at the time, led Canadian rebels to eventually take refuge on a small island on the Niagara River situated between the United States and Canada. The rebels declared themselves a republic while other rebels made their way to Buffalo, New York and attempted to raise money for their cause. This rebel activity strained relations between the United States and Great Britain. Relations would be further tested when an American steamship, the *Caroline*, which was ferrying Canadian rebels to Navy Island on the Niagara River, was seized by the Royal Navy. In seizing the *Caroline*, British Royal Navy Commander Andrew Drew had the ship boarded, set on fire and pulled into current where it eventually went over the Niagara Falls killing one American still on board. The incident, which was first embellished in the press as to the number of Americans killed, sparked outrage and led to the commencement of a series of letters between Secretary of State Daniel Webster and Lord Ashburton, Great Britain's Special Minister to Washington. According to Webster, the British Force would have to show the necessity of self-defense was "instant, overwhelming, leaving no choice of means, and no moment of deliberation."[6] Webster sought an explanation from Ashburton as to Great Britain's justification for self-defense and if no justification was provided demanded reparations be paid to the United States. Lord Ashburton provided a response that contained a stirring defense of the Royal Navy's actions and built on the theme contained in Webster's original statement regarding a nation's use of self-defense and customary international law.[7] In 1842 the Webster-Ashburton Treaty would resolve several matters of land boundaries between the United States and Britain as well as resolving the issues surrounding the *Caroline Affair*. The lasting effect of the *Caroline Affair* was to create the notion of anticipatory self-defense in international law, requiring a showing of "necessity of self-defence, instant, overwhelming, leaving no choice of means, and no moment for deliberation."[8] Does international law support President Lincoln's decision to blockade Southern ports? What did the Court hold with respect to the Southern states as an "enemy"?

3. *Brown v. U.S.*, 12 U.S. 110 (1814) is a case emanating from the War of 1812 that took a restrictive view of the confiscation of enemy property at the start of war. The opinion by Chief Justice Marshall examined established princi-

ples of international law dealing with the confiscation of enemy property, concluding that there must be an express authorization from the legislature for confiscation.[9] The facts of the case result from an embargo in place at the start of the War of 1812 and an American ship, the *Emulous*, owned by Americans but chartered to a company doing business with Great Britain, whose cargo was confiscated.[10] Chief Justice Marshall framed the two issues before the Court: "*1) May enemy's property, found on land at the commencement of hostilities, be seized and condemned as a necessary consequence of the declaration of war? 2) Is there any legislative act which authorizes such seizure and condemnation?*"[11] Marshall inquired as to whether a declaration of war was the requisite law necessary for the condemnation of property. Because war is a matter of hostility between nations it does not follow that it also includes the transfer of property. "*[T]he mere declaration of war,*" Marshall wrote, "*gives the right to confiscate, but does not itself confiscate the property of the enemy.*"[12] That right must emanate from some law provided by the legislature: "*It is urged that in executing the laws of war, the executive may seize and the courts condemn all property which, according to the modern law of nations, is subject to confiscation, although it might require an act of the legislature to justify the condemnation of that property which, according to modern usage, ought not to be confiscated.*"[13] Did the U.S. Supreme Court in *The Prize Cases* extend the authority of the executive branch to seize enemy property? What justification prevailed in the 1863 case that the Court did not find in 1814? Was the naval blockade initiated by President Lincoln of a different character than the embargo in place at the start of the War of 1812?

4. In *The Paquete Habana*, 175 U.S. 677 (1900), the U.S. Supreme Court limited executive power by "firmly establishing customary international law as part of the laws of the United States."[14] The case involved the seizure of two fishing vessels, the *Lola* and the *Paquete Habana*, during the Spanish-American War. The vessels were sailing in and out of Havana, Cuba operating under the Spanish flag, each commanded by a Spanish captain living in Cuba. The crews consisted of Cubans who were entitled to a two-thirds share of the catch with a third of the catch going to the owner. There was no evidence either vessel was engaged in any activity other than fishing. Each ship was captured by a U.S. gunboat and taken to Key West, Florida where they were sold for auction. Claims were made by the owners that the capture and sales of the ships were in error. The opinion by Justice Gray provided an extensive review of international law that was heavily relied upon in the Court's decision: "*International law is part of our law, and must be ascertained and administered by the courts of justice of appropriate jurisdiction as often as questions of right depending upon it are duly presented for their determination. For this purpose, where there is no treaty and no controlling executive or legislative act or judicial decision, resort must be had to the customs and usages of civilized nations, and, as evidence of these, to the works of jurists and commentators who by years of labor, research, and experience have made themselves peculiarly well acquainted with the subjects of which they treat. Such works are resorted to by judicial*

tribunals, not for the speculations of their authors concerning what the law ought to be, but for trustworthy evidence of what the law really is."[15] This review led the Court to exempt fishing vessels from capture, despite orders to the contrary from the President to the Secretary of the Navy in 1898.

5. An early theory of federal statutory construction, which has since been followed by U.S. courts, is what is known as the "Charming Betsy canon" of construction, which holds that ambiguous Congressional statutes should be construed in accordance with international law.[16] The theory came from the case *Murray v. Schooner Charming Betsy*, 6 U.S. 64 (1804), which involved the recapture by an American naval vessel of a ship that had previously been captured by a French privateer. At issue was the Federal Non-Intercourse Act of 1800, which prohibited United States residents, or anyone under the protection of the United States, from trading with France or any or its territories.[17] The captain of the schooner was a natural-born American who became a Danish citizen. The schooner was an American ship sailing under the Danish flag, a neutral in hostilities between the United States and France. The question before the Court was whether the congressional statute applied to the captain and the schooner as being "under the protection" of the United States.[18] Chief Justice Marshall, in deciding for the captain of the schooner and against the claims of the seizing authority, wrote: *"The libel claims this forfeiture under the act passed in February, 1800, further to suspend the commercial intercourse between the United States and France and the dependencies thereof. That act declares "that all commercial intercourse," &c. It has been very properly observed in argument that the building of vessels in the United States for sale to neutrals in the islands is, during war, a profitable business which Congress cannot be intended to have prohibited unless that intent be manifested by express words or a very plain and necessary implication. It has also been observed that an act of Congress ought never to be construed to violate the law of nations if any other possible construction remains, and consequently can never be construed to violate neutral rights or to affect neutral commerce further than is warranted by the law of nations as understood in this country. These principles are believed to be correct, and they ought to be kept in view in construing the act now under consideration."*[19] How much does international law guide U.S. statutory construction today? Has there been a shifting role since the 18th century in U.S. policy with respect to the international community? How does the statement regarding statutory construction in *Murray v. Schooner Charming Betsy* impact the dynamic between Presidential and Congressional power and authority?

The Selective Draft Law Cases
245 U.S. 366 (1918)

Mr. Chief Justice White delivered the opinion of the court.

We are here concerned with some of the provisions of the Act of May 18, 1917, c. 15, 40 Stat. 76, entitled "An Act to authorize the

President to increase temporarily the Military Establishment of the United States." The law, as its opening sentence declares, was intended to supply temporarily the increased military force which was required by the existing emergency, the war then and now flagrant. The clauses we must pass upon and those which will throw light on their significance are briefly summarized:

The act proposed to raise a national army, first by increasing the regular force to its maximum strength and there maintaining it; second, by incorporating into such army the members of the National Guard and National Guard Reserve already in the service of the United States (Act of Congress of June 3, 1916, c. 134, 39 Stat. 211) and maintaining their organizations to their full strength; third, by giving the President power, in his discretion, to organize by volunteer enlistment four divisions of infantry; fourth, by subjecting all male citizens between the ages of twenty-one and thirty to duty in the national army for the period of the existing emergency after the proclamation of the President announcing the necessity for their service, and, fifth, by providing for selecting from the body so called, on the further proclamation of the President, 500,000 enlisted men and a second body of the same number, should the President in his discretion deem it necessary. To carry out its purposes, the act made it the duty of those liable to the call to present themselves for registration on the proclamation of the President, so as to subject themselves to the terms of the act, and provided full federal means for carrying out the selective draft. It gave the President, in his discretion, power to create local boards to consider claims for exemption for physical disability or otherwise made by those called. The act exempted from subjection to the draft designated United States and state officials, as well as those already in the military or naval service of the United States, regular or duly ordained ministers of religion and theological students under the conditions provided for, and, while relieving from military service in the strict sense the members of religious sects as enumerated whose tenets excluded the moral right to engage in war, nevertheless subjected such persons to the performance of service of a noncombatant character to be defined by the President.

The proclamation of the President calling the persons designated within the ages described in the statute was made, and the plaintiffs in error, who were in the class and, under the statute, were obliged to present themselves for registration and subject themselves to the law, failed to do so, and were prosecuted under the statute for the penalties for which it provided. They all defended by denying that there had been conferred by the Constitution upon Congress the power to compel military service by a selective draft, and asserted that, even if such power had been given by the Constitution to Congress, the terms of the particular act for various reasons caused it to be beyond the power and repugnant to the Constitution. The cases are here for review because of the constitutional questions thus raised, convictions having resulted from instructions of the courts that the legal defenses were without merit, and that the statute was constitutional.

The possession of authority to enact the statute must be found in the clauses of the Constitution giving Congress power to declare war; ... to raise and support armies, but no appropriation of money to that use shall be for a longer term than two years; ... to make rules for the government and regulation of the land and naval forces.

Article I, § 8. And, of course, the powers conferred by these provisions, like all other powers given, carry with them, as provided by the Constitution, the authority "to make all laws which shall be necessary and proper for carrying into execution the foregoing powers." Article I, § 8.

As the mind cannot conceive an army without the men to compose it, on the face of the Constitution, the objection that it does not give power to provide for such men would seem to be too frivolous for further notice. It is said, however, that since, under the Constitution as originally framed, state citizenship was primary, and United States citizenship but derivative and dependent thereon, therefore the power conferred upon Congress to raise armies was only coterminous with United States citizenship, and could not be exerted so as to cause that citizenship to lose its dependent character and dominate state citizenship. But the proposition simply denies to Congress the power to raise armies which the Constitution gives. That power, by the very terms of the Constitution being delegated, is supreme. Article VI. In truth, the contention simply assails the wisdom of the framers of the Constitution in conferring authority on Congress, and in not retaining it as it was under the Confederation in the several States. Further, it is said, the right to provide is not denied by calling for volunteer enlistments, but it does not and cannot include the power to exact enforced military duty by the citizen. This however but challenges the existence of all power, for a governmental power which has no sanction to it and which therefore can only be exercised provided the citizen consents to its exertion is in no substantial sense a power. It is argued, however, that, although this is abstractly true, it is not concretely so, because, as compelled military service is repugnant to a free government and in conflict with all the great guarantees of the Constitution as to individual liberty, it must be assumed that the authority to raise armies was intended to be limited to the right to call an army into existence counting alone upon the willingness of the citizen to do his duty in time of public need, that is, in time of war. But the premise of this proposition is so devoid of foundation that it leaves not even a shadow of ground upon which to base the conclusion. Let us see if this is not at once demonstrable. It may not be doubted that the very conception of a just government and its duty to the citizen includes the reciprocal obligation of the citizen to render military service in case of need, and the right to compel it. Vattel, Law of Nations, Book III, c. 1 & 2.

***

In the Colonies before the separation from England, there cannot be the slightest doubt that the right to enforce military service was unquestioned, and that practical effect was given to the power in many cases. Indeed, the brief of the Government contains a list of Colonial acts manifesting the power and its enforcement in more than two hundred cases. And this exact situation existed also after the separation. Under the Articles of Confederation, it is true Congress had no such power, as its authority was absolutely limited to making calls upon the States for the military forces needed to create and maintain the army, each State being bound for its quota as called. But it is indisputable that the States, in response to the calls made upon them, met the situation when they deemed it necessary by directing enforced military service on the part of the citizens. In fact, the duty of the citizen to render military service and the power to compel him against his consent to do so was expressly sanctioned by the constitutions of at least nine of the States, an illustration being afforded by the following provision of the Pennsylvania constitution of 1776.

***

When the Constitution came to be formed, it may not be disputed that one of the recognized necessities for its adoption was the want of power in Congress to raise an army and the dependence upon the States for their quotas. In supplying the power, it was manifestly intended to give it all, and leave none to the States, since, besides the delegation to Congress of authority to raise armies, the Constitution prohibited the States, without the consent of Congress, from keeping troops in time of peace or engaging in war. Article I, § 10.

To argue that, as the state authority over the militia prior to the Constitution embraced every citizen, the right of Congress to raise an army should not be considered as granting authority to compel the citizen's service in the army is but to express in a different form the denial of the right to call any citizen to the army. Nor is this met by saying that it does not exclude the right of Congress to organize an army by voluntary enlistments, that is, by the consent of the citizens, for, if the proposition be true, the right of the citizen to give consent would be controlled by the same prohibition which would deprive Congress of the right to compel unless it can be said that, although Congress had not the right to call because of state authority, the citizen had a right to obey the call and set aside state authority if he pleased to do so. And a like conclusion demonstrates the want of foundation for the contention that, although it be within the power to call the citizen into the army without his consent, the army into which he enters after the call is to be limited in some respects to services for which the militia, it is assumed, may only be used, since this admits the appropriateness of the call to military service in the army and the power to make it, and yet destroys the purpose for which the call is authorized—the raising of armies to be under the control of the United States.

The fallacy of the argument results from confounding the constitutional provisions concerning the militia with that conferring upon Congress the power to raise armies. It treats them as one, while they are different. This is the militia clause:

The Congress shall have power ... to provide for calling forth the militia to execute the laws of the Union, suppress insurrections and repel invasions; To provide for organizing, arming, and disciplining the militia, and for governing such part of them as may be employed in the service of the United States, reserving to the States, respectively, the appointment of the officers, and the authority of training the militia according to the discipline prescribed by Congress. Article I, § 8.

The line which separates it from the army power is not only inherently plainly marked by the text of the two clauses, but will stand out in bolder relief by considering the condition before the Constitution was adopted and the remedy which it provided for the military situation with which it dealt. The right, on the one hand, of Congress under the Confederation to call on the States for forces, and the duty, on the other, of the States to furnish when called, embraced the complete power of government over the subject. When the two were combined and were delegated to Congress, all governmental power on that subject was conferred, a result manifested not only by the grant made, but by the limitation expressly put upon the States on the subject. The army sphere therefore embraces such complete authority. But the duty of exerting the power thus conferred in all its plenitude was not made at once obligatory, but was wisely left to depend upon the discretion of Congress as to the arising of the exigencies which would call it in part or in whole into play. There was left, therefore, under the sway of the States un-delegated, the control of the militia to the extent that such control was not taken away by the exercise by Congress of its power to raise armies. This did not diminish the military power or curb the full potentiality of the right to exert it, but left an area of authority requiring to be provided for (the militia area) unless and until, by the exertion of the military power of Congress, that area had been circumscribed or totally disappeared. This, therefore, is what was dealt with by the militia provision. It diminished the occasion for the exertion by Congress of its military power beyond the strict necessities for its exercise by giving the power to Congress to direct the organization and training of the militia (evidently to prepare such militia in the event of the exercise of the army power), although leaving the carrying out of such command to the States. It further conduced to the same result by delegating to Congress the right to call, on occasions which were specified, for the militia force, thus again obviating the necessity for exercising the army power to the extent of being ready for every conceivable contingency. This purpose is made manifest by the provision preserving the organization of the militia so far as formed when called for such special purposes, although subjecting the militia when so called to the paramount authority of the United States. *Tarble's Case*, 13 Wallace, 397, 408. But because, under the express regulations, the power was given to call for specified purposes without exerting the army power, it cannot follow that the latter power, when exerted, was not complete to the extent of its exertion and dominant. Because the power of Congress to raise armies was not required to be exerted to its full limit, but only as in the discretion of Congress it was deemed the public interest required, furnishes no ground for supposing that the complete power was lost by its partial exertion. Because, moreover, the power granted to Congress to raise armies in its potentiality was susceptible of narrowing the area over which the militia clause operated affords no ground for confounding the two areas which were distinct and separate to the end of confusing both the powers, and thus weakening or destroying both.

And, upon this understanding of the two powers, the legislative and executive authority has been exerted from the beginning. From the act of the first session of Congress carrying over the army of the Government under the Confederation to the United States under the Constitution (Act of September 29, 1789, c. 25, 1 Stat. 95) down to 1812, the authority to raise armies was regularly exerted as a distinct and substantive power, the force being raised and recruited by enlistment. Except for one act formulating a plan by which the entire body of citizens (the militia) subject to military duty was to be organized in every State (Act of May 8, 1792, c. 33, 1 Stat. 271) which was never carried into effect, Congress confined itself to providing for the organization of a specified number distributed among the States according to their quota, to be trained as directed by Congress and to be called by the President as need might require. When the War of 1812 came, the result of these two forces composed the army to be relied upon by Congress to carry on the war. Either because it proved to be weak in numbers or because of insubordination developed among the forces called and manifested by their refusal to cross the border, the Government determined that the exercise of the power to organize an army by compulsory draft was necessary, and Mr. Monroe, the Secretary of War (Mr. Madison being President), in a letter to Congress, recommended several plans of legislation on that subject. It suffices to say that by each of them it was proposed that the United States deal directly with the body of citizens subject to military duty, and call a designated number out of the population between the ages of 18 and 45 for service in the army.

***

Down to the Mexican War, the legislation exactly portrayed the same condition of mind which we have previously stated. In that war, however, no draft was suggested, because the army created by the United States immediately resulting from the exercise by Congress of its power to raise armies, that organized under its direction from the militia and the volunteer commands which were furnished, proved adequate to carry the war to a successful conclusion.

***

Brevity prevents doing more than to call attention to the fact that the organized body of militia within the States as trained by the States under the direction of Congress became known as the National Guard (Act of January 21, 1903, c. 196, 32 Stat. 775; National Defense Act of June 3, 1916, c. 134, 39 Stat. 211). And, to make further preparation from among the great body of the citizens, an additional number to be determined by the President was directed to be organized and trained by the States as the National Guard Reserve. (National Defense Act, *supra.*)

Thus, sanctioned as is the act before us by the text of the Constitution and by its significance as read in the light of the fundamental principles with which the subject is concerned, by the power recognized and carried into effect in many civilized countries, by the authority and practice of the colonies before the Revolution, of the States under the Confederation, and of the Government since the formation of the Constitution, the want of merit in the contentions that the act in the particulars which we have been previously called upon to consider was beyond the constitutional power of Congress is manifest. Cogency, however, if possible, is added to the demonstration by pointing out that, in the only case to which we have been referred where the constitutionality of the Act of 1863 was contemporaneously challenged on grounds akin to, if not absolutely identical with, those here urged, the validity of the act was maintained for reasons not different from those which control our judgment. (**Kneedler v. Lane**, 45 Pa.St. 238.) And as further evidence that the conclusion we reach is but the inevitable consequence of the provisions of the Constitution as effect follows cause, we briefly recur to events in another environment. The seceding States wrote into the constitution which was adopted to regulate the government which they sought to establish, in identical words, the provisions of the Constitution of the United States which we here have under consideration.

***

In reviewing the subject, we have hitherto considered it, as it has been argued, from the point of view of the Constitution as it stood prior to the adoption of the Fourteenth Amendment. But to avoid all misapprehension, we briefly direct attention to that Amendment for the purpose of pointing out...how completely it broadened the national scope of the Government under the Constitution by causing citizenship of the United States to be paramount and dominant, instead of being subordinate and derivative, and therefore, operating as it does upon all the powers conferred by the Constitution, leaves no possible support for the contentions made, if their want of merit was otherwise not so clearly made manifest.

It remains only to consider contentions which, while not disputing power, challenge the act because of the repugnancy to the Constitution supposed to result from some of its provisions. First, we are of opinion that the contention that the act is void as a delegation of federal power to state officials because of some of its administrative features is too wanting in merit to require further notice. Second, we think that the contention that the statute is void because vesting administrative officers with legislative discretion has been so completely adversely settled as to require reference only to some of the decided cases. *Field v. Clark*, 143 U.S. 649; *Buttfield v. Stranahan*, 192 U.S. 470; *Intermountain Rate Cases*, 234 U.S. 476; *First National Bank v. Union Trust Co.*, 244 U.S. 416. A like conclusion also adversely disposes of a similar claim concerning the conferring of judicial power. *Buttfield v. Stranahan*, 192 U.S. 470, 497; *West v. Hitchcock*, 205 U.S. 80; *Oceanic Steam Navigation Co. v. Stranahan*, 214 U.S. 320, 338-340; *Zakonaite v. Wolf*, 226 U.S. 272, 275. And we pass without anything but statement the proposition that an establishment of a religion or an interference with the free exercise thereof repugnant to the First Amendment resulted from the exemption clauses of the act to which we at the outset referred, because we think its unsoundness is too apparent to require us to do more.

Finally, as we are unable to conceive upon what theory the exaction by government from the citizen of the performance of his supreme and noble duty of contributing to the defense of the rights and honor of the nation, as the result of a war declared by the great representative body of the people, can be said to be the imposition of involuntary servitude in violation of the prohibitions of the Thirteenth Amendment, we are constrained to the conclusion that the contention to that effect is refuted by its mere statement.

Affirmed.

* The docket titles of these cases are: *Arver v. United States*, No. 663, *Grahl v. United States*, No. 664, *Otto Wangerin v. United States*, No. 665, *Walter*

Wangerin v. United States, No. 666, in error to the District Court of the United States for the District of Minnesota; *Kramer v. United States,* No. 681, *Graubard v. United States,* No. 769, in error to the District Court of the United States for the Southern District of New York.

Perpich v. Department of Defense
496 U.S. 334 (1990)

Justice Stevens delivered the opinion of the Court.

The question presented is whether the Congress may authorize the President to order members of the National Guard to active duty for purposes of training outside the United States during peacetime without either the consent of a State Governor or the declaration of a national emergency.

A gubernatorial consent requirement that had been enacted in 1952 was partially repealed in 1986 by the "Montgomery Amendment," which provides:

"The consent of a Governor described in subsections (b) and (d) may not be withheld (in whole or in part) with regard to active duty outside the United States, its territories, and its possessions, because of any objection to the location, purpose, type, or schedule of such active duty."

In this litigation the Governor of Minnesota and the State of Minnesota (hereinafter collectively referred to as the Governor), challenge the constitutionality of that amendment. The Governor contends that it violates the Militia Clauses of the Constitution.

In his complaint the Governor alleged that pursuant to a state statute the Minnesota National Guard is the organized militia of the State of Minnesota and that pursuant to a federal statute members of that militia "are also members of either the Minnesota unit of the Air National Guard of the United States or the Minnesota unit of the Army National Guard of the United States (hereinafter collectively referred to as the 'National Guard of the United States')." App. 5. The complaint further alleged that the Montgomery Amendment had prevented the Governor from withholding his consent to a training mission in Central America for certain members of the Minnesota National Guard in January 1987, and prayed for an injunction against the implementation of any similar orders without his consent.

The District Judge rejected the Governor's challenge. He explained that the National Guard consists of "two overlapping, but legally distinct, organizations. Congress, under its constitutional authority to 'raise and support armies' has created the National Guard of the United States, a federal organization comprised of state national guard units and their members." 666 F. Supp. 1319, 1320

(Minn. 1987). The fact that these units also maintain an identity as State National Guards, part of the militia described in Art. I, 8, of the Constitution, does not limit Congress' plenary authority to train the Guard "as it sees fit when the Guard is called to active federal service." Id., at 1324. He therefore concluded that "the gubernatorial veto found in 672(b) and 672(d) is not constitutionally required. Having created the gubernatorial veto as an accommodation to the states, rather than pursuant to a constitutional mandate, the Congress may withdraw the veto without violating the Constitution." Ibid.

A divided panel of the Court of Appeals for the Eighth Circuit reached a contrary conclusion. It read the Militia Clauses as preserving state authority over the training of the National Guard and its membership unless and until Congress "determined that there was some sort of exigency or extraordinary need to exert federal power." App. to Pet. for Cert. A92. Only in that event could the army power dissipate the authority reserved to the States under the Militia Clauses.

In response to a petition for rehearing en banc, the Court of Appeals vacated the panel decision and affirmed the judgment of the District Court. Over the dissent of two judges, the en banc court agreed with the District Court's conclusion that "Congress' army power is plenary and exclusive" and that the State's authority to train the militia did not conflict with congressional power to raise armies for the common defense and to control the training of federal reserve forces. 880 F.2d 11, 17-18 (1989).

Because of the manifest importance of the issue, we granted the Governor's petition for certiorari. 493 U.S. 1017 (1990). In the end, we conclude that the plain language of Article I of the Constitution, read as whole, requires affirmance of the Court of Appeals' judgment. We believe, however, that a brief description of the evolution of the present statutory scheme will help to explain that holding.

I

Two conflicting themes, developed at the Constitutional Convention and repeated in debates over military policy during the next century, led to a compromise in the text of the Constitution and in later statutory enactments. On the one hand, there was a widespread fear that a national standing Army posed an intolerable threat to individual liberty and to the sovereignty of the separate States, while, on the other hand, there was a recognition of the danger of relying on inadequately trained soldiers as the primary means of providing for the common defense. Thus, Congress was authorized both to raise and support a national Army and also to organize "the Militia."

In the early years of the Republic, Congress did neither. In 1792, it did pass a statute that purported to establish "an Uniform Militia throughout the United States," but its detailed command that every able-bodied male citizen between the ages of 18 and 45 be enrolled therein and equip himself with appropriate weaponry was virtually ignored for more than a century, during which time the militia proved to be a decidedly unreliable fighting force. The statute was finally repealed in 1901. It was in that year that President Theodore Roosevelt declared: "Our militia law is obsolete and worthless." The process of transforming "the National Guard of the several States" into an effective fighting force then began.

The Dick Act divided the class of able-bodied male citizens between 18 and 45 years of age into an "organized militia" to be known as the National Guard of the several States, and the remainder of which was then described as the "reserve militia," and which later statutes have termed the "unorganized militia." The statute created a table of organization for the National Guard conforming to that of the Regular Army, and provided that federal funds and Regular Army instructors should be used to train its members. It is undisputed that Congress was acting pursuant to the Militia Clauses of the Constitution in passing the Dick Act. Moreover, the legislative history of that Act indicates that Congress contemplated that the services of the organized militia would "be rendered only upon the soil of the United States or of its Territories." H. R. Rep. No. 1094, 57th Cong., 1st Sess., 22 (1902). In 1908, however, the statute was amended to provide expressly that the Organized Militia should be available for service "either within or without the territory of the United States."

When the Army made plans to invoke that authority by using National Guard units south of the Mexican border, Attorney General Wickersham expressed the opinion that the Militia Clauses precluded such use outside the Nation's borders. In response to that opinion and to the widening conflict in Europe, in 1916 Congress decided to "federalize" the National Guard. In addition to providing for greater federal control and federal funding of the Guard, the statute required every guardsman to take a dual oath—to support the Nation as well as the States and to obey the President as well as the Governor - and authorized the President to draft members of the Guard into federal service. The statute expressly provided that the Army of the United States should include not only "the Regular Army," but also "the National Guard while in the service of the United States," and that when drafted into federal service by the President, members of the Guard so drafted should "from the date of their draft, stand discharged from the militia, and shall from said date be subject to" the rules and regulations governing the Regular Army. 111, 39 Stat. 211.

During World War I, the President exercised the power to draft members of the National Guard into the Regular Army. That power, as well as the power to compel civilians to render military service, was upheld in the **Selective Draft Law Cases**, 245 U.S. 366 (1918). Specifically, in those cases, and in **Cox v. Wood**, 247 U.S. 3 (1918), the Court held that the plenary power to raise armies was "not qualified or restricted by the provisions of the militia clause."

The draft of the individual members of the National Guard into the Army during World War I virtually destroyed the Guard as an effective organization. The draft terminated the members' status as militiamen, and the statute did not provide for a restoration of their prewar status as members of the Guard when they were mustered out of the Army. This problem was ultimately remedied by the 1933 amendments to the 1916 Act. Those amendments created the "two overlapping but distinct organizations" described by the District Court—the National Guard of the various States and the National Guard of the United States.

Since 1933 all persons who have enlisted in a State National Guard unit have simultaneously enlisted in the National Guard of the United States. In the latter capacity they became a part of the Enlisted Reserve Corps of the Army, but unless and until ordered to active duty in the Army, they retained their status as members of a separate State Guard unit. Under the 1933 Act, they could be ordered into active service whenever Congress declared a national emergency and authorized the use of troops in excess of those in the Regular Army. The statute plainly described the effect of such an order:

"*All persons so ordered into the active military service of the United States shall from the date of such order stand relieved from duty in the National Guard of their respective States, Territories, and the District of Columbia so long as they shall remain in the active military service of the United States, and during such time shall be subject to such laws and regulations for the government of the Army of the United States as may be applicable to members of the Army whose permanent retention in active military service is not contemplated by law. The organization of said units existing at the date of the order into active Federal service shall be maintained intact insofar as practicable.*" 18, 48 Stat. 160-161.

"*Upon being relieved from active duty in the military service of the United States all individuals and units shall thereupon revert to their National Guard status.*" Id., at 161.

Thus, under the "dual enlistment" provisions of the statute that have been in effect since 1933, a member of the Guard who is ordered to active duty in the federal service is thereby relieved of his or her status in the State Guard for the entire period of federal service.

Until 1952 the statutory authority to order National Guard units to active duty was limited to periods of national emergency. In that year, Congress broadly authorized orders to "active duty or active duty for training" without any emergency requirement, but provided that such orders could not be issued without gubernatorial consent. The National Guard units have under this plan become a sizable portion of the Nation's military forces; for example, "the Army National Guard provides 46 percent of the combat units and 28 percent of the support forces of the Total Army." Apparently gubernatorial consents to training missions were routinely obtained until 1985, when the Governor of California refused to consent to a training mission for 450 members of the California National Guard in Honduras, and the Governor of Maine shortly thereafter refused to consent to a similar mission. Those incidents led to the enactment of the Montgomery Amendment and this litigation ensued.

II

The Governor's attack on the Montgomery Amendment relies in part on the traditional understanding that "the Militia" can only be called forth for three limited purposes that do not encompass either foreign service or nonemergency conditions, and in part on the express language in the second Militia Clause reserving to the States "the Authority of training the Militia." The Governor does not, however, challenge the authority of Congress to create a dual enlistment program. Nor does the Governor claim that membership in a State Guard unit—or any type of state militia—creates any sort of constitutional immunity from being drafted into the Federal Armed Forces. Indeed, it would be ironic to claim such immunity when every member of the Minnesota National Guard has voluntarily enlisted, or accepted a commission as an officer, in the National Guard of the United States and thereby become a member of the Reserve Corps of the Army.

***

This view of the constitutional issue was presupposed by our decision in the **Selective Draft Law Cases**, 245 U.S. 366 (1918). Although the Governor is correct in pointing out that those cases were decided in the context of an actual war, the reasoning in our opinion was not so limited. After expressly noting that the 1916 Act had incorporated members of the National Guard into the National Army, the Court held that the Militia Clauses do not constrain the powers of Congress "to provide for the common Defence," to "raise and support Armies," to "make Rules for the Government and Regulation of the land and naval Forces," or to enact such laws as "shall be necessary and proper" for executing those powers. Id., at 375, 377, 381-384. The Court instead held that, far from being a limitation on those powers, the Militia Clauses are—as the constitutional text plainly indicates—additional grants of power to Congress.

The first empowers Congress to call forth the militia "to execute the Laws of the Union, suppress Insurrections and repel Invasions." We may assume that Attorney General Wickersham was entirely correct in reasoning that when a National Guard unit retains its status as a state militia, Congress could not "impress" the entire unit for any other purpose. Congress did, however, authorize the President to call forth the entire membership of the Guard into federal service during World War I, even though the soldiers who fought in France were not engaged in any of the three specified purposes. Membership in the militia did not exempt them from a valid order to perform federal service, whether that service took the form of combat duty or training for such duty. The congressional power to call forth the militia may in appropriate cases supplement its broader power to raise armies and provide for the common defense and general welfare, but it does not limit those powers.

The second Militia Clause enhances federal power in three additional ways. First, it authorizes Congress to provide for "organizing, arming and disciplining the Militia." It is by congressional choice that the available pool of citizens has been formed into organized units. Over the years, Congress has exercised this power in various ways, but its current choice of a dual enlistment system is just as permissible as the 1792 choice to have the members of the militia arm themselves. Second, the Clause authorizes Congress to provide for governing such part of the militia as may be employed in the service of the United States. Surely this authority encompasses continued training while on active duty. Finally, although the appointment of officers "and the Authority of training the Militia" is reserved to the States respectively, that limitation is, in turn, limited by the words "according to the discipline prescribed by Congress." If the discipline required for effective service in the Armed Forces of a global power requires training in distant lands, or distant skies, Congress has the authority to provide it. The subordinate authority to perform the actual training prior to active duty in the federal service does not include the right to edit the discipline that Congress may prescribe for Guard members after they are ordered into federal service.

The Governor argues that this interpretation of the Militia Clauses has the practical effect of nullifying an important state power that is expressly reserved in the Constitution. We disagree. It merely recognizes the supremacy of federal power in the area of military affairs. The Federal Government provides virtually all of the funding, the material, and the leadership for the State Guard units.

***

In light of the Constitution's more general plan for providing for the common defense, the powers allowed to the States by existing statutes are significant. As has already been mentioned, several constitutional provisions commit matters of foreign policy and military affairs to the exclusive control of the National Government. This Court in ***Tarble's Case***, 13 Wall. 397 (1872), had occasion to observe that the constitutional allocation of powers in this realm gave rise to a presumption that federal control over the Armed Forces was exclusive. Were it not for the Militia Clauses, it might be possible to argue on like grounds that the constitutional allocation of powers precluded the formation of organized state militia. The Militia Clauses, however, subordinate any such structural inferences to an express permission while also subjecting state militia to express federal limitations.

We thus conclude that the Montgomery Amendment is not inconsistent with the Militia Clauses.

***

The judgment of the Court of Appeals is affirmed.

It is so ordered.

Commentary and Questions

6. The initial army put forth to fight Great Britain in the Revolutionary War was largely a volunteer army. Legislation for a draft was first introduced by Congress in 1814 at the close of the War of 1812.[20] Conscription, the forced service of able-bodied males to fight for the country, was first authorized by Congress with the Union Draft Law of 1863, which called for men between the ages of 18 and 45 to register with the local militia and be ready for service in the war. Exemptions from service could be obtained by paying either a fee of $300.00 to the government or by hiring someone to serve in the draftee's place. Civil War conscription was unpopular based largely on the ability of the wealthy to avoid service and the presence of free African-Americans in the North who were viewed as taking employment from whites who were conscripted to serve. This sentiment led to one of the largest riots in U.S. history, the New York City Draft Riots of 1863. The conscription of men to serve in World War I met its own form of resistance. With the passage of the Selective Service Act on May 17, 1917, Congress sought to mobilize an army to fight in Europe. The Act provided exemptions for individuals involved in essential wartime industries and those who were classified as conscientious objectors. Across the country several challenges to conscription were filed and eventually consolidated in their appeals to the Supreme Court in The Selective Draft Law Cases. What power did the Court state was implied in Congress's authority under Article I, section 8 to raise and support armies? What theories did the appellants put forward in arguing against the draft?

7. President Lincoln, in his 1863 "Opinion on the Constitutionality of the Draft" stated: "[T]he constitution provides that the congress shall have power to raise and support armies; and, by this [1863 draft] act, the Congress has exercised the power to raise and support armies. This is the whole of it. It is a law made in literal pursuance of this part of the United States Constitution ....

    ... The power is given fully, completely, unconditionally. It is not a power to raise armies if State authorities consent; nor if the men to compose the armies are entirely willing; but it is a power to raise and support armies given to

Congress by the Constitution, without an if.[21] This is the plain meaning of Article I, section 8 given by Chief Justice White in *The Selective Draft Law Cases* for upholding the Selective Service Act of 1917. Chief Justice White also explains the position of the states in this scheme. What did he say was the role of the states in federal conscription?

8. *Perpich v. Department of Defense* involves a different challenge to Article I, section 8 of the Constitution—this challenge is to the Militia Clause and presidential power of active duty call up of state National Guard troops for training outside the United States. The challenge within was not from conscripted males but a state governor. What did the Court hold with regard to the congressional authority to call up militias? What relation does it have to its power to raise armies and provide for the common defense?

9. Has the Court eliminated individual liberty arguments in the *Selective Draft Law Cases*?

United States v. Curtiss-Wright Export Corp.
299 U.S. 304 (1936)

Mr. Justice Sutherland delivered the opinion of the Court.

On January 27, 1936, an indictment was returned in the court below, the first count of which charges that appellees, beginning with the 29th day of May, 1934, conspired to sell in the United States certain arms of war, namely fifteen machine guns, to Bolivia, a country then engaged in armed conflict in the Chaco, in violation of the Joint Resolution of Congress approved May 28, 1934, and the provisions of a proclamation issued on the same day by the President of the United States pursuant to authority conferred by § 1 of the resolution. In pursuance of the conspiracy, the commission of certain overt acts was alleged, details of which need not be stated. The Joint Resolution (c. 365, 48 Stat. 811) follows:

Resolved by the Senate and House of Representatives of the United States of America in Congress assembled, That if the President finds that the prohibition of the sale of arms and munitions of war in the United States to those countries now engaged in armed conflict in the Chaco may contribute to the reestablishment of peace between those countries, and if after consultation with the governments of other American Republics and with their cooperation, as well as that of such other governments as he may deem necessary, he makes proclamation to that effect, it shall be unlawful to sell, except under such limitations and exceptions as the President prescribes, any arms or munitions of war in any place in the United States to the countries now engaged in that armed conflict, or to any person, company, or association acting in the interest of either country, until otherwise ordered by the President or by Congress.

Sec. 2. Whoever sells any arms or munitions of war in violation of section 1 shall, on conviction, be punished by a fine not exceeding $10,000 or by imprisonment not exceeding two years, or both.

The President's proclamation (48 Stat. 1744), after reciting the terms of the Joint Resolution, declares:

Now, therefore, I, Franklin D. Roosevelt, President of the United States of America, acting under and by virtue of the authority conferred in me by the said joint resolution of Congress, do hereby declare and proclaim that I have found that the prohibition of the sale of arms and munitions of war in the United States to those countries now engaged in armed conflict in the Chaco may contribute to the reestablishment of peace between those countries, and that I have consulted with the governments of other American Republics and have been assured of the cooperation of such governments as I have deemed necessary as contemplated by the said joint resolution, and I do hereby admonish all citizens of the United States and every person to abstain from every violation of the provisions of the joint resolution above set forth, hereby made applicable to Bolivia and Paraguay, and I do hereby warn them that all violations of such provisions will be rigorously prosecuted.

And I do hereby enjoin upon all officers of the United States charged with the execution of the laws thereof the utmost diligence in preventing violations of the said joint resolution and this my proclamation issued thereunder, and in bringing to trial and punishment any offenders against the same.

And I do hereby delegate to the Secretary of State the power of prescribing exceptions and limitations to the application of the said joint resolution of May 28, 1934, as made effective by this my proclamation issued thereunder.

On November 14, 1935, this proclamation was revoked (49 Stat. 3480), in the following terms:

Now, therefore, I, Franklin D. Roosevelt, President of the United States of America, do hereby declare and proclaim that I have found that the prohibition of the sale of arms and munitions of war in the United States to Bolivia or Paraguay will no longer be necessary as a contribution to the reestablishment of peace between those countries, and the above-mentioned Proclamation of May 28, 1934, is hereby revoked as to the sale of arms and munitions of war to Bolivia or Paraguay from and after November 29, 1935, provided, however, that this action shall not have the effect of releasing or extinguishing any penalty, forfeiture or liability incurred under the aforesaid Proclamation of May 28, 1934, or the Joint Resolution of Congress approved by the President on the same date, and that the said Proclamation and Joint Resolution shall be treated as remaining in force for the purpose of sustaining any proper action or prosecution for the enforcement of such penalty, forfeiture or liability.

Appellees severally demurred to the first count of the indictment on the grounds (1) that it did not charge facts sufficient to show the commission by appellees of any offense against any law of the United States; (2) that this count of the indictment charges a conspiracy to violate the joint resolution and the Presidential proclamation, both of which had expired according to the terms of the joint resolution by reason of the revocation contained in the Presidential proclamation of November 14, 1935, and were not in force at the time when the indictment was found. The points urged in support of the demurrers were, first, that the joint resolution effects an invalid delegation of legislative power to the executive; second, that the joint resolution never became effective, because of the failure of the President to find essential jurisdictional facts, and third, that the second proclamation operated to put an end to the alleged liability under the joint resolution.

The court below sustained the demurrers upon the first point, but overruled them on the second and third points. 14 F.Supp. 230. The government appealed to this court under the provisions of the Criminal Appeals Act of March 2, 1907, 34 Stat. 1246, as amended, U.S.C. Title 18, § 682. That act authorizes the United States to appeal from a district court direct to this court in criminal cases where, among other things, the decision sustaining a demurrer to the indictment or any count thereof is based upon the invalidity or construction of the statute upon which the indictment is founded.

First. It is contended that, by the Joint Resolution, the going into effect and continued operation of the resolution was conditioned (a) upon the President's judgment as to its beneficial effect upon the reestablishment of peace between the countries engaged in armed conflict in the Chaco; (b) upon the making of a proclamation, which was left to his unfettered discretion, thus constituting an attempted substitution of the President's will for that of Congress; (c) upon the making of a proclamation putting an end to the operation of the resolution, which again was left to the President's unfettered discretion; and (d) further, that the extent of its operation in particular cases was subject to limitation and exception by the President, controlled by no standard. In each of these particulars, appellees urge that Congress abdicated its essential functions and delegated them to the Executive.

Whether, if the Joint Resolution had related solely to internal affairs, it would be open to the challenge that it constituted an unlawful delegation of legislative power to the Executive we find it unnecessary to determine. The whole aim of the resolution is to affect a situation entirely external to the United States and falling within the category of foreign affairs. The determination which we are called to make, therefore, is whether the Joint Resolution, as applied to that situation, is vulnerable to attack under the rule that forbids a delegation of the lawmaking power. In other words, assuming (but not deciding) that the challenged delegation, if it were confined to internal affairs, would be invalid, may it nevertheless be sustained on the ground that its exclusive aim is to afford a remedy for a hurtful condition within foreign territory?

It will contribute to the elucidation of the question if we first consider the differences between the powers of the federal government in respect of foreign or external affairs and those in respect of domestic or internal affairs. That there are differences between them, and that these differences are fundamental, may not be doubted.

The two classes of powers are different both in respect of their origin and their nature. The broad statement that the federal government can exercise no powers except those specifically enumerated in the Constitution, and such implied powers as are necessary and proper to carry into effect the enumerated powers, is categorically true only in respect of our internal affairs. In that field, the primary purpose of the Constitution was to carve from the general mass of legislative powers then possessed by the states such portions as it was thought desirable to vest in the federal government, leaving those not included in the enumeration still in the states. **Carter v. Carter Coal Co.**, 298 U.S. 238, 294. That this doctrine applies only to powers which the states had is self-evident. And since the states severally never possessed international powers, such powers could not have been carved from the mass of state powers, but obviously were transmitted to the United States from some other source. During the colonial period, those powers were possessed exclusively by, and were entirely under the control of, the Crown. By the Declaration of Independence, "the Representatives of the United States of America" declared the United [not the several] Colonies to be free and independent states, and, as such, to have full Power to levy War, conclude Peace, contract Alliances, establish Commerce, and to do all other Acts and Things which Independent States may of right do.

As a result of the separation from Great Britain by the colonies, acting as a unit, the powers of external sovereignty passed from the Crown not to the colonies severally, but to the colonies in their collective and corporate capacity as the United States of America. Even before the Declaration, the colonies were a unit in foreign affairs, acting through a common agency -- namely the Continental Congress, composed of delegates from the thirteen colonies. That agency exercised the powers of war and peace, raised an army, created a navy, and finally adopted the Declaration of Independence. Rulers come and go; governments end, and forms of government change; but sovereignty survives. A political society cannot endure without a supreme will somewhere. Sovereignty is never held in suspense. When, therefore, the external sovereignty of Great Britain in respect of the colonies ceased, it immediately passed to the Union. See **Penhallow v. Doane**, 3 Dall. 54, 80-81. That fact was given practical application almost at once. The treaty of peace, made on September 23, 1783, was concluded between his Brittanic Majesty and the "United States of America." 8 Stat.— European Treaties—80.

The Union existed before the Constitution, which was ordained and established, among other things, to form "a more perfect Union." Prior to that event, it is clear that the Union, declared by the Articles of Confederation to be "perpetual," was the sole possessor of external sovereignty, and in the Union it remained without change save insofar as the Constitution, in express terms, qualified its exercise. The Framers' Convention was called, and exerted its powers upon the irrefutable postulate that, though the states were several, their people, in respect of foreign affairs, were one. *Compare* **The Chinese Exclusion Case**, 130 U.S. 581, 604, 606. In that convention, the entire absence of state power to deal with those affairs was thus forcefully stated by Rufus King:

The states were not "sovereigns" in the sense contended for by some. They did not possess the peculiar features of sovereignty—they could not make war, nor peace, nor alliances, nor treaties. Considering them as political beings, they were dumb, for they could not speak to any foreign sovereign whatever. They were deaf, for they could not hear any propositions from such sovereign. They had not even the organs or faculties of defence or offence, for they could not, of themselves, raise troops, or equip vessels, for war. 5 Elliott's Debates 212.

It results that the investment of the federal government with the powers of external sovereignty did not depend upon the affirmative grants of the Constitution. The powers to declare and wage war, to conclude peace, to make treaties, to maintain diplomatic relations with other sovereignties, if they had never been mentioned in the Constitution, would have vested in the federal government as necessary concomitants of nationality. Neither the Constitution nor the laws passed in pursuance of it have any force in foreign territory unless in respect of our own citizens (see **American Banana Co. v. United Fruit Co.**, 213 U.S. 347, 356), and operations of the nation in such territory must be governed by treaties, international understandings and compacts, and the principles of international law. As a member of the family of nations, the right and power of the United States in that field are equal to the right and power of the other members of the international family. Otherwise, the United States is not completely sovereign. The power to acquire territory by discovery and occupation (**Jones v. United States**, 137 U.S. 202, 212), the power to expel undesirable aliens (**Fong Yue Ting v. United States**, 149 U.S. 698, 705 *et seq.*), the power to make such international agreements as do not constitute treaties in the constitutional sense (**Altman & Co. v. United States**, 224 U.S. 583, 600-601; Crandall, Treaties, Their Making and Enforcement,2d ed., p. 102 and note 1), none of which is expressly affirmed by the Constitution, nevertheless exist as inherently inseparable from the conception of nationality. This the court recognized, and, in each of the cases cited, found the warrant for its conclusions not in the provisions of the Constitution, but in the law of nations.

In **Burnet v. Brooks**, 288 U.S. 378, 396, we said,

As a nation with all the attributes of sovereignty, the United States is vested with all the powers of government necessary to maintain an effective control of international relations.Cf. **Carter v. Carter Coal Co.**, supra, p. 295.

Not only, as we have shown, is the federal power over external affairs in origin and essential character different from that over internal affairs, but participation in the exercise of the power is significantly limited. In this vast external realm, with its important, complicated, delicate and manifold problems, the President alone has the power to speak or listen as a representative of the nation. He makes treaties with the advice and consent of the Senate; but he alone negotiates. Into the field of negotiation the Senate cannot intrude, and Congress itself is powerless to invade it. As Marshall said in his great argument of March 7, 1800, in the House of Representatives, "The President is the sole organ of the nation in its external relations, and its sole representative with foreign nations." Annals, 6th Cong., col. 613. The Senate Committee on Foreign Relations, at a very early day in our history (February 15, 1816), reported to the Senate, among other things, as follows:

The President is the constitutional representative of the United States with regard to foreign nations. He manages our concerns with foreign nations, and must necessarily be most competent to determine when, how, and upon what subjects negotiation may be urged with the greatest prospect of success. For his conduct, he is responsible to the Constitution. The committee consider this responsibility the surest pledge for the faithful discharge of his duty. They think the interference of the Senate in the direction of foreign negotiations calculated to diminish that responsibility, and thereby to impair the best security for the national safety. The nature of transactions with foreign nations, moreover, requires caution and unity of design, and their success frequently depends on secrecy and dispatch. U.S. Senate, Reports, Committee on Foreign Relations, vol. 8, p. 24.

It is important to bear in mind that we are here dealing not alone with an authority vested in the President by an exertion of legislative power, but with such an authority plus the very delicate, plenary and exclusive power of the President as the sole organ of the federal government in the field of international relations—a power which does not require as a basis for its exercise an act of Congress but which, of course, like every other governmental power, must be exercised in subordination to the applicable provisions of the Constitution.

***

In the light of the foregoing observations, it is evident that this court should not be in haste to apply a general rule which will have the effect of condemning legislation like that under review as constituting an unlawful delegation of legislative power. The principles which justify such legislation find overwhelming support in the unbroken legislative practice which has prevailed almost from the inception of the national government to the present day.

[The Court goes on to discuss at length, in chronological order, the many legislative acts bolstering its point.]

***

The uniform, long-continued and undisputed legislative practice just disclosed rests upon an admissible view of the Constitution which, even if the practice found far less support in principle than we think it does, we should not feel at liberty at this late day to disturb.

We deem it unnecessary to consider *seriatim* the several clauses which are said to evidence the unconstitutionality of the Joint Resolution as involving an unlawful delegation of legislative power. It is enough to summarize by saying that, both upon principle and in accordance with precedent, we conclude there is sufficient warrant for the broad discretion vested in the President to determine whether the enforcement of the statute will have a beneficial effect upon the reestablishment of peace in the affected countries; whether he shall make proclamation to bring the resolution into operation; whether and when the resolution shall cease to operate and to make proclamation accordingly, and to prescribe limitations and exceptions to which the enforcement of the resolution shall be subject.

Second. The second point raised by the demurrer was that the Joint Resolution never became effective because the President failed to find essential jurisdictional facts, and the third point was that the second proclamation of the President operated to put an end to the alleged liability of appellees under the Joint Resolution. In respect of both points, the court below overruled the demurrer, and thus far sustained the government.

The government contends that, upon an appeal by the United States under the Criminal Appeals Act from a decision holding an indictment bad, the jurisdiction of the court does not extend to questions decided in favor of the United States, but that such questions may only be reviewed in the usual way, after conviction. We find nothing in the words of the statute or in its purposes which justifies this conclusion. The demurrer in the present case challenges the validity of the statute upon three separate and distinct grounds. If the court below had sustained the demurrer without more, an appeal by the government necessarily would have brought here for our determination all of these grounds, since, in that case, the record would not have disclosed whether the court considered the statute invalid upon one particular ground or upon all of the grounds alleged. The judgment of the lower court is that the statute is invalid. Having held that this judgment cannot be sustained upon the particular ground which that court assigned, it is now open to this court to inquire whether or not the judgment can be sustained upon the rejected grounds which also challenge the validity of the statute, and, therefore, constitute a proper subject of review by this court under the Criminal Appeals Act. **United States v. Hastings**, 296 U.S. 188, 192.

***

The judgment of the court below must be reversed, and the cause remanded for further proceedings in accordance with the foregoing opinion.

Reversed.

Youngstown Sheet & Tube Co. v. Sawyer
343 U.S. 579 (1952)

Mr. Justice Black delivered the opinion of the Court.

We are asked to decide whether the President was acting within his constitutional power when he issued an order directing the Secretary of Commerce to take possession of and operate most of the Nation's steel mills. The mill owners argue that the President's order amounts to lawmaking, a legislative function which the Constitution has expressly confided to the Congress, and not to the President. The Government's position is that the order was made on findings of the President that his action was necessary to avert a national catastrophe which would inevitably result from a stoppage of steel production, and that, in meeting this grave emergency, the President was acting within the aggregate of his constitutional powers as the Nation's Chief Executive and the Commander in Chief of the Armed Forces of the United States. The issue emerges here from the following series of events:

In the latter part of 1951, a dispute arose between the steel companies and their employees over terms and conditions that should be included in new collective bargaining agreements. Long-continued conferences failed to resolve the dispute. On December 18, 1951, the employees' representative, United Steelworkers of America, CIO, gave notice of an intention to strike when the existing bargaining agreements expired on December 31. The Federal Mediation and Conciliation Service then intervened in an effort to get labor and management to agree. This failing, the President on December 22, 1951, referred the dispute to the Federal Wage Stabilization Board to investigate and make recommendations for fair and equitable terms of settlement. This Board's report resulted in no settlement. On April 4, 1952, the Union gave notice of a nationwide strike called to begin at 12:01 a.m. April 9. The indispensability of steel as a component of substantially all weapons and other war materials led the President to believe that the proposed work stoppage would immediately jeopardize our national defense and that governmental seizure of the steel mills was necessary in order to assure the continued availability of steel. Reciting these considerations for his action, the President, a few hours before the strike was to begin, issued Executive Order 10340, a copy of which is attached as an appendix, *post*, p. 589. The order directed the Secretary of Commerce to take possession of most of the steel mills and keep them running. The Secretary immediately issued his own possessory orders, calling upon the presidents of the various seized companies to serve as operating managers for the United States. They were directed to carry on their activities in accordance with regulations and directions of the Secretary. The next morning the President sent a message to Congress reporting his action. Cong.Rec. April 9, 1952, p. 3962. Twelve days later, he sent a second message. Cong.Rec. April 21, 1952, p. 4192. Congress has taken no action.

Obeying the Secretary's orders under protest, the companies brought proceedings against him in the District Court. Their complaints charged that the seizure was not authorized by an act of Congress or by any constitutional provisions. The District Court was asked to declare the orders of the President and the Secretary invalid and to issue preliminary and permanent injunctions restraining their enforcement. Opposing the motion for preliminary injunction, the United States asserted that a strike disrupting steel production for even a brief period would so endanger the wellbeing and safety of the Nation that the President had "inherent power" to do what he had done—power "supported by the Constitution, by historical precedent, and by court decisions." The Government also contended that, in any event, no preliminary injunction should be issued, because the companies had made no showing that their available legal remedies were inadequate or that their injuries from seizure would be irreparable. Holding against the Government on all points, the District Court, on April 30, issued a preliminary injunction restraining the Secretary from "continuing the seizure and possession of the plants ... and from acting under the purported authority of Executive Order No. 10340." 103 F.Supp. 569. On the same day, the Court of Appeals stayed the District Court's injunction. 90 U.S.App.D.C. ___, 197 F.2d 582. Deeming it best that the issues raised be promptly decided by this Court, we granted certiorari on May 3 and set the cause for argument on May 12. 343 U.S. 937.

Two crucial issues have developed: First. Should final determination of the constitutional validity of the President's order be made in this case which has proceeded no further than the preliminary injunction stage? Second. If so, is the seizure order within the constitutional power of the President?

I

[The Court discusses here the jurisdictional issue regarding the constitutional issues and the fact that the case has not progressed beyond the preliminary injunction issued by the District Court. The Court resolves the issues by agreeing with the District Court's determination that the constitutional issue was ripe for consideration.]

II

The President's power, if any, to issue the order must stem either from an act of Congress or from the Constitution itself. There is no statute that expressly authorizes the President to take possession of property as he did here. Nor is there any act of Congress to which our attention has been directed from which such a power can fairly be implied.

***

It is clear that, if the President had authority to issue the order he did, it must be found in some provision of the Constitution. And it is not claimed that express constitutional language grants this power to the President. The contention is that presidential power should be implied from the aggregate of his powers under the Constitution. Particular reliance is placed on provisions in Article II which say that "The executive Power shall be vested in a President ... "; that "he shall take Care that the Laws be faithfully executed", and that he "shall be Commander in Chief of the Army and Navy of the United States."

The order cannot properly be sustained as an exercise of the President's military power as Commander in Chief of the Armed Forces. The Government attempts to do so by citing a number of cases upholding broad powers in military commanders engaged in day-to-day fighting in a theater of war. Such cases need not concern us here. Even though "theater of war" be an expanding concept, we cannot with faithfulness to our constitutional system hold that the Commander in Chief of the Armed Forces has the ultimate power as such to take possession of private property in order to keep labor disputes from stopping production. This is a job for the Nation's lawmakers, not for its military authorities.

Nor can the seizure order be sustained because of the several constitutional provisions that grant executive power to the President. In the framework of our Constitution, the President's power to see that the laws are faithfully executed refutes the idea that he is to be a lawmaker. The Constitution limits his functions in the lawmaking process to the recommending of laws he thinks wise and the vetoing of laws he thinks bad. And the Constitution is neither silent nor equivocal about who shall make laws which the President is to execute. The first section of the first article says that "All legislative Powers herein granted shall be vested in a Congress of the United States ...." After granting many powers to the Congress, Article I goes on to provide that Congress may make all Laws which shall be necessary and proper for carrying into Execution the foregoing Powers, and all other Powers vested by this Constitution in the Government of the United States, or in any Department or Officer thereof.

The President's order does not direct that a congressional policy be executed in a manner prescribed by Congress—it directs that a presidential policy be executed in a manner prescribed by the President. The preamble of the order itself, like that of many statutes, sets out reasons why the President believes certain policies should be adopted, proclaims these policies as rules of conduct to be followed, and again, like a statute, authorizes a government official to promulgate additional rules and regulations consistent with the policy proclaimed and needed to carry that policy into execution. The power of Congress to adopt such public policies as those proclaimed by the order is beyond question. It can authorize the taking of private property for public use. It can make laws regulating the relationships between employers and employees, prescribing rules designed to settle labor disputes, and fixing wages and working conditions in certain fields of our economy. The Constitution does not subject this lawmaking power of Congress to presidential or military supervision or control.

It is said that other Presidents, without congressional authority, have taken possession of private business enterprises in order to settle labor disputes. But even if this be true, Congress has not thereby lost its exclusive constitutional authority to make laws necessary and proper to carry out the powers vested by the Constitution "in the Government of the United States, or any Department or Officer thereof."

The Founders of this Nation entrusted the lawmaking power to the Congress alone in both good and bad times. It would do no good to recall the historical events, the fears of power, and the hopes for freedom that lay behind their choice. Such a review would but confirm our holding that this seizure order cannot stand.

The judgment of the District Court is

Affirmed.

Commentary and Questions

10. The Court in *U.S. v. Curtiss-Wright Corporation* found a distinction in the president's authority to act in internal and external affairs. The Joint Resolution of Congress at issue in the case was a delegation of power to the president. The Curtiss-Wright Corporation was criminally charged with

conspiring to sell 15 machine guns to the government of Bolivia, which was involved at the time in an armed conflict in the Chaco,[22] a region in South America bordering Bolivia, Argentina and Paraguay. What did the Court state with regard to Presidential power to conduct foreign affairs? How significant is the sweep of the Court's language with regard to this presidential power?

11. The concurring opinion of Justice Robert Jackson in *Youngstown Sheet & Tube Co. v. Sawyer* is well-known and often cited for its language regarding the emergency powers of the president. Justice Jackson created a trilogy of tests for presidential power:

"1. When the President acts pursuant to an express or implied authorization of Congress, his authority is at its maximum, for it includes all that he possesses in his own right plus all that Congress can delegate. In these circumstances, and in these only, may he be said (for what it may be worth) to personify the federal sovereignty. If his act is held unconstitutional under these circumstances, it usually means that the Federal Government, as an undivided whole, lacks power. A seizure executed by the President pursuant to an Act of Congress would be supported by the strongest of presumptions and the widest latitude of judicial interpretation, and the burden of persuasion would rest heavily upon any who might attack it.
2. When the President acts in absence of either a congressional grant or denial of authority, he can only rely upon his own independent powers, but there is a zone of twilight in which he and Congress may have concurrent authority, or in which its distribution is uncertain. Therefore, congressional inertia, indifference or quiescence may sometimes, at least, as a practical matter, enable, if not invite, measures on independent presidential responsibility. In this area, any actual test of power is likely to depend on the imperatives of events and contemporary imponderables, rather than on abstract theories of law.
3. When the President takes measures incompatible with the expressed or implied will of Congress, his power is at its lowest ebb, for then he can rely only upon his own constitutional powers minus any constitutional powers of Congress over the matter. Courts can sustain exclusive presidential control in such a case only by disabling the Congress from acting upon the subject. Presidential claim to a power at once so conclusive and preclusive must be scrutinized with caution, for what is at stake is the equilibrium established by our constitutional system."[23]

Under which test did President Truman's act of seizing the steel mills fall? How did the issue regarding Executive power to act differ in *Youngstown Sheet & Tube Co.* from that in *Curtiss-Wright Corporation*?

12. How much will the courts defer to executive power, especially in the realm of national security and foreign affairs? It is obvious from several cases this is a recurring issue the Supreme Court has encountered. As Justice Rehnquist wrote at the start of *Dames & Moore v. Regan*, there are funda-

mental questions regarding "the manner in which our Republic is to be governed."[24] Rehnquist, citing *Youngstown Sheet & Tube*, pointed to the lack of helpful guidance in the *"concrete problems of the Executive power as they present themselves" and their recurring nature since "the Framers 'did not make the judiciary the overseer of our government.'"*[25] *Dames & Moore* centered on President Jimmy Carter's declaration of a national emergency and subsequent freezing of Iranian assets in the United States several days after Islamist radicals took over the U.S. Embassy in Tehran and held 52 American hostages. The crisis lasted from November 4, 1979, until January 4, 1981. Carter used his emergency powers under the 1977 International Emergency Economic Powers Act (IEEPA). At the heart of the case was a $3 million debt against the government of the Shah of Iran, which was nullified by Executive Order 12170 issued by President Carter on November 14, 1979. With the termination of the hostage crisis President Carter signed several Executive Orders implementing the terms of an agreement that, among other things, obligated the United States "to terminate all legal proceedings in United States courts involving claims of United States persons and institutions against Iran and its state enterprises, to nullify all attachments and judgments obtained therein, to prohibit all further litigation based on such claims, and to bring about the termination of such claims through binding arbitration."[26] A month after his January 1981 inauguration President Reagan signed Executive Order 12294, which ratified the agreements entered into by President Carter with the Iranian government. Dames & Moore, a private firm, sued Treasury Secretary Donald Regan to recover its $3 million debt from Iran. The Court upheld the executive actions and dismissed the $3 million claim. In doing so the Court found that presidential action backed by Congress was presumptively valid. Justice Rehnquist's *Dames & Moore* opinion cited *Youngstown Sheet & Tube Co.* extensively, including the concurring opinion of Justice Jackson.

13. In *Regan v. Wald*, 468 U.S. 222 (1984) the U.S. Supreme Court upheld Reagan Administration restrictions on travel to Cuba. The Treasury Department put currency control regulations in place in 1982, which limited travel to Cuba by *"prohibiting travel related financial transactions."*[27] The Treasury regulations were challenged on the grounds that the president failed to comply with the International Emergency Economic Powers Act (IEEPA), which limited the president's "power to impose peacetime economic embargoes against another country."[28] The Court found that congressional amendments to the Trading with the Enemy Act provided adequate authority for the president's actions. Justice Rehnquist, writing again for the Court, stated: *"Given the traditional deference to executive judgment [i]n this vast external realm," United States v. Curtiss-Wright Export Corp., 299 U.S. 304, 299 U.S. 319 (1936), we think there is an adequate basis under the Due Process Clause of the Fifth Amendment to sustain the President's decision to curtail the flow of hard currency to Cuba—currency that could then be used in support of Cuban adventurism—by restricting travel. Zemel v. Rusk, supra, at 381 U.S. 14-15; Haig v. Agee, 453 U.S. 280, 453 U.S. 306-307 (1981)."*[29]

14. The War Powers Resolution of 1973, otherwise known as the War Powers Act, was passed into law over the veto of President Nixon. The purpose of the War Powers Resolution was to outline presidential authority to commit U.S. troops to military action abroad. Under the Resolution the president is limited in sending military troops abroad to one of three scenarios: 1) express authorization from Congress; 2) pursuant to statutory authorization; or 3) a direct attack upon the United States, its territories, possessions or armed forces. Since its enactment, the War Powers Resolution has been subject to criticism from successive presidents who considered it an unconstitutional infringement on their Article II powers.[30] This has prompted clashes between the executive and legislative branches with the latter seeking to bring the judiciary into the fray through lawsuits claiming violations of the War Powers Resolution. Many of these lawsuits initiated by congressional members were dismissed on political question grounds, meaning the courts will not be involved in purely political questions involving national security.[31] Others were dismissed on ripeness grounds[32] or on the basis of Congress members' lack of standing to bring suit.[33]

   The 2001 Authorization to Use Military Force (AUMF) granted by Congress to President Bush to carry out "necessary and appropriate force" against those who "planned, authorized, committed or aided" the September 11, 2001 attacks included a specific reference to the War Powers Resolution. The AUMF in section 2 (B)(1) stated that the section was specific statutory authority under the War Powers Resolution. The extent of presidential power to continue to wage war under this authorization remains to be the subject of controversy over a decade after the 9/11 attacks.

   In response to evidence of chemical attacks in 2013 against the Syrian people by the Syrian government of Bashar Assad President Barack Obama sought to introduce U.S. military intervention. President Obama's plan called for limited air strikes against Syria's chemical weapons facilities. On September 10, 2013, on the eve of the 12-year anniversary of the 9/11 attacks, President Obama conducted a televised explanation to the American people of his position toward the chemical attacks in Syria in which he stated the following position with regard to the use of military force:

"... after careful deliberation, I determined that it is in the national security interest of the United State to respond to the Assad regime's use of chemical weapons through a targeted military strike. The purpose of this strike would be to deter Assad from using chemical weapons, to degrade his regime's ability to use them, and to make clear to the world that we will not tolerate their use.

That's my judgment as commander-in-chief, but I'm also the president of the world's oldest constitutional democracy. So even though I possess the authority to order military strikes, I believed it was right in the absence of a direct or imminent threat to our security to take this debate to Congress. I believe our democracy is stronger when the president acts with the support of Congress, and I believe that America acts more effectively abroad when we stand together. This is especially true after a decade that put more and more war-making power in the hands of the president and more and more burdens on the shoulders of our troops, while sidelining the people's representatives from the critical decisions about when we use force."[84]

Is President Obama's statement regarding his ability to use military force against Syria correct? Does his Article II commander-in-chief role authorize such action? What is to be made of President Obama's statement about the role of Congress in the war-making power and the past decade's extension of executive authority in that area? Does the War Powers Resolution support President Obama's assertion that he can unilaterally order military action against Syria?

Endnotes

[1]   6 U.S. 170 (1804).

[2]   *Id.*

[3]   *Id.*

[4]   *Little v. Barreme*, The Oyez Project at IIT Chicago-Kent College of Law, http://www.oyez.org/node/63617.

[5]   *Noriega v. Pastrana*, 559 U.S. ___,130 S.Ct. 1002, 175 L.Ed. 2d 1098 (2010), citing *Boumediene v. Bush*, 553 U.S. 723, 128 S.Ct. 2229, 171 L.Ed. 2d 41 (2008), quoting *Marbury v. Madison*, 5 U.S. 137, 1 Cranch 137, 2 L.Ed. 60 (1803).

[6]   Letter of Secretary of State Daniel Webster to Special Minister Ashburton, dated 27 July 1842, reproduced at http://www.yale.edu/lawweb/avalon/diplomacy/britian/br-1842d.htm.

[7]   See generally, Louis Rouillard, *The Caroline Case: Anticipatory Self-Defence in Contemporary International Law*, Miskolc Journal of International Law, Vol. 1, No.2 (2004).

[8]   Abraham D. Sofaer, On the Necessity of Pre-emption, *The European Journal of International Law*, Vol. 14, No. 2 (2003)

[9]   12 U.S. 110 (1814).

[10]   *Id.*

[11]   *Id.*

[12]   *Id.*

[13]   *Id.*

[14]   Note, *Brown v. United States, The Paquete Habana, and the Executive*, 60 Hastings Law Journal 149 (2008).

[15]   175 U.S. 677 (1900).

[16]   C. Bradley, *The Charming Betsy Canon and Separation of Powers: Re-thinking the Interpretive Role of International Law*, Georgetown Law Journal, Vol. 86, No. 3 (1998).

[17]   Federal Nonintercourse Act, ch. 10, § 1, 2 Stat. 7, 8 (1800).

[18]   Bradley.

[19]   *6 U.S. 64* (1804).

[20]   Michael J. Malbin, *Conscription, the Constitution, and the Framers: An Historical Analysis*, 40 Fordham L. Rev. 805 (1972), http://ir.lawnet.fordham.edu/flr/vol40/iss4/3

[21]   *Id at 807.*

[22]   *United States v. Curtiss-Wright Export Corp.,* The Oyez Project at IIT Chicago-Kent College of Law, http://www.oyez.org/cases/1901-1939/1936/1936_98 (last visited April 9, 2012).

[23]   343 U.S. 579 (1952)

[24]   453 U.S. 654 (1981)

[25]   *Id.*

[26]   *Id.*

[27]   Center for Constitutional Rights, *Our Cases,* http://ccrjustice.org/ourcases/past-cases/reagan-v.-wald

[28]   Note, *Regan v. Wald and the Grandfather Clause of Trading with the Enemy Act: A Lesson in Explicit Vagueness*, 5 Pace L. Rev. 693 (1985).

[29]   468 U.S. at 243 (1984).

[30]   Library of Congress. (2012, April 30). *War Powers.* Retrieved from Library of Congress: http://www.loc.gov/law/help/war-powers.php.

[31]   See, *Crockett v. Reagan,* 558 F. Supp. 893 (D.D.C., 1982) aff'd. per curiam 720 F.2d 1355 (D.C. Cir., 1983) cert. denied 467 U.S. 1251 (1984); *Sanchez-Espinoza v. Reagan,* 568 F.Supp. 596 (D.D.C., 1983) aff'd. 770 F.2d 202 (D.C. Cir., 1985); *Lowry v. Reagan,* 676 F.Supp. 333 (D.D.C., 1987) .

[32]   See, *Dellums v. Bush,* 752 F.Supp. 1141 (D.D.C., 1990).

[33]   See, *Campbell v. Clinton,* 203 F.3d 19 (D.C. Cir., 2000).

[34]   *Fox News. (2013, September 10). Transcript of President Obama's Speech on Syria.* Retrieved from Fox News : http://www.foxnews.com/politics/2013/09/10/transcript-president-obama-speech-on-syria/

Chapter Three
HABEAS CORPUS AND MILITARY TRIBUNALS

Habeas Corpus

Article I, section 9, second clause of the U.S. Constitution contains the following words: *"The Privilege of the Writ of Habeas Corpus shall not be suspended, unless when in Cases of Rebellion or Invasion the public safety may require it."* This is the Suspension Clause of the Constitution that protects the privilege of the writ of habeas corpus, allowing for its denial only in extreme matters of national emergency. The language of the Suspension Clause is significant because it references habeas corpus (Latin for *"you have the body"*) as a "privilege" not as a specific enumerated "right." This provides for the emergency suspension by Congress when public safety may require it. Other than that exception the writ is considered as a right that an individual in custody has against illegal detention. But there are recurring questions that have often been brought before the U.S. Supreme Court for resolution. What constitutes an emergency authorizing suspension and who can suspend the writ? Does the president have unilateral power under his commander-in-chief role or is it left specifically to Congress under Article I, section 9? Once again the power and authority of these two government branches seek their clarification within the judiciary. But this, too, raises separate issue as to whether it is the proper role of the Supreme Court to decide matters that are deemed to relate to national security.

Habeas corpus, or the Great Writ[1] as it has often been called, is actually a variety of writs requiring that an individual be produced before a court or judge.[2] Among the writ's various purposes are to bring a prisoner forward to testify,[3] to bring a defendant from a lower court before a superior court,[4] or to transport the prisoner from one county where confined to another county where the trial is to be held.[5] Generally, when referring to the writ, the reference is to *habeas corpus ad subjiciendum*, which directs the individual detaining another to produce the prisoner in order for the court to determine the legality of the prisoner's confinement.

As indicated in this chapter's case captions these are *ex parte* applications, which mean the cases are brought on the behalf of one party without notice or contest from another party with an adverse interest. It is essentially made by the one party without the presence of another. This is the importance and power of the Great Writ in that it offers a remedy for the individual who believes they have been unlawfully detained and, as originally contemplated in the common law, provides relief from the arbitrary power of the executive authority of government. The cases that follow are *habeas corpus ad subjiciendum* proceedings in which the petitioner is claiming an unlawful detention. A finding of unlawful detention results in the release of the prisoner or the prisoner being brought before the proper tribunal, such as a civilian court if held in military custody, and provided a new trial. Habeas corpus proceedings have, in the past few decades, been generally associated with capital sentencing review in criminal cases.

The First Congress of the United States passed the Judiciary Act of 1789 on September 24, 1789, thus giving effect to Article III of the U.S. Constitution by establishing the federal judiciary. Section 14 of the Judiciary Act provided for federal courts to issue the writ of habeas corpus: *"And that either of the justices of the supreme court, as well as judges of the district courts, shall have power to grant writs of habeas corpus for the purpose of an inquiry into the cause of commitment."*[6] Though it restricted the writ to prisoners held in federal custody: *"Provided, That writs of habeas corpus shall in no case extend to prisoners in gaol, unless where they are in custody, under or by colour of the authority of the United States, or are committed for trial before some court of the same, or are necessary to be brought into court to testify."*[7] The Habeas Corpus Act of 1867[8] would first provide a means for those in state custody to challenge their detentions in federal court. The statute reads as follows:

> *"That the several courts of the United States, and the several justices and judges of such courts, within their respective jurisdictions, in addition to the authority already conferred by law, shall have power to grant writs of habeas corpus in all cases where any person may be restrained of his or her liberty in violation of the constitution, or of any treaty or law of the United States; and it shall be lawful for such person so restrained of his or her liberty to apply to either of said justices or judges for a writ of habeas corpus, which application shall be in writing and verified by affidavit, and shall set forth the facts concerning the detention of the party applying, in whose custody he or she is detained, and by virtue of what claim or authority, if known; and the said justice or judge to whom such application shall be made shall forthwith award a writ of habeas corpus, unless it shall appear from the petition itself that the party is not deprived of his or her liberty in contravention of the constitution or laws of the United States."*[9]

The statute became an opening for subsequent cases of postconviction relief in federal court for convicted state prisoners. This line of habeas corpus cases would develop over time with Supreme Court involvement.[10] By the latter part of the 20th century and into the 21st the writ was seen as a relief for state prisoners who petition the federal courts based on claims rejected at the state level. After the 9/11 attacks the applicability and availability of the Great Writ toward prisoners of war would become a subject of concentrated legal argument not observed since the Civil War and World War II.

Ex Parte Merryman and the Suspension of Habeas Corpus

The Writ of Habeas Corpus was suspended by President Lincoln at the start of the Civil War in 1861. The suspension would lead to a legal showdown between the powers of the executive branch, the military under the president's command, and the judiciary in the form of Chief Justice Roger Taney. After fighting began in April 1861, President Lincoln declared martial law in Maryland when federal troops were attacked in Baltimore by Confederate sympathizers. Maryland was a concern for the federal government at the time because it was a border state but considerably southern in its loyalty and support. It would eventually remain in the union, but Maryland's close proximity to the nation's capital and its position as a slave-holding state created initial safety concerns for the federal government. In an April 27, 1861, letter to General Winfield Scott, commanding general of the United States Army, President Lincoln wrote: *"If at any point on or in the vicinity of any military line which is now or which shall be used between the city of Philadelphia and the city of Washington you find resistance which renders it necessary to suspend the writ of habeas corpus for the public safety, you personally, or through the officer in command at the point where resistance occurs, are authorized to suspend the writ."*[11] One month later on May 25, 1861, federal troops arrested John Merryman in his Maryland home for participating in the destruction of railroad bridges after the April Baltimore riots. Merryman, a Maryland militia member sympathetic to the Confederacy, was taken to Fort McHenry where he was held in custody. Merryman immediately obtained counsel who drafted a petition requesting the writ and presented it to Chief Justice Taney who was then sitting as a local circuit court judge. Taney issued the writ of habeas corpus on May 26 with it being returnable before him in Baltimore on May 27. On that date General Cadwalader, the commander of Fort McHenry, to whom the writ was addressed, did not appear but in his place sent a colonel who explained the charges against Merryman and the fact that General Cadwalader, under authority of the president, had suspended the writ of habeas corpus.[12] Taney subsequently issued an order of attachment against General Cadwalader and instructed a court marshal to deliver it for return the next day. On March 28 the marshal reported to Taney that he went to Fort McHenry, announced his presence and intention and was denied entry.[13] Taney's opinion in ***Ex Parte Merryman*** followed in which he chided the president for acting outside his lawful authority and placing the military between him and the rule of law:

> *"... being thus officially notified that the privilege of the writ has been suspended, under the orders, and by the authority of the president, and believing, as I do, that the president has exercised a power which he does not possess under the constitution, a proper respect for the high office he fills, requires me to state plainly and fully the grounds of my opinion, in order to show that I have not ventured to question the legality of his act, without a careful and deliberate examination of the whole subject.... Even if the privilege*

*of the writ of habeas corpus were suspended by act of congress, and
a party not subject to the rules and articles of war were afterwards
arrested and imprisoned by regular judicial process, he could not
be detained in prison, or brought to trial before a military tribunal,
for the article in the amendments to the constitution immediately
following the one above referred to (that is, the sixth article)
provides, that "in all criminal prosecutions, the accused shall enjoy
the right to a speedy and public trial by an impartial jury of the
state and district wherein the crime shall have been committed,
which district shall have been previously ascertained by law; and
to be informed of the nature and cause of the accusation; to be
confronted with the witnesses against him; to have compulsory
process for obtaining witnesses in his favor; and to have the
assistance of counsel for his defence."*

*The only power, therefore, which the president possesses, where the
"life, liberty or property" of a private citizen is concerned, is the
power and duty prescribed in the third section of the second article,
which requires "that he shall take care that the laws shall be
faithfully executed." He is not authorized to execute them himself,
or through agents or officers, civil or military, appointed by himself,
but he is to take care that they be faithfully carried into execution,
as they are expounded and adjudged by the co-ordinate branch of
the government to which that duty is assigned by the
constitution....With such provisions in the constitution, expressed
in language too clear to be misunderstood by any one, I can see no
ground whatever for supposing that the president, in any
emergency, or in any state of things, can authorize the suspension
of the privileges of the writ of habeas corpus, or the arrest of a
citizen, except in aid of the judicial power. He certainly does not
faithfully execute the laws, if he takes upon himself legislative
power, by suspending the writ of habeas corpus, and the judicial
power also, by arresting and imprisoning a person without due
process of law. Nor can any argument be drawn from the nature of
sovereignty, or the necessity of government, for self-defence in times
of tumult and danger. The government of the United States is one
of delegated and limited powers; it derives its existence and
authority altogether from the constitution, and neither of its
branches, executive, legislative or judicial, can exercise any of the
powers of government beyond those specified and granted; for the
tenth article of the amendments to the constitution, in express
terms, provides that "the powers not delegated to the United States
by the constitution, nor prohibited by it to the states, are reserved
to the states, respectively, or to the people."*

Indeed, the security against imprisonment by executive authority, provided for in the fifth article of the amendments to the constitution, which I have before quoted, is nothing more than a copy of a like provision in the English constitution, which had been firmly established before the declaration of independence. Blackstone states it in the following words: "To make imprisonment lawful, it must be either by process of law from the courts of judicature, or by warrant from some legal officer having authority to commit to prison." 1 Bl. Comm. 137..... But the documents before me show, that the military authority in this case has gone far beyond the mere suspension of the privilege of the writ of habeas corpus. It has, by force of arms, thrust aside the judicial authorities and officers to whom the constitution has confided the power and duty of interpreting and administering the laws, and substituted a military government in its place, to be administered and executed by military officers ... a military officer, stationed in Pennsylvania, without giving any information to the district attorney, and without any application to the judicial authorities, assumes to himself the judicial power in the district of Maryland; undertakes to decide what constitutes the crime of treason or rebellion; what evidence (in indeed he required any) is sufficient to support the accusation and justify the commitment; and commits the party, without a hearing, even before himself, to close custody, in a strongly garrisoned fort, to be there held, it would seem, during the pleasure of those who committed him ... These great and fundamental laws, which congress itself could not suspend, have been disregarded and suspended, like the writ of habeas corpus, by a military order, supported by force of arms. Such is the case now before me, and I can only say that if the authority which the constitution has confided to the judiciary department and judicial officers, may thus, upon any pretext or under any circumstances, be usurped by the military power, at its discretion, the people of the United States are no longer living under a government of laws, but every citizen holds life, liberty and property at the will and pleasure of the army officer in whose military district he may happen to be found.... In such a case, my duty was too plain to be mistaken. I have exercised all the power which the constitution and laws confer upon me, but that power has been resisted by a force too strong for me to overcome. It is possible that the officer who has incurred this grave responsibility may have misunderstood hiB instructions, and exceeded the authority intended to be given him; I shall, therefore, order all the proceedings in this case, with my opinion, to be filed and recorded in the circuit court of the United States for the district of Maryland, and direct the clerk to transmit a copy, under seal, to the president of the United States. It will then remain for that high officer, in fulfillment of his constitutional obligation to "take care that the laws be faithfully executed," to determine what measures he will take to cause the civil process of the United States to be respected and enforced."[14]

The U.S. Supreme Court would subsequently issue opinions in two Civil War habeas corpus cases with very different results in *Ex Parte Vallandigham* and *Ex Parte Milligan*. These cases, including *Merryman* and a World War II habeas corpus case, *Ex Parte Quirin*, would form the cornerstone for later legal arguments involving the detention of post-9/11 detainees in the War on Terror.

This chapter and the cases that follow explore the relationship between habeas corpus relief and the authority of military courts over civilians and alleged saboteurs. Chapter 4 cases and material discuss the access to civilian courts for detainees labeled as either enemy combatants or unlawful enemy combatants.

Ex Parte Vallandigham
68 U.S. 243 (1863)

This case arose on the petition of Clement L. Vallandigham for a certiorari, to be directed to the Judge Advocate General of the Army of the United States, to send up to this court, for its review, the proceedings of a military commission, by which the said Vallandigham had been tried and sentenced to imprisonment; the facts of the case, as derived from the statement of the learned Justice (Wayne) who delivered the opinion of the court, having been as follows:

Major-General Burnside, commanding the military department of Ohio, issued a special order, No. 135, on the 21st April, 1863, by which a military commission was appointed to meet at Cincinnati, Ohio, on the 22d of April, or as soon thereafter as practicable, for the trial of such persons as might be brought before it. There was a detail of officers to constitute it, and a judge advocate appointed.

The same general had, previously, on the 13th of April, 1863, issued a general order, No. 38, declaring, for the information of all persons concerned, that thereafter all persons found within his lines who should commit acts for the benefit of the enemies of our country, should be tried as spies or traitors, and if convicted should suffer death; and among other acts prohibited, was the habit of declaring sympathies for the enemy. The order issued by General Burnside declared that persons committing such offences would be at once arrested, with a view to being tried as above stated, or to be sent beyond his lines into the lines of their friends; that it must be distinctly understood that treason, expressed or implied, would not be tolerated in his department.

On the 5th of May, 1863, Vallandigham, a resident of the State of Ohio, and a citizen of the United States, was arrested at his residence and taken to Cincinnati, and there imprisoned. On the following day, he was arraigned before a military commission on a charge of having expressed sympathies for those in arms against the Government of the United States, and for having uttered, in a speech at a public meeting, disloyal sentiments and opinions, with the object and purpose of weakening the power of the Government in its efforts for the suppression of an unlawful rebellion.

The specification under the charge was, that he, the said Vallandigham, a citizen of Ohio, on the 1st of May, 1863, at Mount Vernon, in Knox County, Ohio, did publicly address a large meeting of persons, and did utter sentiments, in words or to the effect, 'that the present war was a wicked, cruel, and unnecessary war, one not waged for the preservation of the Union, but for the purpose of crushing out liberty and to erect a despotism; a war for the freedom of the blacks and the enslavement of the whites; and that if the administration had not wished otherwise, that the war could have been honorably terminated long ago; that peace might have been honorably made by listening to the proposed intermediation of France; that propositions, by which the Southern States could be won back, and the South guaranteed their rights under the Constitution, had been rejected the day before the late battle of Fredericksburg by Lincoln and his minions, meaning the President of the United States, and those under him in authority. Also charging that the Government of the United States was about to appoint military marshals in every district to restrain the people of their liberties, and to deprive them of their rights and privileges, characterizing General Order No. 38, from headquarters of the Department of the Ohio, as a base usurpation of arbitrary authority, inviting his hearers to resist the same, by saying, the sooner the people inform the minions of usurped power that they will not submit to such restrictions upon their liberties, the better; and adding, that he was at all times and upon all occasions resolved to do what he could to defeat the attempts now being made to build up a monarchy upon the ruins of our free government, and asserting that he firmly believed, as he had said six months ago, that the men in power are attempting to establish a despotism in this country, more cruel and oppressive than ever existed before.'

The prisoner, on being arraigned, denied the jurisdiction of the military commission, and refused to plead either to the charge or specification. Thereon, the members of the commission, after private consultation, directed the judge advocate to enter a plea of Not Guilty, and to proceed with the trial, with an allowance to the petitioner to call witnesses to rebut the evidence which might be introduced against him to establish the charge. The next day the commission proceeded with the trial. Seven members of it were present, and tried the charge in due form of military law.

***

It began with the declaration, that he had been arrested without due process of law, without a warrant from any judicial officer; that he was then in a military prison, and had been served with a charge and specifications, as in a court-martial or military commission; that he was not either in the land or naval forces of the United States, nor in the militia in the actual service of the United States, and, therefore, not triable for any cause by any such court; that he was subject, by the express terms of the Constitution, to arrest only by due process of law or judicial warrant, regularly issued upon affidavit by some officer or court of competent jurisdiction for the trial of citizens; that he was entitled to be tried on an indictment or presentment of a grand jury of such court, to a speedy and public trial, and also by an impartial jury of the State of Ohio, to be confronted with witnesses against him, to have compulsory process for witnesses in his behalf, the assistance of counsel for his defence, by evidence and argument according to the common law and the usages of judicial courts;-all those he demanded as his right as a citizen of the United States, under the Constitution of the United States. He also alleged that the offence of which he is charged is not known to the Constitution of the United States, nor to any law thereof; that they were words spoken to the people of Ohio, in an open and public political meeting, lawfully and peaceably assembled under the Constitution, and upon full notice; that they were words of criticism upon the policy of the public servants of the people, by which policy it was alleged that the welfare of the country was not promoted. That they were used as an appeal to the people to change that policy, not by force, but by free elections and the ballot-box; that it is not pretended that he counselled disobedience to the Constitution or resistance to the law or lawful authority; that he had never done so, and that beyond this protest he had nothing further to submit.

The judge advocate replied, that so far as the statement called in question the jurisdiction of the commission, that had been decided by the authority convening and ordering the trial, nor had the commission, at any time, been willing to entertain the objection; that as far as any implications or inferences designed or contemplated by the statement of the accused, his rights to counsel and to witnesses for his defence, he had enjoyed the allowance of both, and process for his witnesses, which had been issued; and that as to the facts charged in the specification, they were to be determined by the evidence;-that his criminality was a question peculiarly for the commission, and that he had submitted the case to its consideration. The commission was then cleared for consideration.

The finding and sentence were, that Vallandigham was guilty of the charge and specification ... and the commission, therefore, sentenced him to be placed in close confinement in some fortress of the United States, to be designated by the commanding officer of this department, there to be kept during the war.

The finding and sentence were approved and confirmed by General Burnside, in an order bearing date the 16th of May, 1863, and Fort Warren was designated as the place of imprisonment. On the 19th of May, 1863, the President, in commutation of the sentence, directed Major-General Burnside to send the prisoner, without delay, to the headquarters of General Rosecrans, then in Tennessee, to be by him put beyond our military lines; which order was executed.

In support of the motion for the certiorari, and against the jurisdiction of the military commission, it was urged that the latter was prohibited by the act of March 3d, 1863, for enrolling and calling out the national forces (30, 12 Stat. at Large, 736), as the crimes punishable in it by the sentence of a court-martial or military commission, applied only to persons who are in the military service of the United States, and subject to the articles of war. And also, that by the Constitution itself, 3, art. 3, all crimes, except in cases of impeachment, were to be tried by juries in the State where the crime had been committed; and when not committed within any State, at such place as Congress may by law have directed; and that the military commission could have no jurisdiction to try the petitioner, as neither the charge against him nor its specifications imputed to him any offence known to the law of the land, and that General Burnside had no authority to enlarge the jurisdiction of a military commission by the General Order No. 38, or otherwise.

Mr. Justice Wayne, after stating the case, much as precedes, delivered the opinion of the court:

General Burnside acted in the matter as the general commanding the Ohio Department, in conformity with the instructions for the government of the armies of the United States, approved by the President of the United States, and published by the Assistant Adjutant-General, by order of the Secretary of War, on the 24th of April, 1863. It is affirmed in these instructions, that military jurisdiction is of two kinds. First, that which is conferred and defined by statute; second, that which is derived from the common law of war. 'Military offences, under the statute, must be tried in the manner therein directed; but military offences, which do not come within the statute, must be tried and punished under the common law of war. The character of the courts which exercise these jurisdictions depends upon the local law of each particular county.'

In the armies of the United States, the first is exercised by courts-martial, while cases which do not come within the 'rules and regulations of war,' or the jurisdiction conferred by statute or court-martial, are tried by military commissions.

These jurisdictions are applicable, not only to war with foreign nations, but to a rebellion, when a part of a country wages war against its legitimate government, seeking to throw off all allegiance to it, to set up a government of its own.

Our first remark upon the motion for a certiorari is, that there is no analogy between the power given by the Constitution and law of the United States to the Supreme Court, and the other inferior courts of the United States, and to the judges of them, to issue such processes, and the prerogative power by which it is done in England. The purposes for which the writ is issued are alike, but there is no similitude in the origin of the power to do it. In England, the Court of King's Bench has a superintendence over all courts of an inferior criminal jurisdiction, and may, by the plenitude of its power, award a certiorari to have any indictment removed and brought before it; and where such certiorari is allowable, it is awarded at the instance of the king, because every indictment is at the suit of the king, and he has a prerogative of suing in whatever court he pleases. The courts of the United States derive authority to issue such a writ from the Constitution and the legislation of Congress.

***

The appellate powers of the Supreme Court, as granted by the Constitution, are limited and regulated by the acts of Congress, and must be exercised subject to the exceptions and regulations made by Congress. In other words, the petition before us we think not to be within the letter or spirit of the grants of appellate jurisdiction to the Supreme Court. It is not in law or equity within the meaning of those terms as used in the 3d article of the Constitution. Nor is a military commission a court within the meaning of the 14th section of the Judiciary Act of 1789. That act is denominated to be one to establish the judicial courts of the United States, and the 14th section declares that all the 'before- mentioned courts' of the United States shall have power to issue writs of scire facias, habeas corpus, and all other writs not specially provided for by statute, which may be necessary for the exercise of their respective jurisdictions, agreeably to the principles and usages of law. The words in the section, 'the before-mentioned' courts, can only have refer- ence to such courts as were established in the preceding part of the act, and excludes the idea that a court of military commission can be one of them.

Whatever may be the force of Vallandigham's protest, that he was not triable by a court of military commission, it is certain that his petition cannot be brought within the 14th section of the act; and further, that the court cannot, without disregarding its frequent decisions and interpretation of the Constitution in respect to its judicial power, originate a writ of certiorari to review or pronounce any opinion upon the proceedings of a military commission.

***

For the reasons given, our judgment is, that the writ of certiorari prayed for to revise and review the proceedings of the military commission, by which Clement L. Vallandigham was tried, sentenced, and imprisoned, must be denied, and so do we order accordingly.

Certiorari Refused.

Ex parte Milligan
71 U.S. 2 (1866)

Mr. Justice Davis delivered the opinion of the court.

On the 10th day of May, 1865, Lambdin P. Milligan presented a petition to the Circuit Court of the United States for the District of Indiana to be discharged from an alleged unlawful imprisonment. The case made by the petition is this: Milligan is a citizen of the United States; has lived for twenty years in Indiana, and, at the time of the grievances complained of, was not, and never had been, in the military or naval service of the United States. On the 5th day of October, 1864, while at home, he was arrested by order of General Alvin P. Hovey, commanding the military district of Indiana, and has ever since been kept in close confinement.

On the 21st day of October, 1864, he was brought before a military commission, convened at Indianapolis by order of General Hovey, tried on certain charges and specifications, found guilty, and sentenced to be hanged, and the sentence ordered to be executed on Friday, the 19th day of May, 1865.

On the 2d day of January, 1865, after the proceedings of the military commission were at an end, the Circuit Court of the United States for Indiana met at Indianapolis and empaneled a grand jury, who were charged to inquire whether the laws of the United States had been violated. and, if so, to make presentments. The court adjourned on the 27th day of January, having, prior thereto, discharged from further service the grand jury, who did not find any bill of indictment or make any presentment against Milligan for any offence whatever, and, in fact, since his imprisonment, no bill of indictment has been found or presentment made against him by any grand jury of the United States.

Milligan insists that said military commission had no jurisdiction to try him upon the charges preferred, or upon any charges whatever, because he was a citizen of the United States and the State of Indiana, and had not been, since the commencement of the late Rebellion, a resident of any of the States whose citizens were arrayed against the government, and that the right of trial by jury was guaranteed to him by the Constitution of the United States.

The prayer of the petition was that, under the act of Congress approved March 3d, 1863, entitled, "An act relating to habeas corpus and regulating judicial proceedings in certain cases," he may be brought before the court and either turned over to the proper civil tribunal to be proceeded against according to the law of the land or discharged from custody altogether.

With the petition were filed the order for the commission, the charges and specifications, the findings of the court, with the order of the War Department reciting that the sentence was approved by the President of the United States, and directing that it be carried into execution without delay. The petition was presented and filed in open court by the counsel for Milligan; at the same time, the District Attorney of the United States for Indiana appeared and, by the agreement of counsel, the application was submitted to the court. The opinions of the judges of the Circuit Court were opposed on three questions, which are certified to the Supreme Court:

1st. "On the facts stated in said petition and exhibits, ought a writ of habeas corpus to be issued?"

2d. "On the facts stated in said petition and exhibits, ought the said Lambdin P. Milligan to be discharged from custody as in said petition prayed?"

3d. "Whether, upon the facts stated in said petition and exhibits, the military commission mentioned therein had jurisdiction legally to try and sentence said Milligan in manner and form as in said petition and exhibits is stated?"

The importance of the main question presented by this record cannot be overstated, for it involves the very framework of the government and the fundamental principles of American liberty.

During the late wicked Rebellion, the temper of the times did not allow that calmness in deliberation and discussion so necessary to a correct conclusion of a purely judicial question. *Then*, considerations of safety were mingled with the exercise of power, and feelings and interests prevailed which are happily terminated. Now that the public safety is assured, this question, as well as all others, can be discussed and decided without passion or the admixture of any element not required to form a legal judgment. We approach the investigation of this case fully sensible of the magnitude of the inquiry and the necessity of full and cautious deliberation.

***

[The Court proceeds to examine the authority of the Circuit Court of Indiana to certify the issue on appeal and the Court's own jurisdiction in the case. The Court determined it had jurisdiction and that Milligan exercised the remedy available to him at the time.]

***

The controlling question in the case is this: upon the facts stated in Milligan's petition and the exhibits filed, had the military commission mentioned in it jurisdiction legally to try and sentence him? Milligan, not a resident of one of the rebellious states or a prisoner of war, but a citizen of Indiana for twenty years past and never in the military or naval service, is, while at his home, arrested by the military power of the United States, imprisoned, and, on certain criminal charges preferred against him, tried, convicted, and sentenced to be hanged by a military commission, organized under the direction of the military commander of the military district of Indiana. Had this tribunal the legal power and authority to try and punish this man?

No graver question was ever considered by this court, nor one which more nearly concerns the rights of the whole people, for it is the birthright of every American citizen when charged with crime to be tried and punished according to law. The power of punishment is alone through the means which the laws have provided for that purpose, and, if they are ineffectual, there is an immunity from punishment, no matter how great an offender the individual may be or how much his crimes may have shocked the sense of justice of the country or endangered its safety. By the protection of the law, human rights are secured; withdraw that protection and they are at the mercy of wicked rulers or the clamor of an excited people. If there was law to justify this military trial, it is not our province to interfere; if there was not, it is our duty to declare the nullity of the whole proceedings. The decision of this question does not depend on argument or judicial precedents, numerous and highly illustrative as they are. These precedents inform us of the extent of the struggle to preserve liberty and to relieve those in civil life from military trials. The founders of our government were familiar with the history of that struggle, and secured in a written constitution every right which the people had wrested from power during a contest of ages. By that Constitution and the laws authorized by it, this question must be determined. The provisions of that instrument on the administration of criminal justice are too plain and direct to leave room for misconstruction or doubt of their true meaning. Those applicable to this case are found in that clause of the original Constitution which says "That the trial of all crimes, except in case of impeachment, shall be by jury," and in the fourth, fifth, and sixth articles of the amendments. The fourth proclaims the right to be secure in person and effects against unreasonable search and seizure, and directs that a judicial warrant shall not issue "without proof of probable cause supported by oath or affirmation." The fifth declares that no person shall be held to answer for a capital or otherwise infamous crime unless on presentment by a grand jury, except in cases arising in the land or naval forces, or in the militia, when in actual service in time of war or public danger, nor be deprived of life, liberty, or property without due process of law.

And the sixth guarantees the right of trial by jury, in such manner and with such regulations that, with upright judges, impartial juries, and an able bar, the innocent will be saved and the guilty punished. It is in these words:

"In all criminal prosecutions the accused shall enjoy the right to a speedy and public trial by an impartial jury of the state and district wherein the crime shall have been committed, which district shall have been previously ascertained by law, and to be informed of the nature and cause of the accusation, to be confronted with the witnesses against him, to have compulsory process for obtaining witnesses in his favor, and to have the assistance of counsel for his defense."

These securities for personal liberty thus embodied were such as wisdom and experience had demonstrated to be necessary for the protection of those accused of crime. And so strong was the sense of the country of their importance, and so jealous were the people that these rights, highly prized, might be denied them by implication, that, when the original Constitution was proposed for adoption, it encountered severe opposition, and, but for the belief that it would be so amended as to embrace them, it would never have been ratified.

Time has proven the discernment of our ancestors, for even these provisions, expressed in such plain English words that it would seem the ingenuity of man could not evade them, are now, after the lapse of more than seventy years, sought to be avoided. Those great and good men foresaw that troublous times would arise when rulers and people would become restive under restraint, and seek by sharp and decisive measures to accomplish ends deemed just and proper, and that the principles of constitutional liberty would be in peril unless established by irrepealable law. The history of the world had taught them that what was done in the past might be attempted in the future. The Constitution of the United States is a law for rulers and people, equally in war and in peace, and covers with the shield of its protection all classes of men, at all times and under all circumstances. No doctrine involving more pernicious consequences was ever invented by the wit of man than that any of its provisions can be suspended during any of the great exigencies of government. Such a doctrine leads directly to anarchy or despotism, but the theory of necessity on which it is based is false, for the government, within the Constitution, has all the powers granted to it which are necessary to preserve its existence, as has been happily proved by the result of the great effort to throw off its just authority.

Have any of the rights guaranteed by the Constitution been violated in the case of Milligan? and, if so, what are they?

Every trial involves the exercise of judicial power, and from what source did the military commission that tried him derive their authority? Certainly no part of judicial power of the country was conferred on them, because the Constitution expressly vests it "in one supreme court and such inferior courts as the Congress may from time to time ordain and establish," and it is not pretended that the commission was a court ordained and established by Congress. They cannot justify on the mandate of the President, because he is controlled by law, and has his appropriate sphere of duty, which is to execute, not to make, the laws, and there is "no unwritten criminal code to which resort can be had as a source of jurisdiction."

But it is said that the jurisdiction is complete under the "laws and usages of war."

It can serve no useful purpose to inquire what those laws and usages are, whence they originated, where found, and on whom they operate; they can never be applied to citizens in states which have upheld the authority of the government, and where the courts are open and their process unobstructed. This court has judicial knowledge that, in Indiana, the Federal authority was always unopposed, and its courts always open to hear criminal accusations and redress grievances, and no usage of war could sanction a military trial there for any offence whatever of a citizen in civil life in nowise connected with the military service. Congress could grant no such power, and, to the honor of our national legislature be it said, it has never been provoked by the state of the country even to attempt its exercise. One of the plainest constitutional provisions was therefore infringed when Milligan was tried by a court not ordained and established by Congress and not composed of judges appointed during good behavior.

Why was he not delivered to the Circuit Court of Indiana to be proceeded against according to law? No reason of necessity could be urged against it, because Congress had declared penalties against the offences charged, provided for their punishment, and directed that court to hear and determine them. And soon after this military tribunal was ended, the Circuit Court met, peacefully transacted its business, and adjourned. It needed no bayonets to protect it, and required no military aid to execute its judgments. It was held in a state, eminently distinguished for patriotism, by judges commissioned during the Rebellion, who were provided with juries, upright, intelligent, and selected by a marshal appointed by the President. The government had no right to conclude that Milligan, if guilty, would not receive in that court merited punishment, for its records disclose that it was constantly engaged in the trial of similar offences, and was never interrupted in its administration of criminal justice. If it was dangerous, in the distracted condition of affairs, to leave Milligan unrestrained of his liberty because he "conspired against the government, afforded aid and comfort to rebels, and incited the people to insurrection," the law said arrest him, confine him closely, render him powerless to do further mischief, and then present his case to the grand jury of the district, with proofs of his guilt, and, if indicted, try him according to the course of the common law. If this had been done, the Constitution would have been vindicated, the law of 1863 enforced, and the securities for personal liberty preserved and defended.

Another guarantee of freedom was broken when Milligan was denied a trial by jury. The great minds of the country have differed on the correct interpretation to be given to various provisions of the Federal Constitution, and judicial decision has been often invoked to settle their true meaning; but, until recently, no one ever doubted that the right of trial by jury was fortified in the organic law against the power of attack. It is *now* assailed, but if ideas can be expressed in words and language has any meaning, this right—one of the most valuable in a free country—is preserved to everyone accused of crime who is not attached to the army or navy or militia in actual service. The sixth amendment affirms that, "in all criminal prosecutions, the accused shall enjoy the right to a speedy and public trial by an impartial jury," language broad enough to embrace all persons and cases; but the fifth, recognizing the necessity of an indictment or presentment before anyone can be held to answer for high crimes, "*excepts* cases arising in the land or naval forces, or in the militia, when in actual service, in time of war or public danger," and the framers of the Constitution doubtless meant to limit the right of trial by jury in the sixth amendment to those persons who were subject to indictment or presentment in the fifth.

The discipline necessary to the efficiency of the army and navy required other and swifter modes of trial than are furnished by the common law courts, and, in pursuance of the power conferred by the Constitution, Congress has declared the kinds of trial, and the manner in which they shall be conducted, for offences committed while the party is in the military or naval service. Everyone connected with these branches of the public service is amenable to the jurisdiction which Congress has created for their government, and, while thus serving, surrenders his right to be tried by the civil courts. All other persons, citizens of states where the courts are open, if charged with crime, are guaranteed the inestimable privilege of trial by jury. This privilege is a vital principle, underlying the whole administration of criminal justice; it is not held by sufferance, and cannot be frittered away on any plea of state or political necessity. When peace prevails, and the authority of the government is undisputed, there is no difficulty of preserving the safeguards of liberty, for the ordinary modes of trial are never neglected, and no one wishes it otherwise; but if society is disturbed by civil commotion—if the passions of men are aroused and the restraints of law weakened, if not disregarded—these safeguards need, and should receive, the watchful care of those entrusted with the guardianship of the Constitution and laws. In no other way can we transmit to posterity unimpaired the blessings of liberty, consecrated by the sacrifices of the Revolution.

It is claimed that martial law covers with its broad mantle the proceedings of this military commission. The proposition is this: that, in a time of war, the commander of an armed force (if, in his opinion, the exigencies of the country demand it, and of which he is to judge) has the power, within the lines of his military district, to suspend all civil rights and their remedies and subject citizens, as well as soldiers to the rule of *his will*, and, in the exercise of his lawful authority, cannot be restrained except by his superior officer or the President of the United States.

If this position is sound to the extent claimed, then, when war exists, foreign or domestic, and the country is subdivided into military departments for mere convenience, the commander of one of them can, if he chooses, within his limits, on the plea of necessity, with the approval of the Executive, substitute military force for and to the exclusion of the laws, and punish all persons as he thinks right and proper, without fixed or certain rules.

The statement of this proposition shows its importance, for, if true, republican government is a failure, and there is an end of liberty regulated by law. Martial law established on such a basis destroys every guarantee of the Constitution, and effectually renders the "military independent of and superior to the civil power"—the attempt to do which by the King of Great Britain was deemed by our fathers such an offence that they assigned it to the world as one of the causes which impelled them to declare their independence. Civil liberty and this kind of martial law cannot endure together; the antagonism is irreconcilable, and, in the conflict, one or the other must perish.

This nation, as experience has proved, cannot always remain at peace, and has no right to expect that it will always have wise and humane rulers sincerely attached to the principles of the Constitution. Wicked men, ambitious of power, with hatred of liberty and contempt of law, may fill the place once occupied by Washington and Lincoln, and if this right is conceded, and the calamities of war again befall us, the dangers to human liberty are frightful to contemplate. If our fathers had failed to provide for just such a contingency, they would have been false to the trust reposed in them. They knew—the history of the world told them—the nation they were founding, be its existence short or long, would be involved in war; how often or how long continued human foresight could not tell, and that unlimited power, wherever lodged at such a time, was especially hazardous to freemen. For this and other equally weighty reasons, they secured the inheritance they had fought to maintain by incorporating in a written constitution the safeguards which time had proved were essential to its preservation. Not one of these safeguards can the President or Congress or the Judiciary disturb, except the one concerning the writ of habeas corpus.

It is essential to the safety of every government that, in a great crisis like the one we have just passed through, there should be a power somewhere of suspending the writ of habeas corpus. In every war, there are men of previously good character wicked enough to counsel their fellow-citizens to resist the measures deemed necessary by a good government to sustain its just authority and overthrow its enemies, and their influence may lead to dangerous combinations. In the emergency of the times, an immediate public investigation according to law may not be possible, and yet the period to the country may be too imminent to suffer such persons to go at large. Unquestionably, there is then an exigency which demands that the government, if it should see fit in the exercise of a proper discretion to make arrests, should not be required to produce the persons arrested in answer to a writ of habeas corpus. The Constitution goes no further. It does not say, after a writ of habeas corpus is denied a citizen, that he shall be tried otherwise than by the course of the common law; if it had intended this result, it was easy, by the use of direct words, to have accomplished it. The illustrious men who framed that instrument were guarding the foundations of civil liberty against the abuses of unlimited power; they were full of wisdom, and the lessons of history informed them that a trial by an established court, assisted by an impartial jury, was the only sure way of protecting the citizen against oppression and wrong. Knowing this, they limited the suspension to one great right, and left the rest to remain forever inviolable. But it is insisted that the safety of the country in time of war demands that this broad claim for martial law shall be sustained. If this were true, it could be well said that a country, preserved at the sacrifice of all the cardinal principles of liberty, is not worth the cost of preservation. Happily, it is not so.

It will be borne in mind that this is not a question of the power to proclaim martial law when war exists in a community and the courts and civil authorities are overthrown. Nor is it a question what rule a military commander, at the head of his army, can impose on states in rebellion to cripple their resources and quell the insurrection. The jurisdiction claimed is much more extensive. The necessities of the service during the late Rebellion required that the loyal states should be placed within the limits of certain military districts and commanders appointed in them, and it is urged that this, in a military sense, constituted them the theater of military operations, and as, in this case, Indiana had been and was again threatened with invasion by the enemy, the occasion was furnished to establish martial law. The conclusion does not follow from the premises. If armies were collected in Indiana, they were to be employed in another locality, where the laws were obstructed and the national authority disputed. On her soil there was no hostile foot; if once invaded, that invasion was at an end, and, with it, all pretext for martial law. Martial law cannot arise from a *threatened* invasion. The necessity must be actual and present, the invasion real, such as effectually closes the courts and deposes the civil administration.

It is difficult to see how the *safety* for the country required martial law in Indiana. If any of her citizens were plotting treason, the power of arrest could secure them until the government was prepared for their trial, when the courts were open and ready to try them. It was as easy to protect witnesses before a civil as a military tribunal, and as there could be no wish to convict except on sufficient legal evidence, surely an ordained and establish court was better able to judge of this than a military tribunal composed of gentlemen not trained to the profession of the law.

It follows from what has been said on this subject that there are occasions when martial rule can be properly applied. If, in foreign invasion or civil war, the courts are actually closed, and it is impossible to administer criminal justice according to law, *then,* on the theatre of active military operations, where war really prevails, there is a necessity to furnish a substitute for the civil authority, thus overthrown, to preserve the safety of the army and society, and as no power is left but the military, it is allowed to govern by martial rule until the laws can have their free course. As necessity creates the rule, so it limits its duration, for, if this government is continued *after* the courts are reinstated, it is a gross usurpation of power. Martial rule can never exist where the courts are open and in the proper and un-obstructed exercise of their jurisdiction. It is also confined to the locality of actual war. Because, during the late Rebellion, it could have been enforced in Virginia, where the national authority was overturned and the courts driven out, it does not follow that it should obtain in Indiana, where that authority was never disputed and justice was always administered. And so, in the case of a foreign invasion, martial rule may become a necessity in one state when, in another, it would be "mere lawless violence."

We are not without precedents in English and American history illustrating our views of this question, but it is hardly necessary to make particular reference to them. From the first year of the reign of Edward the Third, when the Parliament of England reversed the attainder of the Earl of Lancaster because he could have been tried by the courts of the realm, and declared that, in time of peace, no man ought to be adjudged to death for treason or any other offence without being arraigned and held to answer, and that regularly when the king's courts are open it is a time of peace in judgment of law, down to the present day, martial law, as claimed in this case, has been condemned by all respectable English jurists as contrary to the fundamental laws of the land and subversive of the liberty of the subject.

During the present century, an instructive debate on this question occurred in Parliament, occasioned by the trial and conviction by court-martial, at Demerara, of the Rev. John Smith, a missionary to the negroes, on the alleged ground of aiding and abetting a formidable rebellion in that colony. Those eminent statesmen Lord Brougham and Sir James Mackintosh participated in that debate, and denounced the trial as illegal because it did not appear that the courts of law in Demerara could not try offences, and that, "when the laws can act, every other mode of punishing supposed crimes is itself an enormous crime."

So sensitive were our Revolutionary fathers on this subject, although Boston was almost in a state of siege, when General Gage issued his proclamation of martial law, they spoke of it as an "attempt to supersede the course of the common law, and, instead thereof, to publish and order the use of martial law." The Virginia Assembly also denounced a similar measure on the part of Governor Dunmore as an assumed power which the king himself cannot exercise, because it annuls the law of the land and introduces the most execrable of all systems, martial law.

In some parts of the country, during the war of 1812, our officers made arbitrary arrests and, by military tribunals, tried citizens who were not in the military service. These arrest and trials, when brought to the notice of the courts, were uniformly condemned as illegal.

***

The two remaining questions in this case must be answered in the affirmative. The suspension of the privilege of the writ of habeas corpus does not suspend the writ itself. The writ issues as a matter of course, and, on the return made to it, the court decides whether the party applying is denied the right of proceeding any further with it.

If the military trial of Milligan was contrary to law, then he was entitled, on the facts stated in his petition, to be discharged from custody by the terms of the act of Congress of March 3d, 1863. The provisions of this law having been considered in a previous part of this opinion, we will not restate the views there presented. Milligan avers he was a citizen of Indiana, not in the military or naval service, and was detained in close confinement, by order of the President, from the 5th day of October, 1864, until the 2d day of January, 1865, when the Circuit Court for the District of Indiana, with a grand jury, convened in session at Indianapolis, and afterwards, on the 27th day of the same month, adjourned without finding an indictment or presentment against him. If these averments were true (and their truth is conceded for the purposes of this case), the court was required to liberate him on taking certain oaths prescribed by the law, and entering into recognizance for his good behavior.

But it is insisted that Milligan was a prisoner of war, and therefore excluded from the privileges of the statute. It is not easy to see how he can be treated as a prisoner of war when he lived in Indiana for the past twenty years, was arrested there, and had not been, during the late troubles, a resident of any of the states in rebellion. If in Indiana he conspired with bad men to assist the enemy, he is punishable for it in the courts of Indiana; but, when tried for the offence, he cannot plead the rights of war, for he was not engaged in legal acts of hostility against the government, and only such persons, when captured, are prisoners of war. If he cannot enjoy the immunities attaching to the character of a prisoner of war, how can he be subject to their pains and penalties?

***

Commentary and Questions

1. Clement Vallandigham was denied his petition for habeas corpus based on the Court's interpretation of the language of the Judiciary Act of 1789 and the status of the military commission as a "special authority." What was the basis for the authority of the military commission? How was this authority justified by the Court in the denial of Vallandigham's petition?

2. Justice Wayne references three cases in his *Vallandigham* decision: *Ex Parte Milburn*, *In re Kaine* and *Ex Parte Metzger*. Each deserves an explanatory note. In *Ex Parte Milburn*, 34 U.S. 704 (1835), the petitioner sought habeas relief for his arrest on a bench warrant related to a gambling offense. The charge could potentially lead to imprisonment at hard labor. Milburn had been released after posting a bond but was subsequently arrested when he failed to appear in court. He sought the writ to be released from custody on the charges because he had already posted a bond. Justice Story ruled against Milburn citing the flawed reasoning of the petitioner that his bond in some way alleviated the need to arrest him for failure to appear on the same charge:

    > "And a fortiori it cannot be deemed to apply to a case like the present of a penitentiary offense, for that would be to suppose that the law allowed the party to purge away the offense and the corporeal punishment by a pecuniary compensation ... A discharge of a party under a writ of habeas corpus from the process under which he is imprisoned discharges him from any further confinement under the process, but not under any other process which may be issued against him under the same indictment."[15]

    More to the point, however, Chief Justice Marshall questioned the appellate nature of the petition because the jurisdiction of the Court was one of appellate jurisdiction and not general trial jurisdiction, which was more in line with the issue presented by Milburn. The case of *In re Kaine*, 55 U.S. 103 (1852), involved an individual who attempted to murder another person in Ireland before escaping to the United States. Based on an 1842 treaty between Great Britain and the United States, the English authorities issued an arrest warrant for Kaine. He was apprehended and placed in custody in New York. The issue once again came down to the Court's appellate jurisdiction in the case. The Court, in an opinion by Justice Catron, found jurisdiction to be lacking and the transfer of the case from the circuit court to the Supreme Court to be invalid. The writ of habeas corpus was denied. *Ex parte Metzger*, 46 U.S. 176 (1847), is an earlier case cited in *Kaine* and relied on by the *Vallandigham* Court. In *Metzger* the petitioner was arrested as a fugitive from justice based on a warrant issued by a district court judge from his chambers in New York. Lucien Metzger was wanted by French authorities for the crime of forgery and the 1843 treaty between the United States and France providing for the mutual surrender of fugitives from justice was invoked as the justification for the custody. The Court pointed to the treaty as *"the supreme law of the land and, in regard to rights and responsibilities growing out of it, it may become a subject of judicial cognizance."*[16] Further, the Court delineated the powers of the branches with respect to the matter: *"...the executive, when the late demand of the surrender of Metzger was made, very properly as we suppose, referred it to the judgment of a judicial officer. The arrest which followed and the committal of the accused subject to the order of the executive seems to be the most appropriate, if not the only, mode of giving effect to the treaty."*[17] Again, relying on the Judiciary Act of 1789 and the specific powers of the courts outlined in the Act, the Court dismissed the petition based on the special authority of the district court judge exercised under the terms of the 1843 treaty with France. Each of the three cited cases denied habeas corpus relief on jurisdictional arguments, as the Court did in *Vallandigham*.

3. The case of *Ex parte Bollman*, 8 U.S. 75 (1807), previously discussed in Chapter 1, was cited by Justice McLean in the *Metzger* case. *Bollman* was a habeas corpus case in which the Court not only set the standard for the crime of treason but discussed the Court's power to issue writs of habeas corpus: *"It has been demonstrated at the bar, that the question brought forward on a habeas corpus, is always distinct from that which is involved in the cause itself. The question whether the individual shall be imprisoned is always distinct from the question whether he shall be convicted or acquitted of the charge on which he is to be tried, and therefore these questions are separated, and may be decided in different courts. The decision that the individual shall be imprisoned must always precede the application for a writ of habeas corpus, and this writ must always be for the purpose of revising that decision, and therefore appellate in its nature."*[18] The *Bollman* decision began with an extensive explanation of habeas corpus review prior to its assertion that the particular case was appellate in nature and within the jurisdiction of the Court. Yet we find in subsequent cases like *Metzger* and *Vallandigham* the Court's refusal to exercise any jurisdiction over habeas corpus petitions. The special authority of a treaty was the reason in *Metzger*, whereas the special authority of military commissions was the reason in *Vallandigham*. What would be the Court's rationale in *Ex parte Milligan* for its decision on behalf of Lambdan Milligan? How did Milligan's situation differ from that of Vallandigham?

4. In a concurring opinion to *Ex Parte Milligan* Chief Justice Salmon P. Chase, joined by Justices Wayne, Swayne and Miller, outlined three different kinds of military jurisdiction:

"There are under the Constitution three kinds of military jurisdiction: one to be exercised both in peace and war; another to be exercised in time of foreign war without the boundaries of the United States, or in time of rebellion and civil war within states or districts occupied by rebels treated as belligerents; and a third to be exercised in time of invasion or insurrection within the limits of the United States, or during rebellion within the limits of states maintaining adhesion to the National Government, when the public danger requires its exercise. The first of these may be called jurisdiction under military law, and is found in acts of Congress prescribing rules and articles of war, or otherwise providing for the government of the national forces; the second may be distinguished as military government, superseding, as far as may be deemed expedient, the local law, and exercised by the military commander under the direction of the President, with the express or implied sanction of Congress; while the third may be denominated martial law proper, and is called into action by Congress, or temporarily, when the action of Congress cannot be invited, and in the case of justifying or excusing peril, by the President, in times of insurrection or invasion, or of civil or foreign war, within districts or localities where ordinary law no longer adequately secures public safety and private rights. We think that the power of Congress, in such times and in such localities, to authorize trials for crimes against the security and safety of the national forces, may be derived from its constitutional authority to raise and support armies and to declare war, if not from its constitutional authority to provide for governing the national forces."[19]

These would become important distinctions in later cases such as the World War II case of *Duncan v. Kahanamoku*. But these distinctions and the authority for such jurisdiction is only within the powers of Congress to grant, the execution of these powers is provided for by the president as commander-in-chief. The concurring opinion of Chief Justice Chase differed from the majority opinion in that he did not agree that Congress was without the power to authorize military commissions or provide indemnification from civil liability of officers operating as the military commission. In his opinion the Chief Justice wrote the following:

"We agree in the proposition that no department of the government of the United States—neither President, nor Congress, nor the Courts—possesses any power not given by the Constitution.

We assent, fully, to all that is said, in the opinion, of the inestimable value of the trial by jury, and of the other constitutional safeguards of civil liberty. And we concur, also, in what is said of the writ of habeas corpus, and of its suspension, with two reservations: (1.) That, in our judgment, when the writ is suspended, the Executive is authorized to arrest as well as to detain; and (2.) that there are cases in which, the privilege of the writ being suspended, trial and punishment by military commission, in states where civil courts are open, may be authorized by Congress, as well as arrest and detention.

We think that Congress had power, though not exercised, to authorize the military commission which was held in Indiana.... The Constitution itself provides for military government as well as for civil government. And we do not understand it to be claimed that the civil safeguards of the Constitution have application in cases within the proper sphere of the former.

What, then, is that proper sphere? Congress has power to raise and support armies; to provide and maintain a navy; to make rules for the government and regulation of the land and naval forces; and to provide for governing such part of the militia as may be in the service of the United States.

It is not denied that the power to make rules for the government of the army and navy is a power to provide for trial and punishment by military courts without a jury. It has been so understood and exercised from the adoption of the Constitution to the present time.

Nor, in our judgment, does the fifth, or any other amendment, abridge that power. 'Cases arising in the land and naval forces, or in the militia in actual service in time of war or public danger,' are expressly excepted from the fifth amendment, 'that no person shall be held to answer for a capital or otherwise infamous crime, unless on a presentment or indictment of a grand jury,' and it is admitted that the exception applies to the other amendments as well as to the fifth ....We think, therefore, that the power of Congress, in the government of the land and naval forces and of the militia, is not at all affected by the fifth or any other amendment. It is not necessary to attempt any precise definition of the boundaries of this power. But may it not be said that government includes protection and defense as well as the regulation of internal administration? And is it impossible to imagine cases in which citizens conspiring or attempting the destruction or great injury of the national forces may be subjected by Congress to military trial and punishment in the just exercise of this undoubted constitutional power? Congress is but the agent of the nation, and does not the security of individuals against the abuse of this, as of every other power, depend on the intelligence and virtue of the people, on their zeal for public and private liberty, upon official responsibility secured by law, and upon the frequency of elections, rather than upon doubtful constructions of legislative powers?

But we do not put our opinion, that Congress might authorize such a military commission as was held in Indiana, upon the power to provide for the government of the national forces.

Congress has the power not only to raise and support and govern armies but to declare war. It has, therefore, the power to provide by law for carrying on war. This power necessarily extends to all legislation essential to the prosecution of war with vigor and success, except such as interferes with the command of the forces and the conduct of campaigns. That power and duty belong to the President as commander-in-chief. Both these powers are derived from the Constitution, but neither is defined by that instrument. Their extent must be determined by their nature, and by the principles of our institutions.

The power to make the necessary laws is in Congress; the power to execute in the President. Both powers imply many subordinate and auxiliary powers. Each includes all authorities essential to its due exercise. But neither can the President, in war more than in peace, intrude upon the proper authority of Congress, nor Congress upon the proper authority of the President. Both are servants of the people, whose will is expressed in the fundamental law. Congress cannot direct the conduct of campaigns, nor can the President, or any commander under him, without the sanction of Congress, institute tribunals for the trial and punishment of offences, either of soldiers or civilians, unless in cases of a controlling necessity, which justifies what it compels, or at least insures acts of indemnity from the justice of the legislature.

We by no means assert that Congress can establish and apply the laws of war where no war has been declared or exists.

Where peace exists the laws of peace must prevail. What we do maintain is, that when the nation is involved in war, and some portions of the country are invaded, and all are exposed to invasion, it is within the power of Congress to determine in what states or district such great and imminent public danger exists as justifies the authorization of military tribunals for the trial of crimes and offences against the discipline or security of the army or against the public safety .... We cannot doubt that, in such a time of public danger, Congress had power, under the Constitution, to provide for the organization of a military commission, and for trial by that commission of persons engaged in this conspiracy. The fact that the Federal courts were open was regarded by Congress as a sufficient reason for not exercising the power; but that fact could not deprive Congress of the right to exercise it. Those courts might be open and undisturbed in the execution of their functions, and yet wholly incompetent to avert threatened danger, or to punish, with adequate promptitude and certainty, the guilty conspirators.

In Indiana, the judges and officers of the courts were loyal to the government. But it might have been otherwise. In times of rebellion and civil war it may often happen, indeed, that judges and marshals will be in active sympathy with the rebels, and courts their most efficient allies. We have confined ourselves to the question of power. It was for Congress to determine the question of expediency. And Congress did determine it. That body did not see fit to authorize trials by military commission in Indiana, but by the strongest implication prohibited them. With that prohibition we are satisfied, and should have remained silent if the answers to the questions certified had been put on that ground, without denial of the existence of a power which we believe to be constitutional and important to the public safety, a denial which, as we have already suggested, seems to draw in question the power of Congress to protect from prosecution the members of military commissions who acted in obedience to their superior officers, and whose action, whether warranted by law or not, was approved by that upright and patriotic President under whose administration the Republic was rescued from threatened destruction. We have thus far said little of martial law, nor do we propose to say much.

What we have already said sufficiently indicates our opinion that there is no law for the government of the citizens, the armies or the navy of the United States, within American jurisdiction, which is not contained in or derived from the Constitution. And wherever our army or navy may go beyond our territorial limits, neither can go beyond the authority of the President or the legislation of Congress."[20]

How does the position of Chief Justice Chase's concurring opinion in *Ex parte Milligan* compare with his predecessor's opinion in *Ex parte Merryman*? What was Taney's main criticism of government action in *Merryman*?

5. In a later case, *In re Vidal*, 179 U.S. 126 (1900), municipal officials in the town of Guayama, Puerto Rico filed a petition to review proceedings of the military tribunal that sought to replace them. The tribunal was established by military order of Brigadier-General Davis, the supreme military commander of the island. Citing section 14 of the Judiciary Act of 1789 the Court declined review. *"This court is not thereby empowered to review the proceedings of military tribunals by certiorari. Nor are such tribunals courts with jurisdiction in law or equity, within the meaning of those terms as used in the 3d article of the Constitution, and the question of the issue of the writ of certiorari in the exercise of inherent general power cannot arise in respect of them,"* wrote Justice Fuller. As the Court established in *Vallandigham* and would later confirm in *Ex parte Quirin*, the ability to review the rulings of military tribunals is left to the military authorities who established them. The reviewable authority lies in the lawful power of the commission to try the petitioner for the offense charged.[21] What then is the authority of the court of the United States at the conclusion of war? *The Grapeshot*, 76 U.S. 129 (1869), a post-Civil War case addressing the authority of provisional courts established in insurgent territories during hostilities, found constitutional authority in the Executive's establishment of the provisional court. Once hostilities ended the authority of the military courts reverted back to the circuit courts, thereby clearing way for the appellate jurisdiction of the Supreme Court. An earlier case *Leitensdorfer v. Webb*[22] similarly found provisional military courts established by a conquering authority to be valid.

Ex Parte Quirin
317 U.S. 1 (1942)

Mr. Chief Justice Stone delivered the opinion of the Court.

These cases are brought here by petitioners' several application for leave to file petitions for habeas corpus in this Court, and by their petitions for certiorari to review orders of the District Court for the District of Columbia, which denied their applications for leave to file petitions for habeas corpus in that court.

The question for decision is whether the detention of petitioners by respondent for trial by Military Commission, appointed by Order of the President of July 2, 1942, on charges preferred against them purporting to set out their violations of the law of war and of the Articles of War, is in conformity to the laws and Constitution of the United States.

After denial of their applications by the District Court, 47 F.Supp. 431, petitioners asked leave to file petitions for habeas corpus in this Court. In view of the public importance of the questions raised by their petitions and of the duty which rests on the courts, in time of war as well as in time of peace, to preserve unimpaired the constitutional safeguards of civil liberty, and because, in our opinion, the public interest required that we consider and decide those questions without any avoidable delay, we directed that petitioners' applications be set down for full oral argument at a special term of this Court, convened on July 29, 1942. The applications for leave to file the petitions were presented in open court on that day, and were heard on the petitions, the answers to them of respondent, a stipulation of facts by counsel, and the record of the testimony given before the Commission.

While the argument was proceeding before us, petitioners perfected their appeals from the orders of the District Court to the United States Court of Appeals for the District of Columbia, and thereupon filed with this Court petitions for certiorari to the Court of Appeals before judgment, pursuant to § 240(a) of the Judicial Code, 28 U.S.C. § 347(a). We granted certiorari before judgment for the reasons which moved us to convene the special term of Court. In accordance with the stipulation of counsel, we treat the record, briefs and arguments in the habeas corpus proceedings in this Court as the record, briefs and arguments upon the writs of certiorari.

On July 31, 1942, after hearing argument of counsel and after full consideration of all questions raised, this Court affirmed the orders of the District Court and denied petitioners' applications for leave to file petitions for habeas corpus. By per curiam opinion, we announced the decision of the Court, and that the full opinion in the causes would be prepared and filed with the Clerk.

The following facts appear from the petitions or are stipulated. Except as noted, they are undisputed.

All the petitioners were born in Germany; all have lived in the United States. All returned to Germany between 1933 and 1941. All except petitioner Haupt are admittedly citizens of the German Reich, with which the United States is at war. Haupt came to this country with his parents when he was five years old; it is contended that he became a citizen of the United States by virtue of the naturalization of his parents during his minority, and that he has not since lost his citizenship. The Government, however, takes the position that, on attaining his majority he elected to maintain German allegiance and citizenship, or in any case that he has, by his conduct, renounced or abandoned his United States citizenship. See *Perkins v. Elg*, 307 U.S. 325, 334; *United States ex rel. Rojak v. Marshall*, 34 F.2d 219; *United*

States ex rel. Scimeca v. Husband, 6 F.2d 957, 958; 8 U.S.C. § 801 *and compare* 8 U.S.C. § 808. For reasons presently to be stated we do not find it necessary to resolve these contentions.

After the declaration of war between the United States and the German Reich, petitioners received training at a sabotage school near Berlin, Germany, where they were instructed in the use of explosives and in methods of secret writing. Thereafter petitioners, with a German citizen, Dasch, proceeded from Germany to a seaport in Occupied France, where petitioners Burger, Heinck and Quirin, together with Dasch, boarded a German submarine which proceeded across the Atlantic to Amagansett Beach on Long Island, New York. The four were there landed from the submarine in the hours of darkness, on or about June 13, 1942, carrying with them a supply of explosives, fuses, and incendiary and timing devices. While landing, they wore German Marine Infantry uniforms or parts of uniforms. Immediately after landing, they buried their uniforms and the other articles mentioned and proceeded in civilian dress to New York City.

The remaining four petitioners at the same French port boarded another German submarine, which carried them across the Atlantic to Ponte Vedra Beach, Florida. On or about June 17, 1942, they came ashore during the hours of darkness, wearing caps of the German Marine Infantry and carrying with them a supply of explosives, fuses, and incendiary and timing devices. They immediately buried their caps and the other articles mentioned, and proceeded in civilian dress to Jacksonville, Florida, and thence to various points in the United States. All were taken into custody in New York or Chicago by agents of the Federal Bureau of Investigation. All had received instructions in Germany from an officer of the German High Command to destroy war industries and war facilities in the United States, for which they or their relatives in Germany were to receive salary payments from the German Government. They also had been paid by the German Government during their course of training at the sabotage school, and had received substantial sums in United States currency, which were in their possession when arrested. The currency had been handed to them by an officer of the German High Command, who had instructed them to wear their German uniforms while landing in the United States. The President, as President and Commander in Chief of the Army and Navy, by Order of July 2, 1942, appointed a Military Commission and directed it to try petitioners for offenses against the law of war and the Articles of War, and prescribed regulations for the procedure on the trial and for review of the record of the trial and of any judgment or sentence of the Commission. On the same day, by Proclamation, the President declared that "all persons who are subjects, citizens or residents of any nation at war with the United States or who give obedience to or act under the direction of any such nation, and who during time of war enter or attempt to enter the United States . . . through coastal or boundary defenses, and are charged with committing or attempting or preparing to commit sabotage, espionage, hostile or warlike acts, or violations of the law of war, shall be subject to the law of war and to the jurisdiction of military tribunals." The Proclamation also stated in terms that all such persons were denied access to the courts.

Pursuant to direction of the Attorney General, the Federal Bureau of Investigation surrendered custody of petitioners to respondent, Provost Marshal of the Military District of Washington, who was directed by the Secretary of War to receive and keep them in custody, and who thereafter held petitioners for trial before the Commission.

On July 3, 1942, the Judge Advocate General's Department of the Army prepared and lodged with the Commission the following charges against petitioners, supported by specifications:
1. Violation of the law of war.
2. Violation of Article 81 of the Articles of War, defining the offense of relieving or attempting to relieve, or corresponding with or giving intelligence to, the enemy.
3. of Article 82, defining the offense of spying.
4. Conspiracy to commit the offenses alleged in charges 1, 2 and 3.
The Commission met on July 8, 1942, and proceeded with the trial, which continued in progress while the causes were pending in this Court. On July 27th, before petitioners' applications to the District Court, all the evidence for the prosecution and the defense had been taken by the Commission and the case had been closed except for arguments of counsel. It is conceded that, ever since petitioners' arrest, the state and federal courts in Florida, New York, and the District of Columbia, and in the states in which each of the petitioners was arrested or detained, have been open and functioning normally.

***

Petitioners' main contention is that the President is without any statutory or constitutional authority to order the petitioners to be tried by military tribunal for offenses with which they are charged; that, in consequence, they are entitled to be tried in the civil courts with the safeguards, including trial by jury, which the Fifth and Sixth Amendments guarantee to all persons charged in such courts with criminal offenses. In any case, it is urged that the President's Order, in prescribing the procedure of the Commission and the method for review of its findings and sentence, and the proceedings of the Commission under the Order, conflict with Articles of War adopted by Congress—particularly Articles 38, 43, 46, 50 1/2 and 70—and are illegal and void.

The Government challenges each of these propositions. But regardless of their merits, it also insists that petitioners must be denied access to the courts, both because they are enemy aliens or have entered our territory as enemy belligerents, and because the President's Proclamation undertakes in terms to deny such access to the class of persons defined by the Proclamation, which aptly describes the character and conduct of petitioners. It is urged that, if they are enemy aliens or if the Proclamation has force, no court may afford the petitioners a hearing. But there is certainly nothing in the Proclamation to preclude access to the courts for determining its applicability to the particular case. And neither the Proclamation nor the fact that they are enemy aliens forecloses consideration by the courts of petitioners' contentions that the Constitution and laws of the United States constitutionally enacted forbid their trial by military commission. As announced in our per curiam opinion, we have resolved those questions by our conclusion that the Commission has jurisdiction to try the charge preferred against petitioners. There is therefore no occasion to decide contentions of the parties unrelated to this issue. We pass at once to the consideration of the basis of the Commission's authority.

We are not here concerned with any question of the guilt or innocence of petitioners. Constitutional safeguards for the protection of all who are charged with offenses are not to be disregarded in order to inflict merited punishment on some who are guilty. *Ex parte Milligan*, supra, 119, 132; *Tumey v. Ohio*, 273 U.S. 510, 535; *Hill v. Texas*, 316 U.S. 400, 406. But the detention and trial of petitioners—ordered by the President in the declared exercise of his powers as Commander in Chief of the Army in time of war and of grave public danger—are not to be set aside by the courts without the clear conviction that they are in conflict with the Constitution or laws of Congress constitutionally enacted.

Congress and the President, like the courts, possess no power not derived from the Constitution. But one of the objects of the Constitution, as declared by its preamble, is to "provide for the common defence." As a means to that end, the Constitution gives to Congress the power to "provide for the common Defence," Art. I, § 8, cl. 1; "To raise and support Armies," "To provide and maintain a Navy," Art. I, § 8, cl. 12, 13, and "To make Rules for the Government and Regulation of the land and naval Forces," Art. I, § 8, cl. 14. Congress is given authority "To declare War, grant Letters of Marque and Reprisal, and make Rules concerning Captures on Land and Water," Art. I, § 8, cl. 11, and "To define and punish Piracies and Felonies committed on the high Seas, and Offences against the Law of Nations," Art. I, § 8, cl. 10. And finally, the Constitution authorizes Congress "To make all Laws which shall be necessary and proper for carrying into Execution the foregoing Powers, and all other Powers vested by this Constitution in the Government of the United States, or in any Department or Officer thereof." Art. I, § 8, cl. 18.

The Constitution confers on the President the "executive Power," Art. II, § 1, cl. 1, and imposes on him the duty to "take Care that the Laws be faithfully executed." Art. II, § 3. It makes him the Commander in Chief of the Army and Navy, Art. II, § 2, cl. 1, and empowers him to appoint and commission officers of the United States. Art. II, § 3, cl. 1.

The Constitution thus invests the President, as Commander in Chief, with the power to wage war which Congress has declared, and to carry into effect all laws passed by Congress for the conduct of war and for the government and regulation of the Armed Forces, and all laws defining and punishing offenses against the law of nations, including those which pertain to the conduct of war.

By the Articles of War, 10 U.S.C. §§ 1471-1593, Congress has provided rules for the government of the Army. It has provided for the trial and punishment, by courts martial, of violations of the Articles by members of the armed forces and by specified classes of persons associated or serving with the Army. Arts. 1, 2. But the Articles also recognize the "military commission" appointed by military command as an appropriate tribunal for the trial and punishment of offenses against the law of war not ordinarily tried by court martial. See Arts. 12, 15. Articles 38 and 46 authorize the President, with certain limitations, to prescribe the procedure for military commissions. Articles 81 and 82 authorize trial, either by court martial or military commission, of those charged with relieving, harboring or corresponding with the enemy and those charged with spying. And Article 15 declares that "the provisions of these articles conferring jurisdiction upon courts martial shall not be construed as depriving military commissions ... or other military tribunals of concurrent jurisdiction in respect of offenders or offenses that, by statute or by the law of war may be triable by such military commissions ... or other military tribunals."

Article 2 includes among those persons subject to military law the personnel of our own military establishment. But this, as Article 12 provides, does not exclude from that class "any other person who by the law of war is subject to trial by military tribunals" and who, under Article 12, may be tried by court martial or under Article 15 by military commission.

Similarly, the Espionage Act of 1917, which authorizes trial in the district courts of certain offenses that tend to interfere with the prosecution of war, provides that nothing contained in the act "shall be deemed to limit the jurisdiction of the general courts-martial, military commissions, or naval courts-martial." 50 U.S.C. § 38.

From the very beginning of its history, this Court has recognized and applied the law of war as including that part of the law of nations which prescribes, for the conduct of war, the status, rights and duties of enemy nations, as well as of enemy individuals. By the Articles of War, and especially Article 15, Congress has explicitly provided, so far as it may constitutionally do so, that military tribunals shall have jurisdiction to try offenders or offenses against the law of war in appropriate cases. Congress, in addition to making rules for the government of our Armed Forces, has thus exercised its authority to define and punish offenses against the law of nations by sanctioning, within constitutional limitations, the jurisdiction of military commissions to try persons for offenses which, according to the rules and precepts of the law of nations, and more particularly the law of war, are cognizable by such tribunals. And the President, as Commander in Chief, by his Proclamation in time of war, has invoked that law. By his Order creating the present Commission, he has undertaken to exercise the authority conferred upon him by Congress, and also such authority as the Constitution itself gives the Commander in Chief, to direct the performance of those functions which may constitutionally be performed by the military arm of the nation in time of war.

An important incident to the conduct of war is the adoption of measures by the military command not only to repel and defeat the enemy, but to seize and subject to disciplinary measures those enemies who, in their attempt to thwart or impede our military effort, have violated the law of war. It is unnecessary for present purposes to determine to what extent the President as Commander in Chief has constitutional power to create military commissions without the support of Congressional legislation. For here, Congress has authorized trial of offenses against the law of war before such commissions. We are concerned only with the question whether it is within the constitutional power of the National Government to place petitioners upon trial before a military commission for the offenses with which they are charged. We must therefore first inquire whether any of the acts charged is an offense against the law of war cognizable before a military tribunal, and, if so, whether the Constitution prohibits the trial. We may assume that there are acts regarded in other countries, or by some writers on international law, as offenses against the law of war which would not be triable by military tribunal here, either because they are not recognized by our courts as violations of the law of war or because they are of that class of offenses constitutionally triable only by a jury. It was upon such grounds that the Court denied the right to proceed by military tribunal in *Ex parte Milligan,* supra. But, as we shall show, these petitioners were charged with an offense against the law of war which the Constitution does not require to be tried by jury.

***

By universal agreement and practice, the law of war draws a distinction between the armed forces and the peaceful populations of belligerent nations, and also between those who are lawful and unlawful combatants. Lawful combatants are subject to capture and detention as prisoners of war by opposing military forces. Unlawful combatants are likewise subject to capture and detention, but, in addition, they are subject to trial and punishment by military tribunals for acts which render their belligerency unlawful. The spy who secretly and without uniform passes the military lines of a belligerent in time of war, seeking to gather military information and communicate it to the enemy, or an enemy combatant who without uniform comes secretly through the lines for the purpose of waging war by destruction of life or property, are familiar examples of belligerents who are generally deemed not to be entitled to the status of prisoners of war, but to be offenders against the law of war subject to trial and punishment by military tribunals. *See* Winthrop, Military Law, 2d ed., pp. 11997, 1219-21; Instructions for the Government of Armies of the United States in the Field, approved by the President, General Order No. 100, April 24, 1863, §§ IV and V.

***

Our Government, by thus defining lawful belligerents entitled to be treated as prisoners of war, has recognized that there is a class of unlawful belligerents not entitled to that privilege, including those who, though combatants, do not wear "fixed and distinctive emblems." And, by Article 15 of the Articles of War, Congress has made provision for their trial and punishment by military commission, according to "the law of war."

By a long course of practical administrative construction by its military authorities, our Government has likewise recognized that those who, during time of war, pass surreptitiously from enemy territory into our own, discarding their uniforms upon entry, for the commission of hostile acts involving destruction of life or property, have the status of unlawful combatants punishable as such by military commission. This precept of the law of war has been so recognized in practice both here and abroad, and has so generally been accepted as valid by authorities on international law that we think it must be regarded as a rule or principle of the law of war recognized by this Government by its enactment of the Fifteenth Article of War.

Specification 1 of the first charge is sufficient to charge all the petitioners with the offense of unlawful belligerency, trial of which is within the jurisdiction of the Commission, and the admitted facts affirmatively show that the charge is not merely colorable or without foundation.

Specification 1 states that petitioners, "being enemies of the United States and acting for . . . the German Reich, a belligerent enemy nation, secretly and covertly passed, in civilian dress, contrary to the law of war, through the military and naval lines and defenses of the United States . . . and went behind such lines, contrary to the law of war, in civilian dress . . . for the purpose of committing . . . hostile acts, and, in particular, to destroy certain war industries, war utilities and war materials within the United States."

This specification so plainly alleges violation of the law of war as to require but brief discussion of petitioners' contentions. As we have seen, entry upon our territory in time of war by enemy belligerents, including those acting under the direction of the armed forces of the enemy, for the purpose of destroying property used or useful in prosecuting the war, is a hostile and warlike act. It subjects those who participate in it without uniform to the punishment prescribed by the law of war for unlawful belligerents. It is without significance that petitioners were not alleged to have borne conventional weapons or that their proposed hostile acts did not necessarily contemplate collision with the Armed Forces of the United States. Paragraphs 351 and 352 of the Rules of Land Warfare, already referred to, plainly contemplate that the hostile acts and purposes for which unlawful belligerents may be punished are not limited to assaults on the Armed Forces of the United States. Modern warfare is directed at the destruction of enemy war supplies and the implements of their production and transportation, quite as much as at the armed forces. Every consideration which makes the unlawful belligerent punishable is equally applicable whether his objective is the one or the other. The law of war cannot rightly treat those agents of enemy armies who enter our territory, armed with explosives intended for the destruction of war industries and supplies, as any the less belligerent enemies than are agents similarly entering for the purpose of destroying fortified places or our Armed Forces. By passing our boundaries for such purposes without uniform or other emblem signifying their belligerent status, or by discarding that means of identification after entry, such enemies become unlawful belligerents subject to trial and punishment.

Citizenship in the United States of an enemy belligerent does not relieve him from the consequences of a belligerency which is unlawful because in violation of the law of war. Citizens who associate themselves with the military arm of the enemy government, and, with its aid, guidance and direction, enter this country bent on hostile acts, are enemy belligerents within the meaning of the Hague Convention and the law of war. Cf. **Gates v. Goodloe**, 101 U.S. 612, 615, 617-18. It is as an enemy belligerent that petitioner Haupt is charged with entering the United States, and unlawful belligerency is the gravamen of the offense of which he is accused.

Nor are petitioners any the less belligerents if, as they argue, they have not actually committed or attempted to commit any act of depredation or entered the theatre or zone of active military operations. The argument leaves out of account the nature of the offense which the Government charges and which the Act of Congress, by incorporating the law of war, punishes. It is that each petitioner, in circumstances which gave him the status of an enemy belligerent, passed our military and naval lines and defenses or went behind those lines, in civilian dress and with hostile purpose. The offense was complete when, with that purpose, they entered—or, having so entered, they remained upon—our territory in time of war without uniform or other appropriate means of identification. For that reason, even when committed by a citizen, the offense is distinct from the crime of treason defined in Article III, § 3 of the Constitution, since the absence of uniform essential to one is irrelevant to the other. Cf. *Moran v. Devine*, 237 U.S. 632; *Albrecht v. United States*, 273 U.S. 1, 11-12.

But petitioners insist that, even if the offenses with which they are charged are offenses against the law of war, their trial is subject to the requirement of the Fifth Amendment that no person shall be held to answer for a capital or otherwise infamous crime unless on a presentment or indictment of a grand jury, and that such trials by Article III, § 2, and the Sixth Amendment must be by jury in a civil court. Before the Amendments, § 2 of Article III, the Judiciary Article, had provided, "The Trial of all Crimes, except in Cases of Impeachment, shall be by Jury," and had directed that "such Trial shall be held in the State where the said Crimes shall have been committed."

Presentment by a grand jury and trial by a jury of the vicinage where the crime was committed were, at the time of the adoption of the Constitution, familiar parts of the machinery for criminal trials in the civil courts. But they were procedures unknown to military tribunals, which are not courts in the sense of the Judiciary Article, *Ex parte Vallandigham*, 1 Wall. 243; *In re Vidal*, 179 U.S. 126; cf. *Williams v. United States*, 289 U.S. 553, and which, in the natural course of events, are usually called upon to function under conditions precluding resort to such procedures. As this Court has often recognized, it was not the purpose or effect of § 2 of Article III, read in the light of the common law, to enlarge the then existing right to a jury trial. The object was to preserve unimpaired trial by jury in all those cases in which it had been recognized by the common law and in all cases of a like nature as they might arise in the future, *District of Columbia v. Colts*, 282 U.S. 63, but not to bring within the sweep of the guaranty those cases in which it was then well understood that a jury trial could not be demanded as of right.

The Fifth and Sixth Amendments, while guaranteeing the continuance of certain incidents of trial by jury which Article III, § 2 had left unmentioned, did not enlarge the right to jury trial as it had been established by that Article. *Callan v. Wilson*, 127 U.S. 540, 549. Hence, petty offenses triable at common law without a jury may be tried without a jury in the federal courts, notwithstanding Article III, § 2, and the Fifth and Sixth Amendments. *Schick v. United States*, 195 U.S. 65; *District of Columbia v. Clawans*, 300 U.S. 617. Trial by jury of criminal contempts may constitutionally be dispensed with in the federal courts in those cases in which they could be tried without a jury at common law. *Ex parte Terry*, 128 U.S. 289, 302-304; *Savin, Petitioner*, 131 U.S. 267, 277; *In re Debs*, 158 U.S. 564, 594-596; *United States v. Shipp*, 203 U.S. 563, 572; *Blackmer v. United States*, 284 U.S. 421, 440; *Nye v. United States*, 313 U.S. 33, 48; see *United States v. Hudson and*

Goodwin, 7 Cranch 32, 34. Similarly, an action for debt to enforce a penalty inflicted by Congress is not subject to the constitutional restrictions upon criminal prosecutions. *United States v. Zucker*, 161 U.S. 475; *United States v. Regan*, 232 U.S. 37, and cases cited.

All these are instances of offenses committed against the United States, for which a penalty is imposed, but they are not deemed to be within Article III, §2, or the provisions of the Fifth and Sixth Amendments relating to "crimes" and "criminal prosecutions." In the light of this long-continued and consistent interpretation, we must conclude that § 2 of Article III and the Fifth and Sixth Amendments cannot be taken to have extended the right to demand a jury to trials by military commission, or to have required that offenses against the law of war not triable by jury at common law be tried only in the civil courts.

The fact that "cases arising in the land or naval forces" are excepted from the operation of the Amendments does not militate against this conclusion. Such cases are expressly excepted from the Fifth Amendment, and are deemed excepted by implication from the Sixth. *Ex parte Milligan*, *supra*, 123, 138-139. It is argued that the exception, which excludes from the Amendment cases arising in the armed forces, has also, by implication, extended its guaranty to all other cases; that, since petitioners, not being members of the Armed Forces of the United States, are not within the exception, the Amendment operates to give to them the right to a jury trial. But we think this argument misconceives both the scope of the Amendment and the purpose of the exception.

We may assume, without deciding, that a trial prosecuted before a military commission created by military authority is not one "arising in the land ... forces," when the accused is not a member of or associated with those forces. But even so, the exception cannot be taken to affect those trials before military commissions which are neither within the exception nor within the provisions of Article III, § 2, whose guaranty the Amendments did not enlarge. No exception is necessary to exclude from the operation of these provisions cases never deemed to be within their terms. An express exception from Article III, § 2, and from the Fifth and Sixth Amendments, of trials of petty offenses and of criminal contempt has not been found necessary in order to preserve the traditional practice of trying those offenses without a jury. It is no more so in order to continue the practice of trying, before military tribunals without a jury, offenses committed by enemy belligerents against the law of war.

***

We cannot say that Congress, in preparing the Fifth and Sixth Amendments, intended to extend trial by jury to the cases of alien or citizen offenders against the law of war otherwise triable by military commission, while withholding it from members of our own armed forces charged with infractions of the Articles of War punishable by death. It is equally inadmissible to construe the Amendments—whose primary purpose was to continue unimpaired presentment by grand jury and trial by petit jury in all those cases in which they had been customary—as either abolishing all trials by military tribunals, save those of the personnel of our own armed forces, or, what in effect comes to the same thing, as imposing on all such tribunals the necessity of proceeding against unlawful enemy belligerents only on presentment and trial by jury. We conclude that the Fifth and Sixth Amendments did not restrict whatever authority was conferred by the Constitution to try offenses against the law of war by military commission, and that petitioners, charged with such an offense not required to be tried by jury at common law, were lawfully placed on trial by the Commission without a jury.

Petitioners, and especially petitioner Haupt, stress the pronouncement of this Court in the **Milligan** case, supra, p. 121, that the law of war can never be applied to citizens in states which have upheld the authority of the government, and where the courts are open, and their process unobstructed.

Elsewhere in its opinion, at pp. 118, 121-122 and 131, the Court was at pains to point out that Milligan, a citizen twenty years resident in Indiana, who had never been a resident of any of the states in rebellion, was not an enemy belligerent either entitled to the status of a prisoner of war or subject to the penalties imposed upon unlawful belligerents. We construe the Court's statement as to the inapplicability of the law of war to Milligan's case as having particular reference to the facts before it. From them, the Court concluded that Milligan, not being a part of or associated with the armed forces of the enemy, was a nonbelligerent, not subject to the law of war save as—in circumstances found not there to be present, and not involved here—martial law might be constitutionally established.

The Court's opinion is inapplicable to the case presented by the present record. We have no occasion now to define with meticulous care the ultimate boundaries of the jurisdiction of military tribunals to try persons according to the law of war. It is enough that petitioners here, upon the conceded facts, were plainly within those boundaries, and were held in good faith for trial by military commission, charged with being enemies who, with the purpose of destroying war materials and utilities, entered, or after entry remained in, our territory without uniform—an offense against the law of war. We hold only that those particular acts constitute an offense against the law of war which the Constitution authorizes to be tried by military commission.

Since the first specification of Charge I sets forth a violation of the law of war, we have no occasion to pass on the adequacy of the second specification of Charge I, or to construe the 81st and 82nd Articles of War for the purpose of ascertaining whether the specifications under Charges II and III allege violations of those

Articles, or whether, if so construed, they are constitutional. **McNally v. Hill**, 293 U.S. 131.

There remains the contention that the President's Order of July 2, 1942, so far as it lays down the procedure to be followed on the trial before the Commission and on the review of its findings and sentence, and the procedure in fact followed by the Commission, are in conflict with Articles of War 38, 43, 46, 50 1/2 and 70. Petitioners argue that their trial by the Commission, for offenses against the law of war and the 81st and 82nd Articles of War, by a procedure which Congress has prohibited would invalidate any conviction which could be obtained against them, and renders their detention for trial likewise unlawful (see **McClaughry v. Deming**, 186 U.S. 49; **United States v. Brown**, 206 U.S. 240, 244; **Runkle v. United States**, 122 U.S. 543, 555-556; **Dynes v. Hoover**, 20 How. 65, 80-81); that the President's Order prescribes such an unlawful procedure, and that the secrecy surrounding the trial and all proceedings before the Commission, as well as any review of its decision, will preclude a later opportunity to test the lawfulness of the detention.

Petitioners do not argue, and we do not consider, the question whether the President is compelled by the Articles of War to afford unlawful enemy belligerents a trial before subjecting them to disciplinary measures. Their contention is that, if Congress has authorized their trial by military commission upon the charges preferred— violations of the law of war and the 81st and 82nd Articles of War— it has by the Articles of War prescribed the procedure by which the trial is to be conducted, and that, since the President has ordered their trial for such offenses by military commission, they are entitled to claim the protection of the procedure which Congress has commanded shall be controlling.

We need not inquire whether Congress may restrict the power of the Commander in Chief to deal with enemy belligerents. For the Court is unanimous in its conclusion that the Articles in question could not at any stage of the proceedings afford any basis for issuing the writ. But a majority of the full Court are not agreed on the appropriate grounds for decision. Some members of the Court are of opinion that Congress did not intend the Articles of War to govern a Presidential military commission convened for the determination of questions relating to admitted enemy invaders, and that the context of the Articles makes clear that they should not be construed to apply in that class of cases. Others are of the view that---even though this trial is subject to whatever provisions of the Articles of War Congress has in terms made applicable to "commissions"—the particular Articles in question, rightly construed, do not foreclose the procedure prescribed by the President or that shown to have been employed by the Commission, in a trial of offenses against the law of war and the 81st and 82nd Articles of War, by a military commission appointed by the President.

Accordingly, we conclude that Charge I, on which petitioners were detained for trial by the Military Commission, alleged an offense which the President is authorized to order tried by military commission; that his Order convening the Commission was a lawful order, and that the Commission was lawfully constituted; that the petitioners were held in lawful custody, and did not show cause for their discharge. It follows that the orders of the District Court should be affirmed, and that leave to file petitions for habeas corpus in this Court should be denied.

Duncan v. Kahanamoku
327 U.S. 304 (1946)

Mr. Justice Black delivered the opinion of the Court.

The petitioners in these cases were sentenced to prison by military tribunals in Hawaii. Both are civilians. The question before us is whether the military tribunals had power to do this. The United States District Court for Hawaii in habeas corpus proceedings held that the military tribunals had no such power and ordered that they be set free. The Circuit Court of Appeals reversed, and ordered that the petitioners be returned to prison. 9 Cir., 146 F.2d 576. Both cases thus involve the rights of individuals charged with crime and not connected with the armed forces to have their guilt or innocence determined in courts to law which provide established procedural safeguards, rather than by military tribunals which fail to afford many of these safeguards. Since these judicial safeguards are prized privileges of our system of government we granted certiorari. 324 U.S. 833, 65 S.Ct. 677.

The following events led to the military tribunals' exercise of jurisdiction over the petitioners. On December 7, 1941, immediately following the surprise air attack by the Japanese on Pearl Harbor, the Governor of Hawaii by proclamation undertook to suspend the privilege of the writ of habeas corpus and to place the Territory under 'martial law.' Section 67 of the Hawaiian Organic Act, 31 Stat. 141, 48 U.S.C.A. 532, authorizes the Territorial Governor to take this action 'in case of rebellion or invasion, or imminent danger thereof, when the public safety requires it.' His action was to remain in effect only 'until communication can be had with the President and his decision thereon made known.' The President approved the Governor's action on December 9th. The Governor's proclamation also authorized and requested the Commanding General, 'during ... the emergency and until danger of invasion is removed, to exercise all the powers normally exercised' by the Governor and by 'the judicial officers and employees of the Territory.'

Pursuant to this authorization the Commanding General immediately proclaimed himself Military Governor and undertook the defense of the Territory and the maintenance of order. On December

8th, both civil and criminal courts were forbidden to summon jurors and witnesses and to try cases. The Commanding General established military tribunals to take the place of the courts. These were to try civilians charged with violating the laws of the United States and of the Territory, and rules, regulations, orders or policies of the Military Government. Rules of evidence and procedure of courts of law were not to control the military trials. In imposing penalties the military tribunals were to be 'guided by, but not limited to the penalties authorized by the court martial manual, the laws of the United States, the Territory of Hawaii, the District of Columbia, and the customs of war in like cases.' The rule announced was simply that punishment was 'to be commensurate with the offense committed' and that the death penalty might be imposed 'in appropriate cases.' Thus the military authorities took over the government of Hawaii. They could and did, by simply promulgating orders, govern the day to day activities of civilians who lived, worked, or were merely passing through there. The military tribunals interpreted the very orders promulgated by the military authorities and proceeded to punish violators. The sentences imposed were not subject to direct appellate court review, since it had long been established that military tribunals are not part of our judicial system. ***Ex parte Vallandigham***, 1 Wall. 243. The military undoubtedly assumed that its rule was not subject to any judicial control whatever, for by orders issued on August 25, 1943, it prohibited even accepting of a petition for writ of habeas corpus by a judge or judicial employee or the filing of such a petition by a prisoner or his attorney. Military tribunals could punish violators of these orders by fine, imprisonment or death.

White, the petitioner in No. 15, was a stockbroker in Honolulu. Neither he nor his business was connected with the armed forces. On August 20, 1942, more than eight months after the Pearl Harbor attack, the military police arrested him. The charge against him was embezzling stock belonging to another civilian in violation of Chapter 183 of the Revised Laws of Hawaii. Though by the time of White's arrest the courts were permitted 'as agents of the Military Governor' to dispose of some non-jury civil cases, they were still forbidden to summon jurors and to exercise criminal jurisdiction. On August 22nd, White was brought before a military tribunal designated as a 'Provost Court.' The 'Court' orally informed him of the charge. He objected to the tribunal's jurisdiction but the objection was overruled. He demanded to be tried by a jury. This request was denied. His attorney asked for additional time to prepare the case. This was refused. On August 25th he was tried and convicted. The tribunal sentenced him to five years imprisonment. Later the sentence was reduced to four years.

Duncan, the petitioner in No. 14, was a civilian ship-fitter employed in the Navy Yard at Honolulu. On February 24th, 1944, more than two years and two months after the Pearl Harbor attack, he engaged in a brawl with two armed Marine sentries at the yard. He was arrested by the military authorities. By the time of his arrest the military had to some extent eased the stringency of military rule. Schools, bars and motion picture theatres had been reopened. Courts had been authorized to 'exercise their normal functions.' They were once more summoning jurors and witnesses and conducting criminal trials. There were important exceptions, however. One of these was that only military tribunals were to try 'Criminal Prosecutions for violations of military orders.' As the record shows, these military orders still covered a wide range of day to day civilian conduct. Duncan was charged with violating one of these orders, paragraph 8.01, Title 8, of General Order No. 2, which prohibited assault on military or naval personnel with intent to resist or hinder them in the discharge of their duty. He was therefore, tried by a military tribunal rather than the Territorial Court, although the general laws of Hawaii made assault a crime. Revised L.H.1935, ch. 166. A conviction followed and Duncan was sentenced to six months imprisonment.

Both White and Duncan challenged the power of the military tribunals to try them by petitions for writs of habeas corpus filed in the District Court for Hawaii on March 14 and April 14, 1944, respectively. Their petitions urged both statutory and Constitutional grounds. The court issued orders to show cause. Returns to these orders contended that Hawaii had become part of an active theatre of war constantly threatened by invasion from without; that the writ of habeas corpus had therefore properly been suspended and martial law had validly been established in accordance with the provisions of the Organic Act; that consequently the District Court did not have jurisdiction to issue the writ; and that the trials of petitioners by military tribunals pursuant to orders by the Military Governor issued because of military necessity were valid. Each petitioner filed a traverse to the returns, which traverse challenged among other things the suspension of habeas corpus, the establishment of martial law and the validity of the Military Governor's orders, asserting that such action could not be taken except when required by military necessity due to actual or threatened invasion, which even if it did exist on December 7, 1941, did not exist when the petitioners were tried; and that, whatever the necessity for martial law, there was no justification for trying them in military tribunals rather than the regular courts of law. The District Court, after separate trials found in each case, among other things, that the courts had always been able to function but for the military orders closing them, and that consequently there was no military necessity for the trial of petitioners by military tribunals rather than regular courts. It accordingly held the trials void and ordered the release of the petitioners.

The Circuit Court of Appeals, assuming without deciding that the District Court had jurisdiction to entertain the petitions, held the military trials valid and reversed the ruling of the District Court, 9 Cir.,

146 F.2d 576. It held that the military orders providing for military trials were fully authorized by Section 67 of the Organic Act and the Governor's actions taken under it. The Court relied on that part of the section which as we have indicated authorizes the Governor with the approval of the President to proclaim 'martial law', whenever the public safety requires it. The Circuit Court thought that the term 'martial law' as used in the Act denotes among other things the establishment of a 'total military government' completely displacing or subordinating the regular courts, that the decision of the executive as to what the public safety requires must be sustained so long as that decision is based on reasonable grounds and that such reasonable grounds did exist.

In presenting its argument before this Court the government for reasons set out in the margin abandons its contention as to the suspension of the writ of habeas corpus and advances the argument employed by the Circuit Court for sustaining the trials and convictions of the petitioners by military tribunals. The petitioners contend that 'martial law' as provided for by 67 did not authorize the military to try and punish civilians such as petitioners and urge further that if such authority should be inferred from the Organic Act, it would be unconstitutional. We need decide the Constitutional question only if we agree with the government that Congress did authorize what was done here.

Did the Organic Act during the period of martial law give the armed forces power to supplant all civilian laws and to substitute military for judicial trials under the conditions that existed in Hawaii at the time these petitioners were tried? The relevant conditions, for our purposes, were the same when both petitioners were tried. The answer to the question depends on a correct interpretation of the Act. But we need not construe the Act, insofar as the power of the military might be used to meet other and different conditions and situations. The boundaries of the situation with reference to which we do interpret the scope of the Act can be more sharply defined by stating at this point some different conditions which either would or might conceivably have affected to a greater or lesser extent the scope of the authorized military power. We note first that at the time the alleged offenses were committed the dangers apprehended by the military were not sufficiently imminent to cause them to require civilians to evacuate the area or even to evacuate any of the buildings necessary to carry on the business of the courts. In fact, the buildings had long been open and actually in use for certain kinds of trials. Our question does not involve the well-established power of the military to exercise jurisdiction over members of the armed forces, those directly connected with such forces, or enemy belligerents, prisoners of war, or others charged with violating the laws of war. We are not concerned with the recognized power of the military to try civilians in tribunals established as a part of a temporary military government over occupied enemy territory or territory regained from an enemy where civilian government cannot and does not function. For Hawaii since annexation has been held by and loyal to the United States. Nor need we here consider the power of the military simply to arrest and detain civilians interfering with a necessary military function at a time of turbulence and danger from insurrection or war. And finally, there was no specialized effort of the military, here, to enforce orders which related only to military functions, such as, for illustration, curfew rules or blackouts. For these petitioners were tried before tribunals set up under a military program which took over all government and superseded all civil laws and courts. If the Organic Act, properly interpreted, did not give the armed forces this awesome power, both petitioners are entitled to their freedom.

I.

In interpreting the Act we must first look to its language. Section 67 makes it plain that Congress did intend the Governor of Hawaii, with the approval of the President, to invoke military aid under certain circumstances. But Congress did not specifically state to what extent the army could be used or what power it could exercise. It certainly did not explicitly declare that the Governor in conjunction with the military could for days, months or years close all the courts and supplant them with military tribunals. Cf. **Coleman v. Tennessee**, 97 U.S. 509, 514. If a power thus to obliterate the judicial system of Hawaii can be found at all in the Organic Act, it must be inferred from 67's provision for placing the Territory under 'martial law.' But the term 'martial law' carries no precise meaning. The Constitution does not refer to 'martial law' at all and no Act of Congress has defined the term. It has been employed in various ways by different people and at different times.... The language of 67 thus fails to define adequately the scope of the power given to the military and to show whether the Organic Act provides that courts of law be supplanted by military tribunals.

II.

Since the Act's language does not provide a satisfactory answer, we look to the legislative history for possible further aid in interpreting the term 'martial law' as used in the statute. The government contends that the legislative history shows that Congress intended to give the armed forces extraordinarily broad powers to try civilians before military tribunals. Its argument is as follows: That portion of the language of 67 which prescribes the prerequisites to declaring martial law is identical with a part of the language of the original Constitution of Hawaii. Before Congress enacted the Organic Act the Supreme Court of Hawaii had construed that language as giving the Hawaiian

President power to authorize military tribunals to try civilians charged with crime whenever the public safety required it. *In re Kalanianaole*, 10 Hawaii, 29. When Congress passed the Organic Act it simply enacted the applicable language of the Hawaiian Constitution and with it the interpretation of that language by the Hawaiian Supreme Court.

... when the Organic Act is read as a whole and in the light of its legislative history it becomes clear that Congress did not intend the Constitution to have a limited application to Hawaii. Along with 67 Congress enacted 5 of the Organic Act which provides 'that the Constitution ... shall have the same force and effect within the said Territory as elsewhere in the United States.' 31 Stat. 141, 48 U.S.C.A. 495. Even when Hawaii was first annexed Congress had provided that the Territory's existing laws should remain in effect unless contrary to the Constitution. 30 Stat. 750. And the House Committee Report in explaining 5 of the Organic Act stated: 'Probably the same result would obtain without this provision under Section 1891, chapter 1, Title XXIII, of the Revised Statutes, but to prevent possible question, the section is inserted in the bill.' Congress thus expressed a strong desire to apply the Constitution without qualification.

It follows that civilians in Hawaii are entitled to the Constitutional guarantee of a fair trial to the same extent as those who live in any other part of our country. We are aware that conditions peculiar to Hawaii might imperatively demand extraordinarily speedy and effective measures in the event of actual or threatened invasion. But this also holds true for other parts of the United States. Extraordinary measures in Hawaii, however necessary, are not supportable on the mistaken premise that Hawaiian inhabitants are less entitled to Constitutional protection than others.... Whatever power the Organic Act gave the Hawaiian military authorities, such power must therefore be construed in the same way as a grant of power to troops stationed in any one of the states.

III.

Since both the language of the Organic Act and its legislative history fail to indicate that the scope of 'martial law' in Hawaii includes the supplanting of courts by military tribunals, we must look to other sources in order to interpret that term. We think the answer may be found in the birth, development and growth of our governmental institutions up to the time Congress passed the Organic Act. Have the principles and practices developed during the birth and growth of our political institutions been such as to persuade us that Congress intended that loyal civilians in loyal territory should have their daily conduct governed by military orders substituted for criminal laws, and that such civilians should be tried and punished by military tribunals? Let us examine what those principles and practices have been, with respect to the position of civilian government and the courts and compare that with the standing of military tribunals throughout our history.

People of many ages and countries have feared and unflinchingly opposed the kind of subordination of executive, legislative and judicial authorities to complete military rule which according to the government Congress has authorized here. In this country that fear has become part of our cultural and political institutions. The story of that development is well known and we see no need to retell it all. But we might mention a few pertinent incidents.

***

[The Court proceeds to provide a brief history of American limits on military power in government.]

***

Courts and their procedural safeguards are indispensable to our system of government. They were set up by our founders to protect the liberties they valued. **Ex parte Quirin**, supra, 317 U.S. at page 19, 63 S.Ct. at page 6. Our system of government clearly is the antithesis of total military rule and the founders of this country are not likely to have contemplated complete military dominance within the limits of a Territory made part of this country and not recently taken from an enemy. They were opposed to governments that placed in the hands of one man the power to make, interpret and enforce the laws. Their philosophy has been the people's throughout our history. For that reason we have maintained legislatures chosen by citizens or their representatives and courts and juries to try those who violate legislative enactments. We have always been especially concerned about the potential evils of summary criminal trials and have guarded against them by provisions embodied in the constitution itself. See **Ex parte Milligan**, 4 Wall. 2; **Chambers v. Florida**, 309 U.S. 227, 60 S.Ct. 472. Legislatures and courts are not merely cherished American institutions; they are indispensable to our government.

Military tribunals have no such standing. For as this Court has said before: '... the military should always be kept in subjection to the laws of the country to which it belongs, and that he is no friend to the Republic who advocates the contrary. The established principle of every free people is, that the law shall alone govern; and to it the military must always yield.' **Dow v. Johnson**, 100 U.S. 158, 169. Congress prior to the time of the enactment of the Organic Act had only once authorized the supplanting of the courts by military tribunals. Legislation to that effect was enacted immediately after the South's unsuccessful attempt to secede from the Union. Insofar as that legislation applied to the Southern States after the war was at an end it was challenged by a series of Presidential vetoes as vigorous as any in the country's history. And in order to prevent this Court from passing on the constitutionality of this legislation Congress found it necessary to curtail our appellate jurisdiction. Indeed, prior to the Organic Act, the only time this Court had ever discussed the supplanting of courts by military tribunals in a situation other than that involving the establishment of a military government over recently occupied enemy territory, it had emphatically declared that 'civil liberty and this kind of martial law cannot endure together; the antagonism is irreconcilable; and, in the conflict, one or the other must perish.' **Ex parte Milligan**, 4 Wall. 2, 124, 125.

We believe that when Congress passed the Hawaiian Organic Act and authorized the establishment of 'martial law' it had in mind and did not wish to exceed the boundaries between military and civilian power, in which our people have always believed, which responsible military and executive officers had heeded, and which had become part of our political philosophy and institutions prior to the time Congress passed the Organic Act. The phrase 'martial law' as employed in that Act, therefore, while intended to authorize the military to act vigorously for the maintenance of an orderly civil government and for the defense of the island against actual or threatened rebellion or invasion, was not intended to authorize the supplanting of courts by military tribunals. Yet the government seeks to justify the punishment of both White and Duncan on the ground of such supposed Congressional authorization. We hold that both petitioners are now entitled to be released from custody.

Reversed.

Mr. Justice Jackson took no part in the consideration or decision of these cases.

Commentary and Questions

6. The Court in *Quirin* discussed presidential powers in time of war as well as the law of war, otherwise referred to as *jus belli*, and the difference between lawful and unlawful combatants under the legal guidelines for war. The *Quirin* defendants were deemed to be unlawful combatants pursuant to international rules of war and the Geneva Convention. As a result they were, in addition to being subject to trial and capture, subject to trial and punishment by a military tribunal. What is the basis of the German prisoners' habeas petition and argument to the Court? How does the Court address their main argument? What does the Court state with regard to constitutional rights such as the Fifth and Sixth Amendment as applied to these defendants?

7. The U.S. Supreme Court in the Civil War case of *Ex Parte Milligan* established the "open-court" rule for denial of military tribunal jurisdiction. *Quirin* distinguished the *Milligan* holding by pointing to the fact that the defendants were members of an armed force of a hostile nation.[23] Further supporting the Court's decision was the fact of a declared war by Congress against Germany. Despite one of the defendant's being a dual citizen of the United States and Germany, the Court *"created a declared enemy exception to the open court rule."*[24] Was there a true distinction between the two cases or was the Court seeking to justify the punishment set by the military tribunal?

8. *Duncan v. Kahanamoku* was one of the Japanese detention cases from World War II, joining *Korematsu v. U.S.*, *Ex Parte Endo* and *Hirabayashi v. U.S.*, which will each be discussed in a later chapter. Once again the U.S. Supreme Court was tasked with reviewing the authority of military tribunals except in this instance it was whether the specific grant of power under the Organic Act provided for the replacement of civilian courts. How did the Court interpret the authority of the military commander in Hawaii to establish military tribunals for citizens? According to the Court, what was the authority of military tribunals in relation to the operational civilian court system?

9. The *Duncan* case involved the establishment of martial law over the Hawaiian territory after the December 7, 1941 attack on Pearl Harbor. Martial law is not a specific constitutional grant of power to the president yet it is recognized as a "general emergency power" of the executive.[25] In *United States v. Diekelman*, a case emanating from a Civil War seizure of a foreign vessel's cargo at the Port of New Orleans during a naval blockade instituted by the president, Chief Justice Waite wrote, *"Martial law is the law of military necessity in the actual presence of war. It is administered by the general of the army, and is in fact his will. Of necessity it is arbitrary; but it must be obeyed."*[26] The Court acknowledged civil authority was overthrown by martial law and the military commander's will was the necessary law. This view of martial law, though not founded on any specific constitutional ground, can be logically inferred from the Article II, section 2 power as commander-in-chief along with the section 3 power to *"take care that the laws be faithfully executed."* Martial law, while a total replacement of civil law by military rule, is "local in character."[27] It is distinguishable from habeas corpus suspension, which is specifically mentioned in Article I, section 9 of the Constitution, in that when habeas relief is suspended it is limited to the specific right, thus martial law has broader and more powerful implications.[28]

10. The post-World War II case of *In re Yamashita* was another in which the U.S. Supreme Court dealt with the appropriateness of trial by a military commission. The defendant Tomiyuki Yamashita was the commanding general of the Japanese Imperial Army's 14th Army Group in the Philippines who surrendered to U.S. troops and became a prisoner of war. He was charged by U.S. military authorities for failing to exercise control over his

troops that committed atrocities against civilians and prisoners of war. These were violations of war for which Yamashita was charged, tried, convicted and sentenced to death by hanging. Yamashita challenged his conviction as well as the authority of the military commission to hear his case after the conclusion of hostilities. The Court found the military tribunal to be properly constituted pursuant to an Act of Congress under its Article I, section 8 powers to "define and punish ... offenses against the law of nations." Chief Justice Stone writing for the Court stated: *"We do not here appraise the evidence on which petitioner was convicted. We do not consider what measures, if any, petitioner took to prevent the commission, by the troops under his command, of the plain violations of the law of war detailed in the bill of particulars, or whether such measures as he may have taken were appropriate and sufficient to discharge the duty imposed upon him. These are questions within the peculiar competence of the military officers composing the commission, and were for it to decide. It is plain that the charge on which petitioner was tried charged him with a breach of his duty to control the operations of the members of his command, by permitting them to commit the specified atrocities. This was enough to require the commission to hear evidence tending to establish the culpable failure of petitioner to perform the duty imposed on him by the law of war, and to pass upon its sufficiency to establish guilt. Obviously, charges of violations of the law of war triable before a military tribunal need not be stated with the precision of a common law indictment. But we conclude that the allegations of the charge, tested by any reasonable standard, adequately allege a violation of the law of war, and that the commission had authority to try and decide the issue which it raised."*[29] Aside from holding that the government had the authority to establish and maintain military commissions at the close of hostilities the *Yamashita* Court found the charges of the military tribunal to be sustainable as war crimes. The American Military Commission in *United States v. Yamashita* previously found that General Yamashita had failed to properly supervise his troops. This was the genesis of the *Yamashita standard* of command responsibility, which is that a military commander has the responsibility to control his troops and prevent them from committing war crimes or human rights violations, otherwise the commander, by failing to act, is responsible for the acts of his troops. It is a war crime of omission. Does the Yamashita standard have any applicability to the acts of U.S. soldiers responsible for the care, custody and control of inmates at Abu Ghraib prison in Afghanistan? Does the criminal inquiry by the military end with the actions of the soldiers or should it reach beyond them to higher authority? How far up the military chain of command should such an inquiry proceed? Perhaps this is a discussion better left to Chapter Eight, Detention and Rendition, nonetheless it is worth noting at this point because habeas corpus relief is part of due process and the limits of government power.

Rasul v. Bush
542 U.S. 466 (2004)

Justice Stevens delivered the opinion of the Court.

These two cases present the narrow but important question whether United States courts lack jurisdiction to consider challenges to the legality of the detention of foreign nationals captured abroad in connection with hostilities and incarcerated at the Guantanamo Bay Naval Base, Cuba.

I

On September 11, 2001, agents of the al Qaeda terrorist network hijacked four commercial airliners and used them as missiles to attack American targets. While one of the four attacks was foiled by the heroism of the plane's passengers, the other three killed approximately 3,000 innocent civilians, destroyed hundreds of millions of dollars of property, and severely damaged the U.S. economy. In response to the attacks, Congress passed a joint resolution authorizing the President to use "all necessary and appropriate force against those nations, organizations, or persons he determines planned, authorized, committed, or aided the terrorist attacks ... or harbored such organizations or persons." *Authorization for Use of Military Force, Pub. L. 107 – 40, §§1 – 2, 115 Stat. 224.* Acting pursuant to that authorization, the President sent U.S. Armed Forces into Afghanistan to wage a military campaign against al Qaeda and the Taliban regime that had supported it.

Petitioners in these cases are 2 Australian citizens and 12 Kuwaiti citizens who were captured abroad during hostilities between the United States and the Taliban. Since early 2002, the U.S. military has held them—along with, according to the Government's estimate, approximately 640 other non-Americans captured abroad—at the Naval Base at Guantanamo Bay. *Brief for United States.* The United States occupies the Base, which comprises 45 square miles of land and water along the southeast coast of Cuba, pursuant to a 1903 Lease Agreement executed with the newly independent Republic of Cuba in the aftermath of the Spanish-American War. Under the Agreement, "the United States recognizes the continuance of the ultimate sovereignty of the Republic of Cuba over the [leased areas]," while "the Republic of Cuba consents that during the period of the occupation by the United States ... the United States shall exercise complete jurisdiction and control over and within said areas." In 1934, the parties entered into a treaty providing that, absent an agreement to modify or abrogate the lease, the lease would remain in effect "[s]o long as the United States of America shall not abandon the ... naval station of Guantanamo."

In 2002, petitioners, through relatives acting as their next friends, filed various actions in the U.S. District Court for the District of Columbia challenging the legality of their detention at the Base. All alleged that none of the petitioners has ever been a combatant against the United States or has ever engaged in any terrorist acts. They also alleged that none has been charged with any wrongdoing, permitted to consult with counsel, or provided access to the courts or any other tribunal. App. 29, 77, 108.

The two Australians, Mamdouh Habib and David Hicks, each filed a petition for writ of habeas corpus, seeking release from custody, access to counsel, freedom from interrogations, and other relief. *Id.*, at 98 – 99, 124 – 126. Fawzi Khalid Abdullah Fahad Al Odah and the 11 other Kuwaiti detainees filed a complaint seeking to be informed of the charges against them, to be allowed to meet with their families and with counsel, and to have access to the courts or some other impartial tribunal. *Id.*, at 34. They claimed that denial of these rights violates the Constitution, international law, and treaties of the United States. Invoking the court's jurisdiction under 28 U.S.C. § 1331 and 1350, among other statutory bases, they asserted causes of action under the Administrative Procedure Act, 5 U.S.C. § 555 702, 706; the Alien Tort Statute, 28 U.S.C. § 1350; and the general federal habeas corpus statute, §§2241 – 2243. App. 19.

Construing all three actions as petitions for writs of habeas corpus, the District Court dismissed them for want of jurisdiction. The court held, in reliance on our opinion in **Johnson v. Eisentrager**, 339 U.S. 763 (1950), that "aliens detained outside the sovereign territory of the United States [may not] invok[e] a petition for a writ of habeas corpus." 215 F. Supp. 2d 55, 68 (DC 2002). The Court of Appeals affirmed. Reading **Eisentrager** to hold that " 'the privilege of litigation' does not extend to aliens in military custody who have no presence in 'any territory over which the United States is sovereign,'" 321 F.3d 1134, 1144 (CADC 2003) (quoting **Eisentrager**, 339 U.S., at 777 – 778), it held that the District Court lacked jurisdiction over petitioners' habeas actions, as well as their remaining federal statutory claims that do not sound in habeas. We granted certiorari, 540 U.S. 1003 (2003), and now reverse.

II

Congress has granted federal district courts, "within their respective jurisdictions," the authority to hear applications for habeas corpus by any person who claims to be held "in custody in violation of the Constitution or laws or treaties of the United States." 28 U.S.C. § 2241(a), (c)(3). The statute traces its ancestry to the first grant of federal court jurisdiction: Section 14 of the Judiciary Act of 1789 authorized federal courts to issue the writ of habeas corpus to prisoners "in custody, under or by colour of the authority of the United

States, or committed for trial before some court of the same." *Act of Sept. 24, 1789*, ch. 20, §14, 1 Stat. 82. In 1867, Congress extended the protections of the writ to "all cases where any person may be restrained of his or her liberty in violation of the constitution, or of any treaty or law of the United States." *Act of Feb. 5, 1867*, ch. 28, 14 Stat. 385. See **Felker v. Turpin**, 518 U.S. 651, 659 – 660 (1996).

Habeas corpus is, however, "a writ antecedent to statute, ... throwing its root deep into the genius of our common law." **Williams v. Kaiser**, 323 U.S. 471, 484, n. 2 (1945) (internal quotation marks omitted). The writ appeared in English law several centuries ago, became "an integral part of our common-law heritage" by the time the Colonies achieved independence, **Preiser v. Rodriguez**, 411 U.S. 475, 485 (1973), and received explicit recognition in the Constitution, which forbids suspension of "[t]he Privilege of the Writ of Habeas Corpus ... unless when in Cases of Rebellion or Invasion the public Safety may require it," *Art. I, §9, cl. 2.*

As it has evolved over the past two centuries, the habeas statute clearly has expanded habeas corpus "beyond the limits that obtained during the 17th and 18th centuries." **Swain v. Pressley**, 430 U.S. 372, 380, n. 13 (1977). But "[a]t its historical core, the writ of habeas corpus has served as a means of reviewing the legality of Executive detention, and it is in that context that its protections have been strongest." **INS v. St. Cyr**, 533 U.S. 289, 301 (2001). See also **Brown v. Allen**, 344 U.S. 443, 533 (1953) (Jackson, J., concurring in result) ("The historic purpose of the writ has been to relieve detention by executive authorities without judicial trial"). As Justice Jackson wrote in an opinion respecting the availability of habeas corpus to aliens held in U.S. custody:

"Executive imprisonment has been considered oppressive and lawless since John, at Runnymede, pledged that no free man should be imprisoned, dispossessed, outlawed, or exiled save by the judgment of his peers or by the law of the land. The judges of England developed the writ of habeas corpus largely to preserve these immunities from executive restraint." **Shaughnessy v. United States ex rel. Mezei**, 345 U.S. 206, 218 – 219 (1953) (dissenting opinion).

Consistent with the historic purpose of the writ, this Court has recognized the federal courts' power to review applications for habeas relief in a wide variety of cases involving Executive detention, in wartime as well as in times of peace. The Court has, for example, entertained the habeas petitions of an American citizen who plotted an attack on military installations during the Civil War, **Ex parte Milligan**, 4 Wall. 2 (1866), and of admitted enemy aliens convicted of war crimes during a declared war and held in the United States, **Ex parte Quirin**, 317 U.S. 1 (1942), and its insular possessions, **In re Yamashita**, 327 U.S. 1 (1946).

The question now before us is whether the habeas statute confers a right to judicial review of the legality of Executive detention of aliens in a territory over which the United States exercises plenary and exclusive jurisdiction, but not "ultimate sovereignty."

III

Respondents' primary submission is that the answer to the jurisdictional question is controlled by our decision in *Eisentrager*. In that case, we held that a Federal District Court lacked authority to issue a writ of habeas corpus to 21 German citizens who had been captured by U.S. forces in China, tried and convicted of war crimes by an American military commission headquartered in Nanking, and incarcerated in the Landsberg Prison in occupied Germany. The Court of Appeals in *Eisentrager* had found jurisdiction, reasoning that "any person who is deprived of his liberty by officials of the United States, acting under purported authority of that Government, and who can show that his confinement is in violation of a prohibition of the Constitution, has a right to the writ." *Eisentrager v. Forrestal*, 174 F.2d 961, 963 (CADC 1949). In reversing that determination, this Court summarized the six critical facts in the case:

"We are here confronted with a decision whose basic premise is that these prisoners are entitled, as a constitutional right, to sue in some court of the United States for a writ of habeas corpus. To support that assumption we must hold that a prisoner of our military authorities is constitutionally entitled to the writ, even though he (a) is an enemy alien; (b) has never been or resided in the United States; (c) was captured outside of our territory and there held in military custody as a prisoner of war; (d) was tried and convicted by a Military Commission sitting outside the United States; (e) for offenses against laws of war committed outside the United States; (f) and is at all times imprisoned outside the United States." 339 U.S., at 777.

On this set of facts, the Court concluded, "no right to the writ of habeas corpus appears." *Id.*, at 781.

Petitioners in these cases differ from the *Eisentrager* detainees in important respects: They are not nationals of countries at war with the United States, and they deny that they have engaged in or plotted acts of aggression against the United States; they have never been afforded access to any tribunal, much less charged with and convicted of wrongdoing; and for more than two years they have been imprisoned in territory over which the United States exercises exclusive jurisdiction and control.

Not only are petitioners differently situated from the *Eisentrager* detainees, but the Court in *Eisentrager* made quite clear that all six of the facts critical to its disposition were relevant only to the question of the prisoners' *constitutional* entitlement to habeas corpus. *Id.*, at 777. The Court had far less to say on the question of the petitioners' *statutory* entitlement to habeas review. Its only statement on the subject was a passing reference to the absence of statutory authorization: "Nothing in the text of the Constitution extends such a right, nor does anything in our statutes." *Id.*, at 768.

Reference to the historical context in which *Eisentrager* was decided explains why the opinion devoted so little attention to question of statutory jurisdiction. In 1948, just two months after the *Eisentrager* petitioners filed their petition for habeas corpus in the U.S. District Court for the District of Columbia, this Court issued its decision in *Ahrens v. Clark*, 335 U.S. 188, a case concerning the application of the habeas statute to the petitions of 120 Germans who were then being detained at Ellis Island, New York, for deportation to Germany. The *Ahrens* detainees had also filed their petitions in the U.S. District Court for the District of Columbia, naming the Attorney General as the respondent. Reading the phrase "within their respective jurisdictions" as used in the habeas statute to require the petitioners' presence within the district court's territorial jurisdiction, the Court held that the District of Columbia court lacked jurisdiction to entertain the detainees' claims. *Id.*, at 192. *Ahrens* expressly reserved the question "of what process, if any, a person confined in an area not subject to the jurisdiction of any district court may employ to assert federal rights." *Id.*, 192, n. 4. But as the dissent noted, if the presence of the petitioner in the territorial jurisdiction of a federal district court were truly a jurisdictional requirement, there could be only one response to that question. *Id.*, at 209 (opinion of Rutledge, J.).

When the District Court for the District of Columbia reviewed the German prisoners' habeas application in *Eisentrager*, it thus dismissed their action on the authority of *Ahrens*. See *Eisentrager*, 339 U.S., at 767, 790. Although the Court of Appeals reversed the District Court, it implicitly conceded that the District Court lacked jurisdiction under the habeas statute as it had been interpreted in *Ahrens*. The Court of Appeals instead held that petitioners had a constitutional right to habeas corpus secured by the Suspension Clause, U.S. Const., Art. I, §9, cl. 2, reasoning that "if a person has a right to a writ of habeas corpus, he cannot be deprived of the privilege by an omission in a federal jurisdictional statute." *Eisentrager v. Forrestal*, 174 F.2d, at 965. In essence, the Court of Appeals concluded that the habeas statute, as construed in *Ahrens*, had created an unconstitutional gap that had to be filled by reference to "fundamentals." 174 F.2d, at 963. In its review of that decision, this Court, like the Court of Appeals, proceeded from the premise that "nothing in our statutes" conferred federal-court jurisdiction, and accordingly evaluated the Court of Appeals' resort to "fundamentals" on its own terms. 339 U.S., at 768.

Because subsequent decisions of this Court have filled the statutory gap that had occasioned *Eisentrager's* resort to "fundamentals," persons detained outside the territorial jurisdiction of any federal district court no longer need rely on the Constitution as the source of their right to federal habeas review. In *Braden v. 30th Judicial Circuit Court of Ky.*, 410 U.S. 484, 495 (1973), this Court held, contrary to **Ahrens**, that the prisoner's presence within the territorial jurisdiction of the district court is not "an invariable prerequisite" to the exercise of district court jurisdiction under the federal habeas statute. Rather, because "the writ of habeas corpus does not act upon the prisoner who seeks relief, but upon the person who holds him in what is alleged to be unlawful custody," a district court acts "within [its] respective jurisdiction" within the meaning of §2241 as long as "the custodian can be reached by service of process." 410 U.S., at 494 – 495. **Braden** reasoned that its departure from the rule of **Ahrens** was warranted in light of developments that "had a profound impact on the continuing vitality of that decision." 410 U.S., at 497. These developments included, notably, decisions of this Court in cases involving habeas petitioners "confined overseas (and thus outside the territory of any district court)," in which the Court "held, if only implicitly, that the petitioners' absence from the district does not present a jurisdictional obstacle to the consideration of the claim." *Id.*, at 498 (citing **Burns v. Wilson**, 346 U.S. 137 (1953), rehearing denied, 346 U.S. 844, 851 – 852 (opinion of Frankfurter, J.); **United States ex rel. Toth v. Quarles**, 350 U.S. 11 (1955); **Hirota v. MacArthur**, 338 U.S. 197, 199 (1948) (Douglas, J., concurring)). **Braden** thus established that **Ahrens** can no longer be viewed as establishing "an inflexible jurisdictional rule," and is strictly relevant only to the question of the appropriate forum, not to whether the claim can be heard at all. 410 U.S., at 499 – 500.

Because **Braden** overruled the statutory predicate to **Eisentrager's** holding, **Eisentrager** plainly does not preclude the exercise of §2241 jurisdiction over petitioners' claims.

IV

Putting **Eisentrager** and **Ahrens** to one side, respondents contend that we can discern a limit on §2241 through application of the "long-standing principle of American law" that congressional legislation is presumed not to have extraterritorial application unless such intent is clearly manifested. **EEOC v. Arabian American Oil Co.**, 499 U.S. 244, 248 (1991). Whatever traction the presumption against extra-territoriality might have in other contexts, it certainly has no application to the operation of the habeas statute with respect to persons detained within "the territorial jurisdiction" of the United States. **Foley Bros., Inc. v. Filardo**, 336 U.S. 281, 285 (1949). By the express terms of its agreements with Cuba, the United States exercises "complete jurisdiction and control" over the Guantanamo Bay Naval Base, and may continue to exercise such control permanently if it so chooses. 1903 Lease Agreement, Art. III; 1934 Treaty, Art. III. Respondents themselves concede that the habeas statute would create federal-court jurisdiction over the claims of an American citizen held at the base. Tr. of Oral Arg. 27. Considering that the statute draws no distinction between Americans and aliens held in federal custody, there is little reason to think that Congress intended the geographical coverage of the statute to vary depending on the detainee's citizenship. Aliens held at the base, no less than American citizens, are entitled to invoke the federal courts' authority under §2241.

Application of the habeas statute to persons detained at the base is consistent with the historical reach of the writ of habeas corpus. At common law, courts exercised habeas jurisdiction over the claims of aliens detained within sovereign territory of the realm, as well as the claims of persons detained in the so-called "exempt jurisdictions," where ordinary writs did not run, and all other dominions under the sovereign's control. As Lord Mansfield wrote in 1759, even if a territory was "no part of the realm," there was "no doubt" as to the court's power to issue writs of habeas corpus if the territory was "under the subjection of the Crown." *King v. Cowle*, 2 Burr. 834, 854 – 855, 97 Eng. Rep. 587, 598 – 599 (K. B.). Later cases confirmed that the reach of the writ depended not on formal notions of territorial sovereignty, but rather on the practical question of "the exact extent and nature of the jurisdiction or dominion exercised in fact by the Crown." *Ex parte Mwenya*, [1960] 1 Q. B. 241, 303 (C. A.) (Lord Evershed, M. R.).

In the end, the answer to the question presented is clear. Petitioners contend that they are being held in federal custody in violation of the laws of the United States. No party questions the District Court's jurisdiction over petitioners' custodians. Cf. *Braden*, 410 U.S., at 495. Section 2241, by its terms, requires nothing more. We therefore hold that §2241 confers on the District Court jurisdiction to hear petitioners' habeas corpus challenges to the legality of their detention at the Guantanamo Bay Naval Base.

V

In addition to invoking the District Court's jurisdiction under §2241, the *Al Odah* petitioners' complaint invoked the court's jurisdiction under 28 U.S.C. § 1331 the federal question statute, as well as §1350, the Alien Tort Statute. The Court of Appeals, again relying on *Eisentrager*, held that the District Court correctly dismissed the claims founded on §1331 and §1350 for lack of jurisdiction, even to the extent that these claims "deal only with conditions of confinement and do not sound in habeas," because petitioners lack the "privilege of litigation" in U.S. courts. 321 F.3d, at 1144 (internal quotation marks omitted). Specifically, the court held that because petitioners' §1331 and §1350 claims "necessarily rest on alleged violations of the same category of laws listed in the habeas corpus statute," they, like claims founded on the habeas statute itself, must be "beyond the jurisdiction of the federal courts." *Id.*, at 1144 – 1145.

As explained above, *Eisentrager* itself erects no bar to the exercise of federal court jurisdiction over the petitioners' habeas corpus claims.

It therefore certainly does not bar the exercise of federal-court jurisdiction over claims that merely implicate the "same category of laws listed in the habeas corpus statute." But in any event, nothing in **Eisentrager** or in any of our other cases categorically excludes aliens detained in military custody outside the United States from the "'privilege of litigation'" in U.S. courts. 321 F.3d, at 1139. The courts of the United States have traditionally been open to nonresident aliens. Cf. **Disconto Gesellschaft v. Umbreit**, 208 U.S. 570, 578 (1908) ("Alien citizens, by the policy and practice of the courts of this country, are ordinarily permitted to resort to the courts for the redress of wrongs and the protection of their rights"). And indeed, 28 U.S.C. § 1350 explicitly confers the privilege of suing for an actionable "tort ... committed in violation of the law of nations or a treaty of the United States" on aliens alone. The fact that petitioners in these cases are being held in military custody is immaterial to the question of the District Court's jurisdiction over their non-habeas statutory claims.

VI

Whether and what further proceedings may become necessary after respondents make their response to the merits of petitioners' claims are matters that we need not address now. What is presently at stake is only whether the federal courts have jurisdiction to determine the legality of the Executive's potentially indefinite detention of individuals who claim to be wholly innocent of wrongdoing. Answering that question in the affirmative, we reverse the judgment of the Court of Appeals and remand for the District Court to consider in the first instance the merits of petitioners' claims.

It is so ordered.

Hamdan v. Rumsfeld
548 U.S. 557 (2006)

Justice Stevens announced the judgment of the Court and delivered the opinion of the Court with respect to Parts I through IV, Parts VI through VI–D–iii, Part VI–D–v, and Part VII, and an opinion with respect to Parts V and VI–D–iv, in which Justice Souter, Justice Ginsburg and Justice Breyer join.

Petitioner Salim Ahmed Hamdan, a Yemeni national, is in custody at an American prison in Guantanamo Bay, Cuba. In November 2001, during hostilities between the United States and the Taliban (which then governed Afghanistan), Hamdan was captured by militia forces and turned over to the U. S. military. In June 2002, he was transported to Guantanamo Bay. Over a year later, the President deemed him eligible for trial by military commission for then-unspecified crimes. After another year had passed, Hamdan was charged with one count of conspiracy "to commit ... offenses triable by military commission." App. to Pet. for Cert. 65a.

Hamdan filed petitions for writs of habeas corpus and mandamus to challenge the Executive Branch's intended means of prosecuting this charge. He concedes that a court-martial constituted in accordance with the Uniform Code of Military Justice (UCMJ), 10 U. S. C. §801 et seq. (2000 ed. and Supp. III), would have authority to try him. His objection is that the military commission the President has convened lacks such authority, for two principal reasons: First, neither congressional Act nor the common law of war supports trial by this commission for the crime of conspiracy—an offense that, Hamdan says, is not a violation of the law of war. Second, Hamdan contends, the procedures that the President has adopted to try him violate the most basic tenets of military and international law, including the principle that a defendant must be permitted to see and hear the evidence against him.

The District Court granted Hamdan's request for a writ of habeas corpus. 344 F. Supp. 2d 152 (DC 2004). The Court of Appeals for the District of Columbia Circuit reversed. 415 F. 3d 33 (2005). Recognizing, as we did over a half-century ago, that trial by military commission is an extraordinary measure raising important questions about the balance of powers in our constitutional structure, *Ex parte Quirin*, 317 U. S. 1, 19 (1942) , we granted certiorari. 546 U. S. ___ (2005).

For the reasons that follow, we conclude that the military commission convened to try Hamdan lacks power to proceed because its structure and procedures violate both the UCMJ and the Geneva Conventions. Four of us also conclude, see Part V, *infra*, that the offense with which Hamdan has been charged is not an "offens[e] that by ... the law of war may be tried by military commissions." 10 U. S. C. §821.

I

On September 11, 2001, agents of the al Qaeda terrorist organization hijacked commercial airplanes and attacked the World Trade Center in New York City and the national headquarters of the Department of Defense in Arlington, Virginia. Americans will never forget the devastation wrought by these acts. Nearly 3,000 civilians were killed.

Congress responded by adopting a Joint Resolution authorizing the President to "use all necessary and appropriate force against those nations, organizations, or persons he determines planned, authorized, committed, or aided the terrorist attacks ... in order to prevent any future acts of international terrorism against the United States by such nations, organizations or persons." Authorization for Use of Military Force (AUMF), 115 Stat. 224, note following *50 U. S. C. §1541* (2000 ed., Supp. III). Acting pursuant to the AUMF, and having determined that the Taliban regime had supported al Qaeda, the

President ordered the Armed Forces of the United States to invade Afghanistan. In the ensuing hostilities, hundreds of individuals, Hamdan among them, were captured and eventually detained at Guantanamo Bay.

On November 13, 2001, while the United States was still engaged in active combat with the Taliban, the President issued a comprehensive military order intended to govern the "Detention, Treatment, and Trial of Certain Non-Citizens in the War Against Terrorism," 66 Fed. Reg. 57833 (hereinafter November 13 Order or Order). Those subject to the November 13 Order include any noncitizen for whom the President determines "there is reason to believe" that he or she (1) "is or was" a member of al Qaeda or (2) has engaged or participated in terrorist activities aimed at or harmful to the United States. *Id.*, at 57834. Any such individual "shall, when tried, be tried by military commission for any and all offenses triable by military commission that such individual is alleged to have committed, and may be punished in accordance with the penalties provided under applicable law, including imprisonment or death." *Ibid.* The November 13 Order vested in the Secretary of Defense the power to appoint military commissions to try individuals subject to the Order, but that power has since been delegated to John D. Altenberg, Jr., a retired Army major general and longtime military lawyer who has been designated "Appointing Authority for Military Commissions."

On July 3, 2003, the President announced his determination that Hamdan and five other detainees at Guantanamo Bay were subject to the November 13 Order and thus triable by military commission. In December 2003, military counsel was appointed to represent Hamdan. Two months later, counsel filed demands for charges and for a speedy trial pursuant to Article 10 of the UCMJ, 10 U. S. C. §810. On February 23, 2004, the legal adviser to the Appointing Authority denied the applications, ruling that Hamdan was not entitled to any of the protections of the UCMJ. Not until July 13, 2004, after Hamdan had commenced this action in the United States District Court for the Western District of Washington, did the Government finally charge him with the offense for which, a year earlier, he had been deemed eligible for trial by military commission.

The charging document, which is unsigned, contains 13 numbered paragraphs. The first two paragraphs recite the asserted bases for the military commission's jurisdiction—namely, the November 13 Order and the President's July 3, 2003, declaration that Hamdan is eligible for trial by military commission. The next nine paragraphs, collectively entitled "General Allegations," describe al Qaeda's activities from its inception in 1989 through 2001 and identify Osama bin Laden as the group's leader. Hamdan is not mentioned in these paragraphs.

Only the final two paragraphs, entitled "Charge: Conspiracy," contain allegations against Hamdan. Paragraph 12 charges that "from on or about February 1996 to on or about November 24, 2001,"

Hamdan "willfully and knowingly joined an enterprise of persons who shared a common criminal purpose and conspired and agreed with [named members of al Qaeda] to commit the following offenses triable by military commission: attacking civilians; attacking civilian objects; murder by an unprivileged belligerent; and terrorism." App. to Pet. for Cert. 65a. There is no allegation that Hamdan had any command responsibilities, played a leadership role, or participated in the planning of any activity.

Paragraph 13 lists four "overt acts" that Hamdan is alleged to have committed sometime between 1996 and November 2001 in furtherance of the "enterprise and conspiracy": (1) he acted as Osama bin Laden's "bodyguard and personal driver," "believ[ing]" all the while that bin Laden "and his associates were involved in" terrorist acts prior to and including the attacks of September 11, 2001; (2) he arranged for transportation of, and actually transported, weapons used by al Qaeda members and by bin Laden's bodyguards (Hamdan among them); (3) he "drove or accompanied [O]sama bin Laden to various al Qaida-sponsored training camps, press conferences, or lectures," at which bin Laden encouraged attacks against Americans; and (4) he received weapons training at al Qaeda-sponsored camps. Id., at 65a–67a.

After this formal charge was filed, the United States District Court for the Western District of Washington transferred Hamdan's habeas and mandamus petitions to the United States District Court for the District of Columbia. Meanwhile, a Combatant Status Review Tribunal (CSRT) convened pursuant to a military order issued on July 7, 2004, decided that Hamdan's continued detention at Guantanamo Bay was warranted because he was an "enemy combatant."[1] Separately, proceedings before the military commission commenced.

On November 8, 2004, however, the District Court granted Hamdan's petition for habeas corpus and stayed the commission's proceedings. It concluded that the President's authority to establish military commissions extends only to "offenders or offenses triable by military [commission] under the law of war," 344 F. Supp. 2d, at 158; that the law of war includes the Geneva Convention (III) Relative to the Treatment of Prisoners of War, Aug. 12, 1949, [1955] 6 U. S. T. 3316, T. I. A. S. No. 3364 (Third Geneva Convention); that Hamdan is entitled to the full protections of the Third Geneva Convention until adjudged, in compliance with that treaty, not to be a prisoner of war; and that, whether or not Hamdan is properly classified as a prisoner of war, the military commission convened to try him was established in violation of both the UCMJ and Common Article 3 of the Third Geneva Convention because it had the power to convict based on evidence the accused would never see or hear. 344 F. Supp. 2d, at 158–172.

The Court of Appeals for the District of Columbia Circuit reversed. Like the District Court, the Court of Appeals declined the Government's invitation to abstain from considering Hamdan's challenge. Cf.

Schlesinger v. Councilman, *420 U. S. 738* (1975). On the merits, the panel rejected the District Court's further conclusion that Hamdan was entitled to relief under the Third Geneva Convention. All three judges agreed that the Geneva Conventions were not "judicially enforceable," 415 F. 3d, at 38, and two thought that the Conventions did not in any event apply to Hamdan, *id.*, at 40–42; but see *id.*, at 44 (Williams, J., concurring). In other portions of its opinion, the court concluded that our decision in **Quirin** foreclosed any separation-of-powers objection to the military commission's jurisdiction, and held that Hamdan's trial before the contemplated commission would violate neither the UCMJ nor U. S. Armed Forces regulations intended to implement the Geneva Conventions. 415 F. 3d, at 38, 42–43.

On November 7, 2005, we granted certiorari to decide whether the military commission convened to try Hamdan has authority to do so, and whether Hamdan may rely on the Geneva Conventions in these proceedings.

II

[Section II of the decision dealt with a government motion to dismiss based on the recently enacted Detainee Treatment Act of 2005 (DTA). The Court looked at the enactment of the DTA and the specific statutory provisions as well as the government's argument for retroactive effect of the Act and Hamdan's statutory and constitutional claims. The Court rejected the government's argument.]

III

[Section III of the decision addresses the government's claim that even if the federal courts did have jurisdiction over the case they should abstain in light of the pending military case against Hamdan. The Court rejected the government's argument in this instance and moved onto the merits of Hamdan's challenge.]

IV

The military commission, a tribunal neither mentioned in the Constitution nor created by statute, was born of military necessity. See W. Winthrop, Military Law and Precedents 831 (rev. 2d ed. 1920) (hereinafter Winthrop). Though foreshadowed in some respects by earlier tribunals like the Board of General Officers that General Washington convened to try British Major John André for spying during the Revolutionary War, the commission "as such" was inaugurated in 1847. *Id.*, at 832; G. Davis, A Treatise on the Military Law of the United States 308 (2d ed. 1909) (hereinafter Davis). As commander of occupied Mexican territory, and having available to him no other tribunal, General Winfield Scott that year ordered the establishment of both " *'military commissions'* " to try ordinary crimes committed in the occupied territory and a *"council of war"* to try offenses against the law of war. Winthrop 832 (emphasis in original).

When the exigencies of war next gave rise to a need for use of military commissions, during the Civil War, the dual system favored by General Scott was not adopted. Instead, a single tribunal often took jurisdiction over ordinary crimes, war crimes, and breaches of military orders alike. As further discussed below, each aspect of that seemingly broad jurisdiction was in fact supported by a separate military exigency. Generally, though, the need for military commissions during this period—as during the Mexican War—was driven largely by the then very limited jurisdiction of courts-martial: "The *occasion* for the military commission arises principally from the fact that the jurisdiction of the court-martial proper, in our law, is restricted by statute almost exclusively to members of the military force and to certain specific offences defined in a written code." *Id.*, at 831 (emphasis in original).

Exigency alone, of course, will not justify the establishment and use of penal tribunals not contemplated by Article I, §8 and Article III, §1 of the Constitution unless some other part of that document authorizes a response to the felt need. See **Ex parte Milligan**, 4 Wall. 2, 121 (1866) ("Certainly no part of the judicial power of the country was conferred on [military commissions]"); **Ex parte Vallandigham**, 1 Wall. 243, 251 (1864); see also **Quirin**, 317 U. S., at 25 ("Congress and the President, like the courts, possess no power not derived from the Constitution"). And that authority, if it exists, can derive only from the powers granted jointly to the President and Congress in time of war. See *id.*, at 26–29; **In re Yamashita**, 327 U. S. 1, 11 (1946).

The Constitution makes the President the "Commander in Chief" of the Armed Forces, Art. II, §2, cl. 1, but vests in Congress the powers to "declare War ... and make Rules concerning Captures on Land and Water," Art. I, §8, cl. 11, to "raise and support Armies," *id.*, cl. 12, to "define and punish ... Offences against the Law of Nations," *id.*, cl. 10, and "To make Rules for the Government and Regulation of the land and naval Forces," *id.*, cl. 14. The interplay between these powers was described by Chief Justice Chase in the seminal case of Ex parte Milligan:

"The power to make the necessary laws is in Congress; the power to execute in the President. Both powers imply many subordinate and auxiliary powers. Each includes all authorities essential to its due exercise. But neither can the President, in war more than in peace, intrude upon the proper authority of Congress, nor Congress upon the proper authority of the President.... Congress cannot direct the conduct of campaigns, nor can the President, or any commander under him, without the sanction of Congress, institute tribunals for the trial and punishment of offences, either of soldiers or civilians, unless in cases of a controlling necessity, which justifies what it compels, or

at least insures acts of indemnity from the justice of the legislature." 4 Wall., at 139–140.

Whether Chief Justice Chase was correct in suggesting that the President may constitutionally convene military commissions "without the sanction of Congress" in cases of "controlling necessity" is a question this Court has not answered definitively, and need not answer today. For we held in **Quirin** that Congress had, through Article of War 15, sanctioned the use of military commissions in such circumstances. 317 U. S., at 28 ("By the Articles of War, and especially Article 15, Congress has explicitly provided, so far as it may constitutionally do so, that military tribunals shall have jurisdiction to try offenders or offenses against the law of war in appropriate cases"). Article 21 of the UCMJ, the language of which is substantially identical to the old Article 15 and was preserved by Congress after World War II, reads as follows:

"Jurisdiction of courts-martial not exclusive.

"The provisions of this code conferring jurisdiction upon courts-martial shall not be construed as depriving military commissions, provost courts, or other military tribunals of concurrent jurisdiction in respect of offenders or offenses that by statute or by the law of war may be tried by such military commissions, provost courts, or other military tribunals." 64 Stat. 115.

We have no occasion to revisit **Quirin's** controversial characterization of Article of War 15 as congressional authorization for military commissions. Cf. Brief for Legal Scholars and Historians as *Amici Curiae* 12 – 15. Contrary to the Government's assertion, however, even **Quirin** did not view the authorization as a sweeping mandate for the President to "invoke military commissions when he deems them necessary." Brief for Respondents 17. Rather, the **Quirin** Court recognized that Congress had simply preserved what power, under the Constitution and the common law of war, the President had had before 1916 to convene military commissions—with the express condition that the President and those under his command comply with the law of war. See 317 U. S., at 28 – 29. That much is evidenced by the Court's inquiry, *following* its conclusion that Congress had authorized military commissions, into whether the law of war had indeed been complied with in that case. See ibid.

The Government would have us dispense with the inquiry that the **Quirin** Court undertook and find in either the AUMF or the DTA specific, overriding authorization for the very commission that has been convened to try Hamdan. Neither of these congressional Acts, however, expands the President's authority to convene military commissions. First, while we assume that the AUMF activated the President's war powers, see **Hamdi v. Rumsfeld**, 542 U. S. 507 (2004) (plurality opinion), and that those powers include the authority to convene military commissions in appropriate circumstances, see *id.*, at 518; **Quirin**, 317 U. S., at 28–29; see also **Yamashita**, 327 U. S., at 11, there is nothing in the text or legislative history of the AUMF even hinting that Congress intended to expand or alter the authorization set forth in Article 21 of the UCMJ. Cf. **Yerger**, 8 Wall., at 105 ("Repeals by implication are not favored").

Likewise, the DTA cannot be read to authorize this commission. Although the DTA, unlike either Article 21 or the AUMF, was enacted after the President had convened Hamdan's commission, it contains no language authorizing that tribunal or any other at Guantanamo Bay. The DTA obviously "recognize[s]" the existence of the Guantanamo Bay commissions in the weakest sense, Brief for Respondents 15, because it references some of the military orders governing them and creates limited judicial review of their "final decision[s]," DTA §1005(e)(3), 119 Stat. 2743. But the statute also pointedly reserves judgment on whether "the Constitution and laws of the United States are applicable" in reviewing such decisions and whether, if they are, the "standards and procedures" used to try Hamdan and other detainees actually violate the "Constitution and laws." Ibid.

Together, the UCMJ, the AUMF, and the DTA at most acknowledge a general Presidential authority to convene military commissions in circumstances where justified under the "Constitution and laws," including the law of war. Absent a more specific congressional authorization, the task of this Court is, as it was in Quirin, to decide whether Hamdan's military commission is so justified. It is to that inquiry we now turn.

V

The common law governing military commissions may be gleaned from past practice and what sparse legal precedent exists. Commissions historically have been used in three situations. See Bradley & Goldsmith, Congressional Authorization and the War on Terrorism, 118 Harv. L. Rev. 2048, 2132 – 2133 (2005); Winthrop 831–846; Hearings on H. R. 2498 before the Subcommittee of the House Committee on Armed Services, 81st Cong., 1st Sess., 975 (1949). First, they have substituted for civilian courts at times and in places where martial law has been declared. Their use in these circumstances has raised constitutional questions, see **Duncan v. Kahanamoku**, 327 U. S. 304 (1946); **Milligan,** 4 Wall., at 121 – 122, but is well recognized. See Winthrop 822, 836 – 839. Second, commissions have been established to try civilians "as part of a temporary military government over occupied enemy territory or territory regained from an enemy where civilian government cannot and does not function." **Duncan**, 327 U. S., at 314; see **Milligan**, 4 Wall., at 141–142 (Chase, C. J., concurring in judgment) (distinguishing "Martial Proper" from "Military Government" in occupied territory). Illustrative of this second kind of commission is the one that was established, with jurisdiction to apply the German Criminal Code, in occupied Germany following the end of World War II. See **Madsen v. Kinsella**, 343 U. S. 341, 356 (1952).

The third type of commission, convened as an "incident to the conduct of war" when there is a need "to seize and subject to disciplinary measures those enemies who in their attempt to thwart or impede our military effort have violated the law of war," **Quirin**, 317 U. S., at 28–29, has been described as "utterly different" from the other two. Bickers, Military Commissions are Constitutionally Sound: A Response to Professors Katyal and Tribe, 34 Tex. Tech. L. Rev. 899, 902 (2002–2003). Not only is its jurisdiction limited to offenses cognizable during time of war, but its role is primarily a factfinding one—to determine, typically on the battlefield itself, whether the defendant has violated the law of war. The last time the U. S. Armed Forces used the law-of-war military commission was during World War II. In **Quirin**, this Court sanctioned President Roosevelt's use of such a tribunal to try Nazi saboteurs captured on American soil during the War. 317 U. S. 1 . And in **Yamashita**, we held that a military commission had jurisdiction to try a Japanese commander for failing to prevent troops under his command from committing atrocities in the Philippines. 327 U. S. 1 .

Quirin is the model the Government invokes most frequently to defend the commission convened to try Hamdan. That is both appropriate and unsurprising. Since Guantanamo Bay is neither enemy-occupied territory nor under martial law, the law-of-war commission is the only model available. At the same time, no more robust model of executive power exists; **Quirin** represents the highwater mark of military power to try enemy combatants for war crimes.

The classic treatise penned by Colonel William Winthrop, whom we have called "the 'Blackstone of Military Law,' " **Reid v. Covert**, 354 U. S. 1 , n. 38 (1957) (plurality opinion), describes at least four preconditions for exercise of jurisdiction by a tribunal of the type convened to try Hamdan. First, "[a] military commission, (except where otherwise authorized by statute), can legally assume jurisdiction only of offenses committed within the field of the command of the convening commander." Winthrop 836. The "field of command" in these circumstances means the "theatre of war." Ibid. Second, the offense charged "must have been committed within the period of the war." Id., at 837. No jurisdiction exists to try offenses "committed either before or after the war." Ibid. Third, a military commission not established pursuant to martial law or an occupation may try only "[i]ndividuals of the enemy's army who have been guilty of illegitimate warfare or other offences in violation of the laws of war" and members of one's own army "who, in time of war, become chargeable with crimes or offences not cognizable, or triable, by the criminal courts or under the Articles of war." Id., at 838. Finally, a law-of-war commission has jurisdiction to try only two kinds of offense: "Violations of the laws and usages of war cognizable by military tribunals only," and "[b]reaches of military orders or regulations for which offenders are not legally triable by court-martial under the Articles of war." *Id.*, at 839.

All parties agree that Colonel Winthrop's treatise accurately describes the common law governing military commissions, and that the jurisdictional limitations he identifies were incorporated in Article of War 15 and, later, Article 21 of the UCMJ. It also is undisputed that Hamdan's commission lacks jurisdiction to try him unless the charge "properly set[s] forth, not only the details of the act charged, but the circumstances conferring *jurisdiction.*" *Id.*, at 842 (emphasis in original). The question is whether the preconditions designed to ensure that a military necessity exists to justify the use of this extraordinary tribunal have been satisfied here.

The charge against Hamdan, described in detail in Part I, *supra*, alleges a conspiracy extending over a number of years, from 1996 to November 2001. All but two months of that more than 5-year-long period preceded the attacks of September 11, 2001, and the enactment of the AUMF—the Act of Congress on which the Government relies for exercise of its war powers and thus for its authority to convene military commissions. Neither the purported agreement with Osama bin Laden and others to commit war crimes, nor a single overt act, is alleged to have occurred in a theater of war or on any specified date after September 11, 2001. None of the overt acts that Hamdan is alleged to have committed violates the law of war.

These facts alone cast doubt on the legality of the charge and, hence, the commission; as Winthrop makes plain, the offense alleged must have been committed both in a theater of war and during, not before, the relevant conflict. But the deficiencies in the time and place allegations also underscore—indeed are symptomatic of—the most serious defect of this charge: The offense it alleges is not triable by law-of-war military commission. See *Yamashita*, 327 U. S., at 13 ("Neither congressional action nor the military orders constituting the commission authorized it to place petitioner on trial unless the charge proffered against him is of a violation of the law of war").

There is no suggestion that Congress has, in exercise of its constitutional authority to "define and punish . . . Offences against the Law of Nations," U. S. Const., Art. I, §8, cl. 10, positively identified "conspiracy" as a war crime. As we explained in **Quirin**, that is not necessarily fatal to the Government's claim of authority to try the alleged offense by military commission; Congress, through Article 21 of the UCMJ, has "incorporated by reference" the common law of war, which may render triable by military commission certain offenses not defined by statute. 317 U. S., at 30. When, however, neither the elements of the offense nor the range of permissible punishments is defined by statute or treaty, the precedent must be plain and unambiguous. To demand any less would be to risk concentrating in military hands a degree of adjudicative and punitive power in excess of that contemplated either by statute or by the Constitution. Cf. **Loving v. United States**, 517 U. S. 748, 771 (1996) (acknowledging that Congress "may not delegate the power to make laws"); **Reid**, 354 U. S., at 23–24 ("The Founders envisioned the army as a necessary institution, but one dangerous to liberty if not confined within its essential bounds"); The Federalist No. 47, p. 324 (J. Cooke ed. 1961) (J. Madison) ("The accumulation of all powers legislative, executive and judiciary in the same hands ... may justly be pronounced the very definition of tyranny").

This high standard was met in **Quirin**; the violation there alleged was, by "universal agreement and practice" both in this country and internationally, recognized as an offense against the law of war. 317 U. S., at 30; see *id.*, at 35–36 ("This precept of the law of war has been so recognized in practice both here and abroad, and has so generally been accepted as valid by authorities on international law that we think it must be regarded as a rule or principle of the law of war recognized by this Government by its enactment of the Fifteenth Article of War" (footnote omitted)). Although the picture arguably was less clear in **Yamashita**, compare 327 U. S., at 16 (stating that the provisions of the Fourth Hague Convention of 1907, 36 Stat. 2306, "plainly" required the defendant to control the troops under his command), with 327 U. S., at 35 (Murphy, J., dissenting), the disagreement between the majority and the dissenters in that case concerned whether the historic and textual evidence constituted clear precedent—not whether clear precedent was required to justify trial by law-of-war military commission.

At a minimum, the Government must make a substantial showing that the crime for which it seeks to try a defendant by military commission is acknowledged to be an offense against the law of war. That burden is far from satisfied here. The crime of "conspiracy" has rarely if ever been tried as such in this country by any law-of-war military commission not exercising some other form of jurisdiction, and does not appear in either the Geneva Conventions or the Hague Conventions—the major treaties on the law of war. Winthrop explains that under the common law governing military commissions, it is not enough to intend to violate the law of war and commit overt acts in furtherance of that intention unless the overt acts either are themselves offenses against the law of war or constitute steps sufficiently substantial to qualify as an attempt. See Winthrop 841 ("[T]he jurisdiction of the military commission should be restricted to cases of offence consisting in *overt acts, i.e.*, in unlawful commissions or actual attempts to commit, and not in intentions merely" (emphasis in original)).

***

Finally, international sources confirm that the crime charged here is not a recognized violation of the law of war. As observed above, see *supra*, at 40, none of the major treaties governing the law of war identifies conspiracy as a violation thereof. And the only "conspiracy" crimes that have been recognized by international war crimes tribunals (whose jurisdiction often extends beyond war crimes proper to crimes against humanity and crimes against the peace) are conspiracy to commit genocide and common plan to wage aggressive war, which is a crime against the peace and requires for its commission actual participation in a "concrete plan to wage war." 1 Trial of the Major War Criminals Before the International Military Tribunal: Nuremberg, 14 November 1945–1 October 1946, p. 225 (1947). The International Military Tribunal at Nuremberg, over the prosecution's objections, pointedly refused to recognize as a violation of the law of war conspiracy to commit war crimes, see, e.g., 22 id., at 469, and convicted only Hitler's most senior associates of conspiracy to wage aggressive war, see S. Pomorski, Conspiracy and Criminal Organization, in the Nuremberg Trial and International Law 213, 233–235 (G. Ginsburgs & V. Kudriavtsev eds. 1990). As one prominent figure from the Nuremberg trials has explained, members of the Tribunal objected to recognition of conspiracy as a violation of the law of war on the ground that "[t]he Anglo-American concept of conspiracy was not part of European legal systems and arguably not an element of the internationally recognized laws of war." T. Taylor, Anatomy of the Nuremberg Trials: A Personal Memoir 36 (1992); see also id., at 550 (observing that Francis Biddle, who as Attorney General prosecuted the defendants in **Quirin**, thought the French judge had made a " 'persuasive argument that conspiracy in the truest sense is not known to international law' ").

... Far from making the requisite substantial showing, the Government has failed even to offer a "merely colorable" case for inclusion of conspiracy among those offenses cognizable by law-of-war military commission. Cf. **Quirin**, 317 U. S., at 36. Because the charge does not support the commission's jurisdiction, the commission lacks authority to try Hamdan.

The charge's shortcomings are not merely formal, but are indicative of a broader inability on the Executive's part here to satisfy the most basic precondition—at least in the absence of specific congressional authorization—for establishment of military commissions: military necessity. Hamdan's tribunal was appointed not by a military commander in the field of battle, but by a retired major general stationed away from any active hostilities. Cf. **Rasul v. Bush**, 542 U. S., at 487 (Kennedy, J., concurring in judgment) (observing that "Guantanamo Bay is ... far removed from any hostilities"). Hamdan is charged not with an overt act for which he was caught redhanded in a theater of war and which military efficiency demands be tried expeditiously, but with an agreement the inception of which long predated the attacks of September 11, 2001 and the AUMF. That may well be a crime, but it is not an offense that "by the law of war may be tried by military commission." 10 U. S. C. §821. None of the overt acts alleged to have been committed in furtherance of the agreement is itself a war crime, or even necessarily occurred during time of, or in a theater of, war. Any urgent need for imposition or execution of judgment is utterly belied by the record; Hamdan was arrested in November 2001 and he was not charged until mid-2004. These simply are not the circumstances in which, by any stretch of the historical evidence or this Court's precedents, a military commission established by Executive Order under the authority of Article 21 of the UCMJ may lawfully try a person and subject him to punishment.

VI

Whether or not the Government has charged Hamdan with an offense against the law of war cognizable by military commission, the commission lacks power to proceed. The UCMJ conditions the President's use of military commissions on compliance not only with the American common law of war, but also with the rest of the UCMJ itself, insofar as applicable, and with the "rules and precepts of the law of nations," *Quirin*, 317 U. S., at 28—including, inter alia, the four Geneva Conventions signed in 1949. See *Yamashita*, 327 U. S., at 20–21, 23–24. The procedures that the Government has decreed will govern Hamdan's trial by commission violate these laws.

[The remainder of Section VI reviews the procedural challenges made by Hamdan to the military commission orders of the President as well as Hamdan's claim that the procedures adopted violated the Geneva Convention. The Court sided with Hamdan on his procedural challenges.]

VII

We have assumed, as we must, that the allegations made in the Government's charge against Hamdan are true. We have assumed, moreover, the truth of the message implicit in that charge—viz., that Hamdan is a dangerous individual whose beliefs, if acted upon, would cause great harm and even death to innocent civilians, and who would act upon those beliefs if given the opportunity. It bears emphasizing that Hamdan does not challenge, and we do not today address, the Government's power to detain him for the duration of active hostilities in order to prevent such harm. But in undertaking to try Hamdan and subject him to criminal punishment, the Executive is bound to comply with the Rule of Law that prevails in this jurisdiction.

The judgment of the Court of Appeals is reversed, and the case is remanded for further proceedings.

It is so ordered.

Commentary and Questions

11. The *Quirin* case provided initial justification for the post-9/11 Bush administration's policies with regard to captured enemy combatants. Specifically, President Bush's Executive Order, of November 13, 2001, established a system of military commissions for any "individual subject to this order."[30] John Yoo, a deputy assistant attorney general in the Department of Justice's Office of Legal Counsel and a controversial figure who provided key legal insight to the Bush Administration's detainee policy, wrote of the extensive power that *Quirin* gave to the President in this situation, including that of indefinite detention: *"Quirin flatly declared that the government could detain enemy combatants regardless of whether they were citizens or not ... Military detention is only indefinite because there is no criminal conviction or sentence ... Under the rules of war, nations have always held enemy combatants until 'the cessation of active hostilities.'"*[81] Does *Quirin* support Yoo's argument for the indefinite detention of unlawful enemy combatants? What did *Rasul* and *Hamdan* hold with regard to detainee rights under the President's Executive Order?

12. Bush's Executive Order, of November 13, 2001 provided the following in Section 1: *"(e) To protect the United States and its citizens, and for the effective conduct of military operations and prevention of terrorist attacks, it is necessary for individuals subject to this order pursuant to section 2 hereof to be detained, and, when tried, to be tried for violations of the laws of war and other applicable laws by military tribunals.*
(f) Given the danger to the safety of the United States and the nature of international terrorism, and to the extent provided by and under this order, I find consistent with section 836 of title 10, United States Code, that it is not practicable to apply in military commissions under this order the principles of law and the rules of evidence generally recognized in the trial of criminal cases in the United States district courts.
(g) Having fully considered the magnitude of the potential deaths, injuries, and property destruction that would result from potential acts of terrorism against the United States, and the probability that such acts will occur, I have determined that an extraordinary emergency exists for national defense purposes, that this emergency constitutes an urgent and compelling govern-ment interest, and that issuance of this order is necessary to meet the emergency."[82]

The *Hamdan* decision was a serious rebuke of executive power to act in establishing military commissions without congressional authorization. Justice Stevens' decision also undercut the Bush Administration's argument that presidential authority to act was sanctioned by the international laws of war. In light of the Court's decision regarding the constitutionality of the military commission under which Hamdan was to be tried, and the back-ground facts of his capture and alleged crimes, would the government have been more effective in trying Hamdan in a federal criminal court? As a matter of policy, are there any obstacles to trying terrorist suspects criminally in civilian courts?

13. The issue in *Rasul v. Bush* was whether 28 U.S.C. §2241, the federal statute conferring power upon courts to grant the writ of habeas corpus, applied to the claimed extraterritorial detention of foreign nationals linked to the U.S. War on Terror. 28 U.S.C. §2241 provides the following:

(a) Writs of habeas corpus may be granted by the Supreme Court, any justice thereof, the district courts and any circuit judge within their respective jurisdictions. The order of a circuit judge shall be entered in the records of the district court of the district wherein the restraint complained of is had.

(b) The Supreme Court, any justice thereof, and any circuit judge may decline to entertain an application for a writ of habeas corpus and may transfer the application for hearing and determination to the district court having jurisdiction to entertain it.

(c) The writ of habeas corpus shall not extend to a prisoner unless—

(1) He is in custody under or by color of the authority of the United States or is committed for trial before some court thereof; or

(2) He is in custody for an act done or omitted in pursuance of an Act of Congress, or an order, process, judgment or decree of a court or judge of the United States; or

(3) He is in custody in violation of the Constitution or laws or treaties of the United States; or

(4) He, being a citizen of a foreign state and domiciled therein is in custody for an act done or omitted under any alleged right, title, authority, privilege, protection, or exemption claimed under the commission, order or sanction of any foreign state, or under color thereof, the validity and effect of which depend upon the law of nations; or

(5) It is necessary to bring him into court to testify or for trial.

The *Rasul* Court held that the foreign nationals detained at Guantanamo Bay were within the territorial jurisdiction of the United States by virtue of a prior lease agreement and treaty with Cuba. This essentially provided a continued "sovereignty" over that part of the country subject to the terms of the lease agreement and treaty. Jurisdiction was the sole concern of the case and because the petitioners were not U.S. citizens vested with an automatic right of challenge the next inquiry was court jurisdiction. Justice Stevens's majority opinion in *Rasul* considered the arguments of the respondent government, which relied on the Court's prior holding in *Johnson v. Eisentrager, 399 U.S. 763 (1950)*; however, he differentiated the position of the German war prisoners from that of the unaffiliated foreign nationals in *Rasul*. A significant determinant in the decision, aside from the apparent U.S. sovereignty over Guantanamo Bay granted by agreement and treaty, was interpretation of the language in §2241(a) as provided by the Court in *Braden v. 30th Judicial Circuit Court of Kentucky, 410 U.S. 484 (1973)*. The *Braden* Court held that the phrase *"within their respective jurisdictions"* was not intended to limit the jurisdiction of the courts to those in custody within their territorial jurisdiction. The writ, the Court held, applies to those having custody over the prisoner and who can be reached by process of the court. As such, *Braden* overruled the Court's prior holding in *Ahrens v. Clark, 335 U.S. 188 (1948)*, which based jurisdiction on the physical presence of the prisoner within the territory. The facts in *Braden* involved a state prisoner in Alabama who had a detainer for separate criminal charges filed against him by Kentucky authorities. He petitioned the District Court for the Western District of Kentucky for a writ of habeas corpus to compel the Kentucky court to grant him speedy trial on the charges which were the subject of the detainer. The District Court granted the writ, but it was subsequently overturned by the 6th Circuit Court of Appeals, which held *"the habeas corpus jurisdiction conferred on the federal courts by 28 U.S.C. § 2241(a) is 'limited to petitions filed by persons physically present within the territorial limits of the District Court.'"*[83] Justice Brennan, on behalf of the Court, wrote: *"[R]ead literally, the language of § 2241(a) requires nothing more than that the court issuing the writ have jurisdiction over the custodian. So long as the custodian can be reached by service of process, the court can issue a writ "within its jurisdiction" requiring that the prisoner be brought before the court for a hearing on his claim, or requiring that he be released outright from custody, even if the prisoner himself is confined outside the court's territorial jurisdiction."*[84] Rasul extended this rationale to those noncitizens held in U.S. custody at Guantanamo Bay.

14. As much as *Rasul* and *Hamdan* were about jurisdictional issues—*Rasul*, concerning the extraterritorial reach of habeas relief for foreign nationals, and *Hamdan*, the specific authority of military commissions over foreign nationals—both cases also concerned the extent and limits of executive branch authority. The Court in *Rasul* noted that the great writ of habeas corpus was the product of English jurists' attempts to limit the power of the executive to restrain certain liberties.[35] This question concerning the authority of the president to indefinitely detain a U.S. citizen deemed to be an enemy combatant surfaced in another habeas corpus case over jurisdictional issues. In *Rumsfeld v. Padilla*[36] the Court was confronted first with whether Padilla's petition was properly filed in the Southern District of New York and then the question of whether the president had the authority to detain Padilla militarily. The decision was delivered the same day as *Rasul v. Bush* except the Court in deciding the first issue as to jurisdiction did not reach the second, more important question pertaining to the president's authority. Jose Padilla's legal journey through the federal court system is a multicase study in the questionable nature of executive branch claims of authority to detain American citizens. Padilla's legal troubles began when he was arrested in 2002 at Chicago's O'Hare Airport and held as a material witness in connection with the 9/11 attacks.[37] Shortly thereafter, while a habeas corpus challenge to his detention on the material witness warrant was pending, President Bush determined Padilla was an "enemy combatant." This determination was based on information that Padilla was linked to Al-Qaeda, trained in Afghanistan terror camps, traveled extensively throughout the Middle East, and possessed intelligence related to the 9/11 attacks and

future attacks against the United States. Padilla was alleged to have met with Abu Zubaydah, a close bin Laden associate, who had instructions for Padilla to detonate a radiological material dispersal bomb in an American city.[38] Once he was identified as an "enemy combatant" Padilla was transferred to military custody in South Carolina.

The Non-Detention Act of 1971 prohibits government detention of American citizens arrested within the United States unless specifically provided by an Act of Congress. Padilla challenged his continued detention as an enemy combatant and the Bush Administration's asserted authority under the Congressional Authorization to Use Military Force (AUMF) of 2001. In an early appeal to the Second Circuit Court of Appeals *(Padilla v. Rumsfeld, 352 F.3d 695 (2d. Cir., 2003))*, the court determined that Padilla's detention was not authorized by Congress. The Second Circuit held the AUMF was not the specific congressional authorization required by the Non-Detention Act. The government's appeal to the Supreme Court would result in the Court side-stepping the detention issue in *Rumsfeld v. Padilla* by deciding the case on the jurisdictional question.

In a subsequent case before the federal District Court for South Carolina, Padilla's habeas petition against the navy commander in charge of the detention facility where he was held resulted in the district court granting Padilla's summary judgment motion and ordering his release. The district court in *Padilla v. Hanft, 389 F.Supp. 2d 678 (DSC, 2005)* conducted a review of the *Hamdi, Quirin* and *Milligan* cases as well as the Non-Detention Act and AUMF in deciding that the president did not have the power, either express or implied, constitutionally or statutorily, to detain Padilla as an enemy combatant.[39] Padilla's victory was to be short-lived, however, as the 4th Circuit Court of Appeals overturned the district court 5 months later and held that in the AUMF Congress gave the president all powers "necessary and appropriate to protect American citizens from terrorist acts."[40] Padilla would eventually seek review once again in the U.S. Supreme Court only to have the Court deny certiorari in a brief opinion (see Chapter 8 Detention and Rendition for *Padilla v. Hanft, 547 U.S. 1062*). The certiorari denial would be based on the mootness of the habeas issue because the government had transferred Padilla from military custody to federal law enforcement custody and had made the determination to charge him in a civilian criminal court. The unresolved issue surrounding President Bush's authority under the AUMF to detain American citizens arrested within the United States would remain an open-ended question with no finality from the Supreme Court. However, a hint of the legal uncertainty of the government's position was exposed by the Fourth Circuit in a separate appeal by the government in its attempt to transfer Padilla out of military custody:

"For, as the government surely must understand, although the various facts it has asserted are not necessarily inconsistent or without basis, its actions have left not only the impression that Padilla may have been held for these years, even if justifiably, by mistake—an impression we would have thought the government could ill afford to leave extant. They have left the impression that the government may even have come to the belief that the principle in

reliance upon which it has detained Padilla for this time, that the President possesses the authority to detain enemy combatants who enter into this country for the purpose of attacking America and its citizens from within, can, in the end, yield to expediency with little or no cost to its conduct of the war against terror—an impression we would have thought the government likewise could ill afford to leave extant. And these impressions have been left, we fear, at what may ultimately prove to be substantial cost to the government's credibility before the courts, to whom it will one day need to argue again in support of a principle of assertedly like importance and necessity to the one that it seems to abandon today."[41]

The case of Jose Padilla presents a strange and twisted constitutional journey through the federal courts in an attempt to define the extent of executive authority and power to detain American citizens. It is a government position that the Fourth Circuit indicated may be unsupportable but one that the Supreme Court chose not to address.

Endnotes

[1] Blackstone, *Commentaries* 131: "But the great and efficacious writ in all manner of illegal confinement, is that of habeas corpus ad subjiciendum."

[2] *Black's Law Dictionary*, 837 (4th Edition, 1968); see generally, 3 Blackstone, *Commentaries* 129 – 132.

[3] Habeas corpus ad testificandum.

[4] Habeas corpus ad faciendum et recipiendum.

[5] Habeas corpus ad deliberandum et recipiendum.

[6] Judiciary Act of 1789, Ch. 20, 1 Stat. 73-93 (1789).

[7] Id.

[8] 14 Stat. 385 – 86 (1867).

[9] *Id.*

[10] *See generally*, C. Federman, *Habeas Corpus in the Age of Guantanamo*, Belgrade Law Review, No. 3, 215-234 (2010); *see also*, C. Doyle, *Federal Habeas Corpus: A Brief Legal Overview*, Congressional Research Service Report for Congress, The Library of Congress (2006).

[11] William H. Rehnquist, *All the Laws But One: Civil Liberties in Wartime* (1998).

[12] See generally Id at 33.

[13] Id.

[14] *Ex Parte Merryman*, 17 F. Cas. 144 (1861).

[15] 34 U.S. 704 (1835).

[16] 46 U.S. 176 (1847).

[17] Id.

[18] 8 U.S. 75 (1807).

[19] *71 U.S. 2* (1864).

[20] Id.

[21] *In re Yamashita*, 327 U.S. 1 (1946).

[22] *61 U.S. 176* (1857).

[23] William C. Banks, *The Role of the Courts in Time of War: An Historical Overview*, Syndicus, Syracuse University College of Law, 19 – 23, Fall 2003.

[24] Id.

[25] Stephen C. Neff, *Justice in Blue and Gray: A Legal History of the Civil War*, p. 49, Harvard University Press (2010).

[26] *92 U.S. 520* (1876).

[27] Neff at 41.

[28] Id.

[29] *327 U.S. 1* (1946).

[30] (a) The term "individual subject to this order" shall mean any individual who is not a United States citizen with respect to whom I determine from time to time in writing that: (1) there is reason to believe that such individual, at the relevant times, (i) is or was a member of the organization known as al Qaida; (ii) has engaged in, aided or abetted, or conspired to commit, acts of international terrorism, or acts in preparation therefor, that have caused, threaten to cause, or have as their aim to cause, injury to or adverse effects on the United States, its citizens, national security, foreign policy, or economy; or (iii) has knowingly harbored one or more individuals described in subparagraphs (i) or (ii) of subsection 2(a)(1) of this order; and (2) it is in the interest of the United States that such individual be subject to this order.

[31] John Yoo, *War By Other Means: An Insider's Account of the War on Terror,* pp. 146 – 7, Atlantic Monthly Press (2006).

[32] *http://georgewbush-whitehouse.archives.gov/news/releases/2001/11/20011113-27.html.*

[33] *410 U.S. at 486.*

[34] *Id. at 495.*

[35] 542 U.S. at 474.

[36] *542 U.S. 426* (2004).

[37] Goodnough, A. (2007, August 16). *Jose Padilla Convicted on All Counts in Terror Trial.* Retrieved from The New York Times: http://www.nytimes.com/2007/08/16/us/16cnd-padilla.html.

[38] U.S. Department of Justice. (2004, June 1). *Summary of Jose Padilla's Activities with Al-Qaeda.* Retrieved from Federation of American Scientists: http://www.fas.org/irp/hotdocs.htm.

[39] 389 F.Supp.2d at 691.

[40] *Padilla v. Hanft,* 423 F.3d at 397 (4th, Cir., 2005).

[41] *Padilla v. Hanft,* 432 F.3d 582 (4th Cir., 2005).

Chapter Four
HABEAS CORPUS & ACCESS TO CIVILIAN COURTS

The preceding chapter dealt with the Great Writ of Habeas Corpus and the authority of the federal government to suspend the writ thereby subjecting detainees to the jurisdiction of military tribunals. This chapter continues the habeas corpus discussion but focuses on the specific issue of a detainee's assertion of the writ and access to civilian courts. As noted in Chapter 3, in the Civil War case of *Ex Parte Milligan*, the U.S. Supreme Court established the "open-court rule," which held that martial law does not remove the authority of civilian courts that remain operational. Justice Black further emphasized this point in *Duncan v. Kahanamoku*: "*Legislatures and courts are not merely cherished American institutions; they are indispensable to our government. Military tribunals have no such standing. For as this Court has said before: '... the military should always be kept in subjection to the laws of the country to which it belongs ...'*"[1] Yet, the Court in *Quirin* responded with the "declared enemy exception" to the open court rule. There remain a number of other considerations not the least of which is the legality of attempts to assert the jurisdiction of military tribunals over citizens—as in *Milligan*—and the ability of citizens to challenge their detention by way of a habeas petition. In a similar vein are the rights of non-citizen nationals who are not on American soil but find themselves detained by U.S. authorities. These issues gained heightened attention in several post-9/11 cases challenging the authority of the president to not only label individuals as "enemy combatants" but to detain them under the auspices of military law.

Concerns about judicial review and access to civilian courts for those considered to be enemies of the United States were present in a number of post-World War II cases, particularly *Quirin* and *Yamashita* as outlined in the previous chapter. Interestingly, in two additional cases to reach the Supreme Court, *Hirota v. MacArthur*[2] and *Application of Homma*[3], the Court's concurring and dissenting opinions in each had some prescient views that would mirror later discussions in post-9/11 habeas cases. In each case the Court was presented with habeas petitions by Japanese officials, one an officer the other a diplomat, who had been sentenced to death as a result of their convictions for war crimes. General Homma and Koki Hirota, the Japanese diplomat, were tried by the International Military Tribunal of the Far East. The Supreme Court's per curiam opinion in *Hirota v. MacArthur* held that the military tribunal conducted in Japan was not a tribunal of the United States and therefore the Court had no power to review or intervene in any meaningful way. Justice Douglas's concurring opinion in *Hirota* took a different view of jurisdiction in the case, making the point that the impaneling of the tribunal was an executive decision not subject to judicial review but that a wholesale abdication of the Court's review power in military tribunal cases was a flawed path to tread upon. The Court's per curiam opinion noted: "*We are satisfied that the tribunal sentencing these petitioners is not a tribunal of the United States. The United States and other allied countries conquered, and now occupy and control, Japan. General Douglas MacArthur has been selected and is acting as the Supreme Commander for the Allied Powers. The military tribunal sentencing these petitioners has been set up by General MacArthur as the agent of the Allied Powers. Under the foregoing circumstances, the courts of the United States have no power or authority to review, to affirm, set aside, or annul the judgments and sentences imposed on these petitioners, and, for this reason, the motions for leave to file petitions for writs of habeas corpus are denied."*[4] In response, Douglas indicated *"that statement does not, in my opinion, adequately analyze the problem. The formula which it evolves to dispose of the cases is indeed potentially dangerous. It leaves practically no room for judicial scrutiny of this new type of military tribunal which is evolving. It leaves the power of those tribunals absolute. Prisoners held under its mandates may have appeal to the conscience or mercy of an executive, but they apparently have no appeal to law. The fact that the tribunal has been set up by the Allied Powers should not, of itself, preclude our inquiry. Our inquiry is directed not to the conduct of the Allied Powers, but to the conduct of our own officials. Our writ would run not to an official of an Allied Power, but to our own official. We would want to know not what authority our Allies had to do what they did, but what authority our officials had."*[5] Two years earlier in his *Homma* dissent Justice Murphy expressed similar, though more strenuous objections. The brief dissent is worth presenting here:

> *"This case, like In re Yamashita, 327 U.S. 1, 66 S.Ct. 340, poses a problem that cannot be lightly brushed aside or given momentary consideration. It involves something more than the guilt of a fallen enemy commander under the law of war or the jurisdiction of a military commission. This nation's very honor, as well as its hopes for the future, is at stake. Either we conduct such a trial as this in the noble spirit and atmosphere of our Constitution or we abandon all pretense to justice, let the ages slip away and descend to the level of revengeful blood purges. Apparently the die has been cast in favor of the latter course. But I, for one, shall have no part in it, not even through silent acquiescence.*
>
> *Petitioner, a civilian for the past three and a half years, was the victorious commander of the 14th Army of the Imperial Japanese Army in the Philippines from December 12, 1941, to August 5, 1942. It may well be that the evidence of his guilt under the law of war is more direct and clear than in the case of General Yamashita, though this could be determined only by an examination of the evidence such as we have had no opportunity to make. But neither clearer proof of guilt nor the acts of atrocity of the Japanese troops could excuse the undue haste with which the trial was conducted or the promulgation of a directive containing such obviously unconstitutional provisions as those approving the use of coerced confessions or evidence and findings of prior mass trials. To try the petitioner in a setting of reason and calm, to issue and use constitutional directives and to obey the dictates of a fair trial are not impossible tasks. Hasty, revengeful action is not the American way. All those who act by virtue of the authority of the United States are bound to respect the principles of justice codified in our Constitution. Those principles, which were established after so many centuries of struggle, can*

scarcely be dismissed as narrow artificialities or arbitrary technicalities. They are the very life blood of our civilization.

Today the lives of Yamashita and Homma, leaders of enemy forces vanquished in the field of battle, are taken without regard to due process of law. There will be few to protest. But tomorrow the precedent here established can be turned against others. A procession of judicial lynchings without due process of law may now follow. No one can foresee the end of this failure of objective thinking and of adherence to our high hopes of a new world. The time for effective vigilance and protest, however, is when the abandonment of legal procedure is first attempted. A nation must not perish because, in the natural frenzy of the aftermath of war, it abandoned its central theme of the dignity of the human personality and due process of law."[6]

Justice Murphy's concern was for the quality of justice the United States, as a conquering nation, would align itself with and the enduring effects of that alignment. Clearly, the message was not lost on a later generation of judges to consider the plight of Guantanamo Bay detainees in a post-9/11 world. Consider the dissent of Justice Stevens in *Rumsfeld v. Padilla*: *"At stake in this case is nothing less than the essence of a free society. Even more important than the method of selecting the people's rulers and their successors is the character of the constraints imposed on the Executive by the rule of law. Unconstrained Executive detention for the purpose of investigating and preventing subversive activity is the hallmark of the Star Chamber. Access to counsel for the purpose of protecting the citizen from official mistakes and mistreatment is the hallmark of due process."*[7] His view was echoed by Justice Ginsburg in her *Padilla v. Hanft* dissent two years later.[8] A crucial consideration in this discussion is the extent of executive power to detain individuals in the name of national security. It is a common theme, as outlined in Chapter 2, when discussing homeland security issues. Does the president's commander-in-chief authority under Article II, Section 2 provide him with blanket authority? Do the president's war powers provide the means? And, again, what is the Article III role of the judiciary in this process?

The Court would confront *Hirota* again during the 2007 term when it was relied upon by the government in a case against Mohammed Munaf and Shawqi Omar.[9] U.S. military forces acting as part of the multinational force in Iraq arrested Munaf on suspicion of aiding in the kidnapping of Romanian journalists. Omar was also arrested by the U.S. military as part of multinational forces after a raid on a house in Baghdad. He was suspected of kidnappings in Iraq as well as rendering aid to terrorist groups in Iraq.[10] Both individuals held dual citizenship, Munaf as an Iraqi-American citizen and Omar as a Jordanian-American citizen. Omar was convicted by a multinational force military tribunal which found he committed *"hostile and warlike acts, and that he was an enemy combatant in the war on terrorism."*[11] He obtained review of the decision by the Combined Review and Release Board, a nine-member panel consisting of three multinational force members and six members of the Iraqi government.[12] The review board concluded he was a security threat and should remain in custody of the U.S. military. Munaf was likewise tried by a multinational force military tribunal and found guilty of kidnapping and posing a security threat to multinational forces. Munaf's case was also transferred to the Central Criminal Court of Iraq where he was found guilty of kidnapping.[13] Omar's case had been slated to be transferred to the Central Criminal Court as well but his attorney obtained a preliminary injunction barring removal.[14] Both individuals' cases made their way to U.S. courts on habeas petitions filed by family members and each was eventually appealed to the U.S. Circuit Court of Appeals for the District of Columbia Circuit. The D.C. Circuit in Omar's case held that habeas review was available because he had not yet been convicted in a foreign court and in this way distinguished the case from the holding in *Hirota*. Because Munaf had been convicted in the Central Criminal Court of Iraq the D.C. Circuit denied habeas review. On appeal to the Supreme Court a unanimous Court concluded that U.S. courts have jurisdiction over habeas petitions filed by U.S. citizens being held in another country by U.S. military forces acting as part of a multinational force. Chief Justice Roberts's opinion gave short shrift to the government's reliance on *Hirota*, distinguishing the petitioner in that case as a Japanese citizen seeking review of the International Military Tribunal of the Far East, a tribunal determined by the *Hirota* Court not to be a tribunal of the United States.[15] Though the government in *Munaf* argued the multinational force military tribunal was akin to the Tokyo War Crimes tribunal, Chief Justice Roberts, aside from distinguishing the two forums, indicated that the American citizenship of Omar and Munaf was an essential factor. Referencing *Johnson v. Eisentrager,* the Chief Justice wrote: *"[T]hese cases concern American citizens while Hirota did not, and the Court has indicated that habeas jurisdiction can depend on citizenship."*[16] Although the Court found habeas review available to the petitioners it did not find that habeas corpus provided any remedy for them. The Iraqi government, the Court noted, had a sovereign right to punish those convicted of committing crimes on its soil and this was unreviewable by any U.S. court.[17] Therefore, transfer of the petitioners to Iraqi custody could not be prevented. The decision to transfer prisoners to a sovereign, even if there is the possibility of inhumane treatment, is an executive one and the judiciary is not one to *"second-guess such determinations."*[18] As a habeas corpus case *Munaf v. Geren* was an important decision because the Court was unanimous in its view that U.S. citizens, no matter where they are imprisoned by U.S. authorities have the right to habeas corpus review.

The following two cases in this chapter emanate from the Guantanamo detentions and provide added 21st century dimension to the extensive body of habeas corpus law previously considered by the U.S. Supreme Court.

Hamdi v. Rumsfeld
542 U.S. 507 (2004)

Justice O'Connor announced the judgment of the Court and delivered an opinion, in which the Chief Justice, Justice Kennedy, and Justice Breyer join.

At this difficult time in our Nation's history, we are called upon to consider the legality of the Government's detention of a United States citizen on United States soil as an "enemy combatant" and to address the process that is constitutionally owed to one who seeks to challenge his classification as such. The United States Court of Appeals for the Fourth Circuit held that petitioner's detention was legally authorized and that he was entitled to no further opportunity to challenge his enemy-combatant label. We now vacate and remand. We hold that although Congress authorized the detention of combatants in the narrow circumstances alleged here, due process demands that a citizen held in the United States as an enemy combatant be given a meaningful opportunity to contest the factual basis for that detention before a neutral decisionmaker.

I

On September 11, 2001, the al Qaeda terrorist network used hijacked commercial airliners to attack prominent targets in the United States. Approximately 3,000 people were killed in those attacks. One week later, in response to these "acts of treacherous violence," Congress passed a resolution authorizing the President to "use all necessary and appropriate force against those nations, organizations, or persons he determines planned, authorized, committed, or aided the terrorist attacks" or "harbored such organizations or persons, in order to prevent any future acts of international terrorism against the United States by such nations, organizations or persons." *Authorization for Use of Military Force ("the AUMF")*, 115 Stat. 224. Soon thereafter, the President ordered United States Armed Forces to Afghanistan, with a mission to subdue al Qaeda and quell the Taliban regime that was known to support it.

This case arises out of the detention of a man whom the Government alleges took up arms with the Taliban during this conflict. His name is Yaser Esam Hamdi. Born an American citizen in Louisiana in 1980, Hamdi moved with his family to Saudi Arabia as a child. By 2001, the parties agree, he resided in Afghanistan. At some point that year, he was seized by members of the Northern Alliance, a coalition of military groups opposed to the Taliban government, and eventually was turned over to the United States military. The Government asserts that it initially detained and interrogated Hamdi in Afghanistan before transferring him to the United States Naval Base in Guantanamo Bay in January 2002. In April 2002, upon learning that Hamdi is an American citizen, authorities transferred him to a naval brig in Norfolk, Virginia, where he remained until a recent transfer to a brig in Charleston, South Carolina. The Government contends that Hamdi is an "enemy combatant," and that this status justifies holding him in the United States indefinitely—without formal charges or proceedings—unless and until it makes the determination that access to counsel or further process is warranted.

In June 2002, Hamdi's father, Esam Fouad Hamdi, filed the present petition for a writ of habeas corpus under 28 U.S.C. § 2241 in the Eastern District of Virginia, naming as petitioners his son and himself as next friend. The elder Hamdi alleges in the petition that he has had no contact with his son since the Government took custody of him in 2001, and that the Government has held his son "without access to legal counsel or notice of any charges pending against him." App. 103, 104. The petition contends that Hamdi's detention was not legally authorized. *Id.*, at 105. It argues that, "[a]s an American citizen, ... Hamdi enjoys the full protections of the Constitution," and that Hamdi's detention in the United States without charges, access to an impartial tribunal, or assistance of counsel "violated and continue[s] to violate the Fifth and Fourteenth Amendments to the United States Constitution." *Id.*, at 107. The habeas petition asks that the court, among other things, (1) appoint counsel for Hamdi; (2) order respondents to cease interrogating him; (3) declare that he is being held in violation of the Fifth and Fourteenth Amendments; (4) "[t]o the extent Respondents contest any material factual allegations in this Petition, schedule an evidentiary hearing, at which Petitioners may adduce proof in support of their allegations"; and (5) order that Hamdi be released from his "unlawful custody." *Id.*, at 108–109. Although his habeas petition provides no details with regard to the factual circumstances surrounding his son's capture and detention, Hamdi's father has asserted in documents found elsewhere in the record that his son went to Afghanistan to do "relief work," and that he had been in that country less than two months before September 11, 2001, and could not have received military training. *Id.*, at 188–189. The 20-year-old was traveling on his own for the first time, his father says, and "[b]ecause of his lack of experience, he was trapped in Afghanistan once that military campaign began." *Id.*, at 188–189.

***

II

The threshold question before us is whether the Executive has the authority to detain citizens who qualify as "enemy combatants." There is some debate as to the proper scope of this term, and the Government has never provided any court with the full criteria that it uses in classifying individuals as such. It has made clear, however, that, for purposes of this case, the "enemy combatant" that it is seeking to detain is an individual who, it alleges, was " 'part of or supporting forces hostile to the United States or coalition partners' " in Afghanistan and who " 'engaged in an armed conflict against the United States' " there. We therefore answer only the narrow question before us: whether the detention of citizens falling within that definition is authorized.

The Government maintains that no explicit congressional authorization is required, because the Executive possesses plenary authority to detain pursuant to Article II of the Constitution. We do not reach the question whether Article II provides such authority, however, because we agree with the Government's alternative position, that Congress has in fact authorized Hamdi's detention, through the AUMF.

Our analysis on that point, set forth below, substantially overlaps with our analysis of Hamdi's principal argument for the illegality of his detention. He posits that his detention is forbidden by 18 U.S.C. § 4001(a). Section 4001(a) states that "[n]o citizen shall be imprisoned or otherwise detained by the United States except pursuant to an Act of Congress." Congress passed §4001(a) in 1971 as part of a bill to repeal the Emergency Detention Act of 1950, 50 U.S.C. § 811 *et seq.*, which provided procedures for executive detention, during times of emergency, of individuals deemed likely to engage in espionage or sabotage. Congress was particularly concerned about the possibility that the Act could be used to reprise the Japanese internment camps of World War II. The Government again presses two alternative positions. First, it argues that §4001(a), in light of its legislative history and its location in Title 18, applies only to "the control of civilian prisons and related detentions," not to military detentions. Second, it maintains that §4001(a) is satisfied, because Hamdi is being detained "pursuant to an Act of Congress"—the AUMF. Again, because we conclude that the Government's second assertion is correct, we do not address the first. In other words, for the reasons that follow, we conclude that the AUMF is explicit congressional authorization for the detention of individuals in the narrow category we describe (assuming, without deciding, that such authorization is required), and that the AUMF satisfied §4001(a)'s requirement that a detention be "pursuant to an Act of Congress" (assuming, without deciding, that §4001(a) applies to military detentions).

The AUMF authorizes the President to use "all necessary and appropriate force" against "nations, organizations, or persons" associated with the September 11, 2001, terrorist attacks. 115 Stat. 224. There can be no doubt that individuals who fought against the United States in Afghanistan as part of the Taliban, an organization known to have supported the al Qaeda terrorist network responsible for those attacks, are individuals Congress sought to target in passing the AUMF. We conclude that detention of individuals falling into the limited category we are considering, for the duration of the particular conflict in which they were captured, is so fundamental and accepted an incident to war as to be an exercise of the "necessary and appropriate force" Congress has authorized the President to use.

The capture and detention of lawful combatants and the capture, detention, and trial of unlawful combatants, by "universal agreement and practice," are "important incident[s] of war." ***Ex parte Quirin***, 317

U.S., at 28. The purpose of detention is to prevent captured individuals from returning to the field of battle and taking up arms once again ...

There is no bar to this Nation's holding one of its own citizens as an enemy combatant ... A citizen, no less than an alien, can be "part of or supporting forces hostile to the United States or coalition partners" and "engaged in an armed conflict against the United States"; such a citizen, if released, would pose the same threat of returning to the front during the ongoing conflict.

In light of these principles, it is of no moment that the AUMF does not use specific language of detention. Because detention to prevent a combatant's return to the battlefield is a fundamental incident of waging war, in permitting the use of "necessary and appropriate force," Congress has clearly and unmistakably authorized detention in the narrow circumstances considered here.

Hamdi objects, nevertheless, that Congress has not authorized the *indefinite* detention to which he is now subject. The Government responds that "the detention of enemy combatants during World War II was just as 'indefinite' while that war was being fought." We take Hamdi's objection to be not to the lack of certainty regarding the date on which the conflict will end, but to the substantial prospect of perpetual detention. We recognize that the national security underpinnings of the "war on terror," although crucially important, are broad and malleable. As the Government concedes, "given its unconventional nature, the current conflict is unlikely to end with a formal cease-fire agreement." The prospect Hamdi raises is therefore not far-fetched. If the Government does not consider this unconventional war won for two generations, and if it maintains during that time that Hamdi might, if released, rejoin forces fighting against the United States, then the position it has taken throughout the litigation of this case suggests that Hamdi's detention could last for the rest of his life.

It is a clearly established principle of the law of war that detention may last no longer than active hostilities. See Article 118 of the Geneva Convention (III) ... Hamdi contends that the AUMF does not authorize indefinite or perpetual detention. Certainly, we agree that indefinite detention for the purpose of interrogation is not authorized. Further, we understand Congress' grant of authority for the use of "necessary and appropriate force" to include the authority to detain for the duration of the relevant conflict, and our understanding is based on longstanding law-of-war principles. If the practical circumstances of a given conflict are entirely unlike those of the conflicts that informed the development of the law of war, that understanding may unravel. But that is not the situation we face as of this date. Active combat operations against Taliban fighters apparently are ongoing in Afghanistan ... The United States may detain, for the duration of these hostilities, individuals legitimately determined to be Taliban combatants who "engaged in an armed conflict against the United States." If the record establishes that United States troops are still involved in active combat in Afghanistan, those detentions are part of the exercise of "necessary and appropriate force," and therefore are authorized by the AUMF.

***

To be clear, our opinion only finds legislative authority to detain under the AUMF once it is sufficiently clear that the individual is, in fact, an enemy combatant; whether that is established by concession or by some other process that verifies this fact with sufficient certainty seems beside the point.

***

III

Even in cases in which the detention of enemy combatants is legally authorized, there remains the question of what process is constitutionally due to a citizen who disputes his enemy-combatant status. Hamdi argues that he is owed a meaningful and timely hearing and that "extra-judicial detention [that] begins and ends with the submission of an affidavit based on third-hand hearsay" does not comport with the Fifth and Fourteenth Amendments. Brief for Petitioners 16. The Government counters that any more process than was provided below would be both unworkable and "constitutionally intolerable."

Our resolution of this dispute requires a careful examination both of the writ of habeas corpus, which Hamdi now seeks to employ as a mechanism of judicial review, and of the Due Process Clause, which informs the procedural contours of that mechanism in this instance.

A

Though they reach radically different conclusions on the process that ought to attend the present proceeding, the parties begin on common ground. All agree that, absent suspension, the writ of habeas corpus remains available to every individual detained within the United States. U.S. Const., Art. I, §9, cl. 2 ("The Privilege of the Writ of Habeas Corpus shall not be suspended, unless when in Cases of Rebellion or Invasion the public Safety may require it"). Only in the rarest of circumstances has Congress seen fit to suspend the writ ... At all other times, it has remained a critical check on the Executive, ensuring that it does not detain individuals except in accordance with law. See **INS v. St. Cyr**, 533 U.S. 289, 301 (2001). All agree suspension of the writ has not occurred here. Thus, it is undisputed that Hamdi was properly before an Article III court to challenge his detention under 28

U.S.C. §2241. Further, all agree that §2241 and its companion provisions provide at least a skeletal outline of the procedures to be afforded a petitioner in federal habeas review. Most notably, §2243 provides that "the person detained may, under oath, deny any of the facts set forth in the return or allege any other material facts," and §2246 allows the taking of evidence in habeas proceedings by deposition, affidavit, or interrogatories.

The simple outline of §2241 makes clear both that Congress envisioned that habeas petitioners would have some opportunity to present and rebut facts and that courts in cases like this retain some ability to vary the ways in which they do so as mandated by due process ...

B

First, the Government urges the adoption of the Fourth Circuit's holding below—that because it is "undisputed" that Hamdi's seizure took place in a combat zone, the habeas determination can be made purely as a matter of law, with no further hearing or fact finding necessary. This argument is easily rejected ... Hamdi's seizure cannot in any way be characterized as "undisputed," as "those circumstances are neither conceded in fact, nor susceptible to concession in law, because Hamdi has not been permitted to speak for himself or even through counsel as to those circumstances." 337 F.3d 335, 357 (CA4 2003) (Luttig, J., dissenting from denial of rehearing en banc); see also id., at 371–372 (Motz, J., dissenting from denial of rehearing en banc). Further, the "facts" that constitute the alleged concession are insufficient to support Hamdi's detention. Under the definition of enemy combatant that we accept today as falling within the scope of Congress' authorization, Hamdi would need to be "part of or supporting forces hostile to the United States or coalition partners" and "engaged in an armed conflict against the United States" to justify his detention in the United States for the duration of the relevant conflict. Brief for Respondents 3. The habeas petition states only that "[w]hen seized by the United States Government, Mr. Hamdi resided in Afghanistan." App. 104. An assertion that one resided in a country in which combat operations are taking place is not a concession that one was "captured in a zone of active combat operations in a foreign theater of war," 316 F.3d, at 459 (emphasis added), and certainly is not a concession that one was "part of or supporting forces hostile to the United States or coalition partners" and "engaged in an armed conflict against the United States." Accordingly, we reject any argument that Hamdi has made concessions that eliminate any right to further process.

C

The Government's second argument requires closer consideration. This is the argument that further factual exploration is unwarranted and inappropriate in light of the extraordinary constitutional interests at stake. Under the Government's most extreme rendition of this argument, "[r]espect for separation of powers and the limited institutional capabilities of courts in matters of military decision-making in connection with an ongoing conflict" ought to eliminate entirely any individual process, restricting the courts to investigating only whether legal authorization exists for the broader detention scheme. At most, the Government argues, courts should review its determination that a citizen is an enemy combatant under a very deferential "some evidence" standard ... Under this review, a court would assume the accuracy of the Government's articulated basis for Hamdi's detention ... and assess only whether that articulated basis was a legitimate one...

In response, Hamdi emphasizes that this Court consistently has recognized that an individual challenging his detention may not be held at the will of the Executive without recourse to some proceeding before a neutral tribunal to determine whether the Executive's asserted justifications for that detention have basis in fact and warrant in law. See, e.g., **Zadvydas v. Davis**, 533 U.S. 678, 690 (2001); **Addington v. Texas**, 441 U.S. 418, 425–427 (1979). He argues that the Fourth Circuit inappropriately "ceded power to the Executive during wartime to define the conduct for which a citizen may be detained, judge whether that citizen has engaged in the proscribed conduct, and imprison that citizen indefinitely," Brief for Petitioners 21, and that due process demands that he receive a hearing in which he may challenge the Mobbs Declaration and adduce his own counter evidence. The District Court, agreeing with Hamdi, apparently believed that the appropriate process would approach the process that accompanies a criminal trial. It therefore disapproved of the hearsay nature of the Mobbs Declaration and anticipated quite extensive discovery of various military affairs. Anything less, it concluded, would not be "meaningful judicial review." App. 291.

Both of these positions highlight legitimate concerns. And both emphasize the tension that often exists between the autonomy that the Government asserts is necessary in order to pursue effectively a particular goal and the process that a citizen contends he is due before he is deprived of a constitutional right. The ordinary mechanism that we use for balancing such serious competing interests, and for determining the procedures that are necessary to ensure that a citizen is not "deprived of life, liberty, or property, without due process of law," U.S. Const., Amdt. 5, is the test that we articulated in **Mathews v. Eldridge**, 424 U.S. 319 (1976). See, e.g., **Heller v. Doe**, 509 U.S. 312, 330–331 (1993); **Zinermon v. Burch**, 494 U.S. 113, 127–128 (1990); **United States v. Salerno**, 481 U.S. 739, 746 (1987); **Schall v. Martin**, 467 U.S. 253, 274–275 (1984); **Addington v. Texas**, supra, at 425. **Mathews** dictates that the process due in any given instance is determined by weighing "the private interest that will be affected by the official action" against the Government's asserted interest, "including the function involved" and the burdens the Government would face in providing greater process. 424 U.S., at 335. The **Mathews** calculus then contemplates a judicious balancing of these concerns, through an analysis of "the risk of an erroneous deprivation" of the private interest if the process were reduced and the "probable value, if any, of additional or substitute safeguards." *Ibid*. We take each of these steps in turn.

1

It is beyond question that substantial interests lie on both sides of the scale in this case. Hamdi's "private interest ... affected by the official action," *ibid*., is the most elemental of liberty interests – the interest in being free from physical detention by one's own government.

***

Nor is the weight on this side of the **Mathews** scale offset by the circumstances of war or the accusation of treasonous behavior, for "[i]t is clear that commitment for *any* purpose constitutes a significant deprivation of liberty that requires due process protection," **Jones v. United States**, 463 U.S. 354, 361 (1983) (emphasis added; internal quotation marks omitted), and at this stage in the **Mathews** calculus, we consider the interest of the *erroneously* detained individual.

***

Moreover, as critical as the Government's interest may be in detaining those who actually pose an immediate threat to the national security of the United States during ongoing international conflict, history and common sense teach us that an unchecked system of detention carries the potential to become a means for oppression and abuse of others who do not present that sort of threat ... We reaffirm today the fundamental nature of a citizen's right to be free from involuntary confinement by his own government without due process of law, and we weigh the opposing governmental interests against the curtailment of liberty that such confinement entails.

2

On the other side of the scale are the weighty and sensitive governmental interests in ensuring that those who have in fact fought with the enemy during a war do not return to battle against the United States.... Without doubt, our Constitution recognizes that core strategic matters of war making belong in the hands of those who are best positioned and most politically accountable for making them.

Department of Navy v. Egan, 484 U.S. 518, 530 (1988) (noting the reluctance of the courts "to intrude upon the authority of the Executive in military and national security affairs"); ***Youngstown Sheet & Tube Co. v. Sawyer***, 343 U.S. 579, 587 (1952) (acknowledging "broad powers in military commanders engaged in day-to-day fighting in a theater of war").

***

To the extent that these burdens are triggered by heightened procedures, they are properly taken into account in our due process analysis.

3

Striking the proper constitutional balance here is of great importance to the Nation during this period of ongoing combat. But it is equally vital that our calculus not give short shrift to the values that this country holds dear or to the privilege that is American citizenship. It is during our most challenging and uncertain moments that our Nation's commitment to due process is most severely tested; and it is in those times that we must preserve our commitment at home to the principles for which we fight abroad.

***

With due recognition of these competing concerns, we believe that neither the process proposed by the Government nor the process apparently envisioned by the District Court below strikes the proper constitutional balance when a United States citizen is detained in the United States as an enemy combatant. That is, "the risk of erroneous deprivation" of a detainee's liberty interest is unacceptably high under the Government's proposed rule, while some of the "additional or substitute procedural safeguards" suggested by the District Court are unwarranted in light of their limited "probable value" and the burdens they may impose on the military in such cases.

We therefore hold that a citizen-detainee seeking to challenge his classification as an enemy combatant must receive notice of the factual basis for his classification, and a fair opportunity to rebut the Government's factual assertions before a neutral decision maker. See ***Cleveland Bd. of Ed. v. Loudermill***, 470 U.S. 532, 542 (1985) ("An essential principle of due process is that a deprivation of life, liberty, or property 'be preceded by notice and opportunity for hearing appropriate to the nature of the case'" (quoting ***Mullane v. Central Hanover Bank & Trust Co.***, 339 U.S. 306, 313 (1950)); ***Concrete Pipe & Products of Cal., Inc. v. Construction Laborers Pension Trust for Southern Cal.***, 508 U.S. 602, 617 (1993) ("due process requires a 'neutral and detached judge in the first instance' " (quoting **Ward v. Monroeville**, 409 U.S. 57, 61–62 (1972)). "For more than a century the central meaning of procedural due process has been clear: 'Parties whose rights are to be affected are entitled to be heard; and in order that they may enjoy that right they must first be notified.' It is equally fundamental that the right to notice and an opportunity to be heard 'must be granted at a meaningful time and in a meaningful manner.' **Fuentes v. Shevin**, 407 U.S. 67, 80 (1972) (quoting **Baldwin v. Hale**, 1 Wall. 223, 233 (1864); **Armstrong v. Manzo**, 380 U.S. 545, 552 (1965) (other citations omitted)). These essential constitutional promises may not be eroded.

***

We think it unlikely that this basic process will have the dire impact on the central functions of war-making that the Government forecasts. The parties agree that initial captures on the battlefield need not receive the process we have discussed here; that process is due only when the determination is made to continue to hold those who have been seized. The Government has made clear in its briefing that documentation regarding battlefield detainees already is kept in the ordinary course of military affairs.

***

In sum, while the full protections that accompany challenges to detentions in other settings may prove unworkable and inappropriate in the enemy-combatant setting, the threats to military operations posed by a basic system of independent review are not so weighty as to trump a citizen's core rights to challenge meaningfully the Government's case and to be heard by an impartial adjudicator.

D

In so holding, we necessarily reject the Government's assertion that separation of powers principles mandate a heavily circumscribed role for the courts in such circumstances. Indeed, the position that the courts must forgo any examination of the individual case and focus exclusively on the legality of the broader detention scheme cannot be mandated by any reasonable view of separation of powers, as this approach serves only to condense power into a single branch of government. We have long since made clear that a state of war is not a blank check for the President when it comes to the rights of the Nation's citizens. **Youngstown Sheet & Tube**, 343 U.S., at 587. Whatever power the United States Constitution envisions for the Executive in its exchanges with other nations or with enemy organizations in times of conflict, it most assuredly envisions a role for all three branches when individual liberties are at stake. ***Mistretta v. United States***, 488 U.S. 361, 380 (1989) (it was "the central judgment of the Framers of the Constitution that, within our political scheme, the separation of governmental powers into three coordinate Branches is essential to the preservation of liberty"); ***Home Building & Loan Assn. v. Blaisdell***, 290 U.S. 398, 426 (1934) (The war power "is a power to wage war successfully, and thus it permits the harnessing of the entire energies of the people in a supreme cooperative effort to preserve the nation. But even the war power does not remove constitutional limitations safeguarding essential liberties"). Likewise, we have made clear that, unless Congress acts to suspend it, the Great Writ of habeas corpus allows the Judicial Branch to play a necessary role in maintaining this delicate balance of governance, serving as an important judicial check on the Executive's discretion in the realm of detentions.... Thus, while we do not question that our due process assessment must pay keen attention to the particular burdens faced by the Executive in the context of military action, it would turn our system of checks and balances on its head to suggest that a citizen could not make his way to court with a challenge to the factual basis for his detention by his government, simply because the Executive opposes making available such a challenge. Absent suspension of the writ by Congress, a citizen detained as an enemy combatant is entitled to this process.

Because we conclude that due process demands some system for a citizen detainee to refute his classification, the proposed "some evidence" standard is inadequate. Any process in which the Executive's factual assertions go wholly unchallenged or are simply presumed correct without any opportunity for the alleged combatant to demonstrate otherwise falls constitutionally short. As the Government itself has recognized, we have utilized the "some evidence" standard in the past as a standard of review, not as a standard of proof ... This standard therefore is ill suited to the situation in which a habeas petitioner has received no prior proceedings before any tribunal and had no prior opportunity to rebut the Executive's factual assertions before a neutral decision-maker.

IV

***

The judgment of the United States Court of Appeals for the Fourth Circuit is vacated, and the case is remanded for further proceedings.

It is so ordered.

Boumediene v. Bush
553 U.S. 723 (2008)

Justice Kennedy delivered the opinion of the Court.

Petitioners are aliens designated as enemy combatants and detained at the United States Naval Station at Guantanamo Bay, Cuba. There are others detained there, also aliens, who are not parties to this suit.

Petitioners present a question not resolved by our earlier cases relating to the detention of aliens at Guantanamo: whether they have the constitutional privilege of habeas corpus, a privilege not to be withdrawn except in conformance with the Suspension Clause, Art. I, §9, cl. 2. We hold these petitioners do have the habeas corpus privilege. Congress has enacted a statute, the Detainee Treatment Act of 2005 (DTA), 119 Stat. 2739, that provides certain procedures for review of the detainees' status. We hold that those procedures are not an adequate and effective substitute for habeas corpus. Therefore §7 of the Military Commissions Act of 2006 (MCA), 28 U. S. C. A. §2241(e) (Supp. 2007), operates as an unconstitutional suspension of the writ. We do not address whether the President has authority to detain these petitioners nor do we hold that the writ must issue. These and other questions regarding the legality of the detention are to be resolved in the first instance by the District Court.

I

Under the Authorization for Use of Military Force (AUMF), §2(a), 115 Stat. 224, note following 50 U.S.C. §1541 (2000 ed., Supp. V), the President is authorized "to use all necessary and appropriate force against those nations, organizations, or persons he determines planned, authorized, committed, or aided the terrorist attacks that occurred on September 11, 2001, or harbored such organizations or persons, in order to prevent any future acts of international terrorism against the United States by such nations, organizations or persons."

In **Hamdi v. Rumsfeld**, 542 U.S. 507 (2004), five Members of the Court recognized that detention of individuals who fought against the United States in Afghanistan "for the duration of the particular conflict in which they were captured, is so fundamental and accepted an incident to war as to be an exercise of the 'necessary and appropriate force' Congress has authorized the President to use." *Id.*, at 518 (plurality opinion of O'Connor, J.), *id.*, at 588-589 (*Thomas, J.,* dissenting). After **Hamdi**, the Deputy Secretary of Defense established Combatant Status Review Tribunals (CSRTs) to determine whether individuals detained at Guantanamo were "enemy combatants," as the Department defines that term. See App. to Pet. for Cert. in No. 06-1195, p. 81a. A later memorandum established procedures to implement the CSRTs. See App. to Pet. for Cert. in No. 06-1196, p. 147. The Government maintains these procedures were designed to comply with the due process requirements identified by the plurality in **Hamdi**. See Brief for Respondents 10.

Interpreting the AUMF, the Department of Defense ordered the detention of these petitioners, and they were transferred to Guantanamo. Some of these individuals were apprehended on the battlefield in Afghanistan, others in places as far away from there as Bosnia and Gambia. All are foreign nationals, but none is a citizen of a nation now at war with the United States. Each denies he is a member of the al Qaeda terrorist network that carried out the September 11 attacks or of the Taliban regime that provided sanctuary for al Qaeda. Each petitioner appeared before a separate CSRT; was determined to be an enemy combatant; and has sought a writ of habeas corpus in the United States District Court for the District of Columbia.

The first actions commenced in February 2002. The District Court ordered the cases dismissed for lack of jurisdiction because the naval station is outside the sovereign territory of the United States. See **Rasul v. Bush**, 215 F. Supp. 2d 55 (2002). The Court of Appeals for the District of Columbia Circuit affirmed. See **Al Odah v. United States**, 321 F. 3d 1134, 1145 (2003). We granted certiorari and reversed, holding that 28 U. S. C. §2241 extended statutory habeas corpus jurisdiction to Guantanamo. See **Rasul v. Bush**, 542 U. S. 466, 473 (2004). The constitutional issue presented in the instant cases was not reached in **Rasul**. Id., at 476.

***

While appeals were pending from the District Court decisions, Congress passed the DTA. Subsection (e) of §1005 of the DTA amended 28 U. S. C. §2241 to provide that "no court, justice, or judge shall have jurisdiction to hear or consider ... an application for a writ of habeas corpus filed by or on behalf of an alien detained by the Department of Defense at Guantanamo Bay, Cuba." 119 Stat. 2742. Section 1005 further provides that the Court of Appeals for the District of Columbia Circuit shall have "exclusive" jurisdiction to review decisions of the CSRTs. Ibid.

In **Hamdan v. Rumsfeld**, 548 U. S. 557, 576-577 (2006), the Court held this provision did not apply to cases (like petitioners') pending when the DTA was enacted. Congress responded by passing the MCA, 10 U. S. C. A. §948a et seq. (Supp. 2007), which again amended §2241. The text of the statutory amendment is discussed below. See Part II, infra. (Four Members of the **Hamdan** majority noted that "[n]othing prevent[ed] the President from returning to Congress to seek the authority he believes necessary." 548 U. S., at 636 (Breyer, J., concurring). The authority to which the concurring opinion referred was the authority to "create military commissions of the kind at issue" in the case. *Ibid.* Nothing in that opinion can be construed as an invitation for Congress to suspend the writ.)

Petitioners' cases were consolidated on appeal, and the parties filed supplemental briefs in light of our decision in **Hamdan**. The Court of Appeals' ruling, 476 F. 3d 981 (CADC 2007), is the subject of our present review and today's decision.

The Court of Appeals concluded that MCA §7 must be read to strip from it, and all federal courts, jurisdiction to consider petitioners' habeas corpus applications, *id.*, at 987; that petitioners are not entitled to the privilege of the writ or the protections of the Suspension Clause, *id.*, at 990-991; and, as a result, that it was unnecessary to consider whether Congress provided an adequate and effective substitute for habeas corpus in the DTA.

We granted certiorari. 551 U. S. ___ (2007).

II

As a threshold matter, we must decide whether MCA §7 denies the federal courts jurisdiction to hear habeas corpus actions pending at the time of its enactment. We hold the statute does deny that jurisdiction, so that, if the statute is valid, petitioners' cases must be dismissed.

As amended by the terms of the MCA, 28 U. S. C. A. §2241(e) (Supp. 2007) now provides:

"(1) No court, justice, or judge shall have jurisdiction to hear or consider an application for a writ of habeas corpus filed by or on behalf of an alien detained by the United States who has been determined by the United States to have been properly detained as an enemy combatant or is awaiting such determination...."

III

In deciding the constitutional questions now presented we must determine whether petitioners are barred from seeking the writ or invoking the protections of the Suspension Clause either because of their status, *i.e.*, petitioners' designation by the Executive Branch as enemy combatants, or their physical location, *i.e.*, their presence at Guantanamo Bay. The Government contends that noncitizens designated as enemy combatants and detained in territory located outside our Nation's borders have no constitutional rights and no privilege of habeas corpus. Petitioners contend they do have cognizable constitutional rights and that Congress, in seeking to eliminate recourse to habeas corpus as a means to assert those rights, acted in violation of the Suspension Clause.

We begin with a brief account of the history and origins of the writ. Our account proceeds from two propositions. First, protection for the privilege of habeas corpus was one of the few safeguards of liberty specified in a Constitution that, at the outset, had no Bill of Rights. In the system conceived by the Framers the writ had a centrality that must inform proper interpretation of the Suspension Clause. Second, to the extent there were settled precedents or legal commentaries in 1789 regarding the extraterritorial scope of the writ or its application to enemy aliens, those authorities can be instructive for the present cases.

A

The Framers viewed freedom from unlawful restraint as a fundamental precept of liberty, and they understood the writ of habeas corpus as a vital instrument to secure that freedom. Experience taught, however, that the common-law writ all too often had been insufficient to guard against the abuse of monarchial power. That history counseled the necessity for specific language in the Constitution to secure the writ and ensure its place in our legal system ... Even when the importance of the writ was well understood in England, habeas relief often was denied by the courts or suspended by Parliament. Denial or suspension occurred in times of political unrest, to the anguish of the imprisoned and the outrage of those in sympathy with them.

***

This history was known to the Framers. It no doubt confirmed their view that pendular swings to and away from individual liberty were endemic to undivided, uncontrolled power. The Framers' inherent distrust of governmental power was the driving force behind the constitutional plan that allocated powers among three independent branches. This design serves not only to make Government accountable but also to secure individual liberty ... Because the Constitution's separation-of-powers structure, like the substantive guarantees of the Fifth and Fourteenth Amendments protects persons as well as citizens foreign nationals who have the privilege of litigating in our courts can seek to enforce separation-of-powers principles.

That the Framers considered the writ a vital instrument for the protection of individual liberty is evident from the care taken to specify the limited grounds for its suspension: "The Privilege of the Writ of Habeas Corpus shall not be suspended, unless when in Cases of Rebellion or Invasion the public Safety may require it." Art. I, §9, cl. 2 ... Surviving accounts of the ratification debates provide additional evidence that the Framers deemed the writ to be an essential mechanism in the separation-of-powers scheme ...

***

The Clause protects the rights of the detained by a means consistent with the essential design of the Constitution. It ensures that, except during periods of formal suspension, the Judiciary will have a time-tested device, the writ, to maintain the "delicate balance of governance" that is itself the surest safeguard of liberty. The Clause protects the rights of the detained by affirming the duty and authority of the Judiciary to call the jailer to account ... The separation-of-powers doctrine, and the history that influenced its design, therefore must inform the reach and purpose of the Suspension Clause.

B

The broad historical narrative of the writ and its function is central to our analysis, but we seek guidance as well from founding-era authorities addressing the specific question before us: whether foreign nationals, apprehended and detained in distant countries during a time of serious threats to our Nation's security, may assert the privilege of the writ and seek its protection. The Court has been careful not to foreclose the possibility that the protections of the Suspension Clause have expanded along with post-1789 developments that define the present scope of the writ. See **INS v. St. Cyr**, 533 U. S. 289, 300-301 (2001). But the analysis may begin with precedents as of 1789, for the Court has said that "at the absolute minimum" the Clause protects the writ as it existed when the Constitution was drafted and ratified. *Id.*, at 301.

To support their arguments, the parties in these cases have examined historical sources to construct a view of the common-law writ as it existed in 1789—as have *amici* whose expertise in legal history the Court has relied upon in the past. The Government argues the common-law writ ran only to those territories over which the Crown was sovereign. Petitioners argue that jurisdiction followed the King's officers. Diligent search by all parties reveals no certain conclusions. In none of the cases cited do we find that a common-law court would or would not have granted, or refused to hear for lack of jurisdiction, a petition for a writ of habeas corpus brought by a prisoner deemed an enemy combatant, under a standard like the one the Department of Defense has used in these cases, and when held in a territory, like Guantanamo, over which the Government has total military and civil control.

We know that at common law a petitioner's status as an alien was not a categorical bar to habeas corpus relief. See, e.g., **Sommersett's Case**, 20 How. St. Tr. 1, 80-82 (1772) (ordering an African slave freed upon finding the custodian's return insufficient); see generally **Khera v. Secretary of State for the Home Dept.**, [1984] A. C. 74, 111 ("Habeas corpus protection is often expressed as limited to 'British subjects.' Is it really limited to British nationals? Suffice it to say that the case law has given an emphatic 'no' to the question").

***

IV

Drawing from its position that at common law the writ ran only to territories over which the Crown was sovereign, the Government says the Suspension Clause affords petitioners no rights because the United States does not claim sovereignty over the place of detention.

Guantanamo Bay is not formally part of the United States. See DTA §1005(g), 119 Stat. 2743. And under the terms of the lease between the United States and Cuba, Cuba retains "ultimate sovereignty" over the territory while the United States exercises "complete jurisdiction and control." See Lease of Lands for Coaling and Naval Stations, Feb. 23, 1903, U. S.-Cuba, Art. III, T. S. No. 418 (hereinafter 1903 Lease Agreement); *Rasul*, 542 U. S., at 471. Under the terms of the 1934 Treaty, however, Cuba effectively has no rights as a sovereign until the parties agree to modification of the 1903 Lease Agreement or the United States abandons the base. See Treaty Defining Relations with Cuba, May 29, 1934, U. S.-Cuba, Art. III, 48 Stat. 1683, T. S. No. 866.

The United States contends, nevertheless, that Guantanamo is not within its sovereign control. This was the Government's position well before the events of September 11, 2001. See, e.g., Brief for Petitioners in *Sale v. Haitian Centers Council, Inc.*, O. T. 1992, No. 92-344, p. 31 (arguing that Guantanamo is territory "*outside* the United States"). And in other contexts the Court has held that questions of sovereignty are for the political branches to decide. See *Vermilya-Brown Co. v. Connell*, 335 U. S. 377, 380 (1948) ("[D]etermination of sovereignty over an area is for the legislative and executive departments"); see also *Jones v. United States*, 137 U. S. 202 (1890); *Williams v. Suffolk Ins. Co.*, 13 Pet. 415, 420 (1839). Even if this were a treaty interpretation case that did not involve a political question, the President's construction of the lease agreement would be entitled to great respect. See *Sumitomo Shoji America, Inc. v. Avagliano*, 457 U. S. 176, 184-185 (1982).

We therefore do not question the Government's position that Cuba, not the United States, maintains sovereignty, in the legal and technical sense of the term, over Guantanamo Bay. But this does not end the analysis. Our cases do not hold it is improper for us to inquire into the objective degree of control the Nation asserts over foreign territory.

***

Were we to hold that the present cases turn on the political question doctrine, we would be required first to accept the Government's premise that *de jure* sovereignty is the touchstone of habeas corpus jurisdiction. This premise, however, is unfounded. For the reasons indicated above, the history of common-law habeas corpus provides scant support for this proposition; and, for the reasons indicated below, that position would be inconsistent with our precedents and contrary to fundamental separation-of-powers principles.

A

The Court has discussed the issue of the Constitution's extra-territorial application on many occasions. These decisions undermine the Government's argument that, at least as applied to noncitizens, the Constitution necessarily stops where *de jure* sovereignty ends.

The Framers foresaw that the United States would expand and acquire new territories. See ***American Ins. Co. v. 356 Bales of Cotton***, 1 Pet. 511, 542 (1828). Article IV, §3, cl. 1, grants Congress the power to admit new States. Clause 2 of the same section grants Congress the "Power to dispose of and make all needful Rules and Regulations respecting the Territory or other Property belonging to the United States." Save for a few notable (and notorious) exceptions, e.g., ***Dred Scott v. Sandford***, 19 How. 393 (1857), throughout most of our history there was little need to explore the outer boundaries of the Constitution's geographic reach. When Congress exercised its power to create new territories, it guaranteed constitutional protections to the inhabitants by statute. See, e.g., An Act: to establish a Territorial Government for Utah, 9 Stat. 458 ("[T]he Constitution and laws of the United States are hereby extended over and declared to be in force in said Territory of Utah"); Rev. Stat. §1891 ("The Constitution and all laws of the United States which are not locally inapplicable shall have the same force and effect within all the organized Territories, and in every Territory hereafter organized as elsewhere within the United States"); see generally Burnett, *Untied States: American Expansion and Territorial Deannexation*, 72 U. Chi. L. Rev. 797, 825–827 (2005). In particular, there was no need to test the limits of the Suspension Clause because, as early as 1789, Congress extended the writ to the Territories. See Act of Aug. 7, 1789, 1 Stat. 52 (reaffirming Art. II of Northwest Ordinance of 1787, which provided that "[t]he inhabitants of the said territory, shall always be entitled to the benefits of the writ of habeas corpus").

***

In a series of opinions later known as the Insular Cases, the Court addressed whether the Constitution, by its own force, applies in any territory that is not a State. See ***De Lima v. Bidwell***, 182 U. S. 1 (1901); ***Dooley v. United States***, 182 U. S. 222 (1901); ***Armstrong v. United States***, 182 U. S. 243 (1901); ***Downes v. Bidwell***, 182 U. S. 244 (1901); ***Hawaii v. Mankichi***, 190 U. S. 197 (1903); ***Dorr v. United States***, 195 U. S.

138 (1904). The Court held that the Constitution has independent force in these territories, a force not contingent upon acts of legislative grace. Yet it took note of the difficulties inherent in that position.

***

B

[Part B focuses on the government's sovereignty-based claim regarding Court jurisdiction over Cuba and the Court's discussion of separation of powers.]

C

***

The petitioners ... are not American citizens ... In the instant cases ... the detainees deny they are enemy combatants. They have been afforded some process in CSRT proceedings to determine their status; but ... there has been no trial by military commission for violations of the laws of war ... the procedural protections afforded to the detainees in the CSRT hearings are far more limited, and, we conclude, fall well short of the procedures and adversarial mechanisms that would eliminate the need for habeas corpus review. Although the detainee is assigned a "Personal Representative" to assist him during CSRT proceedings, the Secretary of the Navy's memorandum makes clear that person is not the detainee's lawyer or even his "advocate." The Government's evidence is accorded a presumption of validity. The detainee is allowed to present "reasonably available" evidence, but his ability to rebut the Government's evidence against him is limited by the circumstances of his confinement and his lack of counsel at this stage. And although the detainee can seek review of his status determination in the Court of Appeals, that review process cannot cure all defects in the earlier proceedings.

***

The detainees have been deemed enemies of the United States. At present, dangerous as they may be if released, they are contained in a secure prison facility located on an isolated and heavily fortified military base.

There is no indication, furthermore, that adjudicating a habeas corpus petition would cause friction with the host government. No Cuban court has jurisdiction over American military personnel at Guantanamo or the enemy combatants detained there. While obligated to abide by the terms of the lease, the United States is, for all practical purposes, answerable to no other sovereign for its acts on the base. Were that not the case, or if the detention facility were located in an active theater of war, arguments that issuing the writ would be "impracticable or anomalous" would have more weight. See **Reid**, 354 U. S., at 74 (Harlan, J., concurring in result). Under the facts presented here, however, there are few practical barriers to the running of the writ. To the extent barriers arise, habeas corpus procedures likely can be modified to address them.

It is true that before today the Court has never held that noncitizens detained by our Government in territory over which another country maintains de jure sovereignty have any rights under our Constitution. But the cases before us lack any precise historical parallel. They involve individuals detained by executive order for the duration of a conflict that, if measured from September 11, 2001, to the present, is already among the longest wars in American history. See Oxford Companion to American Military History 849 (1999). The detainees, moreover, are held in a territory that, while technically not part of the United States, is under the complete and total control of our Government. Under these circumstances the lack of a precedent on point is no barrier to our holding.

We hold that Art. I, §9, cl. 2, of the Constitution has full effect at Guantanamo Bay. If the privilege of habeas corpus is to be denied to the detainees now before us, Congress must act in accordance with the requirements of the Suspension Clause ... This Court may not impose a de facto suspension by abstaining from these controversies ... MCA does not purport to be a formal suspension of the writ; and the Government, in its submissions to us, has not argued that it is. Petitioners, therefore, are entitled to the privilege of habeas corpus to challenge the legality of their detention.

V

In light of this holding the question becomes whether the statute stripping jurisdiction to issue the writ avoids the Suspension Clause mandate because Congress has provided adequate substitute procedures for habeas corpus. The Government submits there has been compliance with the Suspension Clause because the DTA review process in the Court of Appeals, see DTA §1005(e), provides an adequate substitute. Congress has granted that court jurisdiction to consider "(i) whether the status determination of the [CSRT] ... was consistent with the standards and procedures specified by the Secretary of Defense ... and (ii) to the extent the Constitution and laws of the United States are applicable, whether the use of such standards and procedures to make the determination is consistent with the Constitution and laws of the United States." §1005(e)(2)(C), 119 Stat. 2742.

The Court of Appeals, having decided that the writ does not run to the detainees in any event, found it unnecessary to consider whether an adequate substitute has been provided. In the ordinary course we would remand to the Court of Appeals to consider this question in the first instance. See **Youakim v. Miller**, 425 U. S. 231, 234 (1976) *(per curiam)*. It is well settled, however, that the Court's practice of declining to address issues left unresolved in earlier proceedings is not an inflexible rule. *Ibid.* Departure from the rule is appropriate in "exceptional" circumstances. See **Cooper Industries, Inc. v. Aviall Services, Inc.**, 543 U. S. 157, 169 (2004); **Duignan v. United States**, 274 U. S. 195, 200 (1927).

The gravity of the separation-of-powers issues raised by these cases and the fact that these detainees have been denied meaningful access to a judicial forum for a period of years render these cases exceptional ... Under the circumstances we believe the costs of further delay substantially outweigh any benefits of remanding to the Court of Appeals to consider the issue it did not address in these cases.

A

Our case law does not contain extensive discussion of standards defining suspension of the writ or of circumstances under which suspension has occurred. This simply confirms the care Congress has taken throughout our Nation's history to preserve the writ and its function. Indeed, most of the major legislative enactments pertaining to habeas corpus have acted not to contract the writ's protection but to expand it or to hasten resolution of prisoners' claims ... There are exceptions, of course. Title I of the Antiterrorism and Effective Death Penalty Act of 1996 (AEDPA), §106, 110 Stat. 1220, contains certain gate-keeping provisions that restrict a prisoner's ability to bring new and repetitive claims in "second or successive" habeas corpus actions.

***

In contrast the DTA's jurisdictional grant is quite limited. The Court of Appeals has jurisdiction not to inquire into the legality of the detention generally but only to assess whether the CSRT complied with the "standards and procedures specified by the Secretary of Defense" and whether those standards and procedures are lawful. DTA §1005(e)(2)(C), 119 Stat. 2742. If Congress had envisioned DTA review as coextensive with traditional habeas corpus, it would not have drafted the statute in this manner ... there has been no effort to preserve habeas corpus review as an avenue of last resort. No saving clause exists in either the MCA or the DTA. And MCA §7 eliminates habeas review for these petitioners.

The differences between the DTA and the habeas statute that would govern in MCA §7's absence, 28 U.S.C. §2241, are likewise telling. In §2241 Congress confirmed the authority of "any justice" or "circuit judge" to issue the writ ... To the extent any doubt remains about Congress' intent, the legislative history confirms what the plain text strongly suggests: In passing the DTA Congress did not intend to create a process that differs from traditional habeas corpus process in name only. It intended to create a more limited procedure ... It is against this background that we must interpret the DTA and assess its adequacy as a substitute for habeas corpus. The present cases thus test the limits of the Suspension Clause ...

B

We do not endeavor to offer a comprehensive summary of the requisites for an adequate substitute for habeas corpus. We do consider it uncontroversial, however, that the privilege of habeas corpus entitles the prisoner to a meaningful opportunity to demonstrate that he is being held pursuant to "the erroneous application or interpretation" of relevant law. *St. Cyr*, 533 U. S., at 302. And the habeas court must have the power to order the conditional release of an individual unlawfully detained—though release need not be the exclusive remedy and is not the appropriate one in every case in which the writ is granted ... These are the easily identified attributes of any constitutionally adequate habeas corpus proceeding. But, depending on the circumstances, more may be required.

Indeed, common-law habeas corpus was, above all, an adaptable remedy. Its precise application and scope changed depending upon the circumstances ...

[The Court proceeds to provide an overview of habeas corpus relief and the historical and legal extent of that review to criminal and non-criminal claims.]

Where a person is detained by executive order, rather than, say, after being tried and convicted in a court, the need for collateral review is most pressing. A criminal conviction in the usual course occurs after a judicial hearing before a tribunal disinterested in the outcome and committed to procedures designed to ensure its own independence. These dynamics are not inherent in executive detention orders or executive review procedures. In this context the need for habeas corpus is more urgent. The intended duration of the detention and the reasons for it bear upon the precise scope of the inquiry. Habeas corpus proceedings need not resemble a criminal trial, even when the detention is by executive order. But the writ must be effective. The habeas court must have sufficient authority to conduct a meaningful review of both the cause for detention and the Executive's power to detain.

To determine the necessary scope of habeas corpus review, therefore, we must assess the CSRT process, the mechanism through which petitioners' designation as enemy combatants became final. Whether one characterizes the CSRT process as direct review of the Executive's battlefield determination that the detainee is an enemy combatant—as the parties have and as we do—or as the first step in the collateral review of a battlefield determination makes no difference in a proper analysis of whether the procedures Congress put in place are an adequate substitute for habeas corpus. What matters is the sum total of procedural protections afforded to the detainee at all stages, direct and collateral.

Petitioners identify what they see as myriad deficiencies in the CSRTs. The most relevant for our purposes are the constraints upon the detainee's ability to rebut the factual basis for the Government's assertion that he is an enemy combatant. As already noted, see Part IV-C, *supra*, at the CSRT stage the detainee has limited means to find or present evidence to challenge the Government's case against him. He does not have the assistance of counsel and may not be aware of the most critical allegations that the Government relied upon to order his detention. The detainee can confront witnesses that testify during the CSRT proceedings. But given that there are in effect no limits on the admission of hearsay evidence—the only requirement is that the tribunal deem the evidence "relevant and helpful," —the detainee's opportunity to question witnesses is likely to be more theoretical than real ...

Even if we were to assume that the CSRTs satisfy due process standards, it would not end our inquiry. Habeas corpus is a collateral process that exists, in Justice Holmes' words, to "cut through all forms and go to the very tissue of the structure. It comes in from the outside, not in subordination to the proceedings, and although every form may have been preserved opens the inquiry whether they have been more than an empty shell." **Frank v. Mangum**, 237 U. S. 309, 346 (1915) (dissenting opinion). Even when the procedures authorizing detention are structurally sound, the Suspension Clause remains applicable and the writ relevant ... Although we make no judgment as to whether the CSRTs, as currently constituted, satisfy due process standards, we agree with petitioners that, even when all the parties involved in this process act with diligence and in good faith, there is considerable risk of error in the tribunal's findings of fact. This is a risk inherent in any process that, in the words of the former Chief Judge of the Court of Appeals, is "closed and accusatorial"... And given that the consequence of error may be detention of persons for the duration of hostilities that may last a generation or more, this is a risk too significant to ignore.

For the writ of habeas corpus, or its substitute, to function as an effective and proper remedy in this context, the court that conducts the habeas proceeding must have the means to correct errors that occurred during the CSRT proceedings. This includes some authority to assess the sufficiency of the Government's evidence against the detainee. It also must have the authority to admit and consider relevant exculpatory evidence that was not introduced during the earlier proceeding. Federal habeas petitioners long have had the means to supplement the record on review, even in the post-conviction habeas setting. See **Townsend v. Sain**, 372 U. S. 293, 313 (1963), overruled in part by **Keeney v. Tamayo-Reyes**, 504 U. S. 1, 5 (1992). Here that opportunity is constitutionally required.

Consistent with the historic function and province of the writ, habeas corpus review may be more circumscribed if the underlying detention proceedings are more thorough than they were here. In two habeas cases involving enemy aliens tried for war crimes, **In re Yamashita**, 327 U. S. 1 (1946), and **Ex parte Quirin**, 317 U. S. 1 (1942), for example, this Court limited its review to determining whether the Executive had legal authority to try the petitioners by military commission. See **Yamashita**, supra, at 8 ("[O]n application for habeas corpus we are not concerned with the guilt or innocence of the petitioners. We consider here only the lawful power of the commission to try the petitioner for the offense charged"); **Quirin**, supra, at 25 ("We are not here concerned with any question of the guilt or innocence of petitioners"). Military courts are not courts of record ...

The extent of the showing required of the Government in these cases is a matter to be determined. We need not explore it further at this stage. We do hold that when the judicial power to issue habeas corpus properly is invoked the judicial officer must have adequate authority to make a determination in light of the relevant law and facts and to formulate and issue appropriate orders for relief, including, if necessary, an order directing the prisoner's release.

C

We now consider whether the DTA allows the Court of Appeals to conduct a proceeding meeting these standards ... We cannot ignore the text and purpose of a statute in order to save it.

The DTA does not explicitly empower the Court of Appeals to order the applicant in a DTA review proceeding released should the court find that the standards and procedures used at his CSRT hearing were insufficient to justify detention. This is troubling. Yet, for present purposes, we can assume congressional silence permits a constitutionally required remedy. In that case it would be possible to hold that a remedy of release is impliedly provided for. The DTA might be read, furthermore, to allow the petitioners to assert most, if not all, of the legal claims they seek to advance, including their most basic claim: that the President has no authority under the AUMF to detain them indefinitely. (Whether the President has such authority turns on whether the AUMF authorizes—and the Constitution permits—the indefinite detention of "enemy combatants" as the Department of Defense defines that term. Thus a challenge to the President's authority to detain is, in essence, a challenge to the Department's definition of enemy combatant, a "standard" used by the CSRTs in petitioners' cases.) ...

The absence of a release remedy and specific language allowing AUMF challenges are not the only constitutional infirmities from which the statute potentially suffers, however. The more difficult question is whether the DTA permits the Court of Appeals to make requisite findings of fact. The DTA enables petitioners to request "review" of their CSRT determination in the Court of Appeals, DTA §1005(e)(2)(B)(i), 119 Stat. 2742; but the "Scope of Review" provision confines the Court of Appeals' role to reviewing whether the CSRT followed the "standards and procedures" issued by the Department of Defense and assessing whether those "standards and procedures" are lawful. Among these standards is "the requirement that the conclusion of the Tribunal be supported by a preponderance of the evidence ... allowing a rebuttable presumption in favor of the Government's evidence." §1005(e)(C)(i).

Assuming the DTA can be construed to allow the Court of Appeals to review or correct the CSRT's factual determinations, as opposed to merely certifying that the tribunal applied the correct standard of proof, we see no way to construe the statute to allow what is also constitutionally required in this context: an opportunity for the detainee to present relevant exculpatory evidence that was not made part of the record in the earlier proceedings.

On its face the statute allows the Court of Appeals to consider no evidence outside the CSRT record ... the DTA review proceeding falls short of being a constitutionally adequate substitute, for the detainee still would have no opportunity to present evidence discovered after the CSRT proceedings concluded.

Under the DTA the Court of Appeals has the power to review CSRT determinations by assessing the legality of standards and procedures. This implies the power to inquire into what happened at the CSRT hearing and, perhaps, to remedy certain deficiencies in that proceeding. But should the Court of Appeals determine that the CSRT followed appropriate and lawful standards and procedures, it will have reached the limits of its jurisdiction. There is no language in the DTA that can be construed to allow the Court of Appeals to admit and consider newly discovered evidence that could not have been made part of the CSRT record because it was unavailable to either the Government or the detainee when the CSRT made its findings. This evidence, however, may be critical to the detainee's argument that he is not an enemy combatant and there is no cause to detain him.

***

By foreclosing consideration of evidence not presented or reasonably available to the detainee at the CSRT proceedings, the DTA disadvantages the detainee by limiting the scope of collateral review to a record that may not be accurate or complete. In other contexts, e.g., in post-trial habeas cases where the prisoner already has had a full and fair opportunity to develop the factual predicate of his claims, similar limitations on the scope of habeas review may be appropriate. In this context, however, where the underlying detention proceedings lack the necessary adversarial character, the detainee cannot be held responsible for all deficiencies in the record.

***

To hold that the detainees at Guantanamo may, under the DTA, challenge the President's legal authority to detain them, contest the CSRT's findings of fact, supplement the record on review with exculpatory evidence, and request an order of release would come close to reinstating the §2241 habeas corpus process Congress sought to deny them. The language of the statute, read in light of Congress' reasons for enacting it, cannot bear this interpretation. Petitioners have met their burden of establishing that the DTA review process is, on its face, an inadequate substitute for habeas corpus.

Although we do not hold that an adequate substitute must duplicate §2241 in all respects, it suffices that the Government has not established that the detainees' access to the statutory review provisions at issue is an adequate substitute for the writ of habeas corpus. MCA §7 thus effects an unconstitutional suspension of the writ. In view of our holding we need not discuss the reach of the writ with respect to claims of unlawful conditions of treatment or confinement.

VI
A

In light of our conclusion that there is no jurisdictional bar to the District Court's entertaining petitioners' claims the question remains whether there are prudential barriers to habeas corpus review under these circumstances.

The Government argues petitioners must seek review of their CSRT determinations in the Court of Appeals before they can proceed with their habeas corpus actions in the District Court. As noted earlier, in other contexts and for prudential reasons this Court has required exhaustion of alternative remedies before a prisoner can seek federal habeas relief. Most of these cases were brought by prisoners in state custody, e.g., **Ex parte Royall**, 117 U. S. 241, and thus involved federalism concerns that are not relevant here. But we have extended this rule to require defendants in courts-martial to exhaust their military appeals before proceeding with a federal habeas corpus action. See **Schlesinger**, 420 U. S., at 758.

The real risks, the real threats, of terrorist attacks are constant and not likely soon to abate. The ways to disrupt our life and laws are so many and unforeseen that the Court should not attempt even some general catalogue of crises that might occur. Certain principles are apparent, however. Practical considerations and exigent circumstances inform the definition and reach of the law's writs, including habeas corpus. The cases and our tradition reflect this precept.

In cases involving foreign citizens detained abroad by the Executive, it likely would be both an impractical and unprecedented extension of judicial power to assume that habeas corpus would be available at the moment the prisoner is taken into custody. If and when habeas corpus jurisdiction applies, as it does in these cases, then proper deference can be accorded to reasonable procedures for screening and initial detention under lawful and proper conditions of confinement and treatment for a reasonable period of time. Domestic exigencies, furthermore, might also impose such onerous burdens on the Government that here, too, the Judicial Branch would be required to devise sensible rules for staying habeas corpus proceedings until the Government can comply with its requirements in a responsible way. Cf. **Ex parte Milligan**, 4 Wall., at 127 ("If, in foreign invasion or civil war, the courts are actually closed, and it is impossible to administer criminal justice according to law, *then*, on the theatre of active military operations, where war really prevails, there is a necessity to furnish a substitute for the civil authority, thus overthrown, to preserve the safety of the army and society; and as no power is left but the military, it is allowed to govern by martial rule until the laws can have their free course"). Here, as is true with detainees apprehended abroad, a relevant consideration in determining the courts' role is whether there are suitable alternative processes in place to protect against the arbitrary exercise of governmental power.

The cases before us, however, do not involve detainees who have been held for a short period of time while awaiting their CSRT determinations. Were that the case, or were it probable that the Court of Appeals could complete a prompt review of their applications, the case for requiring temporary abstention or exhaustion of alternative remedies would be much stronger. These qualifications no longer pertain here. In some of these cases six years have elapsed without the judicial oversight that habeas corpus or an adequate substitute demands. And there has been no showing that the Executive faces such onerous burdens that it cannot respond to habeas corpus actions. To require these detainees to complete DTA review before proceeding with their habeas corpus actions would be to require additional months, if not years, of delay. The first DTA review applications were filed over a year ago, but no decisions on the merits have been issued. While some delay in fashioning new procedures is unavoidable, the costs of delay can no longer be borne by those who are held in custody. The detainees in these cases are entitled to a prompt habeas corpus hearing.

Our decision today holds only that the petitioners before us are entitled to seek the writ; that the DTA review procedures are an inadequate substitute for habeas corpus; and that the petitioners in these cases need not exhaust the review procedures in the Court of Appeals before proceeding with their habeas actions in the District Court. The only law we identify as unconstitutional is MCA §7, 28 U. S. C. A. §2241(e) (Supp. 2007). Accordingly, both the DTA and the CSRT process remain intact. Our holding with regard to exhaustion should not be read to imply that a habeas court should intervene the moment an enemy combatant steps foot in a territory where the writ runs. The Executive is entitled to a reasonable period of time to determine a detainee's status before a court entertains that detainee's habeas corpus petition. The CSRT process is the mechanism Congress and the President set up to deal with these issues. Except in cases of undue delay, federal courts should refrain from entertaining an enemy combatant's habeas corpus petition at least until after the Department, acting via the CSRT, has had a chance to review his status.

B

Although we hold that the DTA is not an adequate and effective substitute for habeas corpus, it does not follow that a habeas corpus court may disregard the dangers the detention in these cases was intended to prevent ... Certain accommodations can be made to reduce the burden habeas corpus proceedings will place on the military without impermissibly diluting the protections of the writ.

In the DTA Congress sought to consolidate review of petitioners' claims in the Court of Appeals. Channeling future cases to one district court would no doubt reduce administrative burdens on the Government. This is a legitimate objective that might be advanced even without an amendment to §2241. If, in a future case, a detainee files a habeas petition in another judicial district in which a proper respondent can be served, see **Rumsfeld v. Padilla**, 542 U. S. 426, 435-436 (2004), the Government can move for change of venue to the court that will hear these petitioners' cases, the United States District Court for the District of Columbia. See 28 U.S.C. §1404(a); **Braden v. 30th Judicial Circuit Court of Ky.**, 410 U. S. 484, 499, n. 15 (1973).

Another of Congress' reasons for vesting exclusive jurisdiction in the Court of Appeals, perhaps, was to avoid the widespread dissemination of classified information. The Government has raised similar concerns here and elsewhere. See Brief for Respondents 55-56; **Bismullah** Pet. 30. We make no attempt to anticipate all of the evidentiary and access-to-counsel issues that will arise during the course of the detainees' habeas corpus proceedings. We recognize, however, that the Government has a legitimate interest in protecting sources and methods of intelligence gathering; and we expect that the District Court will use its discretion to accommodate this interest to the greatest extent possible. Cf. **United States v. Reynolds**, 345 U. S. 1, 10 (1953) (recognizing an evidentiary privilege in a civil damages case where "there is a reasonable danger that compulsion of the evidence will expose military matters which, in the interest of national security, should not be divulged").

These and the other remaining questions are within the expertise and competence of the District Court to address in the first instance.

***

In considering both the procedural and substantive standards used to impose detention to prevent acts of terrorism, proper deference must be accorded to the political branches. See **United States v. Curtiss-Wright Export Corp.**, 299 U. S. 304, 320 (1936). Unlike the President and some designated Members of Congress, neither the Members of this Court nor most federal judges begin the day with briefings that may describe new and serious threats to our Nation and its people. The law must accord the Executive substantial authority to apprehend and detain those who pose a real danger to our security.

Officials charged with daily operational responsibility for our security may consider a judicial discourse on the history of the Habeas Corpus Act of 1679 and like matters to be far removed from the Nation's present, urgent concerns. Established legal doctrine, however, must be consulted for its teaching. Remote in time it may be; irrelevant to the present it is not. Security depends upon a sophisticated intelligence apparatus and the ability of our Armed Forces to act and to interdict. There are further considerations, however. Security subsists, too, in fidelity to freedom's first principles. Chief among these are freedom from arbitrary and unlawful restraint and the personal liberty that is secured by adherence to the separation of powers. It is from these principles that the judicial authority to consider petitions for habeas corpus relief derives.

Our opinion does not undermine the Executive's powers as Commander in Chief. On the contrary, the exercise of those powers is vindicated, not eroded, when confirmed by the Judicial Branch. Within the Constitution's separation-of-powers structure, few exercises of judicial power are as legitimate or as necessary as the responsibility to hear challenges to the authority of the Executive to imprison a person. Some of these petitioners have been in custody for six years with no definitive judicial determination as to the legality of their detention. Their access to the writ is a necessity to determine the lawfulness of their status, even if, in the end, they do not obtain the relief they seek.

Because our Nation's past military conflicts have been of limited duration, it has been possible to leave the outer boundaries of war powers undefined. If, as some fear, terrorism continues to pose dangerous threats to us for years to come, the Court might not have this luxury. This result is not inevitable, however. The political branches, consistent with their independent obligations to interpret and uphold the Constitution, can engage in a genuine debate about how best to preserve constitutional values while protecting the Nation from terrorism. Cf. **Hamdan**, 548 U. S., at 636 (Breyer, J., concurring) ("[J]udicial insistence upon that consultation does not weaken our Nation's ability to deal with danger. To the contrary, that insistence strengthens the Nation's ability to determine—through democratic means--how best to do so").

It bears repeating that our opinion does not address the content of the law that governs petitioners' detention. That is a matter yet to be determined. We hold that petitioners may invoke the fundamental procedural protections of habeas corpus. The laws and Constitution are designed to survive, and remain in force, in extraordinary times. Liberty and security can be reconciled; and in our system they are reconciled within the framework of the law. The Framers decided that habeas corpus, a right of first importance, must be a part of that framework, a part of that law.

The determination by the Court of Appeals that the Suspension Clause and its protections are inapplicable to petitioners was in error. The judgment of the Court of Appeals is reversed. The cases are remanded to the Court of Appeals with instructions that it remand the cases to the District Court for proceedings consistent with this opinion.

It is so ordered.

Commentary and Questions

1. *Hamdi v. Rumsfeld* was decided by the Supreme Court the same day as *Rasul v. Bush*. As discussed in Chapter 3, *Rasul* found that non-citizen detainees held at Guantanamo Bay were within the territorial jurisdiction of the United States and therefore able to secure habeas review. The *Hamdi* opinion, though recognizing the power and authority of the president in defending national security, held that U.S. citizens had a fundamental right to *"be free from involuntary confinement."* Due process is, according to the Court, not only an American ideal but a valued privilege that comes with American citizenship. A basic Fifth Amendment guarantee is that no one may be deprived of liberty without due process of law. This guarantee extends to citizens and non-citizens under the Constitution. Included within the Fifth Amendment due process right is the right for the detained to be brought before a magistrate and for the detained to have the right to counsel to challenge the detention and request bail. *Hamdi* was additional judicial recognition of this important principle. It required the government put into practice this important guarantee even for those it considered the most

heinous of prisoners. But even the designation of Yaser Hamdi was at issue in the case because he challenged his status as "enemy combatant" and sought review of the determination made by the government. Justice O'Connor's plurality opinion considered the arguments of the government and that of *Hamdi* pertaining to the review of the "enemy combatant" determination. How did Justice O'Connor address this particular issue? What did the *Hamdi* Court hold with regard to presidential power to detain individuals, including American citizens, under the Authorization to Use Military Force (AUMF)? What did the Court hold regarding the length of detention of U.S. citizens?

2. As a response to the Court's decisions in *Hamdi* and *Rasul* Congress passed the Detainee Treatment Act of 2005, 42 USC §2000dd, hereinafter referred to as DTA. The DTA, established as Public Law 198-148, was made a part of the Department of Defense Emergency Supplemental Appropriations to Address Hurricanes in the Gulf of Mexico and Pandemic Influenza Act, and contained within Title X Matters Relating to Detainees. Section 1005 of the DTA contains the "Procedures for Status Review of Detainees Outside of the United States" but specifically references in subdivision (a) those detainees held in Guantanamo Bay, Cuba, Afghanistan and Iraq. A significant part of the DTA can be found in section (e) which altered the federal habeas corpus statute:

> *(e) Judicial Review of Detention of Enemy Combatants.*
> *(1) In General.—Section 2241 of title 28, United States Code, is amended by adding at the end the following:*
> *"(e) Except as provided in section 1005 of the Detainee Treatment Act of 2005, no court, justice, or judge shall have jurisdiction to hear or consider—*
> *"(1) an application for a writ of habeas corpus filed by or on behalf of an alien detained by the Department of Defense at Guantanamo Bay, Cuba; or*
> *"(2) any other action against the United States or its agents relating to any aspect of the detention by the Department of Defense of an alien at Guantanamo Bay, Cuba, who—*
> *"(A) is currently in military custody; or*
> *"(B) has been determined by the United States Court of Appeals for the District of Columbia Circuit in accordance with the procedures set forth in section 1005(e) of the Detainee Treatment Act of 2005 to have been properly detained as an enemy combatant."*

The DTA severely limited the ability of aliens in U.S. military custody to challenge their detentions in the wake of *Hamdi* and *Rasul*. In §1005(e)(2) the DTA additionally named the U.S. Court of Appeals for the District of Columbia Circuit as the exclusive court holding jurisdiction to hear detainee claims and further limit detainee claims and scope of court review. These sections stripped the federal courts of habeas corpus review and limited appellate review of Combatant Status Review

Tribunals (CSRT) and military commissions. The Court in *Hamdan v. Rumsfeld* rejected the government's jurisdictional claims based on the DTA; it also noted that neither the AUMF nor the DTA expanded presidential authority to convene military commissions.

3. *Hamdan v. Rumsfeld* determined that the Combatant Status Review Tribunals set up by the Department of Defense were unconstitutional. Military commissions, as established by the Bush administration, were without constitutional authority and not a competent tribunal under the Geneva Convention according to the Court. The Military Commissions Act of 2006[19] was drafted after the *Hamdan* decision in order to *"try alien unlawful enemy combatants engaged in hostilities against the United States for violations of the law of war and other offenses triable by military commission."*[20] The Military Commissions Act (MCA) gave the president power to convene the commissions, established procedures for the tribunals, and dispensed with several procedural protections found in the Uniform Code of Military Justice (UCMJ), such as the right to speedy trial, and rules relating to compulsory self-incrimination.[21] In addition, the MCA specifically provided that *"[N]o alien unlawful enemy combatant subject to trial by military commission under this chapter may invoke the Geneva Conventions as a source of rights."*[22] Congress' enactment of the MCA resulted in far-ranging criticism which excoriated the text of the Act.[23] The U.S. Supreme Court would eventually find the MCA's restriction of habeas corpus relief for detainees unconstitutional in *Boumediene v. Bush.*

4. In *Boumedienne* the Court held the Detainee Treatment Act of 2005 did not provide a proper substitute for habeas corpus relief. The deficiencies of the CSRT were raised by the petitioner with a core criticism being the inability to challenge determinations that an individual is an enemy combatant. In MCA section 948a(1)(ii) one of the definitions of unlawful enemy combatant is *"a person who, before, on, or after the date of the enactment of the Military Commissions Act of 2006, has been determined to be an unlawful enemy combatant by a Combatant Status Review Tribunal or another competent tribunal established under the authority of the President or the Secretary of Defense."* Would this be considered an ex post facto law in violation of the Fifth Amendment? Why or why not?

5. What did Justice Kennedy say in *Boumedienne* regarding the relative powers of the different branches in preventing terrorism? How does the role of the judiciary factor into the discussion as outlined by Justice Kennedy?

6. Two dissenting opinions were written in response to the *Hamdi* plurality opinion of Justice O'Connor. One written by Justice Scalia and joined by Justice Stevens, the other written by Justice Thomas, stood at opposite ends of the decisional divide. Justice Scalia's dissent stated that the role of the Court in reviewing Hamdi's petition was a matter of determining the lawfulness of his detention, not providing that he be given a "meaningful review," a process that he was originally denied and for which he now complains. The Suspension Clause, Article I §9 clause 2, is the only provision

preventing judicial review of Executive decisions in conjunction with detention related to the war-making powers. Absent an express Congressional authorization suspending the writ of habeas corpus Justice Scalia wrote of the following options for the President: *"Hamdi is entitled to a habeas decree requiring his release unless (1) criminal proceedings are promptly brought, or (2) Congress has suspended the writ of habeas corpus."*[24] To Scalia the choice was clear and the Court was exhibiting too much deference to the Executive. Perhaps more pointedly it was avoiding a clear constitutional duty: *"Many think it not only inevitable but entirely proper that liberty give way to security in times of national crisis—that, at the extremes of military exigency, inter arma silent leges. Whatever the general merits of the view that war silences law or modulates its voice, that view has no place in the interpretation and application of a Constitution designed precisely to confront war and, in a manner that accords with democratic principles, to accommodate it. Because the Court has proceeded to meet the current emergency in a manner the Constitution does not envision ..."*[25]

Justice Thomas viewed the argument through the lens of the government and sided with the exercise of presidential power in its war-making function. He wrote in dissent: *"The Founders intended that the President have primary responsibility—along with the necessary power—to protect the national security and to conduct the Nation's foreign relations. They did so principally because the structural advantages of a unitary Executive are essential in these domains ... These structural advantages are most important in the national-security and foreign-affairs contexts ... This Court has long recognized these features and has accordingly held that the President has constitutional authority to protect the national security and that this authority carries with it broad discretion."*[26] Justice Thomas's position was that the Court should have denied Hamdi's petition and upheld the decision of the Fourth Circuit Court of Appeals. Hamdi's liberty interest, he wrote, must give way to national security interests.[27]

These are two very different interpretations of the Constitution as well as Court precedent (both Justices cited *Ex Parte Quirin* and *Ex Parte Milligan* among other Supreme Court cases) and each takes an absolutist approach to the issue. Clearly there was no broad consensus in the Court's plurality opinion. Later in *Boumediene v. Bush*, Justice Scalia would dissent again and this time be joined by Justice Thomas along with Chief Justice Roberts and Justice Alito. In his *Boumediene* dissent Justice Scalia found the provisions of the Detainee Treatment Act to fulfill the review requirements guaranteed in habeas corpus review. Thus, his prior Suspension Clause concern voiced in his *Hamdi* dissent was satisfied by the DTA review process and the subsequent provisions of the Military Commissions Act.

7. *Johnson v. Eisentrager*, 339 U.S. 763 (1950) was a post-World War II case wherein twenty-one German soldiers were arrested for war crimes resulting from their collaboration with Japan after the formal surrender of Germany but prior to the end of the U.S. war with Japan. The formal German surrender prevented German troops from any continued military activity against the United States. The German prisoners were convicted by a U.S.

military tribunal in China and imprisoned in the American-occupied part of Germany. None of the German soldiers claimed American citizenship and at no time were they ever in U.S. sovereign territory. They sought habeas review in the District of Columbia District Court wherein they alleged violation of U.S. Constitution Articles I and II, the Fifth Amendment, and the Geneva Convention. The issue as presented by Justice Jackson at the opening of his six-member majority opinion was *"one of jurisdiction of civil courts of the United States vis-a-vis military authorities in dealing with enemy aliens overseas."*[28] The *Eisentrager* Court went on to find that non-resident enemy aliens have no access to American courts in wartime. In the more recent case of *Al-Maqaleh v. Gates*, 605 F.3d 84 (D.C. Cir., 2010) the District of Columbia Circuit Court of Appeals held that three detainees at Bagram Air Force Base in Afghanistan were also to be denied access to habeas corpus relief in U.S. courts. The *Boumedienne* Court created a three-factor test for determining the reach of the Suspension Clause: 1) the citizenship and status of the detainee and the adequacy of the process through which that status determination was made; 2) the nature of the sites where apprehension and then detention took place; and 3) the practical obstacles inherent in resolving the prisoner's entitlement to the writ.[29] Analyzing each of the factors in relation to the Bagram petitioners the D.C. Circuit Court found that the Bagram petitioners were situated differently than their Guantanamo counterparts. Non-citizenship the court said was not alone a factor to deny relief. Focusing on the location of apprehension and detention the circuit court noted that while the three detainees were captured separately in Afghanistan, Pakistan, and Thailand they were detained at Bagram and the United States does not exercise de facto sovereignty over Bagram as it does at Guantanamo. Lastly, in assessing the third factor, Afghanistan remained an active theater of war, which presented several problems unique to it. Echoing the Court in *Eisentrager* the D.C. Circuit said *"the writ does not extend to the Bagram confinement in an active theater of war in a territory under neither the de facto or de jure sovereignty of the United States and within the territory of another de jure sovereign."*[30]

Endnotes

1   327 U.S. 304, 323 (1946).

2   338 U.S. 197 (1948).

3   327 U.S. 759 (1946).

4   338 U.S. at 198.

5   Id at 204.

6   327 U.S. 759, 760-761.

7   542 U.S. at 455 (2004).

8   547 U.S. at (2006).

9   See, *Munaf v. Geren*, 553 U.S. 674 (2008).

10   Id at 682.

11   Id.

12   Id.

13   Id at 683.

14   Id.

15   Id at 688.

16   Id.

17   See, Id at 694, 695, where the Court references the following two cases: *Schooner Exchange v. McFaddon*, 7 Cranch 116, 136 (1812) ("[t]he jurisdiction of the nation within its own territory is necessarily exclusive and absolute"), and *Wilson v. Girard*, 354 U.S. 524, 529 (1957), ("A sovereign nation has exclusive jurisdiction to punish offenses against its laws committed within its borders, unless it expressly or impliedly consents to surrender its jurisdiction.").

18   Id at 702.

19   Public Law 109-366, October 17, 2006.

20   Section 948b(a).

21   Section 948b(d).

22   Section 948b(g).

23   See eg., Center for Constitutional Rights. (October , 17 2006). *Military Commissions Act of 2006*. Retrieved from http://ccrjustice.org/files/report_MCA.pdf.

24   542 U.S. at 573.

25   Id at 579.

26   Id at 580, 581.

27   Id.

28   339 U.S. at 765.

[29]   553 U.S. at 766.

[30]   605 F.3d at 98.

Chapter Five
GOVERNMENTAL PRIVILEGE & IMMUNITY

The Elements of Privilege from Disclosure under the Law

There are a number of privileges that exist under the common law precluding public disclosure of communications between individuals. The basic privileges relate to confidential communications between attorney-client, physician-patient, priest-penitent, and husband-wife. These basic privileges have been extended in some jurisdictions to include social worker-client, psychologist-patient, parent-child, rape crisis counselor-victim, and accountant-client privileges as well as a limited news reporter privilege. Public policy rationales guide the existence of the privileges with the basic characterization being that the privilege against compelled disclosure is necessary to foster complete and truthful communication between the parties. A physician could not adequately treat a patient if the patient held back relevant information for fear of embarrassing disclosures. Similarly, an attorney must rely on the full cooperation and disclosure of the client to prepare a defense or prosecute a lawsuit. The legal definition of privilege is quite extensive but it generally refers to "a particular benefit or advantage enjoyed by a person, company or class of persons not available to other individuals" or an "exemption," "extraordinary power," or "immunity" held by a person "beyond the course of law"; it is "that which releases one from performance of a duty of obligation, or exempts one from a liability which he would otherwise be required to perform."[1] The existence of a privilege of confidentiality between attorney-client has existed in the common law since at least the 16th century.[2] Over time and custom the legal recognition of other privileges developed. Even the prohibition of compelling testimony against oneself in a criminal proceeding, found in the Fifth Amendment, had its genesis several centuries prior to its modern evolution.[3] The above cited privileges are at least vaguely familiar if not actually well-known to the average layperson. Yet, there exist other privileges that inure to the benefit of the government but are not as readily known. The law enforcement privilege, the national security privilege and the executive privilege are additional privileges from disclosure which have potentially far more impact on civil litigation and individual liberties than the aforementioned privileges. And yet it is these same privileges that have found their home in the language of the law centuries beforehand. In Chapter 7, Book 1 of William Blackstone's *Commentaries on the Laws of England* the prerogatives of the king are laid out in detail emanating as they do from the common law of England. These prerogatives extend to the king with regard to his royal character and royal authority, *"necessary to secure reverence to his person, obedience to his commands ... without all of which it is impossible to maintain the executive power in due independence and vigour."*[4] The superiority of the sovereign over the citizen, even in a free and democratic republic, is deeply imbedded in Anglo-American law. Within our own system of government we have experienced what Alexander Hamilton referred to as the *"salutary boundary between power and privilege"* which *"combines the energy of government with the security of private rights."*[5]

197

The Federal Rules of Evidence place the roots of the evidentiary privilege within the common law.[6] This leaves the courts open to the development and recognition of various privileges not specifically found in statutory law or construed through the Constitution.[7] The most controversial of the privileges in recent years has been the invocation of law enforcement privilege, national security privilege, and executive privilege, specifically for the non-disclosure shield the privileges provide to the government and government officials.

The law enforcement privilege, also referred to as the law enforcement investigatory privilege, serves to protect law enforcement from the disclosure of information that would impede or destroy an agency's efforts in investigating criminal offenses.[8] This prohibition from disclosure extends to testimonial as well as documentary evidence.[9] It is a conditional privilege that must be asserted by the head of the agency or the person within the agency designated with the responsibility. In raising the privilege the agency must particularly allege the information sought to be protected from disclosure and the justification for the information being within the scope of the privilege.[10] The conditional aspect of the privilege relates to the fact that a court upon review may require the information to be disclosed; further the claimed privilege, if non-disclosure is granted, may only last until the investigation is closed. Therefore the privilege may merely act as delay rather than a complete prohibition from disclosure. Even in the context of protecting the identity of a government informer the U.S. Supreme Court has said the disclosure may be necessary when the disclosure of the informer's identity or the contents of his communication is relevant and helpful to the defense of an accused or essential to a fair trial.[11] Arguments against the law enforcement privilege have asserted that the original intent of the privilege was only to protect against the disclosure of the identities of government informants; however, courts have found the privilege to extend to overall enforcement and investigative efforts of a law enforcement agency.[12] Although it is a conditional common law privilege, the law enforcement privilege has found codification at the state and federal levels within Freedom of Information statutes. The federal statute 5 U.S.C. §552(b)(7) provides exceptions to disclosure under the Freedom of Information Act (FOIA) for "records or information compiled for law enforcement purposes." This exception, however, applies only to six enumerated qualifications based on production of the information: 1) it would interfere with law enforcement proceedings; 2) it would deprive a person of a fair trial or impartial adjudication; 3) it would interfere with privacy rights; 4) it would disclose the identity of a confidential source; 5) it would disclose law enforcement procedures and techniques used in investigations; 6) it would endanger the life or safety of an individual. The Illinois freedom of information statute, 5 ILCS §140/7(d)(i), and New York State Public Officers Law §87(2)(e) provide similar protection from disclosure. For litigants against the government or government officials the exercise of the law enforcement privilege can have significant impact upon civil cases seeking damages for wrongdoing. The overall result may be to require dismissal of a pending action because a lack of proof that could otherwise be provided in document or witness discovery from the government entity. In terms of litigation the decision whether or not to allow disclosure is left to the court and requires a careful balancing of the litigant's demand for disclosure of the material against the government's need to maintain confidentiality and secrecy as to its investigative methods. Courts will often apply what is referred to as the *Frankenhauser* factors in assessing this balance and arriving at a determination regarding disclosure. These factors for consideration are:

(1) the extent to which disclosure will thwart governmental processes by discouraging citizens from giving the government information;

(2) the impact upon persons who have given information of having their identities disclosed;

(3) the degree to which governmental self-evaluation and consequent program improvement will be chilled by disclosure;

(4) whether the information sought is factual data or evaluative summary;

(5) whether the party seeking discovery is an actual or potential defendant in any criminal proceeding either pending or reasonably likely to follow from the incident in question;

(6) whether the police investigation has been completed;

(7) whether any interdepartmental disciplinary proceedings have arisen or may arise from the investigation;

(8) whether the plaintiff's suit is non-frivolous and brought in good faith;

(9) whether the information sought is available through other discovery or from other sources;

(10) the importance of the information sought to the plaintiff's case.[13]

The law enforcement privilege is a conditional or qualified privilege that can be frustrating to civil litigants asserting government misconduct; however, it is a narrower privilege than that which can be asserted under a state secrets or executive privilege. Both of these privileges can be claimed, and often are claimed, in the interest of national security thereby foreclosing any disclosure in civil or criminal cases. A general liberality with respect to disclosure exists within the American judicial system but these privileges work against such open disclosure. The issue to contend with then is what effect the assertion of these privileges has upon the due process rights of litigants claiming harm from the government? Further still, what recourse is available to those individuals whose injury resulted from government policy related to national security matters?

Totten v. United States
92 U.S. 105 (1875)

Mr. Justice Field delivered the opinion of the Court.

This case comes before us on appeal from the Court of Claims. The action was brought to recover compensation for services alleged to have been rendered by the claimant's intestate, William A. Lloyd, under a contract with President Lincoln, made in July, 1861, by which he was to proceed south and ascertain the number of troops stationed at different points in the insurrectionary states, procure plans of forts and fortifications, and gain such other information as might be beneficial to the government of the United States, and report the facts to the President; for which services he was to be paid $200 a month.

The Court of Claims finds that Lloyd proceeded under the contract within the rebel lines and remained there during the entire period of the war, collecting and from time to time transmitting information to the President, and that upon the close of the war he was only reimbursed his expenses. But the court, being equally divided in opinion as to the authority of the President to bind the United States by the contract in question, decided, for the purposes of an appeal, against the claim and dismissed the petition.

We have no difficulty at to the authority of the President in the matter. He was undoubtedly authorized during the war, as commander-in-chief of the armies of the United States, to employ secret agents to enter the rebel lines and obtain information respecting the strength, resources, and movements of the enemy, and contracts to compensate such agents are so far binding upon the government as to render it lawful for the President to direct payment of the amount stipulated out of the contingent fund under his control. Our objection is not to the contract, but to the action upon it in the Court of Claims. The service stipulated by the contract was a secret service; the information sought was to be obtained clandestinely, and was to be communicated privately; the employment and the service were to be equally concealed. Both employer and agent must have understood that the lips of the other were to be forever sealed respecting the relation of either to the matter. This condition of the engagement was implied from the nature of the employment, and is implied in all secret employments of the government in time of war or upon matters affecting our foreign relations where a disclosure of the service might compromise or embarrass our government in its public duties or endanger the person or injure the character of the agent. If upon contracts of such a nature an action against the government could be maintained in the Court of Claims whenever an agent should deem himself entitled to greater or different compensation than that awarded to him, the whole service in any case, and the manner of its discharge, with the details of dealings with individuals and officers, might be exposed, to the serious detriment of the public. A secret service, with liability to publicity in this way, would be impossible, and, as such services are sometimes indispensable to the government, its agents in those services must look for their compensation to the contingent fund of the department employing them and to such allowance from it as those who dispense that fund may award. The secrecy which such contracts impose precludes any action for their enforcement. The publicity produced by an action would itself be a breach of a contract of that kind, and thus defeat a recovery.

It may be stated as a general principle that public policy forbids the maintenance of any suit in a court of justice the trial of which would inevitably lead to the disclosure of matters which the law itself regards as confidential and respecting which it will not allow the confidence to be violated. On this principle, suits cannot be maintained which would require a disclosure of the confidences of the confessional, or those between husband and wife, or of communications by a client to his counsel for professional advice, or of a patient to his physician for a similar purpose. Much greater reason exists for the application of the principle to cases of contract for secret services with the government, as the existence of a contract of that kind is itself a fact not to be disclosed.

Judgment affirmed.

United States v. Reynolds
345 U.S. 1 (1953)

Mr. Chief Justice Vinson delivered the opinion of the Court.

These suits under the Tort Claims Act arise from the death of three civilians in the crash of a B-29 aircraft at Waycross, Georgia, on October 6, 1948. Because an important question of the Government's privilege to resist discovery is involved, we granted certiorari.

The aircraft had taken flight for the purpose of testing secret electronic equipment, with four civilian observers aboard. While aloft, fire broke out in one of the bomber's engines. Six of the nine crew members and three of the four civilian observers were killed in the crash.

The widows of the three deceased civilian observers brought consolidated suits against the United States. In the pretrial stages the plaintiffs moved, under Rule 34 of the Federal Rules of Civil Procedure, for production of the Air Force's official accident investigation report and the statements of the three surviving crew members, taken in connection with the official investigation. The Government moved to quash the motion, claiming that these matters were privileged against disclosure pursuant to Air Force regulations promulgated under R. S. 161. The District Judge sustained plaintiffs' motion, holding that good cause for production had been shown. The claim of privilege under R. S. 161 was rejected on the premise that the Tort Claims Act, in making the Government liable "in the same manner" as a private individual, had waived any privilege based upon executive control over governmental documents.

Shortly after this decision, the District Court received a letter from the Secretary of the Air Force, stating that "it has been determined that it would not be in the public interest to furnish this report ..." The court allowed a rehearing on its earlier order, and at the rehearing the Secretary of the Air Force filed a formal "Claim of Privilege." This document repeated the prior claim based generally on R. S. 161, and then stated that the Government further objected to production of the documents "for the reason that the aircraft in question, together with the personnel on board, were engaged in a highly secret mission of the Air Force." An affidavit of the Judge Advocate General, United States Air Force, was also filed with the court, which asserted that the demanded material could not be furnished "without seriously hampering national security, flying safety and the development of highly technical and secret military equipment." The same affidavit offered to produce the three surviving crew members, without cost, for examination by the plaintiffs. The witnesses would be allowed to refresh their memories from any statement made by them to the Air Force, and authorized to testify as to all matters except those of a "classified nature."

The District Court ordered the Government to produce the documents in order that the court might determine whether they contained privileged matter. The Government declined, so the court entered an order, under Rule 37(b)(2)(i), that the facts on the issue of negligence would be taken as established in plaintiffs' favor. After a hearing to determine damages, final judgment was entered for the plaintiffs. The Court of Appeals affirmed, both as to the showing of good cause for production of the documents, and as to the ultimate disposition of the case as a consequence of the Government's refusal to produce the documents.

We have had broad propositions pressed upon us for decision. On behalf of the Government it has been urged that the executive department heads have power to withhold any documents in their custody from judicial view if they deem it to be in the public interest. Respondents have asserted that the executive's power to withhold documents was waived by the Tort Claims Act. Both positions have constitutional overtones which we find it unnecessary to pass upon, there being a narrower ground for decision. *Touhy v. Ragen*, 340 U.S. 462 (1951); *Rescue Army v. Municipal Court of Los Angeles*, 331 U.S. 549, 574 -585 (1947).

The Tort Claims Act expressly makes the Federal Rules of Civil Procedure applicable to suits against the United States. The judgment in this case imposed liability upon the Government by operation of Rule 37, for refusal to produce documents under Rule 34. Since Rule 34 compels production only of matters "not privileged," the essential question is whether there was a valid claim of privilege under the Rule. We hold that there was, and that, therefore, the judgment below subjected the United States to liability on terms to which Congress did not consent by the Tort Claims Act.

We think it should be clear that the term "not privileged," as used in Rule 34, refers to "privileges" as that term is understood in the law of evidence. When the Secretary of the Air Force lodged his formal "Claim of Privilege," he attempted therein to invoke the privilege against revealing military secrets, a privilege which is well established in the law of evidence. The existence of the privilege is conceded by the court below, and, indeed, by the most outspoken critics of governmental claims to privilege.

Judicial experience with the privilege which protects military and state secrets has been limited in this country. English experience has been more extensive, but still relatively slight compared with other evidentiary privileges. Nevertheless, the principles which control the application of the privilege emerge quite clearly from the available precedents. The privilege belongs to the Government and must be asserted by it; it can neither be claimed nor waived by a private party. It is not to be lightly invoked. There must be a formal claim of privilege, lodged by the head of the department which has control over the matter, after actual personal consideration by that officer. The court itself must determine whether the circumstances are appropriate for the claim of privilege, and yet do so without forcing a disclosure of the very thing the privilege is designed to protect. The latter requirement is the only one which presents real difficulty. As to it, we find it helpful to draw upon judicial experience in dealing with an analogous privilege, the privilege against self-incrimination.

The privilege against self-incrimination presented the courts with a similar sort of problem. Too much judicial inquiry into the claim of privilege would force disclosure of the thing the privilege was meant to protect, while a complete abandonment of judicial control would lead to intolerable abuses. Indeed, in the earlier stages of judicial experience with the problem, both extremes were advocated, some saying that the bare assertion by the witness must be taken as conclusive, and others saying that the witness should be required to reveal the matter behind his claim of privilege to the judge for verification. Neither extreme prevailed, and a sound formula of compromise was developed. This formula received authoritative expression in this country as early as the Burr trial. There are differences in phraseology, but in substance it is agreed that the court must be satisfied from all the evidence and circumstances, and "from the implications of the question, in the setting in which it is asked, that a responsive answer to the question or an explanation of why it cannot be answered might be dangerous because injurious disclosure could result." **Hoffman v. United States**, 341 U.S. 479, 486–487 (1951). If the court is so satisfied, the claim of the privilege will be accepted without requiring further disclosure.

Regardless of how it is articulated, some like formula of compromise must be applied here. Judicial control over the evidence in a case cannot be abdicated to the caprice of executive officers. Yet we will not go so far as to say that the court may automatically require a complete disclosure to the judge before the claim of privilege will be accepted in any case. It may be possible to satisfy the court, from all the circumstances of the case, that there is a reasonable danger that compulsion of the evidence will expose military matters which, in the interest of national security, should not be divulged. When this is the case, the occasion for the privilege is appropriate, and the court should not jeopardize the security which the privilege is meant to protect by insisting upon an examination of the evidence, even by the judge alone, in chambers.

In the instant case we cannot escape judicial notice that this is a time of vigorous preparation for national defense. Experience in the past war has made it common knowledge that air power is one of the most potent weapons in our scheme of defense, and that newly developing electronic devices have greatly enhanced the effective use of air power. It is equally apparent that these electronic devices must be kept secret if their full military advantage is to be exploited in the national interests. On the record before the trial court it appeared that this accident occurred to a military plane which had gone aloft to test secret electronic equipment. Certainly there was a reasonable danger that the accident investigation report would contain references to the secret electronic equipment which was the primary concern of the mission.

Of course, even with this information before him, the trial judge was in no position to decide that the report was privileged until there had been a formal claim of privilege. Thus it was entirely proper to rule initially that petitioner had shown probable cause for discovery of the documents. Thereafter, when the formal claim of privilege was filed by the Secretary of the Air Force, under circumstances indicating a reasonable possibility that military secrets were involved, there was certainly a sufficient showing of privilege to cut off further demand for the documents on the showing of necessity for its compulsion that had then been made.

In each case, the showing of necessity which is made will determine how far the court should probe in satisfying itself that the occasion for invoking the privilege is appropriate. Where there is a strong showing of necessity, the claim of privilege should not be lightly accepted, but even the most compelling necessity cannot overcome the claim of privilege if the court is ultimately satisfied that military secrets are at stake. A fortiori, where necessity is dubious, a formal claim of privilege, made under the circumstances of this case, will have to prevail. Here, necessity was greatly minimized by an available alternative, which might have given respondents the evidence to make out their case without forcing a showdown on the claim of privilege. By their failure to pursue that alternative, respondents have posed the privilege question for decision with the formal claim of privilege set against a dubious showing of necessity.

There is nothing to suggest that the electronic equipment, in this case, had any causal connection with the accident. Therefore, it should be possible for respondents to adduce the essential facts as to causation without resort to material touching upon military secrets. Respondents were given a reasonable opportunity to do just that, when petitioner formally offered to make the surviving crew members available for examination. We think that offer should have been accepted.

Respondents have cited us to those cases in the criminal field, where it has been held that the Government can invoke its evidentiary privileges only at the price of letting the defendant go free. The rationale of the criminal cases is that, since the Government which prosecutes an accused also has the duty to see that justice is done, it is unconscionable to allow it to undertake prosecution and then invoke its governmental privileges to deprive the accused of anything which might be material to his defense. Such rationale has no application in a civil forum where the Government is not the moving party, but is a defendant only on terms to which it has consented.

The decision of the Court of Appeals is reversed and the case will be remanded to the District Court for further proceedings consistent with the views expressed in this opinion.

Reversed and remanded.

Tenet v. Doe
544 U.S. 1 (2005)

Mr. Chief Justice Rehnquist delivered the opinion of the Court.

In **Totten v. United States**, 92 U.S. 105 (1876), we held that public policy forbade a self-styled Civil War spy from suing the United States to enforce its obligations under their secret espionage agreement. Respondents here, alleged former Cold War spies, filed suit against the United States and the Director of the Central Intelligence Agency (CIA), asserting estoppel and due process claims for the CIA's alleged failure to provide respondents with the assistance it had promised in return for their espionage services. Finding that Totten did not bar respondents' suit, the District Court and the Court of Appeals for the Ninth Circuit held that the case could proceed. We reverse because this holding contravenes the longstanding rule, announced more than a century ago in Totten, prohibiting suits against the Government based on covert espionage agreements.

Respondents, a husband and wife who use the fictitious names John and Jane Doe, brought suit in the United States District Court for the Western District of Washington. According to respondents, they were formerly citizens of a foreign country that at the time was considered to be an enemy of the United States, and John Doe was a high-ranking diplomat for the country. After respondents expressed interest in defecting to the United States, CIA agents persuaded them to remain at their posts and conduct espionage for the United States for a specified period of time, promising in return that the Government "would arrange for travel to the United States and ensure financial and personal security for life." App. to Pet. for Cert. 122a. After "carrying out their end of the bargain" by completing years of purportedly high-risk, valuable espionage services, *id.*, at 123a, respondents defected (under new names and false backgrounds) and became United States citizens, with the Government's help. The CIA designated respondents with "PL – 110" status and began providing financial assistance and personal security.

With the CIA's help, respondent John Doe obtained employment in the State of Washington. As his salary increased, the CIA decreased his living stipend until, at some point, he agreed to a discontinuation of benefits while he was working. Years later, in 1997, John Doe was laid off after a corporate merger. Because John Doe was unable to find new employment as a result of CIA restrictions on the type of jobs he could hold, respondents contacted the CIA for financial assistance. Denied such assistance by the CIA, they claim they are unable to properly provide for themselves. Thus, they are faced with the prospect of either returning to their home country (where they say they face extreme sanctions), or remaining in the United States in their present circumstances.

Respondents assert, among other things, that the CIA violated their procedural and substantive due process rights by denying them support and by failing to provide them with a fair internal process for reviewing their claims. They seek injunctive relief ordering the CIA to resume monthly financial support pending further agency review. They also request a declaratory judgment stating that the CIA failed to provide a constitutionally adequate review process, and detailing the minimal process the agency must provide. Finally, respondents seek a mandamus order requiring the CIA to adopt agency procedures, to give them fair review, and to provide them with security and financial assistance.

The Government moved to dismiss the complaint under Federal Rules of Civil Procedure 12(b)(1) and 12(b)(6), principally on the ground that **Totten** bars respondents' suit. The District Court dismissed some of respondents' claims but denied the Government's **Totten** objection, ruling that the due process claims could proceed. 99 F. Supp. 2d 1284, 1289 – 1294 (WD Wash. 2000). After minimal discovery, the Government renewed its motion to dismiss based on **Totten**, and it moved for summary judgment on respondents' due process claims. Apparently construing the complaint as also raising an estoppel claim, the District Court denied the Government's motions, ruled again that **Totten** did not bar respondents' claims, and found there were genuine issues of material fact warranting a trial on respondents' due process and estoppel claims. App. to Pet. for Cert. 85a – 94a. The District Court certified an order for interlocutory appeal and stayed further proceedings pending appeal. *Id.*, at 79a – 83a.

A divided panel of the Court of Appeals for the Ninth Circuit affirmed in relevant part. 329 F.3d 1135 (2003). It reasoned that **Totten** posed no bar to reviewing some of respondents' claims and thus that the case could proceed to trial, subject to the Government's asserting the evidentiary state secrets privilege and the District Court's resolving that issue. 329 F.3d, at 1145–1155. Over dissent, the Court of Appeals denied a petition for rehearing en banc. 353 F.3d 1141 (CA9 2004). The Government sought review, and we granted certiorari. 542 U.S. ___ (2004).

***

We think the Court of Appeals was quite wrong in holding that **Totten** does not require dismissal of respondents' claims. That court, and respondents here, reasoned first that **Totten** developed merely a contract rule, prohibiting breach-of-contract claims seeking to enforce the terms of espionage agreements but not barring claims based on due process or estoppel theories. In fact, **Totten** was not so limited: "[P]ublic policy forbids the maintenance of *any suit* in a court of justice, the trial of which would inevitably lead to the disclosure of matters which the law itself regards as confidential." *Id.*, at 107 (emphasis added); see also *ibid.* ("The secrecy which such contracts impose precludes *any action* for their enforcement" (emphasis added)). No matter the clothing in which alleged spies dress their claims, **Totten** precludes judicial review in cases such as respondents' where success depends upon the existence of their secret espionage relationship with the Government.

Relying mainly on **United States v. Reynolds**, 345 U.S. 1 (1953), the Court of Appeals also claimed that **Totten** has been recast simply as an early expression of the evidentiary "state secrets" privilege, rather than a categorical bar to their claims. **Reynolds** involved a wrongful-death action brought under the Federal Tort Claims Act, 28 U.S.C. § 1346 by the widows of three civilians who died in the crash of a military B-29 aircraft. 345 U.S., at 2–3. In the course of discovery, the plaintiffs sought certain investigation-related documents, which the Government said contained "highly secret," privileged military information. *Id.*, at 3–4. We recognized "the privilege against revealing military secrets, a privilege which is well established in the law of evidence," *id.*, at 6–7, and we set out a balancing approach for courts to apply in resolving Government claims of privilege, *id.*, at 7–11. We ultimately concluded that the Government was entitled to the privilege in that case. *Id.*, at 10–12.

When invoking the "well established" state secrets privilege, we indeed looked to **Totten**. **Reynolds**, *supra*, at 7, n. 11 (citing **Totten**, *supra*, at 107). See also Brief for United States in **United States v. Reynolds**, O. T. 1952, No. 21, pp. 36, 42 (citing **Totten** in support of a military secrets privilege). But that in no way signaled our retreat from

Totten's broader holding that lawsuits premised on alleged espionage agreements are altogether forbidden. Indeed, our opinion in ***Reynolds*** refutes this very suggestion: Citing ***Totten*** as a case "where the very subject matter of the action, a contract to perform espionage, was a matter of state secret," we declared that such a case was to be "dismissed *on the pleadings without ever reaching the question of evidence,* since it was so obvious that the action should never prevail over the privilege." 345 U.S., at 11, n. 26

***

There is, in short, no basis for respondents' and the Court of Appeals' view that the ***Totten*** bar has been reduced to an example of the state secrets privilege.

***

We adhere to ***Totten***. The state secrets privilege and the more frequent use of *in camera* judicial proceedings simply cannot provide the absolute protection we found necessary in enunciating the ***Totten*** rule. The possibility that a suit may proceed and an espionage relationship may be revealed, if the state secrets privilege is found not to apply, is unacceptable: "Even a small chance that some court will order disclosure of a source's identity could well impair intelligence gathering and cause sources to 'close up like a clam.'" ***CIA v. Sims***, 471 U.S. 159, 175 (1985). Forcing the Government to litigate these claims would also make it vulnerable to "graymail," *i.e.,* individual lawsuits brought to induce the CIA to settle a case (or prevent its filing) out of fear that any effort to litigate the action would reveal classified information that may undermine ongoing covert operations. And requiring the Government to invoke the privilege on a case-by-case basis risks the perception that it is either confirming or denying relationships with individual plaintiffs.

The judgment of the Court of Appeals is reversed.

Commentary and Questions

1. The *Totten* case was the first U.S. Supreme Court decision to suggest a state secrets privilege. However, the recognition of such a privilege was first raised in a government objection during the treason trial of Aaron Burr to the proffered evidence of a letter to President Thomas Jefferson from General James Wilkinson.[14] Wilkinson, a friend and battle veteran alongside Burr during the Revolutionary War, entered into a plan with Burr in 1804 – 1806 to embark on a military expedition.[15] The expedition had at its roots a plan to annex the western part of the country from the rest of the United States. His chief co-conspirator, James Wilkinson, was the commanding General of the Army at the time and the governor of the Louisiana Territory.

Burr and Wilkinson were engaged in secret, coded communications relating to the conspiracy. At some point in the plan Wilkinson betrayed Burr and forwarded his communications with Burr to President Thomas Jefferson. Upon being made aware of the conspiracy and the plans of Burr, President Jefferson ordered Burr arrested and tried for treason. What ensued was an epic trial of the era and in history with Burr as defendant and Chief Justice John Marshall as the presiding trial judge. At the trial the defense attorneys for Burr sought to subpoena orders issued to U.S. land and naval forces for the apprehension of Burr as well as to obtain the letter from Wilkinson to Jefferson.[16] The subpoena duces tecum was issued to President Jefferson. The prosecution objected on several grounds including the propriety and enforceability of the service of a subpoena upon the president of the United States. An additional objection was based on the content of the letter from Wilkinson to Jefferson and the content of the military orders. Chief Justice Marshall's answer to the prosecution's objection alludes to both an executive privilege and a national security privilege:

"The second objection is, that the letter contains matter which ought not to be disclosed. That there may be matter, the production of which the court would not require, is certain; but, in a capital case, that the accused ought, in some form, to have the benefit of it, if it were really essential to his defence, is a position which the court would very reluctantly deny. It ought not to be believed that the department which superintends prosecutions in criminal cases, would be inclined to withhold it. What ought to be done under such circumstances presents a delicate question, the discussion of which, it is hoped, will never be rendered necessary in this country. At present it need only be said that the question does not occur at this time. There is certainly nothing before the court which shows that the letter in question contains any matter the disclosure of which would endanger the public safety. If it does contain such matter, the fact may appear before the disclosure is made. If it does contain any matter which it would be imprudent to disclose, which it is not the wish of the executive to disclose, such matter, if it be not immediately and essentially applicable to the point, will, of course, be suppressed. It is not easy to conceive that so much of the letter as relates to the conduct of the accused can be a subject of delicacy with the president. Everything of this kind, however, will have its due consideration on the return of the subpoena ... The propriety of requiring the answer to this letter is more questionable. It is alleged that it most probably communicates orders showing the situation of this country with Spain, which will be important on the misdemeanor. If it contain matter not essential to the defence, and the disclosure be unpleasant to the executive, it certainly ought not to be disclosed. This is a point which will appear on the return. The demand of the orders which have been issued, and which have been, as is alleged, published in the Natchez Gazette, is by no means unusual. Such documents have often been produced in the courts of the United States and the courts of England. If they contain matter interesting to the nation, the concealment of which is required by the public safety, that matter will

appear upon the return. If they do not, and are material, they may be exhibited."[17]

Burr would be acquitted by the jury, based largely on the standard for proving treason as laid out by Chief Justice Marshall in an earlier case, *Ex Parte Bollman and Ex Parte Swartwout* (see Chapter One), dealing with two other co-conspirators of Burr's. However, the justification for the withholding of relevant evidence due to the claim of executive or national security privilege, even though there may be adverse implications for a litigant, obtained a legal foundation.

2. *Totten* rested upon the Court's determination on jurisdictional grounds rather than the lower Court of Claims decision that President Lincoln did not have the authority to bind the United States to such a contract. The Court held that secret contracts for espionage services between a government official and another party should not by their nature be the subject of legal claims, especially as those matters pertain to wartime efforts or national security. Such claims are non-justiciable. This is an enduring concept rooted in separation of powers considerations. The judiciary is not appropriately suited to consider matters exclusively within the powers of the executive branch.[18] Extensive criticism has ensued within the last decade that the *Totten* doctrine has been broadened from its original holding and the state secrets privilege expanded to provide a protective shield for government behavior that allows it to operate in near secrecy.[19] John Henry Wigmore, the dean of American evidence law, recognized the existence of a state secrets privilege but wrote that a court that *"abdicates its inherent function of determining the facts upon which the admissibility of evidence depends will furnish to bureaucratic officials too ample opportunities for abusing the privilege."*[20]

Is the invocation of a state secrets privilege by the executive branch of government a usurpation of the power of review belonging to the judiciary? What is the interest and power of the legislative branch in this debate?

3. The state secrets privilege received formal recognition in *United States v. Reynolds*. Since that decision the privilege has been asserted numerous times in matters relating to national security and foreign relations. In the post-9/11 war on terror the federal government has encountered increased criticism and scrutiny for its assertion of the state secrets privilege under both President George Bush and President Barack Obama. The extent of this criticism, and the frequency with which the government asserted the privilege, prompted Attorney General Eric Holder in a 2009 Justice Department memorandum to establish new protocols for the invocation of the privilege.[21] These new procedures included facilitating more meaningful court review, adoption of a more rigorous "significant harm" standard for the invocation of the privilege, a state secrets review committee and Attorney General approval prior to invoking the privilege.[22] Despite the 2009 memorandum the privilege has been used to prevent civil litigation against the government for post-9/11 claims relating to torture, rendition, warrantless electronic eavesdropping and surveillance. In 2012 New York

Congressman Jerrold Nadler introduced legislation, the State Secrets Protection Act, seeking to curb abuses of the state secrets privilege by the Executive branch.[23] The bill called for amendment of the Federal Rules of Evidence to require the government's assertion of the privilege in either federal or state court be based on a showing that disclosure of the information sought will create a significant harm to national security and diplomatic relations of the United States.

The Court in *Reynolds* recognized the need for the privilege, stating it belonged to the government to assert but had to be balanced by judicial review. This judicial review, the Court suggested, would be whether the information sought to be disclosed was of such a nature as to disclose military secrets vital to national defense and thereby present a danger to the country. The *Reynolds* Court asserted that the only way to overcome the privilege was through a showing of necessity by the individual seeking the information to be disclosed. This necessity of proof requirement places the burden on the plaintiff in a civil case or upon the defendant in a criminal case. The proposed State Secrets Protection Act would seemingly shift this burden on the government to show "significant harm" to national security through disclosure. Is this type of legislation the appropriate response to claimed abuses of the state secrets privilege? Would this be an appropriate exercise of congressional authority? Would it interfere in any way with the Executive power?

4. In *CIA v. Sims*, 471 U.S. 159 (1985) the Court was presented with the issue of whether §102(d)(3) of the National Security Act of 1947[24] was a statute specifically incorporated within Exemption 3 of the Freedom of Information Act relating to pre-existing non-disclosure statutes. The *Sims* facts were that from 1953 to 1966 the Central Intelligence Agency ran a research and development project aimed at controlling human behavior. Much of the research was contracted out to research institutions. Code named MKULTRA the program *"was established to counter perceived Soviet and Chinese advances in brainwashing and interrogation techniques. Over the years, the program included various medical and psychological experiments, some of which led to untoward results. These aspects of MKULTRA surfaced publicly during the 1970's, and became the subject of executive and congressional investigations."*[25] A Freedom of Information Act request was filed with the CIA in 1977 by the Public Citizen Health Research Group seeking the grant proposals and names of the institutions and individuals involved in the research. The CIA claimed this information was exempt under the FOIA as "intelligence sources."[26] Chief Justice Warren Burger wrote in the Court's decision's: *"[T]he legislative history of §102(d)(3) also makes clear that Congress intended to give the Director of Central Intelligence broad power to protect the secrecy and integrity of the intelligence process. The reasons are too obvious to call for enlarged discussion; without such protections, the Agency would be virtually impotent. Enacted shortly after World War II, §102(d)(3) of the National Security Act of 1947 established the Agency and empowered it, among other things, "to correlate and evaluate intelligence relating to the national security." 50 U.S.C. §403(d)(3). The*

tragedy of Pearl Harbor and the reported deficiencies in American intelligence during the course of the war convinced the Congress that the country's ability to gather and analyze intelligence, in peacetime as well as in war, must be improved ... Congress expressly made the Director of Central Intelligence responsible for "protecting intelligence sources and methods from unauthorized disclosure." This language stemmed from President Truman's Directive of January 22, 1946, 11 Fed. Reg. 1337, in which he established the National Intelligence Authority and the Central Intelligence Group, the Agency's predecessors. These institutions were charged with "assuring the most effective accomplishment of the intelligence mission related to the national security," and accordingly made "responsible for fully protecting intelligence sources and methods." The fact that the mandate of § 102(d)(3) derives from this Presidential Directive reinforces our reading of the legislative history that Congress gave the Agency broad power to control the disclosure of intelligence sources."[27]

The opinion went on to hold that the Director of the Central Intelligence Agency properly invoked §102(d)(3) of the National Security Act of 1947 to withhold the identities of those institutions and individuals involved in project MKULTRA research as protected "intelligence sources." In so doing the Chief Justice said *"it is the responsibility of the Director of Central Intelligence, not that of the judiciary, to weigh the variety of complex and subtle factors in determining whether disclosure of information may lead to an unacceptable risk of compromising the Agency's intelligence-gathering process."*[28] Herein the Court deferred to agency interpretation as to what constituted an "intelligence source." This was the subject of the concurring opinion by Justice Thurgood Marshall who was joined in the concurrence by his colleague Justice William Brennan. Marshall agreed with the result to limit the disclosure allowed by the Court of Appeals but did not join the opinion because he questioned the Court's wholesale adoption of the CIA's definition of "intelligence source."[29] He found odd the Court's failure to consider Exemption 1 of the FOIA which provides a national security exemption and instead focuses on the argument presented by the government regarding the definition of an "intelligence source." For his part Justice Marshall argued that the Court sidestepped the review process by deferring to the CIA's interpretation of the statute. He wrote: *"This reading of the "intelligence source" language also fits comfortably within the statutory scheme as a whole, as the Court's reading does not. I focus, at the outset, on the recent history of FOIA Exemption 1 and particularly on the way in which recent events reflect Congress' ongoing effort to constrain agency discretion of the kind endorsed today. The scope of Exemption 1 is defined by the Executive, and its breadth therefore quite naturally fluctuates over time. For example, at the time this FOIA action was begun, Executive Order 12065, promulgated by President Carter, was in effect. That Order established three levels of secrecy—top secret, secret, and confidential—the lowest of which, "confidential," was "applied to information, the unauthorized disclosure of which reasonably could be expected to cause identifiable damage to the national security." 3 CFR 191 (1979). The Order also listed categories of information that could be considered for classification, including "military plans, weapons, or operations," "foreign government information," and "intelligence activities and sources." As it is now, nondisclosure premised on Exemption 1 was subject to judicial review. A court reviewing an Agency claim to withholding under Exemption 1 was required to determine de novo whether the document was properly classified and whether it substantively met the criteria in the Executive Order. If the claim was that the document or information in it contained military plans, for example, a court was required to determine whether the document was classified, whether it in fact contained such information and whether disclosure of the document reasonably could be expected to cause at least identifiable damage to national security. The burden was on the Agency to make this showing. At one time, this Court believed that the Judiciary was not qualified to undertake this task. Congress, however, disagreed, overruling both a decision of this Court and a Presidential veto to make clear that precisely this sort of judicial role is essential if the balance that Congress believed ought to be struck between disclosure and national security is to be struck in practice. Today's decision enables the Agency to avoid making the showing required under the carefully crafted balance embodied in Exemption 1 and thereby thwarts Congress' effort to limit the Agency's discretion. The Court identifies two categories of information—the identity of individuals or entities, whether or not confidential, that contribute material related to Agency information gathering, and material that might enable an observer to discover the identity of such a "source"—and rules that all such information is per se subject to withholding as long as it is related to the Agency's "intelligence function." The Agency need not even assert that disclosure will conceivably affect national security, much less that it reasonably could be expected to cause at least identifiable damage. It need not classify the information, much less demonstrate that it has properly been classified. Similarly, no court may review whether the source had, or would have had, any interest in confidentiality, or whether disclosure of the information would have any effect on national security. No court may consider whether the information is properly classified, or whether it fits the categories of the Executive Order. By choosing to litigate under Exemption 3, and by receiving this Court's blessing, the Agency has cleverly evaded all these carefully imposed congressional requirements."*[80]

In the concurrence, Marshall cited *EPA v. Mink*, 410 U.S. 73 (1973) in which the Supreme Court ruled in favor of the government by stating that classified documents did not have to be disclosed nor were they subject to in camera inspection for the courts to "sift out" non-objectionable content. The Court in *Mink* completely deferred to government agency decisions regarding classification of information. *Mink* concerned classified documents related to underground nuclear testing. The documents were sought under the FOIA by a member of Congress. Justice White's decision concentrated on the national security exemption provided in the Act and the broad discretion provided by Exemption 1. Two years later in *Administrator, Federal Aviation Administration v. Robertson*[31] Chief Justice Burger, writing for the majority and foreshadowing his opinion in *Sims*, provided additional deference to the government in applying Exemption 3 of the FOIA, that being administrative

materials specifically exempted by statute. In *Robertson* the material sought
were FAA analyses of commercial airline operation and performance.

After the U.S. Supreme Court decisions in *Mink* and *Robertson* Congress
acted by revising the Freedom of Information Act in 1974 and 1976. The
revisions were made in order to dull the effects of the decisions if not to
completely nullify them and grant broader judicial review.[32] Considering the
Court's subsequent decision in the 1985 *Sims* case and its more recent 2005
decision in *Tenet v. Doe* is judicial review a realistic approach to state secrets
privilege oversight? Has the U.S. Supreme Court's historical deference to the
Executive in this area precluded serious consideration of the Judiciary as a
reviewing body? Will congressional involvement, exemplified in legislation
such as the State Secrets Protection Act, be effective in limiting the reach of
claimed privileges?

5. *United States v. Nixon*, 418 U.S. 683 (1974) held that neither the claim of
    confidentiality of high-level executive communications nor the separation of
    powers could sustain the absolute, unqualified privilege from judicial process
    claimed by the White House. The court ruled 8-0 against President Nixon
    who was attempting to avoid answering a subpoena issued by Watergate
    special prosecutor Leon Jaworski seeking tape-recorded conversations of
    meetings between Nixon and several indicted members of his White House
    staff. The Court did recognize a limited executive privilege pertaining to
    military and diplomatic matters but none as broad as that claimed by
    President Nixon. In doing so the Court asserted its Article III power and
    deliberative voice in deciding issues of law: *"Notwithstanding the deference
    each branch must accord the others, the "judicial Power of the United States"
    vested in the federal courts by Art. III, 1, of the Constitution can no more be
    shared with the Executive Branch than the Chief Executive, for example, can
    share with the Judiciary the veto power, or the Congress share with the
    Judiciary the power to override a Presidential veto. Any other conclusion
    would be contrary to the basic concept of separation of powers and the checks
    and balances that flow from the scheme of a tripartite government. The
    Federalist, No. 47, p. 313 (S. Mittell ed. 1938). We therefore reaffirm that it
    is the province and duty of this Court "to say what the law is" with respect to
    the claim of privilege presented in this case. Marbury v. Madison, supra, at
    177."*[33] Additionally the Court referred to the role of due process within our
    system of government in declaring the executive privilege to be a qualified
    privilege: *"But this presumptive privilege must be considered in light of our
    historic commitment to the rule of law. This is nowhere more profoundly
    manifest than in our view that "the twofold aim of criminal justice is that
    guilt shall not escape or innocence suffer." Berger v. United States, 295 U.S.,
    at 88. We have elected to employ an adversary system of criminal justice in
    which the parties contest all issues before a court of law. The need to develop
    all relevant facts in the adversary system is both fundamental and
    comprehensive. The ends of criminal justice would be defeated if judgments
    were to be founded on a partial or speculative presentation of the facts. The
    very integrity of the judicial system and public confidence in the system
    depend on full disclosure of all the facts, within the framework of the rules of*

evidence. To ensure that justice is done, it is imperative to the function of courts that compulsory process be available for the production of evidence needed either by the prosecution or by the defense."[84] *Nixon* was decided by the same Court that issued the opinions in *Mink* and *Robertson*—do these cases suggest that the state secrets privilege is broader than executive privilege?

6. As indicated in commentary note 3 above the post-9/11 use of the state secrets privilege by the United States government has been extensive and not without equally extensive criticism. The cases of plaintiffs who were subjected to involuntary rendition and then subjected to alleged acts of torture have been dismissed by courts as a result of the government assertion of state secrets privilege. Rendition refers to the "return of a fugitive from one state to the state where the fugitive is accused or convicted of a crime."[35] Its use by the United States government began as a limited CIA program designed as an intelligence gathering program during the presidency of William Jefferson Clinton.[36] After 9/11 the program expanded greatly and subjected individual terror suspects to harsh interrogation methods. In *El-Masri v. United States*, 479 F.3d 296 (2006) a German citizen of Lebanese descent was detained by Macedonian law enforcement, held for 23 days and then turned over to the CIA. He was then flown to a CIA site in Kabul, Afghanistan for interrogation where he was held for another 96 days during which time he was incommunicado, drugged, beaten, transported blindfolded, and kept in a small, unsanitary cell.[37] When he was finally released on May 28, 2004, Khaled El-Masri was transported to and released in a remote area of Albania.[38] El-Masri brought a civil suit in the Eastern District of Virginia alleging, among other things, violation of his Fifth Amendment right to due process as well as violation of international norms against prolonged arbitrary detention.[39] The district court, relying on the state secrets privilege, dismissed the complaint. The Fourth Circuit Court of Appeals followed and dismissed on the same grounds. Certiorari was denied by the U.S. Supreme Court.[40] El-Masri's complaint in the U.S. courts did not receive adjudication on the merits and was summarily dismissed owing to the government's claim of state secrets privilege. He eventually obtained a forum to hear his case and obtain resolution of his complaint when he filed with the European Court of Human Rights against Macedonia. The findings of the court were that El-Masri's rights were violated by the government of Macedonia who acted as an agent for the United States.[41] Specifically, the court found violations of Articles 3, 5, 8, and 13 of the European Convention on Human Rights, which respectively relate to prohibition on torture, right to liberty, right to respect for private life and right to an effective remedy.[42]

   In two related cases, *Arar v. Ashcroft* [43] and *Mohamed v. Jeppesen Dataplan, Inc.*[44], the Second Circuit and Ninth Circuit Court of Appeals also dismissed lawsuits resulting from the U.S. government's rendition program. Mahar Arar, a Canadian citizen stopped while at JFK Airport in New York, alleged Fifth Amendment rights violations based on being subject to torture by a foreign government. In *Jeppesen*, five detainees subjected to rendition and alleged torture sued the Boeing aircraft subsidiary they claimed arranged flights for the CIA. Once again these lawsuits were dismissed based on the state secrets privilege without reaching any of the merits of the individual claims.

Governmental Immunity

Immunity from lawsuit takes various forms. There is the immunity that is historically accorded to the sovereign. An early explanation of this common law theory is once again found in the writings of Sir William Blackstone: *"The law also ascribes to the King in his political capacity absolute perfection. The King can do no wrong."*[45] This common law principle was adopted by the newly formed American government and gained its place in the Eleventh Amendment to the U.S. Constitution. The Eleventh Amendment provides: *"The judicial power of the United States shall not be construed to extend to any suit in law or equity, commenced or prosecuted against one of the United States by citizens of another state, or by citizens or subjects of any foreign state."* Simply stated this means that the government cannot be sued. An exception to this sovereign immunity occurs if the government, whether federal or state, consents to be sued. Pursuant to the Federal Tort Claims Act of 1948 the federal government has made itself subject to civil suit by an individual for torts committed against that individual by anyone acting on behalf of the federal government.[46]

In addition to sovereign immunity, absolute immunity exists as an unqualified immunity usually reserved for judges and prosecutors. Absolute immunity is granted to these individual government functions because they "cut so close to the core of representative democracy or the justice system" that it is present to protect judicial and prosecutorial "freedom of action."[47] Absolute immunity stands in contrast to qualified immunity, which is a conditional type of immunity. Qualified immunity applies to the conduct of state public officials sued under the Civil Rights Statute 42 USC §1983 and federal officials sued in a *Bivens* type action. The §1983 statute was originally enacted in 1871 during the post-Civil War era of Reconstruction. The statute provides: *"Every person who, under color of any statute, ordinance, regulation, custom, or usage, of any State or Territory or the District of Columbia, subjects, or causes to be subjected, any citizen of the United States or other person within the jurisdiction thereof to the deprivation of any rights, privileges, or immunities secured by the Constitution and laws, shall be liable to the party injured in an action at law, suit in equity, or other proper proceeding for redress ..."* The statute does not provide a cause of action of its own; it merely provides a means to remedy government action by state government officials (which extends to those employed by any political subdivision of the state such as a village, town, city, or public corporation). Section 1983 plaintiffs typically allege a claimed civil rights violation based on law enforcement conduct though the statute has been applied to other government related conduct alleged to have infringed upon a right, such as municipal planning board decisions or building department orders and property owner allegations that such actions resulted in an improper Fifth Amendment taking.[48] In its application to law enforcement officer conduct the claims are generally based on violations of enumerated rights protected by the First, Fourth, Fifth, Sixth, Eighth, or Fourteenth Amendments. A cause of action may be based on any of these rights individually or in combination. Because the statute does not have a provision specifically addressing misconduct by federal government officials the U.S. Supreme Court created a comparable right to proceed against federal officials in the 1971 case of *Bivens v. Six Unknown Federal Narcotics Agents.*[49]

For a government defendant in either a §1983 or *Bivens* type action to obtain qualified immunity the defendant's conduct cannot have violated a clearly established constitutional right. Just what is a "clearly established constitutional right" has been a subject of debate in the federal courts. Nevertheless, the U.S. Supreme Court in *Saucier v. Katz* created a two-step analysis for determining whether qualified immunity defenses applied: 1) whether the facts state a constitutional law violation; 2) if so, whether the right was clearly established at the time.[50] A brief eight years after *Saucier* the U.S. Supreme Court modified this two-step analysis in *Pearson v. Callahan* by stating that the rule should not be inflexible and lower courts should have discretion to decide whether rigid analysis is appropriate on a case by case basis.[51] The overall effect of this relaxed standard was to provide trial courts the means by which to more readily dispose of those cases where there was no clearly established constitutional right. In *Pearson* the Court stated that qualified immunity *"balances two important interests—the need to hold public officials accountable when they exercise power irresponsibly and the need to shield officials from harassment, distraction, and liability when they perform their duties responsibly."*[52] As indicated in the prior section on government privilege the ability to hold government officials accountable has increasingly waned in a post-9/11 era. When a claim of privilege is not available claims of immunity serve to provide similar relief from judgment.

Sosa v. Alvarez-Machain
542 U.S. 692 (2004)

Justice Souter delivered the opinion of the Court.

The two issues are whether respondent Alvarez-Machain's allegation that the Drug Enforcement Administration instigated his abduction from Mexico for criminal trial in the United States supports a claim against the Government under the Federal Tort Claims Act (FTCA or Act), 28 U. S. C. §1346(b)(1), §§2671–2680, and whether he may recover under the Alien Tort Statute (ATS), 28 U.S.C. §1350. We hold that he is not entitled to a remedy under either statute.

I

We have considered the underlying facts before, **United States v. Alvarez-Machain**, 504 U. S. 655 (1992). In 1985, an agent of the Drug Enforcement Administration (DEA), Enrique Camarena-Salazar, was captured on assignment in Mexico and taken to a house in Guadalajara, where he was tortured over the course of a 2-day interrogation, then murdered. Based in part on eyewitness testimony,

DEA officials in the United States came to believe that respondent Humberto Alvarez-Machain (Alvarez), a Mexican physician, was present at the house and acted to prolong the agent's life in order to extend the interrogation and torture. Id., at 657.

In 1990, a federal grand jury indicted Alvarez for the torture and murder of Camarena-Salazar, and the United States District Court for the Central District of California issued a warrant for his arrest. 331 F. 3d 604, 609 (CA9 2003) (en banc). The DEA asked the Mexican Government for help in getting Alvarez into the United States, but when the requests and negotiations proved fruitless, the DEA approved a plan to hire Mexican nationals to seize Alvarez and bring him to the United States for trial. As so planned, a group of Mexicans, including petitioner Jose Francisco Sosa, abducted Alvarez from his house, held him overnight in a motel, and brought him by private plane to El Paso, Texas, where he was arrested by federal officers. Ibid.

Once in American custody, Alvarez moved to dismiss the indictment on the ground that his seizure was "outrageous governmental conduct," *Alvarez-Machain*, 504 U.S., at 658, and violated the extradition treaty between the United States and Mexico. The District Court agreed, the Ninth Circuit affirmed, and we reversed, id., at 670, holding that the fact of Alvarez's forcible seizure did not affect the jurisdiction of a federal court. The case was tried in 1992, and ended at the close of the Government's case, when the District Court granted Alvarez's motion for a judgment of acquittal.

In 1993, after returning to Mexico, Alvarez began the civil action before us here. He sued Sosa, Mexican citizen and DEA operative Antonio Garate-Bustamante, five unnamed Mexican civilians, the United States, and four DEA agents. 331 F. 3d, at 610. So far as it matters here, Alvarez sought damages from the United States under the FTCA, alleging false arrest, and from Sosa under the ATS, for a violation of the law of nations. The former statute authorizes suit "for … personal injury … caused by the negligent or wrongful act or omission of any employee of the Government while acting within the scope of his office or employment." 28 U. S. C. §1346(b)(1). The latter provides in its entirety that "[t]he district courts shall have original jurisdiction of any civil action by an alien for a tort only, committed in violation of the law of nations or a treaty of the United States." §1350.

The District Court granted the Government's motion to dismiss the FTCA claim, but awarded summary judgment and $25,000 in damages to Alvarez on the ATS claim. A three-judge panel of the Ninth Circuit then affirmed the ATS judgment, but reversed the dismissal of the FTCA claim. 266 F. 3d 1045 (2001).

A divided en banc court came to the same conclusion. 331 F. 3d, at 641. As for the ATS claim, the court called on its own precedent, "that [the ATS] not only provides federal courts with subject matter jurisdiction, but also creates a cause of action for an alleged violation of the law of nations." Id., at 612. The Circuit then relied upon what it called the "clear and universally recognized norm prohibiting arbitrary arrest and detention," id., at 620, to support the conclusion that Alvarez's arrest amounted to a tort in violation of international law. On the FTCA claim, the Ninth Circuit held that, because "the DEA had no authority to effect Alvarez's arrest and detention in Mexico," id., at 608, the United States was liable to him under California law for the tort of false arrest, id., at 640–641.

We granted certiorari in these companion cases to clarify the scope of both the FTCA and the ATS. 540 U. S. 1045 (2003). We now reverse in each.

II

The Government seeks reversal of the judgment of liability under the FTCA on two principal grounds. It argues that the arrest could not have been tortious, because it was authorized by 21 U. S. C. §878, setting out the arrest authority of the DEA, and it says that in any event the liability asserted here falls within the FTCA exception to waiver of sovereign immunity for claims "arising in a foreign country," 28 U. S. C. §2680(k). We think the exception applies and decide on that ground.

***

The FTCA "was designed primarily to remove the sovereign immunity of the United States from suits in tort and, with certain specific exceptions, to render the Government liable in tort as a private individual would be under like circumstances." ***Richards v. United States***, 369 U.S. 1, 6 (1962); see also 28 U.S.C. §2674. The Act accordingly gives federal district courts jurisdiction over claims against the United States for injury "caused by the negligent or wrongful act or omission of any employee of the Government while acting within the scope of his office or employment, under circumstances where the United States, if a private person, would be liable to the claimant in accordance with the law of the place where the act or omission occurred." §1346(b)(1). But the Act also limits its waiver of sovereign immunity in a number of ways.

***

Here the significant limitation on the waiver of immunity is the Act's exception for "[a]ny claim arising in a foreign country," §2680(k), a provision that on its face seems plainly applicable to the facts of this case. In the Ninth Circuit's view, once Alvarez was within the borders of the United States, his detention was not tortious, see 331 F. 3d, at 636–637; the appellate court suggested that the Government's liability to Alvarez rested solely upon a false arrest claim ... Alvarez's arrest, however, was said to be "false," and thus tortious, only because, and only to the extent that, it took place and endured in Mexico. The actions in Mexico are thus most naturally understood as the kernel of a "claim arising in a foreign country," and barred from suit under the exception to the waiver of immunity.

Notwithstanding the straightforward language of the foreign country exception, the Ninth Circuit allowed the action to proceed under what has come to be known as the "headquarters doctrine." Some Courts of Appeals, reasoning that "[t]he entire scheme of the FTCA focuses on the place where the negligent or wrongful act or omission of the government employee occurred," *Sami v. United States*, 617 F. 2d 755, 761 (CADC 1979), have concluded that the foreign country exception does not exempt the United States from suit "for acts or omissions occurring here which have their operative effect in another country."... Headquarters claims "typically involve allegations of negligent guidance in an office within the United States of employees who cause damage while in a foreign country, or of activities which take place within a foreign country." *Cominotto v. United States*, 802 F. 2d 1127, 1130 (CA9 1986). In such instances, these courts have concluded that §2680(k) does not bar suit.

The reasoning of the Ninth Circuit here was that, since Alvarez's abduction in Mexico was the direct result of wrongful acts of planning and direction by DEA agents located in California, "Alvarez's abduction fits the headquarters doctrine like a glove." 331 F. 3d, at 638.

"Working out of DEA offices in Los Angeles, [DEA agents] made the decision to kidnap Alvarez and ... gave [their Mexican intermediary] precise instructions on whom to recruit, how to seize Alvarez, and how he should be treated during the trip to the United States. DEA officials in Washington, D. C., approved the details of the operation. After Alvarez was abducted according to plan, DEA agents supervised his transportation into the United States, telling the arrest team where to land the plane and obtaining clearance in El Paso for landing. The United States, and California in particular, served as command central for the operation carried out in Mexico." Id., at 638–639.

Thus, the Ninth Circuit held that Alvarez's claim did not "aris[e] in" a foreign country.

The potential effect of this sort of headquarters analysis flashes the yellow caution light. "[I]t will virtually always be possible to assert that the negligent activity that injured the plaintiff [abroad] was the consequence of faulty training, selection or supervision—or even less than that, lack of careful training, selection or supervision—in the United States." *Beattie v. United States*, 756 F. 2d 91, 119 (CADC 1984) (Scalia, J., dissenting). Legal malpractice claims, *Knisley v. United States*, 817 F. Supp. 680, 691–693 (SD Ohio 1993), allegations of negligent medical care, *Newborn v. United States*, 238 F. Supp. 2d 145, 148–149 (DC 2002), and even slip-and-fall cases, *Eaglin v. United States*, Dept. of Army, 794 F. 2d 981, 983–984 (CA5 1986), can all be repackaged as headquarters claims based on a failure to train, a failure to warn, the offering of bad advice, or the adoption of a negligent policy. If we were to approve the headquarters exception to the foreign country exception, the " 'headquarters claim' [would] become a standard part of FTCA litigation" in cases potentially implicating the foreign country exception. *Beattie*, supra, at 119 (Scalia, J., dissenting). The headquarters doctrine threatens to swallow the foreign country exception whole, certainly at the pleadings stage.

The need for skepticism is borne out by two considerations. One of them is pertinent to cases like this one, where harm was arguably caused both by individual action in a foreign country as well as by planning in the United States; the other is suggested simply because the harm occurred on foreign soil.

***

In sum, current flexibility in choice of law methodology gives no assurance against applying foreign substantive law if federal courts follow headquarters doctrine to assume jurisdiction over tort claims against the Government for foreign harm. Based on the experience just noted, the expectation is that application of the headquarters doctrine would in fact result in a substantial number of cases applying the very foreign law the foreign country exception was meant to avoid.

***

III

Alvarez has also brought an action under the ATS against petitioner, Sosa, who argues (as does the United States supporting him) that there is no relief under the ATS because the statute does no more than vest federal courts with jurisdiction, neither creating nor authorizing the courts to recognize any particular right of action without further congressional action. Although we agree the statute is in terms only jurisdictional, we think that at the time of enactment the jurisdiction enabled federal courts to hear claims in a very limited category defined by the law of nations and recognized at common law. We do not believe, however, that the limited, implicit sanction to entertain the handful of international law cum common law claims understood in 1789 should be taken as authority to recognize the right of action asserted by Alvarez here.

***

Judge Friendly called the ATS a "legal Lohengrin," *IIT v. Vencap, Ltd.*, 519 F. 2d 1001, 1015 (CA2 1975); "no one seems to know whence it came,"... and for over 170 years after its enactment it provided jurisdiction in only one case. The first Congress passed it as part of the Judiciary Act of 1789, in providing that the new federal district courts "shall also have cognizance, concurrent with the courts of the several States, or the circuit courts, as the case may be, of all causes where an alien sues for a tort only in violation of the law of nations or a treaty of the United States." Act of Sept. 24, 1789, ch. 20, §9(b), 1 Stat. 79.

The parties and amici here advance radically different historical interpretations of this terse provision. Alvarez says that the ATS was intended not simply as a jurisdictional grant, but as authority for the creation of a new cause of action for torts in violation of international law. We think that reading is implausible. As enacted in 1789, the ATS gave the district courts "cognizance" of certain causes of action, and the term bespoke a grant of jurisdiction, not power to mold substantive law. See, e.g., The Federalist No. 81, pp. 447, 451 (J. Cooke ed. 1961) (A. Hamilton) (using "jurisdiction" interchangeably with "cognizance"). The fact that the ATS was placed in §9 of the Judiciary Act, a statute otherwise exclusively concerned with federal-court jurisdiction, is itself support for its strictly jurisdictional nature ... In sum, we think the statute was intended as jurisdictional in the sense of addressing the power of the courts to entertain cases concerned with a certain subject.

***

We must still, however, derive a standard or set of standards for assessing the particular claim Alvarez raises, and for this case it suffices to look to the historical antecedents. Whatever the ultimate criteria for accepting a cause of action subject to jurisdiction under §1350, we are persuaded that federal courts should not recognize private claims under federal common law for violations of any international law norm with less definite content and acceptance among civilized nations than the historical paradigms familiar when §1350 was enacted ... Thus, Alvarez's detention claim must be gauged against the current state of international law, looking to those sources we have long, albeit cautiously, recognized.

"[W]here there is no treaty, and no controlling executive or legislative act or judicial decision, resort must be had to the customs and usages of civilized nations; and, as evidence of these, to the works of jurists and commentators, who by years of labor, research and experience, have made themselves peculiarly well acquainted with the subjects of which they treat. Such works are resorted to by judicial tribunals, not for the speculations of their authors concerning what the law ought to be, but for trustworthy evidence of what the law really is." The Paquete Habana, 175 U. S., at 700.

To begin with, Alvarez cites two well-known international agreements that, despite their moral authority, have little utility under the standard set out in this opinion. He says that his abduction by Sosa was an "arbitrary arrest" within the meaning of the Universal Declaration of Human Rights (Declaration), G. A. Res. 217A (III), U. N. Doc. A/810 (1948). And he traces the rule against arbitrary arrest not only to the Declaration, but also to article nine of the International Covenant on Civil and Political Rights (Covenant), Dec. 19, 1996, 999 U. N. T. S. 171, to which the United States is a party, and to various other conventions to which it is not. But the Declaration does not of its own force impose obligations as a matter of international law. See Humphrey, The UN Charter and the Universal Declaration of Human Rights, in The International Protection of Human Rights 39, 50 (E. Luard ed. 1967) (quoting Eleanor Roosevelt calling the Declaration " 'a statement of principles ... setting up a common standard of achievement for all peoples and all nations' " and " 'not a treaty or international agreement ... impos[ing] legal obligations' "). And, although the Covenant does bind the United States as a matter of international law, the United States ratified the Covenant on the express understanding that it was not self-executing and so did not itself create obligations enforceable in the federal courts. See supra, at 33. Accordingly, Alvarez cannot say that the Declaration and Covenant themselves establish the relevant and applicable rule of international law. He instead attempts to show that prohibition of arbitrary arrest has attained the status of binding customary international law.

Here, it is useful to examine Alvarez's complaint in greater detail. As he presently argues it, the claim does not rest on the cross-border feature of his abduction. Although the District Court granted relief in part on finding a violation of international law in taking Alvarez across the border from Mexico to the United States, the Court of Appeals rejected that ground of liability for failure to identify a norm of requisite force prohibiting a forcible abduction across a border. Instead, it relied on the conclusion that the law of the United States did not authorize Alvarez's arrest, because the DEA lacked extraterritorial authority under 21 U. S. C. §878, and because Federal Rule of Criminal Procedure 4(d)(2) limited the warrant for Alvarez's arrest to "the jurisdiction of the United States." It is this position that Alvarez takes now: that his arrest was arbitrary and as such forbidden by international law not because it infringed the prerogatives of Mexico, but because no applicable law authorized it.

Alvarez thus invokes a general prohibition of "arbitrary" detention defined as officially sanctioned action exceeding positive authorization to detain under the domestic law of some government, regardless of the circumstances. Whether or not this is an accurate reading of the Covenant, Alvarez cites little authority that a rule so broad has the status of a binding customary norm today. He certainly cites nothing to justify the federal courts in taking his broad rule as the predicate for a federal lawsuit, for its implications would be breathtaking. His rule would support a cause of action in federal court for any arrest, anywhere in the world, unauthorized by the law of the jurisdiction in which it took place, and would create a cause of action for any seizure of an alien in violation of the Fourth Amendment, supplanting the actions under Rev. Stat. §1979, 42 U. S. C. §1983 and **Bivens v. Six Unknown Fed. Narcotics Agents**, 403 U. S. 388 (1971), that now provide damages remedies for such violations. It would create an action in federal court for arrests by state officers who simply exceed their authority; and for the violation of any limit that the law of any country might place on the authority of its own officers to arrest. And all of this assumes that Alvarez could establish that Sosa was acting on behalf of a government when he made the arrest, for otherwise he would need a rule broader still.

***

Whatever may be said for the broad principle Alvarez advances, in the present, imperfect world, it expresses an aspiration that exceeds any binding customary rule having the specificity we require. Creating a private cause of action to further that aspiration would go beyond any residual common law discretion we think it appropriate to exercise. It is enough to hold that a single illegal detention of less than a day, followed by the transfer of custody to lawful authorities and a prompt arraignment, violates no norm of customary international law so well defined as to support the creation of a federal remedy.

***

The judgment of the Court of Appeals is Reversed.

Ashcroft v. al-Kidd
131 S.Ct. 415 (2011)

On writ of certiorari to the United States Court of Appeals for the Ninth Circuit.

Justice Scalia delivered the opinion of the Court.

We decide whether a former Attorney General enjoys immunity from suit for allegedly authorizing federal prosecutors to obtain valid material-witness warrants for detention of terrorism suspects whom they would otherwise lack probable cause to arrest.

I

The federal material-witness statute authorizes judges to "order the arrest of [a] person" whose testimony "is material in a criminal proceeding ... if it is shown that it may become impracticable to secure the presence of the person by subpoena." 18 U. S. C. §3144. Material witnesses enjoy the same constitutional right to pretrial release as other federal detainees, and federal law requires release if their testimony "can adequately be secured by deposition, and if further detention is not necessary to prevent a failure of justice." *Ibid.*

Because this case arises from a motion to dismiss, we accept as true the factual allegations in Abdullah al-Kidd's complaint. The complaint alleges that, in the aftermath of the September 11th terrorist attacks, then-Attorney General John Ashcroft authorized federal prosecutors and law enforcement officials to use the material-witness statute to detain individuals with suspected ties to terrorist organizations. It is alleged that federal officials had no intention of calling most of these individuals as witnesses, and that they were detained, at Ashcroft's direction, because federal officials suspected them of supporting terrorism but lacked sufficient evidence to charge them with a crime.

It is alleged that this pretextual detention policy led to the material-witness arrest of al-Kidd, a native-born United States citizen. FBI agents apprehended him in March 2003 as he checked in for a flight to Saudi Arabia. Two days earlier, federal officials had informed a Magistrate Judge that, if al-Kidd boarded his flight, they believed information "crucial" to the prosecution of Sami Omar al-Hussayen would be lost. Al-Kidd remained in federal custody for 16 days and on supervised release until al-Hussayen's trial concluded 14 months later. Prosecutors never called him as a witness.

In March 2005, al-Kidd filed this **Bivens** action, see **Bivens v. Six Unknown Fed. Narcotics Agents**, 403 U.S. 388 (1971) to challenge the constitutionality of Ashcroft's alleged policy; he also asserted several other claims not relevant here against Ashcroft and others. Ashcroft filed a motion to dismiss based on absolute and qualified immunity, which the District Court denied. A divided panel of the United States Court of Appeals for the Ninth Circuit affirmed, holding that the Fourth Amendment prohibits pretextual arrests absent probable cause of criminal wrongdoing, and that Ashcroft could not claim qualified or absolute immunity. See 580 F. 3d 949 (2009). Judge Bea dissented, 580 F. 3d, at 981, and eight judges dissented from the denial of rehearing en banc, see 598 F. 3d 1129, 1137, 1142 (CA9 2010). We granted certiorari.

II

Qualified immunity shields federal and state officials from money damages unless a plaintiff pleads facts showing (1) that the official violated a statutory or constitutional right, and (2) that the right was "clearly established" at the time of the challenged conduct. **Harlow v. Fitzgerald**, 457 U. S. 800, 818 (1982). We recently reaffirmed that lower courts have discretion to decide which of the two prongs of qualified-immunity analysis to tackle first. See **Pearson v. Callahan**, 555 U. S. 223, 236 (2009).

Courts should think carefully before expending "scarce judicial resources" to resolve difficult and novel questions of constitutional or statutory interpretation that will "have no effect on the outcome of the case." *Id.*, at 236–237; see *Id.*, at 237–242. When, however, a Court of Appeals does address both prongs of qualified-immunity analysis, we have discretion to correct its errors at each step. Although not necessary to reverse an erroneous judgment, doing so ensures that courts do not insulate constitutional decisions at the frontiers of the law from our review or inadvertently undermine the values qualified immunity seeks to promote. The former occurs when the constitutional law question is wrongly decided; the latter when what is not clearly established is held to be so. In this case, the Court of Appeals' analysis at both steps of the qualified-immunity inquiry needs correction.

A

The Fourth Amendment protects "[t]he right of the people to be secure in their persons, houses, papers, and effects, against unreasonable searches and seizures." An arrest, of course, qualifies as a "seizure" of a "person" under this provision, **Dunaway v. New York**, 442 U.S. 200, 207–208 (1979), and so must be reasonable under the circumstances. Al-Kidd does not assert that Government officials would have acted unreasonably if they had used a material-witness warrant to arrest him for the purpose of securing his testimony for trial. See Brief for Respondent 16–17; Tr. of Oral Arg. 20–22. He contests, however (and the Court of Appeals here rejected), the reasonableness of using the warrant to detain him as a suspected criminal.

Fourth Amendment reasonableness "is predominantly an objective inquiry." **Edmond**, *supra*, at 47. We ask whether "the circumstances, viewed objectively, justify [the challenged] action." **Scott v. United States**, 436 U. S. 128, 138 (1978). If so, that action was reasonable "*whatever* the subjective intent" motivating the relevant officials. **Whren v. United States**, 517 U. S. 806, 814 (1996). This approach recognizes that the Fourth Amendment regulates conduct rather than thoughts, **Bond v. United States**, 529 U. S. 334, 338, n. 2 (2000); and it promotes evenhanded, uniform enforcement of the law, **Devenpeck v. Alford**, 543 U. S. 146, 153–154 (2004).

Two "limited exception[s]" to this rule are our special-needs and administrative-search cases, where "actual motivations" do matter. **United States v. Knights**, NK "http://supreme.justia.com/cases/federal/us/534/112/index.html" 534 U. S. 112, 122 (2001) (internal quotation marks omitted). A judicial warrant and probable cause are not needed where the search or seizure is justified by "special needs, beyond the normal need for law enforcement," such as the need to deter drug use in public schools, **Vernonia School Dist. 47J v. Acton**,

515 U. S. 646, 653 (1995) (internal quotation marks omitted), or the need to assure that railroad employees engaged in train operations are not under the influence of drugs or alcohol, **Skinner v. Railway Labor Executives' Assn.**, 489 U. S. 602 (1989); and where the search or seizure is in execution of an administrative warrant authorizing, for example, an inspection of fire-damaged premises to determine the cause, **Michigan v. Clifford**, 464 U. S. 287, 294 (1984) (plurality opinion), or an inspection of residential premises to assure compliance with a housing code, **Camara v. Municipal Court of City and County of San Francisco**, 387 U. S. 523, 535–538 (1967). But those exceptions do not apply where the officer's purpose is not to attend to the special needs or to the investigation for which the administrative inspection is justified. The Government seeks to justify the present arrest on the basis of a properly issued judicial warrant—so that the special-needs and administrative-inspection cases cannot be the basis for a purpose inquiry here.

Apart from those cases, we have almost uniformly rejected invitations to probe subjective intent. See **Brigham City v. Stuart**, 547 U. S. 398, 404 (2006). There is one category of exception, upon which the Court of Appeals principally relied. In **Edmond**, 531 U. S. 32, we held that the Fourth Amendment could not condone suspicionless vehicle checkpoints set up for the purpose of detecting illegal narcotics. Although we had previously approved vehicle checkpoints set up for the purpose of keeping off the road unlicensed drivers, **Delaware v. Prouse**, 440 U. S. 648, 663 (1979), or alcohol-impaired drivers, **Michigan Dept. of State Police v. Sitz**, 496 U. S. 444 (1990); and for the purpose of interdicting those who illegally cross the border, **United States v. Martinez-Fuerte**, 428 U. S. 543 (1976); we found the drug-detection purpose in *Edmond* invalidating because it was "ultimately indistinguishable from the general interest in crime control," 531 U. S., at 44. In the Court of Appeals' view, **Edmond** established that "'programmatic purpose' is relevant to Fourth Amendment analysis of programs of seizures without probable cause." 580 F. 3d, at 968.

That was mistaken. It was not the absence of probable cause that triggered the invalidating-purpose inquiry in **Edmond**. To the contrary, **Edmond** explicitly said that it would approve checkpoint stops for "general crime control purposes" that were based upon merely "some quantum of individualized suspicion." 531 U. S., at 47. Purpose was relevant in *Edmond* because "programmatic purposes may be relevant to the validity of Fourth Amendment intrusions undertaken *pursuant to a general scheme without individualized suspicion*," *Id.*, at 45–46 (emphasis added).

Needless to say, warrantless, "suspicionless intrusions pursuant to a general scheme," *Id.*, at 47, are far removed from the facts of this case. A warrant issued by a neutral Magistrate Judge authorized al-Kidd's arrest. The affidavit accompanying the warrant application (as al-Kidd concedes) gave individualized reasons to believe that he was a material witness and that he would soon disappear. The existence of a judicial warrant based on individualized suspicion takes this case outside the domain of not only our special-needs and administrative-search cases, but of **Edmond** as well.

A warrant based on individualized suspicion in fact grants more protection against the malevolent and the incompetent than existed in most of our cases eschewing inquiries into intent. In **Whren**, 517 U. S., at 813, and **Devenpeck**, 543 U. S., at 153, we declined to probe the motives behind seizures supported by probable cause but lacking a warrant approved by a detached magistrate. **Terry v. Ohio**, 392 U. S. 1, 21–22 (1968), and **Knights**, 534 U. S., at 121–122, applied an objective standard to warrantless searches justified by a lesser showing of reasonable suspicion. We review even some suspicionless searches for objective reasonableness. See **Bond**, 529 U.S., at 335–336, 338, n. 2. If concerns about improper motives and pretext do not justify subjective inquiries in those less protective contexts, we see no reason to adopt that inquiry here.

***

Because al-Kidd concedes that individualized suspicion supported the issuance of the material witness arrest warrant; and does not assert that his arrest would have been unconstitutional absent the alleged pretextual use of the warrant; we find no Fourth Amendment violation. Efficient and evenhanded application of the law demands that we look to whether the arrest is objectively justified, rather than to the motive of the arresting officer.

B

A Government official's conduct violates clearly established law when, at the time of the challenged conduct, "[t]he contours of [a] right [are] sufficiently clear" that every "reasonable official would have understood that what he is doing violates that right." **Anderson v. Creighton**, 483 U. S. 635, 640 (1987). We do not require a case directly on point, but existing precedent must have placed the statutory or constitutional question beyond debate. See *Ibid.;* **Malley v. Briggs**, 475 U. S. 335, 341 (1986). The constitutional question in this case falls far short of that threshold.

***

Qualified immunity gives government officials breathing room to make reasonable but mistaken judgments about open legal questions. When properly applied, it protects "all but the plainly incompetent or those who knowingly violate the law." **Malley**, 475 U.

S., at 341. Ashcroft deserves neither label, not least because eight Court of Appeals judges agreed with his judgment in a case of first impression. See **Wilson**, *supra*, at 618. He deserves qualified immunity even assuming—contrafactually—that his alleged detention policy violated the Fourth Amendment.

***

We hold that an objectively reasonable arrest and detention of a material witness pursuant to a validly obtained warrant cannot be challenged as unconstitutional on the basis of allegations that the arresting authority had an improper motive. Because Ashcroft did not violate clearly established law, we need not address the more difficult question whether he enjoys absolute immunity. The judgment of the Court of Appeals is reversed, and the case is remanded for further proceedings consistent with this opinion.

It is so ordered.

Commentary and Questions

7. In *Alvarez-Machain*, the respondent sought to obtain a claim against the United States government under the Federal Tort Claims Act based on his abduction from Mexico by the DEA. The FTCA, codified at 28 USC §1346(b), as mentioned earlier, is the federal statute by which the U.S. government has made itself amenable to civil actions arising from the tortious acts of its officials, thereby waiving Eleventh Amendment immunity. The Act, however, does grant open access to the government as a defendant and limits the right of a plaintiff to bring a claim. One such exception as discussed in *Alvarez-Machain* is that based on any claim arising in a foreign country. The Ninth Circuit Court of Appeals permitted the claim to go forward under a "headquarters exception" and respondent Alvarez-Machain's attorneys argued in the Supreme Court for recognition of the exception. What was the Court's reasoning for rejecting the respondent's argument and the logic of the Ninth Circuit relative to the "headquarters exception"? What did Justice Souter cite as a principal reason for its rejection? The Court also dispensed with Alvarez-Machain's argument under the Alien Tort Statute—what was the basis of the Court's decision on this ground?

8. The federal Material Witness Statute, 18 USC §3144, provides the following: *"If it appears from an affidavit filed by a party that the testimony of a person is material in a criminal proceeding, and if it is shown that it may become impracticable to secure the presence of the person by subpoena, a judicial officer may order the arrest of the person and treat the person in accordance with the provisions of section 3142 of this title. No material witness may be detained because of inability to comply with any condition of release if the testimony of such witness can adequately be secured by deposition, and if further detention is not necessary to prevent a failure of justice. Release of a*

material witness may be delayed for a reasonable period of time until the deposition of the witness can be taken pursuant to the Federal Rules of Criminal Procedure." Section 3142 refers to the release or detention of criminal defendants pending trial. The statutory construction of section 3144, with its reference to 3142, clearly places material witnesses in situations akin to those of a criminal defendant, though without a requirement of probable cause, if the witnesses presence cannot be guaranteed without the detention. Abdullah al-Kidd alleged that the use of the material witness warrant was part of a pre-textual government plan engineered by then Attorney General John Ashcroft, and put into use whenever there was no probable cause to arrest, in order to incarcerate individuals suspected of having terrorist ties. The opinion by Justice Scalia provides an excellent short tutorial on qualified immunity and the contours of Fourth Amendment requirements.

In finding qualified immunity applied to the actions of the Attorney General how did Justice Scalia determine there was no "clearly established constitutional right" the Attorney General could have known to be violated?

9. *Ashcroft v. Iqbal*, 556 U.S. 662 (2009) is another post-9/11 case initiated by an individual detained by U.S. authorities pursuant to investigation into the terror attacks. The respondent Javaid Iqbal, a Muslim and Pakistani citizen, was arrested on fraud charges. Iqbal pled guilty to the charges but contested the circumstances of his detention, alleging general mistreatment by correctional officials and making specific claims against Attorney General John Ashcroft and FBI Director Robert Mueller that he was deemed a "high value" detainee based on his ethnicity and religion. At the core of Iqbal's complaint was the allegation that Ashcroft and Mueller approved "a policy of holding post-September 11th detainees in highly restrictive conditions of confinement until they were 'cleared' by the FBI."[53] He claimed First and Fifth Amendment violations on the basis of race, religion and national origin. At the District Court Ashcroft and Mueller asserted qualified immunity defenses and moved to dismiss the complaint based on a failure to state a claim against them. The District Court denied the motion to dismiss and the Second Circuit Court of Appeals affirmed the decision. On appeal to the U.S. Supreme Court, the qualified immunity issue was never answered in the ensuing decision because the 5-4 majority said the pleadings were insufficient to state a claim. *Iqbal's* significance in terms of civil rights litigation is the Court's reliance on a "flexible plausibility standard" requiring amplification of "a claim with some factual allegations in those contexts where such amplification is needed to render the claim plausible."[54] Federal Rule of Civil Procedure 8a requires that a pleading, to state a claim for relief, must contain: 1) a short and plain statement of the grounds for the court's jurisdiction, unless the court already has jurisdiction and the claim needs no new jurisdictional support; 2) a short and plain statement of the claim showing that the pleader is entitled to relief; and 3) a demand for the relief sought, which may include relief in the alternative or different types of relief. The decision in *Iqbal*, following on the heels of *Bell Atlantic Corp. v. Twombly*,[55] altered what had been an applied liberality in pleading

practice that allowed claims to move forward as long as the plaintiff could state a conceivably cognizable claim for relief. Although not directly impacting case law relative to qualified immunity claims and avoiding the issue entirely, *Iqbal* did address the claim regarding Ashcroft and Mueller's liability pursuant to a *Bivens* action. The Court noted that a *Bivens* action is akin to asserting liability under 42 USC §1983. Similar to case law under §1983 supervisory liability cannot be established on a theory of respondeat superior. Javaid Iqbal's claim of invidious discrimination had to be based on discriminatory purpose on the behalf of the supervising officials, their "undertaking a course of action," not their simple awareness of a result.[56] The complaint failed because Iqbal did not plead direct action on the part of either Ashcroft or Mueller and because he did not plead violation of a clearly established constitutional right.[57]

10. John Yoo, the Deputy Assistant Attorney General in the U.S. Department of Justice Office of Legal Counsel from 2001–2003, was responsible for the legal memorandum in which he took the legal position that Jose Padilla, an American citizen (refer to Chapter 3 commentary note 14), should be held as an enemy combatant. Additionally, Yoo authored legal memorandums aimed to "evade legal constraints" in detaining and interrogating enemy combatants. Yoo was sued by Padilla for his role as legal counsel in the ensuing war on terror. The complaint alleged that as a result of these policies, which Yoo was complicit in formulating, Padilla suffered constitutional deprivations. The District Court for Northern California originally held that Padilla had made out a plausible complaint,[58] but a three-judge panel of the Ninth Circuit Court of Appeals dismissed Padilla's lawsuit on the grounds that Yoo was entitled to qualified immunity.[59] Circuit Judge Raymond C. Fisher outlined the court's position at the beginning of the opinion by laying out the two reasons on which it found qualified immunity applied: *"First, although during Yoo's tenure at OLC the constitutional rights of convicted prisoners and persons subject to ordinary criminal process were, in many respects, clearly established, it was not "beyond debate" at that time that Padilla—who was not a convicted prisoner or criminal defendant, but a suspected terrorist designated an enemy combatant and confined to military detention by order of the President—was entitled to the same constitutional protections as an ordinary convicted prisoner or accused criminal. Second, although it has been clearly established for decades that torture of an American citizen violates the Constitution, and we assume without deciding that Padilla's alleged treatment rose to the level of torture, that such treatment was torture was not clearly established in 2001– 03."[60]* In an opinion subsequent to *Yoo*, *Vance v. Rumsfeld*, 701 F.3d 193 (7th Cir., 2012), the Seventh Circuit Court of Appeals also extended qualified immunity to former Secretary of Defense Donald Rumsfeld and the U.S. government for the acts of subordinates. In *Vance* two American citizens who were civilian employees of an Iraqi security company were arrested and detained by U.S. military troops in 2006. The arrests and detention were the result of their reports to the FBI of their suspicions that the company they worked for was providing weapons to groups hostile to

U.S. forces. Those individuals against whom the two American workers made reports retaliated by accusing the Americans of being gun dealers. The Americans, Donald Vance and Nathan Ertel, were subsequently arrested by U.S. military personnel. Vance and Ertel's complaint alleged denial of counsel; solitary confinement; sleep deprivation; extended interrogation using enhanced methods; denial of food, water, and medical attention. They were both eventually released after being initially designated as "security detainees." Their lawsuit sought to hold several military personnel accountable as well as Rumsfeld, top military commanders and the U.S government. As in earlier decisions, such as *al-Kidd, Iqbal* and scores of other federal court cases, the Seventh Circuit refused to extend liability in a *Bivens*-type action to government supervisors without direct action on the part of the supervisors. Additionally, the circuit court held that civilian courts should not interfere with military authority and that the Detainee Treatment Act did not provide a cause of action or a damages remedy to the plaintiffs. The circuit court's decision effectively ended the litigation for Vance and Ertel against any subordinate government personnel directly involved in their detention and treatment based on the immunity applied and the deference to military command.

11. During the October 2011 term the Supreme Court heard oral argument in five cases involving §1983 liability and governmental immunity.[61] Each of the decisions sided with the government argument and in two cases expanded the scope of qualified immunity's coverage by allowing the defense for a government official acting as a complaining witness in a grand jury proceeding[62] and for a private contractor hired by the government to perform a government function.[63] In the fifth case, the Court issued a per curiam decision without hearing oral argument.[64] But again in that case, *Ryburn v. Huff*, the Court sided with government officials who were police officers investigating a high school student's threat to "shoot up the school." The Court deferred to the decision making process of police officers involved with an investigation who are confronted with evolving circumstances. In doing so the Court denied the plaintiff's §1983 claim based on Fourth Amendment violations. The preceding cases are interesting and insightful in light of the general conversation relating to governmental immunity as well as the volume of cases on the one subject before the Court in a single term. However, the cases take on added meaning in light of the Court's 2006 decision in *Hudson v. Michigan*[65] and the political debate over the exclusionary rule, particularly within the context of terrorism investigations. In *Hudson*, a case dealing with the Fourth Amendment "knock and announce" requirement, the Court held that a violation of the rule by officers failing to wait a reasonable amount of time prior to forcing entry into a residence, did not require suppression of the evidence obtained. Justice Scalia wrote the 5-4 majority decision in which he stated the following: *"We cannot assume that exclusion in this context is necessary deterrence simply because we found that it was necessary deterrence in different contexts long ago. That would be forcing the public today to pay for the sins and inadequacies of a legal regime that existed almost half a century ago."*[66] Further on Justice Scalia wrote: *"Dollree Mapp*

could not turn to 42 USC §1983 for meaningful relief; Monroe v. Pape, 365 U.S. 167 (1961), which began the slow but steady expansion of that remedy, was decided the same Term as Mapp. It would be another 17 years before the §1983 remedy was extended to reach the deep pocket of municipalities, Monell v. NYC Dept. of Social Services, 436 U.S. 658 (1978). Citizens whose Fourth Amendment rights were violated by federal officers could not bring suit until 10 years after Mapp, with this Court's decision in Bivens v. Six Unknown Federal Narcotics Agents, 403 U.S. 388 (1971)."[67] The point made by Scalia in the above excerpts was that exclusion is not as necessary a remedy now as it was during the time of Dollree Mapp due to the fact that there are presently mechanisms in place which provide recourse against unlawful government action. In the same opinion Justice Scalia also made a point of indicating that law enforcement is much more professional now than it was during the 1960s. How viable an argument is this to use in order limit the effect of a remedy provided a generation earlier by the Court? If the Court is attempting to limit the scope of the exclusionary rule has the Court's recent decisions in the area of governmental immunity along with other relevant precedent made government officials practically judgment proof?

Endnotes

[1] *Black's Law Dictionary*, 4th Ed., West Publishing, p. 1359 (1968).

[2] *Berd v. Lovelace*, 21 Eng. Rep. 33 (Ch. 1577)—this is the earliest known case citing the attorney-client privilege; see also, *Upjohn v. United States*, 449 U.S. 383, 389 (1981) referencing the antiquity of the attorney-client privilege.

[3] Dershowitz, A. M. (2008). *Is There a Right to Remain Silent? Coercive Interrogation and the Fifth Amendment After 9/11*. New York: Oxford University Press.

[4] Blackstone, William. *Commentaries on the Laws of England: A Facsimile of the First Edition of 1765–1769*. Chicago: University of Chicago Press, 1979. Commentaries 1:233.

[5] Alexander Hamilton, "Federalist No. 26," in *The Federalist Papers*, para. 1 at http://thomas.loc.gov/home/fedpapers/fed_10.html.

[6] FRE §501 reads as follows: Except as otherwise required by the Constitution of the United States or provided by Act of Congress or in rules prescribed by the Supreme Court pursuant to statutory authority, the privilege of a witness, person, government, state, or political subdivision thereof shall be governed by the principles of the common law as they may be interpreted by the courts of the United States in the light of reason and experience. However, in civil actions and proceedings, with respect to an element of a claim or defense as to which state law supplies the rule of decision, the privilege of a witness, person, government, state, or political subdivision thereof shall be determined in accordance with state law.

[7] See Notes of the Committee on the Judiciary, House Report No. 93-650 and Notes of the Committee on the Judiciary, Senate Report No. 93-1277.

[8] See *In re Department of Investigation of City of New York v. Myerson*, 856 F.2d 481 (2d Cir., 1988).

[9] See, e.g., *In re Sealed Case*, 856 F.2d 268 (D.C. Cir., 1988).

[10]   See *U.S. v. Winner*, 641 F.2d 825 (10th Cir., 1981).

[11]   *Roviaro v. United States*, 353 U.S. 53 (1957).

[12]   See *In re United States Department of Homeland Security*, 459 F.3d 565 (5th Cir., 2006).

[13]   *Frankenhauser v. Goode*, 59 F.R.D. 339 (E.D. Pa., 1973) (unpublished opinion).

[14]   *United States v. Burr*, 25 F. Cas. 30, 1807 U.S. App. LEXIS 492 (Cir. Ct., Dist. Of Va., 1807).

[15]   Hobson, C. (2006). *The Aaron Burr Treason Trial*. Washington D.C.: The Federal Judicial Center.

[16]   *Burr* at 30.

[17]   *Id.* at 34.

[18]   See, e.g., *Dellwood Farms, Inc. v. Cargill, Inc.*, 128 F.3D 1122 (7th Cir., 1997)—referencing the application of the law enforcement privilege to disclosure of investigative files in an ongoing investigation.

[19]   See, e.g., Telman, J. (2012). *On the Conflation of the State Secrets Privilege and the Totten Doctrine*. American University National Security Law Brief, 1–10; George, B. (2009). *An Administrative Law Approach to Reforming the State Secrets Privilege*. New York University Law Review, 1691–1724; Glasionov, R. (2009). *In Furtherance of Transparency and Litigants' Rights: Reforming the State Secrets Privilege*. George Wasington University Law Review, 458–487; Lyons, C.N. (2007). *The State Secrets Privilege: Expanding Its Scope Through Government Misuse*. Lewis & Clark Law Review, 99–132; Flynn, S.C. (2001). *The Totten Doctrine and Its Poisoned Progeny*. Vermont Law Review, 793–810.

[20]   Wigmore, J.H. (1940) *Evidence in Trials at Common Law*, Boston: Little, Brown.

[21]   See memorandum of Attorney General Eric Holder dated September 28, 2009, titled Policies and Procedures Governing Invocation of the State Secrets Privilege. http://www.fas.org/sgp/news/2009/09/ag092309.pdf.

[22]   Federation of American Scientists (February 6, 2013). *Project on Government Secrecy*. Retrieved from http://www.fas.org/sgp/jud/statesec/.

[23]   H.R. 5956—112th Congress: State Secrets Protection Act. (2012). In www.Gov Track.us. Retrieved from http://www.govtrack.us/congress/bills/112/hr5956

[24]   Section 102(d)(3) as originally passed on July 26, 1947 read as follows: *"For the purpose of coordinating the intelligence activities of the several Government departments and agencies in the interest of national security, it shall be the duty of the Agency, under the direction of the National Security Council—(3) to correlate and evaluate intelligence relating to the national security, and provide for the appropriate dissemination of such intelligence within the Government using where appropriate existing agencies and facilities: Provided, That the Agency shall have no police, subpoena, law-enforcement powers, or internal-security functions: Provided Further, That the departments and other agencies of the Government shall continue to collect, evaluate, correlate, and disseminate departmental intelligence: And Provided Further, That the Director of Central Intelligence shall be responsible for protecting intelligence sources and methods from unauthorized disclosure ..."*

[25]   471 U.S. at 159.

[26] Id.

[27] Id. at 173.

[28] Id. at 181.

[29] Id. at 182.

[30] Id. at 189.

[31] 422 U.S. 255 (1975).

[32] Hughes, M. H. (1985). "CIA v. Sims: Supreme Court Deference to Agency Interpretation of FOIA Exemption 3." *Catholic University Law Review*, 279–313.

[33] 418 U.S. at 705.

[34] Id. at 709.

[35] *Black's Law Dictionary* 1322 (8th Ed., 2004).

[36] American Civil Liberties Union. (2005, December 6). *Fact Sheet: Extraordinary Rendition*. Retrieved from http://www.aclu.org/national-security/fact-sheet-extraordinary-rendition.

[37] Id.

[38] Id.

[39] 479 F.3d at 300.

[40] 2007 US LEXIS 11351 (2007).

[41] *El-Masri v. The Former Yugoslavian Republic of Macedonia*, ECtHR, 39630/09 (2012).

[42] Id.

[43] 585 F.3d 559 (2d Cir., 2009).

[44] 614 F.3d 1070 (9th Cir., 2010).

[45] Blackstone, *Commentaries on the Laws of England*, Book 3, Chapter 17.

[46] 28 USC §1346(b).

[47] Lewis, J. H. (2001). *Civil Rights Law and Practice*. St. Paul: West Group.

[48] See, e.g., *Sullivan v. Town of Salem*, 805 F.2d 81 (2d Cir. 1986); *Coogan v. City of Wixom*, 820 F.2d 170 (6th Cir. 1987).

[49] 402 U.S. 388 (1971).

[50] 533 U.S. 194 (2001).

[51] 553 U.S. 223 (2009).

[52] Id.

[53] 556 U.S. 662.

[54] Id.

[55] 550 U.S. 544 (2007)—*Twombly* was decided two years prior to *Iqbal* was an anti-trust case that first announced the plausibility standard in federal pleading thereby dispensing with the old standard announced in *Conley v. Gibson*, 355 U.S. 41 (1957) that a pleading only need to state a conceivable claim in order to proceed forward. *Iqbal* applied the *Twombly* standard outside the realm of anti-trust cases to all pleadings.

[56] 556 U.S. 662.

[57] See *Hamad v. Gates*, 2012 US Dist LEXIS 52487 (W.D. Wash., 2012).

[58] *Padilla v. Yoo*, 633 F.Supp.2d 1005 (N.D. Cal., 2009).

[59] *Padilla v. Yoo*, 678 F.3d 748 (2011).

[60] 678 F.3d at 751.

[61] *Messerschmidt v. Millender*, 132 S.Ct. 1235 (2012); *Filarsky v. Delia*, 132 S.Ct. 1657 (2012); *Rehberg v. Paulk*, 132 S.Ct. 1497 (2012); *Reichle v. Howards*, 132 S.Ct. 2088 (2012); *Ryburn v. Huff*, 132 S.Ct. 987 (2012).

[62] *Rehberg v. Paulk.*

[63] *Filarsky v. Delia.*

[64] *Ryburn v. Huff*, 132 S.Ct. 987 (2012)

[65] 126 S.Ct. 2159 (2006).

[66] 126 S.Ct. at 2167.

[67] Id.

Chapter Six
GOVERNMENT TAKINGS, DESTRUCTION OF PRIVATE PROPERTY AND EMERGENCY AUTHORITY

The Fifth Amendment to the United States Constitution provides several distinct protections. They have become important enumerated rights in our constitutional framework. Yet there are limits that have been placed on some of these rights, limits that either the Supreme Court has said are necessary in order to give way to wartime or national security exigencies or exceptions existing within the amendment itself such as that found in the opening sentence: *"No person shall be held to answer for a capital, or otherwise infamous crime, unless on a presentment or indictment of a grand jury, except in cases arising in the land or naval forces, or in the militia, when in actual service in time of war or public danger."* The built-in exception to basic procedural protocol in criminal matters gives way in time of national emergency for those serving in the military. The Uniform Code of Military Justice applies and the use of military tribunals serves as the substitute for the civilian court system. But as already discussed in Chapters 3 and 4 there is a due process violation in most instances when a civilian citizen is subjected to those same military tribunals. Unless, of course, the civilian citizen has actively taken up arms against the United States and become an enemy. For the most part though, the Fifth Amendment right to *"presentment or indictment of a grand jury"* remains intact.[1]

The remaining protections found in the Fifth Amendment are: *"...nor shall any person be subject for the same offense to be twice put in jeopardy of life or limb; nor shall be compelled in any criminal case to be a witness against himself, nor be deprived of life, liberty, or property, without due process of law; nor shall private property be taken for public use, without just compensation."* In the context of national security and wartime emergency the property protections found within the Fifth Amendment have been limited or completely curtailed based on a legal justification. As discussed in Chapter 2, there is authority, beginning with the late 18th century admiralty cases and "prize" disputes, for the seizure and confiscation of enemy property or the property of any individual or group aiding the enemy. However, in times of national crisis or emergency there are instances when the property of a non-enemy, possibly even the property of a U.S. citizen, is taken or destroyed. What is the responsibility of the government at that point? Must the property be returned or the owner made financially whole? Does the Fifth Amendment provide a remedy for such government behavior? Students of constitutional law are familiar with the last clause of the Fifth Amendment, the Takings Clause, and the requirement of "just compensation" for any government taking of private property. Cases involving the government's eminent domain power wherein the government can seize private property for public use have been contentious justiciable controversies since the landmark U.S. Supreme Court case of *Barron v. Baltimore* where the issue concerned a wharf owner's claim that the city of Baltimore, through diversion of water and depositing of sand and dirt during road construction, made access to his wharf too shallow for ships.[2] The U.S.

Supreme Court ruled against the wharf owner, John Barron, on the basis of its finding that the Fifth Amendment applied only to the federal government and not the states. It would be 64 years until the Court explicitly stated in *Chicago, Burlington & Quincy Railroad Co. v. Chicago* that the Fifth Amendment's "takings clause" was directly applicable to state government by way of the Fourteenth Amendment.[3] This would be the first of a number of later cases over the course of the following century that would begin to incorporate parts of the Bill of Rights into the Fourteenth Amendment and made enforceable against the states. The early incorporation push would come in a series of cases in the 1920s and 1930s dealing with the First Amendment.[4] Even with the shift in the *Chicago, Burlington & Quincy Railroad Co.* case to a broader view of private property protection from government takings, the U.S. Supreme Court has over the years equally broadened the government's seizure authority. More recently, in the 2005 case of *Kelo v. City of New London* the Court continued to re-shape its eminent domain jurisprudence to justify Fifth Amendment taking authority to include "public purpose" as well as "public use."[5] What the *Kelo* case and similar manifestations of government authority signify are legal justifications for the taking of private property by the government despite an owner's reluctance to part with that property. In a separate but unrelated context, the law also provides for the taking of private property when that property is the proceeds or instrumentality of a crime. Federal and state forfeiture statutes have provided criminal as well as civil forfeiture sanctions for individuals who have obtained property in connection with a criminal offense, chiefly in the ongoing "war on drugs," which began in the 1980s and continued with equal fervor into the new millennium until taking a backseat to the "war on terror." Forfeiture statutes have also been used in driving while intoxicated enforcement and organized crime enforcement. The complexity of the forfeiture laws is evident with the number of federal statutes that provide for forfeiture of private property. Although this has always been a controversial issue, the U.S. Supreme Court has generally sided with the government in forfeiture cases.[6] Even in cases where the seized property has been used in connection with a crime without the knowledge of the owner, the Court has rejected the "innocent owner" defense. In the 1974 case *Calero Toledo v. Pearson Yacht Leasing Co.*, a pleasure yacht leased by the owner to two Puerto Rican residents was seized in Puerto Rico for unlawfully transporting marijuana. The owner was unaware of the illegal use of the yacht and endeavored to regain possession. Justice Brennan, in rejecting the "innocent owner" defense to the forfeiture action, wrote the following: *"At common law the value of an inanimate object directly or indirectly causing the accidental death of a King's subject was forfeited to the Crown as a deodand. The origins of the deodand are traceable to Biblical and pre-Judeo-Christian practices, which reflected the view that the instrument of death was accused and that religious expiation was required. The value of the instrument was forfeited to the King, in the belief that the King would provide the money for Masses to be said for the good of the dead man's soul, or insure that the deodand was put to charitable uses. When application of the deodand to religious or eleemosynary purposes ceased, and the deodand became a source of Crown revenue, the institution was justified as a penalty for carelessness ... The enactment of forfeiture statutes has not abated; contemporary federal and state forfeiture statutes reach virtually any type of property that might be used in the conduct of a criminal enterprise. Despite this proliferation of forfeiture enactments, the innocence of the owner of property subject to forfeiture has almost uniformly been rejected as a defense."[7]* Justice Brennan went on to cite Justice Story in *The Palmyra* who, 147 years earlier, rejected a claim that the absence of a criminal conviction of the owner of a vessel prevented an in rem proceeding against the seized vessel: *"[T]he practice has been, and so this Court understand the law to be, that the proceeding in rem stands independent of, and wholly unaffected by any criminal proceeding in personam."[8]* The *Palmyra* case involved an armed privateer operating under the Spanish flag that was captured by the USS Grampus. The seizure was conducted under the authority of an Act of Congress that *"authorizes the president to instruct the commanders of public armed vessels of the United States, to seize, subdue, and send into any port of the United States, any armed vessel or boat, or any vessel or boat, the crew whereof shall be armed, and which shall have attempted or committed any piratical aggression, search, restraint, depredation or seizure, upon any vessel of the United States, or of the citizens thereof, or upon any other vessel."[9]* Despite the fact that there was no criminal prosecution maintained against the commander and crew of the vessel, Justice Story held that it was still subject to seizure by the United States government. In so doing, Justice Story cited a case from the prior term, the *Marianna Flora*, which found that probable cause was a sufficient reason for the capture of an armed vessel at sea with indications of hostile aggression.[10]

The U.S. Supreme Court in its early days dealt with a number of cases involving the seizure of property belonging to a hostile enemy or aggressor. But what about the non-combatant owner of seized private property? During the Quasi-War with France the merchant vessel *Amelia* was captured by a French military ship. The *Amelia* was subsequently re-captured by the *USS Constitution* whose captain, Silas Talbot, placed a salvage claim on the ship. The ship was sent to New York on the captain's claim and the federal district court allowed the claim to go forward. The district court though was reversed by the circuit court. On appeal to the U.S. Supreme Court there were two questions for the Court to consider: 1) whether the capture of the *Amelia* was justified; and 2) whether there was a meritorious service performed by the captain and crew in seizing the ship. The U.S. Supreme Court held that the capture was justified through the authorization of Congress for the military seizure of French vessels and that a meritorious service was performed by the re-capture of the American merchant vessel thereby entitling the captain to compensation. These were the facts of the 1801 case of *Talbot v. Seeman*,[11] an early "prize" case that was significant because the captured vessel was not atypical enemy property. It was an example of the precarious rights of non-combatant, private property owners in relation to the hostilities of belligerents. The non-combatant private property owner stood in no better relation under the law of seizure than the "innocent owner" would in later Supreme Court cases.

As a general rule of law, the private property of a non-combatant can be seized by a military officer to prevent the property from falling into enemy hands, but in doing so the military officer has to justify the seizure by showing an imminent and impending danger or military necessity.[12] Destruction of the property would also be justified based on a valid showing of military necessity. Absent any of these circumstances a trespass upon property can be maintained. The challenge then is to enforce a claim against the government for the seizure or destruction. In the 1870 case of *Perrin v. United States*[13] the U.S. Supreme Court was faced with a claim for property accidentally destroyed by bombing from a United States warship. The property owner's claim, which was for property that was to be used for the establishment of a commercial business in Central America, was held not to be within the jurisdiction of the U.S. Court of Claims or within any laws of Congress, Executive decree, or contractual agreement. As a result the claim was dismissed. Absent any law or express agreement, the property was a mere casualty of conflict for which no remuneration was due.

The war powers of Congress and the president have subsequently been held to include the power to wage war effectively. During World War II the Court held that this power included the right of the government to collect re-negotiated excess profits on war sub-contracts under the Renegotiation Act.[14] There was no claim, said the U.S. Supreme Court in the World War II case of *Litcher v. U.S.*, of an unlawful taking of property in violation of the Fifth Amendment because it was a "necessary and proper" exercise of congressional power in prosecuting the war.[15] The Court further held the method of collecting excess private profits was a better alternative to the government taking over the production capacity of the nation.[16] This, the Court said, was more in line with the expression of a free people.

As the following cases show, the power of the government in the execution of war or other emergency powers can effect a taking or destruction of an individual's or corporation's private property. Of equal concern but in a different national security perspective is the emergency power of the government. To what extent can the government force evacuation of homes, require vaccinations, or use military troops to respond to domestic incidents of unrest or emergency? Fourth and Fifth Amendment rights are similarly impacted in these situations. Natural disasters, extended civil unrest, and the threats from transnational outbreak of disease call for government response, often beyond the local and state level. This chapter ends with a look at Supreme Court precedent in this area and a discussion of federal legislation.

United States v. Pacific Railroad
120 U.S. 227 (1887)

Mr. Justice Field delivered the opinion of the Court.

The Pacific Railroad Company, the claimant in this case, is a corporation created under the laws of Missouri, and is frequently designated as the Pacific Railroad of that state, to distinguish it from the Central Pacific Railroad Company incorporated under the laws of California, and the Union Pacific Railroad Company incorporated under an act of Congress, each of which is sometimes referred to as the Pacific Railroad Company.

From the 14th of August, 1867, to the 22d of July, 1872, it rendered services by the transportation of passengers and freight, for which the United States are indebted to it in the sum of $136,196.98 unless they are entitled to offset the cost of labor and materials alleged to have been furnished by them at its request for the construction of certain bridges on the line of its road. The extent and value of the services rendered are not disputed. It is only the offset or charge for the bridges which is in controversy, and that charge arose in this wise:

During the civil war, the State of Missouri was the theater of active military operations. It was on several occasions invaded by Confederate forces, and between them and the soldiers of the union conflicts were frequent and sanguinary. The people of the state were divided in their allegiance, and the country was ravaged by guerrilla bands. The railroads of the state as a matter of course were damaged by the contending forces, as each deemed the destruction of that means of transportation necessary to defeat or embarrass the movements of the other. In October, 1864, Sterling Price, a noted Confederate officer at the head of a large force, invaded the state and advanced rapidly toward St. Louis, approaching to within a few days' march of the city. During this invasion, thirteen bridges upon the main line and southwestern branch of the company's road were destroyed. General Rosecrans was in command of the federal forces in the state, and some of the bridges were destroyed by his orders as a military necessity to prevent the advance of the enemy. The record does not state by whom the others were destroyed, but, their destruction having taken place during the invasion, it seems to have been taken for granted that it was caused by the Confederate forces, and this conclusion was evidently correct. All the bridges except four were rebuilt by the company. These four were rebuilt by the government, and it is their cost which the government seeks to offset against the demand of the company. Of the four, two—one over the Osage River and one over the Moreau River—were destroyed by order of the commander of the federal forces. The other two, which were over the Maramec River, it is presumed were destroyed by the Confederate forces.

Soon after the destruction of the bridges, and during the same month, General Rosecrans summoned to an informal conference in St. Louis several gentlemen regarded as proper representatives of the railroad company, being its President, the superintendent, and the engineer of the road, and several of the directors. The court below makes the following findings as to what there occurred:

"By General Rosecrans it was stated that the immediate rebuilding of the bridges was a military necessity; that he should expect and require the company to do all in their power to put the roads in working order at the earliest possible moment, and that he intended to have what work they did not do done by the government and withhold from the freight earnings of the road a sum sufficient to repay the government for such outlays as in law and fact it should be found entitled to have repaid. The gentlemen present assured General Rosecrans that they would do all in their power to rebuild the bridges and put the roads in working order at the earliest moment, but they at the same time represented that several of the bridges, as they believed, had been destroyed by the proper military authority of the United States, and that in such cases the government was properly responsible for the loss, and should replace the bridges. Those which the public enemy had destroyed they conceded that the company should replace."

"General Rosecrans replied in substance:"

"Gentlemen, the question of the liability of the government for repairing damages to this road is one of both law and fact, and it is too early now to undertake the investigation of that question in this stirring time. I doubt myself whether all the damages which you say the government should be responsible for will be found liable to be laid to the charge of the government. Nevertheless, whatever is fair and right I should like to see done. You tell me now, and I have been informed by some of your representatives individually, that the company's means are insufficient to make these large repairs and make them promptly. Therefore I want to say to you that as a military necessity we must have the work done, and shall be glad to have the company do everything it can, and I will undertake to have the remainder done, and we will reserve out of the freights money enough to make the government good for that to which it shall be found to be entitled for rebuilding any or all of the bridges, and we will return the freights to you or settle with you on principles of law and equity."

"The gentlemen interested in the company reiterated their view of the case that the company should pay for bridges destroyed by the public enemy and that the government should replace at its own cost the bridges destroyed by its own military authorities."

The court also finds that these mutual representations and assurances were not intended or understood on either side to form a contract or agreement binding on the government or the company; that no formal action upon them was taken by the board of directors, and that there was no proof that they were ever communicated to the directors except as may be inferred from subsequent facts and circumstances mentioned, but that the company, through its directors and officers, promptly exerted itself to its utmost power to restore the roads to running order, and to that end cooperated with the government.

At the same time, General Rosecrans informed the Secretary of War that the rebuilding of the bridges was "essential and a great military necessity" in the defense of the state, and requested that Colonel Myers should be authorized "to have them rebuilt at once, the United States to be reimbursed the cost out of freight on the road." The Secretary referred the matter to the Quartermaster General, who recommended that General McCallum, Superintendent of Military Roads, be directed to take the necessary measures immediately for that purpose. The Secretary approved the recommendation, and General McCallum was thereupon ordered to cause the bridges to be rebuilt by the quickest and surest means possible. It does not appear that the company had any notice of these communications or of the order.

***

The cost of the four bridges rebuilt by the government amounted to $181,548.89. The question presented is whether the company is chargeable with their cost, assuming that there was no promise on its part, express or implied, to pay for them. That there was no express promise is clear. The representations and assurance at the conference called by General Rosecrans to urge the rebuilding of the bridges were not intended or understood to constitute any contract, and it is so found, as above stated, by the court below. They were rebuilt by the government as a military necessity, to enable the federal forces to carry on military operations, and not on any request of or contract with the company. As to the two bridges destroyed by the federal forces, some of the officers of the company at that conference insisted that they should be rebuilt by the government without charge to the company, and, though they appeared to consider that those destroyed by the enemy should be rebuilt by the company, there was no action of the board of directors on the subject. What was said by them was merely an expression of their individual opinions, which were not even communicated to the board.

***

Nor do we think that any promise can be implied from the fact that the company resumed the management and operation of the road after the bridges were rebuilt, but on that point we will speak hereafter. Assuming for the present that there was no such implication, we are clear that no obligation rests upon the company to pay for work done not at its request or for its benefit, but solely to enable the government to carry on its military operations.

It has been held by this Court in repeated instances that though the late war was not between independent nations, yet as it was between the people of different sections of the country and the insurgents were so thoroughly organized and formidable as to necessitate their recognition as belligerents, the usual incidents of a war between independent nations ensued. The rules of war, as recognized by the public law of civilized nations, became applicable to the contending forces. Their adoption was seen in the exchange of prisoners, the release of officers on parol, the recognition of flags of truce, and other arrangements designed to mitigate the rigors of warfare. The inhabitants of the Confederate states on the one hand, and of the states which adhered to the union on the other, became enemies, and subject to be treated as such without regard to their individual opinions or dispositions, while during its continuance commercial intercourse between them was forbidden, contracts between them were suspended, and the courts of each were closed to the citizens of the other. **Brown v. Hiatts**, 15 Wall. 184.

***

For all injuries and destruction which followed necessarily from these causes no compensation could be claimed from the government. By the well settled doctrines of public law, it was not responsible for them. The destruction or injury of private property in battle, or in the bombardment of cities and towns and in many other ways in the war, had to be borne by the sufferers alone as one of its consequences. Whatever would embarrass or impede the advance of the enemy, as the breaking up of roads or the burning of bridges, or would cripple and defeat him, as destroying his means of subsistence, were lawfully ordered by the commanding general. Indeed, it was his imperative duty to direct their destruction. The necessities of the war called for and justified this. The safety of the state in such cases overrides all considerations of private loss.

***

Vattel, in his Law of Nations, speaks of damages sustained by individuals in war as of two kinds—those done by the state and those done by the enemy. And after mentioning those done by the state deliberately and by way of precaution, as when a field, a house, or a garden belonging to a private person is taken for the purpose of erecting on the spot a town rampart or other piece of fortification, or when his standing corn or his storehouses are destroyed to prevent their being of use to the enemy, and stating that such damages are to be made good to the individual, who should bear only his quota of the loss, he says:

"But there are other damages caused by inevitable necessity, as, for instance, the destruction caused by the artillery in retaking a town from the enemy. These are merely accidents; they are misfortunes which chance deals out to the proprietors on whom they happen to fall. The sovereign, indeed, ought to show an equitable regard for the sufferers if the situation of his affairs will admit of it, but no action lies against the state for misfortunes of this nature—for losses which she has occasioned not willfully, but through necessity and by mere accident, in the exertion of her rights. The same may be said of damages caused by the enemy. All the subjects are exposed to such damages, and woe to him on whom they fall. The members of a society may well encounter such risk of property, since they encounter a similar risk of life itself. Were the state strictly to indemnify all those whose property is injured in this manner, the public finances would soon be exhausted and every individual in the state would be obliged to contribute his share in due proportion—a thing utterly impracticable." Book III, c. 15, § 232.

***

In what we have said as to the exemption of government from liability for private property injured or destroyed during war by the operations of armies in the field or by measures necessary for their safety and efficiency, we do not mean to include claims where property of loyal citizens is taken for the service of our armies, such as vessels, steamboats, and the like for the transport of troops and munitions of war, or buildings to be used as storehouse and places of deposit of war material, or to house soldiers or take care of the sick, or claims for supplies seized and appropriated. In such cases, it has been the practice of the government to make compensation for the property taken. Its obligation to do so is supposed to rest upon the general principle of justice that compensation should be made where private property is taken for public use, although the seizure and appropriation of private property under such circumstances by the military authorities may not be within the terms of the constitutional clause. **Mitchell v. Harmony**, 13 How. 134; **United States v. Russell**, 13 Wall. 623.

While the government cannot be charged for injuries to or destruction of private property caused by military operations of armies in the field or measures taken for their safety and efficiency, the converse of the doctrine is equally true—that private parties cannot be charged for works constructed on their lands by the government to further the operations of its armies. Military necessity will justify the destruction of property, but will not compel private parties to erect on their own lands works needed by the government or to pay for such works when erected by the government. The cost of building and repairing roads and bridges to facilitate the movements of troops, or the transportation of supplies and munitions of war, must therefore be borne by the government.

It is true that in some instances the works thus constructed may afterwards be used by the owner. A house built for a barrack or for the storage of supplies or for a temporary fortification might be converted to some purposes afterwards by the owner of the land, but that circumstance would impose no liability upon him. Whenever a structure is permanently affixed to real property belonging to an individual without his consent or request, he cannot be held responsible because of its subsequent use. It becomes his by being annexed to the soil, and he is not obliged to remove it to escape liability. He is not deemed to have accepted it so as to incur an obligation to pay for it merely because he has not chosen to tear it down, but has seen fit to use it. ***Zottman v. San Francisco***, 20 Cal. 96, 107. Where structures are placed on the property of another or repairs are made to them, he is supposed to have the right to determine the manner, form, and time in which the structures shall be built or the repairs be made and the materials to be used, but upon none of these matters was the company consulted in the case before us. The government regarded the interests only of the army; the needs or wishes of the company were not considered. No liability therefore could be fastened upon it for work thus done.

We do not find any adjudged cases on this particular point—whether the government can claim compensation for structures erected on land of private parties or annexed to their property not by their request, but as a matter of military necessity, to enable its armies to prosecute their movements with greater efficiency, and we are unable to recall an instance where such a claim has been advanced.

It follows from these views that the government can make no charge against the railroad company for the four bridges constructed by it from military necessity. The court will leave the parties where the war and the military operations of the government left them.

The judgment of the Court of Claims must therefore be reversed, and judgment be entered for the full amount claimed by the railroad company for its services, and it is so ordered.

Juragua Iron Co., Ltd. v. United States
212 U.S. 297 (1909)

Mr. Justice Harlan delivered the opinion of the Court.

This action was brought in the Court of Claims to recover from the United States the alleged value of certain property destroyed in Cuba, during the war with Spain, by order of the officer who at the time of its destruction commanded the troops of the United States operating in the locality of the property.

The case depends altogether upon the facts found by the court. We cannot go beyond those facts.

The Court of Claims found that the Juragua Iron Company (Limited) was a corporation of Pennsylvania, having its principal office and place of business in Philadelphia, and was and for many years had been engaged in the business of mining and selling iron ore and other mineral products in the United States, Cuba, and elsewhere, and in manufacturing iron and steel products; that it was so engaged at the opening of the late war with Spain; and, to enable it to carry on business, it owned, leased, and operated mines in Cuba, maintaining offices, works, and the necessary tools, machinery, equipments, and supplies for its business in the Province of Santiago de Cuba at or near Siboney, Firmeza, and La Cruz; that, in addition to its mines, works, and their equipments, the company also owned real estate at or near Siboney, which was improved by 66 buildings of a permanent character, used for the purposes of its business, and occupied by its employees as dwellings and for other purposes; that in the year 1898, and "while the war with Spain was in progress, the lives of the United States troops who were engaged in military operations in the province of Santiago de Cuba, in the belligerent prosecution of the war, became endangered by the prevalence of yellow fever, and it was deemed necessary by the officers in command, in order to preserve the health of the troops and to prevent the spread of the disease, to destroy all places of occupation or habitation which might contain the fever germs;" that, on or about the eleventh of July, 1898, General Miles, commanding the United States forces in Cuba, because of the necessity aforesaid, and by the advice of his medical staff, issued orders to destroy by fire these 66 buildings at Siboney, which belonged to the claimant and had been used for the purposes aforesaid; that, pursuant to that order, such buildings and their contents were destroyed by fire by the military authorities of the United States; that the reasonable value of the buildings at the time and place of destruction was $23,130, and the reasonable value of the drills, furniture, tools, and other personal property so destroyed by fire was seven thousand, nine hundred and eighty-six dollars ($7,986), making a total of thirty-one thousand, one hundred and sixteen dollars ($31,116).

As a conclusion of law, the court found that the United States was not liable to pay any sum to the plaintiff on account of the damage aforesaid, and dismissed the petition.

**

By the Act of March 3d 1887, providing for the bringing of suits against the government of the United States, the Court of Claims was given jurisdiction to hear and determine all claims "founded upon the Constitution of the United States or any law of Congress, except for pensions, or upon any regulation of an executive department, or upon any contract, expressed or implied, with the government of the United States, or for damages, liquidated or unliquidated, in cases not sounding in tort, in respect to which claims the party would be entitled to redress against the United States, either in a court of law, equity, or admiralty if the United States were suable."24 Stat. 505, c. 359.

Manifestly no action can be maintained under this statute unless the United States became bound by implied contract to compensate the plaintiff for the value of the property destroyed, or unless the case—regarding it as an action to recover damages—be one "not sounding in tort."

The plaintiff contends that the destruction of the property by order of the military commander representing the authority and power of the United States was such a taking of private property for public use as to imply a constitutional obligation on the part of the government to make compensation to the owner. Const. Amend. 5.

***

But can such a principle be enforced in respect of property destroyed by the United States in the course of military operations for the purpose, and only for the purpose, of protecting the health and lives of its soldiers actually engaged at the time in war in the enemy's country? We say "enemy's country" because, under the recognized rules governing the conduct of a war between two nations, Cuba, being a part of Spain, was enemy's country, and all persons, whatever their nationality, who resided there, were, pending such war, to be deemed enemies of the United States and of all its people. The plaintiff, although an American corporation, doing business in Cuba, was, during the war with Spain, to be deemed an enemy to the United States with respect of its property found and then used in that country, and such property could be regarded as enemy's property, liable to be seized and confiscated by the United States in the progress of the war then being prosecuted—indeed, subject, under the laws of war, to be destroyed whenever, in the conduct of military operations, its destruction was necessary for the safety of our troops or to weaken the power of the enemy.

In **Miller v. United States**, 11 Wall. 268, 78 U. S. 305, the Court, speaking of the powers possessed by a nation at war, said:

"It is sufficient that the right to confiscate the property of all public enemies is a conceded right. Now what is that right, and why is it allowed? It may be remarked that it has no reference whatever to the personal guilt of the owner of confiscated property, and the act of confiscation is not a proceeding against him. The confiscation is not because of crime, but because of the relation of the property to the opposing belligerent—a relation in which it has been brought in consequence of its ownership. It is immaterial to it whether the owner be an alien or a friend, or even a citizen or subject of the power that attempts to appropriate the property. In either case, the property may be liable to confiscation under the rules of war. It is certainly *enough to warrant the exercise of this belligerent right that the owner be a resident of the enemy's country, no matter what his nationality."*

In **Lamar's Ex'r v. Brown**, 92 U. S. 187, 92 U. S. 194, the Court said:

"For the purposes of capture, property found in enemy territory is enemy property, without regard to the status of the owner. In war, all residents of enemy country are enemies."
"All property within enemy territory," said the Court in **Young v. United States**, 97 U. S. 39, 97 U. S. 60, *"is, in law, enemy property, just as all persons in the same territory are enemies. A neutral owning property within the enemy's lines holds it as enemy property, subject to the laws of war; and if it is hostile property, subject to capture."*

Referring to the rules of war between independent nations as recognized on both sides in the late Civil War, the Court, in **United States v. Pacific Railroad Co.**, 120 U. S. 227, 120 U. S. 233, 120 U. S. 239, said:

*"The rules of war, as recognized by the public law of civilized nations, became applicable to the contending forces ... The inhabitants of the Confederate states, on the one hand, and of the states which adhered to the Union, on the other, became enemies, and subject to be treated as such, without regard to their individual opinions or dispositions; while during its continuance commercial intercourse between them was forbidden, contracts between them were suspended, and the courts of each were closed to the citizens of the other. **Brown v. Hiatt**, 15 Wall. 177, 82 U.S. 184 ... More than a million of men were in the armies on each side. The injury and destruction of private property caused by their operations, and by measures necessary for their safety and efficiency, were almost beyond calculation. For all injuries and destruction which followed necessarily from these causes, no compensation could be claimed from the government. By the well settled doctrines of public law, it was not responsible for them ... The principle that, for injuries to or destruction of private property in necessary military operations during the Civil War, the government is not responsible is thus considered established. Compensation has been made in several such cases, it is true; but it has generally been, as stated by the President in his veto message, 'a matter of bounty, rather than of strict legal right.' See also **The Venus**, 8 Cranch 253, 12 U. S. 278; **The Venice**, 2 Wall. 258, 69 U. S. 275; **The Cheshire**, 3 Wall. 233; **The Gray Jacket**, 5 Wall. 342, 72 U. S. 369; **The Friendschaft**, 4 Wheat. 105, 17 U. S. 107; **Griswold v. Waddington**, 16 Johns. 438, 446, 447; Vattel, Law of Nations, b. 3, c. 5, § 70, and c. 4, § 8; Burlamaqui, Pt. 4, c. 4, § 20."*

So, in Hall's International Law, 5th ed. 500, 504, 533:

"A person, though not a resident in a country, may be so associated with it through having or being a partner in a house of trade as to be affected by its enemy character, in respect at least, of the property which he possesses in the belligerent territory."

***

"A neutral, or a citizen of the United States, domiciled in the enemy's country, not only in respect to his property, but also as to his capacity to sue, is deemed as much an alien enemy as a person actually born under the allegiance and residing within the dominions of the hostile nation."

In view of these principles—if there were no other reason—the plaintiff corporation could not invoke the protection of the Constitution in respect of its property used in business in Cuba during the war, any more than a Spaniard residing there could have done, under like circumstances, in reference to his property then in that island. If the property destroyed by order of General Miles had belonged at the time to a resident Cuban, the owner would not have been heard in any court, under the facts found, to claim, as upon implied contract, compensation from the United States on account of such destruction. How, then, under the facts found, could an obligation based on implied contract arise under the Constitution in favor of the plaintiff, an American corporation which, at the time and in reference to the property in question, had a commercial domicile in the enemy's country? It is true that the Army, under General Miles, was under a duty to observe the rules governing the conduct of independent nations when engaged in war—a duty for the proper performance of which the United States may have been responsible in its political capacity to the enemy government. If what was done was in conformity to those rules—as, upon the facts found, we must assume that it was—then the owner of the property has no claim of any kind for compensation or damages, for, in such a case, the commanding general had as much right to destroy the property in question, if the health and safety of his troops required that to be done, as he would have had if, at the time, the property had been occupied and was being used by the armed troops of the enemy for hostile purposes. In the circumstances disclosed by the record, it cannot reasonably be said that there was, in respect of the destruction of the property in question, any "convention between the parties," any "coming together of minds," or any circumstances from which a contract could be implied. ***Russell v. United States***, 182 U. S. 516, 182 U. S. 530; ***Harley v. United States***, 198 U. S. 229, 198 U. S. 234. Again, if, as contended—without, however, any basis for the contention—the acts of that officer were not justified by the laws of war, then the utmost that could be said would be that what was done pursuant to his order amounted to a tort, and a claim against the government for compensation on account thereof would make a case "sounding in tort." But of such a case the court would, of course, have no jurisdiction under the act of Congress.

In this connection, we may refer to **Hijo v. United States**, 194 U. S. 315, 194 U. S. 322, in which the United States was sued by a Spanish corporation for the value of the use of a merchant vessel taken by the United States in the port of Porto Rico, when that city was captured by our Army and Navy on July 28th, 1898, and kept and used by the Quartermaster's Department for some time thereafter. The Court said:

"There is no element of contract in the case, for nothing was done by the United States, nor anything said by any of its officers, from which could be implied an agreement or obligation to pay for the use of the plaintiff's vessel. According to the established principles of public law, the owners of the vessel, being Spanish subjects, were to be deemed enemies, although not directly connected with military operations. The vessel was therefore to be deemed enemy's property. It was seized as property of that kind, for purposes of war, and not for any purposes of gain."

After observing that the case did not come within the principle announced in **United States v. Great Falls Mfg. Co.**, 112 U. S. 645, 112 U. S. 656, the Court proceeded:

"The seizure, which occurred while the war was flagrant, was an act of war, occurring within the limits of military operations. The action, in its essence, is for the recovery of damages, but, as the case is one sounding in tort, no suit for damages can be maintained under the statute against the United States. It is nonetheless a case sounding in tort because the claim is in form for the use of the vessel after actual hostilities were suspended by the protocol of August 12, 1898. A state of war did not in law cease until the ratification in April, 1899, of the treaty of peace ... If the original seizure made a case sounding in tort, as it undoubtedly did, the transaction was not converted into one of implied contract because of the retention and use of the vessel pending negotiations for a treaty of peace."

In our judgment, there is no element of contract in the claim of the plaintiff. And even if it were conceded that its property was wrongfully and unnecessarily destroyed under the order of the general commanding the United States troops, the concession could mean nothing more, in any aspect of the case, than that a tort was committed by that officer in the interest of the United States. But, as already said, of a cause of action arising from such a tort the Court of Claims could not take cognizance, whatever other redress was open to the plaintiff ...

Having noticed all the questions that require consideration, and finding no error in the record, the judgment of the Court of Claims must be affirmed.

It is so ordered.

United States v. Caltex, Inc.
344 U.S. 149 (1952)

Mr. Chief Justice Vinson delivered the opinion of the Court.

Each of the respondent oil companies owned terminal facilities in the Pandacan district of Manila at the time of the Japanese attack upon Pearl Harbor. These were used to receive, handle and store petroleum products from incoming ships and to release them for further distribution throughout the Philippine Islands. Wharves, rail and automotive equipment, pumps, pipelines, storage tanks, and warehouses were included in the property on hand at the outbreak of the war, as well as a normal supply of petroleum products.

News of the Pearl Harbor attack reached Manila early in the morning of December 8, 1941. On the same day, enemy air attacks were mounted against our forces in the Philippines, and thereafter the enemy launched his amphibious assault.

On December 12, 1941, the United States Army, through its Chief Quartermaster, stationed a control officer at the terminals. Operations continued at respondents' plants, but distribution of the petroleum products for civilian use was severely restricted. A major share of the existing supplies was requisitioned by the Army.

The military situation in the Philippines grew worse. In the face of the Japanese advance, the Commanding General, on December 23, 1941, ordered the withdrawal of all troops on Luzon to the Bataan Peninsula. On December 25, 1941, he declared Manila to be an open city. On that same day, the Chief Engineer on the staff of the Commanding General addressed to each of the oil companies letters stating that the Pandacan oil deposits "are requisitioned by the U.S. Army."

The letters further stated: "Any action deemed necessary for the destruction of this property will be handled by the U.S. Army." An engineer in the employ of one of the companies was commissioned a first lieutenant in the Army Corps of Engineers to facilitate this design.

On December 26, he received orders to prepare the facilities for demolition. On December 27, 1941, while enemy planes were bombing the area, this officer met with representatives of the companies. The orders of the Chief Engineer had been transmitted to the companies. Letters from the Deputy Chief of Staff, by command of General MacArthur, also had been sent to each of the oil companies, directing the destruction of all remaining petroleum products and the vital parts of the plants. Plans were laid to carry out these instructions, to expedite the removal of products which might still be of use to the troops in the field, and to lay a demolition network about the terminals. The representatives of Caltex were given, at their insistence, a penciled receipt for all the terminal facilities and stocks of Caltex.

At 5:40 p.m., December 31, 1941, while Japanese troops were entering Manila, Army personnel completed a successful demolition. All unused petroleum products were destroyed, and the facilities were rendered useless to the enemy. The enemy was deprived of a valuable logistic weapon.

After the war, respondents demanded compensation for all of the property which had been used or destroyed by the Army. The Government paid for the petroleum stocks and transportation equipment which were either used or destroyed by the Army, but it refused to compensate respondents for the destruction of the Pandacan terminal facilities. Claiming a constitutional right under the Fifth Amendment to just compensation for these terminal facilities, respondents sued in the Court of Claims. Recovery was allowed. We granted certiorari to review this judgment.

As reflected in the findings of the Court of Claims, there were two rather distinct phases of Army operations in the Pandacan District in December, 1941. While the military exercised considerable control over the business operations of respondents' terminals during the period between December 12 and December 26, there was not, according to the findings below, an assumption of actual physical or proprietary dominion over them during this period. Bound by these findings, respondents do not now question the holding of the Court of Claims that, prior to December 27, there was no seizure for which just compensation must be paid.

Accordingly, it is the legal significance of the events that occurred between December 27 and December 31 which concerns us. Respondents concede that the Army had a right to destroy the installations. But they insist that the destruction created a right in themselves to exact fair compensation from the United States for what was destroyed.

The argument draws heavily from statements by this Court in **Mitchell v. Harmony**, 13 How. 115 (1852), and **United States v. Russell**, 13 Wall. 623 (1871). We agree that the opinions lend some support to respondents' view.

But the language in those two cases is far broader than the holdings. Both cases involved equipment which had been impressed by the Army for subsequent use by the Army. In neither was the Army's purpose limited, as it was in this case, to the sole objective of destroying property of strategic value to prevent the enemy from using it to wage war the more successfully.

A close reading of the **Mitchell** and **Russell** cases shows that they are not precedent to establish a compensable taking in this case. Nor do those cases exhaust all that has been said by this Court on the subject. In **United States v. Pacific R. Co.**, 120 U. S. 227 (1887), Justice Field, speaking for a unanimous Court, discussed the question at length. That case involved bridges which had been destroyed during the war between the states by a retreating Northern Army to impede the advance of the Confederate Army. Though the point was not directly involved, the Court raised the question of whether this act constituted a compensable taking by the United States, and answered it in the negative:

"The destruction or injury of private property in battle, or in the bombardment of cities and towns, and in many other ways in the war, had to be borne by the sufferers alone, as one of its consequences. Whatever would embarrass or impede the advance of the enemy, as the breaking up of roads or the burning of bridges, or would cripple and defeat him, as destroying his means of subsistence, were lawfully ordered by the commanding general. Indeed, it was his imperative duty to direct their destruction. The necessities of the war called for and justified this. The safety of the state in such cases overrides all considerations of private loss."

It may be true that this language also went beyond the precise questions at issue. But the principles expressed were neither novel nor startling, for the common law had long recognized that, in times of imminent peril—such as when fire threatened a whole community—the sovereign could, with immunity, destroy the property of a few that the property of many and the lives of many more could be saved. And what was said in the *Pacific Railroad* case was later made the basis for the holding in **Juragua Iron Co. v. United States**, 212 U. S. 297, where recovery was denied to the owners of a factory which had been destroyed by American soldiers in the field in Cuba because it was thought that the structure housed the germs of a contagious disease.

Therefore, whether or not the principle laid down by Justice Field was dictum when he enunciated it, we hold that it is law today. In our view, it must govern in this case. Respondents and the majority of the Court of Claims, arguing to the contrary, have placed great emphasis on the fact that the Army exercised "deliberation" in singling out this property, in "requisitioning" it from its owners, and in exercising "control" over it before devastating it. We need not labor over these labels; it may be that they describe adequately what was done, but they do not show the legal consequences of what was done. The "requisition" involved in this case was no more than an order to evacuate the premises which were slated for demolition. The "deliberation" behind the order was no more than a design to prevent the enemy from realizing any strategic value from an area which he was soon to capture.

Had the Army hesitated, had the facilities only been destroyed after retreat, respondents would certainly have no claims to compensation. The Army did not hesitate. It is doubtful that any concern over the legal niceties of the situation entered into the decision to destroy the plants promptly, while there was yet time to destroy them thoroughly. Nor do we think it legally significant that the destruction was effected prior to withdrawal. The short of the matter is that this property, due to the fortunes of war, had become a potential weapon of great significance to the invader. It was destroyed, not appropriated for subsequent use. It was destroyed that the United States might better and sooner destroy the enemy.

The terse language of the Fifth Amendment is no comprehensive promise that the United States will make whole all who suffer from every ravage and burden of war. This Court has long recognized that, in wartime, many losses must be attributed solely to the fortunes of war, and not to the sovereign. No rigid rules can be laid down to distinguish compensable losses from non-compensable losses. Each case must be judged on its own facts. But the general principles laid down in the **Pacific Railroad** case seem especially applicable here. Viewed realistically, then, the destruction of respondents' terminals by a trained team of engineers in the face of their impending seizure by the enemy was no different than the destruction of the bridges in the **Pacific Railroad** case. Adhering to the principles of that case, we conclude that the court below erred in holding that respondents have a constitutional right to compensation on the claims presented to this Court.

Reversed.

Commentary and Questions

1. The preceding cases come from three different historical conflicts—the U.S. Civil War, the Spanish-American War, and World War II. Two of the conflicts—the Spanish-American War and World War II—were actual declared wars by Congress whereas the U.S. Civil War was a response to the act of a belligerent power, the Confederate States of America, but not a declared war. Congress in 1861 declared a state of insurrection three months after the April attack on Fort Sumter, which authorized the continued war against the rebellious states. During times of such conflict loyalty to the government is of utmost importance. The crime of treason is defined in Title 18 United

States Code section 2381 as follows: *"Whoever, owing allegiance to the United States, levies war against them or adheres to their enemies, giving them aid and comfort within the United States or elsewhere, is guilty of treason and shall suffer death, or shall be imprisoned not less than five years and fined under this title but not less than $10,000; and shall be incapable of holding any office under the United States."* Treason's definition is also found in Article III, section 3 of the U.S. Constitution: *"Treason against the United States, shall consist only in levying war against them, or in adhering to their enemies, giving them aid and comfort."* Article III continues by providing for the forfeiture of property upon a conviction of treason but limits the forfeiture to that of the traitor: *"The Congress shall have power to declare the punishment of treason, but no attainder of treason shall work corruption of blood, or forfeiture except during the life of the person attainted."* The concept of corruption of the blood refers to the English common law punishment of the innocent heirs of a traitor and the continuing forfeiture of the traitor's estate. A person against whom there was attainder for a capital crime would lose not only their property and right to hereditary titles but the ability to transfer property to heirs. Blackstone in his *Commentaries on the Laws of England* writes: *"The natural justice of forfeiture or confiscation of property, for treason, is founded in this consideration: that he who hath thus violated the fundamental principles of government, and broken his part of the original contract between king and people, hath abandoned his connections with society; and hath no longer any right to those advantages, which before belonged to him purely as a member of the community: among which social advantages the right of transferring or transmitting property to others is one of the chief. Such forfeitures moreover, whereby his posterity must suffer as well as himself, will help to restrain a man, not only by the sense of his duty, and dread of personal punishment, but also by his passions and natural affections; and will interest every dependent and relation he has, to keep him from offending..."*[17] Corruption of blood was outlawed by statute in England and expressly forbidden in Article I, clause 3 of the U.S. Constitution. Nevertheless the concept of forfeiture for crimes against the government retained its vitality against the offender. In criminal cases forfeiture of property used in connection with a criminal offense is permitted and a forfeiture proceeding is commenced by the prosecutor. Typically the seizure of property as a result of criminal conviction can be maintained by the government in a criminal proceeding, which is considered an in personam action against the person of the defendant who as part of the conviction surrenders property to the government. Or in the alternative a separate civil in rem proceeding is commenced in civil court after the disposition of the criminal case. Both are similar in nature but do vary in the level of proof required with the criminal case seizure requiring a greater evidentiary burden. Although there has been criticism of government overreaching in some instances of property forfeiture, the taking of property as a result of owner misconduct has been sanctioned by the courts.[18]

2. The seizure of private property linked to misconduct of its owner generally stems from a sovereign right, which is to be distinguished from confiscation

or destruction based on a belligerent's right.[19] The belligerent as occupier of a territory stands in place of the sovereign.[20] A U.S. officer of the armed forces as military authority is not liable for damages or injuries resulting from his orders or generally answerable in any civil court when such damage or injury results from military necessity.[21] The Court in *Pacific Railroad* spoke extensively of the law of military necessity in addressing the disputed property claim presented to it. What is the generally accepted legal rule with regard to military necessity and the destruction of property as explained in the decision? Must there be compensation of the owner for use of the property? How did the Court resolve the issue as to the government's claim for reimbursement for the bridges it constructed out of military necessity?

3. In *United States v. Russell*, another Civil War property related case, Justice Clifford wrote the following: "*Private property, the Constitution provides, shall not be taken for public use without just compensation, and it is clear that there are few safeguards ordained in the fundamental law against oppression and the exercise of arbitrary power of more ancient origin or of greater value to the citizen, as the provision for compensation, except in certain extreme cases, is a condition precedent annexed to the right of the government to deprive the owner of his property without his consent. Extraordinary and unforeseen occasions arise, however, beyond all doubt, in cases of extreme necessity in time of war or of immediate and impending public danger, in which private property may be impressed into the public service, or may be seized and appropriated to the public use, or may even be destroyed without the consent of the owner. Unquestionably such extreme cases may arise, as where the property taken is imperatively necessary in time of war to construct defences for the preservation of a military post at the moment of an impending attack by the enemy, or for food or medicine for a sick and famishing army utterly destitute and without other means of such supplies, or to transport troops, munitions of war, or clothing to reinforce or supply an army in a distant field, where the necessity for such reinforcement or supplies is extreme and imperative, to enable those in command of the post to maintain their position or to repel an impending attack, provided it appears that other means of transportation could not be obtained, and that the transports impressed for the purpose were imperatively required for such immediate use. Where such an extraordinary and unforeseen emergency occurs in the public service in time of war no doubt is entertained that the power of the government is ample to supply for the moment the public wants in that way to the extent of the immediate public exigency, but the public danger must be immediate, imminent, and impending, and the emergency in the public service must be extreme and imperative, and such as will not admit of delay or a resort to any other source of supply, and the circumstances must be such as imperatively require the exercise of that extreme power in respect to the particular property so impressed, appropriated, or destroyed. Exigencies of the kind do arise in time of war or impending public danger, but it is the emergency, as was said by a great magistrate, that gives the right, and it is clear that the emergency must be shown to exist before the taking can*

be justified. Such a justification may be shown, and when shown the rule is well settled that the officer taking private property for such a purpose, if the emergency is fully proved, is not a trespasser, and that the government is bound to make full compensation to the owner ... Such a taking of private property by the government, when the emergency of the public service in time of war or impending public danger is too urgent to admit of delay, is everywhere regarded as justified, if the necessity for the use of the property is imperative and immediate, and the danger, as heretofore described, is impending, and it is equally clear that the taking of such property under such circumstances creates an obligation on the part of the government to reimburse the owner to the full value of the service. Private rights, under such extreme and imperious circumstances, must give way for the time to the public good, but the government must make full restitution for the sacrifice."[22] The *Russell* case concerned the Union government's use of three steamboats in the war effort. Justice Clifford wrote of the implied promise of restitution by the government in the commandeering of the boats.

Is there a variance in the Court's opinion in *Pacific Railroad* with that in *Russell*? Would the result in *Russell* differ if there was an additional claim for damage to the steamboats or for total replacement as a result of their being destroyed in the war effort?

4. Unless a government has consented to be sued it retains sovereign immunity and there is no liability for tort related conduct. In *Jaragua Iron Co.* the Court specifically addressed this immunity by referencing an 1887 Act of Congress regarding Court of Claims jurisdiction and stating that no claim could be maintained unless there was an implied contract by the sovereign to be bound to compensate the injured party. The plaintiff sought to make a constitutional claim based on a Fifth Amendment taking of property.

What did the Court state with regard to the plaintiff's asserted takings claim? What was the significance of the plaintiff company's position as an American corporation doing business in Cuba during the conflict? How did this impact the plaintiff's asserted claim?

5. The Court's decision in *Caltex* provided insight into its earlier post-Civil War decision in *Russell* as well as *Mitchell v. Harmony*, a case from the Mexican-American War, both of which vary from the Court's holding in *Pacific Railroad* and subsequent cases.[23] As indicated above the Court in *Russell* held that use of steamboats by the Union army was compensable by the government to the owner. Similarly in *Mitchell* the Court found that the confiscation of property belonging to a trader authorized by the government to travel with the army along with other merchants and trade in a particular territory was also compensable. In *Mitchell* the confiscation by the commanding officer of the army was found not to be of military necessity, *"And the property was seized not to defend his position, nor to place his troops in a safer one, nor to anticipate the attack of an approaching enemy, but to ensure the success of a distant and hazardous expedition upon which he was about to march."*[24] As such the trader had a rightful claim.

What was the basis of the denial of compensation by the Court in *Caltex* and the strength of the government's argument in the case that was lacking in *Mitchell* and *Russell*?

6. Instances of national emergency have resulted in the curtailment of certain property rights in support of the common good. These have included the creation of a price control board for commodities during World War II[25] and the regulation of rents on apartments, hotels, and other properties during wartime.[26] In 1942 President Roosevelt resurrected the National War Labor Board, which was originally created by President Wilson in 1918 to arbitrate labor disputes during World War I. Once again the purpose was to avoid industrial labor-management conflicts that could be detrimental to the war effort. In the 1945 case of *United States v. Montgomery Ward & Co.*, the Seventh Circuit Court of Appeals upheld the government's seizure of seven Montgomery Ward stores and properties throughout the country.[27] In a famous photo, Sewell Avery, the Montgomery-Ward Chairman of the Board, is shown being carried out of his Chicago office by two uniformed U.S. soldiers. At issue was Avery's refusal to honor a union contract that led to a strike and the Montgomery-Ward company's refusal to adhere to a National War Labor Board order to end the strike.[28] The government's claimed authority for the seizure was based on President Roosevelt's Executive Order No. 9017 of January 12, 1942, establishing the National War Labor Board, which was subsequently referred to and sanctioned in Congress' passing in 1943 of the War Labor Disputes Act.[29] In doing so the court found that the "seizure power as the ultimate means of settling war disputes in wartime ... and extended to the entire economy."[30] The resolution in this case differed greatly than that of President Truman's efforts to seize steel mills during the Korean War. As discussed in Chapter 2 the U.S. Supreme Court in *Youngstown Sheet & Tube Co. v. Sawyer* found that Truman acted in excess of his Article II Executive authority in seizing the steel mills. The key difference between the *Montgomery Ward* case and *Youngstown Sheet & Tube Co.* is that in the former case the president acted with the approval of Congress pursuant to its power to regulate commerce.

7. In August 1998, President Clinton ordered the bombing of the El-Shifa Pharmaceutical plant in the Sudan. This order was in response to the terrorist bombing of the U.S. embassies in Kenya and Tanzania. The justification for the bombing was based on claims the plant was financed by Osama bin Laden and produced an ingredient used in chemical weapons. A subsequent lawsuit by the owner of the plant, Salah Idris, sought damages for the destruction of the plant. Additional claims were filed for negligence and trespass under the Foreign Tort Claims Act (FTCA) and defamation based on government allegations after the bombing that Idris had terrorist connections. The FTCA claims were dismissed by the D.C. Circuit Court on sovereign immunity grounds.[31] The surviving claims for the destruction of the property and defamation were later denied by the Circuit Court on a re-hearing; thereby affirming the District Court's holding that recovery was

barred by the political question doctrine.[32] The Circuit Court stated the doctrine as follows: *"It is emphatically the province and duty of the judicial department to say what the law is,"* **Marbury v. Madison**, *5 U.S. (1 Cranch) 137, 177 (1803), but some "[q]uestions, in their nature political," are beyond the power of the courts to resolve, id. at 170. The political question doctrine is "essentially a function of the separation of powers,"* **Baker v. Carr**, *369 U.S. 186, 217 (1962), and "excludes from judicial review those controversies which revolve around policy choices and value determinations constitutionally committed for resolution to the halls of Congress or the confines of the Executive Branch ..."*[83] Particularly in the realms of foreign policy and national security decisions the Court said judicial deference needs to be given to the branches of government tasked with those responsibilities. Further, the Court addressed Executive decisions relating to military action: *"In military matters in particular, the courts lack the competence to assess the strategic decision to deploy force or to create standards to determine whether the use of force was justified or well-founded. The complex, subtle, and professional decisions as to the control of a military force are essentially professional military judgments, subject always to civilian control of the Legislative and Executive Branches. The ultimate responsibility for these decisions is appropriately vested in branches of the government which are periodically subject to electoral accountability."*[84] As a result no claims would be recognized in connection with the bombing destruction of the El-Shifa plant by the United States.

Jacobsen v. Massachusetts
197 U.S. 11 (1905)

Mr. Justice Harlan delivered the opinion of the court.

We pass without extended discussion the suggestion that the particular section of the statute of Massachusetts now in question (§137, c.75) is in derogation of rights secured by the Preamble of the Constitution of the United States. Although that Preamble indicates the general purposes for which the people ordained and established the Constitution, it has never been regarded as the source of any substantive power conferred on the Government of the United States or on any of its Departments. Such powers embrace only those expressly granted in the body of the Constitution and such as may be implied from those so granted. Although, therefore, one of the declared objects of the Constitution was to secure the blessings of liberty to all under the sovereign jurisdiction and authority of the United States, no power can be exerted to that end by the United States unless, apart from the Preamble, it be found in some express delegation of power or in some power to be properly implied therefrom...

We also pass without discussion the suggestion that the above section of the statute is opposed to the spirit of the Constitution ...

We have no need in this case to go beyond the plain, obvious meaning of the words in those provisions of the Constitution which, it is contended, must control our decision.

What, according to the judgment of the state court, is the scope and effect of the statute? What results were intended to be accomplished by it? These questions must be answered.

The Supreme Judicial Court of Massachusetts said in the present case:

"Let us consider the offer of evidence which was made by the defendant Jacobson. The ninth of the propositions which he offered to prove, as to what vaccination consists of, is nothing more than a fact of common knowledge, upon which the statute is founded, and proof of it was unnecessary and immaterial. The thirteenth and fourteenth involved matters depending upon his personal opinion, which could not be taken as correct, or given effect, merely because he made it a ground of refusal to comply with the requirement. Moreover, his views could not affect the validity of the statute, nor entitle him to be excepted from its provisions. **Commonwealth v. Connelly***, 163 Massachusetts 539;* **Commonwealth v. Has***, 122 Massachusetts 40;* **Reynolds v. United States***, 98 U.S. 145;* **Regina v. Downes***, 13 Cox C.C. 111. The other eleven propositions all relate to alleged injurious or dangerous effects of vaccination. The defendant 'offered to prove and show by competent evidence' these so-called facts. Each of them, in its nature, is such that it cannot be stated as a truth, otherwise than as a matter of opinion. The only 'competent evidence' that could be presented to the court to prove these propositions was the testimony of experts, giving their opinions. It would not have been competent to introduce the medical history of individual cases. Assuming that medical experts could have been found who would have testified in support of these propositions, and that it had become the duty of the judge, in accordance with the law as stated in* **Commonwealth v. Anthes***, 5 Gray 185, to instruct the jury as to whether or not the statute is constitutional, he would have been obliged to consider the evidence in connection with facts of common knowledge, which the court will always regard in passing upon the constitutionality of a statute. He would have considered this testimony of experts in connection with the facts, that for nearly a century, most of the members of the medical profession have regarded vaccination, repeated after intervals, as a preventive of smallpox; that, while they have recognized the possibility of injury to an individual from carelessness in the performance of it, or even, in a conceivable case, without carelessness, they generally have considered the risk of such an injury too small to be seriously weighed as against the benefits coming from the discreet and proper use of the preventive, and that not only the medical profession and the people*

generally have for a long time entertained these opinions, but legislatures and courts have acted upon them with general unanimity. If the defendant had been permitted to introduce such expert testimony as he had in support of these several propositions, it could not have changed the result. It would not have justified the court in holding that the legislature had transcended its power in enacting this statute on their judgment of what the welfare of the people demands." **Commonwealth v. Jacobson**, *183 Massachusetts 242.*

***

The authority of the State to enact this statute is to be referred to what is commonly called the police power—a power which the State did not surrender when becoming a member of the Union under the Constitution. Although this court has refrained from any attempt to define the limits of that power, yet it has distinctly recognized the authority of a State to enact quarantine laws and "health laws of every description;" indeed, all laws that relate to matters completely within its territory and which do not, by their necessary operation, affect the people of other States. According to settled principles, the police power of a State must be held to embrace, at least, such reasonable regulations established directly by legislative enactment as will protect the public health and the public safety. **Gibbons v. Ogden**, 9 Wheat. 1, 22 U.S. 203; **Railroad Company v. Husen**, 95 U.S. 465, 95 U.S. 470; **Beer Company v. Massachusetts**, 97 U.S. 25; **New Orleans Gas Co. v. Louisiana Light Co.**, 115 U.S. 650, 115 U.S. 661; **Lawton v. Steele**, 152 U.S. 133. It is equally true that the State may invest local bodies called into existence for purposes of local administration with authority in some appropriate way to safeguard the public health and the public safety. The mode or manner in which those results are to be accomplished is within the discretion of the State, subject, of course, so far as Federal power is concerned, only to the condition that no rule prescribed by a State, nor any regulation adopted by a local governmental agency acting under the sanction of state legislation, shall contravene the Constitution of the United States or infringe any right granted or secured by that instrument. A local enactment or regulation, even if based on the acknowledged police powers of a State, must always yield in case of conflict with the exercise by the General Government of any power it possesses under the Constitution, or with any right which that instrument gives or secures. **Gibbons v. Ogden**, 9 Wheat. 1, 22 U.S. 210; **Sinot v. Davenport**, 22 How. 227, 63 U.S. 243; **Missouri, Kansas & Texas Ry. Co. v. Haber**, 169 U.S. 613, 169 U.S. 626.

We come, then, to inquire whether any right given or secured by the Constitution is invaded by the statute as interpreted by the state court. The defendant insists that his liberty is invaded when the State subjects him to fine or imprisonment for neglecting or refusing to submit to vaccination; that a compulsory vaccination law is unreasonable, arbitrary and oppressive, and, therefore, hostile to the inherent right of every freeman to care for his own body and health in such way as to him seems best, and that the execution of such a law against one who objects to vaccination, no matter for what reason, is nothing short of an assault upon his person. But the liberty secured by the Constitution of the United States to every person within its jurisdiction does not import an absolute right in each person to be, at all times and in all circumstances, wholly freed from restraint. There are manifold restraints to which every person is necessarily subject for the common good. On any other basis, organized society could not exist with safety to its members. Society based on the rule that each one is a law unto himself would soon be confronted with disorder and anarchy. Real liberty for all could not exist under the operation of a principle which recognizes the right of each individual person to use his own, whether in respect of his person or his property, regardless of the injury that may be done to others. This court has more than once recognized it as a fundamental principle that "persons and property are subjected to all kinds of restraints and burdens, in order to secure the general comfort, health, and prosperity of the State, of the perfect right of the legislature to do which no question ever was, or upon acknowledged general principles ever can be, made so far as natural persons are concerned." **Railroad Co. v. Husen**, 95 U.S. 465, 95 U.S. 471; **Missouri, Kansas & Texas Ry. Co. v. Haber**, 169 U.S. 613, 169 U.S. 628, 169 U.S. 629; **Thorpe v. Rutland & Burlington R.R.**, 27 Vermont 140, 148. In **Crowley v. Christensen**, 137 U.S. 86, 137 U.S. 89, we said:

"The possession and enjoyment of all rights are subject to such reasonable conditions as may be deemed by the governing authority of the country essential to the safety, health, peace, good order and morals of the community. Even liberty itself, the greatest of all rights, is not unrestricted license to act according to one's own will. It is only freedom from restraint under conditions essential to the equal enjoyment of the same right by others. It is then liberty regulated by law."

In the constitution of Massachusetts adopted in 1780, it was laid down as a fundamental principle of the social compact that the whole people covenants with each citizen, and each citizen with the whole people, that all shall be governed by certain laws for "the common good," and that government is instituted "for the common good, for the protection, safety, prosperity and happiness of the people, and not for the profit, honor or private interests of anyone man, family or class of men." The good and welfare of the Commonwealth, of which the legislature is primarily the judge, is the basis on which the police power rests in Massachusetts. **Commonwealth v. Alger**, 7 Cush. 53, 84.

Applying these principles to the present case, it is to be observed that the legislature of Massachusetts required the inhabitants of a city or town to be vaccinated only when, in the opinion of the Board of Health, that was necessary for the public health or the public safety. The authority to determine for all what ought to be done in such an emergency must have been lodged somewhere or in some body, and surely it was appropriate for the legislature to refer that question, in the first instance, to a Board of Health, composed of persons residing in the locality affected and appointed, presumably, because of their fitness to determine such questions. To invest such a body with authority over such matters was not an unusual nor an unreasonable or arbitrary requirement. Upon the principle of self-defense, of paramount necessity, a community has the right to protect itself against an epidemic of disease which threatens the safety of its members. It is to be observed that, when the regulation in question was adopted, smallpox, according to the recitals in the regulation adopted by the Board of Health, was prevalent to some extent in the city of Cambridge, and the disease was increasing. If such was the situation—and nothing is asserted or appears in the record to the contrary—if we are to attach any value whatever to the knowledge which, it is safe to affirm, is common to all civilized peoples touching smallpox and the methods most usually employed to eradicate that disease, it cannot be adjudged that the present regulation of the Board of Health was not necessary in order to protect the public health and secure the public safety. Smallpox being prevalent and increasing at Cambridge, the court would usurp the functions of another branch of government if it adjudged, as matter of law, that the mode adopted under the sanction of the State, to protect the people at large was arbitrary and not justified by the necessities of the case. We say necessities of the case because it might be that an acknowledged power of a local community to protect itself against an epidemic threatening the safety of all, might be exercised in particular circumstances and in reference to particular persons in such an arbitrary, unreasonable manner, or might go so far beyond what was reasonably required for the safety of the public, as to authorize or compel the courts to interfere for the protection of such persons. **Wisconsin & c. R.R. Co. v. Jacobson**, 179 U.S. 27, 179 U.S. 301; 1 Dillon Mun. Corp., 4th ed.,§§ 319 to 325, and authorities in notes; Freund's Police Power, § 63 et seq. In **Railroad Company v. Husen**, 95 U.S. 465, 95 U.S. 471-473, this court recognized the right of a State to pass sanitary laws, laws for the protection of life, liberty, heath or property within its limits, laws to prevent persons and animals suffering under contagious or infectious diseases, or convicts, from coming within its borders. But as the laws there involved went beyond the necessity of the case and under the guise of exerting a police power invaded the domain of Federal authority, and violated rights secured by the Constitution, this court deemed it to be its duty to hold such laws invalid. If the mode adopted by the Commonwealth of Massachusetts for the protection of its local communities against smallpox proved to be distressing, inconvenient or objectionable to some—if nothing more could be reasonably affirmed of the statute in question—the answer is that it was the duty of the constituted authorities primarily to keep in view the welfare, comfort and safety of the many, and not permit the interests of the many to be subordinated to the wishes or convenience of the few. There is, of course, a sphere within which the individual may assert the supremacy of his own will and rightfully dispute the authority of any human government, especially of any free government existing under a written constitution, to interfere with the exercise of that will. But it is equally true that, in every well ordered society charged with the duty of conserving the safety of its members the rights of the individual in respect of his liberty may at times, under the pressure of great dangers, be subjected to such restraint, to be enforced by reasonable regulations, as the safety of the general public may demand. An American citizen, arriving at an American port on a vessel in which, during the voyage, there had been cases of yellow fever or Asiatic cholera, although apparently free from disease himself, may yet, in some circumstances, be held in quarantine against his will on board of such vessel or in a quarantine station until it be ascertained by inspection, conducted with due diligence, that the danger of the spread of the disease among the community at large has disappeared. The liberty secured by the Fourteenth Amendment, this court has said, consists, in part, in the right of a person "to live and work where he will," **Allgeyer v. Louisiana**, 165 U.S. 578, and yet he may be compelled, by force if need be, against his will and without regard to his personal wishes or his pecuniary interests, or even his religious or political convictions, to take his place in the ranks of the army of his country and risk the chance of being shot down in its defense. It is not, therefore, true that the power of the public to guard itself against imminent danger depends in every case involving the control of one's body upon his willingness to submit to reasonable regulations established by the constituted authorities, under the sanction of the State, for the purpose of protecting the public collectively against such danger.

***

Whatever may be thought of the expediency of this statute, it cannot be affirmed to be, beyond question, in palpable conflict with the Constitution. Nor, in view of the methods employed to stamp out the disease of smallpox, can anyone confidently assert that the means prescribed by the State to that end has no real or substantial relation to the protection of the public health and the public safety.

***

Since, then, vaccination, as a means of protecting a community against smallpox, finds strong support in the experience of this and other countries, no court, much less a jury, is justified in disregarding the action of the legislature simply because, in its or their opinion, that particular method was—perhaps or possibly—not the best either for children or adults.

***

We are not prepared to hold that a minority, residing or remaining in any city or town where smallpox is prevalent, and enjoying the general protection afforded by an organized local government, may thus defy the will of its constituted authorities, acting in good faith for all, under the legislative sanction of the State. If such be the privilege of a minority, then a like privilege would belong to each individual of the community, and the spectacle would be presented of the welfare and safety of an entire population being subordinated to the notions of a single individual who chooses to remain a part of that population. We are unwilling to hold it to be an element in the liberty secured by the Constitution of the United States that one person, or a minority of persons, residing in any community and enjoying the benefits of its local government, should have the power thus to dominate the majority when supported in their action by the authority of the State. While this court should guard with firmness every right appertaining to life, liberty or property as secured to the individual by the Supreme Law of the Land, it is of the last importance that it should not invade the domain of local authority except when it is plainly necessary to do so in order to enforce that law. The safety and the health of the people of Massachusetts are, in the first instance, for that Commonwealth to guard and protect. They are matters that do not ordinarily concern the National Government. So far as they can be reached by any government, they depend, primarily, upon such action as the State in its wisdom may take, and we do not perceive that this legislation has invaded any right secured by the Federal Constitution.

Before closing this opinion, we deem it appropriate, in order to prevent misapprehension as to our views, to observe—perhaps to repeat a thought already sufficiently expressed, namely—that the police power of a State, whether exercised by the legislature or by a local body acting under its authority, may be exerted in such circumstances or by regulations so arbitrary and oppressive in particular cases as to justify the interference of the courts to prevent wrong and oppression. Extreme cases can be readily suggested. Ordinarily such cases are not safe guides in the administration of the law. It is easy, for instance, to suppose the case of an adult who is embraced by the mere words of the act, but yet to subject whom to vaccination in a particular condition of his health or body, would be cruel and inhuman in the last degree. We are not to be understood as holding that the statute was intended to be applied to such a case, or, if it as so intended, that the judiciary would not be competent to interfere and protect the health and life of the individual concerned. "All laws," this court has said, "should receive a sensible construction. General terms should be so limited in their application as not to lead to injustice, oppression or absurd consequence. It will always, therefore, be presumed that the legislature intended exceptions to its language which would avoid results of that character. The reason of the law in such cases should prevail over its letter." **United States v. Kirby**, 7 Wall. 482; **Lau Ow Bew v. United States**, 144 U.S. 47, 144 U.S. 58. Until otherwise informed by the highest court of Massachusetts, we are not inclined to hold that the statute establishes the absolute rule that an adult must be vaccinated if it be apparent or can be shown with reasonable certainty that he is not at the time a fit subject of vaccination or that vaccination, by reason of his then condition, would seriously impair his health or probably cause his death. No such case is here presented. It is the case of an adult who, for aught that appears, was himself in perfect health and a fit subject of vaccination, and yet, while remaining in the community, refused to obey the statute and the regulation adopted in execution of its provisions for the protection of the public health and the public safety, confessedly endangered by the presence of a dangerous disease

We now decide only that the statute covers the present case, and that nothing clearly appears that would justify this court in holding it to be unconstitutional and inoperative in its application to the plaintiff in error.

The judgment of the court below must be affirmed.

It is so ordered.

Commentary and Questions

8. In the 1902 case of *Compagnie Francaise de Navigation a Vapeur v. State Board of Health, Louisiana* the Supreme Court upheld the police power of the state to protect or control the health and safety of its citizens. The case involved the steamship *Brittania* sailing from the ports of Marseilles, France and Palermo, Italy in 1898 with cargo and 408 passengers to New Orleans and its eventual quarantine upon reaching port in New Orleans.[35]

Quarantine was imposed by the newly created State Board of Health pursuant to a resolution it adopted. The shipping company, a French corporation, sued claiming that on arrival in port none of the ship's passengers, crew, or cargo was under quarantine and that an inspection had cleared the ship for entry. The plaintiff corporation alleged the state action violated the Commerce Clause of the U.S. Constitution by encroaching on an area exclusively reserved for Congress. At the state court level the decision went in favor of the defendant State Board of Health finding that the state statute did not violate the Constitution or any law or treaty of the United States.[36] The state court's decision was eventually sustained by the Supreme Court, which found the police power of the state to be a valid exercise of the state's right to protect the health and welfare of its inhabitants. This police power, even if it may interfere with commerce, is valid until such time as Congress steps in to regulate health and quarantine issues.[37]

Decades earlier the Court established the police power of the state to regulate health, safety, and welfare in *New York v. Miln*, 36 U.S. 102 (1837). *Miln* was another case invoking a state law's alleged violation of the Commerce Clause due to a New York law preventing entry of any ships' passengers who may become public charges. As a way of enforcing the law, ships' captains were required to provide to the port master within 24 hours of arrival a list of passengers with their names, ages, and last known addresses. This was required of any vessel arriving from a foreign port or a United States port other than New York. The ship captain of the *Emily* refused to do so and the state initiated an action to collect penalty fines. The Supreme Court held the state statute was not a regulation of commerce but an exercise of a police power rightfully belonging to the state.[38] The state regulation, the Court said, was *"still more clearly embraced within the general power of the states to regulate their own internal police and to take care that no detriment come to the commonwealth. We think it as competent and as necessary for a state to provide precautionary measures against the moral pestilence of paupers, vagabonds, and possibly convicts as it is to guard against the physical pestilence which may arise from unsound and infections articles imported or from a ship the crew of which may be laboring under an infectious disease."*[89] A portion of the *Miln* decision was later disapproved in *Edwards v. California*, 314 U.S. 160 (1941) to the extent that the *Miln* case indicated a state may exclude individuals on the basis of their indigence, but the doctrine relating to the police power of the state remained untouched.

Jacobsen v. Massachusetts involved much different liberty interests than the quarantine issue in *Compagnie Francaise* and port entry in *Miln*—forced vaccination for smallpox was the health concern cited by the state. Although the Court upheld the police power of the state to require the vaccinations, what did the Court state with regard to the absolute nature of the power and court review? What did the Court say about the nature of individual liberty interests?

9. Subsequent U.S. Supreme Court cases have upheld the police power of the state in a variety of circumstances and have provided greater deference to this authority of the state when regulating for the public health, safety, and

welfare. In *Sligh v. Kirkwood*, 237 U.S. 52 (1915), the Court said *"[T]he limitations upon the police power are hard to define, and its far-reaching scope has been recognized in many decisions of this Court... The police power, in its broadest sense, includes all legislation and almost every function of civil government."*[40]

The implementation of temporary curfews and orders to evacuate are another example of the legitimate exercise of the state's police power. The Eleventh Circuit Court of Appeals in *Smith v. Avino*, 91 F.3d 105 (11th Cir, 1996), wrote *"it is a proper exercise of police power to respond to emergency situations with temporary curfews that might curtail the movement of persons who otherwise would enjoy freedom from restriction ... In such circumstance, governing authorities must be granted the proper deference and wide latitude necessary for dealing with the emergency."*[41] *Smith v. Avino* resulted from an American Civil Liberties Union (ACLU) lawsuit challenging the constitutionality of a curfew imposed by Dade County, Florida and its county manager in the wake of 1992's Hurricane Andrew. The ability to limit individual liberty interests also extends to evacuation orders.[42] As a separate rationale to the police power there is the tort concept of "danger invites rescue."[43] Under this doctrine an individual who creates a dangerous situation causing harm to a third party that invites rescue would be liable for any injuries to the third party and the rescuer. In an evacuation scenario an individual who willingly disregards a lawful evacuation order necessitating rescue creates a foreseeable circumstance posing risks to would be rescuers and a strain on public emergency resources that should be otherwise focused.

10. The role of the military in any domestic law enforcement function is limited by the Posse Comitatus Act found in 18 U.S.C. §1385. The Posse Comitatus Act was passed in 1878 after years of post-Civil War federal intervention in the Reconstruction of the South. Passage of the Act was a result of southern Democrat representatives' weariness of Republican reliance on the military to control southern affairs.[44] After passage of the Posse Comitatus Act the ability of the president or anyone else in federal government to authorize the use of federal military troops in the enforcement of state civil law was limited. The limits of the Act however do not apply to state militias subject to control of governors performing law enforcement functions within their own state.[45] Even though Article I, section 10, clause 3 of the Constitution prevents states from maintaining their own standing armies[46] the right to maintain a ready militia for defense was provided for in the Second Amendment.[47] Other exceptions to the Act apply for quelling domestic disturbance and rebellion,[48] to share equipment and information with civilian law enforcement,[49] natural disaster response[50] and homeland defense.[51]

The Posse Comitatus Act specifically limits the use of the Army and Air Force *"to execute the laws"* but the Navy and Marine Corps are included through Department of Defense Regulations.[52] The Coast Guard, which has a law enforcement mandate, is not included under the Posse Comitatus during peacetime. The Navy, when assisting the Coast Guard in the search and seizure of ships involved in drug smuggling, is also exempted from the Act.[53]

Presidential power to use the military in domestic operations is also limited by the Insurrection Act of 1807. Section 332 of the Insurrection Act, however, does provide the president with the authority to use the military when there is threat of rebellion within the states.[54] Section 333 lists the specific instances when this power is authorized. Attempts to broaden presidential authority and extend the power to include *"natural disaster, epidemic, or other serious public health emergency, terrorist attack or incident"* was temporarily accomplished with a 2006 amendment.[55] This short-lived amendment was repealed by the 2008 Defense Authorization Bill returning the Insurrection Act to its original wording. Concerns over the reach of presidential power, the invasion of the federal government into the realm of state governors and the ability of the president to declare martial law under the amendment led to the backlash.

Should the military, at the initiation of the federal government, have an active role in emergency response to natural disaster and public health emergencies or should that role be limited to state governments to handle and decide upon the extent of federal intervention? What is the significance of concerns regarding the implementation of martial law? Should the Posse Comitatus Act and the Insurrection Act be amended in light of the post-9/11 environment?

11. As indicated in the earlier comments, the Posse Comitatus Act provides certain exceptions to its limits, one of these being the use of the military in natural disaster response. Even though attempts to expand presidential authority to use the military in responding to natural disaster, epidemic and public health emergencies was curtailed by the 2008 Defense Authorization Bill's repeal of amendments providing for this response, the military is still authorized to provide assistance through the Robert T. Stafford Disaster Relief and Emergency Assistance Act. The Stafford Act, signed into law in 1988, amended the Disaster Relief Act of 1974 and gave statutory authority for the federal government to provide disaster response and relief. Section 101(b) of the Stafford Act defined the Congressional intent as *"to provide an orderly and continuing means of assistance by the Federal Government to State and local governments in carrying out their responsibilities to alleviate the suffering and damage which result from such disasters."*[56] To use the military under the authority of the Stafford Act, a request must come from the affected state's governor requesting the assistance of federal troops. This assistance, however, is limited to *"debris removal and road clearance, search and rescue, emergency medical care and shelter, provision of food, water, and other essential needs, dissemination of public information and assistance regarding health and safety measures, and the provision of technical advice to state and local governments on disaster management and control."*[57] The provisions of the Posse Comitatus remain in effect unless the president makes a determination that "preeminently federal interests" are involved.[58]

The Homeland Security Act of 2002 placed emergency management within the scope of federal response creating the position of Under Secretary for Emergency Preparedness and Response.[59] Within the control of the Under Secretary are the Federal Emergency Management Agency (FEMA), Office of Emergency Preparedness and the Department of Health and Human Services, among several other emergency response and disaster control related government offices.

Endnotes

[1] See *Hurtado v. California,* 100 U.S. 516 (1884) where the U.S. Supreme Court held that indictment by way of a prosecutor's information did not violate the Fourteenth Amendment and that a grand jury presentation and indictment is not applicable to the States by way of the Fourteenth Amendment.

[2] 32 U.S. 243 (1833).

[3] 166 U.S. 266 (1897).

[4] See, *Gitlow v. New York,* 268 U.S. 652 (1925), *Fisk v. Kansas,* 274 U.S. 380 (1927), and *Stromberg v. California,* 283 U.S. 359 (1931) regarding freedom of speech; *Near v. Minnesota,* 283 U.S. 697 (1931) regarding freedom of the press; *Dejong v. Oregon,* 299 U.S. 353 (1937) regarding freedom of assembly.

[5] 545 U.S. 469 (2005)

[6] See eg., *Calero Toledo v. Pearson Yacht Leasing Co.,* 416 U.S. 663 (1974) (pre-seizure notice or a hearing not required by due process clause); *Bennis v. Michigan,* 517 U.S. 1163 (1996) (forfeiture order does not offend the due process clause of the Fourteenth Amendment or the takings clause of the Fifth Amendment even for an "innocent owner"); *United States v. Ursery,* 518 U.S. 267 (1996) (civil in rem forfeiture proceeding following a criminal conviction is not punitive and does not violate the Fifth Amendment double jeopardy clause).

[7] 416 U.S. 663, 684.

[8] Id. citing *The Palmyra,* 25 U.S. at 14–15.

[9] 25 U.S. 1.

[10] Id. citing *Marianna Flora,* 24 U.S. 1 (1826).

[11] 5 U.S. 1 (1801).

[12] See e.g., *Mitchell v. Harmony,* 13 How. 115, 14 L.Ed. 75 (1851).

[13] 12 Wall. 315, 79 U.S. 315 (1870).

[14] *Litcher v. United States,* 334 U.S. at 782 (1948).

[15] Id.

[16] Id.

[17] Blackstone, William, *Commentaries on the Laws of England,* 4:373.

18   Reed, Terrance G., *American Forfeiture Law: Property Owner Meets Prosecutor*, Cato Institute, September 29, 1992. https://www.cato.org/pubs/pas/pa-179.html.

19   See, Neff, Stephen C., *Justice in Blue and Gray: A Legal History of the Civil War*, p. 113, Harvard University Press, Cambridge, 2010.

20   See e.g., *Leitensdorfer v. Webb*, 61 U.S. 176 (1857) (*"The effects of the conquest are to confer upon the conquering state the public property of the conquered state, and to invest the former with the rights and obligations of the latter ... Conquest likewise invests the conquering state with sovereignty over the subjects of the conquered state."*); see also, *O'Reilly de Camara v. Brooke*, 209 U.S. 45 (1908), wherein the Court upheld the denial of a tort claim brought by a Spanish subject who was the owner of a cattle slaughterhouse in Havana, Cuba. The claim for compensation was based on the loss of business resulting from U.S. military authority decision to end the company's services. The U.S. military was in control of Cuba at the end of the Spanish-American War and had replaced the prior sovereign government when the decision to end the company's services was made. Plaintiff alleged violation of the treaty ending the war as well as the U.S. Constitution and Spanish law in place prior to U.S. control. Justice Holmes wrote: *"...the jurisdiction of the case depends upon the establishment of a "tort only in violation of the law or nations, or of a treaty of the United States," it is impossible for the courts to declare an act a tort of that kind when the Executive, Congress and the treaty-making power have all adopted the act."* Holmes went on to state that the property right of the plaintiff did not survive the end of Spain's sovereignty.

21   *Dow v. Johnson*, 100 U.S. 158 (1879).

22   80 U.S. 623 (1871).

23   54 U.S. 115 (1851).

24   Id.

25   *Yakus v. U.S.*, 321 U.S. 414 (1944).

26   *Block v. Hirsch*, 256 U.S. 135 (1925); *Bowles v. Willingham*, 321 U.S. 503 (1944).

27   150 F.2d 369 (7th Cir., 1945).

28   Frank, John P., *All's Fair: The Battle Over The Wartime Seizure Power*, 28 Litigation 51, Spring 2002.

29   Id.

30   Frank, p. 51.

31   *El-Shifa Pharmaceutical Industries Co. v. United States*, 559 F.3d at 582 (D.C. Cir., 2009).

32   *El-Shifa Pharmaceutical Industries Co. v. United States*, 607 F.3d 836 (D.C. Cir., 2010).

33   Id.

34   Id.

35   186 U.S. 380 (1902).

36   186 U.S. at 386.

[37]   Id at 392.

[38]   36 at 136.

[39]   Id at 142–143.

[40]   237 U.S. at 258–259.

[41]   91 F.3d at 109.

[42]   See e.g., *Miller v. Campbell County*, 945 F.2d 348 (10th Cir. 1991).

[43]   See, *Wagner v. International Railway*, 232 N.Y. 176 (1926).

[44]   Doyle, C., & Elsea, J. K. (2012). *The Posse Comitatus Act and Related Matters: The
       Use of the Military to Execute Civilian Law.* Washington D.C.: Congressional
       Research Service. p. 19.

[45]   See e.g., 32 U.S.C. §112 regarding the drug interdiction exception.

[46]   "No state shall, without the consent of Congress, lay any duty of tonnage, keep
       troops, or ships of war in time of peace, enter into any agreement or compact with
       another state, or with a foreign power, or engage in war, unless actually invaded, or
       in such imminent danger as will not admit of delay."

[47]   "A well regulated Militia, being necessary to the security of a free State, the right of
       the people to keep and bear Arms, shall not be infringed."

[48]   10 U.S.C. §§331–333.

[49]   10 U.S.C. §§ 371–382.

[50]   42 U.S.C. §§ 5121 et seq.

[51]   32 USC §905.

[52]   32 C.F.R. Section 213.2, 1992.

[53]   Larson, E. V., & Peters, J. E. (2001). *Preparing the U.S. Army for Homeland
       Security: Concepts, Issues and Options.* Santa Monica, CA: RAND Corporation.
       Appendix D, p. 245.

[54]   "Whenever the President considers that unlawful obstructions, combinations, or as-
       semblages, or rebellion against the authority of the United States, make it impractic-
       able to enforce the laws of the United States in any State by the ordinary course of
       judicial proceedings, he may call into Federal service such of the militia of any State,
       and use such of the armed forces, as he considers necessary to enforce those laws or
       to suppress the rebellion."

[55]   Section 1076 of the 2007 Defense Authorization Bill.

[56]   42 U.S.C. §5121.

[57]   Elsea, J. K. (2005). *The Use of Federal Troops for Disaster Assistance: Legal Issues.*
       Washington D.C.: Congressional Research Service. p. 4.

[58]   Id.

[59]   See 6 U.S.C. 311.

Legislation

Alien & Sedition Acts in 1798

Chinese Exclusion Act 1882 — cout case

1918 Wartime measures Act

1941 Wartime measures Act   Passport Act 1926

US const

4th Amendment

Privileges & Immunities Clause (Art 4, Sec 2)

5th Amendment Due Process Right

Chapter Seven
REGULATION OF IMMIGRATION, BORDER SECURITY AND THE RIGHT TO TRAVEL

There is a photograph taken by Daniel Hulshizer, former New Jersey chief photographer for the Associated Press, which is one of several iconic images from September 11, 2001. The photograph is a shot across New York harbor with the Statue of Liberty in the foreground and thick clouds of black smoke billowing in the background from where the World Trade Center towers once stood. It is a photographic statement of contrasts—the obvious being the bright blue sky being choked by the thick dark clouds of smoke rising up from the island of Manhattan. But there is another more subtle contrast and that is the image of Lady Liberty, a symbolic acceptance of all who may come to her shores, watching over the carnage wrought by terrorists who took that acceptance and perverted it for their evil purposes. The Statue of Liberty's welcoming of immigrants to America has been often told by those who came by ship at the turn of the 20th century and passed under her torch upon entering New York harbor. It is also immortalized in the last few lines of the sonnet "The New Colossus" by poet Emma Lazarus written on a bronze plaque at the base of the statue:

"Give me your tired, your poor, / Your huddled masses yearning to breathe free, / The wretched refuse of your teeming shore. / Send these, the homeless, tempest-tossed, to me; / I lift my lamp beside the golden door."

After 9/11 the Statue of Liberty would be closed to visitors for security reasons and remain closed for years except for special occasions. This irony should not be overlooked, because in times of national emergency the open arms of America no longer remain outstretched and the welcoming borders become tougher to cross.

There has always been an immigrant suspicion in the United States dating back to the Quasi-War with France and the Federalist Congress' passing of the Alien and Sedition Acts in 1798. This immigrant suspicion has manifested itself in many ways, some in legitimate protective measures for the sake of national security, and others in more insidious and dubious national security claims. The wholesale internment of West Coast Japanese-Americans during the Second World War certainly falls into the latter category.

As much as America has had a love affair with the rags-to-riches immigrant success stories that have become a fabric of the American Dream, it has also had a distrust of the alien. Prohibition, a failed social experiment, was the culmination of decades-old efforts by rural social reformers who masked an anti-immigrant aversion with claims of benefits to public health and morals.[1] The temperance movement focused its moral outrage on American cities with their densely packed immigrant neighborhoods where alcohol flowed freely. Historically though there were less subtle anti-immigrant measures taken. In 1882 the Chinese Exclusion Act was passed by Congress wherein Chinese laborers were excluded from entering into the United States for a ten-year period. Those who were already residing within the United States when the Act was passed were

275

not permitted to remain. The stated purpose behind the Act, as briefly explained in the opening lines of the legislation, was "in the opinion of the Government of the United States the coming of Chinese laborers to this country endangers the good order of certain localities within the territory thereof."[2] The Chinese Exclusion Act would later be repealed in 1943 with China becoming a U.S. ally in the war against Japan. But this was several decades after the U.S Supreme Court in *The Chinese Exclusion Cases* declared the Act a legitimate exercise of national sovereignty. That right, the Court said, was included in the government's inherent authority to protect the public interest; since immigration was such a vital national interest the authority was absolute.[3]

The area of immigration regulation has always been one of exclusive federal control and local efforts to regulate immigration are voided by the Supremacy Clause of the U.S. Constitution.[4] The Supreme Court in cases like *DeCanas* v. *Bica* held that state or local laws seeking to "regulate" immigration violated the Supremacy Clause and were preempted by federal law.[5] Similarly, the Court in *United States v. Brignoni-Ponce* held that police officers may not arrest individuals for immigration enforcement purposes without probable cause.[6] The Court went on to state that a person's appearance could not be the basis of a probable cause determination.[7] However, the post-9/11 environment brought changes to the exclusivity of federal control, especially in light of the fact that several of the hijackers were in the United States on business, tourist or student visas. In 2002 the Justice Department's Office of Legal Counsel issued a written opinion stating Congress did not preempt the states' "inherent arrest authority" over criminal and civil violations of immigration laws.[8] Federal courts had previously approved the criminal arrest authority of local law enforcement for immigration offenses but not their civil enforcement authority. The Office of Legal Counsel, which would be criticized for its narrow interpretation of torture and expansive interpretation of lawful interrogation techniques, provided a questionable interpretation of local law enforcement's immigration authority in its 2002 immigration enforcement opinion. Nevertheless, a 1996 addition to the Immigration and Nationality Act, section 287(g), provided cross-designation as special U.S. deputy marshals for local police and correction officials. This cross-designation occurs when a local law enforcement agency enters a memorandum of understanding with Immigration and Customs Enforcement and officers receive four weeks of immigration enforcement training at a federal facility. Once the officers complete the training they are authorized to access immigration data bases and enforce immigration laws. This program has not been without criticism and not all local law enforcement have embraced it, although it has resonated with politicians who have campaigned for tougher illegal immigrant controls. In a post-9/11 world, the involvement of local law enforcement efforts in stemming the tide of illegal immigration has increased but the nature and degree of that involvement has been debated. One of the main challenges in dealing with homeland security and policing terrorism is whether or not it can be done in an unbiased, race-neutral manner.[9] Religious profiling concerns have been added onto those of racial and ethnic profiling. Driving While Arab and Flying While Arab, euphemistically referred to as DWA and FWA, have joined Driving While Black ("DWB") in the derogatory vernacular focusing on law enforcement's biased application of the Fourth Amendment.[10] Yet, when it came to selective enforcement claims, the Supreme Court in *Reno v. American-Arab Anti-Discrimination Committee* held the Illegal Immigration Reform and Immigrant Responsibility Act of 1996 deprived the federal courts of jurisdiction related to the Attorney General's deportation orders.[11]

The Fourth Amendment states "no warrants shall issue, but upon probable cause, supported by oath or affirmation" and this language has been interpreted by the Supreme Court to impose a warrant requirement prior to any search or seizure. However, there have developed some exceptions to the absolute warrant requirement allowing for warrantless searches and seizures based on probable cause. The rationale for these searches and seizures has resided in the language of the "reasonableness clause" of the Fourth Amendment. One such applied exception is to searches that take place at a border or the functional equivalent of a border. This exception provides a useful but carefully circumscribed tool for government officials. The U.S. Supreme Court first judicially recognized the exception in *United States v. Ramsey* wherein it upheld the search of envelopes by a customs official in New York.[12] The envelopes were found to contain heroin. Justice Rehnquist, writing for the 6-3 majority, cited *Carroll v. United States* (see Endnote 33) for the proposition that travelers at an international boundary could be stopped based on "national self-protection" and *United States v. Thirty-seven Photographs*[13] to distinguish the privacy interest at a port of entry search by customs officials from a search of one's home by police.[14] In concluding Justice Rehnquist wrote: *"Border searches, then, from before the adoption of the Fourth Amendment, have been considered to be 'reasonable' by the single fact that the person or item in question had entered into our country from outside. There has never been any additional requirement that the reasonableness of a border search depended on the existence of probable cause. This longstanding recognition that searches at our borders without probable cause and without a warrant are nonetheless 'reasonable' has a history as old as the Fourth Amendment itself ... The border search exception is grounded in the recognized right of the sovereign to control, subject to substantive limitations imposed by the Constitution, who and what may enter the country."*[15] The Court would go on to endorse the border search exception in subsequent cases. In the 1985 case of *United States v. Montoya de Hernandez* the Court said the routine searches of entrants at the border were not subject to probable cause or warrant requirements.[16] Custom agents stopped a female traveler suspected of being a "balloon swallower" transporting illegal drugs. She was detained for an extended period of time while a court order to search her was obtained. A search of her rectal area revealed 88 cocaine-filled balloons. The Court held the totality of the circumstances known to the agents at the time and their reasonable inferences supported reasonable suspicion. Additionally, the length of the detention and nature of the intrusion were not unreasonable in light of the method for smuggling the drugs chosen by the defendant and the option left to the agents who would have had to release her to the interior of the country and permit distribution of the drugs. In another case, *United States v. Flores Montano*, the Court held that the Fourth Amendment did not prohibit the suspicion-less border search of a motor vehicle's gas tank.[17] The Court distinguished its holding in *Montoya de Hernandez* and the reasonable suspicion required for an invasive body cavity search from that required to check an incoming vehicle at an international border. It should be noted that along with the *Ramsey* opinion, Justice Rehnquist was the author of the *Montoya de Hernandez*, *Flores Montano*, and *Arvizu* opinion discussed in endnote 6, thereby making him the chief architect of Supreme Court border search case law.

There is no fundamental right of a non-citizen to be admitted to the United States or even to be naturalized, but there exists within the Privileges and Immunities Clause found in Article IV, section 2 of the Constitution an implied right of citizens to travel freely from one state to another.[18] This freedom of movement is no less of a liberty interest than free speech, and the contours of the right to free bodily movement can be derived from the First and Fifth Amendments. No denial of the right to interstate travel can be abridged without due process of law. What about travel outside the country? Is there a liberty interest? Case law suggests a similar liberty interest but one that can be proscribed by the federal government based on prevailing governmental interests. For instance, the 1918 Wartime Measure Act[19] required passports of American citizens leaving or entering the United States during wartime and required any alien leaving or entering the country to comply with the terms of the Act. Similar legislation was passed during World War II, the 1941 Wartime Measure Act,[20] but restricted the issuance of visas to any alien believed to be a potential danger to the United States and extended the wartime passport requirement to include national emergencies.[21] As early as 1835 in *Urtetiqui v. D'Arcy* the Supreme Court addressed the admissibility of a passport as evidence of citizenship: *"There is no law of the United States in any manner regulating the issuing of passports, or directing upon what evidence it may be done, or declaring their legal effect. It is understood as matter of practice that some evidence of citizenship is required by the Secretary of State before issuing a passport. This, however, is entirely discretionary with him. No inquiry is instituted by him to ascertain the fact of citizenship, or any proceedings had that will in any manner bear the character of a judicial inquiry. It is a document which, from its nature and object, is addressed to foreign powers, purporting only to be a request that the bearer of it may pass safely and freely, and is to be considered rather in the character of a political document by which the bearer is recognized in foreign countries as an American citizen, and which, by usage and the law of nations, is received as evidence of the fact."*[22] Not until the Passport Act of 1926 was there a formal process for the issuance of passports by the federal government.[23] The Supreme Court had several occasions to consider the constitutionality of international travel restrictions. *Kent v. Dulles*, 357 U.S. 116 (1958) was an important case wherein the Court formally recognized the right to travel as a liberty interest. The 5-4 decision rebuffed the Secretary of State's attempt to deny a passport to an individual based on suspected Communist ties. Questions pertaining to Communist Party affiliation and whether the travel was to support Communist causes were a First Amendment violation and were unrelated to the authority given to the Secretary of State. Similarly in *Aptheker v. Secretary of State*, 378 U.S. 500 (1964) the Court ruled section 6 of the Subversive Activities Control Act of 1950, which required that once a Communist organization was registered its members could not apply for a passport, was unconstitutional. The law as applied violated Fifth Amendment due process rights. A year later, however, in *Zemel v. Rusk*, 381 U.S. 1 (1965), the Court did approve the Secretary of State's area restriction on travel to Cuba. The Court distinguished the foreign policy considerations presented in *Zemel* from the associational rights at issue in *Kent*. As long as there is some prevailing governmental interest, travel restrictions will not abridge Fifth Amendment due process rights; a distinction to be gleaned from *Haig v. Agee*, which follows. The control of who can enter and lawfully reside within the United States as well as the right of citizens to freely travel outside of the country has been regulated by the federal government in the name of national security. Personal liberty interests are always to be weighed in the balance but if government needs prevail or the intrusion on the liberty interest is minimal the balance will tip toward the governmental interest.

Ludecke v. Watkins
335 U.S. 160 (1948)

Mr. Justice Frankfurter delivered the opinion of the Court.

The Fifth Congress committed to the President these powers:

"Whenever there is a declared war between the United States and any foreign nation or government, or any invasion or predatory incursion is perpetrated, attempted, or threatened against the territory of the United States by any foreign nation or government, and the President makes public proclamation of the event, all natives, citizens, denizens, or subjects of the hostile nation or government, being of the age of fourteen years and upward, who shall be within the United States and not actually naturalized, shall be liable to be apprehended, restrained, secured, and removed as alien enemies. The President is authorized, in any such event, by his proclamation thereof, or other public act, to direct the conduct to be observed, on the part of the United States, toward the aliens who become so liable; the manner and degree of the restraint to which they shall be subject and in what cases, and upon what security their residence shall be permitted, and to provide for the removal of those who, not being permitted to reside within the United States, refuse or neglect to depart therefrom, and to establish any other regulations which are found necessary in the premises and for the public safety."
(Act of July 6, 1798, 1 Stat. 577, R.S. § 4067, as amended, 40 Stat. 531, 50 U.S.C. § 21.)

This Alien Enemy Act has remained the law of the land, virtually unchanged since 1798. Throughout these one hundred and fifty years, executive interpretation and decisions of lower courts have found in the Act an authority for the President which is now questioned, and the further claim is made that, if what the President did comes within the Act, the Congress could not give him such power. Obviously these are issues which properly brought the case here.

Petitioner, a German alien enemy, was arrested on December 8, 1941, and, after proceedings before an Alien Enemy Hearing Board on January 16, 1942, was interned by order of the Attorney General, dated February 9, 1942. Under authority of the Act of 1798, the President, on July 14, 1945, directed the removal from the United States of all alien enemies "who shall be deemed by the Attorney General to be dangerous to the public peace and safety of the United States." Proclamation 2655, 10 Fed.Reg. 8947. Accordingly, the Attorney General, on January 18, 1946, ordered petitioner's removal. Denial of a writ of habeas corpus for release from detention under this order was affirmed by the court below.

As Congress explicitly recognized in the recent Administrative Procedure Act, some statutes "preclude judicial review." Act of June 11, 1946, §10, 60 Stat. 237, 243. Barring questions of interpretation and constitutionality, the Alien Enemy Act of 1798 is such a statute. Its terms, purpose, and construction leave no doubt. The language employed by the Fifth Congress could hardly be made clearer, or be rendered doubtful, by the incomplete and not always dependable accounts we have of debates in the early years of Congress. That such was the scope of the Act is established by controlling contemporaneous construction. "The act concerning alien enemies, which confers on the president very great discretionary powers respecting their persons," Marshall, C.J., in **Brown v. United States**, 8 Cranch 110, 12 U. S. 126, "appears to me to be as unlimited as the legislature could make it." Washington, J., in **Lockington v. Smith**, 15 Fed.Cas. No. 8448 at p. 760. The very nature of the President's power to order the removal of all enemy aliens rejects the notion that courts may pass judgment upon the exercise of his discretion. This view was expressed by Mr. Justice Iredell shortly after the Act was passed, **Case of Fries**, 9 Fed.Cas. No. 5126, and every judge before whom the question has since come has held that the statute barred judicial review. We would so read the Act if it came before us without the impressive gloss of history.

The power with which Congress vested the President had to be executed by him through others. He provided for the removal of such enemy aliens as were "deemed by the Attorney General" to be dangerous. But such a finding at the President's behest was likewise not to be subjected to the scrutiny of courts. For one thing, removal was contingent not upon a finding that in fact an alien was "dangerous." The President was careful to call for the removal of aliens "deemed by the Attorney General to be dangerous." But the short answer is that the Attorney General was the President's voice and conscience. A war power of the President not subject to judicial review is not transmuted into a judicially reviewable action because the President chooses to have that power exercised within narrower limits than Congress authorized.

And so we reach the claim that, while the President had summary power under the Act, it did not survive cessation of actual hostilities. This claim in effect nullifies the power to deport alien enemies, for such deportations are hardly practicable during the pendency of what is colloquially known as the shooting war. Nor does law lag behind common sense. War does not cease with a cease-fire order, and power to be exercised by the President such as that conferred by the Act of 1798 is a process which begins when war is declared but is not exhausted when the shooting stops ...

The political branch of the Government has not brought the war with Germany to an end. On the contrary, it has proclaimed that "a state of war still exists"... The Court would be assuming the functions of the political agencies of the Government to yield to the suggestion that the unconditional surrender of Germany and the disintegration of the Nazi Reich have left Germany without a government capable of negotiating a treaty of peace. It is not for us to question a belief by the President that enemy aliens who were justifiably deemed fit subjects for internment during active hostilities do not lose their potency for mischief during the period of confusion and conflict which is characteristic of a state of war even when the guns are silent but the peace of Peace has not come. These are matters of political judgment for which judges have neither technical competence nor official responsibility.

This brings us to the final question. Is the statute valid as we have construed it? The same considerations of reason, authority, and history, that led us to reject reading the statutory language "declared war" to mean "actual hostilities," support the validity of the statute. The war power is the war power. If the war, as we have held, has not in fact ended, so as to justify local rent control, a fortiori, it validly supports the power given to the President by the Act of 1798 in relation to alien enemies. Nor does it require protracted argument to find no defect in the Act because resort to the courts may be had only to challenge the construction and validity of the statute and to question the existence of the "declared war," as has been done in this case. The Act is almost as old as the Constitution, and it would savor of doctrinaire audacity now to find the statute offensive to some emanation of the Bill of Rights. The fact that hearings are utilized by the Executive to secure an informed basis for the exercise of summary power does not argue the right of courts to retry such hearings, nor bespeak denial of due process to withhold such power from the courts.

Such great war powers may be abused, no doubt, but that is a bad reason for having judges supervise their exercise, whatever the legal formulas within which such supervision would nominally be confined. In relation to the distribution of constitutional powers among the three branches of the Government, the optimistic Eighteenth Century language of Mr. Justice Iredell, speaking of this very Act, is still pertinent:

"All systems of government suppose they are to be administered by men of common sense and common honesty. In our country, as all ultimately depends on the voice of the people, they have it in their power, and it is to be presumed they generally will choose men of this description; but if they will not, the case, to be sure, is without remedy. If they choose fools, they will have foolish laws. If they choose knaves, they will have knavish ones. But this can never be the case until they are generally fools or knaves themselves, which, thank God, is not likely ever to become the character of the American people." (**Case of Fries**, supra, at p. 836.)

Accordingly, we hold that full responsibility for the just exercise of this great power may validly be left where the Congress has constitutionally placed it—on the President of the United States. The Founders, in their wisdom, made him not only the Commander in Chief, but also the guiding organ in the conduct of our foreign affairs. He who was entrusted with such vast powers in relation to the outside world was also entrusted by Congress, almost throughout the whole life of the nation, with the disposition of alien enemies during a state of war. Such a page of history is worth more than a volume of rhetoric.

Judgment affirmed and stay order entered February 2, 1948, vacated

Haig v. Agee
453 U.S. 280 (1981)

Chief Justice Burger delivered the opinion of the Court.

The question presented is whether the President, acting through the Secretary of State, has authority to revoke a passport on the ground that the holder's activities in foreign countries are causing or are likely to cause serious damage to the national security or foreign policy of the United States.

I

A

Philip Agee, an American citizen, currently resides in West Germany. From 1957 to 1968, he was employed by the Central Intelligence Agency. He held key positions in the division of the Agency that is responsible for covert intelligence gathering in foreign countries. In the course of his duties at the Agency, Agee received training in clandestine operations, including the methods used to protect the identities of intelligence employees and sources of the United States overseas. He served in undercover assignments abroad and came to know many Government employees and other persons supplying information to the United States. The relationships of many of these people to our Government are highly confidential; many are still engaged in intelligence gathering.

In 1974, Agee called a press conference in London to announce his "campaign to fight the United States CIA wherever it is operating." He declared his intent "to expose CIA officers and agents and to take the measures necessary to drive them out of the countries where they are operating." Since 1974, Agee has, by his own assertion, devoted consistent effort to that program, and he has traveled extensively in other countries in order to carry it out. To identify CIA personnel in a particular country, Agee goes to the target country and consults sources in local diplomatic circles whom he knows from his prior service in the United States Government. He recruits collaborators and trains them in clandestine techniques designed to expose the "cover" of CIA employees and sources. Agee and his collaborators have repeatedly and publicly identified individuals and organizations located in foreign countries as undercover CIA agents, employees, or sources. The record reveals that the identifications divulge classified information, violate Agee's express contract not to make any public statements about Agency matters without prior clearance by the Agency, have prejudiced the ability of the United States to obtain intelligence, and have been followed by episodes of violence against the persons and organizations identified.

In December, 1979, the Secretary of State revoked Agee's passport and delivered an explanatory notice to Agee in West Germany. The notice states in part:

"The Department's action is predicated upon a determination made by the Secretary under the provisions of [22 CFR] Section 51.70(b)(4) that your activities abroad are causing or are likely to cause serious damage to the national security or the foreign policy of the United States. The reasons for the Secretary's determination are, in summary, as follows: Since the early 1970's, it has been your stated intention to conduct a continuous campaign to disrupt the intelligence operations of the United States. In carrying out that campaign you have traveled in various countries (including, among others, Mexico, the United Kingdom, Denmark, Jamaica, Cuba, and Germany), and your activities in those countries have caused serious damage to the national security and foreign policy of the United States. Your stated intention to continue such activities threatens additional damage of the same kind."

The notice also advised Agee of his right to an administrative hearing and offered to hold such a hearing in West Germany on 5 days' notice.

Agee at once filed suit against the Secretary. He alleged that the regulation invoked by the Secretary, 22 CFR § 51.70(b)(4) (1980), has not been authorized by Congress and is invalid; that the regulation is impermissibly overbroad; that the revocation prior to a hearing violated his Fifth Amendment right to procedural due process; and that the revocation violated a Fifth Amendment liberty interest in a right to travel and a First Amendment right to criticize Government policies. He sought declaratory and injunctive relief, and he moved for summary judgment on the question of the authority to promulgate the regulation and on the constitutional claims. For purposes of that motion, Agee conceded the Secretary's factual averments and his claim that Agee's activities were causing or were likely to cause serious damage to the national security or foreign policy of the United States. The District Court held that the regulation exceeded the statutory powers of the Secretary under the Passport Act of 1926, 22 U.S.C. § 211a, granted summary judgment for Agee, and ordered the Secretary to restore his passport.

B

A divided panel of the Court of Appeals affirmed. It held that the Secretary was required to show that Congress had authorized the regulation either by an express delegation or by implied approval of a "substantial and consistent" administrative practice, **Zemel v. Rusk**, 381 U. S. 1, 381 U. S. 12 (1965). The court found no express statutory authority for the revocation. It perceived only one other case of actual passport revocation under the regulation since it was promulgated, and only five other instances prior to that in which passports were actually denied "even arguably for national security or foreign policy reasons." The Court of Appeals took note of the Secretary's reliance on "a series of statutes, regulations, proclamations, orders and advisory opinions dating back to 1856," but declined to consider those authorities, reasoning that "the criterion for establishing congressional assent by inaction is the actual imposition of sanctions, and not the mere assertion of power." The Court of Appeals held that it was not sufficient that "Agee's conduct may be considered by some to border on treason," since "[w]e are bound by the law as we find it." The court also regarded it as material that most of the Secretary's authorities dealt with powers of the Executive Branch "during time of war or national emergency" or with respect to persons "engaged in criminal conduct."

We granted certiorari sub nom. **Muskie v. Agee**, 449 U.S. 818 (1980), and stayed the judgment of the Court of Appeals until our disposition of the case on the grant of certiorari.

II

The principal question before us is whether the statute authorizes the action of the Secretary pursuant to the policy announced by the challenged regulation.

A

1. Although the historical background that we develop later is important, we begin with the language of the statute. The Passport Act of 1926 provides in pertinent part:

"The Secretary of State may grant and issue passports, and cause passports to be granted, issued, and verified in foreign countries by diplomatic representatives of the United States ... under such rules as the President shall designate and prescribe for and on behalf of the United States, and no other person shall grant, issue, or verify such passports." 22 U.S.C. §211a (1976 ed., Supp. IV). This language is unchanged since its original enactment in 1926.

The Passport Act does not, in so many words, confer upon the Secretary a power to revoke a passport. Nor, for that matter, does it expressly authorize denials of passport applications. Neither, however, does any statute expressly limit those powers. It is beyond dispute that the Secretary has the power to deny a passport for reasons not specified in the statutes. For example, in **Kent v. Dulles**, 357 U. S. 116 (1958), the Court recognized congressional acquiescence in Executive policies of refusing passports to applicants "participating in illegal conduct, trying to escape the toils of the law, promoting passport frauds, or otherwise engaging in conduct which would violate the laws of the United States." Id. at 357 U. S. 127. In **Zemel**, the Court held that "the weightiest considerations of national security" authorized the Secretary to restrict travel to Cuba at the time of the Cuban missile crisis. 381 U.S. at 381 U. S. 16. Agee concedes that, if the Secretary may deny a passport application for a certain reason, he may revoke a passport on the same ground.

2

Particularly in light of the "broad rulemaking authority granted in the [1926] Act," **Zemel**, 381 U.S. at 381 U. S. 12, a consistent administrative construction of that statute must be followed by the courts "unless there are compelling indications that it is wrong.'" **E. I. du Pont de Nemours & Co. v. Collins**, 432 U. S. 46, 432 U. S. 55 (1977), quoting **Red Lion Broadcasting Co. v. FCC**, 395 U. S. 367, 395 U. S. 381 (1969); see **Zemel**, supra, at 381 U. S. 11. This is especially so in the areas of foreign policy and national security, where congressional silence is not to be equated with congressional disapproval. In **United States v. Curtiss-Wright Export Corp.**, 299 U. S. 304 (1936), the volatile nature of problems confronting the Executive in foreign policy and national defense was underscored:

"In this vast external realm, with its important, complicated, delicate and manifold problems, the President alone has the power to speak or listen as a representative of the nation ... As Marshall said in his great argument of March 7, 1800, in the House of Representatives, 'The President is the sole organ of the nation in its external relations, and its sole representative with foreign nations." Id. at 299 U. S. 319.

Applying these considerations to statutory construction, the **Zemel** Court observed:

"[B]ecause of the changeable and explosive nature of contemporary international relations, and the fact that the Executive is immediately privy to information which cannot be swiftly presented to, evaluated by, and acted upon by the legislature, Congress—in giving the Executive authority over matters of foreign affairs—must of necessity paint with a brush broader than that it customarily wields in domestic areas." 381 U.S. at 381 U.S. 17 (emphasis supplied). *Matters intimately related to foreign policy and national security are rarely proper subjects for judicial intervention. In* **Harisiades v. Shaughnessy**, *342 U. S. 580 (1952), the Court observed that matters relating "to the conduct of foreign relations . . . are so exclusively entrusted to the political branches of government as to be largely immune from judicial inquiry or interference."* Id. at 342 U. S. 589; accord, **Chicago & Southern Air Lines, Inc. v. Waterman S.S. Corp.**, 333 U. S. 103, 333 U. S. 111 (1948).

B

1

A passport is, in a sense, a letter of introduction in which the issuing sovereign vouches for the bearer and requests other sovereigns to aid the bearer ...

With the enactment of travel control legislation making a passport generally a requirement for travel abroad, a passport took on certain added characteristics. Most important for present purposes, the only means by which an American can lawfully leave the country or return to it—absent a Presidentially granted exception—is with a passport. See 8 U.S.C. § 1185(b) (1976 ed., Supp. IV). As a travel control document, a passport is both proof of identity and proof of allegiance to the United States. Even under a travel control statute, however, a passport remains, in a sense, a document by which the Government vouches for the bearer and for his conduct.

The history of passport controls since the earliest days of the Republic shows congressional recognition of Executive authority to withhold passports on the basis of substantial reasons of national security and foreign policy. Prior to 1856, when there was no statute on the subject, the common perception was that the issuance of a passport was committed to the sole discretion of the Executive, and that the Executive would exercise this power in the interests of the national security and foreign policy of the United States. This derived from the generally accepted view that foreign policy was the province and responsibility of the Executive. From the outset, Congress endorsed not only the underlying premise of Executive authority in the areas of foreign policy and national security, but also its specific application to the subject of passports. Early Congresses enacted statutes expressly recognizing the Executive authority with respect to passports.

The first Passport Act, adopted in 1856, provided that the Secretary of State "shall be authorized to grant and issue passports ... under such rules as the President shall designate and prescribe for and on behalf of the United States ...." §23, 11 Stat. 60. This broad and permissive language worked no change in the power of the Executive to issue passports, nor was it intended to do so. The Act was passed to centralize passport authority in the Federal Government, and specifically in the Secretary of State ... The President and the Secretary of State consistently construed the 1856 Act to preserve their authority to withhold passports on national security and foreign policy grounds. Thus, as an emergency measure in 1861, the Secretary issued orders prohibiting persons from going abroad or entering the country without passports; denying passports to citizens who were subject to military service unless they were bonded; and absolutely denying passports to persons "on errands hostile and injurious to the peace of the country and dangerous to the Union." 3 J. Moore, A Digest of International Law 920 (1906); U.S. Dept. of State, The American Passport 49-54 (1898). An 1869 opinion of Attorney General Hoar held that the granting of a passport was not "obligatory in any case." 13 Op.Atty.Gen. 89, 92. This was elaborated in 1901 in an opinion of Attorney General Knox, in which he stated:

"Substantial reasons exist for the use by Congress of the word 'may' in connection with authority to issue passports. Circumstances are conceivable which would make it most inexpedient for the public interests for this country to grant a passport to a citizen of the United States." 23 Op. Atty. Gen. 509, 511. In 1903, President Theodore Roosevelt promulgated a rule providing that "[t]he Secretary of State has the right in his discretion to refuse to issue a passport, and will

exercise this right towards anyone who, he has reason to believe, desires a passport to further an unlawful or improper purpose."

Subsequent Executive Orders issued between 1907 and 1917 cast no doubt on this position. This policy was enforced in peacetime years to deny passports to citizens whose conduct abroad was "likely to embarrass the United States" or who were "disturbing, or endeavoring to disturb, the relations of this country with the representatives of foreign countries."

By enactment of the first travel control statute in 1918, Congress made clear its expectation that the Executive would curtail or prevent international travel by American citizens if it was contrary to the national security. The legislative history reveals that the principal reason for the 1918 statute was fear that "renegade Americans" would travel abroad and engage in "transference of important military information" to persons not entitled to it. The 1918 statute left the power to make exceptions exclusively in the hands of the Executive, without articulating specific standards. Unless the Secretary had power to apply national security criteria in passport decisions, the purpose of the Travel Control Act would plainly have been frustrated.

Against this background, and while the 1918 provisions were still in effect, Congress enacted the Passport Act of 1926 ... The Executive construed the 1926 Act to work no change in prior practice, and specifically interpreted it to authorize denial of a passport on grounds of national security or foreign policy. Indeed, by an unbroken line of Executive Orders, regulations, instructions to consular officials, and notices to passport holders, the President and the Department of State left no doubt that likelihood of damage to national security or foreign policy of the United States was the single most important criterion in passport decisions. The regulations are instructive. The 1952 version authorized denial of passports to citizens engaged in activities which would violate laws designed to protect the security of the United States "[i]n order to promote the national interest by assuring that the conduct of foreign relations shall be free from unlawful interference." 17 Fed.Reg. 8013 (1952). The 1956 amendment to this regulation provided that a passport should be denied to any person whose "activities abroad would: (a) violate the laws of the United States; (b) be prejudicial to the orderly conduct of foreign relations; or (c) otherwise be prejudicial to the interests of the United States." 22 CFR § 51.136 (1958). This regulation remained in effect continuously until 1966.

This history of administrative construction was repeatedly communicated to Congress, not only by routine promulgation of Executive Orders and regulations, but also by specific presentations, including 1957 and 1966 reports by the Department of State explaining the 1956 regulation and a 1960 Senate Staff Report which concluded that "the authority to issue or withhold passports has, by precedent and law, been vested in the Secretary of State as a part of his responsibility to protect American citizens traveling abroad, and what he considered to be the best interests of the Nation."

In 1966, the Secretary of State promulgated the regulations at issue in this case. 22 CFR §§ 51.70(b)(4), 51.71(a) (1980). Closely paralleling the 1956 regulation, these provisions authorize revocation of a passport where "[t]he Secretary determines that the national's activities abroad are causing or are likely to cause serious damage to the national security or the foreign policy of the United States. "

***

III

Agee also attacks the Secretary's action on three constitutional grounds: first, that the revocation of his passport impermissibly burdens his freedom to travel; second, that the action was intended to penalize his exercise of free speech and deter his criticism of Government policies and practices; and third, that failure to accord him a pre-revocation hearing violated his Fifth Amendment right to procedural due process.

In light of the express language of the passport regulations, which permits their application only in cases involving likelihood of "serious damage" to national security or foreign policy, these claims are without merit.

Revocation of a passport undeniably curtails travel, but the freedom to travel abroad with a "letter of introduction" in the form of a passport issued by the sovereign is subordinate to national security and foreign policy considerations; as such, it is subject to reasonable governmental regulation. The Court has made it plain that the freedom to travel outside the United States must be distinguished from the right to travel within the United States. This was underscored in *Califano v. Aznavorian*, 439 U. S. 170, 439 U. S. 176 (1978):

"Aznavorian urges that the freedom of international travel is basically equivalent to the constitutional right to interstate travel, recognized by this Court for over 100 years. **Edwards v. California**, *314 U.S. 160;* **Twining v. New Jersey**, *211 U.S. 78, 211 U. S. 97;* **Williams v. Fear**, *179 U.S. 270, 179 U.S. 274;* **Crandall v. Nevada**, *6 Wall. 35, 73 U.S. 43-44;* **Passenger Cases**, *7 How. 283, 48 U.S. 492 (Taney, C.J., dissenting). But this Court has often pointed out the crucial difference between the freedom to travel internationally and the right of interstate travel."*

"The constitutional right of interstate travel is virtually unqualified, **United States v. Guest**, *383 U.S. 745, 383 U.S. 757-758 (1966);* **Griffin v. Breckenridge**, *403 U.S. 88, 403 U.S. 105-106 (1971). By contrast, the right' of international travel has been considered to be no more than an aspect of the 'liberty' protected by the Due Process Clause of the*

Fifth Amendment. As such, this 'right,' the Court has held, can be regulated within the bounds of due process." (Citations omitted.) **Califano v. Torres**, *435 U.S. 1, 435 U. S. 4 n. 6."*

It is "obvious and unarguable" that no governmental interest is more compelling than the security of the Nation. **Aptheker v. Secretary of State**, 378 U.S. at 378 U.S. 509. Protection of the foreign policy of the United States is a governmental interest of great importance, since foreign policy and national security considerations cannot neatly be compartmentalized.

Measures to protect the secrecy of our Government's foreign intelligence operations plainly serve these interests. Thus, in **Snepp v. United States**, 444 U.S. 507, 444 U.S. 509, n. 3 (1980), we held that "[t]he Government has a compelling interest in protecting both the secrecy of information important to our national security and the appearance of confidentiality so essential to the effective operation of our foreign intelligence service." See also id. at 444 U.S. 511-513. The Court in **United States v. Curtiss-Wright Export Corp.** properly emphasized: "[The President] has his confidential sources of information. He has his agents in the form of diplomatic, consular and other officials. Secrecy in respect of information gathered by them may be highly necessary, and the premature disclosure of it productive of harmful results." 299 U.S. at 299 U. S. 320. Accord, **Chicago & Southern Air Lines, Inc. v. Waterman S.S. Corp.**, 333 U.S. at 333 U. S. 111; The Federalist No. 64, pp. 392-393 (Mentor ed.1961).

Not only has Agee jeopardized the security of the United States, but he has also endangered the interests of countries other than the United States—thereby creating serious problems for American foreign relations and foreign policy. Restricting Agee's foreign travel, although perhaps not certain to prevent all of Agee's harmful activities, is the only avenue open to the Government to limit these activities.

Assuming, arguendo, that First Amendment protections reach beyond our national boundaries, Agee's First Amendment claim has no foundation. The revocation of Agee's passport rests in part on the content of his speech: specifically, his repeated disclosures of intelligence operations and names of intelligence personnel. Long ago, however, this Court recognized that "[n]o one would question but that a government might prevent actual obstruction to its recruiting service or the publication of the sailing dates of transports or the number and location of troops." **Near v. Minnesota ex rel. Olson**, 283 U.S. 697, 283 U.S. 716 (1931), citing Z. Chafee, Freedom of Speech 10 (1920). Agee's disclosures, among other things, have the declared purpose of obstructing intelligence operations and the recruiting of intelligence personnel. They are clearly not protected by the Constitution. The mere fact that Agee is also engaged in criticism of the Government does not render his conduct beyond the reach of the law.

To the extent the revocation of his passport operates to inhibit Agee, "it is an inhibition of action," rather than of speech. **Zemel**, 381 U.S. at 381 U.S. 117 (emphasis supplied). Agee is as free to criticize the United States Government as he was when he held a passport—always subject, of course, to express limits on certain rights by virtue of his contract with the Government.

On this record, the Government is not required to hold a pre-revocation hearing. In **Cole v. Young**, supra, we held that federal employees who hold "sensitive" positions "where they could bring about any discernible adverse effects on the Nation's security" may be suspended without a pre-suspension hearing. 351 U.S. at 351 U.S. 546-547. For the same reasons, when there is a substantial likelihood of "serious damage" to national security or foreign policy as a result of a passport holder's activities in foreign countries, the Government may take action to ensure that the holder may not exploit the sponsorship of his travels by the United States. "[W]hile the Constitution protects against invasions of individual rights, it is not a suicide pact." **Kennedy v. Mendoza-Martinez**, 372 U.S. 144, 372 U.S. 160 (1963). The Constitution's due process guarantees call for no more than what has been accorded here: a statement of reasons and an opportunity for a prompt post-revocation hearing.

We reverse the judgment of the Court of Appeals and remand for further proceedings consistent with this opinion.

Reversed and remanded.

United States v. Arvizu
534 U.S. 266 (2002)

Chief Justice Rehnquist delivered the opinion of the Court.

Respondent Ralph Arvizu was stopped by a border patrol agent while driving on an unpaved road in a remote area of southeastern Arizona. A search of his vehicle turned up more than 100 pounds of marijuana. The District Court for the District of Arizona denied respondent's motion to suppress, but the Court of Appeals for the Ninth Circuit reversed. In the course of its opinion, it categorized certain factors relied upon by the District Court as simply out of bounds in deciding whether there was "reasonable suspicion" for the stop. We hold that the Court of Appeals' methodology was contrary to our prior decisions and that it reached the wrong result in this case.

On an afternoon in January 1998, Agent Clinton Stoddard was working at a border patrol checkpoint along U.S. Highway 191 approximately 30 miles north of Douglas, Arizona.

***

Agents use roving patrols to apprehend smugglers trying to circumvent the checkpoint by taking the back roads, including those roads through the sparsely populated area between Douglas and the national forest. Magnetic sensors, or "intrusion devices," facilitate agents' efforts in patrolling these areas. Directionally sensitive, the sensors signal the passage of traffic that would be consistent with smuggling activities.

***

Around 2:15 p.m., Stoddard received a report via Douglas radio that a Leslie Canyon Road sensor had triggered. This was significant to Stoddard for two reasons. First, it suggested to him that a vehicle might be trying to circumvent the checkpoint. Second, the timing coincided with the point when agents begin heading back to the checkpoint for a shift change, which leaves the area unpatrolled. Stoddard knew that alien smugglers did extensive scouting and seemed to be most active when agents were en route back to the checkpoint. Another border patrol agent told Stoddard that the same sensor had gone off several weeks before and that he had apprehended a minivan using the same route and witnessed the occupants throwing bundles of marijuana out the door.

Stoddard drove eastbound on Rucker Canyon Road to investigate. As he did so, he received another radio report of sensor activity. It indicated that the vehicle that had triggered the first sensor was heading westbound on Rucker Canyon Road. He continued east, passing Kuykendall Cutoff Road. He saw the dust trail of an approaching vehicle about a half mile away. Stoddard had not seen any other vehicles and, based on the timing, believed that this was the one that had tripped the sensors. He pulled off to the side of the road at a slight slant so he could get a good look at the oncoming vehicle as it passed by.

It was a minivan, a type of automobile that Stoddard knew smugglers used. As it approached, it slowed dramatically, from about 50–55 to 25–30 miles per hour. He saw five occupants inside. An adult man was driving, an adult woman sat in the front passenger seat, and three children were in the back. The driver appeared stiff and his posture very rigid. He did not look at Stoddard and seemed to be trying to pretend that Stoddard was not there. Stoddard thought this suspicious because in his experience on patrol most persons look over and see what is going on, and in that area most drivers give border patrol agents a friendly wave. Stoddard noticed that the knees of the two children sitting in the very back seat were unusually high, as if their feet were propped up on some cargo on the floor.

At that point, Stoddard decided to get a closer look, so he began to follow the vehicle as it continued westbound on Rucker Canyon Road toward Kuykendall Cutoff Road. Shortly thereafter, all of the children, though still facing forward, put their hands up at the same time and began to wave at Stoddard in an abnormal pattern. It looked to Stoddard as if the children were being instructed. Their odd waving continued on and off for about four to five minutes.

Several hundred feet before the Kuykendall Cutoff Road intersection, the driver signaled that he would turn. At one point, the driver turned the signal off, but just as he approached the intersection he put it back on and abruptly turned north onto Kuykendall. The turn was significant to Stoddard because it was made at the last place that would have allowed the minivan to avoid the checkpoint. Also, Kuykendall, though passable by a sedan or van, is rougher than either Rucker Canyon or Leslie Canyon roads, and the normal traffic is four-wheel-drive vehicles. Stoddard did not recognize the minivan as part of the local traffic agents encounter on patrol, and he did not think it likely that the minivan was going to or coming from a picnic outing. He was not aware of any picnic grounds on Turkey Creek, which could be reached by following Kuykendall Cutoff all the way up. He knew of picnic grounds and a Boy Scout camp east of the intersection of Rucker Canyon and Leslie Canyon roads, but the minivan had turned west at that intersection. And he had never seen anyone picnicking or sightseeing near where the first sensor went off.

Stoddard radioed for a registration check and learned that the minivan was registered to an address in Douglas that was four blocks north of the border in an area notorious for alien and narcotics smuggling. After receiving the information, Stoddard decided to make a vehicle stop. He approached the driver and learned that his name was Ralph Arvizu. Stoddard asked if respondent would mind if he looked inside and searched the vehicle. Respondent agreed, and Stoddard discovered marijuana in a black duffel bag under the feet of the two children in the back seat. Another bag containing marijuana was behind the rear seat. In all, the van contained 128.85 pounds of marijuana, worth an estimated $99,080.

Respondent was charged with possession with intent to distribute marijuana in violation of 21 U.S.C. §841(a)(1) (1994 ed.). He moved to suppress the marijuana, arguing among other things that Stoddard did not have reasonable suspicion to stop the vehicle as required by the Fourth Amendment. After holding a hearing where Stoddard and respondent testified, the District Court for the District of Arizona ruled otherwise ... The Court of Appeals for the Ninth Circuit reversed. In its view, fact-specific weighing of circumstances or other multifactor tests introduced "a troubling degree of uncertainty and unpredictability" into the Fourth Amendment analysis ... It therefore "attempt[ed] ... to describe and clearly delimit the extent to which certain factors may be considered by law enforcement officers in making stops such as the stop involv[ing]" respondent. After characterizing the District Court's analysis as relying on a list of 10 factors, the Court of Appeals proceeded to examine each in turn. It held that 7 of the factors, including respondent's slowing down, his failure to acknowledge Stoddard, the raised position of the children's knees, and their odd waving carried little or no weight in the reasonable-suspicion calculus. The remaining factors-the road's use by smugglers, the temporal proximity between respondent's trip and the agents' shift change, and the use of minivans by smugglers-were not enough to render the stop permissible. We granted certiorari to review the decision of the Court of Appeals because of its importance to the enforcement of federal drug and immigration laws.

The Fourth Amendment prohibits "unreasonable searches and seizures" by the Government, and its protections extend to brief investigatory stops of persons or vehicles that fall short of traditional arrest. **Terry v. Ohio**, 392 U.S. 1,9 (1968); **United States v. Cortez**, 449 U.S. 411, 417 (1981). Because the "balance between the public interest and the individual's right to personal security," **United States v. Brignoni-Ponce**, 422 U.S. 873, 878 (1975), tilts in favor of a standard less than probable cause in such cases, the Fourth Amendment is satisfied if the officer's action is supported by reasonable suspicion to believe that criminal activity "may be afoot," **United States v. Sokolow**, 490 U.S. 1, 7 (1989) (quoting **Terry**, supra, at 30). See also **Cortez**, 449 U.S., at 417 ("An investigatory stop must be justified by some objective manifestation that the person stopped is, or is about to be, engaged in criminal activity").

When discussing how reviewing courts should make reasonable-suspicion determinations, we have said repeatedly that they must look at the "totality of the circumstances" of each case to see whether the detaining officer has a "particularized and objective basis" for suspecting legal wrongdoing. This process allows officers to draw on their own experience and specialized training to make inferences from and deductions about the cumulative information available to them that "might well elude an untrained person." See also **Ornelas v. United States**, 517 U.S. 690, 699 (1996) (reviewing court must give "due weight" to factual inferences drawn by resident judges and local law enforcement officers). Although an officer's reliance on a mere "hunch" is insufficient to justify a stop, **Terry**, supra, at 27, the likelihood of criminal activity need not rise to the level required for probable cause, and it falls considerably short of satisfying a preponderance of the evidence standard, **Sokolow**, supra, at 7.

Our cases have recognized that the concept of reasonable suspicion is somewhat abstract.

***

We think that the approach taken by the Court of Appeals here departs sharply from the teachings of these cases. The court's evaluation and rejection of seven of the listed factors in isolation from each other does not take into account the "totality of the circumstances," as our cases have understood that phrase. The court appeared to believe that each observation by Stoddard that was by itself readily susceptible to an innocent explanation was entitled to "no weight." **Terry**, however, precludes this sort of divide-and-conquer analysis. The officer in **Terry** observed the petitioner and his companions repeatedly walk back and forth, look into a store window, and confer with one another. Although each of the series of acts was "perhaps innocent in itself," we held that, taken together, they "warranted further investigation." 392 U.S., at 22. See also **Sokolow**, supra, at 9 (holding that factors which by themselves were "quite consistent with innocent travel" collectively amounted to reasonable suspicion).

***

Having considered the totality of the circumstances and given due weight to the factual inferences drawn by the law enforcement officer and District Court Judge, we hold that Stoddard had reasonable suspicion to believe that respondent was engaged in illegal activity. It was reasonable for Stoddard to infer from his observations, his registration check, and his experience as a border patrol agent that respondent had set out from Douglas along a little-traveled route used by smugglers to avoid the 191 checkpoint. Stoddard's knowledge further supported a common sense inference that respondent intended to pass through the area at a time when officers would be leaving their back roads patrols to change shifts. The likelihood that respondent and his family were on a picnic outing was diminished by the fact that the minivan had turned away from the known recreational areas accessible to the east on Rucker Canyon Road. Corroborating this inference was the fact that recreational areas farther to the north would have been easier to reach by taking 191, as opposed to the 40-to-50-mile trip on unpaved and primitive roads. The children's elevated knees suggested the existence of concealed cargo in the passenger compartment. Finally, for the reasons we have given, Stoddard's assessment of respondent's reactions upon seeing him and the children's mechanical-like waving, which continued for a full four to five minutes, were entitled to some weight.

***

Respondent argues that we must rule in his favor because the facts suggested a family in a minivan on a holiday outing. A determination that reasonable suspicion exists, however, need not rule out the possibility of innocent conduct. See **Illinois v. Wardlow**, 528 U.S. 119, 125 (2000) (that flight from police is not necessarily indicative of ongoing criminal activity does not establish Fourth Amendment violation). Undoubtedly, each of these factors alone is susceptible to innocent explanation, and some factors are more probative than others. Taken together, we believe they sufficed to form a particularized and objective basis for Stoddard's stopping the vehicle, making the stop reasonable within the meaning of the Fourth Amendment.

The judgment of the Court of Appeals is therefore reversed, and the case is remanded for further proceedings consistent with this opinion.

It is so ordered.

Arizona v. United States
132 S.Ct. 2492 (2012)

Justice Kennedy delivered the opinion of the Court.

To address pressing issues related to the large number of aliens within its borders who do not have a lawful right to be in this country, the State of Arizona in 2010 enacted a statute called the Support Our Law Enforcement and Safe Neighborhoods Act. The law is often referred to as S.B. 1070, the version introduced in the state senate. Its stated purpose is to "discourage and deter the unlawful entry and presence of aliens and economic activity by persons unlawfully present in the United States." The law's provisions establish an official state policy of "attrition through enforcement." The question before the Court is whether federal law preempts and renders invalid four separate provisions of the state law.

I

The United States filed this suit against Arizona, seeking to enjoin S.B. 1070 as preempted. Four provisions of the law are at issue here. Two create new state offenses. Section 3 makes failure to comply with federal alien-registration requirements a state misdemeanor. Section 5, in relevant part, makes it a misdemeanor for an unauthorized alien to seek or engage in work in the State; this provision is referred to as §5(C). Two other provisions give specific arrest authority and investigative duties with respect to certain aliens to state and local law enforcement officers. Section 6 authorizes officers to arrest without a warrant a person "the officer has probable cause to believe ... has committed any public offense that makes the person removable from the United States." Section 2(B) provides that officers who conduct a stop, detention, or arrest must in some circumstances make efforts to verify the person's immigration status with the Federal Government.

The United States District Court for the District of Arizona issued a preliminary injunction preventing the four provisions at issue from taking effect. The Court of Appeals for the Ninth Circuit affirmed. It agreed that the United States had established a likelihood of success on its preemption claims. The Court of Appeals was unanimous in its conclusion that §§3 and 5(C) were likely preempted. Judge Bea dissented from the decision to uphold the preliminary injunction against §§2(B) and 6. This Court granted certiorari to resolve important questions concerning the interaction of state and federal power with respect to the law of immigration and alien status.

II

A

The Government of the United States has broad, undoubted power over the subject of immigration and the status of aliens. This authority rests, in part, on the National Government's constitutional power to "establish an uniform Rule of Naturalization," U.S. Const., Art. I, §8, cl. 4, and its inherent power as sovereign to control and conduct relations with foreign nations.

The federal power to determine immigration policy is well settled. Immigration policy can affect trade, investment, tourism, and diplomatic relations for the entire Nation, as well as the perceptions and expectations of aliens in this country who seek the full protection of its laws. Perceived mistreatment of aliens in the United States may lead to harmful reciprocal treatment of American citizens abroad. It is fundamental that foreign countries concerned about the status, safety, and security of their nationals in the United States must be able to confer and communicate on this subject with one national sovereign, not the 50 separate States. This Court has reaffirmed that "[o]ne of the most important and delicate of all international relationships ... has to do with the protection of the just rights of a country's own nationals when those nationals are in another country." **Hines v. Davidowitz**, 312 U.S. 52, 64 (1941).

Federal governance of immigration and alien status is extensive and complex. Congress has specified categories of aliens who may not be admitted to the United States. See 8 U. S. C. §1182. Unlawful entry and unlawful re-entry into the country are federal offenses. §§1325, 1326. Once here, aliens are required to register with the Federal Government and to carry proof of status on their person. See §§1301–1306. Failure to do so is a federal misdemeanor. §§1304(e), 1306(a). Federal law also authorizes States to deny non-citizens a range of public benefits, §1622; and it imposes sanctions on employers who hire unauthorized workers, §1324a.

Congress has specified which aliens may be removed from the United States and the procedures for doing so. Aliens may be removed if they were inadmissible at the time of entry, have been convicted of certain crimes, or meet other criteria set by federal law. See §1227. Removal is a civil, not criminal, matter. A principal feature of the removal system is the broad discretion exercised by immigration officials...Federal officials, as an initial matter, must decide whether it makes sense to pursue removal at all. If removal proceedings commence, aliens may seek asylum and other discretionary relief allowing them to remain in the country or at least to leave without formal removal. See §1229a(c)(4); see also, e.g., §§1158 (asylum), 1229b (cancellation of removal), 1229c (voluntary departure).

***

B

The pervasiveness of federal regulation does not diminish the importance of immigration policy to the States. Arizona bears many of the consequences of unlawful immigration. Hundreds of thousands of deportable aliens are apprehended in Arizona each year. Dept. of Homeland Security, Office of Immigration Statistics, 2010 Yearbook of Immigration Statistics 93 (2011) (Table 35). Unauthorized aliens who remain in the State comprise, by one es timate, almost six percent of the population. See Passel & Cohn, Pew Hispanic Center, U. S. Unauthorized Immigration Flows Are Down Sharply Since Mid-Decade 3 (2010). And in the State's most populous county, these aliens are reported to be responsible for a disproportionate share of serious crime. See, e.g., Camarota & Vaughan, Center for Immigration Studies, Immigration and Crime: Assessing a Conflicted Situation 16 (2009) (Table 3) (estimating that unauthorized aliens comprise 8.9% of the population and are responsible for 21.8% of the felonies in Maricopa County, which includes Phoenix).

Statistics alone do not capture the full extent of Arizona's concerns. Accounts in the record suggest there is an "epidemic of crime, safety risks, serious property damage, and environmental problems" associated with the influx of illegal migration across private land near the Mexican border ... Phoenix is a major city of the United States, yet signs along an interstate highway 30 miles to the south warn the public to stay away. One reads, "DANGER—PUBLIC WARNING—TRAVEL NOT RECOMMENDED/Active Drug and Human Smuggling Area/Visitors May Encounter Armed Criminals and Smug-gling Vehicles Traveling at High Rates of Speed." ... The problems posed to the State by illegal immigration must not be underestimated.

These concerns are the background for the formal legal analysis that follows. The issue is whether, under pre-emption principles, federal law permits Arizona to implement the state-law provisions in dispute.

III

Federalism, central to the constitutional design, adopts the principle that both the National and State Governments have elements of sovereignty the other is bound to respect. See **Gregory v.**

Ashcroft, 501 U.S. 452, 457 (1991); *U.S. Term Limits, Inc. v. Thornton*, 514 U.S. 779, 838 (1995) (Kennedy, J., concurring). From the existence of two sovereigns follows the possibility that laws can be in conflict or at cross-purposes. The Supremacy Clause provides a clear rule that federal law "shall be the supreme Law of the Land; and the Judges in every State shall be bound thereby, any Thing in the Constitution or Laws of any State to the Contrary notwithstanding." Art. VI, cl. 2. Under this principle, Congress has the power to preempt state law. See *Crosby v. National Foreign Trade Council*, 530 U.S. 363, 372 (2000); *Gibbons v. Ogden*, 9 Wheat. 1, 210–211 (1824). There is no doubt that Congress may withdraw specified powers from the States by enacting a statute containing an express preemption provision. See, e.g., *Chamber of Commerce of United States of America v. Whiting*, 563 U.S. ___, ___ (2011) (slip op., at 4).

State law must also give way to federal law in at least two other circumstances. First, the States are precluded from regulating conduct in a field that Congress, acting within its proper authority, has determined must be regulated by its exclusive governance. See *Gade v. National Solid Wastes Management Assn.*, 505 U.S. 88, 115 (1992). The intent to displace state law altogether can be inferred from a framework of regulation "so pervasive ... that Congress left no room for the States to supplement it" or where there is a "federal interest ... so dominant that the federal system will be assumed to preclude enforcement of state laws on the same subject." *Rice v. Santa Fe Elevator Corp.*, 331 U.S. 218, 230 (1947); see *English v. General Elec. Co.*, 496 U.S. 72, 79 (1990).

Second, state laws are preempted when they conflict with federal law. *Crosby*, supra, at 372. This includes cases where "compliance with both federal and state regulations is a physical impossibility," *Florida Lime & Avocado Growers, Inc. v. Paul*, 373 U.S. 132–143 (1963), and those instances where the challenged state law "stands as an obstacle to the accomplishment and execution of the full purposes and objectives of Congress," *Hines*, 312 U.S., at 67 ...

The four challenged provisions of the state law each must be examined under these preemption principles.

IV

A

Section 3

Section 3 of S. B. 1070 creates a new state misdemeanor. It forbids the "willful failure to complete or carry an alien registration document ... in violation of 8 United States Code section 1304(e) or 1306(a)." Ariz. Rev. Stat. Ann. §11–1509(A) (West Supp. 2011). In effect, §3 adds a state-law penalty for conduct proscribed by federal law. The United

States contends that this state enforcement mechanism intrudes on the field of alien registration, a field in which Congress has left no room for States to regulate ...

The Court discussed federal alien-registration requirements in **Hines v. Davidowitz**, 312 U.S. 52. In 1940, as international conflict spread, Congress added to federal immigration law a "complete system for alien registration." Id., at 70. The new federal law struck a careful balance. It punished an alien's willful failure to register but did not require aliens to carry identification cards. There were also limits on the sharing of registration records and fingerprints. The Court found that Congress intended the federal plan for registration to be a "single integrated and all-embracing system." Id., at 74. Because this "complete scheme ... for the registration of aliens" touched on foreign relations, it did not allow the States to "curtail or complement" federal law or to "enforce additional or auxiliary regulations." Id., at 66–67. As a consequence, the Court ruled that Pennsylvania could not enforce its own alien-registration program. See Id., at 59, 74.

The present regime of federal regulation is not identical to the statutory framework considered in **Hines**, but it remains comprehensive. Federal law now includes a requirement that aliens carry proof of registration. 8 U. S. C. §1304(e). Other aspects, however, have stayed the same. Aliens who remain in the country for more than 30 days must apply for registration and be fingerprinted ...

The framework enacted by Congress leads to the conclusion here, as it did in **Hines**, that the Federal Government has occupied the field of alien registration. See **American Ins. Assn. v. Garamendi**, 539 U.S. 396, n. 11 (2003) (characterizing **Hines** as a field preemption case); **Pennsylvania v. Nelson**, 350 U.S. 497, 504 (1956) (same); see also Dinh, Reassessing the Law of Preemption, 88 Geo. L. J. 2085, 2098–2099, 2107 (2000) (same). The federal statutory directives provide a full set of standards governing alien registration, including the punishment for noncompliance. It was designed as a " 'harmonious whole.' " **Hines**, supra, at 72. Where Congress occupies an entire field, as it has in the field of alien registration, even complementary state regulation is impermissible. Field preemption reflects a congressional decision to foreclose any state regulation in the area, even if it is parallel to federal standards. See **Silkwood v. Kerr-McGee Corp.**, 464 U.S. 238, 249 (1984).

***

There is a further intrusion upon the federal scheme. Even where federal authorities believe prosecution is appropriate, there is an inconsistency between §3 and federal law with respect to penalties. Under federal law, the failure to carry registration papers is a misdemeanor that may be punished by a fine, imprisonment, or a term of probation. See 8 U.S.C. §1304(e) (2006 ed.); 18 U.S.C. §3561. State law, by contrast, rules out probation as a possible sentence (and also eliminates the possibility of a pardon). See Ariz. Rev. Stat. Ann. §13–1509(D) (West Supp. 2011). This state framework of sanctions creates a conflict with the plan Congress put in place. See Wisconsin Dept., supra, at 286 ("[C]onflict is imminent whenever two separate remedies are brought to bear on the same activity" (internal quotation marks omitted)).

These specific conflicts between state and federal law simply underscore the reason for field preemption. As it did in **Hines**, the Court now concludes that, with respect to the subject of alien registration, Congress intended to preclude States from "complement[ing] the federal law, or enforc[ing] additional or auxiliary regulations." 312 U.S., at 66–67. Section 3 is preempted by federal law.

B

Section 5(C)

Unlike §3, which replicates federal statutory requirements, §5(C) enacts a state criminal prohibition where no federal counterpart exists. The provision makes it a state misdemeanor for "an unauthorized alien to knowingly apply for work, solicit work in a public place or perform work as an employee or independent contractor" in Arizona. Ariz. Rev. Stat. Ann. §13–2928(C) (West Supp. 2011). Violations can be punished by a $2,500 fine and incarceration for up to six months. See §13–2928(F); see also §§13–707(A)(1) (West 2010); 13–802(A); 13–902(A)(5). The United States contends that the provision upsets the balance struck by the Immigration Reform and Control Act of 1986 (IRCA) and must be preempted as an obstacle to the federal plan of regulation and control.

When there was no comprehensive federal program regulating the employment of unauthorized aliens, this Court found that a State had authority to pass its own laws on the subject. In 1971, for example, California passed a law imposing civil penalties on the employment of aliens who were "not entitled to lawful residence in the United States if such employment would have an adverse effect on lawful resident workers." 1971 Cal. Stats. ch. 1442, §1(a). The law was upheld against a preemption challenge in **De Canas v. Bica**, 424 U.S. 351 (1976). **De Canas** recognized that "States possess broad authority under their police powers to regulate the employment relationship to protect workers within the State." Id., at 356. At that point, however, the Federal Government had expressed no more than "a peripheral concern with [the] employment of illegal entrants." Id., at 360; see **Whiting**, 563 U.S., at ___ (slip op., at 3).

Current federal law is substantially different from the regime that prevailed when **De Canas** was decided. Congress enacted IRCA as a comprehensive framework for "combating the employment of illegal aliens." **Hoffman Plastic Compounds, Inc. v. NLRB**, PERLINK"

http://www.law.cornell.edu/supremecourt/text/535/137"\o"subref"
535 U.S. 137, 147 (2002). The law makes it illegal for employers to
knowingly hire, recruit, refer, or continue to employ unauthorized
workers. See 8 U.S.C. §§1324a(a)(1)(A), (a)(2). It also requires every
employer to verify the employment authorization status of prospective
employees. See §§1324a(a) (1)(B), (b); 8 CFR §274a.2(b) (2012). These
requirements are enforced through criminal penalties and an
escalating series of civil penalties tied to the number of times an
employer has violated the provisions. See 8 U.S.C. §§1324a(e)(4), (f);
8 CFR §274a.10.

This comprehensive framework does not impose federal criminal
sanctions on the employee side (i.e., penalties on aliens who seek or
engage in unauthorized work). Under federal law some civil penalties
are imposed instead ... The legislative background of IRCA under-
scores the fact that Congress made a deliberate choice not to impose criminal penalties on aliens who seek, or engage in, unauthorized employment. A commission established by Congress to study
immigration policy and to make recommendations concluded these
penalties would be "unnecessary and unworkable." ... In the end,
IRCA's framework reflects a considered judgment that making
criminals out of aliens engaged in unauthorized work—aliens who
already face the possibility of employer exploitation because of their
removable status—would be inconsistent with federal policy and
objectives ...

IRCA's express preemption provision, which in most instances bars
States from imposing penalties on employers of unauthorized aliens,
is silent about whether additional penalties may be imposed against
the employees themselves ... The ordinary principles of preemption
include the well-settled proposition that a state law is preempted
where it "stands as an obstacle to the accomplishment and
execution of the full purposes and objectives of Congress." **Hines**, 312
U.S., at 67. Under §5(C) of S. B. 1070, Arizona law would interfere with
the careful balance struck by Congress with respect to unauthorized
employment of aliens. Although §5(C) attempts to achieve one of the
same goals as federal law—the deterrence of unlawful employment—it involves a conflict in the method of enforcement. The Court
has recognized that a "[c]onflict in technique can be fully as dis-
ruptive to the system Congress enacted as conflict in overt policy."
Motor Coach Employees v. Lockridge, 403 U.S. 274, 287 (1971). The
correct instruction to draw from the text, structure, and history of IRCA
is that Congress decided it would be inappropriate to impose criminal
penalties on aliens who seek or engage in unauthorized employment.
It follows that a state law to the contrary is an obstacle to the
regulatory system Congress chose. See **Puerto Rico Dept. of Consumer
Affairs v. ISLA Petroleum Corp.**, 485 U.S. 495, 503 (1988) ("Where a
comprehensive federal scheme intentionally leaves a portion of the
regulated field without controls, then the pre-emptive inference can

be drawn—not from federal inaction alone, but from inaction joined with action"). Section 5(C) is preempted by federal law.

C

Section 6

Section 6 of S. B. 1070 provides that a state officer, "without a warrant, may arrest a person if the officer has probable cause to believe ... [the person] has committed any public offense that makes [him] removable from the United States." Ariz. Rev. Stat. Ann. §13–3883(A)(5) (West Supp. 2011). The United States argues that arrests authorized by this statute would be an obstacle to the removal system Congress created.

As a general rule, it is not a crime for a removable alien to remain present in the United States. See ***INS v. Lopez-Mendoza***, 468 U.S. 1032, 1038 (1984). If the police stop someone based on nothing more than possible removability, the usual predicate for an arrest is absent. When an alien is suspected of being removable, a federal official issues an administrative document called a Notice to Appear. See 8 U.S.C. §1229(a); 8 CFR §239.1(a) (2012). The form does not authorize an arrest. Instead, it gives the alien information about the proceedings, including the time and date of the removal hearing. See 8 U.S.C. §1229(a)(1). If an alien fails to appear, an in absentia order may direct removal. §1229a(5)(A).

The federal statutory structure instructs when it is appropriate to arrest an alien during the removal process ... warrants are executed by federal officers who have received training in the enforcement of immigration law. See §§241.2(b), 287.5(e)(3). If no federal warrant has been issued, those officers have more limited authority. See 8 U.S.C. §1357(a). They may arrest an alien for being "in the United States in violation of any [immigration] law or regulation," for example, but only where the alien "is likely to escape before a warrant can be obtained." §1357(a)(2).

Section 6 attempts to provide state officers even greater authority to arrest aliens on the basis of possible removability than Congress has given to trained federal immigration officers. Under state law, officers who believe an alien is removable by reason of some "public offense" would have the power to conduct an arrest on that basis regardless of whether a federal warrant has issued or the alien is likely to escape. This state authority could be exercised without any input from the Federal Government about whether an arrest is warranted in a particular case. This would allow the State to achieve its own immigration policy. The result could be unnecessary harassment of some aliens (for instance, a veteran, college student, or someone assisting with a criminal investigation) whom federal officials determine should not be removed.

This is not the system Congress created. Federal law specifies limited circumstances in which state officers may perform the functions of an immigration officer ...

By authorizing state officers to decide whether an alien should be detained for being removable, §6 violates the principle that the removal process is entrusted to the discretion of the Federal Government. See, e.g., *Reno v. American-Arab Anti-Discrimination Comm.*, 525 U.S. 471–484 (1999) ... A decision on removability requires a determination whether it is appropriate to allow a foreign national to continue living in the United States. Decisions of this nature touch on foreign relations and must be made with one voice. See *Jama v. Immigration and Customs Enforcement*, 543 U.S. 335, 348 (2005) ("Removal decisions, including the selection of a removed alien's destination, may implicate [the Nation's] relations with foreign powers and require consideration of changing political and economic circumstances" (internal quotation marks omitted)); see also *Galvan v. Press*, 347 U.S. 522, 531 (1954) ("Policies pertaining to the entry of aliens and their right to remain here are ... entrusted exclusively to Congress ..."); *Truax v. Raich*, 239 U.S. 33, 42 (1915) ("The authority to control immigration—to admit or exclude aliens—is vested solely in the Federal Government").

In defense of §6, Arizona notes a federal statute permitting state officers to "cooperate with the Attorney General in the identification, apprehension, detention, or removal of aliens not lawfully present in the United States." 8 U.S.C. §1357(g)(10)(B). There may be some ambiguity as to what constitutes cooperation under the federal law; but no coherent understanding of the term would incorporate the unilateral decision of state officers to arrest an alien for being removable absent any request, approval, or other instruction from the Federal Government. The Department of Homeland Security gives examples of what would constitute cooperation under federal law. These include situations where States participate in a joint task force with federal officers, provide operational support in executing a warrant, or allow federal immigration officials to gain access to detainees held in state facilities ... State officials can also assist the Federal Government by responding to requests for information about when an alien will be released from their custody. But the unilateral state action to detain authorized by §6 goes far beyond these measures, defeating any need for real cooperation.

Congress has put in place a system in which state officers may not make warrantless arrests of aliens based on possible removability except in specific, limited circumstances. By nonetheless authorizing state and local officers to engage in these enforcement activities as a general matter, §6 creates an obstacle to the full purposes and objectives of Congress. See *Hines*, 312 U.S., at 67. Section 6 is preempted by federal law.

D

Section 2(B)

Section 2(B) of S.B. 1070 requires state officers to make a "reasonable attempt ... to determine the immigration status" of any person they stop, detain, or arrest on some other legitimate basis if "reasonable suspicion exists that the person is an alien and is unlawfully present in the United States." Ariz. Rev. Stat. Ann. §11–1051(B) (West 2012). The law also provides that "[a]ny person who is arrested shall have the person's immigration status determined before the person is released." Ibid. The accepted way to perform these status checks is to contact ICE, which maintains a database of immigration records.

Three limits are built into the state provision. First, a detainee is presumed not to be an alien unlawfully present in the United States if he or she provides a valid Arizona driver's license or similar identification. Second, officers "may not consider race, color or national origin ... except to the extent permitted by the United States [and] Arizona Constitution[s]." Ibid. Third, the provisions must be "implemented in a manner consistent with federal law regulating immigration, protecting the civil rights of all persons and respecting the privileges and immunities of United States citizens." §11–1051(L) (West 2012).

The United States and its amici contend that, even with these limits, the State's verification requirements pose an obstacle to the framework Congress put in place. The first concern is the mandatory nature of the status checks. The second is the possibility of prolonged detention while the checks are being performed.

1

Consultation between federal and state officials is an important feature of the immigration system. Congress has made clear that no formal agreement or special training needs to be in place for state officers to "communicate with the [Federal Government] regarding the immigration status of any individual, including reporting knowledge that a particular alien is not lawfully present in the United States." 8 U. S. C. §1357(g)(10)(A). And Congress has obligated ICE to respond to any request made by state officials for verification of a person's citizenship or immigration status ...

The United States argues that making status verification mandatory interferes with the federal immigration scheme. It is true that §2(B) does not allow state officers to consider federal enforcement priorities in deciding whether to contact ICE about someone they have detained. In other words, the officers must make an inquiry even in cases where it seems unlikely that the Attorney General would have the alien removed. This might be the case, for example, when an alien is an elderly veteran with significant and longstanding ties to the community.

Congress has done nothing to suggest it is inappropriate to communicate with ICE in these situations, however. Indeed, it has encouraged the sharing of information about possible immigration violations. A federal statute regulating the public benefits provided to qualified aliens in fact instructs that "no State or local government entity may be prohibited, or in any way restricted, from sending to or receiving from [ICE] information regarding the immigration status, lawful or unlawful, of an alien in the United States." The federal scheme thus leaves room for a policy requiring state officials to contact ICE as a routine matter.

2

Some who support the challenge to §2(B) argue that, in practice, state officers will be required to delay the release of some detainees for no reason other than to verify their immigration status. Detaining individuals solely to verify their immigration status would raise constitutional concerns. See, e.g., **Arizona v. Johnson**, 555 U.S. 323, 333 (2009); **Illinois v. Caballes**, 543 U.S. 405, 407 (2005) ("A seizure that is justified solely by the interest in issuing a warning ticket to the driver can become unlawful if it is prolonged beyond the time reasonably required to complete that mission"). And it would disrupt the federal framework to put state officers in the position of holding aliens in custody for possible unlawful presence without federal direction and supervision ... The program put in place by Congress does not allow state or local officers to adopt this enforcement mechanism.

But §2(B) could be read to avoid these concerns. To take one example, a person might be stopped for jaywalking in Tucson and be unable to produce identification. The first sentence of §2(B) instructs officers to make a "reasonable" attempt to verify his immigration status with ICE if there is reasonable suspicion that his presence in the United States is unlawful. The state courts may conclude that, unless the person continues to be suspected of some crime for which he may be detained by state officers, it would not be reasonable to prolong the stop for the immigration inquiry ...

To take another example, a person might be held pending release on a charge of driving under the influence of alcohol. As this goes beyond a mere stop, the arrestee (unlike the jaywalker) would appear to be subject to the categorical requirement in the second sentence of §2(B) that "[a]ny person who is arrested shall have the person's immigration status determined before [he] is released." State courts may read this as an instruction to initiate a status check every time someone is arrested, or in some subset of those cases, rather than as a command to hold the person until the check is complete no matter the circumstances. Even if the law is read as an instruction to complete a check while the person is in custody, moreover, it is not clear at this stage and on this record that the verification process would result in prolonged detention. However the law is interpreted, if §2(B) only requires state officers to conduct a status check during the course of an authorized, lawful detention or after a detainee has been released, the provision likely would survive pre-emption—at least absent some showing that it has other consequences that are adverse to federal law and its objectives. There is no need in this case to address whether reasonable suspicion of illegal entry or another immigration crime would be a legitimate basis for prolonging a detention, or whether this too would be preempted by federal law. See, e.g., **United States v. Di Re**, 332 U.S. 581, 589 (1948) (authority of state officers to make arrests for federal crimes is, absent federal statutory instruction, a matter of state law); **Gonzales v. Peoria**, 722 F. 2d 468, 475–476 (CA9 1983) (concluding that Arizona officers have authority to enforce the criminal provisions of federal immigration law), overruled on other grounds in **Hodgers-Durgin v. de la Vina**, 199 F. 3d 1037 (CA9 1999).

The nature and timing of this case counsel caution in evaluating the validity of §2(B). The Federal Government has brought suit against a sovereign State to challenge the provision even before the law has gone into effect. There is a basic uncertainty about what the law means and how it will be enforced. At this stage, without the benefit of a definitive interpretation from the state courts, it would be inappropriate to assume §2(B) will be construed in a way that creates a conflict with federal law. Cf. **Fox v. Washington**, 236 U.S. 273, 277 (1915) ("So far as statutes fairly may be construed in such a way as to avoid doubtful constitutional questions they should be so construed; and it is to be presumed that state laws will be construed in that way by the state courts" (citation omitted)). As a result, the United States cannot prevail in its current challenge. See **Huron Portland Cement Co. v. Detroit**, 362 U.S. 440, 446 (1960) ("To hold otherwise would be to ignore the teaching of this Court's decisions which enjoin seeking out conflicts between state and federal regulation where none clearly exists"). This opinion does not foreclose other preemption and constitutional challenges to the law as interpreted and applied after it goes into effect.

V

Immigration policy shapes the destiny of the Nation ... The history of the United States is in part made of the stories, talents, and lasting contributions of those who crossed oceans and deserts to come here.

The National Government has significant power to regulate immigration. With power comes responsibility, and the sound exercise of national power over immigration depends on the Nation's meeting its responsibility to base its laws on a political will informed by searching, thoughtful, rational civic discourse. Arizona may have understandable frustrations with the problems caused by illegal immigration while that process continues, but the State may not pursue policies that undermine federal law.

***

The United States has established that §§3, 5(C), and 6 of S. B. 1070 are preempted. It was improper, however, to enjoin §2(B) before the state courts had an opportunity to construe it and without some showing that enforcement of the provision in fact conflicts with federal immigration law and its objectives.

The judgment of the Court of Appeals for the Ninth Circuit is affirmed in part and reversed in part. The case is remanded for further proceedings consistent with this opinion.

It is so ordered.

Commentary and Questions

1. The Alien Enemies Act of 1798, part of the Alien and Sedition Acts discussed briefly in Chapter 1, was the authority relied on by the government in *Ludecke v. Watkins* for the arrest and internment of a German alien enemy in the United States during World War II. Actual removal from the United States did not occur until 1946. The Act gave power to the president during a time of war to remove unnaturalized individuals considered to be alien enemies. What did the Court's opinion state with regard to the petitioner Ludecke's claim that removal came after the cessation of hostilities? What about the Court's position as to its review status of who is to be designated an alien enemy?

2. The Alien and Sedition Acts of 1798 were a wartime measure aimed at regulating criticism of the government and control of immigration, particularly among those deemed to be critical of the national government. This would be the advent of a familiar pattern of government behavior in response to war or perceived threats to national security. The events of the latter part of the 19th century, which included increased multinational immigration into the United States, settlement of these immigrants into major city centers, and the rise of the organized labor movement, which not coincidentally counted many immigrant laborers among its members, spawned internal security concerns. These concerns were magnified by events like the Haymarket Square bombing and riots in Chicago in 1886, resulting from an immigrant labor rally, and the 1901 assassination of President William McKinley by an anarchist. The Immigration Act of 1903, also referred to as the Anarchist Exclusion Act, added anarchists to the list of excludable persons, and included prostitutes, epileptics, and beggars to the list. The Act was amended by the Immigration Act of 1918, which better

defined the term anarchist. At this point the United States was coming out of World War I but the xenophobia would continue, especially as it related to anarchist activity.

The Alien Registration Act of 1940, also known as the Smith Act,[24] criminalized advocating the overthrow of the federal government and required adult non-citizens to register with the government. The law also included an anti-sedition section and prohibited any affiliation with groups advocating the overthrow of the government. The affiliation language would be at the center of the Supreme Court's decision in *Bridges v. Wixon*.[25] An alien from Australia, Harry Bridges, was ordered deported under the Smith Act because of his alleged membership and affiliation with the Communist Party of the United States, which included in its teachings the overthrow of the United States government. Bridges had also been active within the labor movement on the West Coast for a number of years and was a frequent target of government investigation. The Court reversed the deportation order because the evidence presented against Bridges was based on unsworn testimony and the immigration hearing board too loosely applied the term "affiliation." The *Bridges* case is an example of the intersection between immigration related legislation and potential First Amendment claims of freedom of association and freedom of speech, the latter will be explored in Chapter Nine.

3. *Haig v. Agee* provides a brief history of passport regulation in the United States as well as the relevant case law. What was the distinction of Philip Agee's situation to warrant the Supreme Court to side with the secretary of state's denial of a passport? How is the Court's opinion to be distinguished from *Kent v. Dulles* and *Aptheker v. Secretary of State*?

4. A novel approach to immigration enforcement was taken in 2005 by police in the New Hampshire towns of New Ipswich and Hudson when several illegal immigrants were arrested for criminal trespass. New Hampshire Revised Statutes Annotated section 635:2 defines the offense of criminal trespass as a violation when a person "knowing that he is not licensed or privileged to do so, he enters or remains in any place." It becomes a misdemeanor offense if the trespass occurs upon a "secured premises." The theory the New Hampshire officers put forth in *New Hampshire v. Barros-Batistele*[26] was that by virtue of being in the country illegally the defendants were not licensed or privileged to be in the United States, particularly the state of New Hampshire, and were therefore guilty of criminal trespass. Prior to this case the court noted that the definition of "place" referred to a "specific parcel or privately-owned real property, rather than any public or private place within the respective town."[27] The defendants argued the arrests and use of the criminal trespass statue were unconstitutional as an infringement on the federal government's regulation of immigration, therefore a violation of the Supremacy Clause. The government's position was that the criminal trespass complaints did not "constitute regulation of immigration" and the officers were merely fulfilling their duty to "protect the security of the citizenry."[28] The New Hampshire state district court, citing

DeCanas v. Bica, found the officers' use of the criminal trespass statute to arrest illegal aliens was federally preempted. The officers, the court wrote, were extending the statute into areas Congress intended to be exclusive to the federal government. Does the Supreme Court's opinion in *Arizona v. United States* support the judge's decision in the *Barros-Batistele* case or does it provide New Hampshire officers added incentive to re-visit their novel arrest approach?

5. No conversation concerning illegal immigration in the United States can take place without discussing border security. U.S. border security issues remain a constant source of news items relating not only to immigration discussions but those involving anti-terrorism enforcement as well.[29] The U.S. Senate Committee on the Judiciary has a subcommittee chaired by New York Senator Charles Schumer on Immigration, Refugees and Border Security. This is an important topic that engenders no less important legal considerations of the extent of government power in enforcing the security of those borders. In a triad of cases in the mid-1970s the U.S. Supreme Court outlined the parameters for law enforcement border searches. The case of *Almeida-Sanchez v. United States,* 413 U.S. 266 (1973) involved a Mexican citizen who was stopped by Border Patrol in his automobile approximately 26 miles north of the border in California. A search of the vehicle revealed a large quantity of marihuana. The Border Patrol agents neither had a warrant nor probable cause to search the vehicle but conducted the search under the authority of section 287(a)(3) of the Immigration and Nationality Act (INA). That section of the INA provides that any officer or employee of the Immigration Service, under the authority of the Attorney General, *"shall have the power without a warrant ... within a reasonable distance from any external boundary of the United States, to board and search for aliens any vessel within the territorial waters of the United States and any railway car, aircraft, conveyance, or vehicle, and within a distance of twenty-five miles from any such external boundary to have access to private lands, but not dwellings for the purpose of patrolling the border to prevent the illegal entry of aliens into the United States ..."*[30] Aside from arguing the border search exception the government also claimed the search was authorized as an automobile search under the *Carroll*[31] doctrine. The Court held the automobile exception did not apply because there was no probable cause to search. Assessing the border search argument the Court addressed the need for border security with the importance of Fourth Amendment protections: *"It is not enough to argue, as does the Government, that the problem of deterring unlawful entry by aliens across long expanses of national boundaries is a serious one. The needs of law enforcement stand in constant tension with the Constitution's protections of the individual against certain exercises of official power. It is precisely the predictability of these pressures that counsels a resolute loyalty to constitutional safeguards. It is well to recall the words of Mr. Justice Jackson, soon after his return from the Nuremberg Trials: "These [Fourth Amendment] rights, I protest, are not mere second-class rights, but belong in the catalog of indispensable freedoms. Among deprivations of rights, none is so effective in cowing a population, crushing the spirit of the*

individual and putting terror in every heart. Uncontrolled search and seizure is one of the first and most effective weapons in the arsenal of every arbitrary government."[32] The border search exception was similarly rejected by the Court. Two years later in *United States v. Brignoni-Ponce*, 422 U.S. 873 (1975) the Court rejected the Border Patrol's assertion of its authority to stop vehicles in the vicinity of the border and question occupants concerning their citizenship and immigration status. Two Border Patrol officers were in a patrol vehicle near the U.S.-Mexican border observing northbound traffic south of San Clemente, California. A vehicle occupied by three individuals who appeared to be of Mexican descent passed. The appearance of the occupants was given as the only reason for the stop of the vehicle. No search of the vehicle was conducted, as in *Almeida-Sanchez*, but the officers did inquire about the citizenship of all three individuals. The inquiry yielded the fact that the two passengers were Mexican nationals who had entered the country illegally and were being transported north by the driver. All three were arrested and the driver, Felix Humberto Brignoni-Ponce, was arrested for knowingly transporting illegal aliens in violation of the INA. Government support for the officers' actions relied on the language of section 287(a)(1) of the INA which provided Immigration Service officers with the power *"to interrogate any alien or person believed to be an alien as to his right to be or to remain in the United States."*[33] Once again the Court rejected the government's argument and reliance on section 287. In limiting the exercise of authority under the statute the Court said it applied only *"at the border and its functional equivalents."*[34] The Court further stated, *"officers on roving patrol may stop vehicles only if they are aware of specific articulable facts, together with rational inferences from those facts, that reasonably warrant suspicion that the vehicles contain aliens who may be illegally in the country."*[35] This would be the crux of a post-9/11 border search Supreme Court case, *United States v. Arvizu*, discussed below.

The *Almeida-Sanchez* and *Brignoni-Sanchez* cases involved roving border patrols. This being one of the three methods of roadway surveillance employed by the Border Patrol, as noted in *Almeida-Sanchez*: permanent checkpoints, temporary checkpoints and roving patrols.[36] In *United States v. Martinez-Fuerte*, 428 U.S. 543 (1976), the Supreme Court was confronted with a challenge to the Border Patrol's use of fixed checkpoints leading to and from the U.S.-Mexican border. Similar to the facts of *Brignoni-Ponce* the Border Patrol stopped a vehicle with three occupants, in this instance the driver Amado Martinez-Fuerte and two female passengers who were illegal Mexican immigrants.[37] The stop occurred at a fixed roadside checkpoint on Interstate 5 in San Clemente, 66 miles north of the Mexican border.[38] Martinez-Fuerte produced documents indicating he was a lawful resident alien but the two female passengers admitted unlawful entry into the United States. All three were arrested and Martinez-Fuerte was charged with two counts of illegally transporting aliens.[39] The Court's prior opinion in *Brignoni-Ponce* was relied upon by the defendant-respondents in arguing that stops in the absence of reasonable suspicion were invalid.[40] Justice Lewis Powell's 7-2 majority opinion acknowledged the checkpoints were "seizures within the meaning of the Fourth Amendment" but, in pointing to the national policy to limit immigration and the formidable law enforcement problem posed with interdicting the illegal flow of immigrants, held the fixed immigration checkpoints to be consistent with the Fourth Amendment and not necessary to be authorized by a warrant. The *Brignoni-Ponce* opinion, written by Justice Powell a year earlier, disapproved of law enforcement's actions in the case but provided clear guidance relating to stops made by roving patrols—as long as there were clearly articulable facts leading to reasonable suspicion a stop could be initiated even if probable cause did not exist. The *Brignoni-Ponce* Court reasoned that "the interference with Fourth Amendment interests was modest while the inquiry served significant law enforcement needs."[41] In *Martinez-Fuerte* the Court took a cue from its prior opinion and found the fixed checkpoints to be reasonable based on the public interest, law enforcement need and minimal intrusion upon the motoring public.

These three cases outlined the permissible Fourth Amendment conduct that could be undertaken by law enforcement in stemming the tide of illegal immigration. A fourth case decided after 9/11 and discussed in the note below further defined this area of Fourth Amendment jurisprudence.

6. *United States v. Arvizu*, 534 U.S. 266 (2002) was argued just 2½ months after 9/11. The case involved a 1998 Border Patrol roving patrol stop. This stop occurred on an unpaved road in a remote area of southeastern Arizona by an agent who made numerous observations that led him to make the stop. The vehicle was operated by an adult male with a female passenger and three children in the rear seat of the vehicle. Among a number of factors that led the agent to make the stop were that the children appeared to be sitting high in their seats, as if they were sitting on something on the seat, and the children began to wave at him in a strange manner. Additionally, the driver was very rigid in his posture behind the steering wheel and slowed the vehicle drastically upon seeing the agent's vehicle. A subsequent stop of the vehicle yielded a duffel bag with 128 pounds of marihuana. The Ninth Circuit on appeal suppressed the marihuana that had been admitted into evidence by the district court. The Ninth Circuit found the factors relied on by the agent were not all individually indicative of reasonable suspicion.[42] The Supreme Court criticized the Ninth Circuit and reaffirmed its position that reviewing courts have to consider the totality of the circumstances when considering the basis of law enforcement reasonable suspicion stops.[43] The unanimous opinion written by Chief Justice Rehnquist noted that certiorari had been granted because of the importance of the case to "enforcement of federal drug and immigration laws."[44] The Court's opinion placed reliance on a law enforcement officers training and experience in making reasonable suspicion judgments.[45] How significantly does *Arvizu* add to immigration enforcement efforts?

7. What is the role of local law enforcement in immigration control? Should immigration enforcement be a legitimate role for police officers? Does the Supreme Court's support of section 2(B) of Arizona's legislation S.B. 1070 indicate a more active role for law enforcement after the Court's opinion in

Arizona v. United States? Consider the nine point position statement in June 2006 released by the *Major Cities Chiefs Immigration Committee Recommendations for Enforcement of Immigration Laws by Local Police Agencies* which said primary immigration enforcement belongs with the federal government.[46] The position statement, involving 57 chiefs of police located in metropolitan areas of over 1.5 million residents and employing 1,000+ officers, included the following nine points: 1) secure the borders; 2) enforce laws prohibiting the hiring of illegal immigrants; 3) consult and involve police agencies in decision making; 4) any immigration involving local agencies has to be completely voluntary; 5) any involvement of local agencies has to be incentive based with full federal funding; 6) no reduction or shifting of current assistance funding; 7) clarification of authority and limitation of liability; 8) removal of civil immigration detainers from the N.C.I.C. system; 9) commitment of continued enforcement against criminal violators regardless of immigration status.[47] The opening statement of the *Major Cities Chiefs* position paper carefully explains the foundational concerns behind their nine point plan:

"Since the horrendous attacks of September 11, 2001, local law enforcement has been called upon to do its part in protecting the nation from future terrorist attacks. The response of local law enforcement to the call to protect the homeland has been tremendous. Today, local police agencies stand as the first line of defense here at home to prevent future attacks. Local law enforcement's unending efforts include providing additional training and equipment to officers, increasing communication and coordination with federal agencies, gathering, assessing and sharing intelligence, modifying patrol methods and increasing security for potential targets such as power plants, airports, monuments, ports and other critical facilities and infrastructure. Much of these efforts have been at a high cost to local budgets and resources.

The federal government and others have also called upon local police agencies to become involved in the enforcement of federal immigration laws as part of the effort to protect the nation. This issue has been a topic of great debate in the law enforcement community since September 11. The call for local enforcement of federal immigration laws has become more prominent during the debate over proposed immigration reform at the national level.

Major city police departments have a long undeniable history of working with federal law enforcement agencies to address crime in the United States whether committed by citizens, visitors, and/or illegal immigrants. Local police agencies have not turned a blind eye to crimes related to illegal immigration. They have and continue to work daily with federal agencies whenever possible and to the extent allowable under state criminal law enforcement authority to address crimes such as human trafficking and gang violence which have a nexus with illegal immigration.

How local agencies respond to the call to enforce immigration laws could fundamentally change the way they police and serve their communities. Local enforcement of federal immigration laws raises many daunting and complex legal, logistical and resource issues for local agencies and the diverse communities they serve. Some in local law enforcement would embrace immigration enforcement as a means of addressing the violation of law represented by illegal immigration across our borders. Many others recognize the obstacles, pitfalls, dangers and negative consequences to local policing that would be caused by immigration enforcement at the local level."[48]

Congress previously attempted to provide legislation to involve law enforcement in immigration control and enforcement efforts by sponsoring the Clear Law Enforcement for Criminal Alien Removal Act of 2003 (HR 2671), otherwise known as the CLEAR Act. The legislation sought to provide state and local law enforcement with full authorization to investigate, apprehend and remove aliens in the United States. This authority included interstate transportation to detention centers. One of the provisions in the CLEAR Act allowed the government to withhold federal funding for detention assistance for states not in compliance within two years of the Act's enactment, thereby essentially mandating participation. The legislation also provided liability coverage and immunity to law enforcement agencies and officers involved in immigration enforcement, access to the National Crime Information Center database of immigration violators and increased criminal penalties and forfeiture provisions under the INA. Intense opposition to the CLEAR Act from the American Civil Liberties Union and immigration rights groups blocked passage of the Act. This undoubtedly left states impacted by illegal immigration, such as Arizona, to rely on internal methods of their own. However, even in law enforcement, legislation such as S.B. 1070 has not been widely embraced. The Arizona Association of Chiefs of Police issued a statement in opposition to the bill when first enacted and several other law enforcement executives and line officers voiced their opinions against the law. The issue remains divisive even among law enforcement professionals. Should states impacted by illegal immigration be permitted to act in the absence of federal assistance?

8. The proper role of the military in illegal immigration control and border security is another politically charged topic. Should the military be utilized in enforcement and security efforts? Consider the summary from the Congressional Research Service report *Border Security and Military Support: Legal Authorizations and Restrictions:* "*The military generally provides support to law enforcement and immigration authorities along the southern border. Reported escalations in criminal activity and illegal immigration, however, have prompted some lawmakers to reevaluate the extent and type of military support that occurs in the border region ... Addressing domestic laws and activities with the military, however, might run afoul of the Posse Comitatus Act [U.S. Code, Title 18, § 1385], which prohibits use of the armed forces to perform the tasks of civilian law enforcement unless explicitly authorized. There are alternative legal authorities for deploying the National Guard, and the precise scope of permitted activities and funds may vary with the authority exercised ...*"[49] The report's introductory paragraph further outlines the placement of the military in the enforcement mechanism: "*The Secretary of the Department of Homeland Security (DHS) is charged with preventing the entry of terrorists, securing the borders, and carrying out immigration enforcement functions.*

The Department of Defense's (DOD) role in the execution of this responsibility is to provide support to DHS and other federal, state and local (and in some cases foreign) law enforcement agencies, when requested. Since the 1980s, the DOD (and National Guard), as authorized by Congress, has conducted a wide variety of counterdrug support missions along the borders of the United States.

After the attacks of September 11, 2001, military support was expanded to include counterterrorism activities. Although the DOD does not have the 'assigned responsibility to stop terrorists from coming across our borders,' its support role in counterdrug and counterterrorism efforts appears to have increased the Department's profile in border security.'[50]

Immigration control is a constitutionally reserved federal power; as such would it not make sense for the military, under the aegis of the Executive, to be patrolling the borders? Or is the direct use of the military a violation of the Posse Comitatus Act? Title 18 United States Code section 1385, the Posse Comitatus statute, states: *Whoever, except in cases and under circumstances expressly authorized by the Constitution or Act of Congress, willfully uses any part of the Army or the Air Force as a posse comitatus or otherwise to execute the laws shall be fined under this title or imprisoned not more than two years, or both.* There are several exceptions to the Act, which include the "drug exception" to the Act under 32 U.S.C. §112 where a state governor can use National Guard troops in drug interdiction; pursuant to presidential order under 10 U.S.C. §§331-333 to quell domestic disturbance or rebellion; and, more recently since 2004, for homeland defense activity under 32 USC §905. These are a few of the exceptions to the general prohibition against use of the army or air force to execute domestic laws. There are several other exceptions, including use of the military for disaster relief, to the posse comitatus. The issue of military use extends beyond border security, but it would appear a military role could be on better legal standing for border intervention than in other interior domestic matters. What are the legal arguments for and against military use?

Endnotes

[1]   Fox, S. (1989). *Blood and Power: Organized Crime in Twentieth Century America.* New York: Penguin Books. p. 16.

[2]   An act to execute certain treaty stipulations relating to the Chinese, May 6, 1882; Enrolled Acts and Resolutions of Congress, 1789–1996; General Records of the United States Government; Record Group 11; National Archives.

[3]   *Chae Chan Ping v. United States (The Chinese Exclusion Case),* 130 U.S. 581, 603 (1888).

[4]   Article VI, clause 2: "*This Constitution, and the Laws of the United States which shall be made in Pursuance thereof; and all Treaties made, or which shall be made, under the Authority of the United States, shall be the supreme Law of the Land; and the Judges in every State shall be bound thereby, any Thing in the Constitution or Laws of any State to the Contrary notwithstanding.*"

[5]   424 U.S. 351 (1976).

[6]   422 U.S. 873 (1975).

[7]   Id.

[8]   Department of Justice, Office of Legal Counsel, *Non-preemption of the Authority of State and Local Law Enforcement Officials to Arrest Aliens for Immigration Violations*, at 8 (Apr. 3, 2002), available at http://www.aclu.org/files/FilesPDFs/ACF27DA.pdf

[9]   Dwyer, T. (2009). A Delicate Balance: Immigration Enforcement, Homeland Security and Policing in the United States. *Journal of Ethics in Policing*, 20–25.

[10]   Id.

[11]   525 U.S. 471 (1999).

[12]   431 U.S. 606 (1977).

[13]   402 U.S. 363 (1971).

[14]   422 U.S. at 618.

[15]   431 U.S. at 619.

[16]   473 U.S. 531 (1985).

[17]   541 U.S. 149 (2004).

[18]   See e.g., *Corfield v. Coryell*, 6 Fed. Cas. 546 (Cir. Ct. E.D.Pa., 1823).

[19]   Pub. L. 65-154, 65th Congress, Ch. 81.

[20]   Pub. L. 77-113, 77th Congress, Ch. 210.

[21]   James, R. C. (1974). The Right to Travel Abroad. *Fordham Law Review*, 838–851.

[22]   34 U.S. 692, 699 (1835).

[23]   22 USC §211(a).

[24]   The Smith Act has been revised many times and is now found in Title 18 U.S. Code §2385, Advocating Overthrow of the Government:
Whoever knowingly or willfully advocates, abets, advises, or teaches the duty, necessity, desirability, or propriety of overthrowing or destroying the government of the United States or the government of any State, Territory, District or Possession thereof, or the government of any political subdivision therein, by force or violence, or by the assassination of any officer of any such government; or
Whoever, with intent to cause the overthrow or destruction of any such government, prints, publishes, edits, issues, circulates, sells, distributes, or publicly displays any written or printed matter advocating, advising, or teaching the duty, necessity, desirability, or propriety of overthrowing or destroying any government in the United States by force or violence, or attempts to do so; or
Whoever organizes or helps or attempts to organize any society, group, or assembly of persons who teach, advocate, or encourage the overthrow or destruction of any such government by force or violence; or becomes or is a member of, or affiliates with, any such society, group, or assembly of persons, knowing the purposes thereof—
Shall be fined under this title or imprisoned not more than twenty years, or both, and shall be ineligible for employment by the United States or any department or agency thereof, for the five years next following his conviction.
If two or more persons conspire to commit any offense named in this section, each

shall be fined under this title or imprisoned not more than twenty years, or both, and shall be ineligible for employment by the United States or any department or agency thereof, for the five years next following his conviction.

As used in this section, the terms "organizes" and "organize", with respect to any society, group, or assembly of persons, include the recruiting of new members, the forming of new units, and the regrouping or expansion of existing clubs, classes, and other units of such society, group, or assembly of persons.

[25]   326 U.S. 135 (1945).

[26]   05-CR-1474, slip op. (Nashua D. Ct., 2005).

[27]   Id.

[28]   Id.

[29]   See e.g., Bennett, B. (2013, April 3). *Radar Shows U.S. Border Security Gap.* Retrieved from L.A. Times: http://articles.latimes.com/2013/apr/03/nation/la-na-border-radar-20130404; Chokshi, N. (2013, April 17). *Why the Immigration Plan Rellay Could Give Us Border Security.* Retrieved from National Journal: YPERLINK"http://www.nationaljournal.com/congress/why-the-immigration-plan-really-could-give-us-border-security-20130417"http://www.nationaljournal.com/congress/why-the-immigration-plan-really-could-give-us-border-security-20130417; Preston, J., & Parker, A. (2013, June 12). *Immigration Amendments Reflect Concern About Border Security.* Retrieved from New York Times: http://www.nytimes.com/2013/06/13/us/politics/immigration-amendments-reflect-concern-about-border-security.html

[30]   8 U.S.C. §1357.

[31]   *Carroll v. United States,* 267 U.S. 132 (1925)—U.S. Supreme Court decision written by Chief Justice William Howard Taft which yielded the automobile exception to the Fourth Amendment search warrant requirement. *Carroll*—a Prohibition era case resulting from federal revenue agents' stop of a bootlegger's vehicle, search and confiscation of illegal gin and whiskey—premised the legality of the warrantless search of the vehicle on the presence of probable cause and the ready mobility of the vehicle thereby making it impractical for law enforcement to obtain a warrant.

[32]   413 U.S. at 274.

[33]   8 U.S.C. §1357

[34]   422 U.S. at 884.

[35]   Id.

[36]   413 U.S. at 268.

[37]   *United States v. Martinez-Fuerte* actually involved three different cases, two emanating from stops in California and appeals of decisions from the Ninth Circuit Court of Appeals, the other from a stop in Texas and an appeal of a decision from the Fifth Circuit Court of Appeals. For narrative simplicity the facts of the other two cases are omitted but they each involved stops by Border Patrol at a fixed checkpoint several miles from the Mexican border.

[38]   428 U.S. at 545.

[39]   Id at 546.

[40]   Id at 556.

[41]   422 U.S. at 880.

[42]   534 U.S. 266.

[43]   Dwyer, T. (2012). Enhancing the Right to Inquire: The Supreme Court's Post- 9/11 Jurisprudence for Police Officer Stop and Inquire Authority. *Criminal Law Bulletin*, 1253–1275.

[44]   534 U.S. 266.

[45]   It should be noted that as a Justice during the *Almeida-Sanchez* case Chief Justice Rehnquist joined the dissenting opinion of Justice White which would have voted to uphold the search of the vehicle and affirmed the decision of the Court of Appeals.

[46]   Chiefs, M. C. (2006, June). *Major Cities Chiefs Immigration Committee Recommend-aitons for Enforcement of Immigration Laws by Local Police Agencies*. Retrieved from www.houstontx.gov/police/pdfs/mcc_position.pdf

[47]   Id.

[48]   Id.

[49]   Vina, S. (2006). *Border Security and Military Support: Legal Authorizations and Restrictions*. Washington D.C.: Congressional Research Service.

[50]   Id.

Chapter Eight
DETENTION AND RENDITION

This chapter begins where the last chapter left off, with immigration, except here the discussion is within the context of detention. It is fitting to introduce this content on the heels of the text's prior chapters on habeas corpus relief and immigration control within the framework of our nation's homeland security defenses. Why start here with immigration detention? As Chapter 7 outlined, the control of our nation's borders and the regulation of who can enter and leave the country is an integral part of homeland security. Although the present immigration debate is heated and intensified in the post-9/11 environment, history has taught us that the debate is neither new nor original. What occurred in the days and weeks after the 9/11 terrorist attacks was a massive nationwide roundup of Middle-Eastern males within the United States. Post-9/11 there was in excess of 1,000 Arab and Muslim males taken into custody.[1] They were eventually deported, released, or processed through the criminal justice system. Of the 1,000 plus detainees, 751 were charged with immigration violations and 134 were charged with federal crimes. Of those arrested 99 were convicted based on guilty pleas or trials. Most of the arrestees' violations were for visa overstays, illegal entry into the United States, or other immigration law violations. These individuals were seized and detained by federal and local law enforcement, some held without charges for an extended period of time. The Migration Policy Institute, an influential thinktank, issued a 165-page report *"America's Challenge: Domestic Security, Civil Liberties and National Unity after September 11,"* which criticized the use of immigration as a proxy for anti-terrorism efforts.[2] The detention policies of the government in this anti-terrorism effort have been the object of additional criticism, calling into question the authority for such detention, especially in light of one of the most sacred and cherished of constitutional amendments, the Fourth Amendment prohibiting searches or seizures without probable cause, a warrant or the presence of a lawful warrant exception based on reasonableness.

The specifics of the issue relate to the rights a non-citizen possesses under our constitutional framework—the answer to that question depends on the circumstances. In *Zadvydas v. Davis*, 533 U.S. 678 (2001), the U.S. Supreme Court heard an appeal from the Fifth Circuit wherein an alien was subject to a final removal order but was unable to be returned to his native country or that of his parents because both countries refused to accept him. He was held beyond the original 90-day removal period while the government sought to place him. Zadvydas filed a habeas corpus petition reasoning that if the government were to never place him he would be kept in detention permanently, which would be a violation of the Constitution. In a companion case out of the Ninth Circuit decided under *Zadvydas*, a Cambodian national convicted of an aggravated felony was held beyond the 90-day removal period as well, and he too filed a §2241 habeas corpus petition. Because Cambodia did not have a repatriation treaty with the United States there would be no return of the alien to his native country. The Ninth Circuit held continued detention was not reasonable because there could be no repatriation. The Fifth Circuit held otherwise because of the existing possibility of placement and the existence of an administrative review process. The Supreme Court said post-removal period detention was limited to a reasonably necessary time during which to place the alien, otherwise the result would be an indefinite detention. The Court further held this reasonable time limitation was subject to judicial review. Circumstances justifying continued detention are limited to the removal of the alien; once the objective cannot be met the rationale for detention disappears, unless a reason independent of the immigration purpose exists. *Zadvydas* involved admitted immigrants who were later subject to deportation; however, a subsequent case, *Clark v. Martinez*, 543 U.S. 371 (2005), posed the issue of whether inadmissible aliens could be indefinitely detained.

    Clark involved two Cuban immigrants seeking admission to the United States as refugees. They arrived to the United States in June 1980 as part of the Mariel Boatlift. Both amassed significant criminal records while in the United States awaiting their adjustment as permanent legal residents. They were deemed nonadmissible and held pending deportation to Cuba. However, they were held beyond the 90-day period required for removal under 8 U.S.C. §1231(a)(1)(a). Following its decision in *Zadvydas*, the Court again held detention was permissible only if removal was reasonably foreseeable and this applied to nonadmissible aliens as well as admitted aliens. Though *Zadvydas* and *Clark* were not related to the 9/11 terrorist attacks, they are important cases relating to detention and immigration issues both of which are inextricably linked to post-9/11 homeland security analysis. One of the more controversial detention policies emanating from 9/11 was the "hold until cleared" policy pertaining to those with suspected terrorism contacts. Although there was no clear genesis for the policy it was understood by both the FBI and INS that these 9/11 detainees were not to be released until it was individually confirmed a detainee had no ties to terrorism.[3] The "hold until cleared" policy, along with the wholesale post-9/11 roundup of illegal immigrants, was faulted in a report issued in 2003 by the Department of Justice Inspector General's Office. In its conclusion the report cited various aspects of the FBI and INS treatment of these detainees: "... *the September 11 attacks changed the way the Department, particularly the FBI and the INS, responded when encountering aliens who were in violation of their immigration status ... While recognizing the difficult circumstances confronting the Department in responding to the terrorist attacks, we found significant problems in the way the September 11 detainees were treated. The INS did not serve notices of the immigration charges on these detainees within the specified timeframes. This delay affected the detainees in several ways, from their ability to understand why they were being held, to their ability to obtain legal counsel, to their ability to request a bond hearing. In addition, the Department instituted a policy that these detainees would be held until cleared by the FBI. Although not communicated in writing, this "hold until cleared" policy was clearly understood and applied throughout the Department. The policy was based on the belief—which turned out to be erroneous—that the FBI's clearance process would proceed quickly. Instead of taking a few days as anticipated, the clearance process took an average of 80 days, primarily because it was understaffed and not given sufficient priority by the FBI."*[4] Despite the negative comments found in the June 2003 report of the Inspector General, a

District of Columbia Circuit Court of Appeals decision, *Center for National Security Studies v. U.S. Department of Justice*, 331 F.3d 918 (O.C.Cir., 2003) issued the same month, held that the law enforcement exemption to the Freedom of Information Act was properly invoked to withhold the names of 9/11 detainees and their lawyers because disclosure could harm ongoing terrorism investigations. The circuit court said *"the dates and locations of arrest, detention, and release of all detainees, including those charged with federal crimes"* were not required to be released by the government. This decision stood in stark contrast to the DOJ Inspector General report critical of the immigration detention program. The D.C. Circuit Court overruled a district court decision requiring disclosure of detainees' and their attorneys' names, but upheld the part of the district court decision withholding disclosure of the dates and locations of arrest. Both courts' reasoning for the latter part of the decision was that the government interest in protecting the integrity and secrecy of investigations outweighed any public interest in disclosure of the information.

Detention in a time of national emergency has been used by the government to counter potential threats to the nation. Historically, looking back to the 18th century Quasi-War with France through to the Civil War suspension of habeas corpus and the World War II internment of Japanese-Americans, preventive detention has been invoked with mixed legal outcomes. This chapter's initial case of *Korematsu v. United States* points to a shameful episode in our country's past wherein preventive detention was approved based on a military assessment of risk. Yet, the case remains untouched, a questionable precedent providing provocative language in a post-911 environment: *"Compulsory exclusion of large groups of citizens from their homes, except under circumstances of direst emergency and peril, is inconsistent with our basic governmental institutions. But when, under conditions of modern warfare, our shores are threatened by hostile forces, the power to protect must be commensurate with the threatened danger."*[5] Preventive detention, seemingly at odds with our Constitution, does provide a limited exception to Fourth Amendment reasonableness and Fifth Amendment due process claims. In *United States v. Salerno*, the Supreme Court decided that the section of the Bail Reform Act of 1984 authorizing pre-trial detention based on a defendant's dangerousness to the community was permissible.[6] In this instance the defendant was a well-known Mafia leader. The Court noted that the Bail Reform Act's preventive detention applied only to certain specified serious felonies, and the government had the burden of showing dangerousness by clear and convincing evidence at a hearing before a judicial officer. Weighing the individual liberty interest against the public safety and prevailing governmental interest the Court reasoned that preventive detention did not violate due process: *"On the other side of the scale, of course, is the individual's strong interest in liberty. We do not minimize the importance and fundamental nature of this right. But, as our cases hold, this right may, in circumstances where the government's interest is sufficiently weighty, be subordinated to the greater needs of society. We think that Congress' careful delineation of the circumstances under which detention will be permitted satisfies this standard. When the Government proves by clear and convincing evidence that an arrestee presents an identified and articulable threat to an individual or the community, we believe that, consistent with the Due Process Clause, a court may disable the arrestee from executing that threat."*[1]

Another critical constitutional issue arising from the post-9/11 war on terror has been the CIA program of extraordinary rendition. Although the detention issues discussed above focus primarily on domestic detention, the extraordinary rendition program involved extraterritorial detentions removed from the laws of the United States. In Chapter Five (commentary note 6) several high-profile rendition cases are discussed, particularly that of Khaled El-Masri. The experiences of these individuals who were forcibly seized on suspicion of terrorism links and subjected to sustained harsh treatment, enhanced interrogations, and torture techniques while being denied basic human rights protections are horrible to comprehend but all too real in modern-day war craft. An initial visceral reaction would seem to indicate this could not—it should not—happen at the direction of a government founded upon an expression of inalienable individual rights and liberties. However, some of the underlying legal precedent concerning criminal justice extradition suggests an analysis more favorable to the actual rendition if not to the detention conditions once the individual was rendered to a foreign country. The Ker-Frisbie Doctrine, emanating from two U.S. Supreme Court cases to be discussed below, holds that a criminal defendant can be tried in a U.S. court despite the fact his presence has been obtained in an extra-judicial manner. If a defendant is kidnapped or the extradition violates a treaty and the defendant is brought within a court's jurisdiction neither fact will have a bearing on the court's ability to preside over the case. This doctrine and its impact in the war on terror, along with its surrounding detention concerns, are explored more fully below in the cases of *United States v. Verdugo-Urquidez* and *United States v. Alvarez-Machain* and the commentary that follow. The question remains, however, if this case law follows general international legal guidelines and agreements regarding extradition and its ancillary results.

Korematsu v. United States
323 U.S. 214 (1944)

Mr. Justice Black delivered the opinion of the Court.

The petitioner, an American citizen of Japanese descent, was convicted in a federal district court for remaining in San Leandro, California, a "Military Area," contrary to Civilian Exclusion Order No. 34 of the Commanding General of the Western Command, U.S. Army, which directed that, after May 9, 1942, all persons of Japanese ancestry should be excluded from that area. No question was raised as to petitioner's loyalty to the United States. The Circuit Court of Appeals affirmed, and the importance of the constitutional question involved caused us to grant certiorari.

It should be noted, to begin with, that all legal restrictions which curtail the civil rights of a single racial group are immediately suspect. That is not to say that all such restrictions are unconstitutional. It is to say that courts must subject them to the most rigid scrutiny. Pressing public necessity may sometimes justify the existence of such restrictions; racial antagonism never can.

In the instant case, prosecution of the petitioner was begun by information charging violation of an Act of Congress, of March 21, 1942, 56 Stat. 173, which provides that

... whoever shall enter, remain in, leave, or commit any act in any military area or military zone prescribed, under the authority of an Executive order of the President, by the Secretary of War, or by any military commander designated by the Secretary of War, contrary to the restrictions applicable to any such area or zone or contrary to the order of the Secretary of War or any such military commander, shall, if it appears that he knew or should have known of the existence and extent of the restrictions or order and that his act was in violation thereof, be guilty of a misdemeanor and upon conviction shall be liable to a fine of not to exceed $5,000 or to imprisonment for not more than one year, or both, for each offense.

Exclusion Order No. 34, which the petitioner knowingly and admittedly violated, was one of a number of military orders and proclamations, all of which were substantially based upon Executive Order No. 9066, 7 Fed. Reg. 1407. That order, issued after we were at war with Japan, declared that the successful prosecution of the war requires every possible protection against espionage and against sabotage to national defense material, national defense premises, and national defense utilities ...

One of the series of orders and proclamations, a curfew order, which, like the exclusion order here, was promulgated pursuant to Executive Order 9066, subjected all persons of Japanese ancestry in prescribed West Coast military areas to remain in their residences from 8 p.m. to 6 a.m. As is the case with the exclusion order here, that prior curfew order was designed as a "protection against espionage and against sabotage." In **Hirabayashi v. United States**, 320 U.S. 81, we sustained a conviction obtained for violation of the curfew order. The **Hirabayashi** conviction and this one thus rest on the same 1942 Congressional Act and the same basic executive and military orders, all of which orders were aimed at the twin dangers of espionage and sabotage.

The 1942 Act was attacked in the **Hirabayashi** case as an unconstitutional delegation of power; it was contended that the curfew order and other orders on which it rested were beyond the war powers of the Congress, the military authorities, and of the President, as Commander in Chief of the Army, and, finally, that to apply the curfew order against none but citizens of Japanese ancestry amounted to a constitutionally prohibited discrimination solely on account of race. To these questions, we gave the serious consideration which their importance justified. We upheld the curfew order as an exercise of the power of the government to take steps necessary to prevent espionage and sabotage in an area threatened by Japanese attack.

In the light of the principles we announced in the **Hirabayashi** case, we are unable to conclude that it was beyond the war power of Congress and the Executive to exclude those of Japanese ancestry from the West Coast war area at the time they did. True, exclusion from the area in which one's home is located is a far greater deprivation than constant confinement to the home from 8 p.m. to 6 a.m. Nothing short of apprehension by the proper military authorities of the gravest imminent danger to the public safety can constitutionally justify either. But exclusion from a threatened area, no less than curfew, has a definite and close relationship to the prevention of espionage and sabotage. The military authorities, charged with the primary responsibility of defending our shores, concluded that curfew provided inadequate protection and ordered exclusion. They did so, as pointed out in our **Hirabayashi** opinion, in accordance with Congressional authority to the military to say who should, and who should not, remain in the threatened areas.

In this case, the petitioner challenges the assumptions upon which we rested our conclusions in the **Hirabayashi** case. He also urges that, by May, 1942, when Order No. 34 was promulgated, all danger of Japanese invasion of the West Coast had disappeared. After careful consideration of these contentions, we are compelled to reject them.

Here, as in the **Hirabayashi** case ... we cannot reject as unfounded the judgment of the military authorities and of Congress that there were disloyal members of that population, whose number and strength could not be precisely and quickly ascertained. We cannot say that the war-making branches of the Government did not have ground for believing that, in a critical hour, such persons could not readily be isolated and separately dealt with, and constituted a menace to the national defense and safety which demanded that prompt and adequate measures be taken to guard against it.

Like curfew, exclusion of those of Japanese origin was deemed necessary because of the presence of an unascertained number of disloyal members of the group, most of whom we have no doubt were loyal to this country. It was because we could not reject the finding of the military authorities that it was impossible to bring about an immediate segregation of the disloyal from the loyal that we sustained the validity of the curfew order as applying to the whole group. In the instant case, temporary exclusion of the entire group was rested by the military on the same ground. The judgment that exclusion of the whole group was, for the same reason, a military imperative answers the contention that the exclusion was in the nature of group punishment based on antagonism to those of Japanese origin. That there were members of the group who retained loyalties to Japan has been confirmed by investigations made subsequent to the exclusion. Approximately five thousand American citizens of

Japanese ancestry refused to swear unqualified allegiance to the United States and to renounce allegiance to the Japanese Emperor, and several thousand evacuees requested repatriation to Japan.

We uphold the exclusion order as of the time it was made and when the petitioner violated it. In doing so, we are not unmindful of the hardships imposed by it upon a large group of American citizens. But hardships are part of war, and war is an aggregation of hardships. All citizens alike, both in and out of uniform, feel the impact of war in greater or lesser measure. Citizenship has its responsibilities, as well as its privileges, and, in time of war, the burden is always heavier. Compulsory exclusion of large groups of citizens from their homes, except under circumstances of direst emergency and peril, is inconsistent with our basic governmental institutions. But when, under conditions of modern warfare, our shores are threatened by hostile forces, the power to protect must be commensurate with the threatened danger.

It is argued that, on May 30, 1942, the date the petitioner was charged with remaining in the prohibited area, there were conflicting orders outstanding, forbidding him both to leave the area and to remain there. Of course, a person cannot be convicted for doing the very thing which it is a crime to fail to do. But the outstanding orders here contained no such contradictory commands.

There was an order issued March 27, 1942, which prohibited petitioner and others of Japanese ancestry from leaving the area, but its effect was specifically limited in time "until and to the extent that a future proclamation or order should so permit or direct." 7 Fed.Reg. 2601. That "future order," the one for violation of which petitioner was convicted, was issued May 3, 1942, and it did "direct" exclusion from the area of all persons of Japanese ancestry before 12 o'clock noon, May 9; furthermore, it contained a warning that all such persons found in the prohibited area would be liable to punishment under the March 21, 1942, Act of Congress. Consequently, the only order in effect touching the petitioner's being in the area on May 30, 1942, the date specified in the information against him, was the May 3 order which prohibited his remaining there, and it was that same order which he stipulated in his trial that he had violated, knowing of its existence. There is therefore no basis for the argument that, on May 30, 1942, he was subject to punishment, under the March 27 and May 3 orders, whether he remained in or left the area.

It does appear, however, that, on May 9, the effective date of the exclusion order, the military authorities had already determined that the evacuation should be effected by assembling together and placing under guard all those of Japanese ancestry at central points, designated as "assembly centers," in order to insure the orderly evacuation and resettlement of Japanese voluntarily migrating from Military Area No. 1, to restrict and regulate such migration. And on May 19, 1942, eleven days before the time petitioner was charged with unlawfully remaining in the area, Civilian Restrictive Order No. 1, 8 Fed. Reg. 982, provided for detention of those of Japanese ancestry in assembly or relocation centers. It is now argued that the validity of the exclusion order cannot be considered apart from the orders requiring him, after departure from the area, to report and to remain in an assembly or relocation center. The contention is that we must treat these separate orders as one and inseparable; that, for this reason, if detention in the assembly or relocation center would have illegally deprived the petitioner of his liberty, the exclusion order and his conviction under it cannot stand.

We are thus being asked to pass at this time upon the whole subsequent detention program in both assembly and relocation centers, although the only issues framed at the trial related to petitioner's remaining in the prohibited area in violation of the exclusion order. Had petitioner here left the prohibited area and gone to an assembly center, we cannot say, either as a matter of fact or law, that his presence in that center would have resulted in his detention in a relocation center. Some who did report to the assembly center were not sent to relocation centers, but were released upon condition that they remain outside the prohibited zone until the military orders were modified or lifted. This illustrates that they pose different problems, and may be governed by different principles. The lawfulness of one does not necessarily determine the lawfulness of the others. This is made clear when we analyze the requirements of the separate provisions of the separate orders. These separate requirements were that those of Japanese ancestry (1) depart from the area; (2) report to and temporarily remain in an assembly center; (3) go under military control to a relocation center, there to remain for an indeterminate period until released conditionally or unconditionally by the military authorities. Each of these requirements, it will be noted, imposed distinct duties in connection with the separate steps in a complete evacuation program. Had Congress directly incorporated into one Act the language of these separate orders, and provided sanctions for their violations, disobedience of any one would have constituted a separate offense. There is no reason why violations of these orders, insofar as they were promulgated pursuant to Congressional enactment, should not be treated as separate offenses ... Since the petitioner has not been convicted of failing to report or to remain in an assembly or relocation center, we cannot in this case determine the validity of those separate provisions of the order. It is sufficient here for us to pass upon the order which petitioner violated. To do more would be to go beyond the issues raised, and to decide momentous questions not contained within the framework of the pleadings or the evidence in this case. It will be time enough to decide the serious constitutional issues which petitioner seeks to raise when an assembly or relocation order is applied or is certain to be applied to him, and we have its terms before us.

Some of the members of the Court are of the view that evacuation and detention in an Assembly Center were inseparable. After May 3, 1942, the date of Exclusion Order No. 34, Korematsu was under compulsion to leave the area not as he would choose, but via an Assembly Center. The Assembly Center was conceived as a part of the machinery for group evacuation. The power to exclude includes the power to do it by force if necessary. And any forcible measure must necessarily entail some degree of detention or restraint, whatever method of removal is selected. But whichever view is taken, it results in holding that the order under which petitioner was convicted was valid.

It is said that we are dealing here with the case of imprisonment of a citizen in a concentration camp solely because of his ancestry, without evidence or inquiry concerning his loyalty and good disposition towards the United States. Our task would be simple, our duty clear, were this a case involving the imprisonment of a loyal citizen in a concentration camp because of racial prejudice. Regardless of the true nature of the assembly and relocation centers—and we deem it unjustifiable to call them concentration camps, with all the ugly connotations that term implies—we are dealing specifically with nothing but an exclusion order. To cast this case into outlines of racial prejudice, without reference to the real military dangers which were presented, merely confuses the issue. Korematsu was not excluded from the Military Area because of hostility to him or his race. He was excluded because we are at war with the Japanese Empire, because the properly constituted military authorities feared an invasion of our West Coast and felt constrained to take proper security measures, because they decided that the military urgency of the situation demanded that all citizens of Japanese ancestry be segregated from the West Coast temporarily, and, finally, because Congress, reposing its confidence in this time of war in our military leaders—as inevitably it must—determined that they should have the power to do just this. There was evidence of disloyalty on the part of some, the military authorities considered that the need for action was great, and time was short. We cannot—by availing ourselves of the calm perspective of hindsight—now say that, at that time, these actions were unjustified.

Affirmed.

Padilla v. Hanft
547 U.S. 1062 (2006)

Petition for writ of certiorari to the United States Court of Appeals for the Fourth Circuit denied.

The petition for a writ of certiorari is denied. Justice Souter and Justice Breyer would grant the petition for a writ of certiorari. Justice Kennedy, with whom The Chief Justice and Justice Stevens join, concurring in the denial of certiorari. The Court's decision to deny the petition for writ of certiorari is, in my view, a proper exercise of its discretion in light of the circumstances of the case. The history of petitioner Jose Padilla's detention, however, does require this brief explanatory statement. Padilla is a United States citizen. Acting pursuant to a material witness warrant issued by the United States District Court for the Southern District of New York, federal agents apprehended Padilla at Chicago's O'Hare International Airport on May 8, 2002. He was transported to New York, and on May 22 he moved to vacate the warrant. On June 9, while that motion was pending, the President issued an order to the Secretary of Defense designating Padilla an enemy combatant and ordering his military detention. The District Court, notified of this action by the Government's *ex parte* motion, vacated the material witness warrant. Padilla was taken to the Consolidated Naval Brig in Charleston, South Carolina. On June 11, Padilla's counsel filed a habeas corpus petition in the Southern District of New York challenging the military detention. The District Court denied the petition, but the Court of Appeals for the Second Circuit reversed and ordered the issuance of a writ directing Padilla's release. This Court granted certiorari and ordered dismissal of the habeas corpus petition without prejudice, holding that the District Court for the Southern District of New York was not the appropriate court to consider it. See **Rumsfeld v. Padilla**, 542 U.S. 426, 124 S.Ct. 2711, 159 L.Ed.2d 513 (2004). The present case arises from Padilla's subsequent habeas corpus petition, filed in the United States District Court for the District of South Carolina on July 2, 2004. Padilla requested that he be released immediately or else charged with a crime. The District Court granted the petition on February 28, 2005, but the Court of Appeals for the Fourth Circuit reversed that judgment on September 9, 2005. Padilla then filed the instant petition for writ of certiorari. After Padilla sought certiorari in this Court, the Government obtained an indictment charging him with various federal crimes. The President ordered that Padilla be released from military custody and transferred to the control of the Attorney General to face criminal charges. The Government filed a motion for approval of Padilla's transfer in the Court of Appeals for the Fourth Circuit. The Court of Appeals denied the motion, but this Court granted the Government's subsequent application respecting the transfer. **Hanft v. Padilla**, 546

U.S. ____, 126 S.Ct. 978, 163 L.Ed.2d 721 (2006). The Government also filed a brief in opposition to certiorari, arguing, among other things, that Padilla's petition should be denied as moot. The Government's mootness argument is based on the premise that Padilla, now having been charged with crimes and released from military custody, has received the principal relief he sought. Padilla responds that his case was not mooted by the Government's voluntary actions because there remains a possibility that he will be re-designated and re-detained as an enemy combatant. Whatever the ultimate merits of the parties' mootness arguments, there are strong prudential considerations disfavoring the exercise of the Court's certiorari power. Even if the Court were to rule in Padilla's favor, his present custody status would be unaffected. Padilla is scheduled to be tried on criminal charges. Any consideration of what rights he might be able to assert if he were returned to military custody would be hypothetical, and to no effect, at this stage of the proceedings. In light of the previous changes in his custody status and the fact that nearly four years have passed since he first was detained, Padilla, it must be acknowledged, has a continuing concern that his status might be altered again. That concern, however, can be addressed if the necessity arises. Padilla is now being held pursuant to the control and supervision of the United States District Court for the Southern District of Florida, pending trial of the criminal case. In the course of its supervision over Padilla's custody and trial the District Court will be obliged to afford him the protection, including the right to a speedy trial, guaranteed to all federal criminal defendants. See, e.g., U.S. Const., Amdt. 6; 18 U.S.C. § 3161. Were the Government to seek to change the status or conditions of Padilla's custody, that court would be in a position to rule quickly on any responsive filings submitted by Padilla. In such an event, the District Court, as well as other courts of competent jurisdiction, should act promptly to ensure that the office and purposes of the writ of habeas corpus are not compromised. Padilla, moreover, retains the option of seeking a writ of habeas corpus in this Court. See this Court's Rule 20; 28 U.S.C. §§ 1651(a), 2241. That Padilla's claims raise fundamental issues respecting the separation of powers, including consideration of the role and function of the courts, also counsels against addressing those claims when the course of legal proceedings has made them, at least for now, hypothetical. This is especially true given that Padilla's current custody is part of the relief he sought, and that its lawfulness is uncontested.

These are the reasons for my vote to deny certiorari.

Commentary and Questions

1. Preventive detention has been approved by the Court in a number of situations. The *Salerno* case cited some of these situations in the cases of *Wong Wing v. United States,* 163 U.S. 228 (1896) and *Carlson v. Landon,* 342 U.S. 524 (1952), wherein detention of potentially dangerous resident aliens was permitted pending deportation. Naturally, the Court's subsequent decision in *Zadvydas* limited the duration of such detention. In *Addington v. Texas,* 441 U.S. 418 (1979) the Court allowed government detention of mentally unstable individuals who presented a danger to the public. But the most interesting citation in *Salerno* was to *Moyer v. Peabody,* 212 U.S. 78 (1909) in which the Court said the detention of an individual without probable cause was warranted when a state of insurrection was declared by a governor. Justice Holmes's opinion stated *"what is due process of law depends on circumstances ... varies with the subject matter and the necessities of the situation."*[8] The *Moyer* facts concern a labor dispute in Colorado and the governor who decided the strikes amounted to an insurrection and sent National Guard troops to suppress the strikes and engage in mass arrests of the strikers. Those arrested were held by the military without probable cause and habeas corpus petitions were ignored. Justice Holmes's unanimous opinion provided exceptional deference to the executive when faced with insurrection: *"So long as such arrests are made in good faith and in the honest belief that they are needed in order to head the insurrection off, the Governor is the final judge and cannot be subjected to an action after he is out of office on the ground that he had not reasonable ground for his belief ... Public danger warrants the substitution of executive process for judicial process."*[9] The Court would later limit its *Moyer* ruling in *Sterling v. Constantin,* 287 U.S. 378 (1932) by stating that executive determinations of insurrection were subject to judicial review. Nonetheless, *Moyer* retained its constitutional footing and was cited more recently by the government in *Hamdi v. Rumsfeld* as well as in Justice Scalia's and Thomas's dissenting opinions in the case. This may signal a renewed vitality for *Moyer* in the war on terror, particularly when it comes to executive decisions regarding detention. Although *Moyer* might seem to be outdated its resurgence is a reminder that it, like *Korematsu*, retains precedential authority. Should *Moyer v. Peabody*, an early 20th century decision, be reconsidered by the Court owing to the nature of the 21st century war on terror? Does this case concerning an intrastate labor conflict have any applicability to homeland security measures and the global war on terror?

2. The *Korematsu* opinion referenced the Court's prior term opinion in *Hirabayashi v. United States,* 320 U.S. 81 (1943), which along with its companion case of *Yasui v. United States,* 320 U.S. 115 (1943), challenged the curfew provisions in President Franklin D. Roosevelt's Executive Order 9066.[10] Issued on February 19, 1942, in the wake of the Japanese attacks on Pearl Harbor Executive Order 9066 gave the secretary of war the authority to designate military areas subject to exclusion of "any and all persons." The Order also gave the secretary of war the authority to take whatever addi-

tional steps he deemed necessary to ensure compliance; as a result the curfews ensued. On May 3, 1942, Exclusion Order No. 34 was issued by Lieutenant General John L. DeWitt, military commander for the western United States. This order required all Japanese in the United States, including Japanese-Americans, to report to offices where they would be taken to relocation centers. Gordon Hirabayashi was a University of Washington student charged with violating the curfew order, requiring individuals to stay in their residence from 8:00 p.m. to 6:00 a.m. Minoru Yasui was a U.S. Army reservist and University of Oregon undergraduate and law school degree recipient who purposely broke the curfew by walking the streets of Portland, Oregon after hours. Both Hirabayashi and Yasui were arrested for the misdemeanor violations and immediately challenged the constitutionality of the law. In both cases the U.S. Supreme Court, citing military necessity, upheld the laws. The *Korematsu* case focused not on the curfew orders but on the exclusion and internment provisions. How did the Court in *Korematsu* address the two glaring issues in the case, that of race and involuntary confinement?

3.   The Court's decision in *Ex Parte Endo*, 383 U.S. 283 (1944) was handed down the same day as *Korematsu* but with a different result for Mitsuye Endo than for Fred Korematsu. Mitsuye Endo was an American citizen subjected to an evacuation order from Sacramento, California in 1942. She was removed to a relocation center and shortly thereafter filed a writ of habeas corpus seeking her freedom. The *Endo* opinion traced the chronological history of the government and military commander's exclusion and removal orders while also outlining the clearance procedures enabling individuals to be indefinitely allowed to leave the relocation centers. Justice William O. Douglas, writing for a unanimous Court, stated that once the loyalty of a citizen is proven the purpose of detention becomes moot. In addition he stressed the race-neutral reading of the Executive Order:

"But we stress the silence of the legislative history and of the Act and the Executive Orders on the power to detain to emphasize that any such authority which exists must be implied. If there is to be the greatest possible accommodation of the liberties of the citizen with this war measure, any such implied power must be narrowly confined to the precise purpose of the evacuation program.

A citizen who is concededly loyal presents no problem of espionage or sabotage. Loyalty is a matter of the heart and mind, not of race, creed, or color. He who is loyal is, by definition, not a spy or a saboteur. When the power to detain is derived from the power to protect the war effort against espionage and sabotage, detention which has no relationship to that objective is unauthorized.

Nor may the power to detain an admittedly loyal citizen or to grant him a conditional release be implied as a useful or convenient step in the evacuation program, whatever authority might be implied in case of those whose loyalty was not conceded or established. If we assume (as we do) that the original evacuation was justified, its lawful character was derived from the fact that it was an espionage and sabotage measure, not that there was community hostility to this group of American citizens. The evacuation program rested explicitly on the former ground, not on the latter, as the underlying legislation shows. The authority to detain a citizen or to grant him a conditional release as protection against espionage or sabotage is exhausted, at least when his loyalty is conceded. If we held that the authority to detain continued thereafter, we would transform an espionage or sabotage measure into something else. That was not done by Executive Order No. 9066 or by the Act of March 21, 1942, which ratified it. What they did not do, we cannot do. Detention which furthered the campaign against espionage and sabotage would be one thing. But detention which has no relationship to that campaign is of a distinct character. Community hostility even to loyal evacuees may have been (and perhaps still is) a serious problem. But if authority for their custody and supervision is to be sought on that ground, the Act of March 21, 1942, Executive Order No. 9066, and Executive Order No. 9102, offer no support. And none other is advanced. To read them that broadly would be to assume that the Congress and the President intended that this discriminatory action should be taken against these people wholly on account of their ancestry even though the government conceded their loyalty to this country. We cannot make such an assumption."[11]

How does the Court's opinion in *Korematsu* rationalize a different result than that in *Endo*?

4. The Subversive Activities Control Act of 1950 (also known as the McCarran Internal Security Act, named after its sponsor Senator Pat McCarran of Nevada) contained two provisions. Part I required the registration of Communist organizations with the U.S. Attorney General's Office and created a Subversive Activities Control Board to investigate individuals suspected of Communist ties (this registration requirement was subsequently held to be unconstitutional by the U.S. Supreme Court; this will be discussed in more detail in Chapter 9). Part II contained the Emergency Detention Act, which provided the president with the authority to detain individuals who he believed may be involved in espionage or sabotage against the United States. The detention provisions of the Internal Security Act were later replaced by the Non-Detention Act of 1971, found at 18 U.S.C. §4001(a), which states: *"No citizen shall be imprisoned or otherwise detained by the United States except pursuant to an Act of Congress."* Was the September 14, 2001 joint resolution of Congress passing the Authorization to Use Military Force (AUMF) the necessary Act of Congress required to detain individuals in the war on terror? This was the question the U.S. Supreme Court avoided in *Rumsfeld v. Padilla*—what arguments can be made for or against detention pursuant to the AUMF?

5. The Court in *Rumsfeld v. Padilla* dismissed Jose Padilla's habeas claim based on a jurisdictional issue. His case would bounce around the Second and Fourth Circuit Courts of Appeal before landing back before the Supreme Court in *Padilla v. Hanft* where the Court denied certiorari. Padilla

challenged his detention, originally premised upon a material witness warrant until deemed to be an unlawful enemy combatant by the Bush administration, seeking habeas corpus review. The government argued the issue was moot because of the transfer of his case to the federal criminal courts. Undoubtedly this did nothing to alleviate his fear of further "unlawful" detention. What relief did the Court state would be available with regard to these detention concerns of Padilla's? Would this be an adequate remedy to challenge his continued detention?

6. In light of the questions posed above consider Justice Ginsburg's brief dissent from the denial of certiorari:

   "This case, here for the second time, raises a question "of profound importance to the Nation," **Rumsfeld v. Padilla,** *542 U.S. 426, 455, 124 S.Ct. 2711, 159L.Ed.2d 513 (2004) (Stevens, J., dissenting): Does the President have authority to imprison indefinitely a United States citizen arrested on United States soil distant from a zone of combat, based on an Executive declaration that the citizen was, at the time of his arrest, an "enemy combatant"? It is a question the Court heard, and should have decided, two years ago. Nothing the Government has yet done purports to retract the assertion of Executive power Padilla protests. Although the Government has recently lodged charges against Padilla in a civilian court, nothing prevents the Executive from returning to the road it earlier constructed and defended. A party's voluntary cessation does not make a case less capable of repetition or less evasive of review ... Satisfied that this case is not moot, I would grant the petition for certiorari."*[12]

   Justice Ginsburg reiterates the concern expressed by Justice Stevens in his *Rumsfeld v. Padilla* dissent and questions presidential authority to detain citizens within the United States as enemy combatants. The unresolved question poses a continuing risk not only to Padilla but to all citizens. Justice Ginsburg, and Justice Stevens before her, believed the issues too important for the court to sidestep on what they viewed as legal technicalities. Was the Court's denial of certiorari in *Padilla v. Hanft* a proper restraint of its Article III powers or should the Court have followed Chief Justice Marshall's lead in *Marbury v. Madison*, specifically that "it is emphatically the province and duty of the courts to say what the law is ...," and decided the central issue of presidential authority to detain?

7. The National Defense Authorization Act for Fiscal Year 2012 contains 565 pages of budget and expenditures for the Department of Defense. Deep within the congressional legislation under the heading "Counter-Terrorism" is controversial section 1021. This section provides legislative affirmation of presidential authority to indefinitely detain individuals under the 2001 Authorization to Use Military Force. Section 1021, along with section 1022 pertaining to military custody for al-Qaeda terrorists, has caused considerable uproar and criticism among civil libertarians and legal commentators. The full text of section 1021 is reproduced here:

Section 1021. Affirmation Of Authority Of The Armed Forces Of The United States To Detain Covered Persons Pursuant To The Authorization For Use Of Military Force.

(a) In General—Congress affirms that the authority of the President to use all necessary and appropriate force pursuant to the Authorization for Use of Military Force (Public Law 107-40; 50 U.S.C. 1541 note) includes the authority for the Armed Forces of the United States to detain covered persons (as defined in subsection (b)) pending disposition under the law of war.

(b) Covered Persons—A covered person under this section is any person as follows:

> *(1) A person who planned, authorized, committed, or aided the terrorist attacks that occurred on September 11, 2001, or harbored those responsible for those attacks.*

> *(2) A person who was a part of or substantially supported al-Qaeda, the Taliban, or associated forces that are engaged in hostilities against the United States or its coalition partners, including any person who has committed a belligerent act or has directly supported such hostilities in aid of such enemy forces.*

(c) Disposition Under Law of War—The disposition of a person under the law of war as described in subsection (a) may include the following:

> *(1) Detention under the law of war without trial until the end of the hostilities authorized by the Authorization for Use of Military Force.*

> *(2) Trial under chapter 47A of title 10, United States Code (as amended by the Military Commissions Act of 2009 (title XVIII of Public Law 111-84)).*

> *(3) Transfer for trial by an alternative court or competent tribunal having lawful jurisdiction.*

> *(4) Transfer to the custody or control of the person's country of origin, any other foreign country, or any other foreign entity.*

(d) Construction—Nothing in this section is intended to limit or expand the authority of the President or the scope of the Authorization for Use of Military Force.

(e) Authorities—Nothing in this section shall be construed to affect existing law or authorities relating to the detention of United States citizens, lawful resident aliens of the United States, or any other persons who are captured or arrested in the United States.

(f) Requirement for Briefings of Congress—The Secretary of Defense shall regularly brief Congress regarding the application of the authority described in this section, including the organizations, entities, and individuals considered to be 'covered persons' for purposes of subsection (b)(2).[13]

What does the above sub-section (e) mean in relation to the full text of section 1021? How does this sub-section impact the enforceability of section 1021 in light of the Non-Detention Act of 1971 and the U.S. Supreme Court's body of habeas corpus case law?

8. In Executive Order 13492 of January 22, 2009, newly elected President
Barack Obama ordered the closure of detention camps at Guantanamo Bay,
Cuba. The same day he issued Executive Order 13493, which created a
Special Interagency Task Force whose mission was to find alternate lawful
options for detainees held at Guantanamo Bay. A little over two years later
on March 7, 2011, President Obama issued Executive Order 13567, which
indicated a much different focus than his Executive Order 13492 aimed at
closing Guantanamo Bay. Outright closing of detention operations and
replacement of detainees held at Guantanamo Bay would have created a
host of legal issues for the administration to contend with, not the least of
which would be the continued detention of detainees, immigration, and
repatriation issues.[14] The Executive Order exhibits the continuing attempts
of the Executive branch to refine its detention policies with the requirements
of international and domestic law. Its full text is contained here:

Executive Order 13567 of March 7, 2011
Periodic Review of Individuals Detained at Guantánamo Bay
Naval Station Pursuant to the Authorization for Use of Military
Force
By the authority vested in me as President by the Constitution and the
laws of the United States of America, including the Authorization for Use
of Military Force of September 2001 (AUMF), Public Law 107-40, and in
order to ensure that military detention of individuals now held at the U.S.
Naval Station, Guantanamo Bay, Cuba (Guantánamo), who were subject
to the interagency review under section 4 of Executive Order 13492 of
January 22, 2009, continues to be carefully evaluated and justified,
consistent with the national security and foreign policy interests of the
United States and the interests of justice, I hereby order as follows:
Section 1. Scope and Purpose. (a) The periodic review described in section
3 of this order applies only to those detainees held at Guantánamo on the
date of this order, whom the interagency review established by Executive
Order 13492 has (i) designated for continued law of war detention; or (ii)
referred for prosecution, except for those detainees against whom charges
are pending or a judgment of conviction has been entered.
(b) This order is intended solely to establish, as a discretionary matter, a
process to review on a periodic basis the executive branch's continued,
discretionary exercise of existing detention authority in individual cases.
It does not create any additional or separate source of detention authority,
and it does not affect the scope of detention authority under existing law.
Detainees at Guantánamo have the constitutional privilege of the writ of
habeas corpus, and nothing in this order is intended to affect the
jurisdiction of Federal courts to determine the legality of their detention.
(c) In the event detainees covered by this order are transferred from
Guantánamo to another U.S. detention facility where they remain in law
of war detention, this order shall continue to apply to them.
Sec. 2. Standard for Continued Detention. Continued law of war detention
is warranted for a detainee subject to the periodic review in section 3 of

this order if it is necessary to protect against a significant threat to the security of the United States.

Sec. 3. Periodic Review. The Secretary of Defense shall coordinate a process of periodic review of continued law of war detention for each detainee described in section 1(a) of this order. In consultation with the Attorney General, the Secretary of Defense shall issue implementing guidelines governing the process, consistent with the following requirements:

(a) *Initial Review.* For each detainee, an initial review shall commence as soon as possible but no later than 1 year from the date of this order. The initial review will consist of a hearing before a Periodic Review Board (PRB). The review and hearing shall follow a process that includes the following requirements:

(1) Each detainee shall be provided, in writing and in a language the detainee understands, with advance notice of the PRB review and an unclassified summary of the factors and information the PRB will consider in evaluating whether the detainee meets the standard set forth in section 2 of this order. The written summary shall be sufficiently comprehensive to provide adequate notice to the detainee of the reasons for continued detention.

(2) The detainee shall be assisted in proceedings before the PRB by a Government-provided personal representative (representative) who possesses the security clearances necessary for access to the information described in subsection (a)(4) of this section. The representative shall advocate on behalf of the detainee before the PRB and shall be responsible for challenging the Government's information and introducing information on behalf of the detainee. In addition to the representative, the detainee may be assisted in proceedings before the PRB by private counsel, at no expense to the Government.

(3) The detainee shall be permitted to (i) present to the PRB a written or oral statement; (ii) introduce relevant information, including written declarations; (iii) answer any questions posed by the PRB; and (iv) call witnesses who are reasonably available and willing to provide information that is relevant and material to the standard set forth in section 2 of this order.

(4) The Secretary of Defense, in coordination with other relevant Government agencies, shall compile and provide to the PRB all information in the detainee disposition recommendations produced by the Task Force established under Executive Order 13492 that is relevant to the determination whether the standard in section 2 of this order has been met and on which the Government seeks to rely for that determination. In addition, the Secretary of Defense, in coordination with other relevant Government agencies, shall compile any additional information relevant to that determination, and on which the Government seeks to rely for that determination, that has become available since the conclusion of the Executive Order 13492 review. All mitigating information relevant to that determination must be provided to the PRB.

(5) The information provided in subsection (a)(4) of this section shall be provided to the detainee's representative. In exceptional circumstances where it is necessary to protect national security, including intelligence sources and methods, the PRB may determine that the representative must receive a sufficient substitute or summary, rather than the underlying information. If the detainee is represented by private counsel, the information provided in subsection (a)(4) of this section shall be provided to such counsel unless the Government determines that the need to protect national security, including intelligence sources and methods, or law enforcement or privilege concerns, requires the Government to provide counsel with a sufficient substitute or summary of the information. A sufficient substitute or summary must provide a meaningful opportunity to assist the detainee during the review process.

(6) The PRB shall conduct a hearing to consider the information described in subsection (a)(4) of this section, and other relevant information provided by the detainee or the detainee's representative or counsel, to determine whether the standard in section 2 of this order is met. The PRB shall consider the reliability of any information provided to it in making its determination.

(7) The PRB shall make a prompt determination, by consensus and in writing, as to whether the detainee's continued detention is warranted under the standard in section 2 of this order. If the PRB determines that the standard is not met, the PRB shall also recommend any conditions that relate to the detainee's transfer. The PRB shall provide a written summary of any final determination in unclassified form to the detainee, in a language the detainee understands, within 30 days of the determination when practicable.

(8) The Secretary of Defense shall establish a secretariat to administer the PRB review and hearing process. The Director of National Intelligence shall assist in preparing the unclassified notice and the substitutes or summaries described above. Other executive departments and agencies shall assist in the process of providing the PRB with information required for the review processes detailed in this order.

(b) Subsequent Full Review. The continued detention of each detainee shall be subject to subsequent full reviews and hearings by the PRB on a triennial basis. Each subsequent review shall employ the procedures set forth in section 3(a) of this order.

(c) File Reviews. The continued detention of each detainee shall also be subject to a file review every 6 months in the intervening years between full reviews. This file review will be conducted by the PRB and shall consist of a review of any relevant new information related to the detainee compiled by the Secretary of Defense, in coordination with other relevant agencies, since the last review and, as appropriate,

information considered during any prior PRB review. The detainee shall be permitted to make a written submission in connection with each file review. If, during the file review, a significant question is raised as to whether the detainee's continued detention is warranted under the standard in section 2 of this order, the PRB will promptly convene a full review pursuant to the standards in section 3(a) of this order.

(d) Review of PRB Determinations. The Review Committee (Committee), as defined in section 9(d) of this order, shall conduct a review if (i) a member of the Committee seeks review of a PRB determination within 30 days of that determination; or (ii) consensus within the PRB cannot be reached.

Sec. 4. Effect of Determination to Transfer. (a) If a final determination is made that a detainee does not meet the standard in section 2 of this order, the Secretaries of State and Defense shall be responsible for ensuring that vigorous efforts are undertaken to identify a suitable transfer location for any such detainee, outside of the United States, consistent with the national security and foreign policy interests of the United States and the commitment set forth in section 2242(a) of the Foreign Affairs Reform and Restructuring Act of 1998 (Public Law 105-277).

(b) The Secretary of State, in consultation with the Secretary of Defense, shall be responsible for obtaining appropriate security and humane treatment assurances regarding any detainee to be transferred to another country, and for determining, after consultation with members of the Committee, that it is appropriate to proceed with the transfer.

(c) The Secretary of State shall evaluate humane treatment assurances in all cases, consistent with the recommendations of the Special Task Force on Interrogation and Transfer Policies established by Executive Order 13491 of January 22, 2009.

Sec. 5. Annual Committee Review. (a) The Committee shall conduct an annual review of sufficiency and efficacy of transfer efforts, including:

> *(1) the status of transfer efforts for any detainee who has been subject to the periodic review under section 3 of this order, whose continued detention has been determined not to be warranted, and who has not been transferred more than 6 months after the date of such determination;*

> *(2) the status of transfer efforts for any detainee whose petition for a writ of habeas corpus has been granted by a U.S. Federal court with no pending appeal and who has not been transferred;*

> *(3) the status of transfer efforts for any detainee who has been designated for transfer or conditional detention by the Executive Order 13492 review and who has not been transferred; and*

> *(4) the security and other conditions in the countries to which detainees might be transferred, including a review of any suspension of transfers to a particular country, in order to determine whether further steps to facilitate transfers are appropriate or to provide a recommendation to the President*

regarding whether continuation of any such suspension is warranted.

(b) After completion of the initial reviews under section 3(a) of this order, and at least once every 4 years thereafter, the Committee shall review whether a continued law of war detention policy remains consistent with the interests of the United States, including national security interests.

Sec. 6. Continuing Obligation of the Departments of Justice and Defense to Assess Feasibility of Prosecution. As to each detainee whom the interagency review established by Executive Order 13492 has designated for continued law of war detention, the Attorney General and the Secretary of Defense shall continue to assess whether prosecution of the detainee is feasible and in the national security interests of the United States, and shall refer detainees for prosecution, as appropriate.

Sec. 7. Obligation of Other Departments and Agencies to Assist the Secretary of Defense. All departments, agencies, entities, and officers of the United States, to the maximum extent permitted by law, shall provide the Secretary of Defense such assistance as may be requested to implement this order.

Sec. 8. Legality of Detention. The process established under this order does not address the legality of any detainee's law of war detention. If, at any time during the periodic review process established in this order, material information calls into question the legality of detention, the matter will be referred immediately to the Secretary of Defense and the Attorney General for appropriate action.

Sec. 9. Definitions. (a) "Law of War Detention" means: detention authorized by the Congress under the AUMF, as informed by the laws of war.

(b) "Periodic Review Board" means: a board composed of senior officials tasked with fulfilling the functions described in section 3 of this order, one appointed by each of the following departments and offices: the Departments of State, Defense, Justice, and Homeland Security, as well as the Offices of the Director of National Intelligence and the Chairman of the Joint Chiefs of Staff.

(c) "Conditional Detention" means: the status of those detainees designated by the Executive Order 13492 review as eligible for transfer if one of the following conditions is satisfied: (1) the security situation improves in Yemen; (2) an appropriate rehabilitation program becomes available; or (3) an appropriate third- country resettlement option becomes available.

(d) "Review Committee" means: a committee composed of the Secretary of State, the Secretary of Defense, the Attorney General, the Secretary of Homeland Security, the Director of National Intelligence, and the Chairman of the Joint Chiefs of Staff.

Sec. 10. General Provisions. (a) Nothing in this order shall prejudice the authority of the Secretary of Defense or any other official to determine the disposition of any detainee not covered by this order.

(b) This order shall be implemented subject to the availability of necessary appropriations and consistent with applicable law

including: the Convention Against Torture; Common Article 3 of the Geneva Conventions; the Detainee Treatment Act of 2005; and other laws relating to the transfer, treatment, and interrogation of individuals detained in an armed conflict.

(c) This order is not intended to, and does not, create any right or benefit, substantive or procedural, enforceable at law or in equity by any party against the United States, its departments, agencies, or entities, its officers, employees, or agents, or any other person.

(d) Nothing in this order, and no determination made under this order, shall be construed as grounds for release of detainees covered by this order into the United States.

[signed:] Barack Obama
The White House,
March 7, 2011.

United States v. Alvarez-Machain
504 U.S. 655 (1992)

Chief Justice Rehnquist delivered the opinion of the Court.

The issue in this case is whether a criminal defendant, abducted to the United States from a nation with which it has an extradition treaty, thereby acquires a defense to the jurisdiction of this country's courts. We hold that he does not, and that he may be tried in federal district court for violations of the criminal law of the United States.

Respondent, Humberto Alyarez-Machain, is a citizen and resident of Mexico. He was indicted for participating in the kidnap and murder of United States Drug Enforcement Administration (DEA) special agent Enrique Camarena-Salazar and a Mexican pilot working with Camarena, Alfredo Zavala-Avelar. The DEA believes that respondent, a medical doctor, participated in the murder by prolonging agent Camarena's life so that others could further torture and interrogate him. On April 2, 1990, respondent was forcibly kidnaped from his medical office in Guadalajara, Mexico, to be flown by private plane to El Paso, Texas, where he was arrested by DEA officials. The District Court concluded that DEA agents were responsible for respondent's abduction, although they were not personally involved in it. **United States v. Caro-Quintero**, 745 F.Supp. 599, 602-604, 609 (CD Cal. 1990).

Respondent moved to dismiss the indictment, claiming that his abduction constituted outrageous governmental conduct, and that the District Court lacked jurisdiction to try him because he was abducted in violation of the extradition treaty between the United States and Mexico ... The District Court rejected the outrageous governmental conduct claim, but held that it lacked jurisdiction to try respondent because his abduction violated the Extradition Treaty. The

District Court discharged respondent and ordered that he be repatriated to Mexico.

The Court of Appeals affirmed the dismissal of the indictment and the repatriation of respondent ... the Court of Appeals affirmed the District Court's finding that the United States had authorized the abduction of respondent, and that letters from the Mexican Government to the United States Government served as an official protest of the Treaty violation. Therefore, the Court of Appeals ordered that the indictment against respondent be dismissed, and that respondent be repatriated to Mexico. We granted certiorari and now reverse.

Although we have never before addressed the precise issue raised in the present case, we have previously considered proceedings in claimed violation of an extradition treaty and proceedings against a defendant brought before a court by means of a forcible abduction. We addressed the former issue in **United States v. Rauscher**, 119 U.S. 407 (1886); more precisely, the issue whether the Webster-Ashburton Treaty of 1842, 8 Stat. 572, 576, which governed extraditions between England and the United States, prohibited the prosecution of defendant Rauscher for a crime other than the crime for which he had been extradited. Whether this prohibition, known as the doctrine of specialty, was an intended part of the treaty had been disputed between the two nations for some time. **Rauscher**, 119 U.S., at 411. Justice Miller delivered the opinion of the Court, which carefully examined the terms and history of the treaty; the practice of nations in regards to extradition treaties; the case law from the States; and the writings of commentators, and reached the following conclusion:

> "[A] person who has been brought within the jurisdiction of the court by virtue of proceedings under an extradition treaty, can only be tried for one of the offences described in that treaty, and for the offence with which he is charged in the proceedings for his extradition, until a reasonable time and opportunity have been given him, after his release or trial upon such charge, to return to the country from whose asylum he had been forcibly taken under those proceedings." Id., at 430 (emphasis added). In addition, Justice Miller's opinion noted that any doubt as to this interpretation was put to rest by two federal statutes which imposed the doctrine of specialty upon extradition treaties to which the United States was a party. Id., at 423.5 Unlike the case before us today, the defendant in Rauscher had been brought to the United States by way of an extradition treaty; there was no issue of a forcible abduction.

In **Ker v. Illinois**, 119 U.S. 436 (1886), also written by Justice Miller and decided the same day as **Rauscher**, we addressed the issue of a defendant brought before the court by way of a forcible abduction. Frederick Ker had been tried and convicted in an Illinois court for larceny; his presence before the court was procured by means of forcible abduction from Peru. A messenger was sent to Lima with the proper warrant to demand Ker by virtue of the extradition treaty between Peru and the United States. The messenger, however, disdained reliance on the treaty processes, and instead forcibly kidnaped Ker and brought him to the United States. We distinguished Ker's case from **Rauscher** on the basis that Ker was not brought into the United States by virtue of the extradition treaty between the United States and Peru, and rejected Ker's argument that he had a right under the extradition treaty to be returned to this country only in accordance with its terms. We rejected Ker's due process argument more broadly, holding in line with "the highest authorities," that such forcible abduction is no sufficient reason why the party should not answer when brought within the jurisdiction of the court which has the right to try him for such an offence, and presents no valid objection to his trial in such court. **Ker**, supra, at 444.

In **Frisbie v. Collins**, 342 U.S. 519, rehearing denied, 343 U.S. 937 (1952), we applied the rule in Ker to a case in which the defendant had been kidnaped in Chicago by Michigan officers and brought to trial in Michigan. We upheld the conviction over objections based on the Due Process Clause and the federal Kidnaping Act, and stated:

> "This Court has never departed from the rule announced in **Ker** that the power of a court to try a person for crime is not impaired by the fact that he had been brought within the court's jurisdiction by reason of a `forcible abduction.' No persuasive reasons are now presented to justify overruling this line of cases. They rest on the sound basis that due process of law is satisfied when one present in court is convicted of crime after having been fairly apprized of the charges against him and after a fair trial in accordance with constitutional procedural safeguards. There is nothing in the Constitution that requires a court to permit a guilty person rightfully convicted to escape justice because he was brought to trial against his will." **Frisbie**, supra, at 522.

The only differences between **Ker** and the present case are that **Ker** was decided on the premise that there was no governmental involvement in the abduction, and Peru, from which Ker was abducted, did not object to his prosecution. Respondent finds these differences to be dispositive ... contending that they show that respondent's prosecution, like the prosecution of Rauscher, violates the implied terms of a valid extradition treaty. The Government, on the other hand, argues that **Rauscher** stands as an "exception" to the rule in **Ker** only when an extradition treaty is invoked, and the terms of the treaty provide that its breach will limit the jurisdiction of a court. Brief for United States 17. Therefore, our first inquiry must be whether the abduction of respondent from Mexico violated the Extradition Treaty between the United States and Mexico. If we conclude that the Treaty does not prohibit respondent's abduction, the rule in Ker applies, and the court need not inquire as to how respondent came before it.

In construing a treaty, as in construing a statute, we first look to its terms to determine its meaning. *Air France v. Saks*, 470 U.S. 392, 397 (1985); *Valentine v. United States ex rel. Neidecker*, 299 U.S. 5, 11 (1936). The Treaty says nothing about the obligations of the United States and Mexico to refrain from forcible abductions of people from the territory of the other nation, or the consequences under the Treaty if such an abduction occurs. Respondent submits that Article 22(1) of the Treaty, which states that it "shall apply to offenses specified in Article 2 [including murder] committed before and after this Treaty enters into force," 31 U.S.T., at 5073-5074, evidences an intent to make application of the Treaty mandatory for those offenses. However, the more natural conclusion is that Article 22 was included to ensure that the Treaty was applied to extraditions requested after the Treaty went into force, regardless of when the crime of extradition occurred.

> More critical to respondent's argument is Article 9 of the Treaty, which provides:
> "1. Neither Contracting Party shall be bound to deliver up its own nationals, but the executive authority of the requested Party shall, if not prevented by the laws of that Party, have the power to deliver them up if, in its discretion, it be deemed proper to do so.
> "2. If extradition is not granted pursuant to paragraph 1 of this Article, the requested Party shall submit the case to its competent authorities for the purpose of prosecution, provided that Party has jurisdiction over the offense." Id., at 5065.

According to respondent, Article 9 embodies the terms of the bargain which the United States struck: If the United States wishes to prosecute a Mexican national, it may request that individual's extradition. Upon a request from the United States, Mexico may either extradite the individual or submit the case to the proper authorities for prosecution in Mexico. In this way, respondent reasons, each nation preserved its right to choose whether its nationals would be tried in its own courts or by the courts of the other nation. This preservation of rights would be frustrated if either nation were free to abduct nationals of the other nation for the purposes of prosecution. More broadly, respondent reasons, as did the Court of Appeals, that all the processes and restrictions on the obligation to extradite established by the Treaty would make no sense if either nation were free to resort to forcible kidnaping to gain the presence of an individual for prosecution in a manner not contemplated by the Treaty ...

We do not read the Treaty in such a fashion. Article 9 does not purport to specify the only way in which one country may gain custody of a national of the other country for the purposes of prosecution. In the absence of an extradition treaty, nations are under no obligation to surrender those in their country to foreign authorities for prosecution. **Rauscher**, 119 U.S., at 411-412; **Factor v. Laubenheimer**, 290 U.S. 276, 287 (1933); cf. **Valentine v. United States ex rel. Neidecker**, supra, at 8-9 (United States may not extradite a citizen in the absence of a statute or treaty obligation). Extradition treaties exist so as to impose mutual obligations to surrender individuals in certain defined sets of circumstances, following established procedures. See 1 J. Moore, A Treatise on Extradition and Interstate Rendition 72 (1891). The Treaty thus provides a mechanism which would not otherwise exist, requiring, under certain circumstances, the United States and Mexico to extradite individuals to the other country and establishing the procedures to be followed when the Treaty is invoked.

The history of negotiation and practice under the Treaty also fails to show that abductions outside of the Treaty constitute a violation of the Treaty. As the Solicitor General notes, the Mexican Government was made aware, as early as 1906, of the **Ker** doctrine, and the United States' position that it applied to forcible abductions made outside of the terms of the United States-Mexico Extradition Treaty. Nonetheless, the current version of the Treaty, signed in 1978, does not attempt to establish a rule that would in any way curtail the effect of Ker ... the language of the Treaty, in the context of its history, does not support the proposition that the Treaty prohibits abductions outside of its terms. The remaining question, therefore, is whether the Treaty should be interpreted so as to include an implied term prohibiting prosecution where the defendant's presence is obtained by means other than those established by the Treaty ...

***

The Court of Appeals deemed it essential, in order for the individual defendant to assert a right under the Treaty, that the affected foreign government had registered a protest ... Respondent agrees that the right exercised by the individual is derivative of the nation's right under the Treaty, since nations are authorized, notwithstanding the terms of an extradition treaty, to voluntarily render an individual to the other country on terms completely outside of those provided in the treaty. The formal protest, therefore, ensures that the "offended" nation actually objects to the abduction, and has not in some way voluntarily rendered the individual for prosecution. Thus, the Extradition Treaty only prohibits gaining the defendant's presence by means other than those set forth in the Treaty when the nation from which the defendant was abducted objects.

This argument seems to us inconsistent with the remainder of respondent's argument. The Extradition Treaty has the force of law, and if, as respondent asserts, it is self-executing, it would appear that a court must enforce it on behalf of an individual regardless of the offensiveness of the practice of one nation to the other nation. In **Rauscher**, the Court noted that Great Britain had taken the position in other cases that the Webster-Ashburton Treaty included the doctrine of specialty, but no importance was attached to whether or not Great Britain had protested the prosecution of Rauscher for the crime of cruel and unusual punishment, as opposed to murder.

More fundamentally, the difficulty with the support respondent garners from international law is that none of it relates to the practice of nations in relation to extradition treaties. In Rauscher, we implied a term in the Webster-Ashburton Treaty because of the practice of nations with regard to extradition treaties. In the instant case, respondent would imply terms in the Extradition Treaty from the practice of nations with regards to international law more generally. Respondent would have us find that the Treaty acts as a prohibition against a violation of the general principle of international law that one government may not "exercise its police power in the territory of another state." There are many actions which could be taken by a nation that would violate this principle, including waging war, but it cannot seriously be contended that an invasion of the United States by Mexico would violate the terms of the Extradition Treaty between the two nations.

In sum, to infer from this Treaty and its terms that it prohibits all means of gaining the presence of an individual outside of its terms goes beyond established precedent and practice. In **Rauscher**, the implication of a doctrine of specialty into the terms of the Webster-Ashburton Treaty which, by its terms, required the presentation of evidence establishing probable cause of the crime of extradition before extradition was required, was a small step to take. By contrast, to imply from the terms of this Treaty that it prohibits obtaining the presence of an individual by means outside of the procedures the Treaty establishes requires a much larger inferential leap, with only the most general of international law principles to support it. The general principles cited by respondent simply fail to persuade us that we should imply in the United States-Mexico Extradition Treaty a term prohibiting international abductions.

Respondent and his amici may be correct that respondent's abduction was "shocking,"... and that it may be in violation of general international law principles. Mexico has protested the abduction of respondent through diplomatic notes ... and the decision of whether respondent should be returned to Mexico, as a matter outside of the Treaty, is a matter for the Executive Branch. We conclude, however, that respondent's abduction was not in violation of the Extradition Treaty between the United States and Mexico, and therefore the rule of **Ker v. Illinois** is fully applicable to this case. The fact of respondent's forcible abduction does not therefore prohibit his

trial in a court in the United States for violations of the criminal laws of
the United States.

The judgment of the Court of Appeals is therefore reversed, and
the case is remanded for further proceedings consistent with this
opinion.

So ordered.

Commentary and Questions

9. The Ker-Frisbie doctrine relating to extradition holds that a criminal
    defendant may be prosecuted in a United States court regardless of the fact
    that his or her presence has been procured in the absence of any agreement
    or treaty regarding the extradition. The doctrine emanates from two
    Supreme Court cases. The first, *Ker v. Illinois*, is a latter 19th century case
    in which a U.S. fugitive was kidnapped by a Pinkerton agent in Lima, Peru
    and returned to Illinois for trial.[15] As outlined in Chief Justice Rehnquist's
    Alvarez-Machain opinion, the Pinkerton agent had the proper extradition
    papers but when he was not met by any Peruvian official he proceeded to act
    extra-judicially and apprehend Ker with force and continually detain him
    during ship transport to the United States. Despite the irregularity with
    which Ker was brought before the trial court in Cook County, Illinois the
    Supreme Court found no reason to nullify the jurisdiction of the court to
    preside over and dispense a verdict in the case: *"The 'due process of law' here
    guaranteed is complied with when the party is regularly indicted by the
    proper grand jury in the state court, has a trial according to the forms and
    modes prescribed for such trials, and when, in that trial and proceedings, he
    is deprived of no rights to which he is lawfully entitled. We do not intend to
    say that there may not be proceedings previous to the trial in regard to which
    the prisoner could invoke in some manner the provisions of this clause of the
    Constitution, but, for mere irregularities in the manner in which he may be
    brought into custody of the law, we do not think he is entitled to say that he
    should not be tried at all for the crime with which he is charged in a regular
    indictment. He may be arrested for a very heinous offense by persons without
    any warrant, or without any previous complaint, and brought before a proper
    officer, and this may be in some sense said to be "without due process of law."
    But it would hardly be claimed that, after the case had been investigated and
    the defendant held by the proper authorities to answer for the crime, he could
    plead that he was first arrested "without due process of law." So here, when
    found within the jurisdiction of the State of Illinois and liable to answer for
    a crime against the laws of that state, unless there was some positive
    provision of the Constitution or of the laws of this country violated in bringing
    him into court, it is not easy to see how he can say that he is there "without
    due process of law" within the meaning of the constitutional provision."[16]*
    Because there was no overt government action involved and the terms of the
    extradition treaty between the United States and Peru were not relied upon,
    the Court found that Ker had no remedy with respect to his appearance
    before the Illinois court but could pursue a separate remedy against his

abductor either in a civil suit for trespass upon the person and false imprisonment or under the criminal laws of Peru. In the doctrine's second headline case, *Frisbie v. Collins*, the respondent Shirley Collins initiated a habeas corpus petition challenging his detention based on a conviction for murder.[17] Collins was living in Chicago when he was "forcibly seized, handcuffed, blackjacked" and brought to Michigan to answer the murder charges.[18] The 1952 opinion of Justice Black relied on the Court's prior holding in *Ker* to deny Collins's petition. Despite allegations of a denial of due process under the Fourteenth Amendment and violation of the Federal Kidnapping Law, which Collins asserted resulted in nullifying his conviction, the Court found no persuasive reason to overturn *Ker* and a similar line of cases supporting the jurisdiction of a state court over an involuntarily rendered defendant. Justice Black noted that *"... due process of law is satisfied when one present in court is convicted of crime after having been fairly apprized of the charges against him, and after a fair trial in accordance with constitutional procedural safeguards. There is nothing in the Constitution that requires a court to permit a guilty person rightfully convicted to escape justice because he was brought to trial against his will."*[19]

10. There was an exception to the Ker-Frisbie doctrine emanating not from the United States Supreme Court but from a Second Circuit Court of Appeals case, *United States v. Toscanino*, 500 F.2d 267 (2d Cir., 1974), wherein the Second Circuit held that due process of law may require a court to dismiss a case where there has been an intentional and unreasonable invasion of a defendant's constitutional rights. The defendant in *Toscanino* was abducted in Uruguay and brought to the United States for drug importation offenses. Toscanino, an Italian citizen, alleged he was beaten, knocked unconscious, drugged, and starved for extended periods by U.S. agents during three weeks prior to being transported to the United States. The Second Circuit, citing several recent U.S. Supreme Court decisions and acknowledging the "due process revolution" that had swept the courts in the past decade, questioned the continued logic of the Ker-Frisbie doctrine: *"[F]aced with a conflict between the two concepts of due process, the one being the restricted version found in Ker-Frisbie and the other the expanded and enlightened interpretation expressed in more recent decisions of the Supreme Court, we are persuaded that to the extent that the two are in conflict, the Ker-Frisbie version must yield. Accordingly we view due process as now requiring a court to divest itself of jurisdiction over the person of a defendant where it has been acquired as the result of the government's deliberate, unnecessary and unreasonable invasion of the accused's constitutional rights. This conclusion represents but an extension of the well-recognized power of federal courts in the civil context to decline to exercise jurisdiction over a defendant whose presence has been secured by force or fraud."*[20] The Second Circuit's strong reaction to the allegations within *Toscanino* would be tempered a year later by its holdings in *Lujan v. Gengler*, 510 F.2d 62 (2d. Cir., 1975) and *United States v. Lira*, 515 F.2d 68 (2d. Cir., 1975), wherein the Circuit Court limited the extent of its *Toscanino* holding. *Lujan* and *Lira* reduced the *Toscanino* exception to cases in which U.S. law enforcement officials or their agents

directly engaged in extreme acts of misconduct toward detainees. Absent proof of such "cruel, inhuman and outrageous treatment" a court would not have to divest itself of jurisdiction.[21] The Supreme Court's later decision in *Alvarez-Machain* re-affirmed the Ker-Frisbie doctrine, although it defied basic assumptions under international law regarding extradition, which led to criticism in the legal community, both domestic and internationally.[22]

11. In *Valentine v. United States*, 299 U.S. 5 (1936) several U.S. citizens wanted in France for serious crimes filed a habeas corpus petition seeking to block their extradition back to France to answer the charges. French authorities had contacted the New York City Police Department who were holding the individuals for extradition. The arrestees subsequently challenged the authority of the police commissioner to extradite them back to France under the Franco-American Treaty of 1909. Further, they argued that the president lacked constitutional authority to render them to France. As U.S. citizens they claimed they were outside the terms of the extradition treaty thereby leaving the president without any lawful authority to extradite. The pertinent parts of the treaty relied upon by the Court were as follows: "*Article I. The Government of the United States and the Government of France mutually agree to deliver up persons who, having been charged with or convicted of any of the crimes or offenses specified in the following article, committed within the jurisdiction of one of the contracting Parties, shall seek an asylum or be found within the territories of the other: Provided That this shall only be done upon such evidence of criminality as, according to the laws of the place where the fugitive or person so charged shall be found, would justify his or her apprehension and commitment for trial if the crime or offense had been there committed ...*

    Article V. Neither of the contracting Parties shall be bound to deliver up its own citizens or subjects under the stipulations of this convention."[23] The Court held that Executive authority to extradite must be found in either law or treaty. In the absence of any authority under the 1909 treaty to extradite United States citizens back to a foreign country the president was powerless to remove the petitioners from the United States. How does the Court's holding in *Valentine* differ from its holding in *Alvarez-Machain*? Is there a consistency to the Court's reasoning or are the cases irreconcilable?

12. There are no United States Supreme Court decisions dealing directly with the practice of extraordinary rendition. The opportunity presented to the Court in the extraordinary rendition case of Khaled El-Masri to provide a statement on the practice was lost when the Court denied certiorari without comment in an appeal from the Fourth Circuit's denial of El-Masri's claim under the state secrets privilege. Similarly in another case focusing on the detention, extraordinary rendition and interrogation practices of the United States government, *Vance v. Rumsfeld*, the Court again denied certiorari without comment. In *Vance* the Seventh Circuit Court of Appeals sitting en banc reversed the lower district court and a panel of the circuit court that both created a private right of action against the military chain of command. Citing *Haig v. Agee*, the Seventh Circuit said that "*matters intimately related*

to ... national security are rarely proper subjects for judicial intervention."[24] The Seventh Circuit dismissed the plaintiffs' *Bivens*-type action against the secretary of defense and the United States government. Other federal circuit courts of appeal have taken the same position in extraordinary rendition cases brought before them, dismissing the cases on either state secrets privilege grounds or deferring to the national security decisions of the executive branch.[25]

In Chapter 3 commentary note 10 a question was posed relating to the Yamashita standard of command responsibility and its applicability to the actions of the soldiers involved in the Abu Ghraib prison scandal. Its relevance, as indicated in Chapter 3, is best explored herein, especially in light of the legal conclusions reached by several United States courts regarding chain of command liability for the civil and human rights violations alleged in those cases to have been committed by U.S. government personnel. It has been established that the CIA program of extraordinary rendition is a program operating outside the boundaries of any extradition treaty. Extradition by the U.S. government can be granted only according to a treaty, providing that Congress has not legislated otherwise. International law of extradition recognizes the principle of specificity in which a demanding country can prosecute the person sought only for the offense for which the extradition was granted. Under the rule the requesting country cannot extradite the wanted individual to a third country for prosecution prior to trial for the initial extraditable offense. Most countries will not extradite to countries where the extradited individual is facing the death penalty or the prospect of torture. These are grounded principles of human rights developed within the international legal community since the end of World War II and the initiation of the first war crimes tribunal in Nuremburg. Yet, the U.S. government's extraordinary rendition program has been documented to have resulted in the torture and deaths of detainees. Although U.S. courts have not been willing to hold government officials accountable to plaintiffs seeking a remedy for their treatment, international tribunals, as in the case of Khaled El-Masri, have been more accessible forums. How far should the reach of the Yamashita Standard extend in holding military and government officials responsible for extraordinary rendition and the abuses associated with the program? Should international law have a broader role in regulating U.S. government conduct? Or is that a path which compromises United States national security interests?

Endnotes

[1]   *Center for National Security Studies v. U.S. Department of Justice, 331 F.3d 918 (D.C. Cir., 2003)*

[2]   Chisti, M., Meissner, D., Papademetriou, D., Peterzell, J., Wishnie, M., & Yale-Loehr, S. (2003). *America's Challenge: Domestic Security, Civil Liberties and National Unity After September 11.* Washington D.C.: Migration Policy Institute.

3   U.S. Department of Justice Office of the Inspector General. (2003). *The September 11 Detainees: A Review of the Treatment of Aliens Held on Immigration Charges in Connection with the Investigation of the September 11 Attacks.* Washington D.C.: U.S. Government Printing Office.

4   *Id.*

5   323 U.S. at 220.

6   481 U.S. 739 (1987).

7   481 U.S. at 751.

8   212 U.S. at 84.

9   212 U.S. at 85.

10 *Executive Order No. 9066*
    The President
    Executive Order
    Authorizing the Secretary of War to Prescribe Military Areas
    Whereas the successful prosecution of the war requires every possible protection against espionage and against sabotage to national-defense material, national-defense premises, and national-defense utilities as defined in Section 4, Act of April 20, 1918, 40 Stat. 533, as amended by the Act of November 30, 1940, 54 Stat. 1220, and the Act of August 21, 1941, 55 Stat. 655 (U.S.C., Title 50, Sec. 104);
    Now, therefore, by virtue of the authority vested in me as President of the United States, and Commander in Chief of the Army and Navy, I hereby authorize and direct the Secretary of War, and the Military Commanders whom he may from time to time designate, whenever he or any designated Commander deems such action necessary or desirable, to prescribe military areas in such places and of such extent as he or the appropriate Military Commander may determine, from which any or all persons may be excluded, and with respect to which, the right of any person to enter, remain in, or leave shall be subject to whatever restrictions the Secretary of War or the appropriate Military Commander may impose in his discretion. The Secretary of War is hereby authorized to provide for residents of any such area who are excluded therefrom, such transportation, food, shelter, and other accommodations as may be necessary, in the judgment of the Secretary of War or the said Military Commander, and until other arrangements are made, to accomplish the purpose of this order. The designation of military areas in any region or locality shall supersede designations of prohibited and restricted areas by the Attorney General under the Proclamations of December 7 and 8, 1941, and shall supersede the responsibility and authority of the Attorney General under the said Proclamations in respect of such prohibited and restricted areas.
    I hereby further authorize and direct the Secretary of War and the said Military Commanders to take such other steps as he or the appropriate Military Commander may deem advisable to enforce compliance with the restrictions applicable to each Military area hereinabove authorized to be designated, including the use of Federal troops and other Federal Agencies, with authority to accept assistance of state and local agencies.
    I hereby further authorize and direct all Executive Departments, independent establishments and other Federal Agencies, to assist the Secretary of War or the said Military Commanders in carrying out this Executive Order, including the furnishing of medical aid, hospitalization, food, clothing, transportation, use of land, shelter, and other supplies, equipment, utilities, facilities, and services.
    This order shall not be construed as modifying or limiting in any way the authority heretofore granted under Executive Order No. 8972, dated December 12, 1941, nor

shall it be construed as limiting or modifying the duty and responsibility of the Federal Bureau of Investigation, with respect to the investigation of alleged acts of sabotage or the duty and responsibility of the Attorney General and the Department of Justice under the Proclamations of December 7 and 8, 1941, prescribing regulations for the conduct and control of alien enemies, except as such duty and responsibility is superseded by the designation of military areas hereunder.
Franklin D. Roosevelt
The White House,
February 19, 1942.

[11]   323 U.S. at 302–304.

[12]   546 U.S. at 1065.

[13]   H.R. 1540—112th Congress: National Defense Authorization Act for Fiscal Year 2012. (2011). http://www.govtrack.us/congress/bills/112/hr1540.

[14]   Garcia, M.J., Elsea, J.K., Mason, R.C., & Liu, E.C. (2011). *Closing the Guantanamo Detention Center: Legal Issues.* Washington D.C.: Congressional Research Service.

[15]   119 U.S. 436 (1886).

[16]   119 U.S. at 440.

[17]   342 U.S. 519 (1952).

[18]   Id.

[19]   342 U.S. at 522.

[20]   500 F.2d at 275.

[21]   510 F.2d at 65.

[22]   See e.g., Ruiz-Bravo, H. (1993). "Monstrous Decision: Kidnapping is Legal." *Hastings Constitutional Law Quarterly*, 833–875; but also see the following for U.S. policy on extradition:

United States Attorney Criminal Resource Manual Chapter 9-15.000 International Extradition and Related Matters, section 9-15.100 Definition and General Principles *"International extradition is the formal process by which a person found in one country is surrendered to another country for trial or punishment. The process is regulated by treaty and conducted between the Federal Government of the United States and the government of a foreign country. It differs considerably from interstate rendition, commonly referred to an interstate extradition, mandated by the Constitution, Article 4, Section 2.*

Generally under United States law (18 USC §3184), extradition may be granted only pursuant to a treaty. However, some countries grant extradition without a treaty. However, every such country requires an offer of reciprocity when extradition is accorded in the absence of a treaty. Further, the 1996 amendments to 18 USC 3181 and 3184 permit the United States to extradite, without regard to the existence of a treaty, persons (other than citizens, nationals or permanent residents of the United States), who have committed crimes of violence against nationals of the United States in foreign countries."

[23]   299 U.S. at 7.

[24]   453 U.S. 280, 292 (1981).

[25] See e.g., *Arar v. Ashcroft*, 585 F.3d 559 (2d Cir., 2009) (no remedy against intelligence officials who sent a terror suspect to another country for interrogation) and *Mohamed v. Jeppesen Dataplan, Inc.*, 614 F.3d 1070 (9th Cir., 2010) (dismissing on the basis of the state secrets privilege a case brought by five extraordinary rendition plaintiffs against an airline company that provided services to the C.I.A. in transferring the plaintiffs to interrogation sites). The United States Supreme Court in 2011 also denied certiorari to the *Jeppesen* plaintiffs.

Chapter Nine
FREE SPEECH AND RIGHT OF ASSOCIATION

The First Amendment to the United States Constitution contains just forty-five words. But they are forty-five words of beautiful simplicity and brevity standing as a bulwark against government interference and oppression. Along with the Fourth Amendment, the First Amendment is the greatest guarantee and symbol of liberty devised in government. Those forty-five words are worth repeating: *"Congress shall make no law respecting an establishment of religion, or prohibiting the free exercise thereof; or abridging the freedom of speech, or of the press; or the right of the people peaceably to assemble, and to petition the government for a redress of grievances."* The cherished right to freedom of religion, freedom of speech, right to assemble and petition the government are explicit along with the implied freedom of association. These rights are seemingly sacrosanct but, much like the Fourth Amendment, the First Amendment has been targeted in times of national emergency and subjected to government restrictions of dubious constitutionality. This chapter explores the treatment of these First Amendment rights during periods in American history when national security was heightened. The institutional legal response to government restrictions of First Amendment rights has been an evolutionary process since the dawning of the nation. Beginning with the Sedition Act of 1798 in which President John Adams endeavored to stifle criticism of the government in anticipation of war with France, the restriction of First Amendment rights during national crisis has been a historical redundancy. Numerous arrests and indictments of newspaper editors and Democrat-Republican politicians critical of the Federalist Adams ensued under the Sedition Act.[1] Similar restrictions followed under President Lincoln during the Civil War. In addition to the suspension of habeas corpus the Lincoln administration suppressed anti-war sentiment and any statements considered disloyal, which extended to the press, particularly the influential New York papers.[2] Because conscription was a necessary aspect of the Union's war effort anti-war sentiment included those who would attempt to dissuade able-bodied males from joining the war effort. Draft resistance and other disloyal activities were subject to arrest without the benefit of habeas corpus.[3] General Ambrose Burnside, the Union army commander in charge of the Military Department of Ohio, issued General Order Number 38, which led to the arrest of Clement Vallandigham. The General Order forbade anyone within the area of the Military Department of Ohio from committing any acts benefitting enemies of the country—criticism of the war effort fell into this category. The defendant Vallandigham, a former Congressman, was arrested by federal troops after making speeches in Columbus and Mount Vernon, Ohio critical of Burnside's order and the Lincoln administration's policies pertaining to free assembly and debate over government policy.[4] Though Vallandigham's U.S. Supreme Court case focused on the Executive's authority to try a citizen before a military tribunal the arrest itself was prompted by a government order restricting First Amendment rights. The arrest of Clement Vallandigham in 1863 set off a torrent of debate surrounding First Amendment rights in wartime.[5] This debate would find itself being repeated during the World War I administration of President Woodrow Wilson. At the advent of U.S. involvement in World War I, Congress passed the Espionage Act of 1917 with the express purpose of preventing interference with national defense operations or the divulgence of military operations. However, section 3 of the Espionage Act criminalized behavior similar to that punished during the Civil War with respect to the dissuasion of purpose for those in the military. Section 3 in its entirety provided the following: *"Whoever, when the United States is at war, shall wilfully make or convey false reports or false statements with intent to interfere with the operation or success of the military or naval forces of the United States or to promote the success of its enemies and whoever when the United States is at war, shall wilfully cause or attempt to cause insubordination, disloyalty, mutiny, refusal of duty, in the military or naval forces of the United States, or shall wilfully obstruct the recruiting or enlistment service of the United States, to the injury of the service or of the United States, shall be punished by a fine of not more than $10,000 or imprisonment for not more than twenty years, or both."*[6] This section, opponents argued, created a restriction on First Amendment activities. Criticism increased the following year when the Wilson administration pushed forward its national security plan and Congress passed an amendment to the 1917 Act, otherwise known as The Sedition Act of 1918. The 1918 amendment in part made changes to section 3 of the Espionage Act, which had a more direct effect on limiting First Amendment protections. Specifically, the 1918 amendments created the crime of sedition, the first since the expiration of the Alien and Sedition Acts of 1798, for anyone who criticized the government. This included negative comments concerning the flag,[7] the military, or the Constitution of the United States. Numerous arrests and convictions followed in the wake of the legislation passing as well as several U.S. Supreme Court opinions upholding the constitutionality of the acts. One of the first of these cases was *Schenck v. United States*, 249 U.S. 47 (1919), in which Justice Oliver Wendell Holmes established his famous "clear and present danger" test.

Schenck, the general secretary of the Socialist Party, distributed 15,000 leaflets critical of conscription and the war. The leaflets urged draft age young men, *"[D]o not submit to intimidation ... [A]ssert your rights."*[8] The leaflets further exhorted *"[I]f you do not assert and support your rights, you are helping to deny or disparage rights which it is the solemn duty of all citizens and residents of the United States to retain."*[9] Schenck was indicted on three criminal counts, the first of which was a violation of the Espionage Act of 1917. The Court was unanimous in its decision against Schenck's First Amendment claims. Justice Holmes's opinion differentiated between the exercise of those rights in times of war and peace time: *"We admit that, in many places and in ordinary times, the defendants, in saying all that was said in the circular, would have been within their constitutional rights. But the character of every act depends upon the circumstances in which it is done ... The most stringent protection of free speech would not protect a man in falsely shouting fire in a theatre and causing a panic. It does not even protect a man from an injunction against uttering words that may have all the effect of force ... The question in every case is whether the words used are used in such circumstances and are of such a nature as to create a clear and present danger that they will bring about the substantive evils that Congress has a right to prevent. It is a question of proximity and degree. When a nation is at war, many things that might be said in time of peace are such a hindrance to its effort that their utterance will not be endured so long as men fight, and that no Court could regard them as protected by any constitutional right.*[10] On the heels of its *Schenck* decision the Court decided two more cases challenging the Espionage and Sedition Acts. In the two opinions issued by Justice Holmes a week after his *Schenck* opinion the Court found the facts in *Frohwerk v. United States*, 249 U.S. 204 (1919), and *Debs v. United States*, 249 U.S. 211 (1919), indistinguishable from those in *Schenck*. The defendant in *Frohwerk* faced a thirteen-count indictment for a series of twelve newspaper articles that were critical of the war and urged against voluntary conscription. Once again, Justice Holmes's opinion upheld the constitutionality of the Espionage Acts and the governmental interests in protecting the war effort: *"It may be that all this might be said or written even in time of war in circumstances that would not make it a crime. We do not lose our right to condemn either measures or men because the country is at war."*[11] In *Debs* the Court followed its prior *Schenck* decision and denied relief to the imprisoned Eugene V. Debs. This case brought before the Court the First Amendment challenge to the Espionage Act of one of history's most colorful and well-known defendants. Eugene V. Debs was a former Socialist Party presidential candidate and high-profile labor leader. Though the labor movement had begun to gain traction in the latter part of the 19th century, it was still a nascent movement in the early 20th century as it suffered brutal opposition not only from employers but the government as well. Criminal syndicalism statutes, which outlaw violence or terrorism with the purpose of bringing about social or political change, were used against organized labor. Debs was no stranger to anti-union animus having served prison time for disobeying a government injunction against a railway union strike. The incident that brought Debs to prison a second time was a speech he gave in Canton, Ohio in 1918 calling for opposition to the war and its draft. Fifty-five years after the arrest of Clement Vallandigham for a similar-themed speech he gave in Ohio and Debs was no more protected under the First Amendment. In a parallel situation to ex-Congressman Vallandigham, Debs was a former Indiana state senator. Nonetheless, Debs was considered a foe to his country and Holmes's opinion gave short consideration to the First Amendment argument, resting once again on the holding of *Schenck*.

Later in 1919 the Court decided *Abrams v. United States*, 250 U.S. 616 (1919), a case challenging the Sedition Act of 1918. Five Russian-born individuals were arrested in New York City for the production and distribution of two leaflets, one criticizing government troops being sent to Russia and the second urging that production of weapons for use in Russia be stopped. In a 7-2 majority decision the Court found that the leaflets called for violent action against the government in direct violation of the Sedition Act. The majority opinion by Justice John H. Clarke crafted a more stringent standard for First Amendment analysis—*"Men must be held to have intended, and to be accountable for, the effects which their acts were likely to produce."*[12] This "bad tendency" test followed in this case by the majority of the Court was the predominant standard in the criminalization of speech. It was the standard applied in the 1907 Supreme Court case of *Patterson v. Colorado* which upheld contempt charges against a newspaperman for *"the publication of certain articles and a cartoon, which, it was charged, reflected upon the motives and conduct of the Supreme Court of Colorado in cases still pending and were intended to embarrass the court in the impartial administration of justice."*[13] The test came from a common law application of Blackstone's views of libel.[14] Any speech tending to harm the public welfare could be sanctioned. In his *Commentaries on the Laws of England*, Blackstone wrote: *"Of a nature very similar to challenges are libels, libelli famosi, which, taken in their largest and most extensive sense, signify any writings, pictures, or the like, of an immoral or illegal tendency; but, in the sense under which we are now to consider them, are malicious defamations of any person, and especially a magistrate, made public by either printing, writing, signs, or pictures, in order to provoke him to wrath, or expose him to public hatred, contempt, and ridicule. The direct tendency of these libels is the breach of the public peace, by stirring up the objects of them to revenge, and perhaps to bloodshed ... in a criminal prosecution, the tendency which all libels have to create animosities, and to disturb the public peace, is the sole consideration of the law."*[15] Justice Holmes wrote the majority opinion in *Patterson* and followed the "bad tendency" test until his articulation of the "clear and present danger" test in *Schenck*. In *Abrams* he wrote a dissenting opinion critical of the "bad tendency" approach of the majority and in doing so found no cause to hold the defendants criminally liable, because their conduct of distributing pamphlets, without more, did not meet the "clear and present danger" test.

The Court's wrestling match with the First Amendment, especially in times of national peril, would continue beyond the confines of World War I into the post-war "red scare" of 1919–20, through World War II, the Korean War, and into the Cold War period's concerns about Communist infiltration in American society. The more restrictive approach taken by the Court during World War I in cases like *Schenck, Frohwerk, Debs,* and *Abrams* would give way to a new test announced in *Brandenburg v. Ohio*. Even though the *Brandenburg* case facts did not involve national security it was a seminal case for free speech rights.

Brandenburg v. Ohio
395 U.S. 444 (1969)

Per Curiam.

The appellant, a leader of a Ku Klux Klan group, was convicted under the Ohio Criminal Syndicalism statute for "advocat[ing] ... the duty, necessity, or propriety of crime, sabotage, violence, or unlawful methods of terrorism as a means of accomplishing industrial or political reform" and for "voluntarily assembl[ing] with any society, group, or assemblage of persons formed to teach or advocate the doctrines of criminal syndicalism." Ohio Rev. Code Ann. 2923.13. He was fined $1,000 and sentenced to one to 10 years' imprisonment. The appellant challenged the constitutionality of the criminal syndicalism statute under the First and Fourteenth Amendments to the United States Constitution, but the intermediate appellate court of

Ohio affirmed his conviction without opinion. The Supreme Court of Ohio dismissed his appeal, sua sponte, "for the reason that no substantial constitutional question exists herein." It did not file an opinion or explain its conclusions. Appeal was taken to this Court, and we noted probable jurisdiction. We reverse.

The record shows that a man, identified at trial as the appellant, telephoned an announcer-reporter on the staff of a Cincinnati television station and invited him to come to a Ku Klux Klan "rally" to be held at a farm in Hamilton County. With the cooperation of the organizers, the reporter and a cameraman attended the meeting and filmed the events. Portions of the films were later broadcast on the local station and on a national network.

The prosecution's case rested on the films and on testimony identifying the appellant as the person who communicated with the reporter and who spoke at the rally. The State also introduced into evidence several articles appearing in the film, including a pistol, a rifle, a shotgun, ammunition, a Bible, and a red hood worn by the speaker in the films.

One film showed 12 hooded figures, some of whom carried firearms. They were gathered around a large wooden cross, which they burned. No one was present other than the participants and the newsmen who made the film. Most of the words uttered during the scene were incomprehensible when the film was projected, but scattered phrases could be understood that were derogatory of Negroes and, in one instance, of Jews. Another scene on the same film showed the appellant, in Klan regalia, making a speech. The speech, in full, was as follows:

> "This is an organizers' meeting. We have had quite a few members here today which are—we have hundreds, hundreds of members throughout the State of Ohio. I can quote from a newspaper clipping from the Columbus, Ohio Dispatch, five weeks ago Sunday morning. The Klan has more members in the State of Ohio than does any other organization. We're not a revengent organization, but if our President, our Congress, our Supreme Court, continues to suppress the white, Caucasian race, it's possible that there might have to be some revengeance taken.
> "We are marching on Congress July the Fourth, four hundred thousand strong. From there we are dividing into two groups, one group to march on St. Augustine, Florida, the other group to march into Mississippi. Thank you."

The second film showed six hooded figures one of whom, later identified as the appellant, repeated a speech very similar to that recorded on the first film. The reference to the possibility of "revengeance" was omitted, and one sentence was added: "Personally, I believe the nigger should be returned to Africa, the Jew returned to Israel." Though some of the figures in the films carried weapons, the speaker did not.

The Ohio Criminal Syndicalism Statute was enacted in 1919. From 1917 to 1920, identical or quite similar laws were adopted by 20 States and two territories. In 1927, this Court sustained the constitutionality of California's Criminal Syndicalism Act, Cal. Penal Code 11400-11402, the text of which is quite similar to that of the laws of Ohio. **Whitney v. California**, 274 U.S. 357 (1927). The Court upheld the statute on the ground that, without more, "advocating" violent means to effect political and economic change involves such danger to the security of the State that the State may outlaw it. Cf. **Fiske v. Kansas**, 274 U.S. 380 (1927). But Whitney has been thoroughly discredited by later decisions. See **Dennis v. United States**, 341 U.S. 494 , at 507 (1951). These later decisions have fashioned the principle that the constitutional guarantees of free speech and free press do not permit a State to forbid or proscribe advocacy of the use of force or of law violation except where such advocacy is directed to inciting or producing imminent lawless action and is likely to incite or produce such action. As we said in **Noto v. United States**, 367 U.S. 290, 297 -298 (1961), "the mere abstract teaching ... of the moral propriety or even moral necessity for a resort to force and violence, is not the same as preparing a group for violent action and steeling it to such action." See also **Herndon v. Lowry**, 301 U.S. 242, 259 -261 (1937); **Bond v. Floyd**, 385 U.S. 116, 134 (1966). A statute which fails to draw this distinction impermissibly intrudes upon the freedoms guaranteed by the First and Fourteenth Amendments. It sweeps within its condemnation speech which our Constitution has immunized from governmental control. Cf. **Yates v. United States**, 354 U.S. 298 (1957); **De Jonge v. Oregon**, 299 U.S. 353 (1937); **Stromberg v. California**, 283 U.S. 359 (1931). See also **United States v. Robel**, 389 U.S. 258 (1967); **Keyishian v. Board of Regents**, 385 U.S. 589 (1967); **Elfbrandt v. Russell**, 384 U.S. 11 (1966); **Aptheker v. Secretary of State**, 378 U.S. 500 (1964); **Baggett v. Bullitt**, 377 U.S. 360 (1964).

Measured by this test, Ohio's Criminal Syndicalism Act cannot be sustained. The Act punishes persons who "advocate or teach the duty, necessity, or propriety" of violence "as a means of accomplishing industrial or political reform"; or who publish or circulate or display any book or paper containing such advocacy; or who "justify" the commission of violent acts "with intent to exemplify, spread or advocate the propriety of the doctrines of criminal syndicalism"; or who "voluntarily assemble" with a group formed "to teach or advocate the doctrines of criminal syndicalism." Neither the indictment nor the trial judge's instructions to the jury in any way refined the statute's bald definition of the crime in terms of mere advocacy not distinguished from incitement to imminent lawless action.

Accordingly, we are here confronted with a statute which, by its own words and as applied, purports to punish mere advocacy and to forbid, on pain of criminal punishment, assembly with others merely to advocate the described type of action. Such a statute falls within the condemnation of the First and Fourteenth Amendments. The contrary teaching of **Whitney v. California**, supra, cannot be supported, and that decision is therefore overruled. Reversed.

New York Times Co. v. United States
403 U.S. 713 (1971)

Per Curiam.

We granted certiorari in these cases in which the United States seeks to enjoin the New York Times and the Washington Post from publishing the contents of a classified study entitled "History of U.S. Decision-Making Process on Viet Nam Policy."

"Any system of prior restraints of expression comes to this Court bearing a heavy presumption against its constitutional validity." **Bantam Books, Inc. v. Sullivan**, 372 U.S. 58, 70 (1963); see also **Near v. Minnesota**, 283 U.S. 697 (1931). The Government "thus carries a heavy burden of showing justification for the imposition of such a restraint." **Organization for a Better Austin v. Keefe**, 402 U.S. 415, 419 (1971). The District Court for the Southern District of New York in the New York Times case and the District Court for the District of Columbia and the Court of Appeals for the District of Columbia Circuit in the Washington Post case held that the Government had not met that burden. We agree.

The judgment of the Court of Appeals for the District of Columbia Circuit is therefore affirmed. The order of the Court of Appeals for the Second Circuit is reversed and the case is remanded with directions to enter a judgment affirming the judgment of the District Court for the Southern District of New York. The stays entered June 25, 1971, by the Court are vacated. The judgments shall issue forthwith.

So ordered.

Mr. Justice Black, with whom Mr. Justice Douglas joins, concurring.

I adhere to the view that the Government's case against the Washington Post should have been dismissed and that the injunction against the New York Times should have been vacated without oral argument when the cases were first presented to this Court. I believe that every moment's continuance of the injunctions against these newspapers amounts to a flagrant, indefensible, and continuing violation of the First Amendment. Furthermore, after oral argument, I agree completely that we must affirm the judgment of the Court of Appeals for the District of Columbia Circuit and reverse the judgment of the Court of Appeals for the Second Circuit for the reasons stated by my Brothers Douglas and Brennan. In my view it is unfortunate that some of my Brethren are apparently willing to hold that the publication of news may sometimes be enjoined. Such a holding would make a shambles of the First Amendment.

Our Government was launched in 1789 with the adoption of the Constitution. The Bill of Rights, including the First Amendment, followed in 1791. Now, for the first time in the 182 years since the founding of the Republic, the federal courts are asked to hold that the First Amendment does not mean what it says, but rather means that the Government can halt the publication of current news of vital importance to the people of this country.

In seeking injunctions against these newspapers and in its presentation to the Court, the Executive Branch seems to have forgotten the essential purpose and history of the First Amendment. When the Constitution was adopted, many people strongly opposed it because the document contained no Bill of Rights to safeguard certain basic freedoms. They especially feared that the new powers granted to a central government might be interpreted to permit the government to curtail freedom of religion, press, assembly, and speech. In response to an overwhelming public clamor, James Madison offered a series of amendments to satisfy citizens that these great liberties would remain safe and beyond the power of government to abridge. Madison proposed what later became the First Amendment in three parts, two of which are set out below, and one of which proclaimed: "The people shall not be deprived or abridged of their right to speak, to write, or to publish their sentiments; and the freedom of the press, as one of the great bulwarks of liberty, shall be inviolable." The amendments were offered to curtail and restrict the general powers granted to the Executive, Legislative, and Judicial Branches two years before in the original Constitution. The Bill of Rights changed the original Constitution into a new charter under which no branch of government could abridge the people's freedoms of press, speech, religion, and assembly. Yet the Solicitor General argues and some members of the Court appear to agree that the general powers of the Government adopted in the original Constitution should be interpreted to limit and restrict the specific and emphatic guarantees of the Bill of Rights adopted later. I can imagine no greater perversion of history. Madison and the other Framers of the First Amendment, able men that they were, wrote in language they earnestly believed could never be misunderstood: "Congress shall make no law ... abridging the freedom ... of the press ... ." Both the history and language of the First Amendment support the view that the press must be left free to publish news, whatever the source, without censorship, injunctions, or prior restraints.

In the First Amendment the Founding Fathers gave the free press the protection it must have to fulfill its essential role in our democracy. The press was to serve the governed, not the governors. The

Government's power to censor the press was abolished so that the press would remain forever free to censure the Government. The press was protected so that it could bare the secrets of government and inform the people. Only a free and unrestrained press can effectively expose deception in government. And paramount among the responsibilities of a free press is the duty to prevent any part of the government from deceiving the people and sending them off to distant lands to die of foreign fevers and foreign shot and shell. In my view, far from deserving condemnation for their courageous reporting, the New York Times, the Washington Post, and other newspapers should be commended for serving the purpose that the Founding Fathers saw so clearly. In revealing the workings of government that led to the Vietnam War, the newspapers nobly did precisely that which the Founders hoped and trusted they would do.

The Government's case here is based on premises entirely different from those that guided the Framers of the First Amendment. The Solicitor General has carefully and emphatically stated:

> "Now, Mr. Justice [Black], your construction of ... [the First Amendment] is well known, and I certainly respect it. You say that no law means no law, and that should be obvious. I can only say, Mr. Justice, that to me it is equally obvious that 'no law' does not mean 'no law', and I would seek to persuade the Court that is true ... . [T]here are other parts of the Constitution that grant powers and responsibilities to the Executive, and ... the First Amendment was not intended to make it impossible for the Executive to function or to protect the security of the United States."

And the Government argues in its brief that in spite of the First Amendment, "[t]he authority of the Executive Department to protect the nation against publication of information whose disclosure would endanger the national security stems from two interrelated sources: the constitutional power of the President over the conduct of foreign affairs and his authority as Commander-in-Chief."

In other words, we are asked to hold that despite the First Amendment's emphatic command, the Executive Branch, the Congress, and the Judiciary can make laws enjoining publication of current news and abridging freedom of the press in the name of "national security." The Government does not even attempt to rely on any act of Congress. Instead it makes the bold and dangerously far-reaching contention that the courts should take it upon themselves to "make" a law abridging freedom of the press in the name of equity, presidential power and national security, even when the representatives of the people in Congress have adhered to the command of the First Amendment and refused to make such a law ... To find that the President has "inherent power" to halt the publication of news by resort to the courts would wipe out the First Amendment and destroy the fundamental liberty and security of the very people the Government hopes to make "secure." No one can read the history of the adoption of the First Amendment without being convinced beyond any doubt that it was injunctions like those sought here that Madison and his collaborators intended to outlaw in this Nation for all time.

The word "security" is a broad, vague generality whose contours should not be invoked to abrogate the fundamental law embodied in the First Amendment. The guarding of military and diplomatic secrets at the expense of informed representative government provides no real security for our Republic. The Framers of the First Amendment, fully aware of both the need to defend a new nation and the abuses of the English and Colonial governments, sought to give this new society strength and security by providing that freedom of speech, press, religion, and assembly should not be abridged. This thought was eloquently expressed in 1937 by Mr. Chief Justice Hughes—great man and great Chief Justice that he was—when the Court held a man could not be punished for attending a meeting run by Communists.

"The greater the importance of safeguarding the community from incitements to the overthrow of our institutions by force and violence, the more imperative is the need to preserve inviolate the constitutional rights of free speech, free press and free assembly in order to maintain the opportunity for free political discussion, to the end that government may be responsive to the will of the people and that changes, if desired, may be obtained by peaceful means. Therein lies the security of the Republic, the very foundation of constitutional government."

Mr. Justice Brennan, concurring.

I

I write separately in these cases only to emphasize what should be apparent: that our judgments in the present cases may not be taken to indicate the propriety, in the future, of issuing temporary stays and restraining orders to block the publication of material sought to be suppressed by the Government. So far as I can determine, never before has the United States sought to enjoin a newspaper from publishing information in its possession. The relative novelty of the questions presented, the necessary haste with which decisions were reached, the magnitude of the interests asserted, and the fact that all the parties have concentrated their arguments upon the question whether permanent restraints were proper may have justified at least some of the restraints heretofore imposed in these cases. Certainly it is difficult to fault the several courts below for seeking to assure that the issues here involved were preserved for ultimate review by this Court. But even if it be assumed that some of the interim restraints were proper in the two cases before us, that assumption has no bearing upon the propriety of similar judicial action in the future. To begin with, there has now been ample time for reflection and judgment; whatever values there may be in the preservation of novel questions for appellate review may not support any restraints in the future. More important, the First Amendment stands as an absolute bar to the imposition of judicial restraints in circumstances of the kind presented by these cases.

II

The error that has pervaded these cases from the outset was the granting of any injunctive relief whatsoever, interim or otherwise. The entire thrust of the Government's claim throughout these cases has been that publication of the material sought to be enjoined "could," or "might," or "may" prejudice the national interest in various ways. But the First Amendment tolerates absolutely no prior judicial restraints of the press predicated upon surmise or conjecture that untoward consequences may result. Our cases, it is true, have indicated that there is a single, extremely narrow class of cases in which the First Amendment's ban on prior judicial restraint may be overridden. Our cases have thus far indicated that such cases may arise only when the Nation "is at war," **Schenck v. United States**, 249 U.S. 47, 52 (1919), during which times "[n]o one would question but that a government might prevent actual obstruction to its recruiting service or the publication of the sailing dates of transports or the number and location of troops." **Near v. Minnesota**, 283 U.S. 697, 716 (1931). Even if the present world situation were assumed to be tantamount to a time of war, or if the power of presently available armaments would justify even in peacetime the suppression of information that would set in motion a nuclear holocaust, in neither of these actions has the Government presented or even alleged that publication of items from or based upon the material at issue would cause the happening of an event of that nature. "[T]he chief purpose of [the First Amendment's] guaranty [is] to prevent previous restraints upon publication." **Near v. Minnesota**, supra, at 713. Thus, only governmental allegation and proof that publication must inevitably, directly, and immediately cause the occurrence of an event kindred to imperiling the safety of a transport already at sea can support even the issuance of an interim restraining order. In no event may mere conclusions be sufficient: for if the Executive Branch seeks judicial aid in preventing publication, it must inevitably submit the basis upon which that aid is sought to scrutiny by the judiciary. And therefore, every restraint issued in this case, whatever its form, has violated the First Amendment—and not less so because that restraint was justified as necessary to afford the courts an opportunity to examine the claim more thoroughly.

Unless and until the Government has clearly made out its case, the First Amendment commands that no injunction may issue.

Mr. Justice Stewart, with whom Mr. Justice White joins, concurring.

In the governmental structure created by our Constitution, the Executive is endowed with enormous power in the two related areas of national defense and international relations. This power, largely unchecked by the Legislative and Judicial branches, has been pressed to the very hilt since the advent of the nuclear missile age. For better or for worse, the simple fact is that a President of the United States possesses vastly greater constitutional independence in these two vital areas of power than does, say, a prime minister of a country with a parliamentary form of government.

In the absence of the governmental checks and balances present in other areas of our national life, the only effective restraint upon executive policy and power in the areas of national defense and international affairs may lie in an enlightened citizenry—in an informed and critical public opinion which alone can here protect the values of democratic government. For this reason, it is perhaps here that a press that is alert, aware, and free most vitally serves the basic purpose of the First Amendment. For without an informed and free press there cannot be an enlightened people.

Yet it is elementary that the successful conduct of international diplomacy and the maintenance of an effective national defense require both confidentiality and secrecy. Other nations can hardly deal with this Nation in an atmosphere of mutual trust unless they can be assured that their confidences will be kept. And within our own executive departments, the development of considered and intelligent international policies would be impossible if those charged with their formulation could not communicate with each other freely, frankly, and in confidence. In the area of basic national defense the frequent need for absolute secrecy is, of course, self-evident.

I think there can be but one answer to this dilemma, if dilemma it be. The responsibility must be where the power is. If the Constitution gives the Executive a large degree of unshared power in the conduct of foreign affairs and the maintenance of our national defense, then under the Constitution the Executive must have the largely unshared duty to determine and preserve the degree of internal security necessary to exercise that power successfully. It is an awesome responsibility, requiring judgment and wisdom of a high order. I should suppose that moral, political, and practical considerations would dictate that a very first principle of that wisdom would be an insistence upon avoiding secrecy for its own sake. For when everything is classified, then nothing is classified, and the system becomes one to be disregarded by the cynical or the careless, and to be manipulated by those intent on self-protection or self-promotion. I should suppose, in short, that the hallmark of a truly effective internal security system would be the maximum possible disclosure, recognizing that secrecy can best be preserved only when credibility is truly maintained. But be that as it may, it is clear to me that it is the constitutional duty of the Executive—as a matter of sovereign prerogative and not as a matter of law as the courts know law—through the promulgation and enforcement of executive regulations, to protect the confidentiality necessary to carry out its responsibilities in the fields of international relations and national defense.

This is not to say that Congress and the courts have no role to play. Undoubtedly Congress has the power to enact specific and appropriate criminal laws to protect government property and preserve government secrets. Congress has passed such laws, and several of them are of very colorable relevance to the apparent circumstances of these cases. And if a criminal prosecution is instituted, it will be the responsibility of the courts to decide the applicability of the criminal law under which the charge is brought. Moreover, if Congress should pass a specific law authorizing civil proceedings in this field, the courts would likewise have the duty to decide the constitutionality of such a law as well as its applicability to the facts proved.

But in the cases before us we are asked neither to construe specific regulations nor to apply specific laws. We are asked, instead, to perform a function that the Constitution gave to the Executive, not the Judiciary. We are asked, quite simply, to prevent the publication by two newspapers of material that the Executive Branch insists should not, in the national interest, be published. I am convinced that the Executive is correct with respect to some of the documents involved. But I cannot say that disclosure of any of them will surely result in direct, immediate, and irreparable damage to our Nation or its people. That being so, there can under the First Amendment be but one judicial resolution of the issues before us. I join the judgments of the Court.

Mr. Justice Marshall, concurring.

The Government contends that the only issue in these cases is whether in a suit by the United States, "the First Amendment bars a court from prohibiting a newspaper from publishing material whose disclosure would pose a `grave and immediate danger to the security of the United States.'" With all due respect, I believe the ultimate issue in these cases is even more basic than the one posed by the Solicitor General. The issue is whether this Court or the Congress has the power to make law.

In these cases there is no problem concerning the President's power to classify information as "secret" or "top secret." Congress has specifically recognized Presidential authority, which has been formally exercised in Exec. Order 10501 (1953), to classify documents and information ... Nor is there any issue here regarding the President's power as Chief Executive and Commander in Chief to protect national security by disciplining employees who disclose information and by taking precautions to prevent leaks.

The problem here is whether in these particular cases the Executive Branch has authority to invoke the equity jurisdiction of the courts to protect what it believes to be the national interest. See **In re Debs**, 158 U.S. 564, 584 (1895). The Government argues that in addition to the inherent power of any government to protect itself, the President's power to conduct foreign affairs and his position as Commander in Chief give him authority to impose censorship on the press to protect his ability to deal effectively with foreign nations and to conduct the military affairs of the country. Of course, it is beyond cavil that the President has broad powers by virtue of his primary responsibility for the conduct of our foreign affairs and his position as Commander in Chief. **Chicago & Southern Air Lines, Inc. v. Waterman S. S. Corp.**, 333 U.S. 103 (1948); **Hirabayashi v. United States**, 320 U.S. 81, 93 (1943); **United States v. Curtiss-Wright Corp.**, 299 U.S. 304 (1936). And in some situations it may be that under whatever inherent powers the Government may have, as well as the implicit authority derived from the President's mandate to conduct foreign affairs and to act as Commander in Chief, there is a basis for the invocation of the equity jurisdiction of this Court as an aid to prevent the publication of material damaging to "national security," however that term may be defined.

It would, however, be utterly inconsistent with the concept of separation of powers for this Court to use its power of contempt to prevent behavior that Congress has specifically declined to prohibit. There would be a similar damage to the basic concept of these co-equal branches of Government if when the Executive Branch has adequate authority granted by Congress to protect "national security" it can choose instead to invoke the contempt power of a court to enjoin the threatened conduct. The Constitution provides that Congress shall make laws, the President execute laws, and courts interpret laws. **Youngstown Sheet & Tube Co. v. Sawyer**, 343 U.S. 579 (1952). It did not provide for government by injunction in which the courts and the Executive Branch can "make law" without regard to the action of Congress. It may be more convenient for the Executive Branch if it need only convince a judge to prohibit conduct rather than ask the Congress to pass a law, and it may be more convenient to enforce a contempt order than to seek a criminal conviction in a jury trial. Moreover, it may be considered politically wise to get a court to share the responsibility for arresting those who the Executive Branch has probable cause to believe are violating the law. But convenience and political considerations of the moment do not justify a basic departure from the principles of our system of government.

In these cases we are not faced with a situation where Congress has failed to provide the Executive with broad power to protect the Nation from disclosure of damaging state secrets. Congress has on several occasions given extensive consideration to the problem of protecting the military and strategic secrets of the United States. This consideration has resulted in the enactment of statutes making it a crime to receive, disclose, communicate, withhold, and publish certain documents, photographs, instruments, appliances, and information. The bulk of these statutes is found in chapter 37 of U.S.C., Title 18, entitled Espionage and Censorship. In that chapter, Congress has provided penalties ranging from a $10,000 fine to death for violating the various statutes.

Thus it would seem that in order for this Court to issue an injunction it would require a showing that such an injunction would enhance the already existing power of the Government to act. See **Bennett v. Laman**, 277 N. Y. 368, 14 N. E. 2d 439 (1938). It is a traditional axiom of equity that a court of equity will not do a useless thing just as it is a traditional axiom that equity will not enjoin the commission of a crime ... Here there has been no attempt to make such a showing. The Solicitor General does not even mention in his brief whether the Government considers that there is probable cause to believe a crime has been committed or whether there is a conspiracy to commit future crimes.

If the Government had attempted to show that there was no effective remedy under traditional criminal law, it would have had to show that there is no arguably applicable statute. Of course, at this stage this Court could not and cannot determine whether there has been a violation of a particular statute or decide the constitutionality of any statute. Whether a good-faith prosecution could have been instituted under any statute could, however, be determined.

At least one of the many statutes in this area seems relevant to these cases. Congress has provided in 18 U.S.C. 793(e) that whoever "having unauthorized possession of, access to, or control over any document, writing, code book, signal book ... or note relating to the national defense, or information relating to the national defense which information the possessor has reason to believe could be used to the injury of the United States or to the advantage of any foreign nation, willfully communicates, delivers, transmits ... the same to any person not entitled to receive it, or willfully retains the same and fails to deliver it to the officer or employee of the United States entitled to receive it ... [s]hall be fined not more than $10,000 or imprisoned not more than ten years, or both." Congress has also made it a crime to conspire to commit any of the offenses listed in 18 U.S.C. 793(e).

It is true that Judge Gurfein found that Congress had not made it a crime to publish the items and material specified in 793 (e). He found that the words "communicates, delivers, transmits ... " did not refer to publication of newspaper stories. And that view has some support in the legislative history and conforms with the past practice of using the statute only to prosecute those charged with ordinary espionage. But see 103 Cong. Rec. 10449 (remarks of Sen. Humphrey). Judge Gurfein's view of the statute is not, however, the only plausible construction that could be given. See my Brother White's concurring opinion.

Even if it is determined that the Government could not in good faith bring criminal prosecutions against the New York Times and the Washington Post, it is clear that Congress has specifically rejected passing legislation that would have clearly given the President the power he seeks here and made the current activity of the newspapers unlawful. When Congress specifically declines to make conduct unlawful it is not for this Court to re-decide those issues—to overrule Congress. See **Youngstown Sheet & Tube Co. v. Sawyer**, 343 U.S. 579 (1952).

On at least two occasions Congress has refused to enact legislation that would have made the conduct engaged in here unlawful and given the President the power that he seeks in this case. In 1917 during the debate over the original Espionage Act, still the basic provisions of 793, Congress rejected a proposal to give the President in time of war or threat of war authority to directly prohibit by proclamation the publication of information relating to national defense that might be useful to the enemy. The proposal provided that:

> "During any national emergency resulting from a war to which the United States is a party, or from threat of such a war, the President may, by proclamation, declare the existence of such emergency and, by proclamation, prohibit the publishing or communicating of, or the attempting to publish or communicate any information relating to the national defense which, in his judgment, is of such character that it is or might be useful to the enemy. Whoever violates any such prohibition shall be punished by a fine of not more than $10,000 or by imprisonment for not more than 10 years, or both: Provided, That nothing in this section shall be construed to limit or restrict any discussion, comment, or criticism of the acts or policies of the Government or its representatives or the publication of the same." *55 Cong. Rec. 1763.*

Congress rejected this proposal after war against Germany had been declared even though many believed that there was a grave national emergency and that the threat of security leaks and espionage was serious. The Executive Branch has not gone to Congress and requested that the decision to provide such power be reconsidered. Instead, the Executive Branch comes to this Court and asks that it be granted the power Congress refused to give.

***

Either the Government has the power under statutory grant to use traditional criminal law to protect the country or, if there is no basis for arguing that Congress has made the activity a crime, it is plain that Congress has specifically refused to grant the authority the Government seeks from this Court. In either case this Court does not have authority to grant the requested relief. It is not for this Court to fling itself into every breach perceived by some Government official nor is it for this Court to take on itself the burden of enacting law, especially a law that Congress has refused to pass.

I believe that the judgment of the United States Court of Appeals for the District of Columbia Circuit should be affirmed and the judgment of the United States Court of Appeals for the Second Circuit should be reversed insofar as it remands the case for further hearings.

Holder v. Humanitarian Law Project
561 U.S. 1 (2010)

Chief Justice Roberts delivered the opinion of the Court.

Congress has prohibited the provision of "material support or resources" to certain foreign organizations that engage in terrorist activity. 18 U. S. C. §2339B(a)(1). That prohibition is based on a finding that the specified organizations "are so tainted by their criminal conduct that any contribution to such an organization facilitates that conduct." *Antiterrorism and Effective Death Penalty Act of 1996 (AEDPA)*, §301(a)(7), 110 Stat. 1247, note following 18 U. S. C. §2339B (Findings and Purpose). The plaintiffs in this litigation seek to provide support to two such organizations. Plaintiffs claim that they seek to facilitate only the lawful, nonviolent purposes of those groups, and that applying the material-support law to prevent them from doing so violates the Constitution. In particular, they claim that the statute is too vague, in violation of the Fifth Amendment, and that it infringes their rights to freedom of speech and association, in violation of the First Amendment. We conclude that the material-support statute is constitutional as applied to the particular activities plaintiffs have told us they wish to pursue. We do not, however, address the resolution of more difficult cases that may arise under the statute in the future.

question to be answ

I

This litigation concerns 18 U. S. C. §2339B, which makes it a federal crime to "knowingly provid[e] material support or resources to a foreign terrorist organization." Congress has amended the definition of "material support or resources" periodically, but at present it is defined as follows:

"[T]he term 'material support or resources' means any property, tangible or intangible, or service, including currency or monetary instrument or financial securities, financial services, lodging, training, expert advice or assistance, safehouses, false documentation or identification, communications equipment, facilities, weapons, lethal substances, explosives, personnel (2 or more individuals who may be or include oneself), and transportation, except medicine or religious materials." §2339A(b)(1); see also §2339B(g)(4).

The authority to designate an entity a "foreign terrorist organization" rests with the Secretary of State. 8 U.S.C. §§1189(a)(1), (d)(4). She may, in consultation with the Secretary of the Treasury and the Attorney General, so designate an organization upon finding that it is foreign, engages in "terrorist activity" or "terrorism," and thereby "threatens the security of United States nationals or the national security of the United States." §§1189(a)(1), (d)(4). "'[N]ational security' means the national defense, foreign relations, or economic interests of the United States." §1189(d)(2). An entity designated a foreign terrorist organization may seek review of that designation before the D. C. Circuit within 30 days of that designation. §1189(c)(1).

In 1997, the Secretary of State designated 30 groups as foreign terrorist organizations. Two of those groups are the Kurdistan Workers' Party (also known as the Partiya Karkeran Kurdistan, or PKK) and the Liberation Tigers of Tamil Eelam (LTTE). The PKK is an organization founded in 1974 with the aim of establishing an independent Kurdish state in southeastern Turkey ... The LTTE is an organization founded in 1976 for the purpose of creating an independent Tamil state in Sri Lanka ... The District Court in this action found that the PKK and the LTTE engage in political and humanitarian activities ... The Government has presented evidence that both groups have also committed numerous terrorist attacks, some of which have harmed American citizens. The LTTE sought judicial review of its designation as a foreign terrorist organization; the D. C. Circuit upheld that designation. The PKK did not challenge its designation.

Plaintiffs in this litigation are two U. S. citizens and six domestic organizations: the Humanitarian Law Project (HLP) (a human rights organization with consultative status to the United Nations); Ralph Fertig (the HLP's president, and a retired administrative law judge); Nagalingam Jeyalingam (a Tamil physician, born in Sri Lanka and a naturalized U. S. citizen); and five nonprofit groups dedicated to the interests of persons of Tamil descent.

***

As relevant here, plaintiffs claimed that the material-support statute was unconstitutional on two grounds: First, it violated their freedom of speech and freedom of association under the First Amendment, because it criminalized their provision of material support to the PKK and the LTTE, without requiring the Government to prove that plaintiffs had a specific intent to further the unlawful ends of those organizations. Second, plaintiffs argued that the statute was unconstitutionally vague. #2

***

In IRTPA, Congress clarified the mental state necessary to violate §2339B, requiring knowledge of the foreign group's designation as a terrorist organization or the group's commission of terrorist acts. §2339B(a)(1). Congress also added the term "service" to the definition of "material support or resources," §2339A(b)(1), and defined "training" to mean "instruction or teaching designed to impart a specific skill, as opposed to general knowledge," §2339A(b)(2). It also defined "expert advice or assistance" to mean "advice or assistance derived from scientific, technical or other specialized knowledge." §2339A(b)(3). Finally, IRTPA clarified the scope of the term "personnel" by providing:

> "No person may be prosecuted under §2339B in connection with the term 'personnel' unless that person has knowingly provided, attempted to provide, or conspired to provide a foreign terrorist organization with 1 or more individuals (who may be or include himself) to work under that terrorist organization's direction or control or to organize, manage, supervise, or otherwise direct the operation of that organization. Individuals who act entirely independently of the foreign terrorist organization to advance its goals or objectives shall not be considered to be working under the foreign terrorist organization's direction or control." §2339B(h).

***

The Government petitioned for certiorari, and plaintiffs filed a conditional cross-petition. We granted both petitions.

Procedure

analysis

II

Given the complicated 12-year history of this litigation, we pause to clarify the questions before us. Plaintiffs challenge §2339B's prohibition on four types of material support—"training," "expert advice or assistance," "service," and "personnel." They raise three constitutional claims. First, plaintiffs claim that §2339B violates the Due Process Clause of the Fifth Amendment because these four statutory terms are impermissibly vague. Second, plaintiffs claim that §2339B violates their freedom of speech under the First Amendment. Third, plaintiffs claim that §2339B violates their First Amendment freedom of association.

Plaintiffs do not challenge the above statutory terms in all their applications. Rather, plaintiffs claim that §2339B is invalid to the extent

It prohibits them from engaging in certain specified activities. With respect to the HLP and Judge Fertig, those activities are: (1) "training members of the PKK on how to use humanitarian and international law to peacefully resolve disputes"; (2) "engaging in political advocacy on behalf of Kurds who live in Turkey"; and (3) "teaching PKK members how to petition various representative bodies such as the United Nations for relief." With respect to the other plaintiffs, those activities are: (1) "training members of the LTTE to present claims for tsunami-related aid to mediators and international bodies"; (2) "offering their legal expertise in negotiating peace agreements between the LTTE and the Sri Lankan government"; and (3) "engaging in political advocacy on behalf of Tamils who live in Sri Lanka."

**

III

Plaintiffs claim, as a threshold matter, that we should affirm the Court of Appeals without reaching any issues of constitutional law. They contend that we should interpret the material-support statute, when applied to speech, to require proof that a defendant intended to further a foreign terrorist organization's illegal activities. That interpretation, they say, would end the litigation because plaintiffs' proposed activities consist of speech, but plaintiffs do not intend to further unlawful conduct by the PKK or the LTTE.

We reject plaintiffs' interpretation of §2339B because it is inconsistent with the text of the statute. Section 2339B(a)(1) prohibits "knowingly" providing material support. It then specifically describes the type of knowledge that is required: "To violate this paragraph, a person must have knowledge that the organization is a designated terrorist organization ..., that the organization has engaged or engages in terrorist activity ..., or that the organization has engaged or engages in terrorism ...." *Ibid.* Congress plainly spoke to the necessary mental state for a violation of §2339B, and it chose knowledge about the organization's connection to terrorism, not specific intent to further the organization's terrorist activities.

**

Finally, plaintiffs give the game away when they argue that a specific intent requirement should apply only when the material-support statute applies to speech. There is no basis whatever in the text of §2339B to read the same provisions in that statute as requiring intent in some circumstances but not others. It is therefore clear that plaintiffs are asking us not to interpret §2339B, but to revise it. "Although this Court will often strain to construe legislation so as to save it against constitutional attack, it must not and will not carry this to the point of perverting the purpose of a statute." ***Scales v. United States***, 367 U.S. 203, 211 (1961).

Scales is the case on which plaintiffs most heavily rely, but it is readily distinguishable. That case involved the Smith Act, which prohibited membership in a group advocating the violent overthrow of the government. The Court held that a person could not be convicted under the statute unless he had knowledge of the group's illegal advocacy and a specific intent to bring about violent overthrow. This action is different: Section 2339B does not criminalize mere membership in a designated foreign terrorist organization. It instead prohibits providing "material support" to such a group ... Nothing about ***Scales*** suggests the need for a specific intent requirement in such a case. The Court in ***Scales***, moreover, relied on both statutory text and precedent that had interpreted closely related provisions of the Smith Act to require specific intent ... Plaintiffs point to nothing similar here.

We cannot avoid the constitutional issues in this litigation through plaintiffs' proposed interpretation of §2339B.

IV

[Part IV addressed the plaintiffs' statutory vagueness argument which the Court found lacked merit.]

V

A

[Court rejects government argument that the intermediate scrutiny test should be applied to the constitutional challenge to §2339B. The Court said a more stringent test was required.]

B

The First Amendment issue before us is more refined than either plaintiffs or the Government would have it. It is not whether the Government may prohibit pure political speech, or may prohibit material support in the form of conduct. It is instead whether the Government may prohibit what plaintiffs want to do—provide material support to the PKK and LTTE in the form of speech.

Everyone agrees that the Government's interest in combating terrorism is an urgent objective of the highest order. Plaintiffs' complaint is that the ban on material support, applied to what they wish to do, is not "necessary to further that interest." The objective of combating terrorism does not justify prohibiting their speech, plaintiffs argue, because their support will advance only the legitimate activities of the designated terrorist organizations, not their terrorism.

Whether foreign terrorist organizations meaningfully segregate support of their legitimate activities from support of terrorism is an empirical question. When it enacted §2339B in 1996, Congress made specific findings regarding the serious threat posed by international terrorism. See AEDPA §§301(a)(1)-(7), 110 Stat. 1247, note following 18 U. S. C. §2339B (Findings and Purpose). One of those findings explicitly rejects plaintiffs' contention that their support would not further the terrorist activities of the PKK and LTTE: "[F]oreign organizations that engage in terrorist activity are so tainted by their criminal conduct that any contribution to such an organization facilitates that conduct." §301(a)(7) (emphasis added).

Plaintiffs argue that the reference to "any contribution" in this finding meant only monetary support. There is no reason to read the finding to be so limited, particularly because Congress expressly prohibited so much more than monetary support in §2339B. Congress's use of the term "contribution" is best read to reflect a determination that any form of material support furnished "to" a foreign terrorist organization should be barred, which is precisely what the material-support statute does. Indeed, when Congress enacted §2339B, Congress simultaneously removed an exception that had existed in §2339A(a) (1994 ed.) for the provision of material support in the form of "humanitarian assistance to persons not directly involved in" terrorist activity. AEDPA §323, 110 Stat. 1255; 205 F. 3d, at 1136. That repeal demonstrates that Congress considered and rejected the view that ostensibly peaceful aid would have no harmful effects.

We are convinced that Congress was justified in rejecting that view. The PKK and the LTTE are deadly groups ... It is not difficult to conclude as Congress did that the "tain[t]" of such violent activities is so great that working in coordination with or at the command of the PKK and LTTE serves to legitimize and further their terrorist means. AEDPA §301(a)(7), 110 Stat. 1247.

Material support meant to "promot[e] peaceable, lawful conduct" can further terrorism by foreign groups in multiple ways. "Material support" is a valuable resource by definition. Such support frees up other resources within the organization that may be put to violent ends. It also importantly helps lend legitimacy to foreign terrorist groups—legitimacy that makes it easier for those groups to persist, to recruit members, and to raise funds—all of which facilitate more terrorist attacks.

Social media use by Terr orgs.

***

Providing foreign terrorist groups with material support in any form also furthers terrorism by straining the United States' relationships with its allies and undermining cooperative efforts between nations to prevent terrorist attacks. We see no reason to question Congress's finding that "international cooperation is required for an effective response to terrorism, as demonstrated by the numerous multilateral conventions in force providing universal prosecutive jurisdiction over persons involved in a variety of terrorist acts, including hostage taking, murder of an internationally protected person, and aircraft piracy and sabotage." AEDPA §301(a)(5), 110 Stat. 1247, note following 18 U. S. C. §2339B (Findings and Purpose). The material-support statute furthers this international effort by prohibiting aid for foreign terrorist groups that harm the United States' partners abroad ...

For example, the Republic of Turkey—a fellow member of NATO—is defending itself against a violent insurgency waged by the PKK. That nation and our other allies would react sharply to Americans furnishing material support to foreign groups like the PKK, and would hardly be mollified by the explanation that the support was meant only to further those groups' "legitimate" activities. From Turkey's perspective, there likely are no such activities.

C

In analyzing whether it is possible in practice to distinguish material support for a foreign terrorist group's violent activities and its nonviolent activities, we do not rely exclusively on our own inferences drawn from the record evidence. We have before us an affidavit stating the Executive Branch's conclusion on that question. The State Department informs us that "[t]he experience and analysis of the US government agencies charged with combating terrorism strongly suppor[t]" Congress's finding that all contributions to foreign terrorist organizations further their terrorism. See **Winter v. Natural Resources Defense Council, Inc.**, 555 U.S. ___, ___ (2008) (slip op., at 14-15). In the Executive's view: "Given the purposes, organizational structure, and clandestine nature of foreign terrorist organizations, it is highly likely that any material support to these organizations will ultimately inure to the benefit of their criminal, terrorist functions—regardless of whether such support was ostensibly intended to support non-violent, non-terrorist activities."

That evaluation of the facts by the Executive, like Congress's assessment, is entitled to deference. This litigation implicates sensitive and weighty interests of national security and foreign affairs. The PKK and the LTTE have committed terrorist acts against American citizens abroad, and the material-support statute addresses acute foreign policy concerns involving relationships with our Nation's allies. See *id.*, at 128-133, 137. We have noted that "neither the Members of this Court nor most federal judges begin the day with briefings that may describe new and serious threats to our Nation and its people." **Boumediene v. Bush**, 553 U.S. 723, 797 (2008). It is vital in this context "not to substitute ... our own evaluation of evidence for a reasonable evaluation by the Legislative Branch." **Rostker v. Goldberg**, 453 U.S. 57,

68 (1981). See **Wald**, 468 U.S. at 242; **Haig v. Agee**, 453 U.S. 280, 292 (1981).

Our precedents, old and new, make clear that concerns of national security and foreign relations do not warrant abdication of the judicial role. We do not defer to the Government's reading of the First Amendment, even when such interests are at stake. We are one with the dissent that the Government's "authority and expertise in these matters do not automatically trump the Court's own obligation to secure the protection that the Constitution grants to individuals." But when it comes to collecting evidence and drawing factual inferences in this area, "the lack of competence on the part of the courts is marked," **Rostker**, *supra*, at 65, and respect for the Government's conclusions is appropriate.

One reason for that respect is that national security and foreign policy concerns arise in connection with efforts to confront evolving threats in an area where information can be difficult to obtain and the impact of certain conduct difficult to assess. The dissent slights these real constraints in demanding hard proof—with "detail," "specific facts," and "specific evidence"—that plaintiffs' proposed activities will support terrorist attacks. See *post*, at 9, 16, 23. That would be a dangerous requirement. In this context, conclusions must often be based on informed judgment rather than concrete evidence, and that reality affects what we may reasonably insist on from the Government. The material-support statute is, on its face, a preventive measure—it criminalizes not terrorist attacks themselves, but aid that makes the attacks more likely to occur. The Government, when seeking to prevent imminent harms in the context of international affairs and national security, is not required to conclusively link all the pieces in the puzzle before we grant weight to its empirical conclusions. See **Zemel v. Rusk**, 381 U.S. at 17 ("[B]ecause of the changeable and explosive nature of contemporary international relations, ... Congress ... must of necessity paint with a brush broader than that it customarily wields in domestic areas").

This context is different from that in decisions like **Cohen**. In that case, the application of the statute turned on the offensiveness of the speech at issue. Observing that "one man's vulgarity is another's lyric," we invalidated Cohen's conviction in part because we concluded that "governmental officials cannot make principled distinctions in this area." 403 U.S. at 25. In this litigation, by contrast, Congress and the Executive are uniquely positioned to make principled distinctions between activities that will further terrorist conduct and undermine United States foreign policy, and those that will not.

We also find it significant that Congress has been conscious of its own responsibility to consider how its actions may implicate constitutional concerns. First, §2339B only applies to designated foreign terrorist organizations. There is, and always has been, a limited number of those organizations designated by the Executive Branch, see, e.g., 74 Fed. Reg. 29742 (2009); 62 Fed. Reg. 52650 (1997), and any groups so designated may seek judicial review of the designation. Second, in response to the lower courts' holdings in this litigation, Congress added clarity to the statute by providing narrowing definitions of the terms "training," "personnel," and "expert advice or assistance," as well as an explanation of the knowledge required to violate §2339B. Third, in effectuating its stated intent not to abridge First Amendment rights, see §2339B(i), Congress has also displayed a careful balancing of interests in creating limited exceptions to the ban on material support. The definition of material support, for example, excludes medicine and religious materials. See §2339A(b)(1). In this area perhaps more than any other, the Legislature's superior capacity for weighing competing interests means that "we must be particularly careful not to substitute our judgment of what is desirable for that of Congress." *Rostker, supra,* at 68. Finally, and most importantly, Congress has avoided any restriction on independent advocacy, or indeed any activities not directed to, coordinated with, or controlled by foreign terrorist groups.

At bottom, plaintiffs simply disagree with the considered judgment of Congress and the Executive that providing material support to a designated foreign terrorist organization—even seemingly benign support—bolsters the terrorist activities of that organization. That judgment, however, is entitled to significant weight, and we have persuasive evidence before us to sustain it. Given the sensitive interests in national security and foreign affairs at stake, the political branches have adequately substantiated their determination that, to serve the Government's interest in preventing terrorism, it was necessary to prohibit providing material support in the form of training, expert advice, personnel, and services to foreign terrorist groups, even if the supporters meant to promote only the groups' nonviolent ends.

We turn to the particular speech plaintiffs propose to undertake. First, plaintiffs propose to "train members of [the] PKK on how to use humanitarian and international law to peacefully resolve disputes." 552 F. 3d, at 921, n. 1. Congress can, consistent with the First Amendment, prohibit this direct training. It is wholly foreseeable that the PKK could use the "specific skill[s]" that plaintiffs propose to impart, §2339A(b)(2), as part of a broader strategy to promote terrorism. The PKK could, for example, pursue peaceful negotiation as a means of buying time to recover from short-term setbacks, lulling opponents into complacency, and ultimately preparing for renewed attacks. See generally A. Marcus, Blood and Belief: The PKK and the Kurdish Fight for Independence 286–295 (2007) (describing the PKK's suspension of armed struggle and subsequent return to violence). A foreign terrorist organization introduced to the structures of the international legal system might use the information to threaten, manipulate, and disrupt. This possibility is real, not remote.

Second, plaintiffs propose to "teach PKK members how to petition various representative bodies such as the United Nations for relief." 552 F. 3d, at 921, n. 1. The Government acts within First Amendment strictures in banning this proposed speech because it teaches the organization how to acquire "relief," which plaintiffs never define with any specificity, and which could readily include monetary aid. See Brief for Plaintiffs 10-11, 16-17, n. 10; App. 58-59, 80-81. Indeed, earlier in this litigation, plaintiffs sought to teach the LTTE "to present claims for tsunami-related aid to mediators and international bodies," 552 F. 3d, at 921, n. 1, which naturally included monetary relief. Money is fungible, *supra*, at 26, and Congress logically concluded that money a terrorist group such as the PKK obtains using the techniques plaintiffs propose to teach could be redirected to funding the group's violent activities.

Finally, plaintiffs propose to "engage in political advocacy on behalf of Kurds who live in Turkey," and "engage in political advocacy on behalf of Tamils who live in Sri Lanka." 552 F. 3d, at 921, n. 1. As explained above, *supra*, at 19-20, plaintiffs do not specify their expected level of coordination with the PKK or LTTE or suggest what exactly their "advocacy" would consist of. Plaintiffs' proposals are phrased at such a high level of generality that they cannot prevail in this pre-enforcement challenge. See *supra*, at 20; **Grange**, 552 U. S., at 454; **Zemel**, 381 U.S. at 20.

In responding to the foregoing, the dissent fails to address the real dangers at stake. It instead considers only the possible benefits of plaintiffs' proposed activities in the abstract. See *post*, at 13-15. The dissent seems unwilling to entertain the prospect that training and advising a designated foreign terrorist organization on how to take advantage of international entities might benefit that organization in a way that facilitates its terrorist activities. In the dissent's world, such training is all to the good. Congress and the Executive, however, have concluded that we live in a different world: one in which the designated foreign terrorist organizations "are so tainted by their criminal conduct that any contribution to such an organization facilitates that conduct." AEDPA §301(a)(7). One in which, for example, "the United Nations High Commissioner for Refugees was forced to close a Kurdish refugee camp in northern Iraq because the camp had come under the control of the PKK, and the PKK had failed to respect its 'neutral and humanitarian nature.'" McKune Affidavit, App. 135-136, ¶13. Training and advice on how to work with the United Nations could readily have helped the PKK in its efforts to use the United Nations camp as a base for terrorist activities.

If only good can come from training our adversaries in international dispute resolution, presumably it would have been unconstitutional to prevent American citizens from training the Japanese Government on using international organizations and mechanisms to resolve disputes during World War II. It would, under the dissent's reasoning, have been contrary to our commitment to resolving disputes through " 'deliberative forces,' " *post*, at 13 (quoting **Whitney v. California**, 274 U.S. 357, 375 (1927) (Brandeis, J., concurring)), for Congress to conclude that assisting Japan on that front might facilitate its war effort more generally. That view is not one the First Amendment requires us to embrace.

All this is not to say that any future applications of the material-support statute to speech or advocacy will survive First Amendment scrutiny. It is also not to say that any other statute relating to speech and terrorism would satisfy the First Amendment. In particular, we in no way suggest that a regulation of independent speech would pass constitutional muster, even if the Government were to show that such speech benefits foreign terrorist organizations. We also do not suggest that Congress could extend the same prohibition on material support at issue here to domestic organizations. We simply hold that, in prohibiting the particular forms of support that plaintiffs seek to provide to foreign terrorist groups, §2339B does not violate the freedom of speech.

VI

Plaintiffs' final claim is that the material-support statute violates their freedom of association under the First Amendment. Plaintiffs argue that the statute criminalizes the mere fact of their associating with the PKK and the LTTE, thereby running afoul of decisions like **De Jonge v. Oregon**, 299 U.S. 353 (1937), and cases in which we have overturned sanctions for joining the Communist Party, see, e.g., **Keyishian v. Board of Regents of Univ. of State of N. Y.**, 385 U.S. 589 (1967); **United States v. Robel**, 389 U.S. 258 (1967).

The Court of Appeals correctly rejected this claim because the statute does not penalize mere association with a foreign terrorist organization. As the Ninth Circuit put it: "The statute does not prohibit being a member of one of the designated groups or vigorously promoting and supporting the political goals of the group.... What [§2339B] prohibits is the act of giving material support...." 205 F. 3d, at 1133. Plaintiffs want to do the latter. Our decisions scrutinizing penalties on simple association or assembly are therefore inapposite. See, e.g., *Robel, supra*, at 262 ("It is precisely because th[e] statute sweeps indiscriminately across all types of association with Communist-action groups, without regard to the quality and degree of membership, that it runs afoul of the First Amendment"); **De Jonge**, *supra*, at 362.

Plaintiffs also argue that the material-support statute burdens their freedom of association because it prevents them from providing support to designated foreign terrorist organizations, but not to other groups. See Brief for Plaintiffs 56; Reply Brief for Plaintiffs 37–38. Any burden on plaintiffs' freedom of association in this regard is justified for the same reasons that we have denied plaintiffs' free speech challenge. It would be strange if the Constitution permitted Congress to prohibit certain forms of speech that constitute material support, but did not permit Congress to prohibit that support only to particularly dangerous and lawless foreign organizations. Congress is not required to ban material support to every group or none at all.

***

The Preamble to the Constitution proclaims that the people of the United States ordained and established that charter of government in part to "provide for the common defence." As Madison explained, "[s]ecurity against foreign danger is ... an avowed and essential object of the American Union." The Federalist No. 41, p. 269 (J. Cooke ed. 1961). We hold that, in regulating the particular forms of support that plaintiffs seek to provide to foreign terrorist organizations, Congress has pursued that objective consistent with the limitations of the First and Fifth Amendments.

The judgment of the United States Court of Appeals for the Ninth Circuit is affirmed in part and reversed in part, and the cases are remanded for further proceedings consistent with this opinion.

It is so ordered.

Commentary and Questions

1. *Brandenburg* and *New York Times Co.* were per curiam opinions from the Supreme Court meaning that no one justice was the author, rather the opinion was from the full court. Per curiam decisions either result with no written opinion or a brief collective statement from a court. *Brandenburg* presented a sweeping change in First Amendment jurisprudence, creating the imminent lawless action test, in a little over 1,100 words with no separate opinion issuing from any justice. However, *New York Times Co. v. United States*, otherwise known as the Pentagon Papers case, resulted in a separate concurring opinion from every justice in the Supreme Court's majority. Chief Justice Warren Burger was joined by Justices Blackmun and Harlan in dissent. Despite the brevity of the per curiam opinion itself, the individual concurrences or dissents of the justices created a lengthy postscript to the decision. The *New York Times* and *Washington Post* both sought to publish articles disclosing classified information that had been leaked to the press. The information was from a study commissioned by Secretary of Defense Robert McNamara into the history of U.S. military involvement in Vietnam. An injunction was applied for by the government seeking prior restraint in the publication of the articles. The government's argument was that publication would compromise national security. The *New York Times* defended its right to publish the information and inform the public, claiming that the injunction would be a prior restraint of speech. The importance of the issues presented by the case were evident in the quick trajectory from the federal district court's denial of the injunction to the Supreme Court's per curiam opinion—a span of seventeen days in June 1971.

2. In *Gitlow v. New York*, 268 U.S. 252 (1925) the Supreme Court had to decide whether a New York state statute criminalizing advocacy to overthrow the government was an unconstitutional infringement on free speech. The defendant, Benjamin Gitlow, a member of the Socialist Party, published an article entitled *"The Left Wing Manifesto"* advocating establishing a socialist government by calling for strikes and any other type of concerted efforts aimed at crippling the government. The old New York Penal Law Criminal Anarchy statute §160 defined the crimes as *"the doctrine that organized government should be overthrown by force or violence, or by assassination of the executive head or of any of the executive officials of government, or by any unlawful means. The advocacy of such doctrine either by word of mouth or writing is a felony."*[16] Section 161, subsection 2 of the Penal Law further defined advocacy as the printing, publishing, editing, issuing or knowing circulation, sale, distribution, or public display of *"any book, paper, document, or written or printed matter in any form, containing or advocating, advising or teaching the doctrine that organized government should be overthrown by force, violence or any unlawful means."*[17] Gitlow challenged his indictment on these charges as *"violating his liberty of speech under the due process clause of the Fourteenth Amendment."*[18] The Court had to decide whether the First Amendment applied to the states. As a threshold issue the Court found *"freedom of speech and of the press—which are protected by the First Amendment from abridgment by Congress—are among the fundamental personal rights and 'liberties' protected by the due process clause of the Fourteenth Amendment from impairment by the States."*[19] Nonetheless, the Court upheld the right of the state in the exercise of its police powers to punish speech or expressive conduct likely to create a public harm or threaten the good order of government. Finding the New York statute to be a constitutional exercise of the police power the Court relied on the "bad tendency" test, citing *Patterson v. Colorado* and *Abrams v. United States* for its earlier positions on the issue. Though *Gitlow* was not expressly overruled by *Brandenburg*, as was *Whitney v. California*, its remaining vitality was in its incorporation of First Amendment protections to the states.[20]

3. Charlotte A. Whitney, a former Socialist Party member, became a founding member and officer of the Communist Labor Party of America in 1919 when she was cast out of the Oakland Socialist Party along with others who were considered "radical." Her activities with the Communist Labor Party led to her being charged and convicted under the California Criminal Syndicalism statute, which made it a crime to organize to advocate, teach, aid, or abet criminal syndicalism as defined by the statute, which includes the use of terrorism as a means of accomplishing political change. Justice Sanford, author of *Gitlow*, once again resorted to the "bad tendency" test to uphold a state statute criminalizing speech. Though *Whitney* was eventually overruled by *Brandenburg*, Justice Louis Brandeis' concurrence still resonates as an impassioned advocacy for free speech. His concurring opinion advocated for a standard of suppressing speech that was much closer to the eventual standard adopted by the Court in *Brandenburg*. His was a concurrence in result though not principle: *"Those who won our independence*

believed that the final end of the State was to make men free to develop their faculties, and that, in its government, the deliberative forces should prevail over the arbitrary. They valued liberty both as an end, and as a means. They believed liberty to be the secret of happiness, and courage to be the secret of liberty. They believed that freedom to think as you will and to speak as you think are means indispensable to the discovery and spread of political truth; that, without free speech and assembly, discussion would be futile; that, with them, discussion affords ordinarily adequate protection against the dissemination of noxious doctrine; that the greatest menace to freedom is an inert people; that public discussion is a political duty, and that this should be a fundamental principle of the American government. They recognized the risks to which all human institutions are subject. But they knew that order cannot be secured merely through fear of punishment for its infraction; that it is hazardous to discourage thought, hope and imagination; that fear breeds repression; that repression breeds hate; that hate menaces stable government; that the path of safety lies in the opportunity to discuss freely supposed grievances and proposed remedies, and that the fitting remedy for evil counsels is good ones. Believing in the power of reason as applied through public discussion, they eschewed silence coerced by law—the argument of force in its worst form. Recognizing the occasional tyrannies of governing majorities, they amended the Constitution so that free speech and assembly should be guaranteed.

Fear of serious injury cannot alone justify suppression of free speech and assembly. Men feared witches and burnt women. It is the function of speech to free men from the bondage of irrational fears. To justify suppression of free speech, there must be reasonable ground to fear that serious evil will result if free speech is practiced. There must be reasonable ground to believe that the danger apprehended is imminent. There must be reasonable ground to believe that the evil to be prevented is a serious one. Every denunciation of existing law tends in some measure to increase the probability that there will be violation of it. Condonation of a breach enhances the probability. Expressions of approval add to the probability. Propagation of the criminal state of mind by teaching syndicalism increases it. Advocacy of law-breaking heightens it still further. But even advocacy of violation, however reprehensible morally, is not a justification for denying free speech where the advocacy falls short of incitement and there is nothing to indicate that the advocacy would be immediately acted on. The wide difference between advocacy and incitement, between preparation and attempt, between assembling and conspiracy, must be borne in mind. In order to support a finding of clear and present danger, it must be shown either that immediate serious violence was to be expected or was advocated, or that the past conduct furnished reason to believe that such advocacy was then contemplated.

Those who won our independence by revolution were not cowards. They did not fear political change. They did not exalt order at the cost of liberty. To courageous, self-reliant men, with confidence in the power of free and fearless reasoning applied through the processes of popular government, no danger flowing from speech can be deemed clear and present unless the incidence of the evil apprehended is so imminent that it may befall before there is oppor-

tunity for full discussion. If there be time to expose through discussion the falsehood and fallacies, to avert the evil by the processes of education, the remedy to be applied is more speech, not enforced silence. Only an emergency can justify repression. Such must be the rule if authority is to be reconciled with freedom. Such, in my opinion, is the command of the Constitution. It is therefore always open to Americans to challenge a law abridging free speech and assembly by showing that there was no emergency justifying it.

Moreover, even imminent danger cannot justify resort to prohibition of these functions essential to effective democracy unless the evil apprehended is relatively serious. Prohibition of free speech and assembly is a measure so stringent that it would be inappropriate as the means for averting a relatively trivial harm to society. A police measure may be unconstitutional merely because the remedy, although effective as means of protection, is unduly harsh or oppressive. Thus, a State might, in the exercise of its police power, make any trespass upon the land of another a crime, regardless of the results or of the intent or purpose of the trespasser. It might, also, punish an attempt, a conspiracy, or an incitement to commit the trespass. But it is hardly conceivable that this Court would hold constitutional a statute which punished as a felony the mere voluntary assembly with a society formed to teach that pedestrians had the moral right to cross unenclosed, un-posted, wastelands and to advocate their doing so, even if there was imminent danger that advocacy would lead to a trespass. The fact that speech is likely to result in some violence or in destruction of property is not enough to justify its suppression. There must be the probability of serious injury to the State. Among free men, the deterrents ordinarily to be applied to prevent crime are education and punishment for violations of the law, not abridgment of the rights of free speech and assembly.[21]

Are there parallels to be drawn from the Brandeis concurrence and that of Justice Potter Stewart in *New York Times Co. v. United States*? What are the interests each Justice references which hold governmental power in check?

4.   The Smith Act of 1940 (see Chapter 7, Endnote 24) contained an anti-sedition section prohibiting affiliation with any group committed to overthrowing the government. *Dennis v. United States*, 341 U.S. 494 (1951) would uphold a conviction of the General Secretary of the Communist Party of the United States under the Smith Act based on the group's advocacy for the violent overthrow of the government. The Court relied on the *Schenck* "clear and present danger test" but the Court would subsequently limit its ruling several years later. In the 1957 case of *Yates v. United States* the Court held that advocacy of violence against the government did not meet the "clear and present danger" test if it was an abstract concept.[22] The *Yates* Court found the jury instructions provided at the trial were *"intended to withdraw from the jury's consideration, any issue as to the character of the advocacy in terms of its capacity to stir listeners to forcible action."*[23] In its decision the Court said *"[T]he distinction between advocacy of abstract doctrine and advocacy directed at promoting unlawful action is one that has been consistently recognized in the opinions of this Court."*[24] The Court relied on an advocacy

of action test in *Yates*, thereby limiting the application of *Dennis* and setting up for its eventual "imminent lawless action" test in *Brandenburg*.

5. Freedom of association is an implied right protected by the First Amendment. The right is an individual one as well as a group right, protecting membership in labor organizations, political parties, and religious affiliations. The right extends to interpersonal relationships and prohibits attempts to limit membership in a group based on impermissible restrictions such as race. Though the associational right is not explicitly mentioned in the First Amendment it has been inferred from the general protections of the amendment which includes expressive conduct. In *NAACP v. Alabama*, 357 U.S. 449 (1958), the Supreme Court recognized the importance of associational rights, finding that it was an essential due process protection. The facts of *NAACP v. Alabama* involved an attempt by the state's attorney general to prevent the group's affiliate from activities in Alabama. The attorney general applied for an injunction to prevent the NAACP from conducting any activity within the state and to remove it from the state. The complaint cited irreparable harm to the state, which criminal or civil prosecution would not be sufficient to remedy. The group was restrained through an ex parte court order and subsequently fined $100,000.00 for contempt when the *NAACP* refused to submit to the court its membership lists. In a unanimous opinion for the Court Justice Harlan wrote: "*It is beyond debate that freedom to engage in association for the advancement of beliefs and ideas is an inseparable aspect of the 'liberty' assured by the Due Process Clause of the Fourteenth Amendment, which embraces freedom of speech. It is hardly a novel perception that compelled disclosure of affiliation with groups engaged in advocacy may constitute as effective a restraint on freedom of association as the forms of governmental action in the cases above were thought likely to produce upon the particular constitutional rights there involved. This Court has recognized the vital relationship between freedom to associate and privacy in one's associations.*"[25]

    Yet, in a subsequent case the Court took a somewhat different position when it came to the registration of Communist Party affiliated organizations. In 1950, Congress passed the Subversive Activities Control Act (see Chapter 8, commentary note 4), which established communism as a viable threat to national security. The Subversive Activities Control Board was created to decide which groups were communist-action or communist-front organizations and as such required to register under section 7 of the Act. Registration requirements included provision of membership lists. The Supreme Court, in *Communist Party of the United States v. Subversive Activities Control Board*, 367 U.S. 1 (1961), held that the registration requirement of the Act did not infringe upon the First Amendment right of association. The Court cited congressional investigative findings into the spread and dangerous propensity of worldwide communism as the basis for the validity of the Act. Justice Frankfurter, writing for the majority, opined that "*[T]he Communist Party would have us hold that the First Amendment prohibits Congress from requiring the registration and filing of information, including membership lists, by organizations substantially dominated or controlled by the foreign powers controlling the world Communist movement and which operate primarily to advance the objectives of that movement: the overthrow of existing government by any means necessary and the establishment in its place of a Communist totalitarian dictatorship ....* We cannot find such a prohibition in the First Amendment. So to find would make a travesty of that Amendment and the great ends for the well-being of our democracy that it serves."[26] Here the Court's majority was unwillingly to trade government intentions in the interest of national security for individual (or collective) liberty interests.

6. *Scales v. United States*, 367 U.S. 203 (1961), involved a prosecution under the Smith Act's membership clause. In this case the defendant, Junius Scales, was criminally convicted of a felony based on his eight-year membership in the Communist Party of the United States. He challenged the conviction, in part, as a violation of his First Amendment rights. Addressing the First Amendment objection the Court distinguished "per se" membership in the Communist Party, which is protected, from more active participation, which leads to knowing and intentional involvement in criminal activity. Scales's participation was more than passive membership and based on this distinction the Court found in favor of the government. Justice Harlan for the majority wrote: *"the advocacy with which we are here concerned is not constitutionally protected speech, and it was further established that a combination to promote such advocacy, albeit under the aegis of what purports to be a political party, is not such association as is protected by the First Amendment. We can discern no reason why membership, when it constitutes a purposeful form of complicity in a group engaging in this same forbidden advocacy, should receive any greater degree of protection from the guarantees of that Amendment .... The clause does not make criminal all association with an organization which has been shown to engage in illegal advocacy. There must be clear proof that a defendant "specifically intends to accomplish the aims of the organization by resort to violence.".... Thus, the member for whom the organization is a vehicle for the advancement of legitimate aims and policies does not fall within the ban of the statute: he lacks the requisite specific intent "to bring about the overthrow of the government as speedily as circumstances would permit." Such a person may be foolish, deluded, or perhaps merely optimistic, but he is not by this statute made a criminal."*[27] Scales's conviction was upheld. This conviction was not based on any overt criminal act. He did not conspire to overthrow the government. The conviction was justified solely on Scales's membership in the Communist Party of the United States, which had an agenda aimed at the overthrow of the government. Criminal complicity was based on his active membership in the party rather than a "per se" affiliation in name only. Although there may have been no conspiracy entered into by Scales to overthrow the government, there was advocacy of such action evidenced by his Communist Party membership. The Court's decision in *Scales* strained its "advocacy of action" test announced in *Yates*. Although the *Scales* Court did not condone *"blanket prohibition of a group having both legal and illegal aims,"* because that would impair First Amendment rights, it did state that

to punish association with such a group there had to be proof of specific intent to accomplish the group's goals by violence.[28]

7. The development of First Amendment jurisprudence in the 20th century progressed through the First World War and the subsequent communist scare, highlighted by the Palmer Raids in 1919–1920, into the Second World War, the post-war House Un-American Activities Committee's investigation into Hollywood's involvement in communist propaganda, followed by the Cold War era's red scare and the Senate Permanent Sub-Committee on Investigation's Communist hunt in government headed by Wisconsin Senator Joseph McCarthy. First Amendment expressive and associational rights would be severely tested during this latter period. Many would agree that First Amendment protections gave way to fear-mongering and paranoia within government and society. Challenges to the meaning and extent of the protection offered by the First Amendment would continue through the Vietnam War years—as exhibited in this chapter's *New York Times* case. Perhaps the greatest challenge to First Amendment rights, particularly as those rights stand in relation to government power, is in our present post-9/11 society. In the *Humanitarian Law Project* case the Supreme Court approved criminalization of speech advocating lawful, non-violent activity. The case resulted from a challenge to §2339B of the PATRIOT Act, which criminalized "material support" to terrorist organizations. To qualify as "material support" the speech had to be in the form of expert advice or assistance provided in coordination with or under the control of a designated foreign terrorist organization. Criminalization of "material support" passed the Court's "strict scrutiny" standard of judicial review. In his opinion Chief Justice Roberts rejected the government's position that the less rigid "intermediate scrutiny" test should be applied. Under a "strict scrutiny" test the government must show a compelling state interest served by the challenged statute and that the statute is necessary to serve that interest. The *Humanitarian Law Project* Court found such compelling interest in the provisions of §2339B. Criticism within the legal community of the *Humanitarian Law Project* decision has been extensive.[29] At the forefront of the criticism is the Court's position on associational rights which, relegates membership in a group permissible provided there is no meaningful involvement if that group finds itself on a government list.

    Do *Humanitarian Law Project* and the Court's 1961 opinion in *Subversive Activities Control Board* provide sufficient constitutional justification for limiting the exercise of associational rights? Has judicial review in *Humanitarian Law Project* adequately addressed the "strict scrutiny" standard?

8. *Humanitarian Law Project* is the only First Amendment U.S. Supreme Court case to surface in the post-9/11 environment that is in any way connected to the war on terror. As a First Amendment case it deals less with direct speech and more so with associational rights. Still, it remains the only war on terror–related First Amendment case to find its way to the Supreme Court. The historical trajectory of free speech cases has resulted in clearly defined decisional law regarding the protected legal status of speech. What has been

less clear is the implied associational aspect of the right, which the Court has seen fit to regulate more closely in the past. The *Humanitarian Law Project* decision brings that jurisprudence to a new and, many argue, more dangerous level. In criminal law, attempts at crimes and conspiracies to commit crimes are punished though they represent incomplete, incipient, or anticipatory offenses. Part of the rationale for their punishment is the dangerousness exhibited by these offenses—the attempt comes close to completion and thus has to be punished and the conspiracy involves two or more additional actors in the anticipated crime thereby increasing the dangerousness of the purpose. Can this same rationale validly be applied to First Amendment expressive conduct such as in the Court's *Humanitarian Law Project* and other opinions? Should First Amendment associational conduct be entitled to different consideration than speech? To what extent do we permit criminalization of personal associations and expressive conduct in favor of national security?

9. Despite the absence of extensive First Amendment litigation in the Supreme Court emanating from the war on terror there have been a number of lower federal court cases challenging government restrictions on First Amendment rights. These cases have involved issues of access,[30] chilling of speech,[31] and associational rights.[32] Among the First Amendment–related concerns expressed has been the effect of government surveillance on expressive and associational conduct. Data mining, National Security Agency surveillance, and the proliferation of national and state-wide intelligence fusion centers have created an atmosphere of feared Orwellian dimensions where "Big Brother is watching." Litigation challenging the creep of the surveillance state has met with limited results. In the Second Circuit Court of Appeals case *Hedges v. Obama* (referenced in Endnote 33) an appeal and reargument resulted in a 3-0 panel reversal of Judge Forrest's original circuit court opinion and order.[33] The circuit court panel overruled the prior order based on the plaintiff 's lack of standing because they could not show that they would be detained in the future under §1021 of the National Defense Authorization Act. A similar challenge to government conduct alleged to impact First Amendment rights was found in *Laird v. Tatum*, 408 U.S. 1 (1972). *Laird* was a case in which a group of citizens sought declaratory and injunctive relief based on their claim that the Army's domestic surveillance program "chilled" their free speech. Although there was no direct claim of infringement upon their rights the claim was that knowledge of Army surveillance would have the effect of "chilling" speech. The Supreme Court dismissed the claim on grounds of ripeness since the case was not ready for litigation. The Court said the outcome depended on future contingent events that were not yet before the Court and none of the plaintiffs were presently proscribed by any government conduct. In dismissing the claim Chief Justice Burger wrote, "... *the issue presented, namely, whether the jurisdiction of a federal court may be invoked by a complainant who alleges that the exercise of his First Amendment rights is being chilled by the mere existence, without more, of a governmental investigative and data-gathering activity that is alleged to be broader in scope than is reasonably necessary for the accom-*

plishment of a valid governmental purpose ... In recent years, this Court has found in a number of cases that constitutional violations may arise from the deterrent, or 'chilling,' effect of governmental regulations that fall short of a direct prohibition against the exercise of First Amendment rights ... In none of these cases, however, did the chilling effect arise merely from the individual's knowledge that a governmental agency was engaged in certain activities or from the individual's concomitant fear that, armed with the fruits of those activities, the agency might in the future take some other and additional action detrimental to that individual. Rather, in each of these cases, the challenged exercise of governmental power was regulatory, proscriptive, or compulsory in nature, and the complainant was either presently or prospectively subject to the regulations, proscriptions, or compulsions that he was challenging. The respondents do not meet this test; their claim, simply stated, is that they disagree with the judgments made by the Executive Branch with respect to the type and amount of information the Army needs, and that the very existence of the Army's data-gathering system produces a constitutionally impermissible chilling effect upon the exercise of their First Amendment rights. That alleged 'chilling' effect may perhaps be seen as arising from respondents' very perception of the system as inappropriate to the Army's role under our form of government, or as arising from respondents' beliefs that it is inherently dangerous for the military to be concerned with activities in the civilian sector, or as arising from respondents' less generalized yet speculative apprehensiveness that the Army may at some future date misuse the information in some way that would cause direct harm to respondents.'[84]* Recently, in the case of *Clapper v. Amnesty International USA*, 133 S.Ct. 1138 (2013), the Court, once again, ruled in favor of the government owing to plaintiff's lack of standing. Amnesty International sought to challenge sections of the Foreign Intelligence Surveillance Act (FISA), which allowed electronic surveillance of foreign agents without probable cause. Reversal of the Second Circuit's finding of standing was based on the plaintiff's speculative claims without any concrete evidence of direct impact upon them *("We hold that respondents lack Article III standing because they cannot demonstrate that the future injury they purportedly fear is certainly impending and because they cannot manufacture standing by incurring costs in anticipation of non-imminent harm."[85])* Clapper was subsequently cited by Judge Lewis Kaplan in his opinion for the 3-0 panel decision in *Hedges v. Obama*.

Endnotes

[1]   Stone, G. (2004). *Perilous Times: Free Speech in Wartime from the Sedition Act of 1798 to the War on Terrorism.* New York: W.W. Norton, p. 63.

[2]   Rehnquist, W. H. (2000). *All The Laws But One: Civil Liberties in Wartime.* New York: Vintage Press, pp. 47–48.

[3]   Id. at 60.

[4]   Id. at 65.

[5]   See e.g., Curtis, M. K. (1998). Lincoln, Vallandigham and Anti-War Speech in the Civil War. *William and Mary Bill of Rights Journal*, 105–191.

[6]   Chapter 30, Title I §3, 40 Stat. 217, 219.

[7]   Although negative comments about the flag were considered seditious activity under the 1918 amendments and the United States Supreme Court subsequently upheld the constitutionality of the Espionage Act of 1917 and the amendments referred to in the Sedition Act of 1918, the Court's First Amendment evolution would reach its zenith in 1989 with the case of *Texas v. Johnson*. In *Texas v. Johnson*, 491 U.S. 397 (1989) the Court held that desecration of the flag is a form of speech protected by the First Amendment. As a means of protesting the policies of the Reagan administration Gregory Lee Johnson burned the flag on the steps of Dallas City Hall in 1984. He was arrested, tried, and convicted under a Texas statute outlawing flag desecration. Justice William Brennan writing for the 5-4 majority found that the actions of Johnson were expressive of a political nature and protected, no matter how offensive the public may find those actions.

[8]   249 at 51.

[9]   Id.

[10]   249 at 52.

[11]   249 U.S. at 208.

[12]   250 U.S. at 621.

[13]   205 U.S. 454 (1907).

[14]   For a fuller history of the "bad tendency" test as applied to the Espionage Act see, "The Origins of the Bad Tendency Test: Free Speech in Wartime," Geoffrey Stone, *The Supreme Court Review*, Volume 2002, pp. 411–453.

[15]   Blackstone, William. *Commentaries on the Laws of England: A Facsimile of the First Edition of 1765–1769*. Chicago: University of Chicago Press, 1979. Commentaries 4:150–153.

[16]   268 U.S. at 254.

[17]   Id.

[18]   268 U.S. at 664.

[19]   268 U.S. at 666.

[20]   See e.g., concurring opinion of Justice Douglas in *Samuels v. Mackell*, 401 U.S. 66 (1971) wherein he wrote, *"Gitlow and its progeny, including Whitney v. California, 274 U.S. 357, went into the discard with our decision in Brandenburg v. Ohio."*

[21]   274 U.S. at 375–8.

[22]   354 U.S. 298 (1957).

[23]   Id. at 315.

[24]   Id. at 318.

[25]   357 U.S. at 460–461.

[26]   367 U.S. at 88.

[27]   367 U.S. at 228-229.

[28]   Id. at 229.

[29]   See e.g., the following law review articles: Chesney, R. (2010). "The Supreme Court, Material Support and the Lasting Impact of Holder v. Humanitarian Law Project." *Wake Forest Law Review Forum*, 13–19; Cole, D. (2012). "The First Amendment's Borders: The Place of Holder v. Humanitarian Law Project in First Amendment Doctrine. *Harvard Law & Policy Review*", 147–177; Inazu, J. D. (2013). Advocacy and Association. *Utah Law Review*, 120–123; Said, W. E. (2011). Humanitarian Law Project and the Supreme Court's Construction of Terrorism. *Brigham Young University Law Review*, 1455–1508.

[30]   See e.g., Detroit Free Press v. Ashcroft, 303 F. 3d 681 (6th Cir. 2002)—where media, defendant, and U.S. representative successfully sued to gain access to immigration hearings that had been closed to the public and the press; but cf.—*North Jersey Media Group v. Ashcroft*, 308 F.3d 198 (3rd Cir. 2002) where the circuit court of appeals decided in favor of the government due to the administrative nature of immigration proceedings.

[31]   See e.g., *Muslim Community Association of Ann Arbor v. Ashcroft*, ED Mich., 459 F. Supp. 592 (2006)—American Civil Liberties Union lawsuit challenging §215 of the PATRIOT Act on First Amendment grounds of prohibiting exercise of free speech and having chilling effect; suit withdrawn by ACLU after Congress revised portions of the PATRIOT Act.

[32]   See e.g., *Hedges v. Obama*, 2012 U.S. App. LEXIS 19880 (2d Cir., 2012)—journalists sued the president and members of Congress over the National Defense Authorization Act for Fiscal Year 2012 and its provision allowing indefinite detention of persons supporting al-Qaeda, the Taliban or other terrorist organizations in conflict with the United States. The journalists argued that the provision affected their reporting ability because by meeting with sources, even those in direct arms against the U.S., in order to obtain a story they could be subject to detention. They claimed this infringed on their First Amendment right as reporters. Judge Katherine Forrest issued a 112- page opinion and order striking down the controversial provision, §1021(b)(2). Her ruling was overturned by a panel of the Second Circuit Court of Appeals in 2013.

[33]   See, 2013 U.S. App. LEXIS 14417 (2d. Cir., 2013).

[34]   408 U.S. at 10–11, 13.

[35]   133 S.Ct. at 1155.

Chapter Ten
SEARCH, SURVEILLANCE & INTERROGATION

Fourth and Fifth Amendment Concerns

Prior chapters have explored various constitutional dimensions to national security within a legal and historical perspective. If there is one constant to the study of these legal issues it is that they are not static but subject to change and development in accordance with the prevailing time and political environment. Each challenge to domestic security that our country faced has been met with responses that, at the time, were considered in the best interest of the country. Hindsight provides us with the view that this was not always the case for certain portions of the population, as Chapter 8 makes clear, or that certain freedoms slowly developed over time to their full realization, as the previous chapter on the First Amendment indicates. Nonetheless, we can be certain that the law does not exist in a vacuum. Even though our common law tradition is based on the lasting value and definiteness of precedent, it is not immutable; the law still takes breath from the events of the day. The concerns of the 18th century United States are not remotely those of its 21st century descendants, yet we rely on the bedrock principles formulated by our distant forebears. Ancient legal principles do survive over time and may have a place in the modern world—a case in point is Justice Scalia's reference in the 2012 case *United States v. Jones* to an 18th century government trespass case, *Entick v. Carrington*, to exclude on Fourth Amendment grounds certain evidence obtained from electronic surveillance using global positioning systems. Such continuing legal vitality has also been exemplified by the renewed interest in the Civil War habeas corpus cases of *Merryman*, *Milligan* and *Vallandigham* (Chapter 3) in response to detention litigation resulting from the war on terror. The challenges faced by our representative democracy are ever changing and the post-9/11 war on terror has introduced a new paradigm of warfare wherein the external threats to national security have encroached upon the homeland. The reality of distant wars remains but the new paradigm introduces not only the threat from nation-states but also coalesced groups united by ideology. Does this change the conversation relating to national security? Perhaps, but it is no different from the threats the country faced from anarchists in the early part of the 20th century. However, this new paradigm has also impacted domestic law enforcement and expanded its mission in relation to national security. A 2010 report by the RAND Institute, *Long-term Effects of Law Enforcement's Post-9/11 Focus on Counterterrorism and Homeland Security*, cited this change: *"The continued threat of terrorism has thrust domestic preparedness obligations to the very top of the law enforcement agenda .... [T]his capacity must be considered as much a staple of law enforcement operations as crime analysis, criminal intelligence, and crime prevention."*[1] This domestic preparedness must of course be carefully balanced with individual and collective liberty interests. Fourth Amendment considerations have extended beyond simple government physical trespass upon property. Technology has rapidly advanced providing greater government access to information in a digitally dependent world. Government agents have the ability to remotely monitor an individual's movements, as exhibited in the facts of the *Jones* case. Resolution of that case relied on the simple concept of trespass to property, thereby avoiding the more difficult and critical issue regarding electronic surveillance. But in the future the Court will have to confront the more difficult Fourth Amendment questions raised by technology and the extent of personal privacy protections. Beyond that remains the issue of terror-related investigations and the Fourth Amendment's role as shield from overbearing government intrusion. Is there an exception when it comes to terror-related investigations? Past Supreme Court cases hint there may be.[2] In separate dissents in *Illinois v. Caballes*[3] Justices Ginsburg and Souter criticized what they viewed as an impermissible search—a dog sniff of the exterior of a stopped vehicle that extended beyond the initial purpose of the stop. But both justices indicated the same dog sniff could be justified if the facts were different, such as an "imminent terrorist attack"[4] or to "detect explosives and dangerous chemical or biological weapons that might be carried by a terrorist."[5] Similarly, Justice O'Connor's opinion in *Indianapolis v. Edmond*,[6] issued five years before Justice Ginsburg's *Caballes* dissent, said a roadway checkpoint to "thwart an imminent terrorist attack" would likely be permissible under the Fourth Amendment.[7] Lower courts have also recognized a rationale, if not exactly an outright exception, to the Fourth Amendment's warrant requirement based on terrorism related law enforcement needs. In *MacWade v. Kelly*[8] the Second Circuit Court of Appeals approved the random search of passengers' bags and other containers at New York City subway stations based on special needs related to deterring a terrorist attack. The First Circuit Court of Appeals in *United States v. Ramos*[9] held that a terrorism alert and the specialized training of officers justified the stop of a van at a commuter bus and rail station. Terrorist-related concerns were the basis of a federal district court granting summary judgment based on qualified immunity for federal agents who transported a forcibly stopped individual to a secure facility for fingerprinting and identification purposes.[10] These cases do not circumvent Fourth Amendment protections but rather extend the concept of reasonableness in light of new national security and law enforcement paradigm.

The Fourth Amendment has been covered in prior chapters on habeas corpus, detention, and rendition, but that coverage does not dent the extent of relevant case law. The law is a movable whole and as much as we may try to compartmentalize subject areas the relevance of seemingly unconnected cases cannot be overlooked. The case of *United States v. Verdugo-Urquidez*, 494 U.S. 259 (1990), is a good example. In *Verdugo-Urquidez* the Supreme Court held that Fourth Amendment protections do not apply to foreign nationals in a foreign country. The case resulted from an investigation into the torture and murder in Mexico of DEA agent Enrique Camarena Salazar. Verdugo-Urquidez was a leader of the drug cartel responsible for Salazar's murder. He was arrested in Mexico by Mexican police officers and turned over to the U.S. Border Patrol at the station in Calexico, California. After Verdugo-Urquidez' involuntary removal from Mexico a DEA agent arranged to search his residences in Mexicali and San Felipe.[11] Authorization to search was granted by the Director General of the Mexican Federal Judicial Police and a subsequent search, conducted alongside Mexican police officers, revealed evidence of marijuana smuggling.[12] The defendant moved at trial to suppress the evidence gathered from the search of his Mexican residences. The district court suppressed the evidence and the Ninth Circuit Court of Appeals affirmed. On appeal to the Supreme Court Chief Justice Rehnquist, writing for the 6-3 majority, said the reference to "people" in the text of the Fourth Amendment *"refers to a class of persons who are part of a national community or who have otherwise developed sufficient connection with this country to be considered part of that community."*[13] Verdugo-Urquidez, despite his involuntary presence in the United States, did not have sufficient connection to obtain the benefits of Fourth Amendment protection unless it was through diplomatic means, treaty, or legislation. This case, decided in connection with a criminal drug case (and during a time period when the government was engaged in a "war" of a different sort, the "war on drugs," which engendered its own array of Fourth Amendment literature), certainly has significance for U.S. global law enforcement and national security operations in rooting out terrorism.

What about Fifth Amendment rights within a similar context? Do they apply? In his *Verdugo-Urquidez* opinion Chief Justice Rehnquist distinguished the Fourth Amendment rights at issue in the case from Fifth Amendment protections which he distinguished as trial rights; however, he did reference prior Court decisions where extension of Fifth Amendment rights outside the "sovereign territory of the United States" were also rejected. Aside from this general statement regarding the Fifth Amendment rights against self-incrimination there remains an unanswered question—would a non-citizen terror suspect captured in a foreign country who provided a compelled statement to law enforcement be able to assert the Fifth Amendment protection against self-incrimination? Two lower federal court cases, discussed later, indicate that the alien suspect could assert the right because it is a trial right belonging to an "accused" individual.

Chavez v. Martinez has a different result when the protections of the Fifth Amendment are not invoked at trial. The impact of *Chavez* and the broader implications of the Court's more recent *Miranda* related jurisprudence have to be considered within the scope of the terrorism investigation landscape. But the debate continues as to whether extraterritorial application of the Fifth Amendment's self-incrimination clause should apply to foreign terror suspects, and within that debate is the issue of whether terrorism is treated as a crime or war-like behavior. President Bush's November 13, 2001 military order, *Detention, Treatment and Trial of Certain Non-Citizens in the War on Terror*, placed terrorism in the war category and limited the procedural rights of terror suspects who would be subject to military commissions rather than Article III courts.[14] Interrogation of terror suspects and "enemy combatants" was guided by a series of memorandums authored in 2002 by Office of Legal Counsel Deputy Assistant Attorney General John Yoo. Office of Legal Counsel Assistant Attorney General Jay Bybee subsequently submitted to President Bush a 50-page memorandum offering justifications for using torture as an interrogation method. Release of these memos brought condemnation within the United States and the international legal community. President Obama released the interrogation memos, written between 2002–2005, in 2009 during the first year of his first term in office and in doing so harshly criticized the policy of the Bush administration for interrogation of high-value detainees. Yet, President Obama's position on *Miranda* protections would eventually come under similar harsh criticism. In a 2010 memorandum the Justice Department, with President Obama's approval, established a policy of delaying *Miranda* warnings for domestic terror suspects.[15] Although the Supreme Court has not determined the status of extraterritorial application of *Miranda* real world events push the question to the forefront of the *Miranda* debate. Within that same debate is the question of whether *Miranda* warnings should be read to domestic terror suspects who are citizens.

Justice Felix Frankfurter once wrote, *"Law triumphs when the natural impulses aroused by a shocking crime yield to the safeguards which our civilization has evolved for an administration of justice at once rational and effective."*[16] This statement closed a majority opinion of the Court excluding a confession resulting from the harsh interrogation of a murder suspect involving solitary confinement, sleeping on the floor and abusive relay questioning by police officers. In finding the due process clause did not sustain such conduct Justice Frankfurter pointed to the historical antecedents of due process: *"In holding that the Due Process Clause bars police procedure which violates the basic notions of our accusatorial mode of prosecuting crime and vitiates a conviction based on the fruits of such procedure, we apply the Due Process Clause to its historic function of assuring appropriate procedure before liberty is curtailed or life is taken. We are deeply mindful of the anguishing problems which the incidence of crime presents to the States. But the history of the criminal law proves overwhelmingly that brutal methods of law enforcement are essentially self-defeating, whatever may be their effect in a particular case."*[17] His words are no less significant today as the country responds to the global threat of terrorism. However, the legal dilemma is what process is actually due a terror suspect committed to destroying the very government from which he may seek legal safe harbor upon capture. The debate remains open.

United States v. United States District Court
407 U.S. 297 (1972)

Mr. Justice Powell delivered the opinion of the Court.

The issue before us is an important one for the people of our country and their Government. It involves the delicate question of the President's power, acting through the Attorney General, to authorize electronic surveillance in internal security matters without prior judicial approval. Successive Presidents for more than one-quarter of a century have authorized such surveillance in varying degrees, without guidance from the Congress or a definitive decision of this Court. This case brings the issue here for the first time. Its resolution is a matter of national concern, requiring sensitivity both to the Government's right to protect itself from unlawful subversion and attack and to the citizen's right to be secure in his privacy against unreasonable Government intrusion.

This case arises from a criminal proceeding in the United States District Court for the Eastern District of Michigan, in which the United States charged three defendants with conspiracy to destroy Government property in violation of 18 U.S.C. § 371. One of the defendants, Plamondon, was charged with the dynamite bombing of an office of the Central Intelligence Agency in Ann Arbor, Michigan.

During pretrial proceedings, the defendants moved to compel the United States to disclose certain electronic surveillance information and to conduct a hearing to determine whether this information "tainted" the evidence on which the indictment was based or which the Government intended to offer at trial. In response, the Government filed an affidavit of the Attorney General, acknowledging that its agents had overheard conversations in which Plamondon had participated. The affidavit also stated that the Attorney General approved the wiretaps to gather intelligence information deemed necessary to protect the nation from attempts of domestic organizations to attack and subvert the existing structure of the Government.

The logs of the surveillance were filed in a sealed exhibit for *in camera* inspection by the District Court.

On the basis of the Attorney General's affidavit and the sealed exhibit, the Government asserted that the surveillance was lawful, though conducted without prior judicial approval, as a reasonable exercise of the President's power (exercised through the Attorney General) to protect the national security. The District Court held that the surveillance violated the Fourth Amendment, and ordered the Government to make full disclosure to Plamondon of his overheard conversations.

The Government then filed in the Court of Appeals for the Sixth Circuit a petition for a writ of mandamus to set aside the District Court order, which was stayed pending final disposition of the case. After concluding that it had jurisdiction, that court held that the surveillance was unlawful, and that the District Court had properly required disclosure of the overheard conversations. We granted certiorari.

I

Title III of the Omnibus Crime Control and Safe Streets Act, 18 U.S.C. §§ 2510-2520, authorizes the use of electronic surveillance for classes of crimes carefully specified in 18 U.S.C. § 2516. Such surveillance is subject to prior court order. Section 2518 sets forth the detailed and particularized application necessary to obtain such an order, as well as carefully circumscribed conditions for its use. The Act represents a comprehensive attempt by Congress to promote more effective control of crime while protecting the privacy of individual thought and expression. Much of Title III was drawn to meet the constitutional

requirements for electronic surveillance enunciated by this Court in
Berger v. New York, 388 U.S. 41 (1967), and **Katz v. United States**, 389
U.S. 347 (1967).

Together with the elaborate surveillance requirements in Title III,
there is the following proviso, 18 U.S.C. § 2511(3):

> "Nothing contained in this chapter or in section 605 of the
> Communications Act of 1934 (48 Stat. 1143; 47 U.S.C. 605) shall limit
> the constitutional power of the President to take such measures as
> he deems necessary to protect the Nation against actual or
> potential attack or other hostile acts of a foreign power, to obtain
> foreign intelligence information deemed essential to the security
> of the United States, or to protect national security information
> against foreign intelligence activities. *Nor shall anything contained
> in this chapter be deemed to limit the constitutional power of the
> President to take such measures as he deems necessary to protect
> the United States against the overthrow of the Government by
> force or other unlawful means, or against any other clear and
> present danger to the structure or existence of the Government.*
> The contents of any wire or oral communication intercepted by
> authority of the President in the exercise of the foregoing powers
> may be received in evidence in any trial hearing, or other
> proceeding only where such interception was reasonable, and
> shall not be otherwise used or disclosed except as is necessary to
> implement that power." (Emphasis supplied.)

The Government relies on § 2511(3). It argues that, in excepting
national security surveillances from the Act's warrant requirement,
Congress recognized the President's authority to conduct such
surveillances without prior judicial approval. The section thus is viewed
as a recognition or affirmance of a constitutional authority in the
President to conduct warrantless domestic security surveillance such
as that involved in this case.

We think the language of § 2511(3), as well as the legislative history
of the statute, refutes this interpretation. The relevant language is that:
"Nothing contained in this chapter ... shall limit the constitutional
power of the President to take such measures as he deems necessary
to protect ... against the dangers specified." At most, this is an implicit
recognition that the President does have certain powers in the
specified areas. Few would doubt this, as the section refers—among
other things—to protection "against actual or potential attack or
other hostile acts of a foreign power." But so far as the use of the
President's electronic surveillance power is concerned, the language
is essentially neutral.

Section 2511(3) certainly confers no power, as the language is
wholly inappropriate for such a purpose. It merely provides that the
Act shall not be interpreted to limit or disturb such power as the

President may have under the Constitution. In short, Congress simply left presidential powers where it found them. This view is reinforced by the general context of Title III. Section 2511(1) broadly prohibits the use of electronic surveillance "[e]xcept as otherwise specifically provided in this chapter." Subsection (2) thereof contains four specific exceptions. In each of the specified exceptions, the statutory language is as follows: "It shall not be unlawful ... to intercept" the particular type of communication described.

The language of subsection (3), here involved, is to be contrasted with the language of the exceptions set forth in the preceding subsection. Rather than stating that warrantless presidential uses of electronic surveillance "shall not be unlawful," and thus employing the standard language of exception, subsection (3) merely disclaims any intention to "limit the constitutional power of the President." The express grant of authority to conduct surveillances is found in § 2516, which authorizes the Attorney General to make application to a federal judge when surveillance may provide evidence of certain offenses. These offenses are described with meticulous care and specificity.

Where the Act authorizes surveillance, the procedure to be followed is specified in § 2518. Subsection (1) thereof requires application to a judge of competent jurisdiction for a prior order of approval, and states in detail the information required in such application. Subsection (3) prescribes the necessary elements of probable cause which the judge must find before issuing an order authorizing an interception. Subsection (4) sets forth the required contents of such an order. Subsection (5) sets strict time limits on an order. Provision is made in subsection (7) for "an emergency situation" found to exist by the Attorney General (or by the principal prosecuting attorney of a State) "with respect to conspiratorial activities threatening the national security interest." In such a situation, emergency surveillance may be conducted "if an application for an order approving the interception is made ... within forty-eight hours." If such an order is not obtained, or the application therefor is denied, the interception is deemed to be a violation of the Act.

In view of these and other interrelated provisions delineating permissible interceptions of particular criminal activity upon carefully specified conditions, it would have been incongruous for Congress to have legislated with respect to the important and complex area of national security in a single brief and nebulous paragraph. This would not comport with the sensitivity of the problem involved, or with the extraordinary care Congress exercised in drafting other sections of the Act. We therefore think the conclusion inescapable that Congress only intended to make clear that the Act simply did not legislate with respect to national security surveillances.

***

If we could accept the Government's characterization of § 2511(3) as a congressionally prescribed exception to the general requirement of a warrant, it would be necessary to consider the question of whether the surveillance in this case came within the exception, and, if so, whether the statutory exception was itself constitutionally valid. But viewing § 2511(3) as a congressional disclaimer and expression of neutrality, we hold that the statute is not the measure of the executive authority asserted in this case. Rather, we must look to the constitutional powers of the President.

II

It is important at the outset to emphasize the limited nature of the question before the Court. This case raises no constitutional challenge to electronic surveillance as specifically authorized by Title III of the Omnibus Crime Control and Safe Streets Act of 1968. Nor is there any question or doubt as to the necessity of obtaining a warrant in the surveillance of crimes unrelated to the national security interest. **Katz v. United States**, 389 U.S. 347 (1967); **Berger v. New York**, 388 U.S. 41 (1967). Further, the instant case requires no judgment on the scope of the President's surveillance power with respect to the activities of foreign powers, within or without this country. The Attorney General's affidavit in this case states that the surveillances were "deemed necessary to protect the nation from attempts of domestic organizations to attack and subvert the existing structure of Government" (emphasis supplied). There is no evidence of any involvement, directly or indirectly, of a foreign power.

Our present inquiry, though important, is therefore a narrow one. It addresses a question left open by **Katz**, supra, at 358 n. 23: Whether safeguards other than prior authorization by a magistrate would satisfy the Fourth Amendment in a situation involving the national security ...

The determination of this question requires the essential Fourth Amendment inquiry into the "reasonableness" of the search and seizure in question, and the way in which that "reasonableness" derives content and meaning through reference to the warrant clause. **Coolidge v. New Hampshire**, 403 U.S. 443, 473-484 (1971).

We begin the inquiry by noting that the President of the United States has the fundamental duty, under Art. II, § 1, of the Constitution, to "preserve, protect and defend the Constitution of the United States." Implicit in that duty is the power to protect our Government against those who would subvert or overthrow it by unlawful means. In the discharge of this duty, the President—through the Attorney General—may find it necessary to employ electronic surveillance to obtain intelligence information on the plans of those who plot unlawful acts against the Government. The use of such surveillance in internal security cases has been sanctioned more or less continuously by various Presidents and Attorneys General since July,

1946. Herbert Brownell, Attorney General under President Eisenhower, urged the use of electronic surveillance both in internal and international security matters on the grounds that those acting against the Government turn to the telephone to carry on their intrigue. The success of their plans frequently rests upon piecing together shreds of information received from many sources and many nests. The participants in the conspiracy are often dispersed and stationed in various strategic positions in government and industry throughout the country.

Though the Government and respondents debate their seriousness and magnitude, threats and acts of sabotage against the Government exist in sufficient number to justify investigative powers with respect to them. The covertness and complexity of potential unlawful conduct against the Government and the necessary dependency of many conspirators upon the telephone make electronic surveillance an effective investigatory instrument in certain circumstances. The marked acceleration in technological developments and sophistication in their use have resulted in new techniques for the planning, commission, and concealment of criminal activities. It would be contrary to the public interest for Government to deny to itself the prudent and lawful employment of those very techniques which are employed against the Government and its law-abiding citizens.

It has been said that "[t]he most basic function of any government is to provide for the security of the individual and of his property." *Miranda v. Arizona*, 384 U.S. 436, 539 (1966) (White, J., dissenting). And unless Government safeguards its own capacity to function and to preserve the security of its people, society itself could become so disordered that all rights and liberties would be endangered. As Chief Justice Hughes reminded us in *Cox v. New Hampshire*, 312 U.S. 569, 574 (1941): Civil liberties, as guaranteed by the Constitution, imply the existence of an organized society maintaining public order without which liberty itself would be lost in the excesses of unrestrained abuses.

But a recognition of these elementary truths does not make the employment by Government of electronic surveillance a welcome development—even when employed with restraint and under judicial supervision. There is, understandably, a deep-seated uneasiness and apprehension that this capability will be used to intrude upon cherished privacy of law-abiding citizens. We look to the Bill of Rights to safeguard this privacy. Though physical entry of the home is the chief evil against which the wording of the Fourth Amendment is directed, its broader spirit now shields private speech from unreasonable surveillance. *Katz v. United States*, *supra*; *Berger v. New York*, *supra*; *Silverman v. United States*, 365 U.S. 505 (1961). Our decision in *Katz* refused to lock the Fourth Amendment into instances of actual physical trespass. Rather, the Amendment governs not only the seizure of tangible items, but extends as well to the recording of oral statements ... without any "technical trespass under ... local property law." *Katz*, *supra*, at 353. That decision implicitly recognized that the broad and unsuspected governmental incursions into conversational privacy which electronic surveillance entails necessitate the application of Fourth Amendment safeguards. National security cases, moreover, often reflect a convergence of First and Fourth Amendment values not present in cases of "ordinary" crime. Though the investigative duty of the executive may be stronger in such cases, so also is there greater jeopardy to constitutionally protected speech.

Historically, the struggle for freedom of speech and press in England was bound up with the issue of the scope of the search and seizure power, ***Marcus v. Search Warrant***, 367 U.S. 717, 724 (1961). History abundantly documents the tendency of Government—however benevolent and benign its motive—to view with suspicion those who most fervently dispute its policies. Fourth Amendment protections become the more necessary when the targets of official surveillance may be those suspected of unorthodoxy in their political beliefs. The danger to political dissent is acute where the Government attempts to act under so vague a concept as the power to protect "domestic security." Given the difficulty of defining the domestic security interest, the danger of abuse in acting to protect that interest becomes apparent ...

The price of lawful public dissent must not be a dread of subjection to an unchecked surveillance power. Nor must the fear of unauthorized official eavesdropping deter vigorous citizen dissent and discussion of Government action in private conversation. For private dissent, no less than open public discourse, is essential to our free society.

III

As the Fourth Amendment is not absolute in its terms, our task is to examine and balance the basic values at stake in this case: the duty of Government to protect the domestic security, and the potential danger posed by unreasonable surveillance to individual privacy and free expression. If the legitimate need of Government to safeguard domestic security requires the use of electronic surveillance, the question is whether the needs of citizens for privacy and free expression may not be better protected by requiring a warrant before such surveillance is undertaken. We must also ask whether a warrant requirement would unduly frustrate the efforts of Government to protect itself from acts of subversion and overthrow directed against it.

Though the Fourth Amendment speaks broadly of "unreasonable searches and seizures," the definition of "reasonableness" turns, at least in part, on the more specific commands of the warrant clause. Some have argued that "[t]he relevant test is not whether it is reasonable to procure a search warrant, but whether the search was reasonable," **United States v. Rabinowitz**, 339 U.S. 56, 66 (1950). This view, however, overlooks the second clause of the Amendment. The warrant clause of the Fourth Amendment is not dead language. Rather, it has been a valued part of our constitutional law for decades, and it has determined the result in scores and scores of cases in courts all over this country. It is not an inconvenience to be somehow "weighed" against the claims of police efficiency. It is, or should be, an important working part of our machinery of government, operating as a matter of course to check the "well-intentioned but mistakenly overzealous executive officers" who are a part of any system of law enforcement. **Coolidge v. New Hampshire**, 403 U.S. at 481. See also **United States v. Rabinowitz**, supra, at 68 (Frankfurter, J., dissenting); **Davis v. United States**, 328 U.S. 582, 604 (1946) (Frankfurter, J., dissenting).

... Inherent in the concept of a warrant is its issuance by a "neutral and detached magistrate." **Coolidge v. New Hampshire**, supra, at 453; **Katz v. United States**, supra, at 356. The further requirement of "probable cause" instructs the magistrate that baseless searches shall not proceed.

These Fourth Amendment freedoms cannot properly be guaranteed if domestic security surveillances may be conducted solely within the discretion of the Executive Branch. The Fourth Amendment does not contemplate the executive officers of Government as neutral and disinterested magistrates. Their duty and responsibility are to enforce the laws, to investigate, and to prosecute. **Katz v. United States**, supra, at 359-360 (Douglas, J., concurring). But those charged with this investigative and prosecutorial duty should not be the sole judges of when to utilize constitutionally sensitive means in pursuing their tasks. The historical judgment, which the Fourth Amendment accepts, is that un-reviewed executive discretion may yield too readily to pressures to obtain incriminating evidence and overlook potential invasions of privacy and protected speech.

It may well be that, in the instant case, the Government's surveillance of Plamondon's conversations was a reasonable one which readily would have gained prior judicial approval. But this Court has never sustained a search upon the sole ground that officers reasonably expected to find evidence of a particular crime and voluntarily confined their activities to the least intrusive means consistent with that end. **Katz**, supra, at 356-357. The Fourth Amendment contemplates a prior judicial judgment, not the risk that executive discretion may be reasonably exercised. This judicial role accords with our basic constitutional doctrine that individual freedoms will best be preserved through a separation of powers and division of functions among the different branches and levels of Government. Harlan, Thoughts at a Dedication: Keeping the Judicial Function in Balance, 49 A.B.A.J. 943-944 (1963). The independent check upon executive discretion is not satisfied, as the Government argues, by "extremely limited" post-surveillance judicial review. Indeed, post-surveillance review would never reach the surveillances which failed to result in prosecutions. Prior review by a neutral and detached magistrate is the time-tested means of effectuating Fourth Amendment rights. *Beck v. Ohio*, 379 U.S. 89, 96 (1964).

It is true that there have been some exceptions to the warrant requirement. *Chimel v. California*, 395 U.S. 752 (1969); *Terry v. Ohio*, 392 U.S. 1 (1968); *McDonald v. United States*, 335 U.S. 451 (1948); *Carroll v. United States*, 267 U.S. 132 (1925). But those exceptions are few in number, and carefully delineated, *Katz*, supra, at 357; in general, they serve the legitimate needs of law enforcement officers to protect their own wellbeing and preserve evidence from destruction. Even while carving out those exceptions, the Court has reaffirmed the principle that the "police must, whenever practicable, obtain advance judicial approval of searches and seizures through the warrant procedure," *Terry v. Ohio*, supra, at 20; *Chimel v. California*, supra, at 762.

The Government argues that the special circumstances applicable to domestic security surveillances necessitate a further exception to the warrant requirement. It is urged that the requirement of prior judicial review would obstruct the President in the discharge of his constitutional duty to protect domestic security. We are told further that these surveillances are directed primarily to the collecting and maintaining of intelligence with respect to subversive forces, and are not an attempt to gather evidence for specific criminal prosecutions. It is said that this type of surveillance should not be subject to traditional warrant requirements which were established to govern investigation of criminal activity, not ongoing intelligence gathering.

The Government further insists that courts as a practical matter would have neither the knowledge nor the techniques necessary to determine whether there was probable cause to believe that surveillance was necessary to protect national security. These security problems, the Government contends, involve "a large number of complex and subtle factors" beyond the competence of courts to evaluate.

As a final reason for exemption from a warrant requirement, the Government believes that disclosure to a magistrate of all or even a significant portion of the information involved in domestic security surveillances would create serious potential dangers to the national security and to the lives of informants and agents.... Secrecy is the essential ingredient in intelligence gathering; requiring prior judicial authorization would create a greater "danger of leaks ... because, in addition to the judge, you have the clerk, the stenographer and some other officer like a law assistant or bailiff who may be apprised of the nature" of the surveillance.

These contentions in behalf of a complete exemption from the warrant requirement, when urged on behalf of the President and the national security in its domestic implications, merit the most careful consideration. We certainly do not reject them lightly, especially at a time of worldwide ferment and when civil disorders in this country are more prevalent than in the less turbulent periods of our history. There is, no doubt, pragmatic force to the Government's position.

But we do not think a case has been made for the requested departure from Fourth Amendment standards. The circumstances described do not justify complete exemption of domestic security surveillance from prior judicial scrutiny. Official surveillance, whether its purpose be criminal investigation or ongoing intelligence gathering, risks infringement of constitutionally protected privacy of speech. Security surveillances are especially sensitive because of the inherent vagueness of the domestic security concept, the necessarily broad and continuing nature of intelligence gathering, and the temptation to utilize such surveillances to oversee political dissent. We recognize, as we have before, the constitutional basis of the President's domestic security role, but we think it must be exercised in a manner compatible with the Fourth Amendment. In this case, we hold that this requires an appropriate prior warrant procedure.

We cannot accept the Government's argument that internal security matters are too subtle and complex for judicial evaluation. Courts regularly deal with the most difficult issues of our society. There is no reason to believe that federal judges will be insensitive to or uncomprehending of the issues involved in domestic security cases. Certainly courts can recognize that domestic security surveillance involves different considerations from the surveillance of "ordinary crime." If the threat is too subtle or complex for our senior law enforcement officers to convey its significance to a court, one may question whether there is probable cause for surveillance.

Nor do we believe prior judicial approval will fracture the secrecy essential to official intelligence gathering. The investigation of criminal activity has long involved imparting sensitive information to judicial officers who have respected the confidentialities involved. Judges may be counted upon to be especially conscious of security requirements in national security cases. Title III of the Omnibus Crime Control and Safe Streets Act already has imposed this responsibility on the judiciary in connection with such crimes as espionage, sabotage, and treason, §§ 2516(1)(a) and (c), each of which may involve domestic as well as foreign security threats. Moreover, a warrant application involves no public or adversary proceedings: it is an ex parte request before a magistrate or judge. Whatever security dangers clerical and secretarial personnel may pose can be minimized by proper administrative measures, possibly to the point of allowing the Government itself to provide the necessary clerical assistance.

Thus, we conclude that the Government's concerns do not justify departure in this case from the customary Fourth Amendment requirement of judicial approval prior to initiation of a search or surveillance. Although some added burden will be imposed upon the Attorney General, this inconvenience is justified in a free society to protect constitutional values. Nor do we think the Government's domestic surveillance powers will be impaired to any significant degree. A prior warrant establishes presumptive validity of the surveillance and will minimize the burden of justification in post-surveillance judicial review. By no means of least importance will be the reassurance of the public generally that indiscriminate wiretapping and bugging of law-abiding citizens cannot occur.

IV

We emphasize, before concluding this opinion, the scope of our decision. As stated at the outset, this case involves only the domestic aspects of national security. We have not addressed, and express no opinion as to, the issues which may be involved with respect to activities of foreign powers or their agents. Nor does our decision rest on the language of § 2511(3) or any other section of Title III of the Omnibus Crime Control and Safe Streets Act of 1968. That Act does not attempt to define or delineate the powers of the President to meet domestic threats to the national security.

Moreover, we do not hold that the same type of standards and procedures prescribed by Title III are necessarily applicable to this case. We recognize that domestic security surveillance may involve different policy and practical considerations from the surveillance of "ordinary crime." The gathering of security intelligence is often long range and involves the interrelation of various sources and types of information. The exact targets of such surveillance may be more difficult to identify than in surveillance operations against many types of crime specified in Title III. Often, too, the emphasis of domestic intelligence gathering is on the prevention of unlawful activity or the enhancement of the Government's preparedness for some possible future crisis or emergency. Thus, the focus of domestic surveillance may be less precise than that directed against more conventional types of crime.

Given these potential distinctions between Title III criminal surveillances and those involving the domestic security, Congress may wish to consider protective standards for the latter which differ from those already prescribed for specified crimes in Title III. Different standards may be compatible with the Fourth Amendment if they are reasonable both in relation to the legitimate need of Government for intelligence information and the protected rights of our citizens. For the warrant application may vary according to the governmental interest to be enforced and the nature of citizen rights deserving protection. As the Court said in **Camara v. Municipal Court**, 387 U.S. 523, 534-535 (1967):

In cases in which the Fourth Amendment requires that a warrant to search be obtained, "probable cause" is the standard by which a particular decision to search is tested against the constitutional mandate of reasonableness... . In determining whether a particular inspection is reasonable—and thus in determining whether there is probable cause to issue a warrant for that inspection—the need for the inspection must be weighed in terms of these reasonable goals of code enforcement.

It may be that Congress, for example, would judge that the application and affidavit showing probable cause need not follow the exact requirements of § 2518, but should allege other circumstances more appropriate to domestic security cases; that the request for prior court authorization could, in sensitive cases, be made to any member of a specially designated court (e.g., the District Court for the District of Columbia or the Court of Appeals for the District of Columbia Circuit); and that the time and reporting requirements need not be so strict as those in § 2518.

The above paragraph does not, of course, attempt to guide the congressional judgment, but, rather, to delineate the present scope of our own opinion. We do not attempt to detail the precise standards for domestic security warrants any more than our decision in **Katz** sought to set the refined requirements for the specified criminal surveillances which now constitute Title III. We do hold, however, that, prior judicial approval is required for the type of domestic security surveillance involved in this case, and that such approval may be made in accordance with such reasonable standards as the Congress may prescribe.

V

As the surveillance of Plamondon's conversations was unlawful, because conducted without prior judicial approval, the courts below correctly held that **Alderman v. United States**, 394 U.S. 165 (1969), is controlling, and that it requires disclosure to the accused of his own impermissibly intercepted conversations. As stated in **Alderman**, the trial court can and should, where appropriate, place a defendant and his counsel under enforceable orders against unwarranted disclosure of the materials which they may be entitled to inspect.

The judgment of the Court of Appeals is hereby Affirmed.

Commentary and Questions

1. The Foreign Intelligence Surveillance Act (FISA) of 1978 provides pro-
    cedures for *"requesting judicial approval of electronic surveillance and
    physical search of persons engaged in espionage or international terrorism
    against the United States on behalf of a foreign power."*[18] The Act was in
    partial response to the Supreme Court's decision in *U.S. District Court*, also
    referred to as the Keith case after U.S. District Court for the Eastern
    District of Michigan Damon Keith who originally ruled against the
    government. It was also the result of the Senate Select Committee to Study
    Governmental Operations with Respect to Intelligence Activities (the
    "Church Committee") report on Nixon administration abuses in conducting
    domestic surveillance.[19] FISA is codified in Title 50 U.S.C. Chapter 36, in
    which section 1803 provides *"[T]he Chief Justice of the United States shall
    publicly designate 11 district court judges from at least seven of the United
    States judicial circuits of whom no fewer than 3 shall reside within 20 miles
    of the District of Columbia who shall constitute a court which shall have
    jurisdiction to hear applications for and grant orders approving electronic
    surveillance anywhere within the United States under the procedures set forth
    in this chapter ..."* The Foreign Intelligence Surveillance Court (FISC) is a
    specialized court with hearings on foreign surveillance matters conducted in
    Washington D.C. Application for a surveillance warrant is usually made by
    attorneys from the National Security Agency (NSA) or Federal Bureau of
    Investigation (FBI) and must contain a certification from the Attorney
    General that the surveillance target is a "foreign power" or "agent of a
    foreign power."[20] Criticisms about the court center on the fact that the court
    operates out of public view and only receives information from the
    government. The Electronic Privacy Information Center (EPIC) reported on
    the number of warrant orders issued by the court since 1979. Since 9/11 the
    number of warrants issued increased threefold. The troubled history of the
    FISA court has included the resignation of a judge in protest over NSA
    domestic surveillance[21] and the leak by NSA contractor Edward Snowden to
    the media of a secret court warrant authorizing Verizon to provide in-
    formation relating to daily domestic telephone metadata.[22]

2. The Fourth Amendment requires a warrant based on probable cause to con-
    duct a search. Exceptions apply under certain circumstances, such as
    automobile searches based on probable cause, hot pursuit and emergency
    situations, but each of these exceptions is guided by the "reasonableness
    clause" of the Fourth Amendment. The Court has consistently cited the
    preference for a warrant issued by a neutral and detached magistrate[23] but
    under the provisions of the reasonableness clause the Supreme Court has
    said that a warrantless search is reasonable and permitted if based upon
    probable cause. A separate exception applies that considers neither probable
    cause nor the issuance of a warrant. The "special needs" exception is
    available in circumstances wherein there is a "special government need
    beyond the normal need for law enforcement," in this scenario a
    determination is made that there exists an impracticality of obtaining a

warrant and probable cause determinations are not suited to the situation. The reasonableness of the search is upheld despite the absence of a warrant, probable cause, or individualized suspicion.[24] However, the search is valid only if conducted for a non-criminal investigative purpose. Governmental interests must be weighed against individual privacy interests when invoking the "special needs" exception. Justice Byron White in *New Jersey v. T.L.O.*, 469 U.S. 325 (1985) provided an overview of this balancing effort while addressing the legitimacy of a school administrator's search of a student's purse pursuant to the school's anti-smoking policy and criminal charges resulting from marijuana and evidence of drug dealing found in the student's purse:

> *"How, then, should we strike the balance between the schoolchild's legitimate expectations of privacy and the school's equally legitimate need to maintain an environment in which learning can take place? It is evident that the school setting requires some easing of the restrictions to which searches by public authorities are ordinarily subject. The warrant requirement, in particular, is unsuited to the school environment: requiring a teacher to obtain a warrant before searching a child suspected of an infraction of school rules (or of the criminal law) would unduly interfere with the maintenance of the swift and informal disciplinary procedures needed in the schools. Just as we have in other cases dispensed with the warrant requirement when "the burden of obtaining a warrant is likely to frustrate the governmental purpose behind the search," Camara v. Municipal Court, 387 U.S. at 387 U.S. 532-533, we hold today that school officials need not obtain a warrant before searching a student who is under their authority.*
>
> *The school setting also requires some modification of the level of suspicion of illicit activity needed to justify a search. Ordinarily, a search—even one that may permissibly be carried out without a warrant—must be based upon "probable cause" to believe that a violation of the law has occurred. See, e.g., Almeida-Sanchez v. United States, 413 U.S. 266, 413 U.S. 273 (1973); Sibron v. New York, 392 U.S. 40, 392 U.S. 62-66 (1968). However, "probable cause" is not an irreducible requirement of a valid search. The fundamental command of the Fourth Amendment is that searches and seizures be reasonable, and although "both the concept of probable cause and the requirement of a warrant bear on the reasonableness of a search, ... in certain limited circumstances neither is required." Almeida-Sanchez v. United States, supra, at 413 U.S. 277 (Powell, J., concurring). Thus, we have in a number of cases recognized the legality of searches and seizures based on suspicions that, although "reasonable," do not rise to the level of probable cause."*[25]

In *New Jersey v. T.L.O.* the Court found that a high school student maintained a privacy interest that was not surrendered on entering the school building as argued by the school district; however, the Court said under the circumstances the individual privacy interest had to give way to the school's interest in maintaining order and a safe environment for students. When confronted with "special needs" search cases the courts are generally addressing Fourth Amendment–related searches conducted by non-law enforcement personnel. But this fact does not exclude law enforcement reliance on the doctrine. As noted in the introduction to this chapter, Justice O'Connor in *Indianapolis v. Edmond* referenced the constitutionality under the Fourth Amendment of a roadblock to stop an imminent terrorist attack. In doing so she cited prior Court opinions which upheld the government's interests over individual privacy concerns specific to situations such as "special needs" searches.[26] Considerations as to the viability of the "special needs" search will focus on the intrusiveness of the search as well as the preventive necessity of the search. Based on the national security needs of the country does the Foreign Intelligence Surveillance Court's ex parte process sufficiently alleviate domestic spying issues? Does the pressing national security agenda of the government meet the "special needs" assessment and trump individual privacy interests?

3. As noted in Chapter 9, commentary note 9, First Amendment challenges to government surveillance programs failed in *Laird v. Tatum* based on the ripeness doctrine. Because the plaintiffs could not show visible injury, the claims they made were speculative relating to the Army's domestic surveillance program. Similar issues relating to Article III standing resulted in dismissal of FISA surveillance challenges in *Clapper v. Amnesty International USA*. Other attempts to challenge government surveillance programs, particularly post-9/11 challenges, have not been successful. In *Dinler v. City of New York (In re City of New York)*, 607 F.3d 923 (2d Cir., 2010) protesters who were arrested after demonstrating at the 2004 Republican National Convention in the Borough of Manhattan initiated a lawsuit under 42 U.S.C. §1983 alleging constitutional violations by the New York City Police Department. During pre-trial discovery the plaintiffs sought a motion to compel disclosure of undercover officers' surveillance notes. The City of New York objected to a federal magistrate's order compelling disclosure. Pursuant to a writ of mandamus initiated by the City of New York the Second Circuit Court of Appeals applied the law enforcement privilege in denying the request for disclosure of the surveillance reports. Judge Jose A. Cabranes, writing for the Circuit Court's three-judge panel, said *"disclosure of the Field Reports could undermine the safety of law enforcement personnel and would likely undermine the ability of a law enforcement agency to conduct future investigations."*[27] The New York City Police Department found itself again at the center of surveillance criticism in 2012 when it was accidentally revealed that NYPD detectives were conducting physical surveillance of Muslims in Newark, New Jersey.[28] Several lawsuits against the NYPD resulted from this disclosure.[29] The NYPD and other major city police departments, however, have had a long history of surveillance squads aimed at political protestors, activists, and criminal groups. In the 1972 case of *Handschu v. Special Services Division*, 16 individuals belonging to various political action groups brought a class action lawsuit under 42 U.S.C. §1983 seeking declaratory judgment and

injunctive relief against the activities of the NYPD's Security and Investigation Section.[30] Their claim centered on allegations of electronic and physical surveillance, infiltration, intelligence gathering, and use of informers over a six-year period against the groups that were aimed at denying them the full enjoyment of their constitutional rights, which included freedom of speech, right to assembly and association, and freedom from unlawful search and seizure. The litigation continued for another 14 years until the Second Circuit of Appeals upheld a district court decision that found for the plaintiffs and held that NYPD surveillance of their political activity violated their First Amendment rights.[31] The result of the litigation was a consent decree establishing a set of guidelines for the NYPD's investigation of political activity. These guidelines circumscribed police surveillance activity. After 9/11 the NYPD returned to court seeking to abolish provisions of the *Handschu* consent decree, claiming that easing the restrictions would enable the NYPD to more effectively combat terrorism. In 2003 federal district court Judge Charles Haight, who presided over the original *Handschu* case, agreed to ease the restrictions under what has become known as the "Modified Handschu Guidelines."[32]

Alliance to End Repression v. City of Chicago was a similar class-action lawsuit initiated by plaintiffs in 1975 against the Chicago Police Department, F.B.I. and C.I.A., among other government defendants, based on "violating the plaintiff's First Amendment rights by overly intrusive and improperly motivated activities of alleged subversive activities."[33] The complaint was dismissed in 1981 in favor of a settlement agreement among the parties.[34] The eventual settlement agreement placed restrictions upon the defendants in conducting domestic security investigations.[35] In 2001 the City of Chicago returned to federal court seeking to modify the decree and ease the restrictions placed on domestic security investigations. The district court refused to modify the decree and the City of Chicago appealed.[36] The Seventh Circuit Court of Appeals modified the decree and in doing so Judge Richard Posner wrote: *"First Amendment rights are secure. But under the decree as written and interpreted, the public safety is insecure and the prerogatives of local government scorned. To continue federal judicial micromanagement of local investigations of domestic and international terrorist activities in Chicago is to undermine the federal system and to trifle with public safety."*[37]

Even with the modifications both the NYPD and Chicago Police Department remain under significant restriction and oversight for their domestic surveillance activities. As Judge Posner noted in *Alliance to End Repression*: *"[T]he modified decree will leave the Chicago police under considerably greater constraints than the police forces of other cities."*[38] What do these modifications reveal about U.S. judicial oversight of government surveillance activities in the war on terror?

4. A National Security Letter (NSL) is a search or surveillance process allowing the Federal Bureau of Investigation to request and obtain, without judicial approval and oversight, customer transactional information from financial institutions, communications companies, and consumer credit agencies in

connection with foreign intelligence or terrorism-related investigations. NSLs were created as an amendment in 1986 to the Right to Financial Privacy Act (12 U.S.C. §3414), but the FBI's NSL powers have been expanded under subsequent legislative extensions, such as the Electronic Communications Privacy Act (18 USC §2709), which allows the FBI to obtain from electronic or wire service communications providers customer subscriber information, toll billing records, and electronic communication transactional records. The information sought under §2709 includes e-mails and historical call information. An NSL request from the FBI includes a non-disclosure provision that prohibits the provider served with the NSL from disclosing the request to the subscriber. The PATRIOT Act provided broader authority to the FBI in issuing NSLs when the requirement that there be specific facts providing a reason to believe there is a connection between the subscriber whose records are requested and foreign intelligence or terrorist activity was eliminated in favor of a bare relevancy standard. As long as there is some relevance to an authorized foreign intelligence or terrorism investigation the NSL can issue.[39]

Challenges to the government's use of National Security Letters have not yet found their way to the U.S. Supreme Court[40]; however, some lower federal court cases have been heard. The most notable of these cases is one from the Southern District of New York, *Doe v. Ashcroft*. In *Doe v. Ashcroft* a communications provider challenged the government's authority to use NSLs to request subscriber information without a court order and to prohibit any disclosure by the communications provider. The Southern District Court of New York struck down the NSL authorizing statute and its non-disclosure provision citing Fourth Amendment issues with the unreviewable nature of the government request for the type and extent of information sought.[41] Additionally, the court said there were First Amendment violations inherent in the statute's nondisclosure provision.[42] Subsequent amendments to the NSL provision of the PATRIOT Act prompted the Second Circuit Court of Appeals to send the case back to the District Court to consider the constitutionality of the amendments.[43] On remand to the District Court the new provisions of the NSL statute were held to be unconstitutional.[44] Part of the District Court's determination was upheld on appeal, but the most important part of the decision required the government to justify its nondisclosure order on the recipient of the NSL.[45]

Government use of National Security Letters continue to generate criticism and will likely lead to more litigation. A core criticism is the lack of judicial oversight. Should NSLs continue to be utilized by the government to gather investigative information on individuals without judicial oversight? Is there any detriment to regulating the use of this investigative device such as by the use of a special reviewing court as required under the Foreign Intelligence Surveillance ACT?

Government Use of Drones

Unmanned aerial vehicles (UAVs), otherwise known as drones, have been used extensively by the military in combat operations in the war on terror.

President Bush initially authorized their use in Afghanistan to provide direct battle support to troops on the ground and to deliver ordnance against human and physical targets. Their increased use under the Obama administration, particularly in countries outside the designated combat zones of Afghanistan, to target terrorist suspects and kill them has been condemned under international law.[46] Separate Fifth Amendment due process violations have been cited in the targeted killed in Yemen of a U.S. citizen, Anwar al-Awlaki, an al-Qaeda propagandist.[47] Equal time though has been given to arguments that the use of drones for these targeted missions is lawful within the context of war operations.[48] Debate over the domestic use of drones by law enforcement and the privacy concerns emanating from such potential use have ensued from the increased reliance on drones in military operations, especially since law enforcement often adopts military technology and weaponry in domestic policing operations. The specter of unmanned drone aircraft with their ability to remotely hover and record intimate details of our lives has many privacy advocates worried about the potential for government abuse. Existing case law seems to provide adequate Fourth Amendment protections from invasive government surveillance; however, as technology rapidly develops the law needs to be able to respond as quickly to the potential privacy infringements new technology creates. The U.S. Supreme Court failed to offer such continued legal development in its 2012 *United States v. Jones* opinion. When police attached a Global Positioning System (GPS) device onto Jones's vehicle without a valid warrant there was a Fourth Amendment search according to a unanimous Court. However, Justice Scalia's opinion reflected only the position of the majority who felt the Fourth Amendment violation occurred when the police trespassed by placing the device onto Jones's vehicle. This majority viewpoint failed to address the more pressing privacy issue presented by the long-term monitoring (28 days) resulting from the use of the GPS device. Justice Alito's concurring opinion presented specific concerns for the privacy ramifications of long-term monitoring, which he said constituted a search. Justice Sotomayor's concurrence adopted Justice Alito's privacy rationale but also sought to extend the reach of Fourth Amendment protections in a digital age by re-considering the third-party records doctrine as developed from the cases of *United States v. Miller*, 425 U.S. 435 (1976) and *Smith v. Maryland*, 442 U.S. 735 (1979). Under the third-party records doctrine a person cannot invoke Fourth Amendment protections from information that is knowingly provided to a third-party such as a bank or telephone company. However, Justice Sotomayor, despite her views on Fourth Amendment privacy interests, joined the majority opinion because Justice Scalia's trespass rationale settled the issue in *Jones*. This was a lost opportunity for the Court to establish an initial strong statement on Fourth Amendment protections and slow the growing technological creep into privacy expectations.

Increased drone use by civil law enforcement, emergency management, and emergency response agencies is rapidly approaching.[49] This will prompt the Court to one day address the *"dragnet-type law enforcement practices"* it alluded to in *United States v. Knotts* as the catalyst for considering the privacy implications in pervasive and intrusive law enforcement surveillance.[50] Until that day the Court's opinions in cases like *Knotts*, *United States v. Karo*,[51] *Kyllo v. United States,*[52] and *Katz v. United States*[53] will have to guide Fourth Amendment privacy applications to digital technology. Aerial surveillance remains covered by the Court's opinions in *Florida v. Riley,*[54] *California v. Ciraolo,*[55] and *Dow Chemical v. United States.*[56] However, technology often out paces the law's ability to keep up and the enhanced nature of electronic surveillance and the government's advance technology enabling it to monitor the more private aspects of a person's daily life raise the issue as to whether the holdings in these earlier cases is still viable. *California v. Ciraolo,* which follows, was the first in the trinity of aerial surveillance cases to set the contours of permissible government conduct in conducting aerial surveillance.

California v. Ciraolo
476 U.S. 207 (1986)

Chief Justice Burger delivered the opinion of the Court.

We granted certiorari to determine whether the Fourth Amendment is violated by aerial observation without a warrant from an altitude of 1,000 feet of a fenced-in backyard within the curtilage of a home.

I

On September 2, 1982, Santa Clara Police received an anonymous telephone tip that marijuana was growing in respondent's backyard. Police were unable to observe the contents of respondent's yard from ground level because of a 6-foot outer fence and a 10-foot inner fence completely enclosing the yard. Later that day, Officer Shutz, who was assigned to investigate, secured a private plane and flew over respondent's house at an altitude of 1,000 feet, within navigable airspace; he was accompanied by Officer Rodriguez. Both officers were trained in marijuana identification. From the overflight, the officers readily identified marijuana plants 8 feet to 10 feet in height growing in a 15- by 25-foot plot in respondent's yard; they photographed the area with a standard 35mm camera.

On September 8, 1982, Officer Shutz obtained a search warrant on the basis of an affidavit describing the anonymous tip and their observations; a photograph depicting respondent's house, the backyard, and neighboring homes was attached to the affidavit as an exhibit. The warrant was executed the next day and 73 plants were seized; it is not disputed that these were marijuana.

After the trial court denied respondent's motion to suppress the evidence of the search, respondent pleaded guilty to a charge of cultivation of marijuana. The California Court of Appeal reversed, however, on the ground that the warrantless aerial observation of respondent's yard which led to the issuance of the warrant violated the Fourth Amendment. That court held first that respondent's backyard marijuana garden was within the "curtilage" of his home, under Oliver v. United States, 466 U.S. 170 (1984). The court emphasized that the height and existence of the two fences constituted "objective criteria from which we may conclude he manifested a reasonable expectation of privacy by any standard." 161 Cal. App. 3d, at 1089, 208 Cal. Rptr., at 97.

Examining the particular method of surveillance undertaken, the court then found it "significant" that the flyover "was not the result of a routine patrol conducted for any other legitimate law enforcement or public safety objective, but was undertaken for the specific purpose of observing this particular enclosure within [respondent's] curtilage." Ibid. It held this focused observation was "a direct and unauthorized intrusion into the sanctity of the home" which violated respondent's reasonable expectation of privacy. Id., at 1089-1090, 208 Cal. Rptr., at 98 (footnote omitted). The California Supreme Court denied the State's petition for review.

We granted the State's petition for certiorari. We reverse.

The State argues that respondent has "knowingly exposed" his backyard to aerial observation, because all that was seen was visible to the naked eye from any aircraft flying overhead. The State analogizes its mode of observation to a knothole or opening in a fence: if there is an opening, the police may look.

The California Court of Appeal, as we noted earlier, accepted the analysis that unlike the casual observation of a private person flying overhead, this flight was focused specifically on a small suburban yard, and was not the result of any routine patrol overflight. Respondent contends he has done all that can reasonably be expected to tell the world he wishes to maintain the privacy of his garden within the curtilage without covering his yard. Such covering, he argues, would defeat its purpose as an outside living area; he asserts he has not "knowingly" exposed himself to aerial views.

II

The touchstone of Fourth Amendment analysis is whether a person has a "constitutionally protected reasonable expectation of privacy." Katz v. United States, 389 U.S. 347, 360 (1967) (Harlan, J., concurring). Katz posits a two-part inquiry: first, has the individual manifested a subjective expectation of privacy in the object of the challenged search? Second, is society willing to recognize that expectation as reasonable? See Smith v. Maryland, 442 U.S. 735, 740 (1979).

Clearly—and understandably—respondent has met the test of manifesting his own subjective intent and desire to maintain privacy as to his unlawful agricultural pursuits. However, we need not address that issue, for the State has not challenged the finding of the California Court of Appeal that respondent had such an expectation. It can reasonably be assumed that the 10-foot fence was placed to conceal the marijuana crop from at least street-level views. So far as the normal sidewalk traffic was concerned, this fence served that purpose, because respondent "took normal precautions to maintain his privacy." Rawlings v. Kentucky, 448 U.S. 98, 105 (1980).

Yet a 10-foot fence might not shield these plants from the eyes of a citizen or a policeman perched on the top of a truck or a two-level bus. Whether respondent therefore manifested a subjective expectation of privacy from all observations of his backyard, or whether instead he manifested merely a hope that no one would observe his unlawful gardening pursuits, is not entirely clear in these circumstances. Respondent appears to challenge the authority of government to observe his activity from any vantage point or place if the viewing is motivated by a law enforcement purpose, and not the result of a casual, accidental observation.

We turn, therefore, to the second inquiry under Katz, i. e., whether that expectation is reasonable. In pursuing this inquiry, we must keep in mind that "[t]he test of legitimacy is not whether the individual chooses to conceal assertedly `private' activity," but instead "whether the government's intrusion infringes upon the personal and societal values protected by the Fourth Amendment." *Oliver, supra,* at 181-183.

Respondent argues that because his yard was in the curtilage of his home, no governmental aerial observation is permissible under the Fourth Amendment without a warrant.1 The history and genesis of the curtilage doctrine are instructive. "At common law, the curtilage is the area to which extends the intimate activity associated with the `sanctity of a man's home and the privacies of life.'" Oliver, supra, at 180 (quoting Boyd v. United States, 116 U.S. 616, 630 (1886)). See 4 Blackstone, Commentaries *225. The protection afforded the curtilage is essentially a protection of families and personal privacy in an area intimately linked to the home, both physically and psychologically, where privacy expectations are most heightened. The claimed area here was immediately adjacent to a suburban home, surrounded by high double fences. This close nexus to the home would appear to encompass this small area within the curtilage. Accepting, as the State does, that this yard and its crop fall within the curtilage, the question remains whether naked-eye observation of the curtilage by police from an aircraft lawfully operating at an altitude of 1,000 feet violates an expectation of privacy that is reasonable.

That the area is within the curtilage does not itself bar all police observation. The Fourth Amendment protection of the home has never been extended to require law enforcement officers to shield their eyes when passing by a home on public thoroughfares. Nor does the mere fact that an individual has taken measures to restrict some views of his activities preclude an officer's observations from a public vantage point where he has a right to be and which renders the activities clearly visible. E.g., United States v. Knotts, 460 U.S. 276, 282

(1983). "What a person knowingly exposes to the public, even in his own home or office, is not a subject of Fourth Amendment protection." Katz, supra, at 351.

The observations by Officers Shutz and Rodriguez in this case took place within public navigable airspace in a physically nonintrusive manner; from this point they were able to observe plants readily discernible to the naked eye as marijuana. That the observation from aircraft was directed at identifying the plants and the officers were trained to recognize marijuana is irrelevant. Such observation is precisely what a judicial officer needs to provide a basis for a warrant. Any member of the public flying in this airspace who glanced down could have seen everything that these officers observed. On this record, we readily conclude that respondent's expectation that his garden was protected from such observation is unreasonable and is not an expectation that society is prepared to honor.

The dissent contends that the Court ignores Justice Harlan's warning in his concurrence in Katz v. United States, 389 U.S., at 361-362, that the Fourth Amendment should not be limited to proscribing only physical intrusions onto private property. Post, at 215-216. But Justice Harlan's observations about future electronic developments and the potential for electronic interference with private communications, see Katz, supra, at 362, were plainly not aimed at simple visual observations from a public place. Indeed, since Katz the Court has required warrants for electronic surveillance aimed at intercepting private conversations. See United States v. United States District Court, 407 U.S. 297 (1972).

Justice Harlan made it crystal clear that he was resting on the reality that one who enters a telephone booth is entitled to assume that his conversation is not being intercepted. This does not translate readily into a rule of constitutional dimensions that one who grows illicit drugs in his backyard is "entitled to assume" his unlawful conduct will not be observed by a passing aircraft - or by a power company repair mechanic on a pole overlooking the yard. As Justice Harlan emphasized, *"a man's home is, for most purposes, a place where he expects privacy, but objects, activities, or statements that he exposes to the `plain view' of outsiders are not `protected' because no intention to keep them to himself has been exhibited. On the other hand, conversations in the open would not be protected against being overheard, for the expectation of privacy under the circumstances would be unreasonable."* Katz, supra, at 361.

One can reasonably doubt that in 1967 Justice Harlan considered an aircraft within the category of future "electronic" developments that could stealthily intrude upon an individual's privacy. In an age where private and commercial flight in the public airways is routine, it is unreasonable for respondent to expect that his marijuana plants were constitutionally protected from being observed with the naked eye from an altitude of 1,000 feet. The Fourth Amendment simply does not require the police traveling in the public airways at this altitude to obtain a warrant in order to observe what is visible to the naked eye.

Reversed.

Commentary and Questions

5. Justice Lewis Powell, joined by Justices William Brennan, Thurgood Marshall and Harry Blackmun, issued a dissent in *Ciraolo v. California* which began with a reminder of Justice Harlan's precautionary warning in his *Katz v. United States* concurring opinion.[57] The *Ciraolo* dissent cited the following,

> "...*any decision to construe the Fourth Amendment as proscribing only physical intrusions by police onto private property 'is, in the present day, bad physics as well as bad law, for reasonable expectations of privacy may be defeated by electronic as well as physical invasion.*"[58]

As the dissent further explained, *Katz* recognized that the old physical intrusion standards for Fourth Amendment protection as outlined in *Olmstead v. United States*, 277 U.S. 438 (1928), were ineffective against modern technology. Powell further wrote,

> "[L]ooking to the Fourth Amendment for protection against such "broad and unsuspected governmental incursions" into the "cherished privacy of law-abiding citizens," ... the Court in Katz abandoned its inquiry into whether police had committed a physical trespass."[59]

The *Katz* inquiry, as the dissent noted, involved a two-prong inquiry of whether an individual, by his conduct, has exhibited a subjective expectation of privacy, followed by a determination of whether that expectation is legitimate under the Fourth Amendment. This second inquiry is referred to as the objective test of privacy, that is, whether it is an expectation of privacy objectively reasonable under typical Fourth Amendment analysis. Since *Ciraolo* involved surveillance of a home, an area granted greater protection from government intrusion under the Fourth Amendment,[60] the dissent questioned the majority opinion's exception for aerial surveillance at 1,000 feet of an area it determined was within the homeowner's expectation of privacy. For its part the bare 5-4 majority stated the test for an expectation of privacy's legitimacy was not based on whether an individual decides to conceal private activity but *"whether the government's intrusion infringes upon the personal and societal values protected by the Fourth Amendment."*[61] Chief Justice Burger's opinion went on to chide the dissent by acknowledging Justice Harlan's Katz caution but pointing out his warning was relevant to electronic surveillance not visual observations made in public.

6. *Dow Chemical Co. v. United States* was a companion case to *Ciraolo,* both argued on December 10, 1985 and decided May 19, 1986. The facts in *Dow Chemical* were similar to those in *Ciraolo* in that the government conducted aerial surveillance over property in conjunction with an investigation. However, in this case the property involved was commercial property and the government was conducting an administrative investigation. The federal Environmental Protection Agency (EPA) had statutory jurisdiction to conduct an on-site inspection of the Dow property which, the Court said, included all modes of investigation and inquiry which it may use in furtherance of its statutory authority. The Court also said the open area of a large industrial complex was more like an open field and therefore not subject to the same privacy demands. In this instance the plant was 2,000 acres. It was not akin to the "curtilage" of a home which has been defined as the immediate area surrounding a home to which the intimate activities of the home extend.[62] Thus, the Court disposed of the curtilage issue, one of the two issues raised by Dow Chemical. The second issue was the government's use of an aerial mapping camera which the Court also dismissed by stating enhancement of human vision did not create a constitutional problem. However, the Court did distinguish this type of enhancement from technology capable of penetrating *"walls or windows so as to hear and record confidential discussions of chemical formulae or other trade secrets"* which *"would raise very different and far more serious questions."*[63]

7. While aerial surveillance from a fixed-wing aircraft at 1,000 feet to detect a marijuana growing operation in the yard of a private residence was held constitutional in *Ciraolo* the Court encountered a similar, albeit nuanced, challenge to its aerial surveillance ruling 3 years after Ciraolo. In *Florida v. Riley,* 488 U.S. 445 (1989), the Court considered the question as to whether a helicopter occupied by sheriff's deputies as it flew 400 feet over the respondent Riley's residence (a mobile home on 5 acres of property) was an illegal search. The Florida state trial court originally thought so and suppressed the marijuana evidence seized. The trial court's suppression order was reversed by the State Court of Appeals which sent the case to the State Supreme Court to determine whether helicopter surveillance from 400 feet was a search requiring a warrant. The State Supreme Court held it was a search and reinstated the trial court's suppression order. On appeal to the U.S. Supreme Court a bare 5-4 majority held for the state and reversed the Florida Supreme Court. In a brief opinion Justice White said the use of a helicopter instead of a plane and navigation at the minimum level of FAA airspace was not significant enough to alter the outcome from its *Ciraolo* decision.

   Do the Court's aerial surveillance cases provide adequate Fourth Amendment protection for restricting government use of drones in domestic surveillance programs? Does the ready accessibility of commercial drones diminish privacy arguments?

8. The following cases offer further insight into the Supreme Court's prevailing privacy related jurisprudence which may provide guidance in determining

the contours of Fourth Amendment protection from overly invasive government surveillance: *U.S. v. Knotts*, 460 U.S. 276 (1983), the Court held an individual traveling in public has no expectation of privacy in his/her movements even when monitored through the use of a beeper transmitter; *U.S. v. Karo*, 468 U.S. 705 (1984), the government's monitoring of a beeper place within a container located inside a private residence provided intimate details of the inside of the residence which violated the Fourth Amendment; *Kyllo v. U.S.*, 533 U.S. 27 (2001), the government conducted a Fourth Amendment search when using technology not commonly available to the public, in this instance a thermal-imaging device, to explore details of a private home that would be otherwise unknowable without a physical intrusion. More recently in *United States v. Jones* (discussed in previous brief) the Court rejected the government's argument that, despite the installation of a GPS tracking device on his vehicle, Antoine Jones did not have a reasonable expectation of privacy in his public movements. The Court focused on the government trespass to Jones' property (the vehicle he was driving) which was protected by the Fourth Amendment, but in so doing the Court did not address whether Jones had an expectation of privacy from extended government surveillance. This was the issue prompting the separate concurrences by Justices Sotomayor and Alito. Justice Sotomayor agreed there was a trespass to Jones' property but viewed the case as a broader Fourth Amendment concern focusing on what is a reasonable subjective expectation of privacy in a technological time when physical trespass is not required for prolonged surveillance. For his part, Justice Alito criticized the trespass analysis and preferred to see the issue framed as to whether or not the government violated Jones' expectation of privacy.

Interrogation, Self-Incrimination and Torture

Whether or not someone is familiar with the criminal justice system there is little doubt that the concept behind *Miranda* warnings is known to the lay person. Since the 1966 case of *Miranda v. Arizona* the warnings crafted by the U.S. Supreme Court have become ingrained in popular culture through a mixture of news media, popular television and reality police shows. The protections afforded by the Fifth Amendment, chiefly those against self-incrimination, are required to be made known to a criminal suspect once in custody along with the separate Sixth Amendment right to request an attorney. These are cherished rights, those which distinguish our form of government. The scales of justice theoretically reflect a balance and this balance is achieved by respecting the rights of even those whom society has accused of a heinous crime. But, *Miranda* only extends to those in custody who are accused of a crime and even with respect to that right it only applies if custodial statements are to be used at trial (more on that in the case and commentary that follows). A person not in custody can be questioned by the police and that person has two options, either to submit to the questioning or to invoke the right to remain silent. However, what becomes of the individual who is held in custody by the police and questioned for an extended period of time, makes incriminating statements but is never charged? Again, the case that follows, *Chavez v. Martinez*, provides the answer. Except let us extend the scenario a bit further and introduce more than coercive questioning on the part of the police, let us assume that in order to prod the information from their suspect the police use some force. We can work this scenario through a range of force scenarios from some light contact and threats to more physical conduct to increased, prolonged intensity in the use of force. Yet, at the end of all of this whatever incriminating statements the suspect makes none are used against him in a trial. Would such a scenario ever occur in 21st century United States of America? Could such a scenario ever occur? *Chavez v. Martinez* is a post-9/11 case and one cannot read it without considering its impact upon the scenario presented above. Justice Clarence Thomas, author of the *Chavez* opinion, while finding no substantive right of the respondent Oliverio Martinez within the Fifth Amendment, does cite the Fourteenth Amendment due process clause as the basis for any perceived constitutional violation. Though the Court states there was no due process violation in the case of Martinez it does reiterate its position from earlier cases that Fourteenth Amendment substantive due process claims can be asserted for government conduct which "shocks the conscience." This of course begs the follow-up question – what government conduct rises to the level which can be said to "shock the conscience"? Would police use of force on a terrorism suspect who is believed to be part of a terror cell operating within a large American city be conduct that would satisfy the "shock the conscience" test? Would it depend on the level of force used? Would it depend on the type of information being sought from the suspect – intelligence as opposed to the location of explosive devices set to detonate within a populated city center? These have so far been purely academic questions posed in the context of the theoretical within the safe confines of classrooms and think tanks but questions which have the alarming potential for actuality.

The contemplation of these scenarios and the potential impact of cases like *Chavez* must first rest upon understanding what the Court has defined as conduct that meets the "shocks the conscience" test. First developed by the Supreme Court in *Rochin v. California*, 342 U.S. 165 (1952) the test resulted from a drug case in which a suspect swallowed capsules on his nightstand after three police officers illegally entered his room. The officers had received information that Antonio Rochin was selling drugs, acted upon this information and upon their unlawful entry saw the capsules prior to Rochin swallowing them. The officers tried to force the capsules from Rochin's mouth but when it was apparent he swallowed the capsules the officers brought him to a nearby hospital to have him forcefully administered a solution to cause vomiting. The solution was forced into Rochin via a tube inserted into his stomach. When he vomited the police recovered two morphine capsules. A subsequent appeal of his criminal conviction to the Supreme Court had Justice Frankfurter, writing for the Court's majority, observe that *"[R]egard for the requirements of the Due Process Clause 'inescapably imposes upon this Court an exercise of judgment upon the whole course of the proceedings [resulting in a conviction] in order to ascertain whether they offend those canons of decency and fairness which express the notions of justice of English-speaking peoples even toward those charged with the most heinous offenses.'"*[64] Rochin's conviction would be overturned based on the method by which it was obtained—*"Illegally breaking into the privacy of the petitioner, the struggle to open his mouth and remove what was there, the forcible extraction of his stomach's contents—this course of proceeding by agents of government to obtain evidence is bound to offend even hardened sensibilities. They are methods too close to the rack and the screw to permit of constitutional differentiation"*[65] — because it offended fundamental concepts of ordered liberty. Rochin's case was the result of conscience-shocking government behavior leading to an arrest and conviction. Would there be a different outcome had there not been an arrest and conviction? Can such behavior of the police in the use of force to extract information from an individual be justified if for a legitimate law enforcement purpose? Would terrorism-related investigations provide an exception to some constitutional protections?

When re-visiting the "shocks the conscience" test in *County of Sacramento v. Lewis*, 523 U.S. 833 (1998), the Court made clear that in order to meet the standard for holding the government accountable for its conduct a plaintiff would have to allege something more than ordinary tort liability. The "shocks the conscience" test's high burden requires government conduct of a deliberate nature intending to deprive a person of life, liberty or property.[66] This has evolved to the point where the federal circuit courts require a detained person to show unnecessary and wanton infliction of pain.[67] The Lewis Court described such conduct as *"arbitrary in the constitutional sense."*[68] Which once again brings us back to the hypothetical scenarios presented above and the question as to how far can the police go without engaging in constitutionally arbitrary conduct? If we look at the position of the Office of Legal Counsel with regard to high value Al-Qaeda detainees on non-U.S. soil, the tolerance level for enhanced interrogation techniques goes quite far. In a May 30, 2005 memorandum from Steven G. Bradbury, Principal Deputy Assistant Attorney General in the Office of Legal Counsel, to John A. Rizzo, Deputy General Counsel for the Central Intelligence Agency, wrote: *"[F]ar from being constitutionally arbitrary, the interrogation techniques at issue here are employed by the CIA only as reasonably deemed necessary to protect against grave threats to United States interests, a determination that is made at CIA Headquarters, with input from the on-scene interrogation team, pursuant to careful screening procedures, that ensure that the techniques will be used as little as possible on as few detainees as possible. Moreover, the techniques have been carefully designed to minimize the risk of suffering or injury and to avoid inflicting any serious or lasting physical or psychological harm. Medical screening, monitoring, and ongoing evaluations further lower such risk. Significantly, you have informed us that the CIA believes that this program is largely responsible for preventing a subsequent attack within the United States. Because the CIA interrogation program is carefully limited to further a vital government interest and designed to avoid unnecessary or serious harm, we conclude that it cannot be said to be constitutionally arbitrary."*[69] This memorandum's legal opinion focused on the United States' obligations under Article 16 of the Convention Against Torture (CAT) and its use of certain enhanced techniques to question high value Al-Qaeda targets in U.S. custody. These enhanced techniques involved water-boarding, stress positions, sleep deprivation and restricted diet in order for the CIA to obtain information in the war on terror. Despite subsequent criticism from diverse groups the OLC memos relied on a series of U.S. Supreme Court decisions to justify conduct the international community has decried as torture. If we consider the extent to which legal argument and justification was relied upon to validate conduct many consider to be international violations, can the same type of legal reasoning ever be used to justify domestic use of non-conventional enhanced interrogation techniques? Again, this is a hypothetical but one which cannot be ignored in light of real-world events, past and present. Justice Souter, quoting *Graham v. Connor*, noted in Lewis that the Court was reluctant to expand the concept of substantive due process, relying mainly on the explicit textual source of constitutional protection found within a particular amendment. The following case of *Chavez v. Martinez* provides further material for contemplation in considering the extent to which the government will be allowed to stretch the boundaries of interrogation practices.

Chavez v. Martinez
538 U.S. 760 (2003)

Justice Thomas announced the judgment of the Court and delivered an opinion.

This case involves a §1983 suit arising out of petitioner Ben Chavez's allegedly coercive interrogation of respondent Oliverio Martinez. The United States Court of Appeals for the Ninth Circuit held that Chavez was not entitled to a defense of qualified immunity because he violated Martinez's clearly established constitutional rights. We conclude that Chavez did not deprive Martinez of a constitutional right.

I

On November 28, 1997, police officers Maria Peña and Andrew Salinas were near a vacant lot in a residential area of Oxnard, California, investigating suspected narcotics activity. While Peña and Salinas were questioning an individual, they heard a bicycle approaching on a darkened path that crossed the lot. They ordered the rider, respondent Martinez, to dismount, spread his legs, and place his hands behind his head. Martinez complied. Salinas then conducted a patdown frisk and discovered a knife in Martinez's waistband. An altercation ensued.

There is some dispute about what occurred during the altercation. The officers claim that Martinez drew Salinas' gun from its holster and pointed it at them; Martinez denies this. Both sides agree, however, that Salinas yelled, "'He's got my gun!'" Peña then drew her gun and shot Martinez several times, causing severe injuries that left Martinez permanently blinded and paralyzed from the waist down. The officers then placed Martinez under arrest.

Petitioner Chavez, a patrol supervisor, arrived on the scene minutes later with paramedics. Chavez accompanied Martinez to the hospital and then questioned Martinez there while he was receiving treatment from medical personnel. The interview lasted a total of about 10 minutes, over a 45-minute period, with Chavez leaving the emergency room for periods of time to permit medical personnel to attend to Martinez.

At first, most of Martinez's answers consisted of "I don't know," "I am dying," and "I am choking." Later in the interview, Martinez admitted that he took the gun from the officer's holster and pointed it at the police. He also admitted that he used heroin regularly. At one point, Martinez said "I am not telling you anything until they treat me," yet Chavez continued the interview. At no point during the interview was Martinez given **Miranda** warnings under **Miranda v. Arizona**, 384 U.S. 436 (1966).

Martinez was never charged with a crime, and his answers were never used against him in any criminal prosecution. Nevertheless, Martinez filed suit under 42 U.S.C. §1983 maintaining that Chavez's actions violated his Fifth Amendment right not to be "compelled in any criminal case to be a witness against himself," as well as his Fourteenth Amendment substantive due process right to be free from coercive questioning. The District Court granted summary judgment to Martinez as to Chavez's qualified immunity defense on both the Fifth and Fourteenth Amendment claims. Chavez took an interlocutory appeal to the Ninth Circuit, which affirmed the District Court's denial of qualified immunity. **Martinez v. Oxnard**, 270 F.3d 852 (2001). Applying **Saucier v. Katz**, 533 U.S. 194 (2001), the Ninth Circuit first concluded that Chavez's actions, as alleged by Martinez, deprived Martinez of his rights under the Fifth and Fourteenth Amendments. The Ninth Circuit did not attempt to explain how Martinez had been "compelled in any criminal case to be a witness against himself."... As to Martinez's due process claim, the Ninth Circuit held that "a police officer violates the Fourteenth Amendment when he obtains a confession by coercive conduct, regardless of whether the confession is subsequently used at trial."

The Ninth Circuit then concluded that the Fifth and Fourteenth Amendment rights asserted by Martinez were clearly established by federal law, explaining that a reasonable officer "would have known that persistent interrogation of the suspect despite repeated requests to stop violated the suspect's Fifth and Fourteenth Amendment right to be free from coercive interrogation."

We granted certiorari.

II

In deciding whether an officer is entitled to qualified immunity, we must first determine whether the officer's alleged conduct violated a constitutional right. See **Katz**, 533 U.S., at 201. If not, the officer is entitled to qualified immunity, and we need not consider whether the asserted right was "clearly established." We conclude that Martinez's allegations fail to state a violation of his constitutional rights.

A

1

The Fifth Amendment, made applicable to the States by the Fourteenth Amendment, *Malloy v. Hogan*, 378 U.S. 1 (1964), requires that "[n]o person ... shall be compelled *in any criminal case* to be a *witness* against himself." U.S. Const., Amdt. 5 (emphases added). We fail to see how, based on the text of the Fifth Amendment, Martinez can allege a violation of this right, since Martinez was never prosecuted for a crime, let alone compelled to be a witness against himself in a criminal case.

Although Martinez contends that the meaning of "criminal case" should encompass the entire criminal investigatory process, including police interrogations, we disagree. In our view, a "criminal case" at the very least requires the initiation of legal proceedings ... We need not decide today the precise moment when a "criminal case" commences; it is enough to say that police questioning does not constitute a "case" any more than a private investigator's pre-complaint activities constitute a "civil case." Statements compelled by police interrogations of course may not be used against a defendant at trial, see *Brown v. Mississippi*, 297 U.S. 278, 286 (1936), but it is not until their use in a criminal case that a violation of the Self-Incrimination Clause occurs, see *United States v. Verdugo-Urquidez*, 494 U.S. 259, 264 (1990) ("The privilege against self-incrimination guaranteed by the Fifth Amendment is *a fundamental trial right* of criminal defendants. Although conduct by law enforcement officials prior to trial may ultimately impair that right, *a constitutional violation occurs only at trial*" (emphases added; citations omitted)); *Withrow v. Williams*, 507 U.S. 680, 692 (1993) (describing the Fifth Amendment as a " 'trial right' ...

Here, Martinez was never made to be a "witness" against himself in violation of the Fifth Amendment's Self-Incrimination Clause because his statements were never admitted as testimony against him in a criminal case. Nor was he ever placed under oath and exposed to "'the cruel trilemma of self-accusation, perjury or contempt.'" *Michigan v. Tucker*, 417 U.S. 433, 445 (1974) (quoting *Murphy v. Waterfront Comm'n of N. Y. Harbor*, 378 U.S. 52, 55 (1964)). The text of the Self-Incrimination Clause simply cannot support the Ninth Circuit's view that the mere use of compulsive questioning, without more, violates the Constitution.

2

Nor can the Ninth Circuit's approach be reconciled with our case law. It is well established that the government may compel witnesses to testify at trial or before a grand jury, on pain of contempt, so long as the witness is not the target of the criminal case in which he testifies. See **Minnesota v. Murphy**, 465 U.S. 420, 427 (1984); **Kastigar v. United States**, 406 U.S. 441, 443 (1972). Even for persons who have a legitimate fear that their statements may subject them to criminal prosecution, we have long permitted the compulsion of incriminating testimony so long as those statements (or evidence derived from those statements) cannot be used against the speaker in any criminal case ... By contrast, no "penalty" may ever be imposed on someone who exercises his core Fifth Amendment right not to be a "witness" against himself in a "criminal case."

... Our holdings in these cases demonstrate that, contrary to the Ninth Circuit's view, mere coercion does not violate the text of the Self-Incrimination Clause absent use of the compelled statements in a criminal case against the witness.

We fail to see how Martinez was any more "compelled in any criminal case to be a witness against himself" than an immunized witness forced to testify on pain of contempt. One difference, perhaps, is that the immunized witness *knows* that his statements will not, and may not, be used against him, whereas Martinez likely did not. But this does not make the statements of the immunized witness any less "compelled" and lends no support to the Ninth Circuit's conclusion that coercive police interrogations, absent the use of the involuntary statements in a criminal case, violate the Fifth Amendment's Self-Incrimination Clause. Moreover, our cases provide that those subjected to coercive police interrogations have an *automatic* protection from the use of their involuntary statements (or evidence derived from their statements) in any subsequent criminal trial ... This protection is, in fact, coextensive with the use and derivative use immunity mandated by **Kastigar** when the government compels testimony from a reluctant witness. See 406 U.S., at 453. Accordingly, the fact that Martinez did not *know* his statements could not be used against him does not change our view that no violation of Fifth Amendment's Self-Incrimination Clause occurred here.

3

Although our cases have permitted the Fifth Amendment's self-incrimination privilege to be asserted in non-criminal cases ... that does not alter our conclusion that a violation of the constitutional right against self-incrimination occurs only if one has been compelled to be a witness against himself in a criminal case.

In the Fifth Amendment context, we have created prophylactic rules designed to safeguard the core constitutional right protected by the Self-Incrimination Clause ... Among these rules is an evidentiary privilege that protects witnesses from being forced to give incriminating testimony, even in noncriminal cases, unless that testimony has been immunized from use and derivative use in a future criminal proceeding before it is compelled ...

Rules designed to safeguard a constitutional right, however, do not extend the scope of the constitutional right itself, just as violations of judicially crafted prophylactic rules do not violate the constitutional rights of any person. As we explained, we have allowed the Fifth Amendment privilege to be asserted by witnesses in noncriminal cases in order to safeguard the core constitutional right defined by the Self-Incrimination Clause—the right not to be compelled in any criminal case to be a witness against oneself. We have likewise established the **Miranda** exclusionary rule as a prophylactic measure to prevent violations of the right protected by the text of the Self-Incrimination Clause—the admission into evidence in criminal case of confessions obtained through coercive custodial questioning ... Accordingly, Chavez's failure to read **Miranda** warnings to Martinez did not violate Martinez's constitutional rights and cannot be grounds for a §1983 action ... And the absence of a "criminal case" in which Martinez was compelled to be a "witness" against himself defeats his core Fifth Amendment claim. The Ninth Circuit's view that mere compulsion violates the Self-Incrimination Clause ... finds no support in the text of the Fifth Amendment and is irreconcilable with our case law. Because we find that Chavez's alleged conduct did not violate the Self-Incrimination Clause, we reverse the Ninth Circuit's denial of qualified immunity as to Martinez's Fifth Amendment claim.

Our views on the proper scope of the Fifth Amendment's Self-Incrimination Clause do not mean that police torture or other abuse that results in a confession is constitutionally permissible so long as the statements are not used at trial; it simply means that the Fourteenth Amendment's Due Process Clause, rather than the Fifth Amendment's Self-Incrimination Clause, would govern the inquiry in those cases and provide relief in appropriate circumstances.

B

The Fourteenth Amendment provides that no person shall be deprived "of life, liberty, or property, without due process of law." Convictions based on evidence obtained by methods that are "so brutal and so offensive to human dignity" that they "shock the conscience" violate the Due Process Clause. **Rochin v. California**, 342 U.S. 165, 172, 174 (1952) (overturning conviction based on evidence obtained by involuntary stomach pumping) ... Although **Rochin** did not establish a civil remedy for abusive police behavior, we recognized in **County of Sacramento v. Lewis**, 523 U.S. 833, 846 (1998), that deprivations of liberty caused by "the most egregious official conduct," may violate the Due Process Clause. While we rejected, in **Lewis**, a §1983 plaintiff's contention that a police officer's deliberate indifference during a high-speed chase that caused the death of a motorcyclist violated due process we left open the possibility that unauthorized police behavior in other contexts might "shock the conscience" and give rise to §1983 liability.

We are satisfied that Chavez's questioning did not violate Martinez's due process rights. Even assuming, arguendo, that the persistent questioning of Martinez somehow deprived him of a liberty interest, we cannot agree with Martinez's characterization of Chavez's behavior as "egregious" or "conscience shocking." As we noted in **Lewis**, the official conduct "most likely to rise to the conscience-shocking level," is the "conduct intended to injure in some way unjustifiable by any government interest." Here, there is no evidence that Chavez acted with a purpose to harm Martinez by intentionally interfering with his medical treatment. Medical personnel were able to treat Martinez throughout the interview, and Chavez ceased his questioning to allow tests and other procedures to be performed. Nor is there evidence that Chavez's conduct exacerbated Martinez's injuries or prolonged his stay in the hospital. Moreover, the need to investigate whether there had been police misconduct constituted a justifiable government interest given the risk that key evidence would have been lost if Martinez had died without the authorities ever hearing his side of the story.

The Court has held that the Due Process Clause also protects certain "fundamental liberty interests" from deprivation by the government, regardless of the procedures provided, unless the infringement is narrowly tailored to serve a compelling state interest. **Washington v. Glucksberg**, 521 U.S. 702, 721 (1997). Only fundamental rights and liberties which are "deeply rooted in this Nation's history and tradition" and "implicit in the concept of ordered liberty" qualify for such protection ...

Glucksberg requires a "careful description" of the asserted fundamental liberty interest for the purposes of substantive due process analysis; vague generalities, such as "the right not to be talked to," will not suffice. 521 U.S., at 721. We therefore must take into account the fact that Martinez was hospitalized and in severe pain during the interview, but also that Martinez was a critical non-police witness to an altercation resulting in a shooting by a police officer, and that the situation was urgent given the perceived risk that Martinez might die and crucial evidence might be lost. In these circumstances, we can find no basis in our prior jurisprudence, see, e.g., **Miranda**, 384 U.S., at 477 – 478 ("It is an act of responsible citizenship for individuals to give whatever information they may have to aid in law enforcement"), or in our Nation's history and traditions to suppose that freedom from unwanted police questioning is a right so fundamental that it cannot be abridged absent a "compelling state interest." **Flores**, *supra*, at 302. We have never required such a justification for a police interrogation, and we decline to do so here. The lack of any "guideposts for responsible decision-making" in this area, and our oft-stated reluctance to expand the doctrine of substantive due process, further counsel against recognizing a new "fundamental liberty interest" in this case.

We conclude that Martinez has failed to allege a violation of the Fourteenth Amendment, and it is therefore unnecessary to inquire whether the right asserted by Martinez was clearly established.

III

Because Chavez did not violate Martinez's Fifth and Fourteenth Amendment rights, he was entitled to qualified immunity. The judgment of the Court of Appeals for the Ninth Circuit is therefore reversed and the case is remanded for further proceedings.

It is so ordered.

Commentary and Questions

9. *Chavez v. Martinez* clearly presents the Fifth Amendment right against self-incrimination as a trial right. If a statement elicited from a suspect is not presented at trial there is no Fifth Amendment violation even though there may be objectionable police conduct in the questioning of the suspect. The Court refused to include the privilege against self-incrimination among the list of substantive constitutional rights. Justice Thomas' opinion was careful to point out that the Court's *"views on the proper scope of the Fifth Amendment's Self-Incrimination Clause do not mean that police torture or other abuse that results in a confession is constitutionally permissible so long as the statements are not used at trial."* The Court then noted that the proper remedy in those police abuse cases would be through the Fourteenth Amendment's due process clause. In light of the Court's "shock the conscience" standard for Fourteenth Amendment violations does the *Chavez v. Martinez* case provide U.S. law enforcement with the means to use force, short of conscience-shocking behavior, to question terror suspects? What behavior on the part of domestic law enforcement would "shock the conscience" to the point of making it a constitutional violation?

10. Prior to *Miranda v. Arizona* the Supreme Court used a voluntariness test to determine the admissibility of a suspect's statement. If it was determined the statement was not the product of a suspect's free will, that there had been coercion on the part of the government, then the statement was suppressed and, usually, the resulting conviction overturned. In the 1964 case *Malloy v. Hogan* the Court held that the Fourteenth Amendment protected a state witness's guarantee against self-incrimination in a criminal

proceeding.[70] Malloy, who pled guilty to gambling offenses in Connecticut and placed on two years' probation, was ordered by a specially appointed court referee to testify about gambling activities in Hartford County. Malloy refused to testify and was arrested and charged with contempt of court. In a narrow 5-4 decision the Supreme Court found in favor of Malloy and included the right against self-incrimination as one of those incorporated by the Fourteenth Amendment and applied to the states as well as the federal government. Justice Brennan's majority opinion noted *"that the American system of criminal prosecution is accusatorial, not inquisitorial, and that the Fifth Amendment privilege is its essential mainstay."*[71] In another case decided a few years prior to *Malloy* the Court, in *Spano v. New York*, began its shift away from the voluntariness test when it decided a criminal suspect undergoing police questioning had a right to counsel he had already retained and requested.[72] Vincent Spano, a young Italian immigrant, shot another person in the Bronx after a bar fight in which Spano was seriously injured. After the shooting Spano fled and went into hiding but eventually contacted a lawyer and with the lawyer turned himself into the police. Spano was taken into custody, away from his attorney, and subjected to continuous interrogation during which he repeatedly declined to make a statement and asked for his attorney. Over the course of his custody Spano was moved to several police precincts and subjected to different attempts to obtain his confession before he finally submitted to the entreaties of his friend, a New York City police academy recruit, to confess. On eventual appeal to the Supreme Court Chief Justice Warren's unanimous 9-0 opinion reflected the Court's dissatisfaction with police procedures used to obtain the confession. Spano's limited exposure to the criminal justice system, his lack of formal education, emotional instability, his being subject to multiple interviewers, the denial of his attorney's presence and the use of his police recruit friend to extract a confession, led to the Court's determination that Spano's Fourteenth Amendment due process rights were violated because his confession was involuntary. Presaging the Court's eventual move toward *Miranda* protection Chief Justice Warren wrote *"as law enforcement officers become more responsible and the methods used to extract confessions more sophisticated, our duty to enforce federal constitutional protections does not cease. It only becomes more difficult because of the more delicate judgments to be made."*[73]

Spano and *Malloy* reflected the Court's disapproval of non-physical coercive government means to extract a confession. However, in cases decided nearly two decades before either case, the Court also rejected overt physical means employed to overcome a suspect's resistance to confess. Beginning with *Brown v. Mississippi*, 297 U.S. 278 (1936), the Supreme Court found unconstitutional the confession-based murder conviction of two black defendants. The confessions were obtained after the defendants were brutally whipped, including the hanging by rope from a tree of one of them, by investigating police officers. Four years later in *Chambers v. Florida*, 309 U.S. 227 (1940), the Court examined the extent to which police pressure on a suspect to obtain a confession violates the due process clause of the Fourteenth Amendment. The *Chambers* Court found continual police threats against and mistreatment of the four defendants to violate due process. Police interrogation tactics continued to come under Supreme Court scrutiny in *Ashcraft v. Tennessee*, 322 U.S. 143 (1944) and *Watts v. Indiana*, 338 U.S. 49 (1949). In *Ashcraft* the Court nullified the conviction of the defendant for the murder of his wife due to the nature in which his confession was obtained. After being taken into custody by police Ashcraft was subjected to 36 hours of continual questioning by relays of different officers with only one 5 minute break. The defendant became weary and strained, subsequently confessing to his involvement in the crime. Because the confession was coerced it violated due process. Justice Black, author of the 6-3 majority opinion, closed out his comments on the Ashcraft interrogation by writing: *"There have been, and are now, certain foreign nations with governments dedicated to an opposite policy: governments which convict individuals with testimony obtained by police organizations possessed of an unrestrained power to seize persons suspected of crimes against the state, hold them in secret custody, and wring from them confessions by physical or mental torture. So long as the Constitution remains the basic law of our Republic, America will not have that kind of government."*[74] Similarly, in *Watts* the Court reversed the murder conviction of another defendant who was held incommunicado for several days and subjected to relay questioning by the police. Additionally the defendant was held in a solitary cell with no place to sit or sleep other than on the floor. In his plurality opinion Justice Felix Frankfurter spoke to the Court's disapproval of coercive police interrogation tactics: *"Disregard of rudimentary needs of life—opportunities for sleep and a decent allowance of food—are also relevant, not as aggravating elements of petitioner's treatment, but as part of the total situation out of which his confessions came and which stamped their character. A confession by which life becomes forfeit must be the expression of free choice. A statement, to be voluntary, of course need not be volunteered. But if it is the product of sustained pressure by the police, it does not issue from a free choice. When a suspect speaks because he is overborne, it is immaterial whether he has been subjected to a physical or a mental ordeal. Eventual yielding to questioning under such circumstances is plainly the product of the suction process of interrogation, and therefore the reverse of voluntary. We would have to shut our minds to the plain significance of what here transpired to deny that this was a calculated endeavor to secure a confession through the pressure of unrelenting interrogation. The very relentlessness of such interrogation implies that it is better for the prisoner to answer than to persist in the refusal of disclosure, which is his constitutional right. To turn the detention of an accused into a process of wrenching from him evidence which could not be extorted in open court, with all its safeguards, is so grave an abuse of the power of arrest as to offend the procedural standards of due process."*[75]

The preceding cases all involve the Court's consideration of police conduct which resulted in a criminal conviction. Does *Chavez v. Martinez* weaken constitutional protection from similar police conduct when there is no criminal trial and therefore no use of a coerced statement results? Does Justice Thomas' assurance of Fourteenth Amendment protection even though there was no Fifth Amendment self-incrimination violation offer legitimate constitutional safeguard in light of the existing case law?

11. After the failed attempt in 2010 by Faisal Shahzad to detonate a car bomb in New York City's Times Square, the NYPD was criticized because Shahzad was read his *Miranda* rights after being arrested.[76] Opinion on the subject rested on two opposing positions—one that terror suspects should be denied the basic procedural rights provided to criminal suspects, another that Shahzad, as a citizen, could not be denied his basic constitutional rights nor should the Constitution be shelved when it becomes convenient. Prior to reading Shahzad his *Miranda* warnings law enforcement authorities questioned him about other potential devices or suspects. Once it was determined that there was no longer an immediate danger he was read the warnings. The pre-*Miranda* questioning of Shahzad was permitted based on the 1984 Supreme Court case *New York v. Quarles*.[77]

According to *Quarles* law enforcement questioning of a suspect pertaining to a public safety concern does not violate *Miranda*. When New York City police officers on patrol received a complaint from a woman that she was raped by a man who had just entered into a supermarket they pursued the suspect into the market. Upon stopping the suspect in the crowded market an officer conducted a frisk and felt an empty shoulder holster. The police officer inquired into the location of the gun and the suspect, Benjamin Quarles, said "the gun is over there" while nodding in the direction of empty cartons.[78] The gun was retrieved, Quarles was placed under arrest and read his *Miranda* warnings. After waiving his right to have an attorney present, Quarles admitted to owning the gun and purchasing it in Miami, Florida. At a later trial, Quarles moved to have the gun suppressed based on a violation of *Miranda*, arguing that his statement, "the gun is over there," along with the gun should be suppressed. The trial court granted his motion and it was affirmed by the Appellate Division and eventually the state Court of Appeals. In its decision, the New York Court of Appeals held that Quarles was in custody for *Miranda* purposes when the officer asked him about the location of the gun; the Court refused to recognize any exigency for the officer's questioning of Quarles.[79] On appeal to the U.S. Supreme Court the Court held the gun should not have been suppressed because there is a "public safety" exception to the *Miranda* requirement. The narrow 5-4 majority found there was a custodial situation when Quarles was first stopped by the officer in the supermarket, but that *"there is a "public safety" exception to the requirement that Miranda warnings be given before a suspect's answers may be admitted into evidence, and that the availability of that exception does not depend upon the motivation of the individual officers involved."*[80] Justice Rehnquist's opinion continues, *"In a kaleidoscopic situation such as the one confronting these officers, where spontaneity rather than adherence to a police manual is necessarily the order of the day, the application of the exception which we recognize today should not be made to depend on post hoc findings at a suppression hearing concerning the subjective motivation of the arresting officer. Undoubtedly most police officers, if placed in Officer Kraft's position, would act out of a host of different, instinctive, and largely unverifiable motives—their own safety, the safety of others, and perhaps as well the desire to obtain incriminating evidence from the suspect. Whatever the motivation of individual officers in such a situation, we do not believe that the doctrinal underpinnings of Miranda require that it be applied in all its rigor to a situation in which police officers ask questions reasonably prompted by a concern for the public safety. The Miranda decision was based in large part on this Court's view that the warnings which it required police to give to suspects in custody would reduce the likelihood that the suspects would fall victim to constitutionally impermissible practices of police interrogation in the presumptively coercive environment of the station house."*[81]

Shahzad would continue to cooperate with law enforcement and answer questions after he was read his *Miranda* rights. On June 21, 2010, a month and a half after his arrest, he pled guilty to all ten counts in the federal indictment against him, including charges of attempting to use a weapon of mass destruction and an attempted act of terrorism.[82] On October 5, 2010, he was sentenced to life imprisonment.[83]

The *Miranda* debate begun with the Shahzad case was re-ignited in April 2013 after the bombing at the Boston Marathon. This time the controversy centered on the FBI's invocation of the "public safety" exception to conduct a pre-*Miranda* interview of suspect Dzohkar Tsarnaev several days after his arrest. Despite the Boston Police Department's "all-clear" notice to city residents after the death of Tamerlan Tsarnaev and capture of Dzohkar Tsarnaev, the FBI maintained that "public safety" was still at risk. The *Quarles* "public safety" exception, like other exceptions the Court has created, lasts only as long as the exigent circumstance exists. Critics of the FBI's tactics in questioning Dzohkar Tsarnaev believed the FBI to be disingenuous in its stated reason for holding off on reading Tsarnaev his *Miranda* warnings. The FBI relied in part on a Justice Department memorandum (see endnote 15), which identified exceptional cases where even though public safety is no longer a concern unwarned questioning may continue.

Both Faisal Shahzad and Dzohkar Tsarnaev were U.S. citizens at the time of their arrest; they were also both active terror suspects. Are there any viable legal arguments to refuse to provide these types of suspects their *Miranda* warnings and extend to them Fifth Amendment protections against self-incrimination?

12. The April 16, 2009 release by the Justice Department of a series of memorandums written between 2002-2005 by Office of Legal Counsel staff attorneys to President Bush, which provided a justification for harsh interrogation techniques by the CIA in the questioning of terror suspects (known as "The Torture Memos"), disclosed questionable legal reasoning and sanctioning of interrogation tactics that resulted in worldwide criticism and condemnation. In a January 25, 2002, memorandum to President Bush, White House counsel Alberto Gonzales wrote that the president had the constitutional authority to determine, as he did, that the Geneva Convention for the treatment of prisoners of war did not apply to the conflict with al-

Qaeda. Gonzales further wrote that the U.S. global war on terror's *"new paradigm renders obsolete Geneva's strict limitations on questioning of enemy prisoners and renders quaint some of its provisions."*[84] In a subsequent memorandum dated August 1, 2002, Deputy Assistant Attorney General Jay Bybee provided a narrow definition of torture under U.S. and international law. Bybee also reached the conclusion that presidential commander-in-chief authority trumped the provisions of the federal statute, 18 U.S.C. §2340A, outlawing torture. Bybee wrote: *"Even if an interrogation method arguably were to violate Section 2340A, the statute would be unconstitutional if it encroached on the President's constitutional power to conduct a military campaign. As Commander-in-Chief, the President has the constitutional authority to order interrogations of enemy combatants to gain intelligence information concerning the military plans of the enemy. The demands of the Commander-in-Chief power are especially pronounced in the middle of a war in which the nation has already suffered a direct attack. In such a case, the information gained from the interrogations may prevent future attacks by foreign enemies. Any effort to apply Section 2340A in a manner that interferes with the President's direction of such core war matters as the detention and interrogation of enemy combatants would be unconstitutional."*[85] How does Bybee's legal conclusion regarding presidential commander-in-chief power compare with the U.S. Supreme Court's decision in *Little v. Barreme*? What about Bybee's statement that presidential commander-in-chief power trumps not only U.S. statutory law regarding torture but international law as well? What significance does the U.S. Supreme Court holding in *The Paquete Habana* have to this discussion? Does the Bybee memo find support in these Court decisions?

13. Geneva Convention Common Article 3 bans torture, cruel, inhumane, and degrading treatment, as well as outrages against the dignity of prisoners of war. These basic guidelines initiated for the care of those wounded in battle were eventually extended to treatment of prisoners of war, civilians in war zones, and generally agreed upon international legal principles for the conduct of lawful armed conflict. Despite the legal opinions of the Office of Legal Counsel during the Bush administration that al-Qaeda and other unlawful enemy combatants were not covered under the Geneva rules, the U.S. Supreme Court declared otherwise in *Hamdan v. Rumsfeld*. The *Hamdan* Court said the military commissions set up by the Bush administration violated the Geneva Convention and the Uniform Code of Military Justice. Although the *Hamdan* decision focused on detention issues and congressional authority to strip the courts of review power under the Detainee Treatment Act of 2005, the decision's extension of Geneva Convention coverage to unlawful enemy combatants weakened government arguments that enhanced interrogation methods could lawfully be utilized against unlawful enemy combatants since they operated outside Geneva protections. Geneva Convention Common Article 3 does not define torture, but the United Nations Convention Against Torture (C.A.T.), ratified in 1987, provides a definition in Article I, Part 1: *"any act by which severe pain or suffering, whether physical or mental, is intentionally inflicted on a person*

for such purposes as obtaining from him or a third person information or a confession, punishing him for an act he or a third person has committed or is suspected of having committed, or intimidating or coercing him or a third person, or for any reason based on discrimination of any kind, when such pain or suffering is inflicted by or at the instigation of or with the consent or acquiescence of a public official or other person acting in an official capacity. It does not include pain or suffering arising only from, inherent in or incidental to lawful sanctions."[86] Title 18 United States Code §2340A was enacted during the term of the 103rd Congress in the 1993–1994 legislative session in order to implement into U.S. law the provisions of the UN Convention Against Torture. The statute, as enacted, provides: *"Whoever outside the United States commits or attempts to commit torture shall be fined under this title or imprisoned not more than 20 years, or both, and if death results to any person from conduct prohibited by this subsection, shall be punished by death or imprisoned for any term of years or for life."*[87] Section 2340 defines torture as *"an act committed by a person acting under the color of law specifically intended to inflict severe physical or mental pain or suffering (other than pain or suffering incidental to lawful sanctions) upon another person within his custody or physical control."* It is within the specific intent language of the statute that the Bybee memorandum relied upon in crafting U.S. policy excepting common legal understandings of what constitutes torture from the actual implementation by the C.I.A. in the questioning of unlawful enemy combatants. The basic Bybee rationale was that if the use of certain interrogation techniques were for a purpose other than the specific intention to cause gratuitous pain or suffering then it did not fall within the strict legal definition of torture. What are the inherent inconsistencies between the U.N. Convention Against Torture's definition of torture and the Bybee rationale? How does U.S. statute's definition of torture in §2340 constrict the C.A.T. definition?

14. The question of whether or not Fifth Amendment protections against self-incrimination apply to a foreign subject outside the United States has never been determined by the U.S. Supreme Court. As noted in the introduction to this chapter, the Court in *Verdugo-Urquidez* did point to specific wording in the Fourth Amendment to deny an alien defendant's suppression motion. But the *Verdugo-Urquidez* Court, while generally referencing Fifth Amendment rights, did not provide explicit guidance regarding the right against self-incrimination, though it did imply that an alien arrested outside the United States did not have access to the right. Two years prior to *Verdugo-Urquidez*, a special concurring opinion in *United States v. Yunis*, a District of Columbia Circuit Court of Appeals case, provided an argument for extra-territorial application of the self-incrimination clause to alien defendants.[88] D.C. Circuit Judge Abner Mikva wrote the court opinion, then in his special concurrence separately wrote: *"We need not decide whether the trial judge is right as to the constitutional strictures imposed on our government when it acts against aliens outside the territory of the United States. My analysis of the constitutional issue is somewhat different from the district court's, but I*

reach the same conclusion: Yunis' confession must be suppressed if it was obtained in violation of the fifth amendment.

At least since the landmark decision in Miranda v. Arizona, 384 U.S. 456, 86 S.Ct. 1602, 16 L.Ed.2d 694 (1966), courts have protected the right against self-incrimination primarily by circumscribing police interrogation. It bears reemphasizing, however, that the fifth amendment's text does not refer to custodial interrogation. Rather, it focuses on the period of trial and prosecution, proclaiming that "[n]o person ... shall be compelled in any criminal case to be a witness against himself."

The Supreme Court has explained its extension of the self-incrimination clause to cover testimony given in situations not literally encompassed by the amendment's text in this fashion: [A] defendant's right not to be compelled to testify against himself at his own trial might be practically nullified if the prosecution could previously have required him to give evidence against himself before a grand jury ... In more recent years this concern—that compelled disclosures might be used against a person at a later criminal trial—has been extended to cases involving police interrogation. Michigan v. Tucker, 417 U.S. 433, 440-41, 94 S.Ct. 2357, 2362, 41 L.Ed.2d 182 (1974). As this statement makes clear, the focus of the fifth amendment protection continues to be the use of compelled, self-incriminatory evidence against the defendant at trial.

This fact was made clear in one of the Supreme Court's earliest decisions enforcing the self-incrimination clause. In Bram v. United States, 168 U.S. 532, 18 S.Ct. 183, 42 L.Ed. 568 (1897), the Court excluded a confession from an American trial, notwithstanding that the coercive interrogation was conducted by a foreign police officer in a foreign country. As the Ninth Circuit subsequently explained this result, it is not until the statement is received in evidence that the violation of the Fifth Amendment becomes complete. For this reason we believe that if the statement is not voluntarily given, whether given to a United States or foreign officer—the defendant has been compelled to be a witness against himself when the statement is admitted. Brulay v. United States, 383 F.2d 345, 349 n. 5 (9th Cir.), cert. denied, 389 U.S. 986, 88 S.Ct. 469, 19 L.Ed.2d 478 (1967); cf. United States v. Wolf, 813 F.2d 970, 972 n. 3 (9th Cir.1987) (fifth amendment may not require exclusion when confession is obtained abroad by foreign police, without involvement of American officials). I conclude, then, that the circumstances surrounding Yunis' interrogation by FBI agents aboard the Butte should be subjected to fifth amendment scrutiny.[89]

Thirteen years later and a few months before the 9/11 attacks, Judge Leonard Sand, Southern District of New York, came to a similar conclusion in *United States v. Bin Laden.*[90] The case involved a 302 count indictment against four foreign nationals charged in connection with the 1998 bombings of U.S. embassies in Kenya and Tanzania. Judge Sand ruled that *Miranda* warnings applied to the foreign interrogations of these suspects: *"Our analysis of Defendants' motions to suppress statements turns chiefly on the constitutional standard we adopt today, as a matter of first impression, concerning the admissibility of a defendant's admissions at his criminal trial in the United States, where that defendant is a non-resident alien and his statements were the product of an interrogation conducted abroad by U.S. law enforcement representatives. We conclude that such a defendant, insofar as he is the present subject of a domestic criminal proceeding, is indeed protected by the privilege against self-incrimination guaranteed by the Fifth Amendment, notwithstanding the fact that his only connections to the United States are his alleged violations of U.S. law and his subsequent U.S. prosecution. Additionally, we hold that courts may and should apply the familiar warning/waiver framework set forth in Miranda v. Arizona, 384 U.S. 437, 16 L. Ed. 2d 694, 86 S. Ct. 1602 (1996), to determine whether the government, in its case-in-chief, may introduce against such a defendant evidence of his custodial statements—even if that defendant's interrogation by U.S. agents occurred wholly abroad and while he was in the physical custody of foreign authorities ... it bears noting that the Government incorrectly frames the legal inquiry as one dependent on the extraterritorial application of the Fifth Amendment. Whether or not Fifth Amendment rights reach out to protect individuals while they are situated outside the United States is beside the point. This is because any violation of the privilege against self-incrimination occurs, not at the moment law enforcement officials coerce statements through custodial interrogation, but when a defendant's involuntary statements are actually used against him at an American criminal proceeding. (See United States v. Verdugo-Urquidez, 494 U.S. 259, 264, 108 L. Ed. 2d 222, 110 S. Ct. 1056 (1990) ("Although conduct by law enforcement officials prior to trial may ultimately impair [the privilege against self-incrimination], a constitutional violation occurs only at trial.") (citing Kastigar v. United States, 406 U.S. 441, 453, 32 L. Ed. 2d 212, 92 S. Ct. 1653 (1972)); Deshawn E. by Charlotte E. v. Safir, 156 F. 3d 340, 346 (2d Cir., 1998) ("Even if it can be shown that a statement was obtained by coercion, there can be no Fifth Amendment violation until that statement is introduced against the defendant in a criminal proceeding.")). Indeed, were the opposite the case—that is, if instead the Fifth Amendment injury resulted from the forcible extraction of a statement and not its later evidentiary use--then no statute compelling witness testimony under grants of immunity could withstand constitutional challenge ... The violation of Defendants' rights here, if any, is clearly prospective, and so the relevant question is the scope of the privilege against self-incrimination as to non-resident aliens presently inside the United States and subject to domestic criminal proceedings.*[91]

Is the judicial reasoning in *Yunis* and *Bin Laden* still persuasive in light of the Supreme Court's collective decisions in *Verdugo-Urquidez* and *Chavez*?

Endnotes

[1]   Davis, Lois M., Michael Pollard, Kevin Ward, Jeremy M. Wilson, Danielle M. Varda, Lydia Hansell, and Paul Steinberg. *Long-Term Effects of Law Enforcement's Post-9/11 Focus on Counterterrorism and Homeland Security.* Santa Monica, CA: RAND Corporation, 2010. http://www.rand.org/pubs/monographs/MG1031. Also available in print form.

[2]   For a fuller exposition of Fourth Amendment terror investigation exceptionalism in "stop and frisk" encounters see, Dwyer, T. (2012). "Enhancing the Right to Inquire: The Supreme Court's Post-9/11 Jurisprudence for Police Officer Stop and Inquire Authority." *Criminal Law Bulletin*, 1253–1275.

[3]   543 U.S. 405 (2005).

[4]   543 U.S. at 424.

[5]   543 U.S. at 416, fn. 7.

[6]   531 U.S. 32 (2000).

[7]   531 U.S. at 42.

[8]   460 F.3d 260 (2d Cir, 2006).

[9]   629 F.3d 60 (1st Cir., 2010).

[10] *Shah v. Czellecz*, 2010 U.S. Dist. LEXIS 134843 (D. Mass.).

[11] 494 U.S. at 262.

[12] Id.

[13] 494 U.S. at 265.

[14] President Bush's military commissions were later ruled unconstitutional by the Supreme Court in *Hamdan v. Rumsfeld*, 548 U.S. 547 (2006) and replaced with the *Military Commissions Act of 2006.*

[15] Text of the FBI memo regarding *Miranda* warnings, N.Y. Times, Mar. 25, 2011, http://www.nytimes.com/2011/03/25/us/25miranda-text.html

U.S. Department of Justice
Federal Bureau of Investigation

October 21, 2010

Custodial Interrogation for Public Safety and Intelligence-Gathering Purposes of Operational

Terrorists Inside the United States[1]

Identifying and apprehending suspected terrorists, interrogating them to obtain intelligence about terrorist activities and impending terrorist attacks, and lawfully detaining them so that they do not pose a continuing threat to our communities are critical to protecting the American people. The Department of Justice and the FBI believe that we can maximize our ability to accomplish these objectives by continuing to adhere to FBI policy regarding the use of Miranda warnings for custodial interrogation of operational terrorists[2] who are arrested inside the United States:

1. If applicable, agents should ask any and all questions that are reasonably prompted by an immediate concern for the safety of the public or the arresting agents without advising the arrestee of his Miranda rights.[3]

2. After all applicable public safety questions have been exhausted, agents should advise

the arrestee of his Miranda rights and seek a waiver of those rights before any further interrogation occurs, absent exceptional circumstances described below.

3. There may be exceptional cases in which, although all relevant public safety questions have been asked, agents nonetheless conclude that continued unwarned interrogation is necessary to collect valuable and timely intelligence not related to any immediate threat, and that the government's interest in obtaining this intelligence outweighs the disadvantages of proceeding with unwarned interrogation.[4] In these instances, agents should seek SAC approval to proceed with unwarned interrogation after the public safety questioning is concluded. Whenever feasible, the SAC will consult with FBI-HQ (including OGC) and Department of Justice attorneys before granting approval. Presentment of an arrestee may not be delayed simply to continue the interrogation, unless the defendant has timely waived prompt presentment.

The determination whether particular unwarned questions are justified on public safety grounds must always be made on a case-by-case basis based on all the facts and circumstances. In light of the magnitude and complexity of the threat often posed by terrorist organizations, particularly international terrorist organizations, and the nature of their attacks, the circumstances surrounding an arrest of an operational terrorist may warrant significantly more extensive public safety interrogation without Miranda warnings than would be permissible in an ordinary criminal case. Depending on the facts, such interrogation might include, for example, questions about possible impending or coordinated terrorist attacks; the location, nature, and threat posed by weapons that might post an imminent danger to the public; and the identities, locations, and activities or intentions of accomplices who may be plotting additional imminent attacks.

As noted above, if there is time to consult with FBI-HQ (including OGC) and Department of Justice attorneys regarding the interrogation strategy to be followed prior to reading the defendant his Miranda rights, the field office should endeavor to do so. Nevertheless, the agents on the scene who are interacting with the arrestee are in the best position to assess what questions are necessary to secure their safety and the safety of the public, and how long the post-arrest interview can practically be delayed while interrogation strategy is being discussed.

[1] This guidance applies only to arrestees who have not been indicted and who are not known to be represented by an attorney. For policy on interrogation of indicted defendants, see Legal Handbook for Special Agents (LHBSA) Section 7-3.2 For policy on contact with represented persons, see LHBSA Sections 7-4.1 and 8-3.2.2.

[2] For these purposes, an operational terrorist is an arrestee who is reasonably believed to be either a high-level member of an international terrorist group; or an operative who has personally conducted or attempted to conduct a terrorist operation that involved risk to life; or an individual knowledgeable about operational details of a pending terrorist operation.

[3] The Supreme Court held in New York v. Quarles, 467 U.S. 649 (1984), that if law enforcement officials engage in custodial interrogation of an individual that is "reasonable prompted by a concern for the public safety," any statements the individual provides in the course of such interrogation shall not be inadmissible in any criminal proceeding on the basis that the warnings described in Miranda v. Arizona 384 U.S. 436 (1966), were not provided. The court noted that this exception to the Miranda rule is a narrow one and that "in each case it will be circumscribed by the [public safety] exigency which justifies it." 467 U.S. at 657.

[4]The Supreme Court has strongly suggested that an arrestee's Fifth Amendment right against self-incrimination is not violated at the time a statement is taken without Miranda warnings, but instead may be violated only if and when the government introduces an unwarned statement in a criminal proceeding against the defendant. See Chavez v. Martinez, 538 U.S. 760, 769 (2003) (plurality op.); id. at 789 (Kennedy, J., concurring in part and dissenting in part); cf. also id. at 778-79 (Souter, J., concurring

in the judgment); see also United States v. Patane, 542 U.S. 630, 641 (2004) (plurality opinion) ("[V]iolations [of the Fifth Amendment right against self-incrimination] occur, if at all, only upon the admission of unwarned statements into evidence at trial.")); United States v. Verdugo-Urquidez, 494 U.S. 259, 264 (1990) ("[A] violation [of the Fifth Amendment right against self-incrimination] occurs only at trial.").

[16] *Watts v. Indiana*, 338 U.S. 49, 55 (1949).

[17] Id.

[18] Federation of American Scientists. (July 31, 2013). *Foreign Intelligence Surveillance Act*. Retrieved from Federation of American Scientists: https://www.fas.org/irp/agency/doj/fisa/.

[19] Federal Judicial Center. (n.d.). *History of the Federal Judiciary*. Retrieved July 14, 2013 from Federal Judicial Center: http://www.fjc.gov/history/home.nsf/page/courts_special_fisc.html.

[20] Id.

[21] Shawl, J. (2005, December 21). *FISC judge resigns in protest over NSA domestic surveillance*. Retrieved July 14, 2013 from Jurist: http://jurist.law.pitt.edu/paperchase/2005/12/fisc-judge-resigns-in-protest-over-nsa.php.

[22] Drury, I., & Robinson, M. (June 19, 2013). *U.S. Senators demand 'traitor' NSA whistleblower be extradited from Hong Kong to face trial in America after he reveals why he exposed online spy scandal*. Retrieved July 14, 2013, from Mail Online: http://www.dailymail.co.uk/news/article-2338534/Edward-Snowden-speaks-NSA-contractor-leaked-details-surveillance-scheme-reveals-himself.html.

[23] *Coolidge v. New Hampshire*, 403 U.S. 443 (1971).

[24] *New Jersey v. T.L.O.*, 469 U.S. 325, 341 (1985)—*"Where a careful balancing of governmental and private interests suggests that the public interest is best served by a Fourth Amendment standard of reasonableness that stops short of probable cause, we have not hesitated to adopt such a standard."*

[25] 469 U.S. at 340–341.

[26] Dwyer at 1265–1266; see also, *Treasury Employees v. Von Raab,* 489 U.S. 656 (1989) and *Skinner v. Railway Labor Executives' Assn.*, 489 U.S. 602 (1989) for the "special needs" related cases referenced by Justice O'Connor.

[27] 607 F.3d at 945.

[28] Gonzalez, J. (February 24, 2012). *Wholesale surveillance of Muslims in Newark, NJ shows NYPD's fight against terrorism has gone wild*. Retrieved July 15, 2013, from Daily News: http://www.nydailynews.com/news/wholesale-surveillance-muslims-newark-n-shows-nypd-fight-terrorism-wild-article-1.1027882.

[29] Goldman, A., & Sullivan, E. (June 18, 2013). *NYPD Muslim Surveillance Lawsuit Seeks to End Religious Profiling*. Retrieved July 15, 2013, from Huffington Post: http://www.huffingtonpost.com/2013/06/18/nypd-muslim-surveillance-spying-lawsuit-_n_3460079.html.

[30] 349 F. Supp. 766 (SDNY, 1972).

[31] 605 F. Supp. 1384, affm'd 787 F.2d 828.

[32] See *Handschu v. Special Services Division*, 288 F. Supp 2d. 575 (SDNY, 2003).

33 237 F.3d 799 (7th Cir., 2001).

34 91 F.R.D. 182 (N.D. Ill., 1981).

35 561 F. Supp. 575 (N.D. Ill., 1983).

36 See *Alliance to End Repression v. City of Chicago*, 237 F.3d 799 (7th Cir., 2001).

37 237 F.3d at 802.

38 Id.

39 The overview of National Security Letters is from Electronic Privacy Information Center. (n.d.). *National Security Letters.* Retrieved September 15, 2013, from Electronic Privacy Information Center: http://epic.org/privacy/nsl/.

40 *Doe v. Gonzalez,* 126 S.Ct. 1 (2005) did reach the U.S. Supreme Court as an emergency application to vacate a stay by the Second Circuit Court of Appeals of a preliminary injunction against enforcement of 18 U.S.C. §2709(c). Justice Ginsburg, sitting as a circuit court justice to hear the emergency application, denied the application in light of the expedited appeal schedule in place to hear the parties on the central case issue, that being the constitutionality of §2709(c) and its nondisclosure provision. Justice Ginsburg also wrote that the applicants had not shown sufficient extraordinary cause to vacate the stay while the merits of the case were swiftly proceeding within the Second Circuit.

41 334 F.Supp. 2d 471 (SDNY, 2004).

42 Id.

43 See *Doe I v. Gonzalez,* 449 F.3d 415 (2d Cir., 2006).

44 See *Doe v. Gonzalez,* 500 F.Supp. 2d 379 (SDNY, 2007).

45 See *Doe v. Mukasey,* 549 F.3d 861 (2d Cir., 2008).

46 See e.g., O'Connell, M. E. (2012, August 6). *When Are Drone Killings Illegal.* Retrieved August 22, 2013, from CNN: http://www.cnn.com/2012/08/15/opinion/oconnell-targeted-killing/index.html; Bowcott, O. (2012, June 21). *Drone Strikes Threaten 50 Years of International Law, Says U.N. Rapporteur.* Retrieved August 22, 2013, from The Guardian: http://www.theguardian.com/world/2012/jun/21/drone-strikes-international-law-un.

47 See e.g., Martinez, M. (2011, September 30). *U.S. drone killing of American Anwar al-Awlaki prompts legal, moral debate.* Retrieved August 22, 2013, from CNN: http://www.cnn.com/2011/09/30/politics/targeting-us-citizens/index.html; Coll, S. (2012, August 2). *Kill or Capture.* Retrieved August 22, 2013, from The New Yorker: http://www.newyorker.com/online/blogs/comment/2012/08/kill-or-capture.html.

48 See e.g., Groves, S. (2013, April 10). *Drone Strikes: The Legality of Targeting Terrorists Abroad.* Retrieved August 22, 2013, from The Heritage Society: http://www.heritage.org/research/reports/2013/04/drone-strikes-the-legality-of-us-targeting-terrorists-abroad; Kramer, C. (2011). The Legality of Targeted Drone Attacks as U.S. Policy. *Santa Clara Journal of International Law* , 375–398; Lewis, M. W. (June 3, 2011). "The Use of Drones and Targeted Killing in Counterterrorism." *Engage* , pp. 73–76.

49 See e.g., Francescani, C. (2013, March 3). *Domestic drones are already reshaping U.S. crime-fighting.* Retrieved August 20, 2013, from Reuters:

http://www.reuters.com/article/2013/03/03/us-usa-drones-lawenforcement-idUSBRE92208W20130303; Wood, C. (2013, March 1). *The Case for Drones*. Retrieved August 20, 2013, from Emergency Management: http://www.emergencymgmt.com/safety/Case-for-Drones.html.

[50]   The facts in *United States v. Knotts*, 460 U.S. 276 (1983) involve the police placing a beeper transmitter in a 5-gallon drum containing chloroform to be purchased by a criminal suspect in the manufacture of controlled substances. Police tracked the public movements of the suspects upon their purchase of the chloroform from a chemical company that was cooperating with the police. One of the defendants who was arrested and charged with conspiracy to manufacture a controlled substance challenged the admissibility of the evidence gained from the use of the beeper transmitter. Justice Rehnquist rejected the privacy argument of the respondent Knotts and in dicta wrote: *"... though he expresses the generalized view that the result of the holding sought by the Government would be that "twenty-four hour surveillance of any citizen of this country will be possible, without judicial knowledge or supervision." But the fact is that the "reality hardly suggests abuse," Zurcher v. Stanford Daily, 436 U.S. 547, 566 (1978); if such dragnet-type law enforcement practices as respondent envisions should eventually occur, there will be time enough then to determine whether different constitutional principles may be applicable. Ibid. Insofar as respondent's complaint appears to be simply that scientific devices such as the beeper enabled the police to be more effective in detecting crime, it simply has no constitutional foundation. We have never equated police efficiency with unconstitutionality, and we decline to do so now."*

[51]   468 U.S. 705 (1984).

[52]   533 U.S. 27 (2001).

[53]   389 U.S. 347 (1967).

[54]   488 U.S. 485 (1989).

[55]   476 U.S. 207 (1986).

[56]   476 U.S. 227 (1986).

[57]   See, 476 U.S. at 216 (1986).

[58]   476 U.S. at 216 (citing *Katz*, 389 U.S. at 362).

[59]   476 U.S. at 219.

[60]   476 U.S. at 21.

[61]   476 U.S. at 212.

[62]   See, *Oliver v. United States*, 466 U.S. 170, 180 (1984).

[63]   Id at 239.

[64]   342 U.S. at 169.

[65]   Id at 172.

[66]   See, *Daniels* v. *Williams*, 474 U. S. at 331 (1986).

[67]   See e.g., *Walton v. Gomez*, 745 F.3d 405, 426 (10th Cir., 2014) ("force ... inspired by malice of excessive zeal that shocks the conscience"); *Burgess v. Fischer*, 735 F.3d 462, 473 (6th Cir., 2013) ("no evidence deputies acted maliciously or sadistically");

Porter v. Osborn, 546 F.3d 1131, 1137 (9th Cir., 2008) ("use of force shocks the conscience only if the officer had a 'purpose to harm' for reasons unrelated to legitimate law enforcement objectives").

[68]   523 U.S. at 846.

[69]   *United States Department of Justice* (n.d.). Retrieved August 20, 2013, from OLC FOIA Electronic Reading Room: http://www.justice.gov/sites/default/files/olc/legacy/2013/10/21/memo-bradbury2005.pdf.

[70]   378 U.S. 1 (1964).

[71]   Id at 8.

[72]   360 U.S. 315 (1959).

[73]   Id at 321.

[74]   322 U.S. at 155.

[75]   338 U.S. at 53, 54.

[76]   See e.g., Baker, P. (May 5, 2010). A Renewed Debate Over Suspect Rights. *New York Times*, p. A28; Bazelon, E. (May 5, 2010). *Miranda Worked! The bizarre criticism of the Faisal Shahzad interrogation.* Retrieved July 15, 2013 from Slate: http://www.slate.com/articles/news_and_politics/jurisprudence/2010/05/miranda_worked.single.html; Murphy, P. (May 4, 2010). *Shahzad Arrest Ignites Debate Over Miranda Warnings for Accused Terrorists.* Retrieved from Politics Daily: http://www.politicsdaily.com/2010/05/04/steny-hoyer-defends-miranda-warning-to-terror-suspect-faisal-sha/.

[77]   467 U.S. 649 (1984).

[78]   467 U.S. at 652.

[79]   467 U.S. at 653.

[80]   467 U.S. at 655.

[81]   467 U.S. at 655–657.

[82]   CNN. (June 21, 2010). *Shahzad pleads guilty to Times Square bombing charges.* Retrieved from CNN: http://www.washingtonpost.com/wp-dyn/content/article/2010/06/21/AR2010062102468.html; Markon, J. (June 22, 2010). *Shahzad pleads guilty in failed Times Square bombing, warns of future attacks.* Retrieved from Washington Post: http://www.washingtonpost.com/wp-dyn/content/article/2010/06/21/AR20100 62102468.html.

[83]   Wilson, M. (October 6, 2010). Shahzad Gets Life Term for Times Square Bombing Attempt. *New York Times* , p. A25.

[84]   The New York Times. (2005). *NY Times International.* Retrieved from A Guide to the Memos on Torture: http://www.nytimes.com/ref/international/24MEMO-GUIDE.html?_r=0.

[85]   Id.

[86]   United Nations. (December 12, 1984). *Convention Against Torture and other Cruel, Inhuman or Degrading Treatment or Punshment* . Retrieved August 20, 2013, from United Nations General Assembly: http://www.un.org/documents/ga/res/39/a39r046.htm.

[87] Cornell University School of Law. (n.d.). *18 USC Section 2340A -- Torture*. Retrieved August 20, 2013, from Legal Information Institute: http://www.law.cornell.edu/uscode/text/18/2340A.

[88] See 859 F.2d 953 (D.C. Cir., 1988).

[89] 859 F. 2d at 970–971.

[90] 132 F.Supp. 2d 168 (SDNY, 2001).

[91] 132 F. Supp. 2d at 181–182.

INDEX

OTHER TITLES OF INTEREST
FROM LOOSELEAF LAW PUBLICATIONS, INC.

Organized Crime Conspiracies
Investigator Strategies & Tactics
by Thomas E. Baker

Terrorism Prevention and Response – *3rd Edition*
The Definitive Counter-Terrorism Guide for Law Enforcement
by Cliff Mariani

Constitutional Police Procedure – *2nd Edition*
An Instructional Dialogue
by Michael A. Petrillo

Contemporary Issues in Criminal Justice
A Research-Based Introduction
An anthology by Carolyn D'Argenio, David Owens & Jeffrey Chin

Criminal Investigative Function - *2nd Edition*
A Guide for New Investigators
by Joseph L. Giacalone

Detecting Deception
The Science of Communication
by Inv. Paul S. McCormick

Gangs, Outlaw Bikers, Organized Crime & Extremists
Who They Are, How They Work and the Threats They Pose
by Philip J. Swift

International Sex Trafficking of Women & Children – 2nd Edition
Understanding the Global Epidemic
An anthology by Leonard Territo

Invasion of Privacy & the Law
28 Cornerstone Court Decisions Every Officer & P.I. Should Know
by Ron Hankin

Processing Under *Pressure*
  Stress, Memory and Decision-Making in Law Enforcement
  by Matthew J. Sharps

Real World Search & Seizure – *2ⁿᵈ Edition*
  by Matthew J. Medina

Safe Overseas Travel
  Maximizing Enjoyment by Minimizing Risk
  by Brian Johnson & Brian Kingshott

Use of Force – *2ⁿᵈ Edition*
  Expert Guidance for Decisive Force Response
  by Brian A. Kinnaird

The Verbal Judo Way of Leadership
  Empowering the Thin Blue Line from the Inside Up
  by Dr. George Thompson & Gregory A. Walker

Winning Court Testimony for Law Enforcement Officers
  The Law, Art & Science of Effective Court Communication
  by Matthew J. Medina

(800) 647-5547   **www.LooseleafLaw.com**